THE RISALAH

PRINCIPLES OF SUFISM

Abū-l-Qāsim ᶜAbd-al-Karīm bin Hawāzin al-Qushayrī

TRANSLATED BY
RABIA HARRIS

EDITED BY
LALEH BAKHTIAR

SERIES EDITOR
SEYYED HOSSEIN NASR

GREAT BOOKS OF THE ISLAMIC WORLD

Printed in the United States of America.

Library of Congress Cataloging-in-Publication Data

Abu-l-Qasim Abd-al-Karim bin Hawazin al-Qushayri
The Risalah: Principles of Sufism
  1. Sufism. I. Title.

ISBN: 1-930637-22-5

Cover design: Liaquat Ali
  Cornerstones are Allah and Muhammad connected by *Bismillāh al-Rahmān al-Rahīm* (In the Name of God, the Merciful, the Compassionate).

Logo design by Mani Ardalan Farhadi
  The cypress tree bending with the wind, the source for the paisley design, is a symbol of the perfect Muslim, who, as the tree, bends with the wind of God's Will.

Published by
Great Books of the Islamic World, Inc.

Distributed by
KAZI Publications, Inc.
3023 W. Belmont Avenue
Chicago IL 60618
Tel: 773-267-7001; FAX: 773-267-7002
email: info@kazi.org /www.kazi.org

CONTENTS

FOREWORD

God's last plenar revelation to present humanity came in the form of a book, al-Qurʾan, which for Muslims is also *the* book and is in fact known also as *Umm al-kitāb* or Mother of All Books. While the peerless majesty of the revelation reduced the first generation of Muslims to silence, the echo of the Noble Book and its encouragement of acquiring knowledge could not but result in a culture which cherished books and honored scholars. This unmistakable emphasis of the Noble Quran on knowledge, combined with the synthetic power of Islam to absorb the learning of older civilizations to the extent that they conformed to the doctrine of unity (*al-tawḥīd*), gave rise to a vast and diversified intellectual life which for the past thirteen centuries has produced millions of works dealing with nearly every field of knowledge from the religious sciences, theology and philosophy to the natural sciences, from law to music, and from poetry to politics.

Islamic civilization was a lake into which flowed streams from many civilizations: Greek, Roman, Egyptian, Mesopo- tamian, Byzantine, Persian, Indian and even Chinese. In this lake the various elements became synthesized into a new body of water which itself became the source for numerous tributaries that have watered the various lands of *Dār al-islām*. Furthermore, Islamic civilization created works which had profound influence upon at least three major civilizations outside of the Islamic world: the Far Eastern, the Indian and the Western besides creating numerous masterly works whose influence has remained confined within the Islamic world. Such works in both categories contain a precious message for humanity as a whole and need to be made known by the world at large today.

Most treatises in Islamic civilization were written in the language of the Quranic revelation, Arabic, followed by the only other universal language of Islamic civilization, Persian. But important works have also been written in Turkish, Urdu, Bengali, Malay, Swahili, Berber, and numerous other languages including Chinese and, during this century, even English and French. Nor have all the works in Arabic been written by Arabs nor all the works in Persian by Persians. Numerous treatises in Arabic were written by Persians and later Turks, Indians, Berbers and Black Africans while many books in the Persian language were composed by Indians, Turks and Central Asians. The body of works written within the confines of Islamic civilization belongs to the whole of that civilization and in classical times, in fact, important books became known rapidly from Morocco to India and later Southeast Asia.

The Great Books of the Islamic World series seeks to make some of the most important works produced in Islamic civilization, primarily in Arabic and Persian, available in English so that these treasures of Islamic thought can be appreciated by those who do not possess the facility to benefit from them in the original languages. The audience to which the series addresses itself is predominantly the Western English reading public, but the series is also meant for Muslims themselves who have facility with the English language and also for non-Muslim and non-Westerners who are now becoming ever more knowledgeable in English and who might wish to gain deeper knowledge of the Islamic intellectual universe.

We hope that with the help of God, Exalted is His Majesty, this series will be successfully completed and that by providing a clear and readable translation of some of the great masterpieces of Islamic thought in English, this series will be able to create better understanding of Islam in the world at large and make accessible some of the treasures of traditional thought which, although Islamic in genesis, belong to all human beings who are interested in true knowledge in whatever form it appears. *wa mā tawfīqunā illā bi'Llāh*

Seyyed Hossein Nasr
Washington DC, June, 1997

TRANSLATOR'S PREFACE

In the Name of Allah, Most Beneficent, Most Merciful

When this translation was originally completed in 1984, I had no inkling that seventeen years would pass before it would find its way to the audience for whom it was intended. Yet "for every message there is a moment," and Allah is the best of planners. Perhaps this is the moment in which Imam Qushayri's message will yield us, the English-reading Muslim public, its deepest and most lasting gifts—gifts of which it has a plentiful store. In any case, it is an honor to set before you now the *Risalah Qushayriyyah,* one of the most broadly influential books in Islamic history.

Compiled by a master teacher in response to a moral and political crisis nearly a thousand years ago, the *Risalah* has lost little of its relevance. In his time, as in ours, the Muslim community was involved in a long and complex struggle to reinvent itself as a viable social entity. And in his time, as in ours, the temptations to intolerance and abuse of power on the one hand, and to grandiose fantasies on the other, posed regular challenges to the efforts of Muslims to forge a life together that was at once rational, pious, and warmly humane. It was the task of a whole century's worth of writers (among whom Abu-l-Qasim al-Qushayri was arguably the greatest) to support this effort with a great marshalling of traditional evidence for the centrality of personal humility, social responsibility, and spiritual profundity to the success of an Islamic life.

Many of the people most deeply engaged in this work were of the sort called Sufis. The grand design of the *Risalah* is to make it clear just who such people are and with what issues they have regularly concerned themselves. It accomplishes this through an anecdotal recollection of eighty-four exemplary Sufi masters, together with an encyclopedic elucidation of subjects of Sufi discourse. The point of all this scholarship, however, was never academic. It was to stimulate the religious imagination of ordinary literate Muslims, while focusing their aspirations upon an ideal both achievable and benign: an ever-deepening human awareness of service to God.

I thank editor Laleh Bakhtiar for undertaking the formidable logistical effort of bringing such a large work to press (an effort that defeated several predecessors), and, even more importantly, for ensuring that this translation of the *Risalah* would come within reach of the broad Muslim readership its author intended. It is also necessary to recall here the encouragement of Prof. Jeannette Wakin of Columbia University, under whose supervision the introduction to this volume was originally written as a Master's thesis. Dr. Wakin was a better scholar of Islamic law than many a Muslim scholar, and a true friend of the community: were she still alive, she would certainly have made me update my research!

The merit of any act is in its intention, and the merit of any book is in its inspiration. I would never have dared turn my hand to the *Risalah* had it not been for the inspiration and direct request of two extraordinary men: al-Hajj Shaykh Muzaffer Ozak al-Jerrahi al-Halveti, of Istanbul (may Allah sanctify his secret), and his inheritor in the Americas, al-Hajj Shaykh Tosun Bayrak al-Jerrahi al-Halveti, of New York. Shaykh Muzaffer was an astonishment and a priceless privilege to encounter. Out of Tosun Efendi's endlessly flowing generosity over more than two decades I have gained what little insight I have managed to keep. Together they have taught me, by direct example, what this book is really all about.

Rabia Terri Harris al-Jerrahi
January 2001/Dhu-l-Qidah 1421
Chestnut Ridge, New York

TRANSLATOR'S INTRODUCTION

> Know, may God have mercy upon you, that the best
> of the Muslims after the Messenger of God (ﷺ) were not
> called, in their own time, by any special name, but were
> known only as those who kept company with the Messenger.
> Since there is no excellence greater than that, they came to
> be spoken of as the Companions. In the second generation,
> those who kept company with the Companions were called
> the Followers, and saw in this the noblest of titles; the ones
> who came after them were called the Following of the
> Followers. After this people began to differ and levels of
> development became distinguishable, so the elite, who had
> been given an intense concern for matters of religion, were
> called the Ascetics and the Devotees. Then destructive inno-
> vation appeared and parties began to contend with each
> other, each group claiming that the Ascetics were within its
> own ranks. So the elite of the people of the *Sunnah*, who
> held each of their breaths accountable to God Most High
> and protected their hearts from the disasters of negligence,
> came to be specified by the word *tasawwuf*, Sufism. This
> name became prevalent for these great ones before the close
> of the second century Hijrah.[1]

With this brief definition of the people called Sufis, Abu-l-Qasim
Abd-al-Karim bin Hawazin al-Qushayri opens the biographical section of his *Risalah*. In his view, a view shared almost universally by
the shaykhs whose writings have come down to us, Sufism is a direct
inheritance from the earliest Muslim community and represents the
fullest and most ardent inward affirmation of the Prophetic message.
People of all-embracing spirituality, who held each of their breaths
accountable to God Most High and protected their hearts from the dis-

asters of negligence, were common in the original community because of the overwhelming effect of the presence of the Prophet, and hence required no special name. Only after several generations of distance had taken their toll did such concerns become remarkable, and only after the claim of such concerns became an item of sectarian polemic did Islamic mysticism as an entity arise. Sufism, to such a perspective, developed organically from the earliest community practice, and in essence is simply living Islam.

The standard view in the West—even among scholars—has been rather different. In this theater of opinion, despite an occasional nod in the direction of early Muslim spiritual practice, "Sufism" and "orthodoxy" stand opposed.[1] The former, held to be essentially anti-*Shariah*, is understood as the result of a concatenation of foreign influences, while the latter-"real" Islam is ultimately a form of legalistic and political puritanism.

Such a bifurcation would have alarmed Qushayri, but it would not have surprised him. It is not a new problem. The century and a half that preceded the composition of the *Risalah* saw the first positing of an illusory dichotomy of orthodoxy and mysticism that had previously never manifested itself in Islam. It is this presumption that he and the whole body of "manual writers" attempted to explode. The destruction of such misconceptions-and the imaginary Sufism they produce-was one of the major motivations of the *Risalah*.

I. A Brief History of Early Sufism

1. Transmission from the Prophet

The intense spiritual commitment that eventually came to be called Sufism originated, according to Qushayri and almost all Sufi writers, with the Companions of the Prophet, and derived ultimately from the Prophet himself. It was transmitted by association, by means of living examples, from generation to generation. It is therefore a vital aspect of the practice of the Prophet.

Until very recently, the trend of Western Islamic studies has been first, to minimize or deny an inward spiritual basis to the community at Medina, overemphasizing instead the idea of a political theocracy; and second, to attempt to challenge the whole idea of extra-Quranic transmission from the Prophet.

There are reasons for both these views-some intellectually conscionable, others less so. Many earlier scholars frankly state their low opinion of the moral and spiritual level of the original Islamic community and preclude "higher" concerns by definition. Such concerns must then, by scholarly fiat, be imported, and influences can always be found to account for them. Goldziher[1] attempted to moderate this point of view, but nevertheless held much in common with it. Even Watt, a splendid historian and political analyst to whose work I shall often refer, startles us by admitting his belief in an Arab mind—a "true" Islamic mind—incapable of real spirituality. He speaks of "the difficulty experienced by the Arabs in observing the internal or mental aspects of human life." For such, "Responsibility is external and not in any way . . . moral."[2] Many more such examples, unfortunately, could be given. The arrogance of such statements is breathtaking, and should make an unbiased reader very wary. Yet there is a real incomprehension here, and that is precisely how, in view of later history, spirituality could have been coordinated with politics in the original Islamic community: a very central issue, as we shall see. The challenge to the transmission of the practices of the Prophet (*sunnat al-nabi*) while it has its aspects of cultural chauvinism, is largely based upon an honest critique of written Traditions (*ahadith*), the history of which is complex. Yet it is a pitfall of research that what has not yet been discovered can too easily be theorized not to exist, and it is a substantial leap from the theoretical nonexistence of early Tradition (*hadith*) reports to the equally presumed nonexistence of the whole principle of practices of the Prophet. What is involved here is again a lack of understanding of the spiritual status of the Prophet in his community.

William Graham, in his important study, *Divine Word and Prophetic Word in Early Islam*, argues against both of these conceptions on the basis of the latest research on the Traditions and the implications of very early examples of the Sacred Traditions (*hadith qudsi*) for the attitudes of the primitive Muslim community. Such Traditions, first of all, are notable for their devotional and moral, rather than theological and juridical, content.[3] These latter interests, hypothesized (most notably by Schacht)[4] to have been the major motivators for the later invention of the principle of Prophetic practices (*Sunnah*) and of individual written Traditions, are not stressed in the early material. Instead, early Sacred Traditions demonstrate both the importance and the transmission of the Prophetic spiritual example. On Schact's hypothesis Graham comments: "It would . . . be a mistake to see this living *Sunnah* of the community of the Companions and early Followers as ever having been consciously set up as a standard different from what was understood to be the *Sunnah* of the Prophet."

What the post-Prophetic community practiced was perceived as but the continuation of what the community in the Prophet's time had practiced. The relatively recent scholarly theory that the stress on the practices of the Prophet developed only after A.H. 150 in legal circles as an *ex post facto* confirmation of the living *Sunnah* of the community must be modified in light of the most recent investigations into the early history of the development of the Traditions. This theory rests not only upon a rather selective reading of the early legal sources, but also upon a mis-perception of the basis of Muslim traditionalism, which is the conviction of the sacred nature of the prophetic-revelatory event. Whatever the number of late Traditions ascribed to the Prophet, or however late the development of the practices of the Prophet as a conscious legal principle, the community always and ever understood its authoritative source of knowledge and guidance to lie in the Revelation and the practice of its bearer.[5]

According to Graham, then, the living *Sunnah* of the early community was seen to be the transmission of the *Sunnah* of the Prophet. Formal mechanisms of definition and verification were simply not necessary while the impact of the Prophetic witness was still so close. Fazlur Rahman also argues for this understanding of transmission (though lacking Graham's evidence, simply from common sense).[6] It is also, as we have seen, the thesis of Qushayri: transmission by companionship.

The *Sunnah* that was transmitted was originally a unitary attitude, unfragmented into inner and outer. Even so traditional a scholar as Wensinck notes that *islam* and *iman* were at first identical, a split between them developing only with the growing necessity for a political definition of a Muslim.[7] Very significantly, according to his research the earliest available Traditions (even though later than those accessible to Graham) are marked by an absence of any distinction between the ritual duties and the inner relation of man to God.[8] At that period, then, they were understood as indivisible.

Equally revealing is Watt's observation that theological issues that dramatically divided later generations had little interest for earlier ones. "For example," he writes, "there were elements in the Quranic text from which it might be inferred with a show of plausibility that the Quran was created and others from which it might be similarly inferred that it was uncreated. For over a century, so far as

we can tell, sound Muslim scholars made neither of the sets of infer-
ences, though they accepted all the elements as part of the Quranic
text."9 It has sometimes been assumed by Western writers on the
Quran that the earliest Muslims were not sharp enough thinkers to
see the "intrinsic conflicts" in the material of the revelation.10 It is far
more plausible that the primitive community simply did not see any
profit in attempting to fit the revelation into a neat intellectual package, but rather sought to benefit from what Rahman calls the "moral
tensions necessary for creative human action"11 so crucial to the function of the Quran as an active guide rather than as a passive text.

In fine, as Graham argues, ". . . the early Muslims were less concerned with theological categories of religious guidance.. .than with
seeking all possible guidance as to what islam, submission to God,
involves in a post-prophetic, post-revelation world."12

If then we establish the existence of extra-Quranic guidance from
the Prophet (made strikingly clear by the early presence of nonscrip-
tural Divine Word), transmitted by association, dealing with personal
responsibility to God rather than points of law or theology, and characterized by a unitary, non-discursive attitude, we have a very good
description of the origins of Sufism according to the great shaykhs.
Graham draws this conclusion from his research: ". . .the Divine
Saying is one specific genre of early material that reflects those specific concerns that were at a later date subsumed under the rubric of
Sufism. Not only is the Divine Saying not a late blossom of some
"movement" called "Sufism," it is a strong argument for the deep roots
of Sufi piety in early Muslim spirituality and the prophetic revelatory
event itself."13

2. The Circle of Hasan al-Basri

As Islam became politically successful, it gained multitudes of
adherents whose interest was primarily to be on the victorious side.
The social ideal of Islam has always been the Community (*ummah*),
the mutually devoted community of believers. Yet it became evident
from the time of the Wars of Apostasy that there were strong objections on many sides to committing oneself to the Community. Men
whose immemorial social horizon was the tribe balked at overriding
what they conceived to be their self-interest for the sake of an utterly
novel social entity. Those who had not received the impact of the
Prophetic example needed a powerful motivator to keep them within
the embryonic new society, and that motivator was found in the enor-

mous power and wealth generated by the Arab conquests.

Governmental structure and the skeleton of a state developed within the Community under the pressure of necessity. Means for management of the fruits of expansion had to be devised. Yet these means rapidly became independent of the community of feeling and participation they were originally intended to support, and the Community of the believers metamorphosed into the Umayyad Arab state.

The rise of the Umayyads, the tardiest converts to Islam and for years among the fiercest enemies of its Prophet, required, as Wensinck points out,[14] considerable rethinking, for the rift between the ideal Community and the real state institution was deeply troubling. This is the era in which, as Qushayri puts it, "people began to differ and levels of development became distinguishable," and those for whom the life of God was paramount were called Ascetics and Devotees rather than simply Muslims.

Of great importance in these transitional times was the circle of Hasan al-Basri. Hasan al-Basri, born of Persian freedmen in 21/642 and raised outside of Medina, moved in his fifteenth year to Basra in Iraq where he eventually gained great fame and universal respect as a scholar of insight and compassion who unswervingly practiced what he preached.

His scholarship was comprehensive. He was a famous preacher who took seriously the Islamic scholar's duty to admonish rulers. He was a student of the first practitioner of Quranic commentary (*tafsir*), the Prophet's cousin Abd-Allah bin Abbas,[15] and transmitted this science to his own pupils. He was the founder of theological argumentation.[16] Out of his following also developed the passionate pursuit of anecdotes of Prophetic example that became the Traditionist movement, the *ahl al-hadith*.[17] His circle was perhaps the intellectual center of the early 2nd/8th century, and he has been called the prototype of later Sunnism.[18]

Yet his so-called "ascetic" writings are the most famous and best preserved of Hasan's works. Their asceticism took form from his moral opposition to the thoroughly worldly course that Umayyad society was taking. It was not founded on mortification, but on a poignant awareness of the danger of losing spiritual priorities in the midst of material luxury. Hasan emphasized not eremitic withdrawal, but the necessity of a fully religious life in the world in view of the inevitability of death and judgment. Watt summarizes that Hasan ". . . is constantly aware of the eschatological relevance of this-worldly acts, that is, the possibility of employing them in fulfilling God's commands."[19] His unitary view of inward and outward spiritual responsibility, his commitment to practice rather than theory and to the integrity of the Community as Community place him fully in accord with the Islamic spiritual origins we have examined. According to general Sufi opinion he was also the first Sufi.

Qushayri does not list Hasan in the *Risalah* among the early Sufi shaykhs. Perhaps, since Hasan antedated the period of multiple schism which particularized Sufism, Qushayri considered him one of the Ascetics. (Qushayri's master Sulami, from whose work he drew the names of almost all those to whom the *Risalah* devotes biographies, also counted Hasan as predating the specifically Sufi schools.)[20] According to Sarraj, however, Hasan was the first to use the term,[21] and according to Makki and the first historian of Sufism, bin al-Arabi (d.341/952), he was the first to be so identified.[22] In any case, most later Sufi orders trace themselves to him, and members of his circle were among the founders of the distinctively Sufi ancient schools." As Massignon points out, two hundred years later the disciples of Hasan may have held the monopoly on the cloak initiation by which a Sufi was invested.[23]

Outside of Basra itself, Hasan's student Abd al-Wahid bin Zayd (d. 178/794) founded a famous ascetic community at Abbadan[24] that produced many mystics, among them that Sahl al-Tustari (d.283/896) with whom Hallaj lived for a time.[25] Another disciple of Abd al-Wahid, the influential early teacher Abu Sulayman al-Darani (d. 215/830) together with his student Ahmad bin Abi-l-Hawari (d. 236/851) inaugurated a circle of what were now identified as Sufis in Syria;[26] there other communities were also founded by a parallel Sufi influence out of Kufa.[27] Groups proliferated in cities throughout the Islamic world. But the most important centers that formed in the two generations after Hasan were the schools of Khurasan (where Hasan, during his employment as secretary to the governor[28] himself may have once taught) and Baghdad, the capital of the new Abbasid dynasty.

3. The Abbasid Religious Environment

The accession of the Abbasids in 133/750 introduced a new dynamic into religious life, for while the Umayyads had provided a frankly secular style of administration, the Abbasids claimed themselves to be an explicitly Islamic government. One consequence of this ideological foundation was the growth of law and the formalization of Traditions in response to the "religious" form of the far more institutionalized Abbasid state.[29] Another was that theology developed even further as the natural rhetoric for political positions, a rhetoric that would become increasingly heated and increasingly divisive.

One of the major conflicts of the time centered around the legitimacy of logical argumentation in religion, or theology (*kalam*). Theology, as well as what was now to be called Sufism, had developed out of the circle of Hasan al-Basri. Logical argumentation had first been employed for debate with the Christians and dualists of 2nd/8th century Iraq, upon whom citations from the Quran would have no convincing effect.[30] It seems that originally there was little interest in expanding the technique into philosophy. As Schimmel observes, "The first ascetic tendencies in Basra and its environs (i.e., the community of Hasan) were almost exclusively devotional and lacked any interest in speculative thought."[31]

One may suppose that the possibilities for developing distinctive intellectual positions were attractive to some members of the circle even then, but Hasan's insistence on the inclusive brotherhood of the community was so strong that unity was maintained for a considerable period. Watt notes, "For a time after his death the scholars of his following remained on friendly terms with one another, even when their views diverged. . . . This state of affairs may have lasted forty years or longer after al-Hasan's death in 728. . . ."[32]

It was then in the early years of the Abbasids, in the era of the first great doctor of the Law, Abu Hanifah, that the intellectual doctrines of the Mutazilah were first separately articulated. The origin of the name is obscure, but one explanation traces it to "those who withdrew themselves" from Hasan's circle—which what historical evidence we have shows they, in fact, did.

The Mutazilah for the most part lived ascetic lives and concerned themselves, as did other serious Muslims, with righteousness. They made a fierce defense of the unity of God—a priority drawn from the original Basran debates with dualist Manicheans and trinitarian Christians—and of divine justice, but their arguments were intellectual and their final criterion became the intellect. The universe, the divine order, and the nature of God Himself had above all things to be rationally comprehensible. This premise, developed with the logic of theology, led them to several conclusions. Unity, rationally conceived, required that divine attributes be created, and that the Quran be created. Justice, rationally conceived, required that God must inevitably reward the good and punish the wicked, and that He had no capacity of grace to transform nonbelievers into believers. God, according to them, was bound to act in certain ways because it was rational for Him to do so.

They were drawn to the Greek philosophers, and in the interests of defending religion became the first group in the Islamic world to promulgate the Greek idea of Reason. Many Western orientalists, fond of the Greek heritage, have been drawn to them and attempted to see them as enlightened liberals (with comfortably familiar intellectual assumptions). But as Goldziher points out, they were "the very founders of theological dogmatism in Islam."[33]

Though devoted to championing the divine unity, the Mutazilah made intellect a principle beyond God. This scandalized many, and their insistence on their moral primacy deeply involved them in the complex religio-political polemic of the times. The great jurist Ibn Yusuf, expounder of Hanafi law in the reign of Harun, ruled theology to be dualist heresy (*zandaqah*) dangerous to the state.[34] That very popularly based school of opinion, the *ahl al-hadith*—enthusiasts, moralists, and believers in the absoluteness of the text of Quran and Traditions (and another set of inheritors of Hasan!)—at the same time took it upon themselves to persecute the Mutazilah.[35] The Mutazilites, for their part, declared that all those holding views other than their own were nonbelievers. When under Harun's successor al-Mamun the state changed political tactics and came to espouse the Mutazilite view the unprecedented episode of the rationalist inquisition (*mihnah*), began.

Ahmad bin Hanbal, famously upright and politically intransigent founder of the Hanbali school of law and a leader of the *ahl al-hadith*, actively opposed the Mutazilites and all they stood for. He was consequently imprisoned and scourged for insisting that the Quran was uncreated. At the death of Mamun he emerged a public hero. Many others were similarly arrested and tortured in the state's effort to impose its own theological view. For as Hodgson has elucidated, the belief in an uncreated Quran ". . . stressed the immediate accessibility of the Divine Law to every believer, which was very appropriate to the *Shariah*-minded conception of social equality and individual dignity; but by the same token it was ill-suited to the ideal of absolute monarchy."[36] To declare that the Quran is uncreated is to insist on an ultimate moral and legal authority beyond the caliph and his administration, while to declare that it is created allows caliphal absolutism undisputed authority.

The Mutazilites were interested in the triumph of intellectually pure religion. The caliph was interested in consolidating state power. The Hanbalis were interested in maintaining an independent and uncontaminated source of validity for the ummah. All could say they were acting for the sake of Islam.

> "Then destructive innovation appeared," wrote Qushayri, "and parties began to contend with each other, each group claiming that the Ascetics were within its own ranks. So the elite of the people of the *Sunnah* . . . came to be specified by the word Sufism. This name became prevalent . . . before the close of the second century Hijrah."

4. The Ancient Schools of Sufism

> "When God loves His servant," said that Sufi of the close of the second century Hijrah, Marif al-Karkhi, "He opens for him the door of actions and closes the door of theological disputations."[37]

Maruf al-Karkhi was one of the founders of the Baghdad School of Sufism, whose central concern was the affirmation of unity in practice, rather than theory.[38] Though Sufism was now a thing with a name, it was understood simply as an element of the general religious scene. Even Fazlur Rahman, despite his great wish to brand Sufism as thoroughly counter-Islamic, admits that in the ninth century the "Sufi ceremony" of *dhikr* was routinely performed in mosques, with no objections raised. He writes (rather reluctantly!), ". . . still at this stage . . . Sufi practice was not, and was not regarded as, a rival growth challenging the formal disciplines of Islam."[39]

It was, in fact, well integrated into the general educational life of the times. "*Il etait tres important*," as Pedersen puts it in his introduction to Sulami's *Tabaqat*, "*que l'etude de sufisme se constituat en une science propre lui, comme par ex. le hadith, etait professee dans les mosquees.*"[40] The verbal teaching of this science rapidly became specialized into a number of specific studies, known as *usul al-tasawwuf*, the fundamentals of Sufism, and most particularly as the sciences of conduct, *ulum al-muamalat*. These included such topics as the flaws of the ego (*uyub al-nafs*), weaknesses of personality and intention that destroy the benefit of religious works (*afat al-amal,* ethical character (*akhlaq*), sincerity (*ikhlas*), religious experience in terms of spontaneous authenticity of response (*awqat*) and type (*ahwal*), generosity in social relations (*futuwah*), refined spiritual perception (*marif*), underlying principles of the religious enterprise (*haqaiq*), transformation (*ilm al-fana wa-l-baqa*), and exemplary biography (*ulum al-qawm*).[41] All of these studies were tools for the evaluation and correction of daily life. This was the Sufi curriculum, which proceeded side by side with, and was considered an outgrowth of, the fundamental study of Quran, Traditions, and the Divine Law (*Shariah*).

Yet as Pedersen points out, it would be a mistake to see the formal Sufi teaching in the mosques as an academic affair. Though organized discourses were given, they were only one aspect of a life that laid great emphasis simultaneously on brotherly companionship—exteriorized in communal prayer, *dhikr,* and recitation as well as simple social intercourse—and on the pursuit of inner and outer closeness to the master.[42] "*L'exigence de vie commune,*" he writes, "*apparait constamment dans les ecrits sufis.*"[43] This close community life, attached to the mosques and running fluidly through the private houses of its many participants, was an intrinsic feature of Islamic urban society in the ninth century.

5. Early Controversies

Though their ranks held many shades of political and theological opinion, the Baghdad Sufis were inheritors of Hasan's policy of avoiding political involvement and cultivating concrete brotherhood, and such differences were de-emphasized. Given the climate of the times, however, members of the school inevitably found themselves involved in controversial situations. Any religious statement beyond the Five Pillars was likely, at this period, to become a subject of violent dispute, and accusations of heresy and nonbelief were to be found on all sides. Charges of heterodoxy were laid at the door of the Sufis too.

It was the Hanbalis who took exception to one of the teachers of Junayd, later the inspiration of Ghazzali and Harith al-Muhasibi. Muhasibi was appalled by fragmentation in the Muslim community, and according to Arberry[44] may have been the first to comment on what later became a recurrent Sufi theme-the decay of Islam. He wrote:

> It has come to pass in our days, that this

Community is divided into more than seventy sects: of these,
one only is in the way of salvation, and for the rest, God
knows best concerning them. Now I have not ceased, not so
much as one moment of my life, to consider well the differences into which the Community has fallen, and to search
after the clear way and the true path.. . . Of all this I understood as much as was appointed for me to understand: and I
saw that their divergence was as it were a deep sea, where-
in many had been drowned, and but a small band therefrom
escaped; and I saw every party of them asserting that salvation was to be found in following them, and that he would
perish who opposed them.[45]

Harith had been born in Basra in 164/781, in a milieu in which
Hasan's influence was still active, and Hasan, credited to be the
founder of the "science of hearts," was the most frequent citation in his
works.[46] What earned Muhasibi the opposition of Ahmad bin Hanbal
himself was his use of that other weapon from Hasan's armory, the
kalam.

Muhasibi's concern for the *ummah*, coupled with his alarm at the
rise of dogmatism, caused him to attempt to fight fire with fire. But
this style of argumentation, now thoroughly identified with the
Mutazilite position, was to many an alien intrusion into Islamic practice, a dangerous *bidah*. Thus, though Muhasibi shared much with the
ahl al-hadith, his very use of the disputed technique made him suspect. "Beware of al-Harith," Ahmad bin Hanbal was related to have
said, "beware, for he is at the root of the trouble (i.e., the prevalence
of speculation). He is like a lion which is chained up; be on the look-
out for the day when he will spring upon men."[47]

Yet Harith was scarcely a speculator. His title, al-Muhasibi, was
derived from self-examination (*muhasabah*), and his method centered
upon observing and recognizing one's true motivations. He gave special attention to the uncovering of unconscious manifestations of
hypocrisy. Even Ahmad bin Hanbal, brought to listen to one of his discourses in secret, was said to have been greatly moved.[48] For all that,
his opposition did not waver. He banned Muhasibi's works and forced
him for awhile to leave the city. When Muhasibi died, a year after lbn
Hanbal, in 243/857, only four people dared attend his funeral.[49]

Yet significantly, Ahmad bin Hanbal did not oppose Sufism *per se.*
(Or, one should note, the practice of *dhikr*, which recent generations

of his intellectual descendants have anathematized as *bidah*.) It was human reason's gaining an edge on divine revelation that he attempted to wipe out in all dimensions. He routinely referred those who came to him with certain types of questions to Bishr al-Hafi, another early Sufi uninvolved with theology.[50] And even among Sufis theology produced strenuous differences of opinion. Muhasibi's own student, Junayd, remarked on his master's anti-theological argumentation that "the least danger of speculation on matters of dogmatic theology is that the heart loses its reverence for the Lord Most High, and when the heart loses its reverence, it also loses its faith."[51]

Theology remained a very live issue for centuries after.

Maruf al-Karkhi, whose view of theology has been quoted above, was a younger contemporary of the famous Rabiah al- Adawiyah (d. 185/801). Her powerful realization of the divine love described in the verse, *"He loves them and they love Him"* (5:59) was a strong influence on him, as it was on the whole spiritual atmosphere of Baghdad.[52] He both spoke of love and transmitted its importance to his students. One of them was Sari al-Saqat (d. 253/867), a contemporary of Ahmad bin Hanbal and Muhasibi, and the uncle and major teacher of Junayd. In the atmosphere of persecution and counter-persecution prevalent at the time, he was the first to discourse publicly on divine love defined as "real mutual love between man and God."[53] This was, as Schimmel comments, "a scandal."[54] Love was only to be understood in the sense of obedience, a view (deriving perhaps from a deep nervousness about human feeling, the puritanism of repression that cannot differentiate love and lust and is standing guard over the revolutionary potential of desire) which soon was to develop political implications of its own.

Sari lived a life blameless in the eyes of the Divine Law (*Shariah*)-minded, and seems to have escaped active persecution. (When his name came up before Ibn Hanbal, the latter is said to have remarked, "Oh, you mean the shaykh who is well-known for his scrupulousness about food?")[55] Perhaps the content of his discourse was not as provocative in his time as it would seem in one more generation, or perhaps he moderated his expression, for Sulami calls him "the leader of the Baghdadis in symbolic utterances."[56]

The late ninth century, when the Abbasid caliphate grew ever more unstable and religious discourse grew ever more loaded, was a time for careful speech and the precautionary limiting of certain topics to audiences that would understand them. It was at this point, as Massignon records, that the students of Maruf, Bishr al-Hafi, and

Muhasibi built the first separate Sufi meeting house on the west bank of the Tigris, in Shuniz.[57]

6. Disaster in Baghdad

The crisis came in the generation of Junayd, and grew not out of Muhasibi's controversy, but out of Sari's. Now that the Sufis had to an extent separated themselves out of general public life by creating their own institutions, though some of their transactions could be conducted more privately, it was all the easier for them to be focused upon as an entity. Junayd, "Peacock of the Knowers," Thawri legist and the pivotal Sufi master of the time, was well aware of the vulnerability of the community. Yet despite his sensitivity to what could and could not be openly discussed, the Baghdad School was eventually brought before the caliph al-Muwaffaq on charges of heresy dangerous to the public order.

The accusation, brought by one Ghulam al-Khalil in 272/885, had two principal parts. The first was one of sexual misconduct. According to Sarraj:

> Sumnun, a friend of Junayd, was called "the lover."
> He was handsome and talked with charm. It is related that
> a woman disciple of Sumnun's fell in love with him. When he
> knew that she loved him, he turned her out of his circle. This
> woman then went to al-Junayd and asked him: "What do
> you think of a man who was my way to God, but then God
> vanished and the man remained?" Junayd knew what she
> meant and did not answer her. The woman had wished to
> marry Sumnun, but, when he turned her out in a haughty
> way, she went to Ghulam al-Khalil, his adversary, saying:
> "These men," mentioning some names, "did not behave cor-
> rectly towards me." So Ghulam al-Khalil took up this and
> other complaints and took the case before the caliphate.[58]

The other charge was doctrinal. Ghulam al-Khalil held that love between God and man was impossible, that love was a human weakness rather than a divine attribute, and that to say "I love God and He loves me" was heresy (he also charged pantheism and promoting superstition).[59]

Junayd, known as a jurist, was not charged, but five members of the Baghdad School—Nuri, Abu Hamzah, Raqqam, Shahham and

Sumnun—were brought before the court. The caliph ruled against them and the executioner was called. In one of the most famous of all examples of magnanimity in the Sufi annals, Nuri, another student of Sari, another specialist in
love, volunteered himself to be beheaded first so that his brothers might have another few moments to live. This astounded the caliph, who halted the execution and referred the case back to the judge. On personal investigation, he acquitted them all." If the Sufis are heretics," Hujwiri reported him as commenting, "who in the world is a unitarian?"[60]

Though a narrow escape, it was a sobering indication of the state of things. Junayd grew even more circumspect. But some years later a young correspondent of his, twenty-five at the time of the Ghulam al-Khalil affair, would find he had no time for circumspection. This was Hallaj, perhaps the most celebrated and controversial of all Sufis, the quintessential devotee of love.

Though his story is widely known, and has been examined in painstaking detail in Massignon's masterwork, *The Passion of al-Hallaj*, I will give Hodgson's summary here:

> Aware of the horror which . . . talk of awareness of God aroused in the *Shariah*-minded, who wanted no emotive extravagance to intervene between a man and his daily duties, Junayd took great pains to avoid any scandal in his private conversations with and letters to the like-minded. One of his disciples, al-Hallaj, lost patience with such caution. Convinced that all people could and should open themselves up to the love of God, he wandered about the lands of Islamdom preaching among the common people the ideal of an immediate loving responsiveness to God's presence as being better than any amount of ritual or other external proprieties. His teaching about human nature and divine love was subtle as well as poetic-and he put it in poetry—but it was, above all, rash.When he began making disciples in high places in Baghdad, the authorities found reason to imprison him as a heretic. Eventually he was tried, condemned as having taught that a symbolic and spiritual fulfillment of the law was as good as the actual rites, crucified with his hands and feet cut off, quartered, and burned. It is said that in his agony he expressed his delight that he was suffering

so for God's sake, but acknowledged that his judges were as
right to condemn him, so as to safeguard the Community
life, as he was right to express paradoxes so as to proclaim
the love of God.[61]

Hallaj's practice "was founded on a method of interiorization of the
strictly followed Islamic rituals of worship,"[62] but his intentions were
far from understandable to many of lesser depth. The very dangers
Junayd guarded against, he courted. As Hallaj's determination to
"tear the veils" grew more and more manifest, the members of the
Baghdad school grew more and more horrified, and Junayd himself
ruled against him. But he persisted in a course that must have been
transparently bound for disaster-and not only for himself, but for all
the Sufis. The implications of his activities were substantial.
Schimmel writes:

> Aside from the subtle problems of mystical love,
> political and social problems were at stake. Hallaj was a
> friend of the chamberlain Nasr al- Qushuri, who favored bet-
> ter administration and juster taxation, dangerous ideas in a
> time when the caliph was almost powerless and the viziers,
> though all-powerful for a short period, changed frequently. .
> . . All the political factions were afraid that the effect on the
> people of a spiritual revival might have repercussions on the
> social organization and even on the political structure. The
> idea of converting the hearts of all Muslims and teaching
> them the secret of personal sanctification and not just of
> blind acceptance would certainly have been dangerous for a
> society whose religious and political leaders lived in a state
> of stagnation with neither the strength nor the intention to
> revitalize the Muslim Community.[63]

The time from Hallaj's imprisonment until his execution was a full
ten years. Junayd did not live to see the eventual fate of his former
student, for he died the same year that Hallaj was arrested, 299/912.
By the end of his life every single member of the Baghdad School had
been publicly accused of heresy, and sometimes of belief in reincarna-
tion and even atheism.[64] Sarraj notes that despite the general
acknowledgement of his intellectual and moral stature, his deep
knowledge and religious performance, Junayd himself was declared to

be an infidel.[65] His dying wish was to be buried beside Nuri. This was not carried out.[66] He spent his last breath in recitation of the Quran.[67]

Hallaj had prayed at the grave of Ahmad bin Hanbal, and when he was arrested the Hanbalis rioted in his support.[68] For them, at least, the most orthodox of the orthodox, his Islam had not been in question. They were a populist movement, and Hallaj had put his spirituality before the people. On his execution, the city of Taleqan in Khurasan revolted and proclaimed him Mahdi.[69] Eighty years later, the Syrian poet Maarri observed,[70] people in Baghdad would still stand on the banks of the Tigris, into which his ashes had been thrown, and wait for him to reappear.

Ten years after Hallaj's death, caliphal power began to collapse. By 333/945 the Buyids, three warrior brothers from the remote highlands of Daylam, had occupied the whole of the western Iranian domains, and then took the capital itself; the caliph was maintained as a figurehead. The Abbasid state ceased to exist.

II. After the Abbasids

1. Sunnism

The seeming tragedy of the early 4th/10th century had paradoxical effects. The collapse of the Abbasid state and the crisis of the Baghdad School were to result in a new and effective vehicle for Islam-an international Sunni culture.

From one perspective it is possible to say that the Islam of the *ahl al-sunnah wal-jamaah*—"the people of Tradition and Consensus"— derives directly from the original practice at Medina. From another perspective, it arose at the Abbasid revolution. And from still another, before the fill of the Abbasids it did not exist.

Watt points the issue: For the traditional Muslim scholar there is no problem; Islam has always been Sunnite, Sunnite Islam has always existed. That is true, of course, in the sense that the elements of Sunnism always existed; but it is also true that other elements existed contrary to Sunnism, and that it had not become clear and explicit that the good Muslim chose the Sunnite elements and interpretations and rejected the others.[1]

Part of the difficulty in defining Sunnism as an entity, as Hodgson observes, is that "Sunni" is a slippery term. In usage, it is roughly equivalent to "orthodox."[2] And what does orthodoxy mean? It can be understood as communal solidarity, or as common doctrine. It can also mean faithfulness to the original object of association. Each of these emphases will yield a somewhat different understanding.

In terms of solidarity, Sunnism first manifested itself at the beginning of Abbasid times in the decision to accept the government of the community, whatever its faults, for the sake of unity among Muslims. This decision placed the sheer existence of the community above the demand that it assume a special political form. By it the *ahl al-jamaah*, the consensus, became distinct from the Shia—and as the Shia came to power in the 4th/10th century, the cohesiveness of this consensus became important as never before.

In terms of dogma, Watt's special concern, Sunnism had formed implicitly by the fall of the empire—but explicitly not until more than a century and a half later. By around 340/950, as he says, ". . . the doctrines of the creed had assumed more or less their final form . . . . At the same time . . . the legal rites or schools had taken definite shape, the canon of Tradition had been formed, and there had been agreement about the text of the Quran."[3] Yet though all the principal doctrinal elements were present by the mid-tenth century, one crucial item was missing: There was as yet no generally recognized name for "Sunnites"; and there was still intense rivalry between certain legal and theological schools.[4]

Fundamental tolerance, which had been at the root of the first manifestation of Sunnism, was not yet universally accepted as the necessary basis of a common identity within the Sunnis.

The birth of a new unifying self -awareness required a kind of social shock. While the Abbasid framework existed to "stand in" for the unity of the community, aggressive contest of opinion could be afforded among those whose business was the theory of Islamic life. Through all the vigorous moral challenge from the inside, the Sunnis had remained identified with the empire. But without an active center, and threatened from without, the maintenance of social organization had to depend more and more on common dedication and principles. *Ijma,* the process of consensus, which had always been operative, now pressed strongly for both closure and tolerance. The Community had to become independent of the state. This did not happen overnight. It was in the late 4th/10th and the 5th/11th centuries that the importance of a working agreement became paramount, and the events of those hundred and fifty years brought this agreement into effect.

Thus at the beginning of the eleventh century it could be said merely that the other mainstream legal schools had come closer to the Hanafites and "there was some feeling of belonging together."[5] By its end, however, al-Pazdawi (d. 492/1099) could declare that the religion of the Sunnis was that of "the jurists, the textual scholars, the Sufiyya, and the Ashab al-Hadith. . . ."[6]

The age of this coalescence of Sunnism was the era of Qushayri, whose life (376-465/986-1072) fell across the central span of a period that was transitional in several respects.

In politics, it comprised the successive "guardianship" of Baghdad and the caliph by the Daylami Buyids (333-436/945- 1045), Shias, and the Turkish Seljuks (447-512/1055-1118), fervent Hanafis; and the heyday (358-487/969-1094) of their opponents, the Egyptian Fatimi vanguard of the Ismaili movement: the last glimmering of the old state ideal.

In theology, it stretched from the death of Ashari (935)—the ex-Mutazilite, converted by three dreams, who, dedicating himself to the spirit of Ahmad bin Hanbal, attempted to tame theology to the service of the Quran, and won the hatred of the Hanbalis for it—to the death of Ghazzali (d. 505/1111), Asharite theologian and Sufi popularizer, whose enormously influential synthesis removed both theology and Sufism from the realm of controversy.

In Sufism itself, it was the time between the death (in 309/922) of Hallaj, the people's mystic, and the birth (in 470/1077) of Abd-al-Qadir al-Jilani, patron saint of the most widely disseminated and popular of the Sufi orders.

In this era in all its dimensions doctrinal Sunnism—the systematization by consensus of Islamic law, thought, and religious practice—became the basis for a new Islamic social order. Sunni self-awareness was defined by the internal challenge of Shiism, while the Islamic solidarity at its heart was sharpened by external confrontations with India (the conquests of Mahmud of Ghazna, (389-421 /999-1030)), Byzantium (Anatolia opened to the Turkmen by the battle of Malazgirt, 463/1071), and Western Christendom (First Crusade, 489/1096). According to Hodgson, the new structure was firmly in place by the dawn of the 6th/12th century.[7]

> The new society was based neither on a state nor on regional sympathies. As it developed, an individual's identity as a Muslim began to take priority over all more limited

social identifications. A Muslim, whatever his origin, could take his place anywhere in the *dar al-islam* on the basis of his established position according to the *Shariah*, which prevailed irrespective of the local political-military power and reduced the shifting boundaries of the various states to insignificance.[8]

The older trend of opinion in Western Islamic studies[9] has been to see this transformation as "manifest decay."[10] The development of a static society and the predominance of a static formalist theology led to a decline in independent speculation and research. Yet the "static" quality perceived by such critics is deceptive. Even where formalism was most insistent, for instance in law, "there was often a pragmatic flexibility under the apparently rigid framework,"[11] as Gilsenan observed in a contemporary context. Though the Divine Law was a universal ideal constitution, no pattern of living was ever absolute, for one of the critical virtues to develop in the new society was the simultaneous existence of multiple viewpoints—"differences within the community are a mercy" (*ikhtilaf al-ummah rahmah*). And the supposed decline of independent intellectual enterprise is a flagrant misconception: certain fields receded, but others emerged, and much of the greatest Islamic literature was produced in the post-Abbasid era.

Viewed from the perspective of the Sassanian imperial inheritance, the period was undoubtedly one of decline. The absolutism had failed; government was decentralized, rudimentary, and in the hands of shifting military regimes. Yet as Hodgson points out, if looked at in terms of other underlying social ideals (the traditions of prophetic monotheism), the time "would show not a breakdown but rather a culmination":[12]

> The result . . . was the attrition of the pre-Islamic cultural tradition and the reconstitution of not just the empire but the whole society on more openly structured, more egalitarian and contractual, bases, appealing to Islam for legitimation.[13] The living *Sunnah* of the early community had been encapsulated in *hadiths*; the *hadiths*, through the process of *ijma*, had formed the foundation of an articulated, comprehensive moral and social rule; this rule, now mature enough to stand on its own, became again the basis of the living *Sunnah*. But the social and doctrinal orthodoxy

that now took hold drew their meaning from the other aspect of orthodoxy: faithfulness to the original object. And it was here that Sunnism faced its greatest test.

2. The Shiah: Radical Alternatives

From the Umayyad era on through the Abbasid period and after, opposition to the general consensus of the Islamic community had found its most widespread and potent form in Shiism. Shiism, which Hodgson calls "the piety of protest,"[14] was based on the fundamental presupposition that the dominant society had gone astray; that the truth had been lost to all but an elect remnant, and that these, by divinely ordained historical imperative, would inherit the earth at the end of time, when the reign of true justice would finally manifest. It thus became the umbrella for a vast amount of social disaffection of various kinds, from moderate to revolutionary.

The truth that was to underlie the perfect social order was conceived as a secret teaching, a special science passed from the Prophet to Ali and his line, either in doctrine or in a special quality of essence. This truth was, or would be, shared out among the faithful according to their ability to receive it-according to their devotion to the Imam, the only true teacher.

Shiism thus denied legitimacy of political and religious leadership to any but the proper divinely empowered descendant of Ali. The infallibility and necessity of this Imam was of prime doctrinal importance, guaranteeing as it did the rightness of the protesting minority. The numerous Shii factions split over who the Imam was—that is, just what view had actually received the sanction of divine guidance. All of them, however, refused to grant authenticity to Traditions or the Divine Law reasoning that was not originated by the elect line of Imams—-though Shii Traditions and Divine Law were in substance almost identical to those they condemned.[15] Likewise the basic theology underlying the many variations of Shii esoteric teaching was Mutazilite in all but name. That the Shias could not be reconciled with the larger body of Muslims was far less a matter of religious substance than one of political stance: the determination to exclude rather than include.

On ideological grounds the Shii factions defined themselves as outside the majority, and in the days of the Abbasids the majority was identified with the economic and political structure of the state. This structure was crumbling long before Baghdad fell and the caliph was reduced to being the client of tribesmen. The late 3rd/9th and the 4th/10th century had seen increasing decentralization as control was lost both over the outlying provinces and over the caliph's own Turkish Praetorian Guard, while the life of the people both inside and outside of the capital grew precarious. In this atmosphere millenarian hopes flourished. The Ismailis—who had long recruited through a highly efficient secret apparatus based on levels of initiation—found their moment.

3. The Fatimids

In the midst of the general fragmentation, Hodgson notes, One movement was an exception, that of the Ismailis. It did presuppose an all-Islamic framework, but not on the basis of the generally recognized leaders of Muslim piety. It proposed to substitute at once a new political and a new religious elite, and based itself, to this end, on malcontents of any class.[16]

The effects of this movement included the Qarmathian social rebellion in the deserts of Iraq, which the caliph had put down with difficulty; the foundation of the remarkable communistic republic of Qarmathians in Bahrayn, whose theft of the Black Stone from the Kabah in 318/930 was the *coup de grace* to the spiritual legitimacy of the empire;[17] and the establishment of the Fatimid anti-caliphate in North Africa. This last, gaining power in Egypt in 969, after the Abbasid collapse, was to have considerable impact throughout the era of Qushayri.

The challenge of the Shiah was double-sided. On the surface, it directly attacked the legitimacy, or even the welfare, of the consensus. But more subtly, it provoked violent reaction that, if not subdued by conscious affirmation of principle, might prove far more damaging than any outward opponent.

Sufism, according to Qushayri, essentially left Egypt with the death of Junayd's contemporary Abu Bakr Ahmad al- Zaqqaq.[18] Instead, under the influence of the Fatimids symbolic, mythological, and occult thought dominated a whole body of city intelligentsia, the Cairenes, and was extended outward through the propagation into all the Islamic lands.

This attitude, proposing itself as true Muslim spirituality and so far from the Clan of old Medina, was energetically spread in the eleventh century.

4. A Moderate Imami Regime in Baghdad

Ironically, with the accession of the Buyids, Imami Shias, in Baghdad, the local power of Shiism was substantially defused. With the central authority broken, "opposition" Shiism made little sense,[19] and the complex internal politics in which the Baghdad Shiah had taken part were disrupted.[20]

In Abbasid Baghdad Shiism was the long-established doctrine of a stratum of merchants, bureaucrats, and intellectuals[21] whose Shii identification may have traced back to Umayyad times and the ancient core community of Kufa.[22] These, accepting the inevitability of a wicked world, for perhaps with expressly cynical motivations[23] had largely reconcile their convictions with the advantages of service to the regime. They formed a powerful bloc in the caliphal administration. Their financial position may have helped motivate the riots that were periodically directed against them.[24]

In theology they, like the Ismailis, were essentially Mutazilite, giving primacy to a rational model of God. Also like the Ismailis, they rejected non-Shii sources of religious knowledge. In the midst of Ismaili revolutions their politics had been extremely delicate, and their doctrine was hated by the mainstream religious scholars, *ahl al-hadith* and Divine Law lawyers alike. And this likely suited them well, for even the moderate Shii mystique was founded on being an oppressed minority, the rejected guardians of the truth.

In 201/817 al-Mamun, who would later originate the Mutazilite inquisition, had been engaged in a civil war. In an attempt to solidify his base of power and undercut provincial opposition, he had designated the eighth Imam of the Shias, Ali al-Rida, as his heir to the caliphate. Riots broke out all over Baghdad and throughout Iraq. Ali al-Rida died the following year, and Mamun retrieved the situation, but from that point on the penetration of Shias into positions of power became an obsession in the capital.[25]

This then was the situation when the Abbasid collapse brought a Shii dynasty to power in Baghdad. The Buyids, however, were warriors, and neither administrators nor ideologues. They installed their own caliph and maintained him and his household as a defense against a general revolt.[26] They allowed what was left of the old imperial territory to fall into a family consortium of smaller realms (to be attacked and finally lost piecemeal), but did not attempt to rearrange the social structure of their predominantly non-Shii domains. They attempted no interference with the Divine Law they found in force—a major sign of the degree of independent authority and cohesion it had developed by this time.[27] An effort-which failed-was even made to classify Imami Shiism as simply an alternative, "Jafari," school of jurisprudence.[28] The caliph was also permitted to patronize non-Shii learning, which he did "in a dogmatically narrow way."[29]

The Buyids did, however, impart a Shii devotional tone to public life. They instituted public Shii festivals and endowed a Shii school; Shii intellectuals, already well-established in Baghdad, prospered; all forms of speculation thrived.

Despite this, as Hodgson summarizes, "external conditions for intellectual life continued not very dissimilar to those under the High Caliphate."[30] But Baghdad, once the hub of empire, was no longer the focus of the Islamic world.

The position of the Baghdad Sufis during this critical interval has not been well researched.

In the early stages, Shiism and Sufism had been intertwined, and their complex interrelations have not been adequately studied. Syria in the 2nd/8th century had held mystical communities drawing their guidance from Kufa, the epicenter of Shiism, as well as those emanating from Basra,[31] and the first individual actually to be named al-Sufi was a Kufan, Abu Hashim.[32] The Quranic commentary of the sixth imam, Jafar al-Sadiq, was read and highly valued in Sufi circles,[33] and Jafar himself is cited in a number of later spiritual chains of transmission. Ali al-Rida, Mamun's heir-designate, was credited with having brought the teacher of Sari, Maruf al-Karkhi, from Manicheanism to Islam.[34] The general attachment of the Sufis to the family of Ali is and was well-known.

5. Khurasan

"Syria is the home of chivalry, Iraq of eloquence,
and Khurasan of sincerity"
—Junayd (d. 299/912)[35]

"Khurasan is the land whose product is saints."
—Abu Yazid al-Bistami (d. 260/874)[36]

Khurasan, home of both a native Iranian population and a large stratum of Arab settlers dating back to the earliest days of the Islamic conquest, had originally been instrumental in bringing the Abbasids to power. After the initial religious expectations accompanying the change of dynasty had been disappointed, it had harbored a millenarian resistance centered around the figure of Abu Muslim, the charismatic propagandist who had raised the people in support of the Abbasids, only to be executed afterwards as a threat to the regime. The revolt was put down by 163/780, and the region settled into the status of a province of the empire. It existed in a kind of counterpoint to Baghdad, and continued to provide some of the finest soldiers: Mamun's faction at the time of the Abbasid civil war had been based there, and the consequent prestige of the Khurasanis greatly annoyed the capital.[37]

This prestige led to the semi-independent and then fully independent governorship of the region under a succession of military families, who functioned autonomously but continued to acknowledge the caliph. The last of these to come to power before the collapse of the empire was the Samanids, who governed Khurasan through three quarters of the tenth century; Hodgson calls them "The most loyal or at least respectful to the caliphate of all the new powers that were arising."[38] Their importance was their preservation of the old social and administrative patterns,[39] and very likely something of the old spirit, despite the disappearance of the empire.

In their time the Turkish influx into the central Islamic lands was underway; Turkish cohesiveness and military prowess would soon make Turks the rulers of most of the fragments of the empire. By 3561916 a Turkish slave garrison in the Afghan hills gained independence from Samani control-much as the predecessors of the Samanids themselves had from the caliphs-and assumed power in Khurasan. These were the Ghaznavids. During their reign Qushayri was born. When he was a child of eleven the second Ghaznavid ruler reached the throne-the famous conqueror and Sunni zealot Mahmud of Ghazna, who opened the Indian plains to Islam as well as expanding his power westward in Iran and persecuting Shias at Rayy.[40] His court was a celebrated center of patronage, but his son and successor Masud lost the support of Khurasani gentry whose lands he could not protect from the depredations of oncoming Turkish tribes. The gentry then negotiated on their own, and in 428/1037—Qushayri was 51—rulership of Khurasan passed to the nomad aristocracy the Seljuks. These Seljuks were to have an important role in the consolidation of Sunnism and the growth of Sufism.

Khurasan had early developed a distinctive spiritual tone that eventually focused as a school of Sufism. The views and approaches of the Khurasan School often differed from those of the school in Baghdad, with whom the Khurasanis were in touch.

Its first stages are hard to trace. Hasan al-Basri had served as secretary to the governor there in Umayyad times, but whether he had a circle, and if his influence survived the troubles following the Abbasid revolution, has not been established, though he is often credited in a general way with the ultimate origin of the school. Within fifty years or so of his time arose the legendary Ibrahim bin Adham (c. 99 166/718-782), a prince of Balkh who resigned his state to become a wandering ascetic. His association with Sufyan al-Thawri may have put him in touch with Jafar al-Sadiq,[41] whose commentary on the Quran the Sufis used; in any case, he stayed awhile in the Shii center of Kufa, sitting with the great Doctor of the law Abu Hanifah, before leaving to found a community in the Syrian desert (where the outposts off the Basra circle were also established).[42]

Following the time of Ibrahim and Sufyan names of famous Sufis begin to cluster around Khurasan, particularly the cities of Nishapur and Balkh—Shaqiq, Fudayl, Shah Shuja, Hatim al-Asamm, Hamdun al-Qassar—and the special attitudes of the school became known: ascetic discipline as a tool to educate the ego out of arrogance; the "blameworthy" (*malamati*) technique of "courting blame" in order to develop indifference to human appreciation or the lack thereof; poverty, culturing awareness of the absolute need of God. This focus on self-purification led Junayd to call the Khurasan School "the people of the heart."[43] In the generation that saw Sari al-Saqati in Baghdad, the old Khurasani approach produced its crowning example in Abu Yazid al-Bistami (d. 260/874), the supreme embodiment of utter unmitigated thirst for God, the "spiritual drunkenness" against which Junayd and the Baghdad school set their "sobriety." In a famous anecdote, Abu Yazid received a letter from another Khurasanian Sufi, Yahya bin Muadh (d. 257/871), who wrote: "I am intoxicated from having drunk so deeply of the cup of His love."—Abu Yazid wrote to him in reply: "Someone else has drunk up the seas of heaven and earth, but his thirst is not yet slaked; his tongue is hanging out and he is crying, 'Is there any more'?"[44]

While Abu Yazid became famous to the later Islamic world for his depth, Yahya bin Muadh's dimension was breadth. He took a course out of line with the direction of the Khurasan School of his time, but one that was to bear substantial fruit a few generations later: he became a public preacher. "He was the first of the Shaykhs of this sect," commented Hujwiri, "after the Orthodox Caliphs, to mount the pulpit."[45] Massignon notes that in this period, when the Sufis were drawn in closely to themselves, Yahya appears to have been the only one to hold open sessions for cultured people.[46] He also discoursed in the Karramiyyah, the school of a sect related to both the Sufis and the *ahl al-hadith* that had devoted itself to popular spiritual teaching in Khurasan.[47]

His themes were gentler than those of the rigorous Khurasan School—he spoke constantly about hope, God's love of Creation, and His forgiveness, principles that could be cultivated at the level of ordinary life—and it would seem this was not entirely approved by his mystical peers. Hujwiri records that "Yahya held the doctrine that wealth is superior to poverty" and follows it by a story of how he was robbed of a hundred thousand dirhems given him by the people of Balkh.[48] He also relates that Shah Shuja, of the "old school," temporarily refused to accept one of Yahya's former students, saying, "You have been nursed . . . in the doctrine of hope on which Yahya takes his stand. No one who has imbibed this doctrine can tread the path of purgation, because a mechanical belief in hope produces indolence."[49] Yet other Sufis accounted him a saint,[50] and significantly, Hujwiri records, "He was always honored and held in respect by the people."[51]

It was the temporarily rejected student of Yahya, Abu Uthman al-Hiri (d.297/910), who brought the teaching tradition in Khurasan to a second phase. He had had three masters: Yahya, Shah Shuja, and finally the extremely venerable Abu Hafs al-Haddad, accounted by the Baghdadis "the Grand Shaykh of Khurasan";[52] he also studied with the Baghdad School, including Junayd, and managed to unite all of this in a striking synthesis: says Hujwiri, "No Shaykh ever derived as much spiritual advantage from his directors as he did."[53] Though more rigorous than Yahya, he made himself generally available to the people: the Nishapuris established him in a mosque to publicly teach Sufism,[54] and he was one of the very first to set up a strict educational system for students.[55] He was in fact credited with the solid establishment of Sufism in Nishapur and Khurasan;[56] he set in motion those forces that would produce the first embryonic Sufi orders in the generation of Qushayri.

Hallaj had also preached publicly in Khurasan, and his influence must have helped to increase the popular interest in Sufism there.

But as had happened in the days of Abu Muslim, his charismatic figure took on mythological dimensions. The revolt at Taleqan, near
Balkh, was based on the conviction that Halls could not be killed; the
Abbasids sent his head on display to convince the rebels otherwise.[57]
Yet a number of his students more familiar with the human person of
their master also moved to Khurasan to escape the persecutions in
Baghdad[58] and continued his teaching in secret. All that we know of
what he actually taught derives from manuscripts that were secretly
preserved there.[59]

Though he remained controversial, Hallaj was more favorably
viewed in Khurasan than he was in post-Abbasid Baghdad. He had
been perhaps the first to attempt to preach Islam on a large scale to
the Turks and had met Turkish amirs in the region,[60] and it was now
Turks who were ruling Khurasan.

In contrast to the Buyids, the Turkish Khurasani regimes favored
the Sufis.[61] A disciplined tradition had existed in the region since
early days; a popular base had begun to form under the influence of
Yahya, Abu Uthman al-Hiri, and finally Hallaj; the political pressure
had sent many heirs of the Baghdad School into the region as well. By
Qushayri's time, Khurasan was the center of the Sufi world. His contemporary, Hujwiri, wrote:

> It would be difficult to mention all the Shaykhs of
> Khurasan. I have met three hundred in that province alone
> who had such mystical endowments that a single man of
> them would have been enough for the whole world. This is
> due to the fact that the sun of love and the fortune of the Sufi
> Path is in the ascendant in Khurasan.[62]

Not coincidentally, the new Islamic society would also take
form in Khurasan.

III. The Object of the *Risalah*

1. Qushayri's Spiritual Environment

Abd-al-Karim bin Hawazin al-Qushayri Abd al-Malik bin Talha
Abu-l-Qasim al-Qushayri[1] was born in the town of Ustuva near
Nishapur in July AD 986 (AH Rabi-l-Awwal 376, ten years after the

Ghaznavids won the rulership of Khurasan. His *nisbah* derived from Qushayr, one of the Arab tribes who settled in Khurasan after the first conquests. Through his mother he was also related to the important Arab tribe of Sulaym, and his mother's brothers were local landlords. He was, therefore, born into the mixed Arab and old Iranian aristocracy known as the *buyutat*, who in Nishapur "were very preoccupied with Islamic solidarity and its great intellectual activity."[2]

As a child he received a thorough Arabic literary education which included memorization of the Quran as a matter of course. He was known not only for his beautiful writing in poetry and prose but also for his courage as a rider and a swordsman. His father died when he was still quite young. He inherited a village and from the income of that village he moved into Nishapur, where he studied mathematics with the hope of a job in the Ghaznavid financial administration. Mahmud of Ghaznah had only been in power a few years.

Nishapur was a city just coming into its own as "the capital of the East and even the center of Sunni Islam."[3] Its intellectual life was now glorified by Ghaznavid military exploits. Mahmud made Sunnism his banner, and his Indian conquests in its name gained him enormous prestige. A Turk himself, his patronage was instrumental in bringing Persian language and culture to a point where it would soon be of international importance. The *Shahnamah* (*Book of Kings*), the foundation of Persian literature, was written during his reign.

Balkh had been the intellectually dominant city in the Samanid period, but Nishapur's influence had been growing among both legal and theological scholars and Sufis for perhaps fifty years.[4] Hallaj had preached there and been well received.[5]

Some years before Qushayri's birth in AD 970/AH 359, the Hallajians of the city had split with those of Bukhara by abandoning an "incarnationist" (*hululi*)[6] interpretation of his teaching[6] for a more centrist one. This view was very compatible with the Ashari theology which also found a home in Nishapur. In the days of Hallaj, the city's younger followers of the Traditions (*Hadith*) had been less conservative than those in Baghdad[7] and had accepted intellectual arguments parallel to those of Muhasibi. This trend, though persecuted at first, eventually led to Asharism finding a firm position in Khurasani intellectual life and to Ashari-trained Sufis becoming the inheritors of Hallaj.

Asharism was basically "a rational defense of a non-rationalistic kerygmatic position."[8] It logically supported many difficult Quran and

Hadith statements concerning the attributes of God, divine omnipotence, and other thorny topics by adopting a very subtle and seemingly counter-intuitive model of the universe. This model first contested the reliability of sense perception as an ultimate criterion. Next, by tracing all secondary causes back to the First Cause, it denied the secondaries true causality, seeing them instead as means for the manifestation of the effects of the First Cause, which alone was genuinely active. The obvious uniformities visible in nature, then, were not the result of independent and unbreakable "natural laws," but instead were the traces left by the habitual action of the First Cause itself. This action, being a free creative adaptation unlimited by any law higher than itself, could be altered. Hence, miracles were possible. Finally, the action of the First Cause was not distanced from its effect, the universe, by any chain of intermediaries, but each instant, each event, was an immediate direct creation.[9]

Though Asharite theologians came in the course of time to be more and more bound up with the niceties of logical argumentation and less and less concerned with substance, the basic view itself was hadith-derived and congenial to the Sufis. According to Wensinck, a typical Asharite creed stated: Faith is believing in God and His Messengers in accordance with what Tradition reports concerning them, and this belief is not sound unless it rests on knowledge (*marifah*) of God.[10]

While thoroughgoing theologians may have held this know-ledge to be the result of theology, Asharite Sufis took it rather another way. By chance, it appears, while pursuing his financial studies in Nishapur, young Qushayri found himself at one of the sessions of just such an Asharite Sufi, Abu Ali al-Hasan bin Muhammad al-Daqqaq. Abu Ali, according to Hujwiri, was "the leading authority in his department (of science) and had no rival among his contemporaries. He was lucid in exposition and eloquent in speech as regards the revelation of the way to God."[11]

Under the impact of that lucid and eloquent discourse, Qushayri changed his plans and attached himself to the shaykh as a Sufi novice. Abu Ali al-Hasan bin Muhammad al-Daqqaq had been the student of the master-teacher Nasrabadhi. Nasrabadhi himself, "like a king in Nishapur, save that the glory of kings is of this world,"[12] had sat with Shibli (Junayd's student and perhaps Hallaj's sincerest friend). Through him the writings of Hallaj had been carefully preserved.[13] Abu Ali received these influences and passed them on to his student, four generations from the time of Abu Uthman al-Hiri and Junayd.

The shaykh took a special interest in Qushayri. He did not, however, call him out of worldly life but had him intensively educated as a scholar. On Daqqaq's advice, Qushayri began to read jurisprudence with Abu Bakr Muhammad bin al-Hasan bin Tusi, then Asharite theology with the famous Abu Bakr Muhammad bin al-Hasan bin Furak (d. AD 1015/AH 406), and then jurisprudence, again on an advanced level of independent reading and questioning with Abu Ishaq al-Isfarayani (d. AD 1027/AH 417). Daqqaq undoubtedly occupied himself personally with the young man's inner education. When all seemed at a satisfactory level, he married Qushayri to his daughter, Fatimah, who was herself independently known as a scholar, a Sufi, and a transmitter of Traditions.[14]

On the death of Abu Ali al-Daqqaq (in either AD 1021/AH 412 or possibly AD 1014/AH 405), Qushayri sat briefly with the master of Daqqaq's master, Abu Abd-al-Rahman al-Sulami (d. AD 1021) who was then about eighty-five years old. If Daqqaq formed Qushayri as a teacher, Sulami formed him as a writer.

Sulami was a famous author. Among other works, he had composed the first comprehensive biographical history of Sufism, originally written in two volumes. The first volume, on the years between the Prophet and the generation of Sari al-Saqati, has been lost.[15] The second volume, the *Tabaqat al-sufiyah* (*Grades of Sufis*), remains and has been extremely influential. An authoritative compilation of Sufi lives, it is distinguished by the careful attention it gives to transmission (*isnad*) documentation.[16] Qushayri quotes Sulami often in the *Risalah*.

Sulami was the product of a change in policy that had resulted from the Baghdad disaster. Schimmel observes, "The case of Hallaj had confronted the Sufis with the danger of persecution, and even without his tragic death one might well have felt that the path had to be made accessible to people who could never reach the abysses of mystical experience Hallaj had reached, or who could not be compared in sobriety to Junayd, in burning love to Nuri, or in paradoxical speech to Shibli. It was left to men like Ibn Khafif of Shiraz (d. AD 982, at about 100 years of age) and similar mystics to teach the path, to make it understandable—at least in part—to the intellectuals, and to set an example to larger groups of the faithful."[17]

Ibn Khafif, Asharite, ascetic, and testifier to the truth of Hallaj, was an associate of all the old masters of the Baghdad School. He became the teacher of Abu Nasr al-Tusi al-Sarraj (d. AD 988/AH

378),[18] author of the first of the Sufi "manuals," *Kitab al-lumah li-l tasawwuf* (*Glimmers of Sufism*)." Both Sarraj[19] and Ibn Khafif himself[20] had been teachers of Sulami.

Qushayri, heir to all the major forces in Sufism in his time, was gradually "elevated to the position of the greatest teacher of Sufism not only in the city of Nishapur, but in all of Khurasan."[21]

2. Qushayri and the Seljuks

When Qushayri was fifty-one and at the height of his maturity and influence (he had already written his Great Commentary on the Quran, *al-Tafsir al-kabir lataif al-isharat bi tafsir al-quran*[22]), Toghril Bey, leader of the Seljuks, first captured the city of Nishapur. He held the city a year, lost it again to the Ghaznavid Masud, then recovered it two years later, in AD 1040/AH 432, when his control of all of Khurasan became firm.

The Seljuks were already Muslim and fervently Hanafi when they came to power. They also (under an influence dating perhaps from the days of Hallaj) favored the Sufis. This tendency did not in itself, however, prevent them from intolerance and especially fierce anti-Shiism. In this they continued the attitude of the Ghaznavids. The great Seljuk vizier, Nizam al-Mulk, would later write, "In the days of Mahmud, Masud, Toghril Bey, and Arp-Arslan (may God have mercy upon them) no Zoroastrian or Jew or Rafidi would have had the audacity to appear in a public place or to present himself before a great man. Those who administered the affairs of the Turks were all professional civil servants and secretaries from Khurasan who belonged to the orthodox Hanafi or Shafii sects. The heretics of Iraq were never admitted as secretaries and tax collectors. In   fact, the Turks never used to employ them at all. They said, 'These men are of the same religion as the Dailamites [Buyids] and their supporters. If they get a firm footing they will injure the interests of the Turks and cause distress to the Muslims. It is better that enemies should not be in our midst.'" Consequently they lived free from disaster.[23]

Such an attitude was certainly understandable when the Sunnis felt threatened by fragmentation on every side and needed, at all costs, to maintain themselves as a coherent unit. It was, in fact, very politically effective. Yet it activated the shadow side of consensus, the maintenance of conformity by force. Mahmud had vented his wrath on the Shias of Rayy. Nizam al-Mulk records that even in the intellectual life of Nishapur, in many ways a far more liberal city than for instance Baghdad, Hanafi and Shafii legal scholars joined to prevent other opinions from being heard.[24] Hodgson makes such motivations clear, ". . . if the safety and good order of society depended on the strength and coherence of the religious community, then everything else must, at need, be sacrificed to this. Even pity for an honest but misguided man should not divert one from one's duty to prevent him from corrupting society with his misguided ideas."

In such an atmosphere even personally magnanimous men, able to resist the impulse to protect their own intellectual security by silencing a threatening voice, might become persecutors. For they might feel it their duty to support intolerance for the sake of others who could not endure the threat so easily.[25]

Toghril Bey was one such personally magnanimous man who felt it his duty to protect the orthodox Sunnis. The dangerous element brought to his attention was not the Sufis per se, as had been the case in the Baghdad disaster. It was the Asharites.

Amid al-Mulk al-Kunduri, Toghril Bey's vizier, on the advice of the head of Nishapur's Shafii jurists, received permission from his prince to have the Shia and instigators of innovation publicly cursed from the *minbar*s of the mosques of Nishapur. He then had this permission extended to Abul-Hasan al-Ashari.

This was a provocative move as the Asharites were numerous and well established in the city, especially among the Shafiis. Quite possibly some internal Shafii power struggle was involved. The curse was an extension of the cursing of the Shia, and given the predominance of the surrounding Shia regimes, the action has a resounding political ring: it as much as called the Asharis agents of subversion. The connection was probably taken to be the theologians, for the Shia sect at that time was essentially Mutazilite. The old argument against theology as innovation reappeared.

Yet what underlay this argument was now different. In Ahmad bin Hanbal's time, combating theology had involved, on the one hand, resisting the power of an absolutist state and, on the other, defending the supremacy of revelation. Now, the transcendence of revelation was not in question. It was the state itself that was attacking theology. A coercive manipulation of Sunnism was being attempted, and this the Sufis, and many others, could not accept.

Qushayri responded to this state of affairs. As Hasan al-Basri had done centuries before, he assumed the duty of admonition, "commanding the right and forbidding the wrong." In AD 1044/AH 436 he

passed an edict arguing that Ashari was a great leader of the followers of the Traditions whose creed was Sunni and entirely congruent
with the faith of the Sunnis. He and his followers could not be cursed.
Still pressure on the Asharis continued and in AD 1054/AH 446 or a
little earlier, Qushayri wrote a long letter addressed to all the scholars of the Islamic world entitled "Complaint of the People of the
Sunnah with Reports of the Trials That Have Afflicted Them." Within
a short while the situation appeared threatening to the regime and
the crackdown came. Kunduri received an order from Toghril Bey to
have several of the leading scholars of Nishapur arrested and deport-
ed. The names specified were al-Rais al-Furati, Abu Sahl bin al-
Muwaffaq (who had succeeded to the leadership of the Shafiis and was
well-known at court), Juwayni (the later theological teacher of
Ghazzali), and Qushayri. Juwayni fled to Makkah whence he would
attain wide renown. Qushayri and Furati were arrested and imprisoned in the old citadel of Nishapur.

They did not stay there long. Abu Sahl, who had been out of
Nishapur when the arrest order arrived from Rayy, put his influence
to work. He gathered a body of men. With them, he demanded Furati
and Qushayri from the governor of the city. When their release was
not forthcoming, he entered Nishapur, dispersed the governor's soldiers by force of arms, and rescued the prisoners. In a surprising gesture—seemingly for the sake of the unity of the Sunnis—he then proceeded to Rayy and surrendered himself to Toghril Bey.

Qushayri could not stay in Nishapur. He went on the pilgrimage.
He took the Baghdad road and apparently reached the old capital just
after the Buyids finally lost it. According to Ates, Khatib al-Baghdadi's
contemporary history places him in Baghdad in AD 1056/AH 448. The
triumphant Toghril Bey had been invited into Baghdad as protector of
the caliph in AD 1055/AH 447.

The current caliph was al-Qaim bi-Amrillah (AD 1031-75/AH 422-
467). Under the Buyids, the caliphate had worked at developing what
little power was left to it by playing upon its moral authority as the
symbolic center of the Sunni community. The residual prestige of the
office was still strong and the Seljuks, as its liberators from the Shias,
received unprecedented honor and acceptance in the Islamic world. A
new political theory was introduced—namely, Mawardi, AD 1058/AH
450), whereby the caliph was seen as the source of legitimacy of the
military regimes that served as his executive lieutenants (and held
the actual power).

This retrieval of the caliphate's spiritual existence by giving temporal power to the Turks had been engineered by al-Qaim's vizier, Ali bin al-Muslimah. At his investiture in 437/1046—still under the Buyids—this vizier had stopped the official procession to pray at the site of Hallaj's martyrdom.[26] This was the first public official recognition of the center of so much controversy. It marked a change of feeling in the caliphal court.

Thus when Qushayri arrived in the city, he found al-Qaim well-disposed. Though Toghril Bey was master of Baghdad, the caliph stubbornly maintained his local authority. It was Toghril Bey's vizier—the persecutor of the Asharis, Kunduri—who was instrumental in keeping the caliph subordinate to the Turks.[27] Those fleeing from Kunduri's action were good candidates for caliphal protection. Al-Qaim built Qushayri a school where he received a wide audience. According to Massignon, it was in Baghdad that he published the *Risalah*, which had been written in AD 1046/AH 437, at the beginning of the persecutions.[28]

Qushayri apparently stayed in Baghdad about seven years—through the temporary Fatimid seizure of the capital in AD 1058/AH 450 and its recapture a year later[29]—not completing his pilgrimage until AD 1063/AH 455.[30] While he was in Makkah, some 400 religious judges and scholars arrived, also escaping from the persecution. They were in turmoil as to their future. It is said that Qushayri received a mystical insight that Kunduri would die and advised them to go home. He himself started back on the Baghdad road. That same year Toghril Bey died and Alp Arslan came to the throne. He promptly (AD 1064/AH 456) had Kunduri executed. The great Nizam al-Mulk became vizier.

Qushayri lived eight peaceful years in Nishapur, writing and transmitting hadiths. Some twenty works are credited to him. Fatimah, who lived on until 481/1088[31] had borne him six sons, all called Qushayri like their father. One became a scholar (as did a grandson). Another wrote of the Sufis. A student of his, Shaykh al-Shuyukh Abu Ali al-Farmadi (who sat with several other important teachers of the time) later was the master of Ghazzali.[32] He died on 31 December AD 1072/16 Rabi I AH 465. The tomb of his shaykh and father-in-law, Abu Ali al-Daqqaq, was in his traditional school (*madrasah*), and he was buried there. His *Risalah*—written two years before the "*Complaint*" as an affirmation of Islamic spirituality in the midst of political abuse—became the most widely disseminated handbook of Sufism in the Islamic world.[33]

3. The Manuals

Massignon, listing futile early efforts toward Islamic universalization, includes the Sufis. "The third attempt was that of the Sufis, those ascetics who from Muhasibi to Hallaj developed through self-examination and an interiorization of the acts of worship, a method of guidance capable of morally purifying the life of society by spreading recollection and communal centers of spiritual and fraternal mutual aid. This attempt collapsed too, since it was caught in a vise between the large banking capitalism of the Shiite businessmen and the urban bedouin communism of the Ismaili revolutionaries, both the declared enemies of the universal Sunni caliphate."[34]

While this analysis is probably correct, what it actually describes is the political dimensions of the Baghdad disaster. The Sufis, as has been shown, existed as such well before Muhasibi, are still in existence, and were pivotally active in the generations after Hallaj. Their "attempt," rather than collapsing, decentralized. After the disaster and the fall of the Abbasids, Sufi meeting-houses (*khanqah*), began to be founded in numbers throughout Iraq, Transoxania, and, as already discussed, Khurasan.[35] In them the life of "spiritual and fraternal mutual aid" was maintained. From them, it would spread.

As has also been shown, even before Hallaj action began to be taken by Yahya bin Muadh and Abu Uthman al-Hiri in Khurasan to draw the general populace into connection with the Sufi life. The Karrami "evangelists" in the same region widened the base of interest. One impact of Hallaj was to make the nature of sincerity a popular issue.

In the AD 10th/AH 4th century, paper, which previously had been an expensive Chinese import, began to be manufactured in Iraq, Syria, Egypt, and even Arabia.[36] Further, by the AD 11th/AH 8th century Arabic had become the common tongue of culture and exchange from Spain to Persia, superseding the old local languages.[37] Wide dissemination of written work began to become practical.

The old AD 9th/AH 3rd century mosque curriculum started to be organized and recorded in books. A new science, the science of Sufism or *ilm al-tasawwuf*, took form. Pedersen describes it in his introduction to Sulami's *Tabaqat*.[38]

The science of Sufism served to aid Sufi aspirants in testing the soundness of their practice and their state. Its criteria and comparisons help deflate fantasies of attainment that vitiate moral and spiritual character, while indicating directions for real development. This approach, made accessible in written form, can be valuable not just for geniuses of the spirit, but for all those who take their inner integrity seriously. Qushayri received from Sulami the importance of the transmission of this knowledge.

Sulami's teacher, Sarraj (d. AD 988/AH 378), had belonged to the generation in which this type of transmission began to be undertaken by the so-called "manual writers." Among his contemporaries were Kalabadhi (d. c. AD 990/AH 380), author of the *Kitab al- taarruf li madhhab ahl al-tasawwuf* (Book of Familiarization with Sufi Doctrine), and Abu Talib al-Makki (d. AD 996), who produced the comprehensive *Qut al-qulub* (Food of Hearts). Sulami's *Tabaqat* found a companion-piece in the ten-volume compilation of Abu Nuaym al-Isfahani (d. AD 1037/AH 428), *Hilyat al-awliya* (*Ornament of Saints*). Qushayri's fellow in the undertaking was Hujwiri of Lahore (d. AD 1074/AH 466), whose *Kashf al-Mahjub*, (*Unveiling of the Hidden*), has often been quoted here.

The manuals emerged to argue for what Islamic spirituality was intended to be. They based their authority on the Quran and *Hadith*, proof-texts for the transmission of the unitary and non-discursive attitude of Madinah. It was precisely this that the Sufis claimed to be preserving. The manual writers did not see themselves as the mouthpiece of a sect but as guardians of the heart of the whole Islamic enterprise. This is made particularly explicit by the inclusion in several of the manuals[39] of many of the Companions, the four rightly-guided caliphs, the Shia Imams, and the four founders of Sunni law among the founders of the Sufis.

The writers on the science of Sufism are particularly concerned to show the unbreakable relationship that must exist between the outward manifestation of form and the inward realization of being in order for religion to be real. Hujwiri comments, "Two parties err in this matter: firstly, the formal theologians, who assert that there is no distinction between *Shariah* (law) and *Haqiqah* (truth), since the Law is the Truth and the Truth is the Law; secondly, some heretics, who hold that it is possible for one of these things to subsist without the other, and declare that when the Truth is revealed the Law is abolished."[40]

These are the twin poles that threaten the Islam of an individual

or a community with disintegration: the reduction of religious responsibility to a shell of procedure maintained by force and the rejection of
concrete duties owed to God and humanity in favor of imaginary
epiphanies.

Both these heterodoxies calling themselves orthodoxies had come
into focus in the days of Junayd, with the Sufis, accused as heretics for
the first time, caught in the middle. The situation was then compli-
cated by the appearance of new sects taking the name of Sufi for themselves. Hallaj's magnetism and his growing legend had merged with
the millenarian atmosphere to produce antinomian groups.They still
existed in Qushayri's time.

Hujwiri records, "I have seen at Baghdad and in the adjoining dis-
tricts a number of heretics who pretend to be the followers of al-Hallaj
and make his sayings an argument for their heresy and call themselves Hallajis. They spoke of him in the same terms of exaggeration
as the Rafidis apply to Ali."[41]

He speaks of another such group attached to the figure of Abu
Hulman of Damascus, whom he exonerates, as he does Hallaj, from
personal responsibility for the beliefs attached to his name.[42] Further,
his "Rafidis" must include not just the Ismailis, whose doctrine was
spreading on every side, but the Nusayris of Khurasan, another Shia
splinter, who believed Ali to be the incarnation of God.[43] Many more
exotic doctrines could be described.

Amid so much mythologizing enthusiasm and so much violent
reaction, a spirituality of discipline and balance had to be actively
affirmed. The old goods had to be put back on public display. The manual writers and the generation of Qushayri struck the return blow. It
has become common place among modern writers in Islamic studies to
see Ghazzali as having achieved for the first time a meeting or fusion
of Sufism with orthodoxy. Because of this, nearly every influential earlier Sufi writer is likely to be tagged as the "precursor of Ghazzali"—
for instance, Qushayri, Sulami, Kalabadhi, Junayd, and even
Muhasibi.[44] In point of fact, however, the Sufis never stopped being
orthodox. Whether in terms of maintaining the solidarity of the
Community (*ummah*), holding to the primacy of the Quran and
Traditions in the definition of Muslim life, or clinging to the spirit of
the Prophetic example and the impulse of the community of Madinah,
they were orthodox from the very beginning. Ghazzali was simply in
a unique position to give authority to this recognition. His success was
really the success of a 150 years of Sufi effort.

That universalizing effort—which did not fail in Baghdad as Massignon describes—was to have substantial social effects.

4. The Social Impact of the Sufis

Sufism, Fazlur Rahman notes, was an urban phenomenon until the AD 10th/AH 4th century, but from the AH 11th/AH 5th was the "religion of the masses."[45] This expansion was simultaneous with the consolidation of Sunnism, and the Seljuk domains were its cradle.[46] The international network of schools which helped to unify the forming Sunni society (*madrasahs*), grew from the model of Karrami spiritual schools (where Yahya bin Muadh had taught) already established in Khurasan. The integration of theology—which had been fought for by Qushayri at the head of the Asharite Sufis and which alone would make theological consensus and consequent peace possible—was also first achieved in Khurasan.[47] The Sufi orders, the teaching lines that would carry the culture and attitudes of the great shaykhs through the whole of the Islamic world, originated here as well. The manuals would be their textbooks. The most effective of these, for purposes of broadening general understanding, was the *Risalah*. "It was accounted such a blessing for the Muslims," Ates quotes Subki, "that a copy was found in every home."[48]

After the manuals, the consensus of the community recognized the Sufi inheritance as its own. It is likely that the existence of Sufism as a tolerated aspect of Islamic life gave strong support to Sunnism in the process of establishing itself. The existence of Sufism and its toleration implied the validity, at least in certain cases, of the religious experience of individuals, and Sunnism was largely based on ordinary men.[49] The Seljuk rulers were aware of this legitimizing function of Sufism and encouraged it, while simultaneously fostering the legal and theological scholarship of the religious scholars, giving the latter an unprecedented institutional basis and state support.

Nizam al-Mulk, the vizier of Alp Arslan, was the architect of these arrangements. It was he who founded the great universities, the Nizamiyyahs, centers for the study of the Divine Law in the two cities of Qushayri, Baghdad and Nishapur. According to Muhammad bin Munawwar, who wrote his *Asrar al-tawhid* in the latter half of the 8th/12th century,[50] Nizam al-Mulk had been, as a youth, a student of Abu Said bin Abi-l-Khayr (b. 356/967)—another illustrious disciple of Sulami and the first Sufi to draw up a rule for his pupils, marking the formative stage of that other great unifying institution, the Sufi orders.[51]

The body of opinion that insists on invoking a separation between Sufism and orthodoxy finds this policy of the Seljuks a remarkable rather than a natural development and perhaps even slightly suspect: "The Turkish sultans, although outwardly zealous patrons of orthodoxy, nevertheless paid real homage and honor to the Sufi shaykhs."[52] The Seljuks' devotion to Sunnism can scarcely be doubted, and it is significant that Fazlur Rahman would rather hesitate over their orthodoxy than admit that of the Sufis. His reluctance to recognize how intrinsic the Sufis were to the Sunni synthesis stems from his distaste for situations that were to develop in India half a millennium later, when the name of "Sufi" was taken up by late inheritors of the Ismaili pattern of thought.[53] But the spiritual outreach of the Sufis was probably instrumental in limiting the spread of this pattern in the era of Qushayri. The Sufi shaykhs could do this in a way that the partisans of legal or theological uniformity could not—by insisting on the spirit of the *Shariah* animating its letter, making the consensus of faith and practice attractive rather than insistent, a way of life rather than a dogmatic structure. Where the persecutions of a Mamun or a Kunduri could never create consensus, the tolerance of the Sufis could bridge differences and build unity. In this they materially aided the work of the religious scholars by bringing the popular religious consensus to assent to the theoretical one. Hodgson notes, "It is probable that without the subtle leaven of the Sufi orders . . . the mechanical arrangements of the *Shariah* would not have maintained the loyalty essential to their effectiveness."[54]

It was this loyalty that made the international Sunni society outlast its competitors. The seemingly formidable Fatimid state was based on allegiances that were unstable at best. From the late AD 11th/AH 5th, through the AD 12th/AH 6th centuries, group after local Ismaili group withdrew support deciding that the Imam at Cairo was not the real Imam—first the Berbers, then the Druzes in Syria and Egypt itself, then the Iranians, and finally the Arabians and Indians withdrew.[55] The Qarmathian republic of townsmen in Bahrain was destroyed in the latter half of the AD 11th/AH 5th century by the surrounding peasants it had exploited. The *Shariah* was put back into force.[56] The most powerful of the local Ismaili factions, the famous Nizaris or "Assassins," in AD 1090/AH 482 seized the fortress of Alamut and surrounding towns in the south of Khurasan from which it conducted campaigns of strategic terror and led piecemeal uprisings against the Turks. It too was overthrown in AD 1107/AH 500,[57] and the movement withered to a handful of supporters.

Yet though the Nizaris had succeeded in assassinating Nizam al-Mulk and demoralizing the Seljuk regime (which began to collapse in AD 1092/AH 485 and finally fell, some twenty-five years later, into a series of transient military governments without structure or ideas)[58] the network of relationships which underlay what was now Sunni society did not fail. The last outbreak of Ismaili force, in fact, only cemented it and brought into the consensus even the Shias.[59] The orthodox Sunnis found their form, and the religion found its proper agent.

During the three centuries following the initial spread of Muslim rule, the boundaries of Muslim territory had varied little. In the many centuries after 945, on the contrary, there was an almost constant expansion of the area in which the religion and even the civilization flourished, often with no dependence on any previously Muslim state. This expansion has indeed continued, in some sense, down to our own time.[60] Islam is like a banquet to which everyone is invited, and when the Community (*ummah*) shows its universality, many accept the invitation. But the feast is found in the point of gathering together, and not in the mere gathering itself. It is for the service of God that the Community was constituted. That the believers should be enabled to dine at the table of the Prophet, rather than eating scraps in a cellar, was the whole object of *The Risalah*.

Notes to Translator's Introduction

1. A major exception to this rule is to be found in the admirable work of Annemarie Schimmel.

Notes to Part I: A Brief History of Early Sufism

1 Ignaz Goldziher, *Introduction to Islamic Theology and Kalam*, trans. Andras and Ruth Hamori, introduction and additional notes by Bernard Lewis (Princeton: Princeton University Press, 1981).

2 W. M. Watt, *The Formative Period of Islamic Thought* (Edinburgh: Edinburgh University Press, 1973), p. 238.

3 Graham, *Divine Word and Prophetic Word In Early Islam* (The Hague: Mouton, 1978) p. 95.

4 Joseph Schacht, *An Introduction to Islamic Law* (Oxford: Oxford University Press, Clarendon Press ed., 1982).

5 Graham, p. 26.

6 Fazlur Rahman, *Islam*. (Garden City, NY: Doubleday and Co., Anchor Books ed., 1968) p. 57.

7 A. J. Wensinck, *The Muslim Creed: Its Genesis and Historical Development* (New York: Barnes & Noble, 1932; 2nd printing 1965), p. 23.

8 *Ibid.*, p. 22.

9 Watt, p. 265.

10 See for instance R.A. Nicholson, *A Literary History of the Arabs*, cited in A.J. Arberry, *The Koran Interpreted* (New York: Macmillan Publishing Co., 1955) 2:9-and Nicholson was notable in his time for generosity of view-or Richard Bell, quoted 2:12 of the same work.

11 Rahman p. 32.

12 Graham, p.107.

13 *Ibid.*, pp. 109-10.

14 Wensinck, p. 37.

15 H. Gatje, *The Quran and Its Exegesis. Selected Texts and Modern Muslim Interpretation*, trans. A. T. Welch (Berkeley and Los Angeles: University of California Press, 1976), p.119.

16 Seyyid Hossein Nasr, "Sufism," in *Cambridge History of Iran* vol. 4: The Period from the Arab Invasion to the Seljuks, ed. R. N. Frye (Cambridge: Cambridge University Press, 1982), p. 449. (Hereafter Camb. Iran 4).

17 Marshall G.S. Hodgson, *The Venture of Islam: Conscience and History in a World Civilization*, 3 vols. (Chicago and London: University of Chicago Press, 1974), p. 1:386.

18 Watt, p.81.

19 *Ibid.*, p. 79.

20 Abu Abd- al-Rahman Muhammad bin al-Husayn b. Muhammad b. Musa al-Sulami, Tabaqat al-sufiyah, ed. with an intro. and index by Johannes Pedersen (Leiden: E.J. Brill, 1960) p. 14.

21 Abu Nasr al-Sarraj, *Kitab al-lumah li-l tasawwuf* p. 22, quoted in *Camb. Iran* 4:443.

22 Johannes Pedersen, Introduction to Sulami, *Tabaqat*, p. 24.

23 Qushayri, quoted in Louis Massignon, *The Passion of al- Hallaj, Mystic and Martyr of Islam*, 3 vols., trans. Herbert Mason, Bollingen Series 98 (Princeton: Princeton University Press, 1982), 1:72. Massignon does, however, query this statement, which contradicts his theory on the origins of the rituals of the Sufi orders.

24 Annemarie Schimmel, *Mystical Dimensions of Islam* (Chapel Hill: University of North Carolina Press, 1975) p. 31.

25 *Ibid.*, p. 56.

26 *Ibid.*, p. 31.

27 Massignon, 1:68.

28 Watt, p. 78.

29 Goldziher, p. 46.

30 Watt, p. 186.

31 Schimmel, p. 31.

32 Watt, p. 212.

33 Goldziher, p. 101.

34 Watt, p. 186.

35 Hodgson, I:387.

36 *Ibid.*, I:480.

37 Sulami, *Tabaqat*, quoted in Schimmel, p. 32.

38 Ali Hassan Abd al-Kader, *The Life. Personality. and Writings of Al-Junayd*, E. J. W. Gibb Memorial Series, New Series 22 (London: Luzac and Co., 1976), p. 35.

39 Rahman, p. 159.

40 Pedersen, p. 25.

41 These and more listed in Pedersen, p. 27.

42 Pedersen, p. 28.

43 *Ibid.*, p. 29.

44 A. J. Arberry, *Introduction to Abu Bakr al-Kalabadhi, The Doctrine of the Sufis*, trans. A. J. Arberry (Cambridge: Cambridge University Press, paperback ed., 1977) p. xvi. 45 Harith al-Muhasibi, Nasaih, quoted *ibid.*

46 Margaret Smith, *An Early Mystic of Baghdad* (New York: AMS Press ed., 1973), p. 68.

47 From Hajji Khalifah, *Kashf al-zunun*, p. 471, quoted in Smith, p. 256.

48 Smith, p. 240.

49 Abd al-Kader, p. 25.

50 Ali bin Uthman al-Jullabi al-Hujwiri, *Kashf al-Mahjub of Al-Hujwiri: The Oldest Persian Treatise on Sufism*, trans. Reynold A. Nicholson, E. J. W. Gibb Memorial Series 17 (London: Luzac, new ed. 1976), p. 117.

51 Smith, 257.

52 Schimmel, p. 53. It is interesting to speculate that the persistent matching of the two Basrans Rabiah and Hasan in Sufi legend, despite the eighty years between them in historical time, may reflect their status as the two major influences on the Baghdad School in this formative period.

53 *Ibid.*, p. 32.

54 *Ibid*.
55 Ab] Nuaym al-Isfahani, *Hilyat-al-awliya*, quoted in Abd al Kader, p. 9.
56 Sulami, *Tabaqat*, quoted *ibid*.
57 Massignon, *Hallaj* I, p. 68.
58 Sarraj, quoted in Abd al-Kader, p. 39.
59 *Ibid*., pp. 38-9.
60 Hujwiri, p.191.
61 Hodgson, 1:409.
62 Massignon, 1:193.
63 Schimmel, p. 68.
64 Abd al-Kader, p. 57.
65 Sarraj, p.9, cited in Abd al-Kader, p.37-8.
66 Khatib al-Baghdadi, *Tarikh Baghdad,* 5:30, cited in *ibid*.,
p. 41.
67 Qushayri, p. 90.
68 Massignon, 1:30, 278.
69 Massignon, 1:309.
70 Schimmel, p. 73.

Notes to Part II: After the Abbasids

1 Watt, p. 265
2 Hodgson 1:278.
3 *Ibid*., 1:317.
4 *Ibid*.
5 *Ibid*., 1:142.
6 *Ibid*., 1:267.
7 *Ibid*.
8 *Ibid*., 2:57.
9 Bernard Lewis, *The Arabs in History* (New York: Harper and Row, Harper Torchbooks, 2nd ed., 1966), p. 144.
10 *Ibid*., p. 159-60.
11 Michael Gilsenan, *Recognizing Islam* (New York: Pantheon Books, 1982), p. 34.
12 Hodgson, 2:68-9.
13 *Ibid*., 2:65.
14 *Ibid*., 1:372.
15 *Ibid*., 1:38.
16 *Ibid*., 1:490.
17 They took it out of protest at "idolatry," thinking to disrupt the pilgrimage. It was returned, via Cairo, five years after the Abbasids had fallen, in 951.
18 Qushayri, p. 107.
19 Hodgson, 2:36-8.
20 Massignon, 1: 321.
21 Hodgson, 1:390.
22 Hodgson, 2:37.

23 Massignon, 1:305.

24 Hodgson, 1:390.

25 Massignon, 1:251.

26 A. Bausani, "Religion in the Saljuq Period," in *Cambridge History of Iran* vol. 5: The Seljuk and Mongol Periods, ed. J. A. Boyle (Cambridge: Cambridge University Press, 1968), p. 449. (Hereafter Camb. Iran 5.)

27 Watt, 245.

28 Hodgson, 2:39.

29 Hodgson, 2:35.

30 *Ibid.*, 2:153.

31 Massignon, 1:68.

32 *Camb. Iran* 4:443.

33 Schimmel, p.41.

34 Hujwiri, *Kashf*, p. 114. And Karkh was the Shii quarter of Baghdad, according to Hodgson, 1:153.

35 Qushayri, p. 103, quoted in Hujwiri, p. 11.

36 *Camb. Iran.*, 4:456.

37 Hodgson, 1:475.

38 *Ibid.*, 1:492.

39 *Ibid.*, 2:33.

40 *Ibid.*, 2:41-2.

41 *Camb. Iran*, 5:450.

42 Massignon, 1:68.

43 *Camb. Hist.* Iran, 5:450.

447 Abu Nuaym al-Isfahani, Hilyat al-awliya, quoted in Schimmel, p. 51.

45 Hujwiri, p. 123.

46 Massignon, 1:346.

47 *Camb. Iran* 4:456-7.

48 Hujwiri, p. 123.

49 *Ibid.*, p. 133.

50 *Ibid.*, p. 122.

51 *Ibid.*, p. 123.

52 *Ibid.*

53 *Ibid.*, p. 134.

54 *Ibid.*

55 Schimmel, p. 53.

56 Hujwiri, p. 134; Schimmel, p. 52.

57 Massignon, 1:637.

58 Schimmel, p. 74.

59 Massignon, 1:641.

60 *Ibid.*, 1:83-4.

61 Hodgson, 2:42.

62 Hujwiri, p. 174.

Notes to Part III: The Object of the *Risalah*

1 Where not otherwise noted, biographical facts are drawn from the arti-

cle "Kusheyri" by Ahmad Ates, in *Islam Ansiclopedisi* (Istanbul: Milli Egitim
Basimevi, 1977), s.v .(hereafter IA.)

2 Massignon, 1:170.

3 *Ibid.*

4 Massignon, 1:173.

5 *Ibid.*, 1:170-72.

6 *Ibid.*, 1:39.

7 *Ibid.*, 1:172.

8 Hodgson, 2:178.

9 The essentials are laid out in Goldziher, p. 112, with rather a different
understanding. Orientalists have tended to see Asharite cosmology as preposterous, and certainly "anti-scientific." But in light of major questions of contemporary physics-quantum and probability theory, and the provocative issue
of the origins of physical laws-it would seem to hold up rather well.

10 Baghdadi, *Usul*, p. 248, quoted in Wensinck, p. 134.

11 Hujwiri, p. 162.

12 Hujwiri, p. 159.

13 Massignon, 1:641.

14 Schimmel, p. 427.

15 Pedersen, p. 50.

16 *Ibid.*, p. 25.

17 Schimmel, p. 83.

18 Schimmel, p. 84

19 Tosun Bayrak, Foreword, Muhammad bin al-Husayn al-Sulami, *The
Book of Sufi Chivalry: Futuwa*. Tosun Bayrak, trans. (New York: Inner
Traditions International, 1983), p. 5

20 Pedersen, p. 24.

21 IA.

22 In about AD 1019/AH 410 according to Ates. Reputed to be one of the
best, not a copy survives.

23 Nizam al-Mulk, *Siyasat-namah*, quoted in *Camb. Iran.*, 5:292.

24 Hodgson, 2:194.

25 *Ibid.*, 2:193.

26 Massignon, 1:40.

27 Hodgson, 2:43.

28 Massignon, 2:104.

29 According to Massignon (1:40-41), Ibn al-Muslimah was captured and
executed by the Fatimids during this year. His family was saved along with
the caliph's grandson and on this account a cenotaph was erected on the spot
where he had honored Hallaj with a prayer. This marker stood in 1945 and
may still stand.

30 The chronology of these events is reconstructed from indications in
Ates and Massignon.

31 Schimmel, p. 427.

32 *Camb. Iran* 5:287.

33 Schimmel, p. 88.

34 Massignon 1:379.

35 *Camb. Iran*, 5:296.

36 Lewis, p. 87.

37 Lewis, p. 132.

38 Pedersen, p. 23.

39 Hujwiri is the best example in translation.

40 Hujwiri, p. 383.

41 *Ibid.*, p. 152.

42 *Ibid.*, p. 260.

43 *Camb. Iran*, 5:290.

44 Qushayri, according to *IA*; Sulami, according to Pedersen, p, 23; Kalabadhi, according to Arberry, p. xii; Junayd, according to Abd al-Kader, p. 34; Muhasibi, according to Rahman, p. 164.

45 Rahman, *Islam*, pp. xxi-xxii.

46 Hodgson, 2:203.

47 *Ibid.*, 2:210-11.

48 Subki 1:246, quoted in *IA*.

49 Watt, pp. 264-5.

50 *Camb. Iran* 5:301.

51 Schimmel, p. 241

52 Rahman, p. xxii.

53 In fact, Hindu-Muslim syncretism and the abandonment of Divine Law practice in some regions appear to have been mediated precisely by the Ismailis (who established one of their last few strongholds in India), according to Annemarie Schimmel, *Pain and Grace:. A Study of Two Mystic Writers of Eighteenth Century India* (Leiden: E. J. Brill, 1976), p. 24. It is interesting that just as in the earliest days the terms *zuhhad* and *ubbad* were abandoned as they lost the meaning they were intended to convey, eminent 18th century Indian Sufis like Shah Waliullah, Mazhar Janjanan and Mir Dard began to refuse the "Sufi" label. (Schimmel, *Pain and Grace*, p. 10-18.)

54 Hodgson, 2:125.

55 Hodgson, 2:26-28.

56 *Ibid.*, 1:491.

57 *Ibid.*, 2:58-59.

58 *Ibid.*, 2:53.

59 *Ibid.*, 2:61.

60 Hodgson, 2:272.

Selected Bibliography

Abd al-Kader, Ali Hassan *Junayd*. E. J. W. Gibb Memorial Series, New Series 22. London: Luzac G Co., 1976.

Cambridge History of Islam. 4 vols. Cambridge: Cambridge University Press, 1970. Vol. la: The Central Lands from Pre-Islamic Times to the first World War, edited by P.M. Holt, Ann K.S. Lambton, and Bernard Lewis.

Cambridge History of Iran. 6 vols. Cambridge: Cambridge University Press, 1968. Vol. 4: The Period from the Arab Invasion to the Saljuks, edited by R.N. Frye. "Religion in the Saljuq Period," by A. Bausani. Vol. 5: The Saljuq and Mongol Periods, edited by J.A. Boyle. Sufism," by S.H. Nasr.

Gatje, H. *The Quran and Its Exegesis. Selected Texts and Modern Muslim Interpretation*. Translated by A. T. Welch. Berkeley and Los Angeles: University of California Press, 1976.

Gilsenan, Michael. *Recognizing Islam*. New York: Pantheon Books, 1982.

Goldziher, Ignaz. *Introduction to Islamic Theology and Law*. Translated by Andras and Ruth Hamori. Introduction and additional notes by Bernard Lewis. Princeton: Princeton University Press, 1981.

Graham, William. *Divine Word and Prophetic Word In Early Islam*. The Hague: Mouton, 1977.

Hodgson, Marshall, *The Venture of Islam: Conscience and History in a World Civilization*, 3 vols. Chicago and London: University of Chicago Press, 1974.

al-Hujwiri, Ali bin Uthman al-Jullabi. *Kashf al-mahjub of al-Hujwiri: The Oldest Persian Treatise on Sufism*. Translated by Reynold R. Nicholson. E.J.W. Gibb Memorial Series 17. London: Luzac, new ed., 1976.

Islam *Ansiclopedisi*. Istanbul: Milli Egitim Basimevi, 1977. "Kusheyri" by Ahmad Ates.

al-Kalabadhi, Abu Bakr. *The Doctrine of the Sufis*. Translated by A. J. Arberry. Cambridge: Cambridge University Press, paperback ed., 1977

EXORDIUM

All praise is to due God whose dominion through invisible causes is unequalled in majesty, Whose immense power transcending all causes is unique in beauty, Whose unapproachable unity is exalted in loftiness, Whose all-embracing sufficiency is sanctified in holiness, Whose essence is unparalleled, Whose attributes are flawless; to Whom belong the attributes befitting His Reality, and the signs bespeaking His creation's incomparability with Him.

Exalted is He, the Most Rare. No boundary contains Him, no number encompasses Him, no end limits Him; no one helps Him, no son intercedes with Him, nothing countable exceeds His oneness. There is no place which holds Him nor time which overtakes Him; no understanding measures Him and no imagination conceives His form.

Exalted is He beyond such questions as What is He? And Where is He?, beyond the thought that His work acquires for Him some new perfection or dispels from Him some imperfection or flaw. For, "*There is nothing like unto Him, The Seeing and The Hearing,*" [Sura 11] and no living creature prevails over Him, the Aware, Capable of All.

I praise Him for what He charges and performs, and thank Him for what He grants and forbids. I trust in Him and am content with Him, satisfied with what He may give or refuse.

I bear witness that there is no god but God, alone, without a partner; the testimony of one certain of His unity and seeking aid from the excellence of His confirmation. And I bear witness that our master Muhammad is His chosen servant, His elect Trustworthy One, and His Messenger sent to the whole of humanity. May the blessings of God be upon him and upon his family, who are lamps in the darkness, and his companions, the keys of guidance; and may God send them abundant peace.

This book was written by one in need of God Most High, Abd-al-Karim bin Hawazin bin Abd-al-Malik bin Talhah Abu-l-Qasim al-Qushayri, and addressed to the Sufi community in the domains of Islam, in the year 1046 AD/437 AH.

God has made this group [the Sufis] the elite among His friends, caused them to excel all the rest of His friends, caused them to excel all the rest of His servants except the prophets and Messengers (☙), made their hearts the mines of His secrets, and selected them out of the community of Islam by the dawning of His lights. Therefore, they are the helpers of creation, and circle through all their states with the Truth, through the Truth. God has purified them from the turbulence of the human condition. With the truths of divine unity which He has revealed to them, He has raised them to levels of direct witnessing of the real. He has caused them to act with the finest conduct of servants, while showing them the operation of the principles of lordship, so that they are firm in fulfilling the obligations of service which rest upon them, while verifying the works of transformation and free disposal which proceed to them from Him. In all this they refer themselves entirely to God Most High, sincere in their knowledge of their poverty before Him, and with all self-regard entirely tamed. They do not depend upon what works they have produced or the clarity of their states, for they know that God, magnified and exalted, does what He wills, and chooses whomever He pleases from among His servants. No creation dominates Him, and no created being has a right to His special favor. His reward is a grace without cause, His punishment is a just judgment, and His command ordains the discrimination between them.

Then know—may God have mercy on you—that most of the true examples of this group have passed away, and in our time only their traces remain. As it is said:

As for these tents, they are like those tents of theirs
But I see that the women of this tribe are not those women.

This Way has been enfeebled—no, in actuality the Way has been blotted out. The teachers through whom guidance came have passed, and few are the students whose attitudes and behavior follow their example. Moral heedfulness has rolled up its carpet and left, while greed has reinforced its shackles and grown strong. Reverence for the Divine Law has vanished from their hearts, so that [those who call themselves Sufis] consider ignoring religion to be the best way of reaching their ends. They discard the distinction between lawful and unlawful and are debased by the abandonment of respect and the casting aside of shame. They attach no importance to devotional service and scorn fasting and prayer, while racing [to excel each other] in the field of negligence and unconsciousness. They rely upon following their appetites and do not hesitate to pursue forbidden things, getting whatever profit they can out of the rabble, women, and the companions of kings.

Yet they are not satisfied with the evil of their acts until they point to the highest states and realities, and claim that they are free of the bonds to servitude to worldly things, have confirmed in themselves the realities of divine union, and are established in truth, so that its principles flow through them while they themselves are negated. They claim that the secrets of divine unity have been revealed to them, and all multiplicity torn away. They say that the principles determining the human condition have left them so that after their self-extinction they continue only through the lights of the Absolute. That which speaks through them, they claim, is other than they, and that which acts when they act is not themselves. Rather, they have strayed entirely from the path.

The trial in which we find ourselves through the sort of thing I have described above has grown prolonged, and out of jealousy I have not opened my mouth to criticize it before. I did not wish that the people of this Way should be mentioned together with evil, or that opposition should arise through their slander, since the difficulty caused by opponents and deniers of the Way in these lands is intense. Moreover, I had hoped that this lassitude [which besets us] would be cut off at the root, and that perhaps God out of His grace would grant guidance to those who have turned aside from ideal conduct through neglect of the behavior and courtesy of this Way. The time, further, has not appeared favorable. Most of the people of this age in these lands are only persisting in habits to which they have grown accustomed, and are full of delusion and conceit about what they do. However, I am concerned about the hearts which believe that this business is based on such principles as those currently put forth, or that its founders conducted themselves in such a way.

So I dedicate this book to you, may God be generous to you. In it I have recalled the life stories of some of the teachers of this Way: their conduct, their character, their relationships, the beliefs of their hearts, what they have hinted was revealed to them, and the manner of their increasing perfection, from beginning to end. May it be a source of strength for sincere seekers of this Way and may you bear witness to me of its rectification.

I have found consolation in publishing this complaint: blessing and reward are from God the Generous. I seek the help of God in what I have mentioned, and ask that the work may be sufficient and preserved from error. I beg His forgiveness and seek His indulgence. All credit belongs to Him, and He is Able to do what He wills.

Qushayri's Introduction: Explaining the Beliefs of the Sufis Concerning Questions of the Fundamentals of Faith

Know, may God have mercy upon you, that the teachers of this group base their methods upon sound principles for affirming God's Unity (*tawhid*), and by means of these protect their beliefs from degeneration. They are indebted to the early Muslims and the preservers of the traditions of the Prophet for an affirmation of Unity that contains neither a likening of God to any created thing nor a denial of His attributes. They understand the truth of God's eternity, and realize the nature of creatures brought into existence form nothing. Thus the master of this Way, Junayd, said, " To affirm the Unity means to distinguish the eternal from the ephemeral." They strengthen the basic elements of belief with clarifying illustrations and suggestive evidence. As Abu Muhammad al-Jurayri said, "If someone does not seek to acquire the knowledge of the Unity through some kind of evidence, the foot of his delusion will slip into an abyss of destruction." He meant by this that whoever relies upon mere imitation and does not reflect upon the indications pointing to God's Unity slips from the path of salvation and falls into ruin.

Anyone who examines the pronouncements of these masters and ponders their words will find reassurance, in their sayings and comments, that these people did not fall short of the goal in realization, or abandon the search in failure.

In this section we will first recall a number of miscellaneous sayings of Sufi masters concerning issues of the foundations of faith. Subsequently we will set out in an orderly fashion—briefly and concisely, God willing—the implications of these sayings for the requirements of belief.

*****

I heard Abu Abd-al-Rahman al-Sulami say[1] . . . that I heard Abu Bakr al-Shibli say, "The Unique One is known before limits and before letters. This is a clear statement from Shibli that the essence of the Eternal One is without limitations, and His speech is beyond words.

I heard Abu Hatim al-Sufi say that Abu Nasr al-Tusi said that Ruwaym was asked, "What is the first obligation that God Almighty and Glorious has imposed upon His creation?" He answered, "Gnosis of Him (*marifah*), according to His great word, *'We have not created the jinn and humanity except to serve'* (51:56). Ibn Abbas said, 'That is, to "know" God.'"[2]

Junayd said, "The first tenet of wisdom that the servant needs is gnosis (*marifah*) of the Maker of the thing made, so that he knows the attribute of the Creator from that of the created and the attribute of the Eternal from that of the ephemeral, humbles himself to His summons, and acknowledges the duties of obedience to Him. For whoever does not recognize his Owner does not concede sovereignty to the One entitled to it."

Muhammad ibn al-Husayn informed me[3] . . . that Abu-l-Tayyib al-Maraghi said, "Intellect reads signs, wisdom senses indications, and gnosis (*marifah*) sees proof. So intellect suggests, wisdom points out, and gnosis bears witness that purity of worship is only granted when Unity is purely affirmed."

Junayd was asked about affirming Unity and said, "It is to recognize the uniqueness of He Whose oneness is affirmed. You realize Him to be alone in the perfection of His Unity—that He is indeed the Unique One, Who does not beget and is not begotten—and refuse to assign Him opposites, equals, or parallels. You attribute to Him neither resemblance, means, form, nor analogy. *'There is nothing like unto Him, and He is The Hearing, The Seeing'* (42:11)."

Muhammad bin Ahmad bin Muhammad bin Yahya al-Sufi told us[4] . . . that Abu Bakr al-Zahrabadhi was asked about the gnosis of God. He said, "Gnosis is a word whose meaning is a glorification of God that, when it exists in the heart, prevents you from either denying Him attributes or attributing Him resemblances."

Abu-l-Hasan Ali bin Ahmad bin Sahl al-Bushanji said, "Affirmation of the Unity is when you know that no being resembles Him, but do not deny His qualities."

Abu Abd-al-Rahman al-Sulami told me[4] . . . that al-Husayn bin Mansur [al-Hallaj] said, "He has imposed on everything existence in time, for eternity belongs to Him. So whatever appears in physical form is subject to contingency, joined to instruments and intermediaries and held by their power. The created being is sometimes close to God, sometimes separated from Him and occupied with other than He, so that it falls into dire need. It is overpowered by imagination so that it attempts to conceive of Him. It takes shelter in a place subject to 'Where?' and takes on a nature understandable by 'Of what sort?'

"He, glory to Him, is not overshadowed by above, is not supported by below. He does not face a direction; location does not enclose Him; behind does not drive Him, in front of does not limit Him; before does not make Him appear nor after cause Him to vanish. All does not encompass Him, being does not make Him exist, nonexistence is not deprived of Him.

"His description is that He has no description and His distinguishing act is that He has no cause. His form of existence is that He is without duration. He is far above the conditions of His creation. He possesses no nature in common with His creation, and His action involves no labor. He is set apart from them by His eternity, as they are set apart from Him by their temporality.

"If you ask, 'When?', His existence preceded time, and if you say, "He,' the 'H' and 'e' are His creations. If you ask, 'Where?', His being is prior to place. The words themselves are His manifest signs, His existence is its own affirmation, and to know Him is to declare His Unity. To declare His Unity is to discriminate Him from His creation. Whatever the imagination may form, He is other than that.

"How can what has appeared from Him re-enter Him? And how can that which He brought into existence return to Him of itself? Eyes do not see Him; thoughts do not encounter Him. Nearness to Him is His blessing; distance from Him is His humiliation. His highness exists without His rising up, and His manifesting Himself to His creation occurs without His changing place. He is the First and the Last, the Manifest and the Hidden, the Near, the Distant, of Whom it is written, "There is nothing like unto Him, and He is The Hearing, The Seeing."

I heard Abu Hatim al-Sijistani say[5] . . . that Yusuf bin al-Husayn said that a man came before Dhu-l-Nun al-Misri and asked, "Tell me about affirming the Unity. What is it?" He answered, "It is your knowing that God's power over things is absolute, unmixed, and that He creates without means. The cause of everything is His creative act, and His creative act has no cause. Neither in the highest heavens nor in the lowest earths is there any orderer of things except God, and whatever takes form in your imagination—God is other than that."

Junayd said, "Declaring the Unity is your knowledge and affirmation that God is alone in His eternal existence before all things, that there is no second together with Him, and that nothing performs His action."

Abu Abd Allah bin Khafif al-Shirazi said, "Faith is the heart's confirmation of what the Truth has taught about the Unseen." Abu-l-Abbas al-Sayyari said, "His gifts are of two kinds: special grace (*karamah*) and misleading favors (*istidraj*). Special grace: He maintains in you permanently; misleading favors: He causes to pass over you and removes. So say, 'I am a believer, if God Most High wills.'" Abu-l-Abbas al-Sayyari was the pre-eminent shaykh of his time. I heard Abu Ali al-Daqqaq say, "A man touched the foot of Abu Abbas al-Sayyari. He remarked, 'You have touched a foot that has never moved in disobedience to God Almighty and Glorious.'"

Abu Bakr al-Wasiti commented, "If anyone said, 'I am truly a believer in God,' he was told, 'The state of truth requires total vision, full familiarity, and comprehensive knowledge. If someone falls short of that, his claim is false.'" He means by this what all the Sunnis say—that the true believer is he for whom paradise is decided. If someone has not learned this from the secret of God's wisdom, his claim to be 'truly' a believer is not correct."

I heard Abu Abd-al-Rahman al-Sulami say[6] . . . that Sahl bin Sahl bin Abd Allah al-Tustari said, "The believers will gaze on Him [in the next life] without encompassing Him and without perceiving an end." And Abu-l-Husayn al-Nuri said, "The Truth observed the hearts and saw none more desirous of Him than the heart of Prophet Muhammad. So He honored him with the Ascension, hastening his seeing and speaking with His Lord."

*****

I heard the Imam Abu Bakr Muhammad bin al-Hasan bin Furak say that he heard Muhammad bin al-Mahbub, the servant of Abu Uthman al-Maghribi, say that one day Abu Uthman al-Maghribi said to him, "O Muhammad! If someone asked you, 'Where is that which you serve?' what would you say?" I answered, "I would say, 'Where He always was.'" "And if you were asked, 'Where was He eternally?' what would you say?" I replied, "I would say, 'Where He is now!'" (meaning that He was, while there were no places, and He is now as He was.) On account of this he was pleased with him, took off his shirt and gave it to him.

I heard Abu Bakr Muhammad bin al-Hasan bin Furak say that he heard Abu Uthman al-Maghribi say that he used to be inclined to believe that God was qualified by a direction, but when he entered Baghdad this passed out of his heart. So he wrote to his friends in Makkah that he had now accepted Islam anew.

*****

I heard Abd-al-Rahman Muhammad bin al-Husayn al-Sulami say that when Abu Uthman al-Maghribi was asked about the creation, he said, "It is shapes and apparitions upon which act the principles of divine power."

Al-Wasiti remarked, "Since souls and bodies were established by God and their manifestation is through Him and not through their own essences, thoughts and actions also are established by God and not by themselves. For actions and thoughts are outgrowths of bodies and souls."

He makes clear in this statement that the qualities acquired by the servant are created by God. Thus there is no creator of substances except God Most High, and there is also no creator of accidents except God Most High.

*****

I heard Abd-al-Rahman Muhammad bin al-Husayn al-Sulami say[7] . . . that Abu Said al-Kharraz said, "Whoever thinks that he can attain his object by the expenditure of effort is bringing useless trouble upon himself. Whoever thinks that he can attain it without effort is dreaming."

Al-Wasiti said, "The spiritual stations are shares appointed and qualities bestowed. So how can they be gained by actions, or granted on account of efforts?"[7]

*****

Al-Wasiti was asked about unbelief. He said, "Unbelief and faith, and this world and the next, are from God, to God, through God, and belonging to God: from God in their beginning and growth, to God in their returning and end, through God in their permanence and passing away, belonging to God in their being His kingdom and creation."

*****

Junayd was asked by some scholars about the affirmation of the Unity. He said, "It is certainty." "Explain to me in detail what it is," pursued a questioner. Junayd continued, "It is your realization that the motion and rest of creation are the action of God Almighty and Glorious—alone, without a partner. If you have done that, then you have affirmed His Unity."

*****

I heard Muhammad bin al-Husayn say[8]. . .that when a man came to him saying "Pray for me," Dhu-l-Nun al-Misri said, "If you were strengthened by knowledge of the unseen through sincerely affirming the Unity, how many of your prayers would have been preceded by their answers! As it is, crying out, by itself, will not save a drowning man."

*****

"Pharaoh laid claim to divine lordship explicitly," al-Wasiti observed. "The Mutazilites, [arguing the supremacy of reason], do it implicitly, by saying 'What I will, I do.'"

*****

Abu-l-Husayn al-Nuri said, "Every thought directed toward God Most High partakes of the affirmation of Unity, when thoughts of associating things with Him do not compete." Abu Abu Abd-al-Rahman al-Sulami told me[9] . . . that Abu Ali al-Rudhbari was asked about affirming the Unity and said, "Affirmation of Unity is the continuous sincerity of a heart that has proven its refusal to associate God with anything, and that has abandoned its denial of the existence of God. In a word, affirmation of Unity is the knowledge that however thought and imagination have conceived Him, God, glory to Him, is something else—as in His saying "Nothing is like unto Him, and He is the Hearing, the Seeing."

*****

Abu-l-Qasim al-Nasrabadhi said, "Paradise remains in existence through His preservation of it, while His remembrance of you, His mercy, and His love for you remain in existence through their own permanence. What a difference between that which continues through its own eternity and that which continues because it is maintained!"

What Abu-l-Qasim al-Nasrabadhi has mentioned is the goal of gnosis. As the people of Truth say, the attributes of the essence of the Eternal One, glory to Him, are permanent through His permanence. Nasrabadhi calls our attention to this issue and explains that what is rightfully called enduring (*baqi*) is only what is permanent through its own permanence. This is in contrast to the teaching of those who differ from the people of Truth—"And they differ from the Truth."

Muhammad bin al-Husayn told me that he heard al-Nasrabadhi say, "I wavered between the attributes of action and the attributes of essence. Both of them are in reality His attributes. But when He bewilders you in the stage of separation, He attaches you to the qualities of His action, and when He transports you to the stage of union He attaches you to the qualities of His essence." Abu-l-Qasim al-Nasrabadhi was the preeminent shaykh of his time.

I heard Imam Abu Ishaq al-Isfarayani say, "When I left Baghdad I used to teach questions of the soul in the mosque of Nishapur. I explained the statement that it was created. Abu-l-Qasim al-Nasrabadhi used to sit apart from us, listening to my words. After a few days he came to see us. He said to Muhammad al-Furra, 'Bear witness that I have submitted to Islam anew at the hands of that man'—and he pointed to me."

*****

I heard Muhammad bin al-Husayn al-Sulami say[10] . . . that Junayd said, "How should That which possesses no comparison or equal unite with that which has comparisons and equals? Preposterous! This is an amazing thought, save through the graciousness of the subtle one, concerning which there can be no perception, no imagination, and no comprehension except the guidance of certainty and the realization of faith."

*****

Muhammad bin al-Husayn told him[11] . . . that Tahir bin Ismail al-

Razi said that Yahya bin Muadh was asked, "Inform us about God Almighty and Glorious." He said, "One God." He was asked, "What is He like?" He said, "Possessor of all, Capable of all." He was asked, "Where is He?" He said, "Where you cannot escape Him." The questioner said, "I did not ask you about this!" He said, "Anything other than this is a description of created being. We have not informed you of its description."

Muhammad bin al-Husayn told me[12] . . . that Abu Ali al-Rudhbari said, "Whatever an imaginer, in ignorance, tries to imagine Him to be, intellect shows to be other than He."

*****

Ibn Shahin asked Junayd about the meaning of being "with" God. Junayd said, "'With' has two significances. If it refers to the prophets, He is 'with' them through His help and protection, as when He said '*I am with you; I hear and see*' (20:46). If it refers to the majority of people, He is 'with' them through His knowledge and comprehension, as when He said '*There is no meeting of three except that He is the fourth of them*' (58:7)." Ibn Shahin said, "Your example is fit to guide the community of God."

Dhu-l-Nun al-Misri was asked about His saying "*The Beneficent One is established upon the Throne*" (20:5). He said, "It attests to His essence and denies His being bound by a location, for He is existent through His own essence, while material things [which, in their totality, come under the Throne] are existent through His rule, as He wills, glory to Him."

Shibli was questioned about His saying, "*The Beneficent One is established upon the Throne*," and replied, "The Beneficent One does not cease, and the Throne is established by the Beneficent One."

Jafar al-Sadiq said, "Whoever asserts that God is 'in' something, or 'from' something, or 'upon' something has assigned partners to Him and is a polytheist, since if He were upon something He would be carried by it, if He were in something He would be restricted by it, and if He were from something He would be originated by it." He also remarked on His saying, "*Then He drew near and descended*" (53:4): "whoever imagines that He literally drew near sets up an imaginary distance. Rather this coming together signifies that, to the extent to which one becomes intimate with Him, He draws one away from all knowledge of the world and everything that belongs to it."

I saw in the handwriting of Abu Ali that a Sufi was asked "Where is God?" and replied, "May God send you no good! Do you search for 'where' with your eyes?"

Abu Abd-al-Rahman al-Sulami told us[13] . . . that al-Kharraz said, "The true "nearness" to God is the heart's loss of the sense of worldly things, and tranquility of mind toward God Most High."

*****

I heard Muhammad bin al-Husayn say[14] . . . that Ibrahim al-Khawwas said, "I came across a man whom the Satan had thrown to the ground in a fit. I began to recite the call to prayer in his ear, and Satan cried out to me from his belly, "Let me kill him, for he says that the Quran is created!"

Ibn Ata said, "When God Most High created words, He made them a secret, and when He created Adam (ﷺ) He unfolded that secret within him, while He did not unfold it in any of His angels. So words came easily to the tongue of Adam in all their varieties and all the varieties of language, and God made them significant forms."

Ibn Ata here declares that the letters were created. [Therefore, the recitation and the words of the Quran are also created.]

Sahl bin Abd Allah said, "The letters express God's action, they do not express His essence, because they are themselves a divine action within the realm of effects." This is also a unequivocal statement that the letters are created.

Junayd said, in "*Answers to the Questions of the Damascenes*," "Trust is the work of the heart, and affirming the Unity is the speech of the heart."

*****

In "*Answers to the Questions of the Damascenes*," Junayd also said, "Only the Truth possesses knowledge of the unknown things, so that He knows what was, what is, and what is not; and if a thing were, how it would have to be."

Husayn bin Mansur [al-Hallaj] said, "When someone understands the truth of Unity, 'why' and 'how' fall away from him."

*****

Muhammad bin al-Husayn informed us[15] . . . that Junayd said,

"The noblest and most exalted of gatherings is to be seated in contemplation in the court of Unity."

Al-Wasiti said, "God has not originated anything more noble than the spirit (*al-ruh*)." He thus declares the spirit to be created.

*****

The ornament of Islam, the Imam Abu-l-Qasim Abd-al-Karim bin Hawazin al-Qushayri said: These accounts indicate that the beliefs of the Sufi shaykhs are in agreement with Sunni teaching on questions of the fundamentals of faith.

We have limited ourselves to this much only for fear of departing from the brevity and conciseness we prefer.

Summary of the Doctrine of Unity

These pages are concerned with the clarification of Sufi beliefs in questions of the Unity. We will recapitulate them here in an orderly fashion. As is indicated by their various statements, the collections of their discourses, and their writings on the Unity, shaykhs of this Way have said that the Truth, may He be exalted and magnified, is:

mawjud, existent
qadim, eternal and prior to all being
wahid, single
hakim, the determiner of the proper place and degree of
    everything
qadir, all-capable, the determiner of the destiny of everything
alim, all-knowing
qahir, all-powerful
rahim, compassionate
murid, willing
sami, hearing
majid, glorious
rafi, exalted above the creation
mutakallim, speaking
basir, seeing
mutakabbir, so great as to overpower all greatness
qadir, able to do precisely what He wills
hayy, alive
baqi, permanent, while all else passes away
samad, the absolute source of all.

and that He is The Knower through possessing knowledge; The Able through possessing ability; The Willer through possessing will; The Hearer through possessing hearing, The Seer through possessing sight; The Speaker through possessing speech; The Living One through possessing life; The Permanent One through possessing permanence.

He possesses two Hands which are two attributes with which He creates exactly what He wills. He possesses a Face, and essential attributes specific to His being, of which it cannot be said that they are He, or that they are other than He. They are pre-existent attributes and eternal qualities, while He is absolutely single in essence.

None of the originated or created things may be compared with Him, neither in body nor substance nor accident. His attributes are not phenomena or accidents. He is not conceived by any imagination nor weighed by any intellect. He has neither direction nor place, is not subject to time or duration, cannot be qualified by excess or deficiency.

Form and measure do not specify Him, end and boundary do not define Him. No event brings Him about, no cause sets Him in motion. Quality and entity do not pertain to Him, help and assistance lend Him no aid. No destiny is outside His omnipotence and no originated thing is apart from His rule. No object of knowledge is concealed from His knowledge, and about His action—what He performs and how He performs it—He cannot be reproached.

"Where," "how" and "because" cannot be addressed to Him. His existence does not begin, so that one could say when it was, nor does His permanence end, so that one could state that the time and span were complete. One cannot ask, "Why did He do what He did?" since His actions are not subject to cause, nor can one ask, "Of what sort is He?", since He belongs to no category that can be distinguished by characteristics from similar categories.

He is seen without being met with, and sees what is other than He without eyes. He works without effort or toil. His are the most beautiful names and the most exalted attributes.

He does what He wishes and subdues the servants to His rule. Nothing takes place within His authority except what He wills, and nothing occurs in His kingdom other than what was previously ordained. Whatever is known to be, in the realm of events, He willed that it be, and whatever among possible things is known not to be, He willed that it not exist.

He is the creator of the acquired traits and moral characters of His servants, both the good and the bad of them, and the producer of whatever important men and important works are in the world, whether they are few or many.

He is the sender of the Messengers to their communities, without there having been any necessity for Him to have done so.

He is the one who made humanity devoted to divine service through the tongue of the prophets (peace and blessing be upon them) with acts that no one could accomplish, with argument and remonstrance.

He is the one who aided our Prophet Muhammad (ﷺ) with evident miracles and the dazzling verses of the Quran, removing any excuse for unbelief and bringing to light both certainty and denial.

Through the Rightly-Guided Caliphs, the Truth protected the domain of Islam after the Prophet passed away. Thereafter He guarded and helped Islam with proofs of religion upon the tongues of His saints. He has made the upright community secure against coming to a consensus in error, and has cut off the root of falsehood and vanity with the guidance He has established. He has fulfilled the promise of help to the religion given in His saying, *"He is placing it over all religions, though the polytheists be averse"* (9:33).

These pages have briefly indicated the principles of the shaykhs. And success is from God.

PART I: ON THE SHAYKHS OF THIS WAY: HOW THEIR LIVES AND TEACHINGS SHOW THEIR REGARD FOR THE DIVINE LAW

Know, may God have mercy upon you, that the best of the Muslims after the Messenger of God were not called, in their own time, by any special name, but were known only as those who kept company with the Messenger. Since there is no excellence greater than that, they came to be spoken of simply as the Companions. In the second generation, those who kept company with the Companions were called the Followers, and saw in this the noblest of titles. The ones who came after them were called the Followers of the Followers. After this people began to differ and levels of development became distinguishable. The elite, who had been given an intense concern for matters of religion, were called ascetics and devotees. Then a new and alien element appeared and parties began to contend with each other, each group claiming that the ascetics were within its own ranks. So the elite of the people of the *Sunnah*, who held each of their breaths accountable to God Most High and protected their hearts from the disasters of negligence, came to be specified by the word *tasawwuf*, Sufism. This name became prevalent for these great ones before the close of the second century AH.

In this section, if God wills, we will recall the names of a number of shaykhs of this Way, from the first generation up to the present time, together with many of their histories and their sayings. These will serve to draw attention to their principles and behavior.

1 Abu Ishaq Ibrahim bin Adham bin Mansur

He was from the region of Balkh. He was a king's son. He went out hunting one day and came across the tracks of an animal, a fox or a rabbit. While he was following it, a voice from the unseen called to him, "O Ibrahim! Is it for this that you were created? Is it to this that you were commanded?" Then it called again, from the pommel of his saddle, "By God, it is not for this that you were created, and it is not to this that you were commanded!" He got off his horse and, meeting with one of his father's shepherds, took the man's woolen garment, put it on, and gave him in exchange his horse and all he had with him. Then he went into the desert. Later he came to Makkah, where he met Sufyan al-Thawr and al-Fudayl bin Iyad, and went on to Damascus, where he died.

He used to eat from the work of his own hands, serving as a reaper and a watchman over orchards and so forth, although in the desert he had met a man who had taught him the Greatest Name of God, so that he prayed by it. Then he met Khidr [the immortal guide and protector of seekers], who told him, "It was my brother the prophet David who taught you the Greatest Name."

(We were told this by Shaykh Abd-al-Rahman Muhammad bin al-Husayn al-Sulami who said[1] . . . that Ibrahim bin Bashshar related, "I met Ibrahim bin Adham and asked, 'Tell me how you became involved with all this.' And he recalled what is given above.)

Ibrahim bin Adham had great care for the moral impact of every action. It is reported that he said, "Heal your eating, and you need not pray all night and fast all day." It is said that he mostly prayed, "O my God, transport me from the humiliation of disobedience to You to the honor of obedience to You."

Someone told Ibrahim bin Adham, "The price of meat has become high." He said, "Cut the price!"—meaning, "Don't buy it!"—and he recited:

When something turned expensive for me I abandoned it
And what used to be expensive became cheap.

Muhammad bin al-Husayn told us[2] . . . that Ibrahim bin Adham said to a man circumambulating the Kabah, "Know that you will not attain the degree of the righteous until six difficult things become possible for you. The first: closing the door of ease and opening the door of hardship. The second: closing the door of honor and opening the door of humiliation. The third: closing the door of comfort, and opening the door of effort. The fourth: closing the door of sleep and opening the door of wakefulness. The fifth: closing the door of wealth and opening the door of poverty. The sixth: closing the door of expectations, and opening the door of readiness for death."

While Ibrahim bin Adham was guarding a vineyard a soldier passed by and demanded, "Give me some of these grapes." He refused. "Their owner did not so order me." The soldier began to beat him with his whip. Ibrahim bowed his head, saying, "Strike a head that has so often revolted against God!" The man was unable to continue, and went away.

Sahl bin Ibrahim said, "I was a friend of Ibrahim bin Adham, and I fell sick. He took upon himself the expense of my illness. I developed a craving for something, so he sold his donkey and spent the price of it on me. When I recovered, I asked, 'O Ibrahim, where is your donkey?' He said, 'We sold it.' I said, 'Then on what shall I ride?' He said, 'O my brother, on my shoulders.' And he carried me three days' journey."

2 Abu-l-Fayd Dhu-l-Nun al-Misri

His given name was Thawban bin Ibrahim. He was also called Fayd bin Ibrahim. His father was a Nubian. He died in the year 859 AD/245 AH. He was remarkable in this undertaking, unique in his time for knowledge, moral attention, spiritual state, and action perfectly suited to each circumstance.

He was reported to the caliph al-Mutawakkil, who summoned him from Egypt. Brought before the caliph, Dhu-l-Nun al-Misri reproached him for his sins. Al-Mutawakkil wept, and returned him to Egypt in honor. Thereafter when pious men were mentioned before al-Mutawakkil, he used to weep and say, "When the pious are remembered, haste to Dhu-l-Nun al-Misri!"

Dhu-l-Nun al-Misri was a lean man with a reddish complexion. His beard never turned white. I heard Ahmad bin Muhammad say[1] . . . that Dhu-l-Nun al-Misri said, "There are four things worth talking about: love of the sublime, hatred of the trivial, following what has been revealed, fear of changing for the worse."

I heard Muhammad bin al-Husayn say[2] . . . that Dhu-l-Nun al-Misri said, "One of the marks of the lover of God is his following the Beloved of God in his character, his actions, his advice, and his habits."

Dhu-l-Nun al-Misri was asked about the lowliest of men and said, "Whoever neither knows the way to God, nor seeks to know it."

I heard Abu Abd-al-Rahman al-Sulami say[3] . . . that Yusuf bin al-Husayn said, "One day I was present at one of Dhu-l-Nun al-Misri's gatherings when Salim al-Maghribi came to him and said, 'O Abu-l-

Fayd! What was the cause of your turning to God?' 'A marvel that you would not be able to bear,' he replied.

'By your Lord, you must tell me!' Salim insisted. So Dhu-l-Nun al-Misri answered, 'I was returning from a journey from Egypt to some villages when I fell asleep on the road in the middle of the desert. When I opened my eyes, there beside me was a blind lark, fallen from its nest onto the ground. The ground split and out of it came two bowls, one gold and one silver. In one of them was sesame seed and in the other water, and the bird began to eat and drink from this. I said, 'It is enough. I have repented.' So I remained at the door until I was received by God Almighty and Glorious.'"

I heard Muhammad bin al-Husayn say[4] . . . Dhu-l-Nun al-Misri said, "Wisdom does not dwell in a belly full of food." Dhu-l-Nun al-Misri was asked about repentance, and said, "The repentance of the majority of people is from sins; the repentance of the elite is from unconsciousness."

3 Abu Ali al-Fudayl bin Iyad

He was from Khurasan, from the region of Merv. It is said that he was born in Samarkand and grew up in Abiward. He died in Makkah in the month of Muharram in the year 802 AD/187 AH.

I heard Muhammad bin al-Husayn say[1] . . . that Abu Ammar related [the following] about al-Fudayl bin Musa, "Fudayl was a brigand who worked the road between Abiward and Dusarkhas. His repentance came about in the following way. He had developed a passion for a serving girl. He was scaling a wall to get to her when he heard a reciter of the Quran chant, '*Has the time not come for those who believe, that their hearts will be humble for the remembrance of God?*' (57:16). He said, 'O Lord, the time has come.' So he abandoned what he was doing and took shelter for the night in a ruin. Unexpectedly, a group of people was already there. Some of them said, 'Let us leave,' but another party said, 'Not until morning, for Fudayl is on the road and will fall upon us.' So Fudayl repented [before them] and reassured them. He then went to live near the sacred precincts in Makkah until he died."

Fudayl bin Iyad said, "When God loves a servant He increases his pain, and when He hates a servant He makes this world wide for him." Ibn al-Mubarak remarked, "When Fudayl bin Iyad died, sadness passed out of this world."

Fudayl said, "If the whole of this world were spread before me and

I was not accountable for what I did with it, I would still shun it, just as one of you shuns the gutter when you pass by it, lest it soil your clothes." And, "If you should swear that I am a hypocrite, I would prefer it to my swearing that I am not one."

He also said, "To give up working for the sake of human beings is hypocrisy; to work for the sake of human beings is polytheism."

Abu Ali al-Razi recalled, "I was with Fudayl for thirty years and never saw him laughing or smiling except on the day his son Ali died. I asked him about this and he said, "If if pleases God, how can it not be pleasing for me?" Fudayl said, "I revolt against God, and know it from the misbehavior of my donkey and my servant."

4 Abu Mahfuz Maruf bin Firuz al-Karkhi

He was one of the greatest shaykhs, whose prayers were always granted and whose tomb is sought out for its healing influence. The Baghdadis say, "The tomb of Maruf is a proven remedy." He came to Islam under the protection of Ali bin Musa al-Rida. He died in the year 200 [815], or according to some, in 816 AD/201AH.

He was the master of Sari al-Saqati, and said to him one day, "When you have need of anything from God, adjure Him by me." I heard Abu Ali al-Daqqaq say, "The parents of Maruf al-Karkhi were Christians, so when Maruf was a young boy they sent him to a Christian religious instructor. The teacher used to say to him, 'Say [God is] the third of three,' and he would answer, 'No, He is One.' One day the teacher struck him a violent blow, and Maruf ran away. His parents said, "Oh, if only he would come back to us, we would agree with him on whatever religion he might choose!" Meanwhile he had become a Muslim at the hands of Ali bin Musa al-Rida. He returned to his home and knocked on the door. 'Who is it?' 'Maruf,' he said. 'In what religion have you come?' they asked. 'In the true and upright religion.' So his parents became Muslims.

Muhammad bin al-Husayn said[1] . . . that Sari al-Saqati said, "I saw Maruf al-Karkhi in a dream as if he were under the Divine Throne. God Almighty and Glorious was saying to his angels, 'Who is this?' and they replied, 'You know best, O Lord.' He said, 'This is Maruf al-Karkhi, drunken with My love, and he will not recover except by meeting with Me.'

Maruf said, 'One of the companions of Dawud al-Tai said to me, "Take care not to neglect a work that will bring you closer to the pleasure of your master." I said, 'And what is that work?' He said, 'To obey your Lord continually, and to serve and advise the Muslims.'"

I heard Muhammad bin al-Husayn say that his father said:
I saw Maruf al-Karkhi in a dream, and I asked him, "How did God deal with you?" He said, "He forgave me." I asked, "Because of your asceticism and fear?" He said, "No, because of my acceptance of the advice of Ibn Sammak, my need of poverty, and my love of the poor."

Maruf gave an account of the advice of Ibn Sammak, "I was passing though Kufah and stopped in front of a man known as Ibn Sammak. He was addressing the people, and said during this speech, 'Whoever turns away from God entirely, God turns away from him entirely. Whoever turns his heart toward God, God turns toward him His mercy and the faces of all His creatures. Whoever is sometimes one way and sometimes the other, God has mercy upon him from time to time.' His speech struck upon my heart, and I turned to God Most High, abandoning all of what I was occupied with except the service of my master, Ali bin Musa al-Rida. I related this speech to my master, and he said, 'This advice, if you heed it, will suffice you.'" This story was told me by Muhammad bin al-Husayn, who said[2] . . . that Sari al-Saqat said, "I heard Maruf say that."

In his last illness, Maruf was told, "Make your will." He said, "When I die, give my shirt to charity. As I came into this world naked, I want to leave it naked."

While making a voluntary fast, Maruf passed a water-seller who was saying, "May God have mercy upon the one who drinks!" He went up and drank. "Aren't you fasting?" they asked him. "Indeed, but I had hopes of his prayer," he replied.

5 Abu-l-Hasan Sari bin al-Mughallis al-Saqati

The uncle and teacher of Junayd, he was the student of Maruf al-Karkhi. He was unique in his time for moral attentiveness, states in harmony with the *Sunnah*, and the sciences of unity. I heard Muhammad bin al-Husayn say[1] . . . that Abu-l-Abbas Ahmad bin Muhammad bin Masruq said, "It was reported to me that while Sari was one of the companions of Maruf al-Karkhi, he used to do business in the marketplace. One day Maruf went to him accompanied by an orphan boy, and said, 'Clothe this orphan.'

'So I clothed him,' Sari related. 'And Maruf was pleased by this. He said, May God make this world hateful to you, and free you from the state in which you find yourself!' 'So I got up from the shop,' Sari continued. 'And indeed there is nothing more hateful to me than this world, and the whole of my state is through the blessing of Maruf.'"

I heard Shaykh Abu Abd-al-Rahman al-Sulami say[2] . . . that Junayd said, "I never say anyone more devoted to service than Sari, 'Ninety-eight [years of life] passed over him; he was not seen lying down except in his final illness.

It is related that Sari said, "Sufism is a word with three implications. A person is a Sufi when the light of his realization does not extinguish the light of his moral evaluation of his acts; when he does not discuss esoterically a knowledge invalidated by the practical application of the Book and the *Sunnah*; when miracles do not induce him to tear the veils of God's hidden secrets." Sari died in the year 870 AD/257 AH.

I heard Abu Ali al-Daqqaq relate that Junayd said, "One day Sari asked me about love. I said, 'Some people say it is to act in harmony with one's beloved; some people say it is to prefer the beloved to oneself; some people say . . .' and so on and on.
Sari took hold of the skin of his arm and pulled it, and it did not stretch. Then he said, "By the might of the Exalted, if you had said, 'This skin has dried to these bones from love,' you would have spoken the truth!" He fainted, and his face became like a rising moon. He shone white.

It is said of Sari that he said, "For thirty years I have been asking forgiveness for saying 'May God be praised!' once."

When asked "How can this be?" he replied, "A fire broke out in Baghdad. A man came to see me and said to me, 'Your shop has been saved.' I said, 'May God be praised!' For thirty years I have regretted what I said, because I wanted for myself something better than what had befallen the Muslims." Abd Allah bin Yusuf told me about this, saying[3] . . . that Abu Bakr al-Harbi said, "I heard Sari say that."

It is related that Sari said, "I look at my nose time after time each day, for fear that it will have become black. I am afraid that God will darken my face because of [the disgrace of] the things with which I occupy myself."

I heard Muhammad bin al-Husayn say[4] . . . that Junayd said, that he heard Sari say, "I know a special road that goes direct to Paradise." "What is it?" I asked him. "Do not ask anything from anyone, do not take anything from anyone, and do not keep with you anything that you can give to anyone," he said.

I heard Abd Allah bin Yusuf al-Ispahani say[5] . . . Junayd bin Muhammad said that he heard Sari say, "I wish to die in a land other than Baghdad." Asked "Why is that?" he answered, "I am afraid that my grave will not receive me [on account of my sins], and I would be publicly disgraced."

I heard Abd Allah bin Yusuf al-Ispahani say[6] . . . Sari prayed, "O God, however much you may punish me with something, do not punish me with the humiliation of the veil [between You and me]."

I heard Abd Allah bin Yusuf al-Ispahani say[7] . . . that Junayd said, One day I came in on Sari while he was weeping. I asked, "What is making you cry?" He said, "Yesterday my little girl came to me and said, 'Father, it is a hot night; I will hang this jug here.' Then drowsiness overcame me and I slept. [In my dream] I saw a serving-maid of the greatest beauty descend from the sky. I asked, 'To whom do you belong?' 'To the one who does not drink cold water in jugs!' she answered. Then she picked up the jug, struck it against the earth, and broke it."

Junayd said, {I saw the shards. He did not pick them up, or touch them, until they had been completely covered over by dust."

6 Abu Nasr Bishr bin al-Harith al-Hafi

His family was from Merv, but he lived and died in Baghdad. He was the son of the sister of Ali bin Khashram. He died in the year 842 AD/227 AH, and had great influence.

He turned to God in the following way. He came upon a piece of paper on which was written the Name of God. It had been trodden underfoot in the road. He picked it up, bought perfume with a dirham he had with him, perfumed it, and put it in a crack in a wall. Then, as if he were asleep, he had a vision. It seemed someone was saying to him, "O Bishr! You have made My name fragrant; I will make your name fragrant in this world and the next!"

I heard Abu Ali al-Daqqaq say that Bishr passed by some people who were saying, "Such-and-such a man does not sleep the whole night and breaks his fast only once in three days." Bishr wept. When asked why, he said, "I do not recall that I ever stayed awake one full night, or that I fasted a day when I did not end the fast the same evening. But God, may He be exalted and magnified, out of His kindness and generosity places in the heart more than the servant can accomplish." Then he related the beginning of his own experience, as we have related it above.

I heard Abu Abd-al-Rahman al-Sulami say[1] . . . that Bishr al-Hafi said, "I saw the Prophet in a dream. He said to me, 'Bishr, do you know why God has raised you up from among your fellows?' 'No, O Messenger of God,' I said. He said, 'Because of your adherence to my *Sunnah*, your service to the righteous, your advice to your brethren and your love of my Companions and my family. This is what has brought you to the degree of the pious.'"

I heard Muhammad bin al-Husayn say[2] . . . that Bilal al-Khawwas said, "I was in the desert of the Children of Israel when suddenly there was a man walking beside me. I was amazed. Then it came to me that this was Khidr. So I said to him, 'By the truth of the Truth, who are you?' He said, "Your brother Khidr.' 'I want to ask you something,' I said. 'Ask,' he replied. 'What do you say about al-Shafii, [who made written Traditions the first principle of legal interpretation] may God have mercy upon him?' 'He was one of the pillars of the world.' 'What do you say about [the great defender of the literal Quran] Ahmad bin Hanbal, may God be pleased with him?' 'A man of perfect integrity.' 'And what do you say about Bishr al-Hafi?' 'His like was not created after him.' I asked, How has it come about that I see you?' 'Through your kindness to your mother,' he replied.

I heard Abu Ali al-Daqqaq say, "Bishr al-Hafi came and knocked on the door of Muafi bin Imran. Someone said, 'Who is it?' 'Bishr al-Hafi,' he answered. From inside the house a little girl called to him, 'If you bought yourself a shoe for two danaqs you would lose the name of Hafi ['barefoot']!"

Muhammad bin Abd Allah al-Shirazi told me the story. He said[3] . . . al-Mughazili said, "I heard Bishr al-Hafi recall this story."

I heard Muhammad bin al-Husayn say[4] . . .that Ahmad bin Ali al-Dimashqi said that Abd Allah bin al-Jalla said to me, "I saw Dhu-l-Nun al-Misri, and he possessed the power of clear explanation. I saw Sahl al-Tustari, and he possessed the power of symbolic intimation. I saw Bishr bin al-Harith, and he possessed moral wakefulness. Someone asked him, "Whom did you prefer?" He answered, "Our master Bishr al-Harith."

It is said that for years Bishr craved beans, but did not eat them. After his death someone saw him in a dream and asked him, "How has God dealt with you?" "He forgave me," he replied, "and said, 'Eat, O you who did not eat, and drink, O you who did not drink!'"

Abu Abd-al-Rahman al-Sulami told us[5] . . . that Bishr bin al-Harith said, "I craved roast meat for forty years, but its price was never lawful for me." Bishr was asked, "With what do you eat your bread?" He said, "I remember health and make that my condiment!"

Muhammad bin al-Husayn told us[6] . . . that Ibn Abi-l-Dunya said, "A man said to Bishr . . ." and so on, the above-mentioned story. Bishr said, "The lawful cannot be wasted."

Bishr was seen in a dream, and asked, "How did God deal with you?" He said, "He forgave me, and allowed me half of paradise, and said to me, 'O Bishr, if you had prostrated yourself to Me on hot coals, you would not have discharged your debt of gratitude for what was attributed to you in the hearts of my servants.'" Bishr said, "A man who loves people to know who he is will not find the sweetness of the next world."

7 Abu Abd Allah al-Harith bin Asad al-Muhasibi

He was without equal in his time for knowledge, moral awareness, the conduct of human relationships, and spiritual state. He was originally from Basra, and died in Baghdad in 857 AD/243 AH.

It is said that he inherited seventy thousand dirhams from his father and never touched any of it. This is supposed to have been because his father used to hold views [denying the existence of] destiny. He felt ethically unable to take anything from his inheritance, and said, "The report is trustworthy that the Prophet said, 'People who have differences of opinion in their religion cannot inherit from each other.'"

I heard Muhammad bin al-Husayn say[1] . . . that I heard Muhammad bin Masruq say that al-Harith bin Asad al-Muhasibi died penniless. His father had left him property and estates, but he had taken nothing from them.

I heard Abu Ali al-Daqqaq say that when al-Harith al-Muhasibi passed his hand over food in which there was something not entirely lawful, a vein in his finger would stir, and he would abstain from it.

Abu Abd Allah bin Khafif al-Shirazi said, "Copy five of our shaykhs, and leave the others alone—al-Harith al-Muhasibi, Junayd bin Muhammad, Abu Muhammad Ruwaym, Abu-l-Abbas bin Ata, and Amr bin Uthman al-Makki. They joined knowledge with the realities."

I heard Abu Abd-al-Rahman Muhammad bin al-Husayn al-Sulami say[2] . . . that Harith al-Muhasibi said, "When someone sets right his inner being through self-examination and sincerity, God will adorn his outer being with spiritual effort and adherence to the *Sunnah*.

Junayd related, "One day al-Harith al-Muhasibi passed by me and I saw the signs of hunger in him, so I called, 'Uncle, won't you come into the house and have something to eat?' He said yes. I went inside to look for something to offer him and found some food that had been brought to me from a wedding feast. I gave it to him. He took a bite, turned it in his mouth a few times, and then stood up, threw it into the courtyard, and went away. When I saw him a few days later I spoke to him about it. 'I was hungry, and I wanted to please you by eating and not hurt your feelings,' he said, 'but between God, glory to Him, and me there is a sign—He will not permit me to eat food that is in any way doubtful. So He makes me incapable of swallowing it. From where did you get that food?' 'It was brought to me from the house of one of my neighbors, from a wedding feast,' I said. Then I asked, 'Will you come and visit today?' 'Yes,' he said. So I offered him some slices of dry bread that we had, and he ate, and said, 'When you give something to one of God's poor, let it be something like this.'"

8 Abu Sulayman Dawud bin Nusayr al-Tai

He was of great importance. Abu Abd al-Rahman al-Sulami told us[1] . . . that Yusuf bin Asbat said that Dawud al-Tai inherited twenty dinars and it took him twenty years to spend them.

I heard Abu Ali al-Daqqaq say that the origin of Dawud al-Tai's asceticism was that one day as he was walking through Baghdad, as was his custom, the attendants of Hamid al-Tusi pushed him aside while clearing the road for the governor to pass. He looked and saw Hamid and said to himself, "Shame on this world that gives precedence to Hamid over you!" So he withdrew to his house and began to engage in spiritual struggle and devotion.

I heard a dervish in Baghdad say that Dawud al-Tai came to asceticism through hearing a hired mourner lament. She said:

In which of your cheeks does decay appear?
And which of your eyes, then, is melting?

His asceticism is also said to have originated from his association with Abu Hanifah [the great jurist, founder of the oldest surviving school of interpretation of Islamic law]. One day Abu Hanifah said to him, "Abu Sulayman, we have mastered the instrument." "So what remains to be done?" Dawud asked. He replied, "Putting it to use." Dawud al-Tai said, "My ego desired solitude and fought with me. I said to it, 'Not until you can keep company with these people and not argue with them about anything.' So I sat with them a year in which

I did not discuss any matter, and the issues passed before me while I struggled terribly with the desire to discuss them, a desire greater than that of a thirsty man craving cold water. But I did not discuss them." Then his state became what it became.

It is said that Dawud was bled by Junayd the cupper, and gave him a dinar. The man said, "This is extravagance!" He said, "There is no devotion to God in the man who has no generosity."

Dawud used to say, "At night my preoccupation with You, my God, suspends my worldly cares and comes between me and sleep."

I heard Muhammad bin Abd Allah al-Sufi say[2] . . . that Ismail bin Ziyad al-Tai told us, "Dawud's woman servant, Dayah, [having served him two dishes], said to him, "Don't you want the bread?" He said, "Between drinking the broth and chewing the bread comes the recitation of fifty verses."

When Dawud passed away, a righteous man saw him in a dream. He was running. The man asked him, "What are you doing?" He said, "I have just escaped from prison!" The man awoke from his dream, and people were raising the cry, "Dawud is dead!"

A man said to Dawud, "Counsel me." He said to him, "The army of death awaits you!" Someone went to see Dawud and saw a jar of water upon which the sun had fallen. "Won't you move it into the shade?" the visitor asked. Dawud said, "When I put it there, there was no sun, and I am ashamed that God should see me move toward what gives pleasure to my lower self."

A man came into Dawud's presence and began to stare at him. Dawud said, "Don't you know that the Prophet's Companions used to dislike too much looking, as they disliked too much speaking?" Abd Allah bin Yusuf al-Ispahani told us[3] . . . that Abu Rabi al-Wasiti said, "I said to Dawud, 'Counsel me.' He said, 'Fast from this world and let your breaking of fast be death, and flee from the people as you would flee from a beast of prey.'"

9 Abu Ali Shaqiq bin Ibrahim al-Balkhi

He was among the shaykhs of Khorasan. He spoke eloquently on trust in God, and was the teacher of Hatim al-Asamm.

Here is how his repentance was said to have come about. He was a rich man's son, and when he was young he went on a trading expedition to the land of the polytheists. He entered an idol-temple and saw there an idol-server with a shaven head and face, dressed in a bright red robe. Shaqiq said to the server, "You have a Maker who is

Living, Knowing, and All-Capable, so worship Him, not these idols that can do you neither harm nor good!" The man retorted, "If it is as you say, then He is capable of providing for you in your own country. Why did you trudge all the way here for trade?" Shaqiq was spiritually awakened, and started upon the path of asceticism.

It is also said that his asceticism began when, at a time when food was scarce, he encountered a slave who was playful and merry though everyone else was overcome by anxiety. "What is this liveliness you have in you?" Shaqiq asked. "Don't you see what a state everyone is in on account of the drought and famine?" "And what is that to me," the slave said, "while my master has a village of his own from which everything we need comes to him?" Shaqiq, in realization, said, "His master owns a village, so he has no worries about his sustenance. But his master is only a poor creature! How should a Muslim worry about sustenance, while his Master is rich?"

I heard Abu Abd al-Rahman al-Sulami say[1] . . . that Hatim al-Asamm said, "Shaqiq bin Ibrahim was a prosperous man. He used to pursue the ideals of chivalry and was well-known in the chivalrous brotherhoods."

Ali bin Isa bin Mahan, the ruler of Balkh, loved hunting dogs. One day he lost one of his dogs and accused one of Shaqiq's neighbors of having it. He started looking for the man, who fled and sought protection in Shaqiq's house. Shaqiq went to the amir and said,"Let him be. I have the dog and will return it to you in three days." The ruler left the man alone, but Shaqiq began worrying about what he had done. When the third day arrived, one of Shaqiq's friends, who had been out of Balkh, returned. On the road he had found a dog in a collar and taken it, saying to himself, "I will lead it to Shaqiq, since he follows the code of chivalry so closely." So he brought it to him, and Shaqiq saw that it was indeed the dog of the amir, and rejoiced. He took the dog to the amir and was released from standing surety for it. Then God bestowed awareness upon him, and he turned away from all his affairs and sought the path of asceticism.

It is related that Hatim al-Asamm said, "We were with Shaqiq in the line of battle, fighting the Turks, on a day when you could see nothing but heads falling, spears shattering and swords being sliced. Shaqiq said to me, 'How do you see yourself on this day, Hatim? Do you see yourself as you were on the night your bride was led to you?' 'No, by God,' I said. 'But, by God,' he went on, 'I see myself this day as I was that night.' Then he slept between the ranks, with his head on his shield, [so soundly that] I heard his snoring."

Shaqiq said, "When you want to know a man, look at what God has promised him and what men have promised him—on which of the two does his heart rely the more?" He also said, "The piety of a man is known by three things: what he accepts, what he refuses, and what he says."

10 Abu Yazid bin Tayfur bin Isa al-Bistami

His grandfather accepted Islam from Zoroastrianism. There were three brothers, Adam, Tayfur, and Ali, and all of them were renunciates and devoted worshippers. The state of Abu Yazid was the most sublime. He is said to have died either in 875 AD/261 AH or in 848 AD/234AH.

I heard Muhammad bin al-Husayn say[1] . . . that al-Hasan bin Ali said that Abu Yazid was asked, "Through what thing is this realization to be found?" He replied, "Through an empty belly and and a naked body."

I heard Muhammad bin al-Husayn say[2] . . . that Abu Yazid said, "I struggled thirty years and never found anything more difficult for me than knowledge and conforming to knowledge. If it were not for the differences among scholars I would have remained [attached to these things]. Differences among scholars are a mercy, except in establishing the abstract idea of the unity of God."

It is said that Abu Yazid did not leave this world until he had memorized the entire Quran. Abu Hatim al-Sijistani related to us[3] . . . that the father of a friend of Abu Yazid's uncle said that Abu Yazid said to him, "Let's go and see this man who has distinguished himself for saintliness." This was a man much imitated, who was famous for asceticism. So they went to see him. When the man left his house to go to the mosque he spit in the direction of prayer. Abu Yazid turned away without even greeting him. He said, "This man is not trustworthy with regard to one of the practices of the Prophet. How then can he be trustworthy with regard to what he is said to be?"

According to this same chain of narrators, Abu Yazid said, "I intended to ask God Most High for protection from the burden of food and the burden of women. Then I said to myself, 'How can I ask God for this while the Messenger of God never asked it?' So I did not request it. At that, God Exalted and Magnified spared me from the burden of women to such an extent that I did not care whether what faced me was a woman or a wall."

I heard Abu Abd al-Rahman al-Sulami say[4] . . . that al-Hasan bin Ali's great-uncle said, "I asked Abu Yazid about the beginnings of his practice and his asceticism. He said, 'There is nowhere to rest in asceticism.' 'Why?' I asked. 'Because I spent three days in asceticism,' he told me, 'and on the fourth I left it. The first day I gave up this world and what is in it. The second day I gave up the next world and what is in it. The third day I gave up what is other than God. The fourth day nothing remained to me except God, so I understood. I heard a voice say, "O Abu Yazid! You will not be able to endure with Me!" I said, 'That is what I desire.' And I heard the One that spoke reply, "You have found it! You have found it!"'"

Abu Yazid was asked, "What is the most difficult thing you have undergone in the Way of God?" He answered, "It is not possible to describe it." "And what is the easiest thing your ego has undergone?" "As for that, certainly!" he said. "I called it to the performance of a religious duty and it did not answer me, so I forbade it water for a year."

Abu Yazid said, "For thirty years I prayed, though in each prayer the conviction within me was no better than it would have been had I been a fire-worshiper, wrapped about the waist with the belt of dualism. I wanted to cut the belt."

I heard Muhammad bin al-Husayn say[5] . . . that Abu Yazid said, "Even if you see a man who has been granted such power to work miracles that he rises into the air, do not let him deceive you. Wait until you find out his attitudes toward the command of good and the prohibition of evil, the preservation of the limits set by God, and the performance of the duties of the Divine Law (*Shariah*)."

My uncle from Bistam related that his father said, "Abu Yazid went out one night to the fortress, in order to invoke the name of God upon its walls. He remained until morning and did not invoke. I asked him about this, and he said, 'I remembered a word that used to come to my tongue when I was a boy, and I was ashamed to invoke God, the Magnified and Exalted.'"

11 Abu Muhammad Sahl bin Abd Allah al-Tustari

He first among the imams of the Sufis, unequaled in his time for the quality of his daily life and his precise moral awareness, he possessed the power of miracles. He met Dhu-l-Nun al-Misri in Makkah the year he went on the prescribed pilgrimage. The year of his death is said to have been 886 AD/283 AH, or alternatively 896 AD/273 AH.

Sahl said, "When I was a boy of three I used to stay awake to watch my uncle, Muhammad bin Suwar, stay up at night and pray. Sometimes he would say to me, 'Sahl, go to sleep. You are distracting my heart.'"

I heard Muhammad bin al-Husayn say[1] . . . Sahl bin Abd Allah said, "One day my uncle said to me, 'Don't you remember God who created you?' I asked, 'How should I remember Him?'" He answered, 'When you go to bed, say three times—in your heart, without moving your tongue—"God is my witness." I said this for three days, and then told him about it.

He said to me, 'Say it every night seven times.' I did, and then spoke to him again. He said, 'Say it every night eleven times.' I did this, and sweetness came into my heart. When a year had passed, my uncle said to me, 'Preserve what I have taught you, and continue with it until you enter your grave, and it will profit you in this world and the next.' I continued without ceasing for some years, and the sweetness of it came into my innermost awareness.

Then one day my uncle said, 'Sahl, when God is with someone, looking at him, as his witness, does that person disobey Him? Beware of disobedience!' I used to go into seclusion. They tried to send me to school, but I would say, 'I am afraid of breaking my concentration!' Finally they arranged with the teacher that I should go to him for an hour and study, and then return. So I went to school and memorized the Quran. I was six or seven years old. Until I was twelve I used to fast for long periods of time, and make my nourishment barley bread.

When I was thirteen years old a question developed in me, and I asked my family if they would send me to Basra so that I could inquire into the answer. I went to Basra and asked all of the scholars about it, and none of them could satisfy me at all. Then I went to Abadan, to a man known as Abu Habib Hamzah bin Abd Allah al-Abadani. I asked about it and he answered me. So I stayed with him a long time, profiting from his talk and learning his ways. Then I returned to Tustar. I limited my nourishment to a dirham's worth of barley. I milled it, baked it, and breakfasted after staying awake all night on one measure of it only, without salt or condiment, and that dirham used to suffice me for a year. Next I determined to pass three nights fasting and then break for a night. I extended this to five, then seven, then twenty-five nights. I continued in this way for twenty years. Then I went out to travel in the earth for two years. Finally I returned to Tustar and undertook to stand in prayer the entire night."

I heard Muhammad bin al-Husayn say[2] . . . that Sahl bin Abd

Allah al-Tustari said, "Every action the servant performs that is not in emulation of the Prophet, whether it be an act of obedience or dis- obedience, is food for the ego. But every action he performs by imita- tion of that example is punishment for the ego."

12 Abu Sulayman Abd al-Rahman bin Atiyah al-Darani

He came from Daran, one of the villages of Damascus. He died in the year 830 AD/215 AH. I heard Muhammad bin al-Husayn say[1] . . . that Abu Sulayman said, "Whoever does good by day is rewarded at night, and whoever does good at night is rewarded by day. If someone is sincere in abandoning a desire, God will make it disappear from his heart, for God Most High is too noble to punish a heart with a desire that was given up for Him." By the same chain of narrators, "When this world settles into a heart, the next world emigrates out of it."

I heard Abu Abd al-Rahman al-Sulami say[2] . . . that Abu Sulayman al-Darani said, "Sometimes one of the subtle sayings of the Sufis stays in my heart for days, but I will not accept it save on [the testimony of] two just witnesses: the Quran and the *Sunnah*."

Other sayings of Abu Sulayman include: The most excellent work is to oppose the desires of the ego; everything has a sign, and the sign of being turned away in prayer is to give up weeping; there is a rust for everything, and the rust for the light of the heart is the satisfac- tion of the belly; everything that distracts you from God Most High, whether it be wives, property, or children, is a misfortune for you."

Abu Sulayman said, "One chilly night I was in the prayer niche. The cold disturbed me, so I wrapped one of my hands [in my clothing], while I kept the other open and extended for prayer. I was overcome by sleep, and a voice from nowhere addressed me, 'O Abu Sulayman! We have placed in this hand that which it reaches for—as for the other, We would have given to it as well!' So I swore to myself that I would not pray except with both hands out, whether the weather were hot or cold."

Abu Sulayman said, "I neglected my devotions, and suddenly I found myself with a *huri*, who said to me, 'You sleep,while I have been waiting for you behind the veil for five hundred years!'"

Abd Allah bin Yusuf al-Ispahani informed us[3] . . . that Ahmad bin Abi-l-Hawari reported that he came in on Abu Sulayman one day while he was crying. He asked him, "What makes you weep?" Abu Sulayman answered, "Ahmad, why should I not weep? When the night has overspread, and eyes are closed, and every lover is alone with his beloved, and the people of love stretch out their feet, their tears flowing down their cheeks and trickling into their places of prayer, the Sublime One looks down, and calls,'O Gabriel! By My Essence,those who delight in My Word, and rest in My remembrance—certainly I watch over them in their seclusion. I hear their moans and see their weeping. Why do you not call to them, O Gabriel, and say, "What is this weeping? Have you ever seen a beloved who punished his lovers?" How could it be fitting for Me to punish a people who, when night conceals them, speak words of love to Me? I swear by Myself that when they reach Me on the day of judgment I will reveal to them my precious face, so that they will look on Me and I will look on them.'"

13 Abu Abd al-Rahman Hatim bin Ulwan

He was called Hatim bin Yusuf al-Asamm, "the deaf." He was one of the greatest shaykhs of Khurasan. He was the student of Shaqiq and the teacher of Ahmad bin Khadruyah. It is said that he was not deaf, but pretended to be deaf on one occasion, which gave rise to his name.

Abu Ali al-Daqqaq said, "A woman came and asked Hatim a question, and it so happened that in this circumstance a certain sound came out of her, and she was embarrassed. Hatim said, 'Speak louder!'—pretending that he was deaf. The woman was delighted at this, and said, 'He did not hear the sound, for the name of deafness has prevailed over him!'"

Abu Abd al-Rahman al-Sulami informed us[1] . . . that Hatim al-Asamm said, "No morning arrives without Satan asking me,'What will you eat?' and 'What will you wear?' and 'Where will you find shelter?' So I say to him, 'I will eat death, and wear my shroud, and find shelter in the grave.'" By the same chain of narrators it is reported that Hatim was asked, "Don't you desire anything?" He said, "I desire health day and night." "Aren't all your days healthy?" they inquired. "My day of health is one in which I do not disobey God," said he.

It is related that Hatim al-Asamm said, "I was in a battle for religion when somebody seized me and threw me down for slaughter. My heart did not become distraught—instead, I contemplated what God Most High was ordaining for me. Then, while my opponent was groping for the knife in his boot, he was struck by an arrow unawares. It killed him; so I threw him off me and got up."

I heard Abd Allah bin Yusuf al-Ispahani say[2] . . . that it is reported that Hatim said, "Whoever enters this path of ours shall bring about in himself four kinds of death: a white death, which is hunger; a black death, which is bearing affronts from people; a red death, which is uncontaminated effort in opposing one's desires; a green death, which is wearing patch upon patch."

14 Abu Zakariya Yahya bin Muadh al-Razi al-Waiz

He was unique in his time. He spoke particularly on hope, and discussed gnosis (*marifah*). He traveled to Balkh and lived there for some time, then returned to Nishapur and died there in the year 872 AD/258 AH.

I heard Muhammad bin al-Husayn say[1] . . . that Yahya bin Muadh said, "How can he who has no moral carefulness become an ascetic? First be cautious in regard to what is not yours— then be abstinent in regard to what is yours." Through the same narrators, he said, "The hunger of penitents is an experiment, the hunger of renunciates is a policy, and the hunger of the sincere is an honor from God."

Yahya said, "Separation is worse than death, because separation is to be cut off from the Truth, while death is only to be cut off from the creation." He also said, "Asceticism is three things: making do with little, withdrawing from the world, and hunger." And, "Nothing will give you a greater advantage over your ego than to occupy it at every moment with what is worthier for it."

It is said that in Balkh Yahya bin Muadh argued on the superiority of wealth to poverty. He was given thirty thousand dirhams. One of the shaykhs said to him, "May God not bless this money!" He left for Nishapur. A thief came upon him on the road and took the money from him.

Abd Allah bin Yusuf al-Ispahani informed us[2] . . . that Yahya bin Muadh said, "Whoever betrays God in secret, God exposes his secret in public."

I heard Abd Allah bin Yusuf say[3] . . . that Yahya bin Muadh said, "Testimonials from bad people are a defect, and their liking you is a shame upon you. Someone who is in need of others is lowly in their eyes.

15 Abu Hamid Ahmad bin Khadruyah al-Balkhi

He was one of the great shaykhs of Khurasan, an associate of Abu Turab al-Nakhshabi. He arrived at Nishapur and visited Abu Hafs [al-Haddad], then left for Bistam to visit Abu Yazid al-Bistami. He was great in the cultivation of spiritual chivalry (*futuwah*). Abu Hafs said, "I have not seen anyone with greater zeal, or a sounder spiritual state, than Ahmad bin Khadruyah."

Abu Yazid used to say, "Ahmad is our master." I heard Muhammad bin al-Husayn say[1] . . . that Muhammad bin Hamid said, "I sat with Ahmad bin Khadruyah when he was in his death-agony. He was ninety-five years old. One of his disciples asked him a question. Tears came to his eyes, and he said, 'O my dear son, a door that I have been knocking upon for ninety-five years is about to be opened to me this very hour. I do not know whether it will open to joy or to misery. How should I have time to give an˘ answer?'

He related that Ahmad ibn Khadruyah owed seven hundred dinars. His creditors were all around him. He looked at them and prayed, "O God, You have placed things in pawn with men of property, and now You are taking away what they count as security. So You pay my debts!" Just then someone knocked on the door and said, "Where are the creditors of Ahmad?" And he settled his debts.

He died, may God have mercy upon him, in the year 854 AD/240 AH. Ahmad bin Khadruyah said, "There is no slumber heavier than heedlessness and no slavery more dominating than desire. If heedlessness did not weigh upon you, desire would not be victorious over you."

16 Abu-l-Husayn Ahmad bin Abi-l-Hawari

He was from Damascus. He kept company with Abu Sulayman al-Darani and others. He died in the year 845 AD/230 AH. Junayd used to say, "Ahmad bin Abil-Hawari is the sweet-smelling herb of Damascus."

I heard Abu Abd al-Rahman al-Sulami say[1] . . . that Ahmad bin Abil-Hawari said, "If someone looks at the world with ambition and desire, God makes the light of certainty and renunciation leave his heart." And by the same narrators, "Whoever undertakes a work that is not in emulation of the *Sunnah* of the Messenger of God—his undertaking is in vain."

According to these narrators, Ahmad bin Abil-Hawari said, "The best of crying is the servant's crying over the time he has wasted on what is not in conformity with the *Sunnah*." Ahmad said, "God does not try a servant by anything harder than heedlessness and hard-heartedness."

17 Abu Hafs Umar bin Maslamah al-Haddad

He was from a village called Kurdabadh, outside the gate of the city of Nishapur, on the Bukhara road. He was first among the imams and the sayyids, the descendants of the Prophet. He died around the year 874 AD/260 AH.

Abu Hafs said, "Rebellion is the messenger of unbelief, as fever is the messenger of death." He also said, "When I see a seeker who loves the spiritual concert, I know there is a remnant of idleness in him." And, "The best of exterior courtesy is the reflection of the best of interior courtesy." And again, "Spiritual chivalry *(futuwah)* is to act fairly, and to give up looking for fair treatment."

I heard Muhammad bin al-Husayn say[1] . . . that Abu Hafs used to say, "Whoever does not weigh his actions and states at every moment by the Book and the *Sunnah*, and does not question his thoughts, is not counted in the ranks of men."

18 Abu Turab Askar bin Husayn al-Nakhshabi

He was a companion of Hatim al-Asamm and Abu Hatim al-Attar al-Misri. He died in the year 859 AD/245 AH. It is said that he died in the desert and his body was torn apart by beasts of prey. Ibn al-Jalla said, "I sat with six hundred shaykhs, and did not encounter among them the likes of four. The first of these was Abu Turab al-Nakhshabi."

Abu Turab said, "The dervish is he whose food is whatever he finds, whose clothing is what covers him, and whose shelter is where he alights." Abu Turab said, "When a servant sincerely performs his duty in an action, he finds its sweetness before he undertakes it, and when he is purely devoted to God in it, he finds its sweetness and deliciousness at the very moment of acting."

I heard Abu Abd al-Rahman al-Sulami say that he heard his grandfather, Ismail bin Nujayd, say, "When Abu Turab al-Nakhshabi saw anything that he found objectionable among his students, he increased his own efforts and reviewed his repentance, saying, 'It is through my evils that they have been driven to what they have been driven to, since God Almighty and Glorious says, *"God will not alter the circumstances of a people until they alter themselves""'* (13:11).

Abu Abd al-Rahman al-Sulami said that he also heard his grandfather, Ismail bin Nujayd, say to his students, "Whoever among you wears rags is a beggar, whoever sits idly in a house of dervishes or a mosque is a beggar, and whoever reads the Quran in a book, or recites it so that people can hear, is a beggar." He also heard [his grandfather] say that Abu Turab used to say, "There is a compact between God and me that I shall not stretch out my hand toward anything unlawful without that hand being unable to reach it."

One day Abu Turab looked at a Sufi among his students who reached for a watermelon rind. The man had gone hungry for three days. Abu Turab said to him, "You stretch out your hand to a watermelon rind? Sufism is not proper for you. Stick to the marketplace!"

I heard Muhammad bin al-Husayn say[1] . . . that he heard Abu Turab al-Nakhshabi say, "My lower self has not exhausted me in anything at all except once, when it wore me out about some bread and eggs. I was traveling, and turned off the road to go to a village. Thereupon a man jumped on me, grabbed me, and said, 'This one was with the thieves!' People threw me down on the ground and beat me, seventy strokes. Then a man of the Sufis stopped by us, and yelled out, 'But this is Abu Turab al-Nakhshabi!' They freed me and apologized to me, and the man led me to his house, where he brought me bread and eggs. So I said to myself, 'Eat, after seventy lashes!'"

Ibn al-Jalla reported, "Abu Turab came into Mecca with a sweet breath, and I asked him, 'Where have you eaten, Master?'
He said, 'A bite in Basra, and a bite in Nabaj, and a bite here.'"

19 Abu Muhammad Abd Allah bin Khubayq

He was one of the ascetics of the Sufi way, an associate of Yusuf bin Asbat. His family was from Kufah, but he lived in Antakya.

I heard Muhammad bin al-Husayn say[1]. . . that he heard Fath bin Shakhraf say that the first time he met him, Abd Allah ibn Khubayq said to him, "O Khorasani! There are only four things, no more: your eye, your tongue, your heart, and your desire. Guard your eye: do not use it to gaze on what is not lawful. Guard your tongue: do not use it to say anything whose opposite God Most High knows to be in your heart. Guard your heart: let there not be in it malice nor hatred toward any of the Muslims. Guard your desire: do not desire with it any bad thing. If these four traits are not in you, pour ashes on your head—you are wretched."

Ibn Khubayq said, "Do not worry about anything but what will injure you tomorrow, and do not rejoice about anything but what will please you tomorrow." He also said, "Estrangement of servants from the Truth causes the estrangement of the hearts of others from them. If they were to be at ease with their Lord, everyone would be at ease with them." And, "The most beneficial fear is that which holds you back from rebellion, prolongs your sorrow over opportunities lost, and forces you to think about the remainder of your life. The most benefi-cial hope is that which makes the work easy for you." He also said, "Long listening to foolishness smothers the sweetness of obedience in the heart."

20 Abu Ali Ahmad bin Asim al-Antaki

He was one of the intimates of Bishr bin al-Harith, Sari al-Saqati, and al-Harith al-Muhasibi. Abu Sulayman al-Darani used to call him "the spy of the heart" on account of the keenness of his insight into people's thoughts. Ahmad bin Asim said, "If you seek soundness of heart, turn to guarding your tongue." He also said, "God Most High has said, '*Your wealth and your children are [only] a trial*' (8:28; 102:15), yet we seek to increase the trial!"

21 Abu-l-Sari Mansur Ibn Ammar

He was from Merv, from a village called Yaranqan. It is also said that he came from Bushanj. He established himself in Basra and became one of its greatest preachers.

Mansur bin Ammar said, "When someone worries about worldly troubles, misfortune turns into his religion." He also said, "The best of garments for the servant is humility and contrition, and the best of garments for the Knower of God is awe of God (*taqwa*), for God Most High has said, '*The garment of God-wariness, that is the best*' (7:36)."

It is related that the cause of his turning to God was his finding a scrap of paper in the road on which was written, "In the Name of God, the Merciful, the Compassionate." He picked it up, and not finding any place to put it, ate it. Then someone appeared to him in a dream and said, "God has opened the door of wisdom for you because of your respect for that scrap."

I heard Abu Abd al-Rahman al-Sulami say[1] . . . that Abu-l-Hasan al-Sharani said that he saw Mansur bin Ammar in a dream, and asked him, "What did God do with you?" He replied, "He asked me, 'Are you Mansur bin Ammar?' 'Yes, O Lord,' I replied. He said, 'You are the one who urged men to abstain from the world while coveting it yourself?' 'It was so, O Lord; but I never held a session that did not begin with Your praise, continue with blessings upon Your Prophet, and proceed to good advice for Your servants.' He said, 'It is true. Set up a pulpit for him! You will glorify Me in My heaven among My angels as you used to glorify Me on My earth among My servants.'"

22 Abu Salih Hamdun bin Ahmad bin Umarah al-Qassar

He was from Nishapur, and through him the Malamati school [of those who manifest blameworthy qualities while maintaining their purity in secret] was spread in Nishapur. He was a student of Salman al-Barusi and Abu Turab al-Nakhshabi. He died in the year 884 AD/271 AH.

Hamdun was asked, "When is it permissible for a man to preach to the people?" He replied, "When on account of his knowledge he has been assigned to discharge an obligatory duty imposed by God Most High, or when he fears that men may be destroyed by deviating from the truth, while hoping that God Most High may save them."

He said, "Whoever thinks that his ego is better than Pharaoh's ego has shown arrogance." And he said, "Since I learned that the King has insight into evildoers, fear of the King has not left my heart." And, "If you see a drunkard, do not hasten to judge him, lest you do him wrong; you would then be afflicted to the same degree that he has been."

Abd Allah bin Munazil said, "I asked Abu Salih, 'Advise me.' He said, 'If you are capable of not getting angry at anything in the world, then do it.'"

A friend of his died while Hamdun was at his side. Hamdun extinguished the lamp. They exclaimed, "At a time like this oil should be added to the lamp!" Hamdun answered, "Up until this time, the oil was his. From now on, it belongs to his heirs."

Hamdun said, "Whoever looks at the histories of earlier generations knows his own backwardness and falling short of the lowest degree of manhood." He also said, "Do not divulge something about somebody else that you would want veiled if it were about you."

23 Abu-l-Qasim al-Junayd bin Muhammad

He was the prince and imam of this group. His family was from Nahawand, but his birth and upbringing was in Iraq. His father used to sell glass, and on account of this Junayd was known as al-Qawariri, "vendor of glass vessels." He was a legal scholar of the school of Abu Thawr, and used to give opinions to Abu Thawr's circle, in the master's presence, when he was only twenty years old. He was among the companions of his maternal uncle Sari [al-Saqati], al-Harith al-Muhasibi, and Muhammad bin Ali al-Qassab. He died in the year 910 AD/297 AH.

I heard Muhammad bin al-Husayn say[1] . . . that when asked, "Who is a gnostic (*arif*)?" Junayd said, "Whoever speaks of your innermost self, though you remain silent."

I heard Shaykh Abu Abd al-Rahman al-Sulami say[2] . . . that Junayd said, "We have not derived Sufism from idle chatter, but from hunger, and abandoning the world, and cutting off pleasant and familiar habits."

I heard Muhammad bin al-Husayn say[3] . . . that Abu Ali al-Rudhbari said that he heard a man speak thus of knowledge, *marifah*, to Junayd, "The people of knowledge of God come to abandon all action for the sake of righteousness and seeking closeness to God Almighty and Glorious."

Junayd said, "This is the talk of people who say that works are meaningless! With me this is an enormity; someone who steals or fornicates is in a better state than whoever says such a thing. The gnostics receive their works from God, and return to Him by means of them. If I were to live for a thousand years, I would not diminish the works of righteousness one atom, unless I were actively prevented from them."

Junayd said, "If it is possible for you to get by with no household goods but an earthen jar, do it." He also said, "All roads are closed to everyone, save whosoever follows the track of the Messenger."

I heard Muhammad bin al-Husayn say[4] . . . that Junayd said, "If a sincere person were to approach God for a thousand, thousand years, and then turn aside from Him for an instant, what he lost would be greater than what he had gained." Junayd said, "Whoever has not learned the Quran by heart nor written *hadiths* should not be taken for a model in this affair, because this knowledge of ours is bound by the Book and the *sunnah*."

I heard Muhammad bin al-Husayn say[5] . . . that Abu Ali al-Rudhbari quoted Junayd, "This school of ours is bound by the principles of the Book and the *sunnah*." Junayd also said, "This knowledge of ours is constructed upon the *hadiths* of the Messenger of God."

Muhammad bin al-Husayn informed us[6] . . . that Abu-l-Husayn Ali bin Ibrahim al-Haddad said that he was present at a session held by the judge Abu-l-Abbas bin Shurayh when he spoke of the fundamentals and subordinate branches of the Law using a beautiful argument which amazed me. When he saw my astonishment, he asked, 'Do you know where this comes from?'
I said, 'Perhaps the judge will tell me.' He said, 'It is through the blessing bestowed by the sessions of Abu-l-Qasim al-Junayd.'"

Junayd was asked, "Where did you acquire this knowledge?" He replied, "From sitting before God for thirty years under that stair," and he pointed to a staircase in his house.

I heard Abu Ali al-Daqqaq relate this. I also heard him say that Junayd was seen with prayer beads in his hand. "You, with all your eminence, still take prayer beads in hand?" it was asked. "It is a road by which I reached my Lord," he replied. "I will not abandon it."

I heard Abu Ali say that every day Junayd used to enter his shop, let fall the curtain, and pray four hundred cycles of prostration. Then he returned to his house. Abu Bakr al-Atawi said, "I was with Junayd at the time of his death. I saw him recite the whole Quran, then begin again at Surah al-Baqarah. He recited seventy verses, and then died, may God have mercy upon him."

24 Abu Uthman Said bin Ismail al-Hiri

He lived in Nishapur, though he came from Rayy, where he kept company with Shah al-Kirmani and Yahya bin Muadh al-Razi. He came to Nishapur with Shah al-Kirmani to see Abu Hafs al-Haddad, and remained with him. Abu Hafs trained him, and married his daughter to him. He died in the year 298 AH, surviving Abu Hafs by thirty and one half years.

I heard Muhammad bin al-Husayn say[1] . . . that Abu Uthman said, "A person's faith is not perfect until four things are equal in his heart: refusal and permission, and honor and humiliation." Muhammad bin al-Husayn also say[2] . . . that Abu Uthman said, "I had been in Abu Hafs's company for a while, as a youth, when a time came that he drove me away, saying, 'Do not sit with me!' I got up, not turning my back to him, and moved away backwards, my face to his face, until I passed out of his sight. I decided to dig a pit by his door, and not leave it except by his order. When he saw this, he brought me close, and made me one of his special friends. He said, 'It is said that the world holds three who have no fourth: Abu Uthman in Nishapur, Junayd in Baghdad, and Abu Abd Allah bin al-Jalla in Damascus.'"

Abu Uthman said, "For forty years God Most High did not establish me in a state which I hated, nor did He transport me to another one which I resented."

I heard Abu Abd al-Rahman al-Sulami say[3] . . . that Abu Uthman said that when Abu Uthman [fell ill and] his state worsened, his son Abu Bakr tore his shirt [in grief]. Abu Uthman opened his eyes and said, "Outer divergence from the *Sunnah*, my son, is the sign of some inner hypocrisy."

I heard Muhammad bin al-Husayn say[4] . . . that Abu Uthman said that the conditions for companionship with God are beautiful courtesy, continuous awe, and deep receptivity. The conditions for companionship with the Messenger are adherence to his *Sunnah* and a recognition of the need for an exterior form for knowledge. The conditions for companionship with the Friends of God Most High are reverence and service. The condition for companionship with developed Sufis is fine character. The condition for companionship with the brotherhood of aspirants is continuous joy without offense. The conditions for companionship with the ignorant are prayer for them and mercy upon them."

I heard Abd Allah bin Yusuf al-Ispahani say[5] . . . that Abu Uthman said, "Whoever puts himself under the authority of the *Sunnah* in word and deed speaks wisdom, and whoever puts himself under the authority of his desires in word and deed speaks deviation. God Most High said, '*If you obey him, you are rightly guided*' (24:54).'

25 Abu-l-Hasan bin Muhammad al-Nuri

He was born and raised in Baghdad, of a Baghawi family. He was among the companions of Sari al-Saqati and Ibn Abi-l-Hawari, and one of the contemporaries of Junayd. He died in the year 908 AD/295 AH. He was of great importance, and was known for the beauty of his ordinary transactions with people and for his discourse. Nuri said, "Sufism is to abandon every pleasure of the ego." He also said, "In our time, the most powerful and honorable things [to be] are two: a knower of the divine Command who puts his knowledge to work, and a gnostic who speaks the truth."

I heard Abu Abd Allah al-Sufi say[1] . . . that Nuri said, "Whenever you see someone claim, before God, a state exempting him from the limits imposed by knowledge of the divine Ordinance—have nothing whatsoever to do with him."

I heard Abu Abd al-Rahman al-Sulami say[2] . . . that Junayd said that since Nuri died, no one has brought word of true integrity. Abu Ahmad al-Mughazili said, "I never saw anyone more devoted to worship and service than Nuri." He was asked, "Even Junayd?" and replied, "Even Junayd."

Nuri said, "The patched cloak of Sufism used to be a wrapper covering pearls, but today it has become a trash heap covering corpses." It is said that Nuri used to leave his house every day with a loaf of bread, which he would distribute in charity on the road. He would enter the mosque and pray until nearly noon, then leave and open up his shop, all of this while fasting. His family supposed he would eat in the marketplace, and his associates in the marketplace supposed that he had eaten at home. He carried on in this way, from the time he began this practice, for twenty years.

26 Abu Abd Allah Ahmad bin Yahya al-Jalla

From a Baghdadi family, he lived in Ramlah and Damascus, and is counted one of the greatest shaykhs of Syria. He kept company with Abu Turab [al-Nakhshabi], Dhu-l-Nun, Abu Ubayd al-Busra, and his father Yahya al-Jalla.

I heard Muhammad bin al-Husayn say[1] . . . that Ibn al-Jalla said that he had said to my father and mother, "I want you to give me to God Almighty and Glorious." They said, "We have now given you to God Almighty and Glorious." So I left them for awhile. When I returned it was a rainy night. I knocked on the door, and my father said to me, "Who is it?" I answered, "Your son Ahmad." He replied, "We had a son, but we gave him to the Almighty. We are Arabs; we will not take back what we have given." And he did not open the door.

Ibn al-Jalla said, "He for whom praise and blame are equal is a true ascetic. He who takes care of religious obligations immediately as they fall due is a true devotee. He who sees all actions as proceeding from God is a true monotheist, who sees only One."

When Ibn al-Jalla died they looked in on him, and he was laughing. The doctor said, "He is alive." Then he took his pulse and exclaimed, "He is dead!" Then he uncovered his face, and stated, "I cannot tell whether he is dead or alive." On the surface of Ibn al-Jalla's skin was a vein in the shape of the Arabic letters *"lil-lah"*— God's."

Ibn al-Jalla said, "I was walking with my teacher when I saw a beautiful young man. I said, 'O Master, do you think that God could punish such a form?' He said, 'Do you look upon it? See the result!' After that, I forgot the Koran [I had memorized] for twenty years."

27 Abu Muhammad Ruwaym bin Ahmad

He was of Baghdad, and is one of the most revered of shaykhs. He died in the year 915 AD/303 AH. He was a reciter of the Quran and a legal scholar of the school of Dawud [al-Zahiri]. Ruwaym said, "Part of the wise man's wisdom is in allowing a broad interpretation of the rules to his spiritual brothers while enforcing a narrow one upon himself. For granting latitude to them follows from knowledge, while being exacting towards himself is one guideline of moral responsibility."

I heard Abu Abd al-Rahman al-Sulami say[1] . . . that Abu Abd Allah bin Khafif said that he asked Ruwaym to counsel me. He said, "This business consists of giving your whole soul, fully and freely. So if it is possible for you to enter into it in this way, [do it]. If not, then do not occupy yourself with mockeries of Sufism." Ruwaym said, "To sit with any class of people is safer than your sitting with the Sufis. For everybody sits with outward forms, but this group sits with the realities; everybody requires of themselves an outer appearance in conformity with the Law, but these require of themselves real morality and enduring sincerity. If someone sits with them and opposes them in something they know to be true, God will strike the light of faith from his heart."

Ruwaym said, "I was passing through Baghdad at midday by the back streets when I became thirsty and stopped at a house to ask for something to drink. The door was opened by a young girl carrying a jug. When she saw me, she exclaimed, 'A Sufi, drinking by day!' After that I never broke my fast by day again."

Ruwaym said, "When God provides you with words and action, if He takes from you the words and lets you keep the action, it is a blessing. If He takes from you the action and lets you keep the words, it is a misfortune. If he takes both of them from you, it is a punishment and an affliction."

28 Abu Abd Allah Muhammad bin al-Fadl al-Balkhi   He

made his home in Samarkand. His family was from Balkh, but he was banished from there and went to Samarkand, where he died. He shared companionship with Ahmad bin Khadruyah and others; Abu Uthman al-Hiri was very fond of him. The year of his death was 931 AD/319 AH.

I heard Abu Abd al-Rahman al-Sulami say[1] . . . that Abu Bakr bin Uthman said that Abu Uthman al-Hiri wrote to Muhammad bin al-Fadl asking, "What is the sign of spiritual failure?" He answered, "Three things: if one is provided with knowledge and made incapable of acting upon it; or if one is provided with action but made incapable of sincerity in it; or if one is provided with the companionship of the righteous servants of God and does not treat them with respect."

Abu Uthman al-Hiri said, "Muhammad bin al-Fadl is a broker of men," [who knows their value as a broker appraises his commodities]. I heard Muhammad bin al-Husayn say[2] . . . that Muhammad bin al-Fadl said, "To be comfortable in the dungeon is a dream of the lower self." Muhammad bin al-Husayn also said[3] . . . that Muhammad bin al-Fadl said, "The disappearance of Islam is due to four attitudes: people not acting on what they know; their taking action on what they do not know; their not seeking knowledge of what they do not know; and their preventing people from seeking to know." According to the same chain of narrators, he said, "Isn't it amazing that somebody would cross over deserts to reach the Kabah and see the signs of prophecy, but would not cross over his ego and his desires to reach his heart and see the signs of his Lord Almighty and Glorious?" And he said, "If you see a student seeking increase in this world, that is one of the signs of his retreat [from the business of Sufism]."

Asked about asceticism, Muhammad bin al-Fadl remarked, "It is to look at the worldly and see its inferiority, and to turn away from the pursuit of power, success, and honor that it entails."

29 Abu Bakr Ahmad Nadr al-Zaqqaq al-Kabir

He was a contemporary of Junayd and one of the great men of Egypt. I heard Muhammad bin al-Husayn say[1] . . . that al-Kattani said that when al-Zaqqaq died, the pretext for spiritual aspirants' coming to Egypt was cut off.

Zaqqaq said, "Whoever takes up the dervish life unaccompanied by fear of God eats what is outright forbidden." I heard Abu Abd al-Rahman al-Sulami say[2] . . . that al-Zaqqaq said, "I was lost in the desert of the Children of Israel for fifteen days. When I found the road again a soldier came across me and gave me a drink of water. The veil from this was over my heart for thirty years."

30 Abu Abd Allah Amr bin Uthman al-Makki

He met Abu Abd Allah al-Nabaji and kept company with Abu Said al-Kharraz and others. He was a shaykh for developed Sufis, and a leader of this group in the fundamentals of religion and the practices of the mystical way. He died in Baghdad in the year 903 AD/291 AH.

I heard Muhammad bin al-Husayn say[1] . . . that Amr bin Uthman al-Makki said, "Whatever goodness or splendor or intimacy or beauty or brilliance or apparition or light or personality or subtle form your heart imagines, or that permeates the flow of your thought, or occurs among the conflicting opposites in your heart—God Most High is far from it. Have you not heard the word of the Exalted, 'Nothing is like unto Him, and He is The Hearing, The Seeing' (42:11), and 'He does not beget and is not begotten and nothing is like unto Him' (112:3-4).

According to the same narrators, he said, "Knowledge leads, and fear drives, and the ego is obstinate between them, in its defiance, treachery, and deceit. So protect yourself from it through the policy of knowledge, and drive it with the threat of fear; you will accomplish what you desire." He also said, "The ecstatic cannot directly express his state, because ecstasy is a secret between God and the believers."

31 Sumnun bin Hamzah

He was known as Abu-l-Hasan, but he was called Abu-l-Qasim. He kept company with Sari [al-Saqati], Abu Ahmad al-Qalanasi, Muhammad bin Ali al-Qassar, and others. It is said that he recited,

I have no portion in what is other than You
Try me howsoever You will!

and was afflicted from that hour with retention of the urine. He used to go about among the schools saying "Pray for your uncle the liar!"

Now it appears that after he had recited these lines, one of his students told the others, "Yesterday I was out in the country, and I heard the voice of our master Sumnun praying to God, imploring Him and asking to be cured." Somebody said, "I also heard that yesterday, but I was somewhere else!" Then a third spoke, and a fourth, relating the same thing. News of this came to Sumnun. All the while he had been suffering from the illness of retention of the urine patiently and without anxiety. When he heard them saying this, while he had not so prayed or said anything of the sort, he knew that the object of it was that he should show anxiety, as a refinement of servanthood and as a veil for his state. So he began to go around among the schools saying, "Pray for your uncle the liar!"

I heard Muhammad bin al-Husayn say[1] . . . that Abu Ahmad al-Mughazili said, "There was a man in Baghdad who distributed forty thousand dirhams to the dervishes. Sumnun said to me, 'Abu Ahmad, don't you see what this man has given, what he has done? And we have nothing [to give]! Come with me to somewhere where we can pray a prostration for each dirham.' So I continued with him into Madain, and we prayed forty thousand ritual prayers."

Sumnun had a graceful and elegant disposition. The greater part of his discourse concerned love, and he was very influential. He died before Junayd, it is said.

32 Abu Ubayd al-Busra

He was one of the oldest among shaykhs, and kept company with Abu Turab al-Nakhshabi. I heard Muhammad bin al-Husayn say[1] . . . that Ibn al-Jalla said that he met six hundred shaykhs, and never saw the like of four: Dhu-l-Nun al-Misri, my father [Yahya al-Jalla], Abu Turab [al-Nakhshabi], and Abu Ubayd al-Busra.

I heard Abu Abd al-Rahman al-Sulami say[2] . . . that Abu Zaraah al-Hasani said that one day Abu Ubayd al-Busra was threshing wheat. It was three days before the time of the prescribed pilgrimage. Two men came him and said, 'Abu Ubayd, don't you wish you were going with us on the prescribed pilgrimage?' 'No,' he replied. Then he turned to me and said, 'Your shaykh is more easily able to do that than they are,' meaning himself.

33 Abu-l-Fawaris Shah bin Shuja al-Kirmani

He was the son of a king, and kept company with Abu Turab al-Nakhshabi, Abu Ubayd al-Busra, and others of that generation. He was pre-eminent among those who pursued the ideal of manly nobility (*futuwah*), and was very influential. He died before 912 AD/300 AH. Shah said, "The sign of awe of God is a vigilant morality, and the sign of vigilant morality is to hold back in doubtful situations." He used to say to his companions, "Avoid lying, treachery, and slander, and then do what seems right to you."

I heard Abu Abd al-Rahman al-Sulami say[1] . . . that Shah al-Kirmani said, "Whoever lowers his gaze before the forbidden things, restrains his lower self from desires, strengthens his inner being with continuous meditation and his outer being with adherence to the *Sunnah*, and accustoms himself to eating what is lawful—his insight will not err.

34 Yusuf bin al-Husayn

He was the shaykh of Rayy and the Caucasian mountains in his time, and was without equal for eliminating affectation. A scholar and literary man, he was one of the companions of Dhu-l-Nun al-Misri and Abu Turab al-Nakhshabi, and a close friend of Abu Said al-Kharraz. He died in the year 916 AD/304 AH.

Yusuf bin al-Husayn said, "I would rather meet God Most High full of every sort of disobedience than meet Him with an atom's worth of affectation." He also said, "When you see a student occupy himself with permissions for lightening the stringency of practice, know that nothing will come of him." He wrote to Junayd, "May God not cause you to taste the food of your ego. Because if you taste it yourself, you will never again afterwards taste any good." Yusuf bin al-Husayn also said, "I see the bane of the Sufis in companionship with youths, association with adversaries, and intimate friendships with women."

35 Abu Abd Allah Muhammad bin Ali al-Tirmidhi

He was one of the great shaykhs, and composed works on the Quranic sciences. He kept company with Abu Turab al-Nakhshabi, Ahmad bin Khadruyah, Ibn al-Jalla, and others.

Muhammad bin Ali was asked about the characteristic state of humanity. He said, "Obvious weakness and vast pretense." Muhammad bin Ali also said, "I never wrote one word by plan, or in order that anything be attributed to me. But when life was difficult for me, that was how I consoled myself."

36 Abu Bakr bin Umar al-Warraq al-Tirmidhi

He lived in Balkh, and kept company with Ahmad bin Khadruyah and others. He was the author of works on ascetic discipline and the training of character.

I heard Abu Abd al-Rahman say[1] . . . that Abu Bakr al-Warraq said, "Whoever satisfies the body with the objects of desire has planted the tree of regrets in his heart." I heard Abu Abd al-Rahman al-Sulami say[2] . . . that Abu Bakr al-Warraq said, "If greed were asked, 'Who is your father?' it would reply, 'Doubt of what is destined.' If it were asked, 'What is your profession?' it would reply, 'Earning humiliation.' And if it were asked, 'What is your purpose?' it would say, 'Deprivation.'"

Abu Bakr al-Warraq used to forbid his followers to travel and visit other Sufi centers. He would say, "The key of every blessing is patient endurance where your studies began until your will becomes sound; for when your will becomes sound, the origins of blessing will have manifested in you."

37 Abu Said Ahmad bin Isa al-Kharraz

He was one of the people of Baghdad. He kept company with Dhu-l-Nun al-Misri, al-Nabaji, Abu Ubayd al-Busra, Sari [al-Saqati], Bishr [al-Hafi], and others. He died in the year 890 AD/277 AH.

Abu Said al-Kharraz said, "Anything esoteric that is contradicted by something exoteric is falsehood." I heard Muhammad bin al-Husayn say[1] . . . that Abu Said al-Kharraz said, "I saw satan in a dream, and he was going off to one side of me. 'Come here! What's wrong with you?' I demanded. 'How am I supposed to work on you people?' he complained. 'You cast off from yourselves what I use to deceive everybody!' 'What is that?' 'The world.' He turned away. Then he turned around to face me. 'Nonetheless I have something subtle to use on you.' 'And what is that?' 'The companionship of youths.'

Abu Said al-Kharraz said, "As much as I kept company with the Sufis, no opposition ever arose between them and me." They asked him why. He said, "Because I was with them, against myself."

38 Abu Abd Allah Muhammad bin Ismail al-Maghribi

He was the teacher of Ibrahim bin Shayban and the student of Ali bin Ruzayn. He lived 120 years, and died in 912 AD/299 AH. His affair was extraordinary: for many years he ate nothing that reached him through human hands. He used to obtain things from the roots of herbs, which he accustomed himself to eat.

Abu Abd Allah al-Maghribi said, "The most excellent of works is to fill one's moments with actions acceptable to God." He said, "The basest of people is a poor man who flatters a rich one and becomes his parasite, while the noblest of people is a rich man who humbles himself to the poor and maintains respect for them."

39 Abu-l-Abbas Ahmad bin Muhammad bin Masruq

His family was from Tus, but he lived in Baghdad and associated with al-Harith al-Muhasibi and Sari al-Saqati. He passed away in Baghdad in the year 912 AD/299 AH, or according to some, 911 AD/298 AH.

Ibn Masruq said, "If someone fears God Most High with regard to the thoughts of his heart, God will preserve him from evil in the actions of his limbs." He also said, "Deep reverence for the believers comes from deep reverence for God Most High; through it the servant arrives at the place of true piety." And, "The tree of realization is watered with the water of reflection. The tree of unconsciousness is watered with the water of ignorance. The tree of repentance is watered with the water of remorse. The tree of love is watered with the water of seeking harmony and the acceptable act." He further said, "When you are greedy for realization without having previously mastered the degrees of studenthood, you are ignorant. When you seek to be a spiritual student before being soundly established in the stage of repentance, you are unconscious of what you seek."

40 Abu-l-Hasan Ali bin Sahl al-Ispahani

He was a contemporary of Junayd. Amr bin Uthman al-Makki contracted a debt and went to him about it. He settled it for him; it came to thirty thousand dirhams. He met Abu Turab al-Nakhshabi and the others of his generation.

I heard Muhammad bin al-Husayn say[1] . . . that Ali bin Sahl said, "To hasten to acts of obedience is a sign of spiritual success. To stand aloof from arguments is a sign of mindfulness. To show respect for secrets is a sign of being awake. The manifestation of pretense is part of human frivolity. Whoever does not make the foundations of his spiritual effort firm will not be safe from the ultimate consequences.

41 Abu Muhammad Ahmad Ibn Muhammad bin al-Husayn al-Jurayri

He was one of the greatest students of Junayd, and kept company with Sahl bin Abd Allah [al-Tustari]. After Junayd's time he was seated in his place. He was learned in the sciences of this group, and his state was profound. He died in the year 923 AD/311 AH.

I heard Abd Allah al-Shirazi say that he heard Ahmad bin Ata al-Rudhbari say that Jurayri died in the Year of al-Habir. I passed by him a year later, and he was leaning, sitting with his knee against his chest, indicating the unity of God with his outstretched finger.

I heard Muhammad bin al-Husayn say[1] . . . that Abu Muhammad al-Jurayri said, "Whoever is overwhelmed by the ego becomes a captive under the the the power of desires, imprisoned in the dungeon of lust. God Most High forbids his heart the inner things, so that he finds no delight or sweetness in the word of the Truth, may He be exalted, even if he repeats it with his tongue over and over again; as in His saying, *'I will turn from My signs those who make themselves great in the land without right'* (7:146)."

Jurayri said, "A clear vision of the fundamentals of religion comes about through the application of their derivative principles, and the derivatives are corrected by comparing them against the original sources. There is no way to the stage of the contemplation of states except by esteeming as great the means and principles that God has esteemed to be great."

42 Abu-l-Abbas Ahmad bin Muhammad bin Sahl bin Ata al-Admi

He was a great shaykh and scholar of the Sufis. Al- Kharraz used to speak of the importance of his work. He was one of the contemporaries of Junayd, and kept company with Ibrahim al-Maristani. He died in the year 921 AD/309 AH.

I heard Muhammad bin al-Husayn say[1] . . . that Ibn Ata said, "If someone requires of himself the conduct prescribed by the divine Command, God will illuminate his heart with the light of realization. There is no station nobler than the station of following the Beloved in the orders he gave, the actions he took, and the character he possessed."

Ibn Ata said, "The most serious heedlessness is the servant's heedlessness of his Lord Almighty and Glorious, of His commands and prohibitions, and of His rules for daily behavior."

I heard Abd Allah al-Shirazi say[2] . . . that Ahmad bin Ata said, "Search for what you are asked about in the sanctuary of knowledge, and if you do not find it there, then in the battlefield of wisdom. If you still do not find it, weigh it with the Unity. If it is not to be found in any of these three places, strike Satan in the face with it."

43 Abu Ishaq Ibrahim bin Ahmad al-Khawwas

He was one of the contemporaries of Junayd and Nuri and possessed a large share of trust in God and ascetic discipline. He died in Rayy in the year 904 AD/291 AH. He developed an intestinal ailment so that he was always getting up to make an ablution, then returning to the mosque and offering two cycles of prescribed prayer. On one such occasion, when he had gone into the water [to make total ablution], he died, may God have mercy upon him.

I heard Muhammad bin al-Husayn say[1] . . . that al-Khawwas said, "Knowledge is not in how many formal reports one acquires from others. Rather the learned man is he who, though he may have only a little knowledge, acts in accordance with it and applies it, and models himself on the *sunnah*."

I heard Muhammad bin al-Husayn say[2] . . .that al-Khawwas said, "The remedy of the heart is five things: reading and pondering the Quran; keeping an empty stomach; standing in prayer by night; imploring God at dawn; and sitting in the company of the righteous."

44 Abu Muhammad Abd Allah bin Muhammad al-Kharraz

He was from Rayy. He settled near Makkah, and was a companion of Abu Hafs [al-Haddad] and Abu Imran al-Kabir. He was one of those who center their effort on the pursuit of moral scrupulosity. He died before 310 AH[922 AD].

I heard Abu Abd al-Rahman al-Sulami say[1] . . . that al-Duqqi said, "I hadn't eaten for four days, and I went in to see Abd Allah al-Kharraz. He said, 'When one of you goes hungry for four days, being hungry begins to obsess him! If every living person risked everything he had for the sake of what he hoped from God, would that really be much?'"

Abu Muhammad Abd Allah al-Kharraz said, "Hunger is the food of ascetics; remembrance of God is the food of those who know Him."

45 Abu-l-Hasan Bunnan bin Muhammad al-Hammal

He was originally from Wasit, lived in Egypt, and died in the year 928 AD/316 AH. He was very influential and possessed the power of miracles.

Bunnan was asked about the sublimest state of the Sufis. He said, "Trust in what is guaranteed, perseverance in what is commanded, safeguarding the inner secret, and renunciation of the two worlds."

I heard Muhammad ibn al-Husayn say[1] . . . that Abu Ali al-Rudhbari said, "Bunnan al-Hammal was thrown before a lion. The animal began to sniff him, and did not injure him. When he was brought out, they asked him, 'What was in your heart while the creature sniffed you?' 'I was thinking about the differences of opinion among scholars about the legality of food left by beasts of prey,' said he.

46 Abu Hamzah al-Baghdadi al-Bazzaz

He died before Junayd, was one of his contemporaries, and kept company with Sari al-Saqati and al-Hasan al-Musuhi. He was learned in the variant forms of recitation of the Quran and in Quranic law. He was one of the children of Isa bin Aban. Ahmad bin Hanbal used to remark, "The questions proper to him are those in which you say, 'O Sufi!'" It is said that he was addressing a session one Friday when his state of health changed and he fell from the pulpit. He died the following Friday. This is supposed to have occurred in 902 AD/289 AH.

Abu Hamzah said, "Someone who knows the road of the true One, may He be exalted, finds it easy to travel upon. There is no guide upon the road to God Most High except to follow the Messenger in his states, actions, and his words."

Abu Hamzah said, "Whoever has been provided with three things has been delivered from disasters: an empty stomach accompanied by a contented heart; continual poverty accompanied by ready renunciation; perfect patience accompanied by constant remembrance of God."

47 Abu Bakr bin Musa al-Wasiti

He was of Khurasanian origin, from Farghana, and was one of the company of Junayd and Nuri. An influential scholar, he lived in Merv and died there after 932 AD/320 AH.

Al-Wasiti said, "Fear and hope are two bridles holding the servant back from bad behavior." He also said, "Looking for the reward for acts of obedience comes from forgetfulness of grace." And he said, "When God wishes to disgrace a servant he throws him to these stinking corpses." He intended by this the companionship of youths.

I heard Muhammad bin al-Husayn say[1] . . . that al-Wasiti said, "[Hypocrites] assert that their bad behavior is sincerity, that the voracity of their egos is boldness, that the vileness of their ambitions is toughness. So they are blind to the Way and look for narrowness and difficulty in it. No life vivifies their 'contemplation' and no devotional service grows in their 'gatherings before God.' If they discuss privately it is for the sake of extortion; if they discourse publicly it is for the sake of pride. The way their egos pounce shows the filth of their consciences; the greed with which they eat shows what is in their innermost beings. *'May God destroy them! How they are turned aside from the path!'* (63:4)."

I heard Abu Ali al-Daqqaq say that one of the people of Merv heard an apothecary say that one Friday al-Wasiti passed by the door of his shop, intending to go to the congregational mosque, when his sandal strap broke. The apothecary said, "O Shaykh! Will you permit me to fix your sandal?" "Go ahead and fix it," he said. So he repaired the strap. Al-Wasiti told him [the apothecary], "Do you know why the strap of my sandal broke?" "Until you tell, [no]" the apothecary replied. "Because I have not made the full ablution for the Friday congregational prayer!" said he. The apothecary said, "Sir, there is a bathhouse here—come in!" "Good!" he said. So he brought al-Wasiti into the bathhouse, and he performed a total ablution.

48 Abu-l-Hasan ibn al-Saigh

He was named Ali bin Muhammad bin Sahl al-Dinawari. One of the great shaykhs, he lived and died in Egypt. Abu Uthman al-Maghribi said, "I have not seen among the shaykhs any more full of light than Abu Yaqub al-Nahrajuri, nor any more full of awe than

Abu-l-Hasan bin al-Saigh." He died in 942 AD/330 AH.

Ibn al-Saigh was asked about a visible human object of devotion as evidence of the invisible one. He said, "How can the qualities of one who possesses like and equal give evidence of One Who has neither like nor equal?"

Asked about the characteristic of the spiritual aspirant, he replied, "It is as God Almighty and Glorious said—'*The earth, wide as it is, became narrow to them, and their souls became narrow to them and they knew there was no refuge from God but in Him. Then He turned to them so that they might turn. Surely God is the Oft-return - ing to mercy, the Merciful*' (9:118). He said, "The states are like lightning flashes. If they become fixed, it is self-deception and indulging one's temperament."

49 Abu Ishaq Ibrahim bin Dawud al-Raqqi

He was one of the great shaykhs of Damascus, a contemporary of Junayd and Ibn al-Jalla. He had a long life, living until 938 AD/326 AH.

Ibrahim al-Raqqi said, "Realization is sure knowledge of the Truth as He is, outside of all of that is imagined." He also said, "God's power is obvious and the eyes are open—but the lights of inner vision are weak." And, "The weakest of people is he who is weak in resisting his desires, and the strongest of people is he who is strong in resisting them." He further said, "The sign of loving God is to choose obedience to Him and adherence to His Prophet."

50 Mumshad al-Dinawari

He was one of the great Sufi shaykhs, and died in the year 912 AD/299 AH. Mumshad said, "In the spiritual aspirant, beautiful behavior means his commitment to respecting the shaykhs and to serving the brotherhood, his abandoning reliance upon the apparent worldly causes of events, and his protecting the usages of the divine Command against his lower self."

Mumshad said, "I never went to see a single one of my shaykhs unless I was free of everything that occupied me and looking for the blessings that would befall me through seeing him and hearing him speak. Whoever comes to a shaykh in order to test him, cuts himself off from the blessings of seeing him, sitting in his presence, and hearing his talk."

51 Khayr al-Nassaj

He kept company with Abu Hamzah al-Baghdadi and met Sari [al-Saqati] and was one of the contemporaries of Abu-l-Hasan al-Nuri. He had a very long life, living, it is said, 120 years. Shibli and al-Khawwas turned conclusively to God while in his circle. He was the teacher of the congregation of Sufis.

His name is said to have been Muhammad bin Ismail, from Samirah, but he was only called Khayr al-Nassaj, Khayr the Weaver. [Khayr, "good," was a common slave name.] He had left home for the prescribed pilgrimage when a man seized him by the Kufah gate, exclaiming, "You are my slave, and your name is Khayr!" He was black: he did not contradict him. The man employed him at the weaving of silk, and when he would call "Khayr!" Khayr would answer, "*Labbayk!*" ["I am here, at your service"—the cry of the pilgrims to God throughout the prescribed pilgrimage]. After several years, the man told him, "I was wrong. You are not my slave, and your name is not Khayr!"

Saying, "I will not change a name by which a Muslim man has called me," Khayr left him and went away.

Khayr said, "Fear is the lash of God by which He corrects an ego accustomed to bad behavior."

I heard Abu Abd al-Rahman al-Sulami say[1] . . . that Abu-l-Husayn al-Maliki said, "I asked someone who had been present at the death of Khayr al-Nassaj about what happened. He said,

'When the time for the evening prescribed prayer came, he lost consciousness. Then he opened his eyes, pointed to a corner of the house, and cried, "Stop! May God forgive you—you are only a servant under orders and I am only a servant under orders. What you have been ordered to do will not escape you, while what I have been ordered to do is escaping me!" He called for water and made the ablution for the prescribed prayer. Afterwards he stretched himself out, closed his eyes, repeated the profession of faith, and died. Later he was seen in a dream and asked, 'What did God do with you?' 'Don't ask me about that!' he told his questioner. 'But I have been delivered from this filthy world of yours.'"

52 Abu Hamzah al-Khurasani

He was from Nishapur, his family being from the neighborhood of Malqabadh. One of the contemporaries of Junayd, al-Kharraz, and Abu Turab al-Nakhshabi, he was highly developed in morality and religion.

Abu Hamzah said, "When someone is filled with the remembrance of death, God makes dear to him everything permanent, and makes hateful to him everything ephemeral." He said, "The gnostic strives for his livelihood day after day, and receives his livelihood from one day to another." A man said to him, "Advise me." He replied, "Make ready your provision for the journey that is before you!"

I heard Muhammad bin al-Husayn say[1] . . . that Abu Hamzah al-Khurasani said, "He remained in the sacred state [*ihram*, the consecrated state of the pilgrims entering Mecca, likened to the condition of a corpse in its shroud] in a single garment] and traveled every year a thousand farsangs. The sun rose and set upon me, and whenever I came out of the consecrated state, I went back into it." He passed away in the year 903 AD/290 AH.

53 Abu Bakr Dulaf bin Jahdar al-Shibli

His family was from Usrushnah although he born and raised in Baghdad. He kept company with Junayd and the others of his generation, and was the pre-eminent shaykh of his time for state, delicacy of behavior, and knowledge. The legal interpretation to which he adhered was that of the Maliki school. He lived eighty-seven years and died in 849 AD/234 AH. His grave is in Baghdad.

After Shibli [who was a government official] had turned decisively to God in a meeting of the circle of Khayr al-Nassaj, he went to Damavand and said, "I have been the governor of this country of yours; now set me free from responsibility for it!"
The effort he made in his earliest days passed beyond the furthest limit of effort eventually reached by others.

I heard Abu Ali al-Daqqaq say that he had been told that Shibli, in order to become accustomed to wakefulness and not be overpowered by sleep, used to put much salt on his eyes, like collyrium (*kohl*). If there had been nothing more to his magnification of the divine ordinances than what Bukran al-Dinawari had related about the end of his life, it would have been much.

I heard Abu Abd al-Rahman al-Sulami say[1] . . . that at the end of his days, Shibli recited,

How many the places which, if I had died in them,
I would have been but a warning example to the tribe!

I heard Abu Ali relate of him, "When the month of Ramadan came, Shibli used to display a diligence in devotion beyond that of the others of his age. He used to say, 'This month has been declared great by my Lord, and I am the first of those who shall hold it great.'"

54 Abu Muhammad Abd Allah bin Muhammad al-Murtaish

He was from Nishapur, from the neighborhood of Hira; or, it is said, from Malqabadh. He was among the companions of Abu Hafs [al-Haddad] and Abu Uthman [al-Hiri], and met Junayd. He was very influential. He used to live in the Shuniziyyah mosque [established by the Sufis in Baghdad], and died in Baghdad in the year 940 AD/328 AH.

Al-Murtaish said, "Will exists in restraining the ego from the objects of its desire, responding to the orders of God Most High, and being satisfied with the ways in which destiny comes upon you."

He was told, "So-and-so walks on water." He replied, "It seems to me that a person whom God Most High has made able to oppose his desires is greater than somebody who walks on air!"

55 Abu Ali Ahmad bin Muhammad al-Rudhbari

He was from Baghdad. He lived in Egypt and died there in the year 934 AD/322 AH. He kept company with Junayd, Nuri, Ibn al-Jalla, and others of that generation. He was the most expressive and knowledgeable of the shaykhs in matters related to the rule of life of aspirants.

I heard Abu Abd al-Rahman al-Sulami say that he heard Abu-l-Qasim al-Dimashqi say that Abu Ali al-Rudhbari was asked about someone who would listen to musical instruments and say, "It is lawful for me, for I have arrived at a degree that is not affected by the variation of states." He said, "Yes, he has certainly arrived—but in hell!" Asked about Sufism, he said, "This school is entirely serious. No element of frivolity is mixed into it."

I heard Muhammad ibn al-Husayn say[1] . . . that Abu Ali al-Rudhbari said, "One of the signs of self-deception is: if you do evil, and God does good to you, you abandon repentance and contrition, imagining that you are indulged in your slips, and believing that this is from the expansiveness of the Truth towards you."

He said, "My master in Sufism is Junayd, in law is Abu-l-Abbas bin Shurayh, in literature is Thalab, and in *hadith* is Ibrahim al-Harbi."

56 Abu Muhammad Abd Allah bin Munazil

A shaykh of the Malamatis [those whose discipline is to draw blame upon themselves while secretly remaining free of everything blamable], unique in his time, he kept company with Hamdun al-Qassar. He was a scholar, and recorded many Traditions. He died in Nishapur in 941 or 942 AD/329 or 330 AH.

I heard Muhammad bin al-Husayn say[1] . . . that Abd Allah bin Munazil said, "No one omits a religious obligation before God Most High has tried him with neglect of the *Sunnah*, and no one is tried with neglect of the *Sunnah* who was not on the verge of being afflicted with heresy."

I heard Abu Abd al-Rahman al-Sulami say[2] . . . Abd Allah bin Manazil said, "The finest moments are those in which you are safe from the random thoughts of your ego and the evil of your opinions."

57 Abu Ali Muhammad bin Abd-l-Wahhab al-Thaqafi

He was the imam of his time and one of the companions of Abu Hafs [al-Haddad] and Hamdun al-Qassar. Through him Sufism appeared in Nishapur. He died in the year 940 AD/328 AH.

I heard Muhammad bin al-Husayn say[1] . . . that Abu Ali al-Thaqafi said, "Even if a person were to gather together all of knowledge and keep company with all classes of people, he would not mature except by means of training of character at the hands of a shaykh or an imam or a sincere teacher of behavior. If someone has not received his conduct from a master who shows him the flaws of his work and the stupidities of his ego, his example cannot be followed in the correction of one's daily life."

Abu Ali said, "A time will come upon this community in which no comfortable livelihood will be possible for a believer without his having to depend upon hypocrites." And he remarked, "Fie on the distractions of this world when things go well, and fie on its anxieties when things go badly! An intelligent person does not value something that, when it courts you, is a chore, and when it avoids you, is a worry."

58 Abu-l-Khayr al-Aqta

He originally from North Africa, he lived in Tinat. He possessed the power of miracles and insight into people's thoughts, and was very influential. He died halfway through the year 951 AD/340 AH.

Abu-l-Khayr said, "No one grows into a condition of nobility except through maintaining harmony with the divine will and command, embracing the rule of beautiful behavior, fulfilling the obligatory duties, and keeping company with the righteous."

59 Abu Bakr Muhammad ibn Ali al-Kattani

He was originally from Baghdad, he kept company with Junayd, al-Kharraz, and Nuri, and lived in the vicinity of Mecca until he died in the year 322AH [934 AD]. I heard Abu Abd al-Rahman al-Sulami say that he heard Abu Bakr al-Razi say that al-Kattani looked at an old man, white of hair and beard, who was begging from people. He said, "This man neglected the right of God in his youth, so God has neglected him in his old age." Al-Kattani said, "Lust is the halter of Satan, and whomever he seizes with his halter is his slave."

60 Abu Yaqub Ishaq bin Muhammad al-Nahrajuri

He was a companion of Abu Amr al-Makki, Abu Yaqub al-Susi, Junayd, and others. He died in Makkah, near the Holy Places, in the year 942 AD/330 AH. I heard Muhammad bin al-Husayn say[1] . . . that Nahrajuri said, "This world is an ocean, and the next world is a shore. The ship is awe of God, and humanity are travelers." I heard Muhammad bin al-Husayn say[2] . . . that Nahrajuri said, "I saw a one-eyed man making the circumambulation of the Kabah. He was repeating, 'I seek refuge with You from You.' 'What is this prayer?' I asked. 'One day I looked at somebody and found her attractive,' he said. 'Suddenly a blow struck my vision and my eyes ran, and I heard an invisible voice say, "A blow for a look—if you increase [such looks], We shall increase [such blows]!"'" I heard Muhammad bin al-Husayn say[3] . . . that Nahrajuri said. "The best of states is that which goes together with knowledge."

61 Abu Ali bin al-Katib

He was called al-Hasan bin Ahmad. He was one of the companions of Abu Ali al-Rudhbari, Abu Bakr al-Misri, and others; his state was very advanced. He died halfway through 951 AD/340 AH.

Ibn al-Katib said, "When fear of God dwells in the heart the tongue speaks nothing but what it means." He also said, "[The philosophical school of] the Mutazilites declares the transcendence of God Most High from the point of view of reason [by dissociating Him from His creation], and they err. The Sufis declare His transcendence from the point of view of knowledge, and they hit the mark."

62 Muzaffar al-Qirmisini

He was one of the shaykhs of Azerbaijan, and kept company with Abd Allah al-Kharraz and others. Muzaffar al-Qirmisini said,

"Fasting has three aspects: the fast of the spirit is in the curtailment of expectations; the fast of the intellect is in the opposition of desires; and the fast of the animal self is in abstinence from food and forbidden things." He also said, "The worst of gifts is the gift of women, in whatever form it may be." And, "Hunger supported by contentment is the meadow of reflection, the spring of wisdom, the life of intelligence, and the lamp of the heart." Further, he said, "The best work for servants of God is to guard the present moment, so as not to neglect an order, nor exceed a limit." And, "Whoever does not receive proper behavior from a wise man will not be able to use it to educate a seeker."

63 Abu-l-Hasan Ali bin al-Muzayyin

He was one of the people of Baghdad, a companion of Sahl bin Abd Allah [al-Tustari], Junayd, and others of that generation. He died in Makkah, near the Kabah, in the year 940 AD/328 AH. He was a great moralist. I heard Abu Abd al-Rahman al-Sulami say[1] . . . that al-Muzayyin said, "A sin committed after another sin is the punishment for the first sin, and a good deed performed after another good deed is the reward of the first good deed."

He was asked about the recognition of Unity, and said, "It is your knowing His attributes to be distinct from the attributes of His creations. He is distinguished from them by His eternal attributes, as they are distinguished from Him by their temporal attributes." He also said, "If someone is not satisfied with God, God Most High puts him in need of the creation. If someone is satisfied with God, God puts the creation in need of him."

64 Abu Bakr Abd Allah bin Tahir al-Abhari

He was a contemporary of Shibli, one of the shaykhs of Azerbaijan, a scholar, a moralist; he kept company with Yusuf bin al-Husayn and others, and died in approximately 942 AD/330 AH. I heard Abu Abd al-Rahman al-Sulami say[1] . . . that Abu Bakr bin Tahir said, "One of the rules of the dervish is not to wish for things. But if he does, if it can't be helped, then his wish ought not to go beyond what is sufficient for him, meaning what he needs." According to the same chain of narrators, he said. "When you love a brother in God, help him decrease his involvement with the world."

65 Abu-l-Husayn bin Bunan

He was related to Abu Said al-Kharraz, and was one of the great shaykhs of Egypt. [d. 932 AD/320 AH]. Ibn Bunan said, "If worry about his sustenance is rooted in the heart of a Sufi, it is better for him to go to work for a living. The sign of the heart's resting in God is that whatever is in God's hands is depended upon more than what is in one's own hands." He said, "Avoid baseness of character as you avoid what is unlawful."

66 Abu Ishaq Ibrahim ibn Shayban al-Qirmisini

The preeminent shaykh of his time associated with Abu Abd Allah al-Maghribi al-Khawwas and others. I heard Muhammad bin al-Husayn say[1] . . . that Ibrahim bin Shayban said, "If someone wants to stop working or to waste his time, let him make a practice of exceptions to the rules!" By the same narrators, "The knowledge of mystical annihilation and subsistence, *fana* and *baqa*, turns on pure devotion to the Unity and sound servanthood. Anything else is error and heresy." Ibrahim said, "The lowest of men is one who disobeys God."

67 Abu Bakr al-Husayn bin Ali bin Yazdanyar

He was an Armenian, and was distinguished by a path in Sufism peculiar to himself. A cautious scholar, he used to disagree with some of the gnostics over their terminology and forms of expression. Ibn Yazdanyar said, "Beware of coveting intimacy with God while you love intimacy with people. Beware of coveting the love of God while you love the superfluous. Beware of coveting a place with God while you love a place with the people."

68 Abu Said bin al-Arabi

He was Ahmad bin Muhammad bin Ziyad al-Basri. He lived near the Holy Places in Makkah and died there in the year 952 AD/341 AH. He kept company with Junayd, Amr bin Uthman al-Makki, Nuri, and others. Ibn al-Arabi said, "The loser of losers shows off to people the righteousness of his own works, vilely competing with the One who is closer to him than his jugular vein."

69 Abu Amr Muhammad bin Ibrahim al-Zajjaji al-Nishapuri

He lived in Makkah for many years, and died there. He was a companion of Junayd, Abu Uthman [al-Hiri] Nuri, Khawwas, and Ruwaym. He passed away in the year 959 AD/ 348 AH. I heard Shaykh Abu Abd al-Rahman al-Sulami say that he heard his grandfather, Abu Amr bin Nujayd, said that someone asked Abu Amr al-

Zajjaji, "What happens to you? At the first announcement of the obligatory prayer, you change!" "I am afraid," he replied, "of beginning my duty dishonestly. When someone declares 'God is greater' while, in his heart, something is greater than Him—or if during that passage of time he should hold anything other than Him to be great—his own ego will have made a liar of his tongue." He also said, "The words of someone who talks of a state he has not attained are a trial for whoever listens to him. Pretension has been generated in the speaker's heart, and God prohibits him from attaining that state." He lived in Makkah for many years and never performed his ablution in the Holy Precincts. He used to go out beyond the boundary that marks off the sacred site, and purify himself there.

70 Abu Muhammad Jafar bin Muhammad bin Nusayr

He was born and raised in Baghdad. He kept company with Junayd, whom he followed closely, and with Nuri, Ruwaym, Sumnun, and others of that generation. He died in Baghdad in the year 9569 AD/348 AH. Jafar said, "The servant will not find the joy of a relationship with God together with the joy of the lower self. Those who know the realities of life break their ties to what cuts them off from the Truth, before those ties break them."

I heard Muhammad bin al-Husayn say[1] . . . that Jafar said, "What joins the servant to real being is that awe of God and of his duty to God dwells in his heart. When such awe dwells in his heart the blessings of knowledge descend upon him, and the desire for this world passes out of him."

71 Abu-l-Abbas al-Sayyari

He was named al-Qasim bin al-Qasim, and he came from Merv. He kept company with al-Wasiti, and was like a son to him in the Sufi sciences. A scholar, he died in the year 953 AD/342 AH.

Abu-l-Abbas al-Sayyari was asked, "How does the spiritual student tame his ego?" He said, "With patience in performing the things that God commands and avoiding those He prohibits; with the companionship of the righteous; with service to the dervish brotherhood." And he said, "A rational person finds no personal pleasure whatsoever in the contemplation of the Truth, because contemplation of the Truth is an extinction of the lower self. There can be no personal pleasure in it."

72 Abu Bakr Muhammad bin Dawud al-Dinawari

He was known as al-Duqqi. He made his home in Damascus, and lived to be more than a hundred years old, dying in Damascus after 961 AD/350 AH. He was a companion of Ibn al-Jalla and al-Zaqqaq.

Abu Bakr al-Duqqi said, "The stomach is the place that gathers together foods. When you cast into it what is lawful, righteous works will arise in all your limbs. When you cast into it what is doubtful, the way to God Most High will become doubtful to you. And when you cast into it damages extracted from people, between you and the command of God will be a veil."

73 Abu Muhammad Abd Allah bin Muhammad al-Razi

He was born and raised in Nishapur. He kept company with Abu Uthman al-Hiri, Junayd, Yusuf bin al-Husayn, Ruwaym, Sumnun, and others. He died in the year 961 AD/350 AH.

I heard Muhammad bin al-Husayn say that when asked, "Why is it that some people know their faults yet do not return to what is right?" I heard Abd Allah al-Razi say, "It is because they have competed against each other with knowledge rather than applying it, and have been preoccupied with the external aspect of the rules of religion rather than with the conduct to be derived from their inner meanings. So God has blinded their hearts and held back their limbs from acts of worship."

74 Abu Amir Ismail bin Nujayd

He kept company with Abu Uthman [al-Hiri] and met Junayd, and was very influential. The last of Abu Uthman's companions to die, he passed away in Makkah in the year 977 AD/366 AH.

I heard Abu Abd al-Rahman al-Sulami say that he heard his grandfather Abu Amr bin Nujayd say, "Any mystical state that is not the fruit of formal religious knowledge brings more trouble than benefit to the one who experiences it." And [al-Sulami] said he used to hear him say, "If on one occasion someone willfully neglects an obligatory duty enjoined upon him by God, the delight of that duty will be forbidden to him, even long after the event." [Sulami] said, "Questioned about Sufism, he replied, "It is patience under the command and the prohibition." And he said, "The bane of the servant is his satisfaction with himself as he is."

75 Abu-l-Hasan Ali bin Ahmad bin Sahl al-Bushanji

Bushanji was the first Khorasanian practitioner of the code of moral reasonableness *(muruwah)*. He met Abu Uthman [al-Hiri], Ibn Ata, Jurayri, and Abu Amr al-Dimashqi, and died in the year 348˙[960].

Asked about moral reasonableness *(muruwah)*, he said it is abandoning the use of what is forbidden to you by [consciousness of] the presence of the two recording angels at your sides."

A man said to him, "Pray to Allah for me."

He said, "May Allah protect you from your own sedition!"

Bushanji said, "The beginning of faith hangs upon its end."

76 Abu Abd Allah bin Khafif al-Shirazi

He was a companion of Ruwaym, Jurayri, Ibn Ata and others. He died in the year 981 AD/371 AH. He was a shaykh of shaykhs, and unique in his time.

Ibn Khafif said, "To be a spiritual student is to work hard continuously and abandon ease." He also said, "The worst thing for students is to allow the ego's pursuit of exemptions and indulgences, and its capacity for making legitimizing interpretations."

About nearness to God *(qurb)* he said, "Your nearness to Him is your acting in harmony with His will, while His nearness to you is the constant assistance for your work *(tawfiq)*."

I heard Abu Abd Allah al-Sufi say that he heard Abu Abd Allah bin Khafif say, "In the beginning of my undertaking I sometimes used to recite 'Say: He, God, is One' [*Surah Ikhlas*] ten thousand times in one cycle of prostration in prayer. Sometimes I used to recite the entire Quran in one cycle. Sometimes I used to pray, between the early morning and the afternoon, a thousand cycles." I also heard Abu Abd Allah bin Bakuyah al-Shirazi say that he heard Abu Ahmad al-Saghir say, "One day a dervish came in and told Abu Abd Allah bin Khafif, 'I suffer from destructive imaginings.' The shaykh said, 'I well know that the Sufis once laughed at Satan—and now satan laughs at them!'"

And I heard him say[1] . . . that Abu Abd Allah bin Khafif said, "I grew too weak to stand while making voluntary prayers, so in my private devotions I began to substitute two cycles of prayer made sitting down for each ordinary cycle, in accordance with the hadith, 'The prayer of the person who sits is worth half the prayer of the person who stands.'"

77 Abu-l-Husayn Bundar bin Husayn al-Shirazi

He was a scholar of the Quran and *Sunnah*; his state of inner experience was great. He kept company with Shibli, and died in Arrajan in the year 964 AD/353 AH.

Bundar bin al-Husayn said, "Do not argue with your ego; that is not for you to do. Summon it to its Owner—He will do with it what He wills." He also said, "Associating with people who deviate from the teaching brings on avoidance of the truth." And, "Leave what you fancy for what you hope."

78 Abu Bakr al-Tamastani

He kept company with Ibrahim al-Dabbagh and others. He was unparalleled in his time for knowledge and state. He died in Nishapur after the year 951 AD/340 AH.

Abu Bakr al-Tamastani said, "The greatest good fortune is to escape from the ego, for the ego is the greatest veil between you and God." I heard Abu Abd Allah al-Shirazi say[1] . . . that Abu Bakr al-Tamastani said, "When the heart has felt anxious, it has been punished in that moment." And he said, "The Way is plain, and the Book and the *sunnah* are clear in our midst. The excellence of the Companions of the Prophet, which came of their early emigration from Makkah to join the Prophet in Madinah and their keeping company with him, is well known. So the one among us who keeps company with the Book and the *Sunnah*, leaving his own ego and worldly life to emigrate in his heart to God, is the real man of sincerity."

79 Abu-l-Abbas Ahmad bin Muhammad al-Dinawari   He was

a companion of Yusuf bin al-Husayn, Ibn Ata, and Jurayri. He was an excellent scholar. He came to Nishapur and stayed there awhile, preaching to the people there and discoursing with words of divine wisdom; then he went to Samarkand where he died after 951 AD/340 AH.

Abu-l-Abbas al-Dinawari said, "The lowest form of remembrance of God (*dhikr*)—the practice and state of the remembrance of God—is that you forget everything else. The goal of remembrance is that the one who performs it be absent in the remembrance from the remembrance." He also said, "Outward expression does not change the inner law." He observed, "They pull down the pillars of Sufism and tear up its road; they alter its meanings with names they have invented. They call covetousness 'growth,' bad behavior 'sincerity,' departing from the truth 'ecstatic utterance,' and taking pleasure in the objectionable 'good nature.' The pursuit of desires is 'testing,' returning to the world is 'union,' bad temper is 'forcefulness,' avarice is 'endurance,' begging is 'work,' foul language is 'calling blame upon oneself.' This is not the way of the people."

80 Abu Uthman Said bin Sallam al-Maghribi

He was singular in his age; his like was not known before him. He was among the companions of Ibn al-Katib, Habib al-Maghribi, Abu Amr al-Zujjaji, Ibn al-Saigh and others. He died in Nishapur in the year 983 AD/373 AH. He asked that Abu Bakr bin Furak lead his funeral prayer.

I heard Master Abu Bakr bin Furak say, "I was with Abu Uthman al-Maghribi when his time approached, and Ali, the little singer of hymns, was chanting. When the shaykh's state changed [from the imminence of death], we signaled Ali to be quiet. So Abu Uthman opened his eyes and asked, 'Why isn't Ali singing?' I said to one of those present, 'Ask him, "How should a person seeking ecstasy from spiritual music listen to it?" I am ashamed to ask, at such a time.' So they asked him. He said, 'He can only listen in the way that he is made to listen." He was very effective in the training of character.

Abu Uthman said, "The fear of God is to stop at the limits set by divine Law, not falling short of them and not crossing beyond them." And he said, "Whoever prefers the company of the rich to the gatherings of the poor will be tried by God with the death of the heart."

81 Abu-l-Qasim Ibrahim bin Muhammad al-Nasrabadhi

The shaykh of Khorasan in his time, he kept company with Shibli, Abu Ali al-Rudhbari, and al-Murtaish. He moved to Makkah in the year 977 AD/366 AH and died there in 978 AD/367 AD. He was a scholar of hadith who collected many accounts.

I heard Abu Abd al-Rahman al-Sulami say that he heard al-Nasrabadhi say, "When something of the manifestation of the Truth has appeared to you, you care nothing for any garden, or any fire. But when you return from this state, then treat as important that which God treats as important."

I heard Muhammad bin al-Husayn say that al-Nasrabadhi was asked about someone who would sit with women and say, "I am blameless in seeing them." He replied, "As long as human individuals exist, the command and the prohibition remain, and they address themselves to the lawfulness and unlawfulness of things. People do not venture upon doubtful actions except when they are willing to risk forbidden ones."

I heard Muhammad bin al-Husayn say, "Al-Nasrabadhi said, 'The foundation of Sufism is the observance of the Book and the *Sunnah*; the abandonment of schisms and of deviation from the teaching; reverence for the shaykhs; seeing people's excuses; continuing private devotions; and giving up indulging oneself in exemptions and interpretations.'"

82 Abu-l-Hasan Ali bin Ibrahim al-Husri al-Basri

He lived in Baghdad. Extraordinary in state and discourse, he was the shaykh of his time; he was a close follower of Shibli. He died in Baghdad in the year 982 AD/371 AH.

Al-Husri remarked, "People say, 'Al-Husri never has anything to say about additional voluntary prayers.' But since my youth certain private devotions have been incumbent upon me. Had I missed a single cycle of prostration, I would have been punished." He also said, "If someone lays false claim to some part of the Truth, the evidence of the proofs he will show will brand him a liar."

83 Abu Abd Allah Ahmad bin Ata al-Rudhbari

He was the son of the sister of Abu Ali al-Rudhbari. The shaykh of Damascus in his time, he died in Sur in the year 980 AD/369 AH.

I heard Muhammad bin al-Husayn say[1] . . . that Ahmad bin Ata al-Rudhbari said, "I was riding a camel, and the camel's feet sank into the sand. I said, 'Exalted be God!' and the camel said, 'Exalted be God!'"

Abu Abd Allah al-Rudhbari used to call his companions to come with him when he was invited to eat at the houses of ordinary people who were not attached to Sufism. He would not notify the dervishes that they were invited somewhere. He used to feed the dervishes something himself, and only when they had finished would he tell them about the invitation and go with them. On such occasions, having already eaten, they could no longer stretch out their hands toward the host's food except with an effort. He only used to do that so that people would not hold bad opinions of this group, and fall into sin on account of them.

It is said that one day, while they were on their way to a meal to which they had been invited, Abu Abd Allah al-Rudhbari was walking in the footsteps of the dervishes, as was his habit. A grocer [whom they passed, unaware of the presence of the shaykh, whom he would have expected to walk in front] shouted, "These are they who hold other people's property lawful!" And he began to abuse them, saying in the course of his tirade, "One of these asked me for a loan of a hundred dirhams, and didn't return it to me—and I haven't known where to go looking for him!"

When they entered the house to which they had been invited, Abu Abd Allah al-Rudhbari said to the owner of the house, who was an affiliate of this group, "If you wish the quiet of my heart, give me a hundred dirhams!" He gave them to him immediately, and Abu Abd Allah said to one of his companions, "Take this to such-and-such a grocer, and say to him, 'This is the hundred dirhams that one of our company borrowed from you. He was unavoidably delayed, but he has sent it now, so please accept his excuse.'" The man went and did it. As they returned from their visit they crossed in front of the shop of the grocer, and the grocer began to praise them, saying, "They are the God-fearing, the trustworthy, the righteous!" Abu Abd Allah al-Rudhbari said, "The most repulsive of all repulsive people is a stingy Sufi."

*****

Thus far the recollection of a number of shaykhs of this group. The object of mentioning them in this place has been to demonstrate that they are united in declaring the greatness of the *Shariah*, characterized by traveling the paths of inner discipline and training of character, and established in adherence to the *Sunnah*. They do not omit any of the usages of religion, but agree that whoever lacks proper conduct in daily life and self-confrontation and correction, and who does not base his undertaking on the foundations of moral care and responsibility to God, has invented a lie against God, Exalted and Glorified; his pretensions are madness. He has destroyed himself and will lead to destruction whoever is misled by him and relies upon his false and futile ideas.

If we were to deeply investigate all that has reached us about these shaykhs—their words, the stories about them, the description of their lives from the evidence about their states—this book would become too long, and produce weariness. But there is plenty within the range of things to which we have alluded while meeting our goal—and success is from God.

As for contemporary shaykhs whom we have come to know, whether or not we have happened to meet them—as for instance the martyr Abu Ali al-Hasan bin Ali al-Daqqaq, the voice of his time, unique in his age; Abu Abd al-Rahman al-Sulami, unparalleled in his time; Abu-l-Hasan Ali bin Jahdam, dweller near the holy place; Abu-l-Abbas al-Qassab of Tabaristan; Ahmad al-Aswad of Dinawar; Abu-l-Qasim al-Sayyir of Nishapur; Abu Sahl al-Khashshab al-Kabir, also of Nishapur; Mansur bin Khalaf al-Maghribi; Abu Said al-Malini; and Abu Tahir al-Khawzandi, may God sanctify their spirits, and others as well—if we had occupied ourselves with their recollection and the detailing of their states we would have gone beyond the bounds of the brevity we have intended. Their states show indisputably the beauty of their lives [reflected] in their transactions. We will present some of their stories in other places in this Treatise (*Risalah*), if God so wills

PART II: AN EXPLANATION OF EXPRESSIONS IN USE AMONG THE SUFIS WITH A CLARIFICATION OF WHAT IS OBSCURE IN THEM

It is common knowledge that every group of learned people has special expressions that they employ among themselves, whose use distinguishes them from other people. They have agreed upon such usage so that those whom they address might reach a more precise understanding, and others interested in their art might find it easier to grasp what they mean.

The members of this group, however, employ expressions among themselves with the object of disclosing their meanings to each other in summary form, while veiling them from those whose ways differ from their own. Therefore the meanings of their expressions are ambiguous to outsiders.

This is done out of caution for fear that their secrets might be divulged to people to whom they do not belong. For these truths are not gathered by some sort of applied effort nor acquired through any kind of personal initiative. Rather they are significances that God Most High has entrusted to the hearts of certain people, and for the realities of which He has selected the inner awareness of certain people. We wish, in the explanation of these expressions, to facilitate the understanding of those who, following the paths of the Sufis and adhering to their customs, desire to comprehend what they mean.

*****

This has been a section explaining the application of Sufi terms, and clarifying their expressions in usages that are unique to them. We have dealt with this as brevity requires. We will now turn to some chapters elucidating the stations (*maqamat*), which are stages of the development of spiritual travelers. After that will be some chapters detailing the states, insofar as God Most High makes it possible by His grace—if He so wills—our secrets might be divulged to people to whom they do not belong. For these truths are not gathered in the inner awareness but in the explanation of these expressions, to facilitate the understanding of those who, following the patand adhering to their customs, desire to comprehend what they mean.

1 THE PRESENT MOMENT (WAQT)

According to philologists, the lexical definition of moment—*waqt*, locus in time—is: When the occurrence of a projected event is tied to a definite event, the definite event is the moment of the projected one. For example, if you say, "I will come to you at the beginning of the month," the act of coming is projected, but the time of the beginning of the month is definite, so the beginning of the month is the moment of the coming.

I heard Abu Ali al-Daqqaq say that the "now"—*waqt*—is that in which you are. If you are in this world, your "now" is this world. If you are in the next world, your "now" is the next world. If you are in joy, your "now" is joy. If you are in sorrow, your "now" is sorrow. He means by this that the the present moment is that which has dominance over a person.

Waqt may refer [specifically] to the time in which one is. Some people say that the the present moment is what is between the two times, that is, the past and the future. And they say that the Sufi is the "son of his moment." This means that he occupies himself immediately with whatever sort of devotion should come first in a given moment. He bases himself upon what is required of him at the time. It is said, "The dervish cares for neither the past nor the future of his moment; he cares for the moment in which he is." And regarding this, "To be preoccupied with what escaped you in a moment that has passed is to waste a second moment."

The Sufis also may use *waqt* to mean the power and direction of the Truth when it comes over them regardless of their own will. They say, "So-and-so is under the rule of the now," (*bi hukm il-waqt*)—that is, he has surrendered himself without preference to whatever appears to him from the unknown. This can apply only to circumstances where God Most High has given no order, and where there is no model in the Divine Ordinance that one is obliged to follow. For to neglect that to which you have been ordered, to make an order an object of surmise, and to be indifferent to your falling short of your duty, is to depart from the religion.

One of the sayings of the Sufis is, "The moment is a sword." That is, in just the way that a sword severs, the present moment shows forth the influence of God's action, ending things and bringing them to be. It is said, "The touch of the flat of a sword is temperate, but its blade cuts"—the one who treats it gently is safe and the one who treats it rudely is destroyed. Thus with the "now": Whoever submits himself to its authority is saved and whoever resists it deteriorates and declines. They have recited about this:

> Like a sword, if you polish it, its touch is soothing
> But its edge, if you are harsh to it, is harsh.
> If the moment makes someone happy, it is just a moment to him.
> If it makes him miserable, it becomes something hateful.

I heard Abu Ali al-Daqqaq say:

> The moment is harsh:
> It grinds you down but doesn't wipe you out.

He means that if it were to obliterate and annihilate your isolated personal existence, you would be freed when you were annihilated, but it takes from you [bit by bit] while not effacing you entirely. With this in mind he used to recite:

> Every day that goes by takes part of me.
> It brings down a sorrow upon the heart and then passes away.

He also used to recite:

> Like the inmates of hell—when their skins peel away
> Other skins grow from their torment.

And with this meaning:

> Not the person who dies—for dying has given him rest.
> The only actual corpse is the living man who is dead.

The shrewd person is he who is under the rule of his "now." If his "now" is sobriety. He is steadfast in the divine command. If his "now" is obliteration of self, the principles of reality rule him.

2 STATION (*MAQAM*)

A station consists of certain forms of behavior actualized by the servant through his struggles. He gains access to these through some kind of voluntary effort and makes them a reality through a sort of striving and the endurance of constraints upon his nature. Everyone's station is the place that he occupies in this way and with the discipline of which he concerns himself. The necessary condition involved is that no one may proceed from one station to another without fulfilling the requirements of the first station. For instance, he who has no contentment cannot properly possess trust. He who has no trust cannot properly possess the quality of surrender. Likewise he who has not turned to God cannot properly know penitence. He who has no vigilance over the morality of his actions cannot properly know renunciation.

The station, place of stay, is the act of staying (*iqamah*), just as the word *madkhal*, entry, has the sense of the act of entering (*idkhal*) and the word *makhraj*, exit, has the sense of the act of leaving (*ikhraj*). If his affair is to be firmly constructed upon a sound basis, no one may remain in a given station unless there is evidence that it is the act of God Most High [and not his own act] that causes him to stay in that station.

I heard Abu Ali al-Daqqaq say, "When al-Wasiti entered Nishapur, he asked the companions of Abu Uthman [al-Hiri], 'What did your shaykh use to order you to do?' They replied, 'He used to order us to realize the necessity of acts of obedience and to see clearly how we fell short in them.' Al-Wasiti exclaimed, 'He ordered you to sheer fire-worship! Why did he not command you to be absent from these acts in the vision of their Originator and Further?'" Al-Wasiti only intended to safeguard these people against complacency, not to turn aside into realms of negligence or to authorize the infringement of a single one of the usages of religion.

3 STATE (*HAL*)

According to the Sufis, a state is a spiritual influence that arrives in the heart without their intending, contriving or earning it, such as joy or sorrow or expansion or contraction or desire or agitation, or awe, or need. While the stations are earned, the states (*ahwal*) are gifts. The stations are attained through the expenditure of effort, but the states appear from the fount of generosity. The possessor of a station is confirmed in it. The possessor of a state is transported beyond it. Dhu-l-Nun al-Misri was asked about the gnostic and said, "He was here, and he left."

Some of the shaykhs have said, "The states are like lightning-flashes: if one [seems to] continue, it is self-deception." And they have said, "The states are as their name," [the verb *hala* means "to change" or "to pass"], meaning that immediately as they come upon the heart, they vanish. They recite:

Did it not change, it would not be called a state
And everything that changes vanishes.
Look at the shadow whenever it draws to an end.
It begins its diminution when it has grown long.

Another party does speak of the continuation and perpetuation of the states. These Sufis have said that when states are not perpetual and constant, they are to be called flashes (*lawaih*), and surprises (*bawadih*) and that the one who experiences them does not thereupon arrive at the states. [According to this terminology, only] at the time that this characteristic becomes constant is it to be called state.

Abu Uthman al-Hiri says, "For forty years God has not established me in a state to which I objected." He points to the persistence of *rida*, satisfaction (*rida*) with God's will. Satisfaction is counted among the states.

It is necessary to mention that—assuming the one claiming continuation of states is correct in what he says—it is possible for a spiritual influence to become a sustaining condition for someone, so that he is educated and developed within it. Whoever possesses this sort of state, however, will experience other states beyond the states that have become his given condition and which are occurrences that do not persist. When these occurrences have become continual for him, as the preceding states were continual for him, he will advance to yet other states, above and subtler than these. Thus he will be engaged in endless progressive development.

I heard Abu Ali al-Daqqaq speak about the meaning of the saying of the Prophet, "Something covers my heart so that I ask forgiveness of God Most High seventy times a day." [He said that] the states of the Prophet were always in progressive development. When he moved from one condition to a higher one, it would sometimes happen that his attention returned to what he had advanced beyond. He used to count this "a covering" compared to what he was attaining in the immediate condition, for his states were always in increase.

The Truth's capacities for depth and subtlety are without end. And since honor is due to the Truth. It is impossible to fully attain this, the servant is always involved in the refinement of his states. No spiritual significance is conveyed to anyone unless there is in his destiny something beyond it, to which it may transport him. This is the point of the saying, "What is good in the righteous is bad in those brought closer to God."

Junayd was asked about this, and recited:

Explosions of light glitter when they appear
Making a secret visible and giving news of a unification.

4 CONTRACTION (QABD) AND EXPANSION (BAST)

These are two states that occur after the servant has advanced from the condition of fear and hope. Contraction is to the gnostic what fear is to the beginner, and expansion is to the gnostic what hope is to the beginner. The distinction between contraction and fear and expansion and hope, is that fear only relates to something in the future, whether it be the loss of something dear or the onset of something dreaded. Hope likewise only relates to future events—the anticipation of something one likes or the awaited disappearance of something one dreads, the expected end of something one hates. Contraction, however, is a subtle impact produced in the moment itself and the same is the case with expansion. The heart of the one who experiences fear and hope is attached by its two states to the future, while the "now" of the one who experiences contraction and expansion is captured by a feeling that overpowers him in the present.

As the Sufis' states differ, the quality of their contraction and expansion also differs. Under one sort of influence, which is not total, contraction is produced but the possibility of outside concerns remains. Other people in a state of contraction may find that the influence affecting them permits no access to outside concerns. Thus one of these said, "I am a barrier"—that is, "There is no means of entry in me."

This is also how it is for people in the state of expansion. There may be an expansion in someone that widens his nature but does not cut him off from the majority of ordinary things. And there may be someone in bast who will not be affected by anything at all.

I heard Abu Ali al-Daqqaq say, "A dervish came to visit Abu Bakr al-Qahti who had a son who conducted himself as young boys will. The visitor passed by this boy while he was with his playmates, involved in his games. He felt sorry and suffered for al-Qahti, saying to himself, 'The poor shaykh! How has he endured the annoyances of this boy?' When he came in to al-Qahti, he found him seemingly unaware of the distractions going on around him. The visitor was amazed at this, and remarked, 'Let my life be sacrificed for someone whom even mountains cannot move!' Al-Qahti said, 'We have been eternally freed from the bondage of things.'"

One of the lowest causes of contraction is the arrival in the heart of a feeling brought on by a sign of divine reproof or a hint that one deserves punishment. This inevitably produces a contraction in the heart. Other feelings may be prompted by an indication, through a sort of kindness and welcome, of approach to God or response from Him. This produces an expansion in the heart.

In general, the degree of contraction of which someone is capable is the same as his potential expansion and his expansion is to the degree of his contraction. There may be a contraction whose cause is unclear to the one who experiences it. He finds in his heart a state of contraction for which he perceives no reason or motive. The proper course of action for such a one is submission until that moment passes from him. If he were to try to refuse it by his efforts or to bring on the moment [of the conclusion of this state] before it comes upon him of itself, his contraction would increase, and [his efforts] might be counted against him as an infringement of the principles of spiritual conduct. But if he surrenders to the rule of the moment, before long the state of contraction will vanish. As God, may He be exalted, said, "*And God brings about contraction and expansion*" (2:245).

And there may be an expansion that comes on suddenly — the one who experiences this encounters it unexpectedly, without knowing any reason for it. It shakes him and makes him giddy. The proper course of action for someone in this circumstance is silence and the observance of correct behavior, for there is at that moment a great danger for him. Such a person must beware of a hidden scheme, a test in the form of a gift. Thus one of the Sufis said, "A door of expansion was opened upon me. I slipped so I was veiled from my station." And on account of this they say, "Stay on the prayer-rug (*bisat*), and beware of delight (*inbisat*)!"

People with experience of truth have counted the two states of contraction and expansion in the class of things from which they seek the protection of God, for in comparison to what is beyond them they are the destruction of the servant. Their classification, in reality, is poverty and harm.

I heard Abu Abd al- Rahman al-Sulami say[1]. . . that Junayd said, 'Fear of God contracts me while hope of Him expands me. The real nature of things (*haqiqah*) unifies me [in His Presence], while the Truth of His Being (*haqq*) separates me [from Him in essence]. When He contracts me through fear He makes me pass away from myself, and when He expands me through hope, He returns me to myself. When He unifies me through the real nature of things, He raises me to His Presence and when He separates me [from Him] through His Unique Truth, He makes me witness what is other than myself, and so veils me from Him. He, may He be exalted, in all of that moves me [from state to state], not holding me back. He estranges me [from all else] but does not make me familiar with Him. It is in His Presence that I taste the food of my being. Would that He would annihilate me from myself and so gratify me, or take me away from myself and so revive me!

5 AWE (HAYBAH) AND INTIMACY (UNS)

These two states are above the states of contraction (awe, haybah) and expansion, in the same way that contraction is above the level of fear and expansion is above the degree of hope. Awe is higher than contraction and uns is more perfect than expansion.

The true nature of awe is absence (*ghaybah*), absence, being carried beyond oneself. Everyone in awe is lost to himself. What is more, Sufis in a state of awe differ in degree according to their detachment from or attachment to ordinary awareness. Some of them [are greatly detached] and some of them [are less so].

The true nature of intimacy, is rightly sobriety (*sahw*). In truth, the condition of balance after mystical experience. Everyone who becomes intimate with God becomes sober and clear. Such people vary according to the strength of their experience. About this the Sufis say, "The lowest stage of intimacy with God is that if one were thrown into a blazing fire, one's intimacy would not be disturbed."

Junayd said that he used to hear Sari say, "The servant reaches a degree where if he were struck in the face with a sword, he would feel nothing." Some [reservations about this remained] in my heart, until it became clear to me that the matter was exactly thus.

My father related that Muqatil al-Akki said, "I came in upon Shibli while he was plucking hairs from his eyebrow with a tweezers. 'Master!' I cried, 'You are doing this to yourself and the pain of it is reaching my heart!' 'Woe to you!' he returned. 'Reality is manifest to me and I have not been able to bear it and so—this. I am bringing pain upon myself so that perhaps I will feel it and Reality will be veiled from me. But I have not felt pain, it has not been veiled from me, and I have not the capacity for it!'

The states of awe and intimacy, while they are sublime, are counted as deficient by people with experience of truth, because the variability of the servant is responsible for them both. The states of those who gain stability are beyond change. They are erased in Being Itself, so for them there is neither awe nor intimacy, neither understanding nor sensation.

In a well-known account, Abu Said al-Kharraz said:

Once, lost in the desert, I recited:
I wander, and in bewilderment do not know who I am
Save for what people say of me and my kind.
I wander through the *jinn* of this country and its men.
Finding no one, I wander in myself.
Then I heard a voice from nowhere address me. It said:
O one who sees cause and effect as the highest level of his being
And delights in the miserable desert and in intimacy!
Did you truly belong to the People of Being
You would disappear from the worlds,
From the Throne and the Footstool of God.
You would be, without state, with God indeed
Preserved from the counsels of the *jinn* and men.

The servant only advances from this way-station through *wujud* — finding, being.

6 IMITATING ECSTASY (TAWAJUD), ECSTASY (WAJD), BEING (WUJUD)

Imitating Ecstasy means trying to attain ecstasy by an act of will. Someone who does this does not possess the perfection of ecstasy. People who know perfect ecstasy are called *wajid*, while the grammatical form of the word imitating ecstasy generally implies the showing forth of a quality that does not actually exist.

The poet said:

I closed one eye to appear one-eyed.
I was put to shame without anything to be ashamed of.

Some say that imitating ecstasy is not accepted from those who practice it because of the element of pretense it contains and how far it is from being real. Others say that it is accepted from dervishes who are free of attachments and who closely observe the excitement of this condition [that is, who have witnessed true being.] The justification for this view is the saying of the Prophet, "Cry, and if you cannot cry, pretend to cry."

There is a well-known account that Abu Muhammad al-Jurayri said that he was with Junayd, together with Ibn Masruq and others, when there was a singer present. Ibn Masruq and the others got up [moved by the music], but Junayd was still. I asked, "Master, do you not partake of anything in the sacred recital?" Junayd replied, "'And you will see the mountains, which you think firmly fixed, passing as clouds pass.' (27:88)" Then he added, "And you, Abu Muhammad, do you not partake of anything in the sacred recital?" I answered, "Master, when I am present in a place where there is a sacred recital, if there is a shy person there, I keep my ecstasy to myself. But when I am alone, I will liberate my ecstasy and strive after ecstasy." In this account he used the word imitating ecstasy and Junayd did not disapprove of it.

I heard Abu Ali al-Daqqaq say that when Abu Muhammad upheld the conduct of the great ones regarding recitals of sacred music, God preserved his moment for him through the blessing of that conduct. Thus he could say, "I keep my ecstasy to myself, but when I am alone, I will liberate my being, and strive after Being." For it is not possible to let ecstasy loose when you wish, after the moment has passed and been overcome. But since he was sincere in observing respect for the shaykhs, God preserved his moment for him until he could set free his ecstasy in solitude.

So, according to the description given above, imitating ecstasy is the preface to ecstasy. After it comes ecstasy proper. Ecstasy, befalls the heart suddenly and unexpectedly, coming upon it without design or artificial prompting. Of this the shaykhs have said, "Ecstasies are sudden events, but they are the fruits of assigned devotions." God increases His kindnesses toward all who increase their spiritual practice.

I heard Abu Ali al-Daqqaq say that inner events arise out of systematic private devotions. He who has no assigned litany, in his outer being, has no spiritual influx in his inner being. An ecstasy that owes anything to the one who experiences it is not true ecstasy.

Just as, in outward life, it is the ordinary daily transactions in which the servant engages that produce for him the sweetness of acts of worship, so, in inward life, the guidelines the servant confronts are what bring on his ecstasies. The sweetnesses of worship are the fruits of outer dealings; ecstasies are the results of inner efforts.

As for being or finding—it follows on advancement out of *wajd*. There is no finding the Truth save after the extinction of the ordinary human condition, because when the power of reality manifests, the perception of material things cannot endure. This is the meaning of the saying of Abu-l-Husayn al-Nuri, "For twenty years I have been between finding and losing—when I have found my Lord, I have lost my heart, and when I have found my heart, I have lost my Lord." It is also the meaning of the saying of Junayd, "The knowledge of Unity is contrary to its existence, and its existence is contrary to the knowledge of it."

With this sense they recite:

I find my true existence in vanishing from existence
And from all apparent evidence I see.

Imitating ecstasy is the beginning, being is the end, and wajd is the connection between the beginning and the end. I heard Abu Ali al-Daqqaq say, "*Tawajud* brings about the capacity of the servant. *Wajd* brings about the overwhelming of the servant. *Wujud* brings about the destruction of the servant." It is like someone who sees the sea, then sails upon the sea, then drowns in the sea. The order of this undertaking is: intention; arrival; witnessing; motionlessness; extinction.

And the extinction that takes place is to the extent of the real existence that will follow.

The man of Being possesses both sober balance (*sahw*), and obliteration of self (*mahw*). His state of sobriety (*sahw*) is his continuing existence (*baqa*) in the Real. His state of obliteration (*mahw*) is his annihilation (*fana*) in the Real. These two states always come upon him in succession. When sobriety in the Real overcomes him, he acts and speaks in Truth. The Prophet reported from God Most High, [relating a non-Quranic divine utterance or *hadith qudsi*], ". . . so with Me he hears and with Me he sees."

I heard Abu Abd al-Rahman al-Sulami say that he heard Mansur bin Abd allah say that a man stopped by the circle of Shibli and asked, "Do signs of soundness of Being show upon those who possess it?"

He answered, "Yes. A light deriving from the lights of yearning arises and shines upon the physical frames. The traces of it are as Ibn Mutazz says:

Water from the pitchers rained upon the cup
And made a seed of gold sprout in the earth.
The people gave praise for the wonder they saw—
A light from water within a fire from the grape.
A wine whose heirs are [the disobedient] Ad from Iram
Is only a broken relic from an ancestor—so yearn!"

[The following story is told] of Abu Bakr al-Duqqi. Jahm al-Duqqi, in a state brought on by a recital of sacred music, seized a tree in his hand and in violent excitement tore it up by the roots. The two of them —he and Abu Bakr—had come together to a banquet. [Abu Bakr] al-Duqqi was blind. When Jahm stood up and began to whirl in a state of great agitation, al-Duqqi ordered, "When he comes near me, let me know." Now al-Duqqi was a physically weak man. Jahm passed by him, and as he came close they said to Abu Bakr, "Here he is!" Al-Duqqi took hold of Jahm's leg and stopped him so that he was unable to move. Jahm cried, "O Shaykh! Repentance! Repentance!" And he gave up his state.

The excitement of Jahm was in truth (*fi haqq*), while al-Duqqi's holding him by the leg was through truth (*bi-haqq*). When Jahm knew that the state of al-Duqqi was above his state, he returned to balance and submitted. Thus whoever acts through truth is not opposed by anything.

When that which overcomes [the man of Being] is obliteration of self *(mahw)*, there is no knowledge, no intellect, no understanding, and no sensation. I heard Abu Abd al-Rahman al-Sulami recall with an authenticating chain of narrators that Abu Iqal al-Maghribi remained in Makkah for four years neither eating nor drinking, until he died.

A spiritual student came to Abu Iqal and greeted him, saying, "Peace be upon you." Abu Iqal replied, "Upon you be peace." The man said, "I am so-and-so." Abu Iqal answered, "You are so-and-so. How are you? What is going on with you?" Then he became unconscious, absent from himself. The man reported, "I gave him greeting and he returned it as if he had never seen me before. This happened repeatedly. So I knew that the man was absent from himself. I went away and left his presence."

I heard Muhammad bin al-Husayn say[2] . . . that he heard the wife of Abu Abd allah al-Tarughandi say that there was a famine. People were dying of starvation. Abu Abd allah al-Tarughandi came into his house and saw there two measures of wheat. He cried, "The people dying of hunger, and wheat in my house!" He became disordered in mind and did not recover except at the times of prayer. He would pray the prescribed prayer and then return to his condition. He continued in that way until he died.

This account shows that the usages of religion were preserved for this man even in the face of the overwhelming effect of the principles of reality. This is the characteristic of those who attain Truth. Furthermore, the reason for his becoming absent from his common sense and discernment was loving sympathy for the Muslims. That is the strongest sign ascertaining his state.

7 GATHERING *(JAM)* AND SEPARATION *(FARQ)*

The expression "*jam* and *tafriqah* [or *farq*]" is often used by the Sufis. Abu Ali al-Daqqaq used to say, "Separation *(farq)* is what you are given a share in. Gathering *(jam)* is what is removed from your power." His meaning was that whatever pertains to servanthood and is attributed to the servant, whatever is linked to the conditions of being human, is a form of *farq*, the separation between worshiper and Worshiped. Whatever proceeds from the Truth—the generation of spiritual meaning and experience, the gifts of grace—is a form of gathering (*jam*), the coming together of worshiper and Worshiped.

This is the lowest state of the Sufis in gathering and separation since it originates in the perception of actions [rather than attributes or essence]. When the Truth makes someone see his acts of obedience and disobedience as personal, that servant has the quality of separation (*tafriqah*). But when the Truth makes someone see these acts as divine actions entrusted to him, that servant bears witness to the synthesis of Lord and servant, gathering (*jam*). So the affirmation of the creation belongs to the domain of separation and the affirmation of the Truth is the property of gathering. Both of these are necessary to the servant, for he who has no separation has no servanthood and he who has no gathering has no knowledge of God.

God Most High's saying [in the Opening Chapter of the Quran and most frequently repeated of prayers], "You we worship" (*iyyaka na budu*), points to separation (*farq*) and His saying "To You we turn for aid" (*iyyaka nastain*) points to gathering (*jam*). When the servant addresses the Truth in intimate conversation, whether asking, invoking, praising, thanking, renouncing faults, or making humble supplication, he has taken his position in separation. But when he attends with his innermost awareness to that which his Lord confides to him, listening closely with his heart to what He says to him—His calling, His telling of secrets, His teaching, His giving signs to the heart, His wish—it is "with the witness of gathering," of synthesis.

I heard Abu Ali al-Daqqaq say that a singer chanted before Master Abu Sahl al-Suluki:

I made my pleasure my gazing upon you.
(Arabic from the original)

Abu-l-Qasim al-Nasrabadhi was present. Master Abu Õl Sahl said [correcting the singer], "*Jaalta*, with a final '*a*' —'you made' [my pleasure my gazing upon you]." Al-Nasrabadhi said, "No, rather *jaal - tu* with final '*u*'—'I made.'" Abu Sahl said, "Is not the eye of gathering (*jam*) more perfect?" Al-Nasrabadhi was silent. I also heard Abu Abd al-Rahman al-Sulami relate this account in this way.

The meaning of this is that if someone says "I made," it is an announcement of his own state. The servant appears to be saying that his condition has proceeded from himself. But if someone says "You made," it is like his clearing himself of tying the event to his own contrivance. Instead he addresses his Lord, saying, "You are He who has chosen me thus—not I by my own doing."

The first formulation runs the danger of pretension. The second has the quality of freeing one from [the arrogation of] power, confirming the grace and might of God. There is a difference between one who says, "By my effort I worship You," and one who says, "By Your grace and kindness I witness You."

8 GATHERING OF THE GATHERING (JAM AL-JAM)

The gathering of the gathering is higher than what has just been described. People of this sort are to be distinguished by the differences in their states and their various levels. The level of a person who affirms himself and the creation, but beholds everything established in Truth, is gathering (*jam*). But if someone is seized from his experience of the creation, carried off from himself, completely taken away from the perception of everything else by the power of the reality that has manifested and overwhelmed him, it is the ultimate synthesis. So *tafriqah* is to behold things and events as belonging to God, *jam* is to behold things and events in God, and the gathering of the gathering or the ultimate synthesis is to be completely absorbed—it is the vanishing of the perception of what is other than God Almighty and Glorious in the face of the overpowering force of reality.

After this comes an exalted condition known to the Sufis as the second separation (*al-farq al-thani*). It is when the servant is returned to sobriety at the times of the performance of religious obligations, so that it is possible for him to undertake those obligations in their proper course. And this is due to God and through Him, not due to the servant and through himself. In this condition the servant looks upon himself as under the control of the Truth. He sees the origin of his essence and intrinsic form in God's Omnipotence, and experiences that his actions and states come upon him through God's Knowledge and will.

Some of the Sufis use the expression "gathering and separation" to point to God's unrestricted power over the whole creation. All are comprehended (*jama*) in His freedom of action and government of events, inasmuch as He is the originator of the essences and the source of the attributes of everyone. Then He separates (*farraqa*) everyone by making them of different sorts: a portion of them He makes happy and a portion of them He makes distant from Him and miserable; a portion He guides and a portion He leads astray and blinds; a portion He veils from Himself and a portion He draws to Himself; a portion He makes intimate with His union and a portion He makes despair of His mercy; a portion He honors with His acceptance and a portion He causes to lose themselves in the realization of their desire; a portion He grants clear sobriety and a portion He obliterates; a portion He draws close and a portion He sends away; a portion He brings near Him and into His presence, then gives them to drink and makes them drunk; a portion He hinders and sets back, then drives them away and leaves them behind. The varieties of His actions cannot be confined by any boundary, and neither explanation nor recounting can approach them in detail.

On the meaning of gathering and separation, they recited to Junayd:

I affirmed Your Reality in my innermost self
While my tongue confided in You
So we came together in some senses and were separated in others.
If glorifying You should make You absent from the glance of my
    eye
Then ecstasy would draw You near me from within.
And they recited:

When it shows itself to me I am lost in magnificence
Then I'm back to the state of someone who hasn't arrived.
It's You who thus gathers me up and breaks me away.
There's one in the uniting, two in the reckoning!

9 *ANNIHILATION (FANA) AND SUBSISTENCE (BAQA)*

By their use of the term annihilation (*fana*)— passing away—the Sufis indicate the disappearance of blameworthy characteristics. By the term subsistence (*baqa*)—abiding in God—they indicate the establishment of praiseworthy characteristics. If the servant be not entirely devoid of one of these classes of traits [he cannot be fully possessed by the other], for it is well known that where one of these two is not, the other undoubtedly is. So if someone passes away from his blameworthy characteristics, praiseworthy qualities appear to him, and if someone is dominated by his blameworthy traits, from him praiseworthy qualities are hidden.

Know that the attributes of the servant are acts, character, and states. Acts (*afal*) are his behaviors by his choice. Character (*akhlaq*) is an inborn disposition that is alterable by the cultivation of constant habit. States (*ahwal*) come upon the servant [without his active involvement] initially, but their clarity appears after the purification of his actions. They are like character to this extent. If the servant combats the character in his heart, refusing by his efforts its shallownesses and trivialities, God will grant him the refinement of his character. Just so, if he continually takes pains to purify his actions to the best of his ability, God in His grace will grant him the purification of his states —in fact, even the complete development of his states.

In the language of the divine command, one who has abandoned what is blameworthy in his acts is said to have passed away (*faniya*) from his lusts, and when he has passed away from the desires of his flesh he abides (*baqiya*) in his intention and the sincerity of his servanthood. One who has renounced the world in his heart is said to have passed away from his passions (appetites, desires) and when he has passed away from his passions for it he abides in the authenticity of his repentance. One who has cultivated his character, expelling from his heart envy and hatred, greed and avarice, anger and pride, and the like of these intoxications of the ego, is said to have passed away from bad characteristics, and when he has passed away from bad characteristics he abides in nobility (*futuwah*) and integrity (*sidq*). One who observes the play of Omnipotence in the changing order of the world is said to have passed away from attributing causality to the creation, and when he has passed away from imagining effects to arise from what is other than God, he abides through the attributes of the Real. And one who is overwhelmed by the power of Reality so that he perceives nothing other than God, neither essence nor effect, form nor remnant, is said to have passed away from the creation and to abide in the Real.

The servant's annihilation from his contemptible actions and low states is in the disappearance of these actions, and his annihilation from himself and other people is in his giving up the perception of himself and of them. When he has passed away from actions, character, and states, it is not possible for the things from which he has passed away to further exist.

[It may be argued that while] he is said to have passed away from himself and the people, his self exists, and the people exist. [The reply is] that he has no knowledge, nor perception, nor information about either of them. His self exists, and people exist, but he is unconscious of himself and other people altogether, without a sensation of himself or of them.

Look at the case of a man who enters the presence of a very powerful or venerable person, and who is distracted from himself and the gathering by awe. He may even be distracted from the venerable person, so that if after leaving his presence he were asked about the gathering, the demeanor of that leader, or even his own demeanor, he would not be able to give any information about anything. God Most High said [of the Egyptian women to whom the beauty of Joseph was suddenly exhibited], *"And when they saw him, they extolled him, and cut their hands [distracted by his beauty]."* Though the weakest of people, they did not feel the pain of cutting their hands when they suddenly encountered Joseph. They said, *"This is not a human being!"* though he was a human being, and *"This can only be a noble angel!"* though he was not an angel (12:31). This is a creature's becoming heedless of his own condition through meeting another creature. How do you suppose it is for one to whom is disclosed the vision of the Truth, glory to Him? If he were to become oblivious to his perceptions of himself and his fellows, what is strange in that?

He who has passed away from ignorance abides in knowledge, he who has passed away from lust abides in repentance, he who has passed away from the passions abides in renunciation, and he who has passed away from his own wish abides in the will of the Most High. This is the way it is with all of one's qualities.

When the servant has passed away from his worldly qualities as described, he advances further by passing away from his vision of passing away. It is to this that a Sufi poet has pointed:

One party has lost its way in a desert land
And one party has lost its way in the court of His love.
They passed away, then passed away, then passed away
Then remained, abiding in nearness to their Lord.

At first the annihilation [of the servant] is from himself and his attributes, through his subsistence in the attributes of the Real.

Then his annihilation is from the attributes of the Real, through his witnessing of the Real. Then his annihilation is from his witnessing his annihilation, through his being absorbed in the existence of the Real.

10 ABSENCE (GHAYBAH) AND PRESENCE (HUDUR)

Absence is the heart's absence from knowledge of what is going on in ordinary human affairs, due to the absorption of the senses in something else that is influencing them. The heart may be made absent from its sense of itself and others by the influence of remembering eternal reward or of thinking about eternal punishment. For instance, it is said that Rabi bin Khaytham was going to visit Ibn Masud when he passed by the shop of a blacksmith and saw hot iron in the forge. He lost consciousness and did not come to himself until the next day. Having awakened, he was asked about what happened, and said, "Through that fire, the existence of the People of the Fire came to my mind." This is an absence that exceeded its bounds and became a faint. It is also told that a fire broke out in the house of Ali ibn Husayn while he was in prostration, but he did not turn away from his prayer. When asked about what had happened, he said, "The remembrance of hellfire protected me from that fire."

Sometimes absence from one's senses may be brought on by the Truth's disclosure of an inner meaning. Those who experience this are differentiated according to their states. It is well known that the state of Abu Hafs al-Nishapuri al-Haddad (the Blacksmith) began with his leaving his trade. He was in his shop when a reciter of the Quran chanted a verse, and an influence came over his heart that made Abu Hafs lose awareness of his senses. He put his hand into the fire and drew out the hot iron. One of his students saw this and exclaimed, "Master! What is this?" Abu Hafs looked at what had manifested through him, abandoned his trade, and left his shop.

Junayd was sitting with his wife when Shibli came in. His wife wished to go behind the curtain, but Junayd said to her, "Shibli has no awareness of you, so sit down." Not long after he said this, Shibli wept. When the weeping began, Junayd told his wife, "Now go and veil yourself—Shibli has awakened from his absence."

I heard Abu Nasr, the muezzin of Nishapur, who is a righteous man, say, "When Abu Ali al-Daqqaq was in Nishapur I used to recite the Quran at his meetings. He would often speak about the greater pilgrimage, and his words moved me, so I went out on the greater pilgrimage that year, leaving my shop and trade. Abu Ali also went on the pilgrimage that year. I had waited upon him during the time of his stay in Nishapur, and had devoted myself to Koran recitation in his sessions.

One day, in the desert, I saw him performing his ablutions. He forgot a bottle that he had in his hand, so I picked it up. When I went to his camp and placed it near him, he said, "May God reward you for bringing this." Then he looked at me a long time, as if he had never seen me before and said, "I saw you somewhere once. Who are you?"

"All help is from God!" I exclaimed. "I kept company with you for such a long while, left my home and property because of you, crossed the desert because of you, and now you say, 'I saw you somewhere once'!"

As for presence, it means that one is present with the Real, because if one is absent from creation one is present with the Real. [The term] implies that [the state] resembles being [physically] present: the remembrance of the Real captures one's heart, and one is present within one's heart before the Lord Most High.

Presence with God, is to the degree of absence from oneself and the world. When it is said that so-and-so is "present," it means that he is present in his heart with his Lord, not unconscious of Him and not distracted, in continuous recollection of Him. In that state, and according to his degree, the Truth reveals to him the spiritual meanings and secrets for which he has been chosen.

"Present," with the sense of being back from an absence, may also be used for the servant's return to his perception of his own condition and human situations. This, however, refers to presence with the creation, while the first use of the term refers to presence with the truth. States of absence vary—for some Sufis, absence is not prolonged, while for others it is continuous.

It is related that Dhu-l-Nun al-Misri sent one of his companions to Abu Yazid [al-Bistami] so that the man could bring him word of Abu Yazid's quality. When he reached Bistam, the messenger inquired after the house of Abu Yazid and went in to see him. Abu Yazid asked, "What do you want?" "I want Abu Yazid," he said. "Who is Abu Yazid?" was the reply, "and where is Abu Yazid? I myself am in search of Abu Yazid!"

The man went away, saying to himself, "This one is mad!" He returned to Dhu-l-Nun and informed him of what he had seen. Dhu-l-Nun wept. "My brother Abu Yazid has left with those who go to God," said he.

11 SOBRIETY (SAHW) AND INTOXICATION (SUKR)

Sobriety is returning to one's senses after the state of absence. Intoxication, is absence through a powerful influence. Intoxication in one aspect goes further than absence. The man of intoxication [in its lesser degree] may be simply elated, expanded but not fully overtaken by his state of intoxication. Still, thoughts of things may vanish from his heart in such a state. This is the condition of the the one who strives for spiritual drunkenness (*mutasakir*). Inspiration does not entirely fill him, so he has the possibility of ordinary perception. On the other hand, one's intoxication may strengthen until it goes beyond absence. When his intoxication grows powerful, the man of intoxication may know a more intense absence than the man of the state of absence. Yet someone who experiences absence may know a more thorough absence than the one who experiences intoxication—that is, if the latter is *mutasakir* and not one of those who has reached a perfect state of intoxication.

Absence may come to all servants of God with the effects of desire and dread, the consequences of hope and fear, that overwhelm their hearts. Intoxication, however, comes only to those who experience ecstasy. When an aspect of the beauty of God is disclosed to the servant, spiritual intoxication ensues — the spirit is thrilled and moved, the heart is enraptured. It is with this meaning that they recite:

Your soberness—from the sight of Me—is entirely union.
Your intoxication—from the sight of Me—permits you the wine.
Neither its cupbearer becomes weary nor the one who drinks.
The dregs of the sights of His cup make drunken the souls.

And they recite:
People became intoxicated from passing the cup
But the One who passed it made them still more intoxicated.

And they recite:

I have two intoxications, my drinking companions have only one.
The thing distinguishing me from them is One.

And:

Two intoxications: An intoxication of love and an intoxication of
    wine.
When shall a youth who is intoxicated twice over
Ever come to his senses?

Know that sobriety is in proportion to intoxication. He whose
intoxication is in truth, his sobriety will be in truth also. He whose
intoxication is adulterated by a portion of worldly pleasure, his sobriety will also be attended by a share of the world. And he whose state
is correct [in sobriety] will be protected in his intoxication.

Intoxication and sobriety indicate the extreme limit of the state of
separation of worshiper and Worshiped. When a token of the power of
reality appears, the servant's attribute becomes destruction and overwhelming force. With this meaning they recite:

When the dawn broke upon the star of my wine
In it the intoxication man and the sober one were the same.

The Most High said, "*When his Lord manifested Himself to the
mountain, it turned into dust, and Moses fell down in a swoon*" (7:143).
The one, for all his prophethood and the majesty of his destiny, fell
into a swoon. The other, for all its solidity and strength, became shattered and broken.

In his state of intoxication, the servant is "in the witness of state,"
lost in mystical experience. In his state of sobriety he is "in the witness of knowledge," reasoning in accordance with religion. Therefore,
in intoxication he is protected by God, not by his own contrivance,
while in sobriety he is preserved by his own conduct.

Intoxication and sobriety occur after tasting and drinking.

12 SPIRITUAL TASTING (DHAWQ) AND SPIRITUAL DRINKING (SHURB)

The terms tasting and drinking occur in the discourse of the Sufis.
They use these words to express their experience of the fruits of divine
manifestation, the results of the disclosure of secrets, and the appearance of subtle inner conditions. When this experience begins, it is
called tasting. Later comes drinking, and then quenching of thirst
(*riyy*).

The Sufis' purification of their daily lives grants them the taste of spiritual things. Their fulfillment of the requirements of their level grants them deep drinking. The continuity of their communion with God ordains for them the quenching of thirst.

The person who tastes is trying to become intoxicated (*mutasakir*). The person who drinks is intoxicated. The person whose thirst is quenched is sober. One whose love is strong drinks endlessly. If this quality continues, drinking will no longer produce intoxication. Such a person will be sober through the Real, having passed away from every portion of worldly desire. Nothing that comes over him will affect him or change him from what he is. If someone has clarified his inner awareness, drinking will not cloud it. One for whom the wine has become food will not give it up, and will not endure without it. They recite:

The cup is nursing at the breast for us.
If we do not taste it, we will not live.

And they recite:
I am amazed at whoever says I have remembered my Lord.
Do I forget, that I should remember what was forgotten?
I have drunk love, cup after cup.
The cup is not exhausted, nor have I drunk my fill.

It is said that Yahya bin Muadh wrote to Abu Yazid al-Bistami, "Here is one who has drunk from the cup of love till he no longer thirsts." Abu Yazid wrote back to him, "I am surprised at the weakness of your state. Here is one who drinks the oceans of existence, and his mouth is open asking for more!" Know that the cups of closeness to God appear from the Unseen. They are only sent round to inner awarenesses with conviction in faith and spirits liberated from attachment to things.

13 ERASURE OF SELF (MAHW) AND AFFIRMATION OF TRUE BEING (ITHBAT)

Erasure of self is the suspension of the characteristics of the habitual life. Affirmation of true being, is the establishment of the principles of the life of service. If a person expels blameworthy qualities from among his states and brings praiseworthy actions and states to replace them, he possesses the characteristics of erasure of self (*mahw*) and affirmation of true being (*ithbat*). I heard Abu Ali al-

Daqqaq say that a shaykh asked somebody, "When do you erase? When do you affirm?"

The man was silent. The shaykh asked, "Don't you know that each moment is a self-erasure and an affirmation, since whoever lacks both of these is idle and heedless?"

Erasure of self is subdivided into the erasure of lapses in the exterior aspects of behavior, the erasure of negligence from conscience, and the erasure of infirmity from one's inner being. When outward lapses are erased, right relationships are affirmed. When negligence is erased, spiritual warfare is affirmed. When inner infirmity is erased, constant aspiration to God is affirmed. This is erasure and affirmation from the perspective of servanthood.

In reality erasure of self and affirmation of true being both issue from divine Omnipotence. "Erasure" is what the Truth has veiled and negated. "Affirmation" is what the Truth [not the servant] has manifested and displayed. Both erasure and affirmation pertain to God's will. God Most High has said, "*God abrogates and affirms what he wills*" (13:39). It is said, "He wipes the remembrance of other-than-God from gnostics' hearts. He sets the remembrance of God on seekers' lips."

The Truth's erasure and affirmation of each individual is what is suitable for his state. When He erases the witnessing [of apparencies] in someone, He affirms for that person the truth of His truth. When He erases someone's affirmation of Him, He returns that person to witnessing the other-than-God, and fixes (*athbata*) him in the valleys of separation.

A man said to Shibli, "Why do I see you agitated? Is not He with you and are not you with Him?" Shibli answered, "If I were 'with' Him I would be I, but I am erased in what He is." Obliteration is above erasure for erasure allows traces to remain, but obliteration leaves no trace. The object of the aspirations of the Sufis is that the Truth obliterate what they ordinarily perceive, and then not return them to themselves after having released them from themselves.

14 VEILING (SITR) AND SELF-DISCLOSURE (TAJALLI)

Ordinary people are within the concealment of the veil. The elite are within a continuous divine Self-disclosure. According to a saying of the Prophet, "When God manifests to something, He humbles it to

Him." The one who sees the veil has the quality of what he sees. The one who sees God's Self-disclosure always has the quality of humility before the Truth.

Veiling is a punishment for most people, but for the elite it is a mercy. If what is revealed to them were not then veiled from them, they would be destroyed by the power of reality. But just as God discloses to them, He also covers them.

I heard Mansur al-Maghribi say that a dervish came to a tribe of Bedouins. A young man of the tribe attached himself to him. One day while the youth was in the service of that dervish, he lost consciousness. The dervish inquired into his condition and was told that the young man had a cousin with whom he had fallen in love. She had been walking in her tent when he had seen the dust raised by the trailing hem of her dress, and had fainted. The dervish went to the door of her tent and said, "By the right and respect that a stranger has among you, I have come to intercede with you in the matter of this young man. Favor him and show him your affection, for the sake of the desire for you that is in him!" She replied, "Glory be to God! You are of sound heart, [what do you think?] If he is not able to endure seeing the dust of my hem, how will he be able to endure my company?"

The majority of Sufis find their life in God's Self-disclosure and their difficulty in His veiling. The elite, however, are between life and recklessness. When He discloses to them, they become reckless of living, and when He is veiled from them, they are returned to their share of this world, and continue to live. It is told that the Truth said to Moses, *"What is that in your hand, O Moses?"* [referring to his staff — the question is asked during the revelation of the Burning Bush, Ta Ha 17] only in order to veil him, by means of something familiar to him, from some of the divine disclosure's impact, produced by the suddenness of hearing [the words of his Lord].

The Prophet said, "Something comes over my heart so that I ask forgiveness of God seventy times a day." To ask forgiveness (*istighfar*) is to seek the veil, because [the root of the verb "to forgive," *ghafara*, has the sense of "to cover," and provides the noun] *ghafr*, which is the veil. (From it derive *ghafar al-thawb*, the nap or pile of a garment, and *mighfar*, a helmet, and other [derivatives with similar implications].) Thus he has reported that he sought to veil his heart from the assaults of reality, since human nature cannot continue to exist together with the being of the Truth. According to another Tradition, "Were His Face unveiled, the glories of His Face would burn whatever His vision reached."

15 AWARENESS (MUHADARAH), UNVEILING (MUKASHAFAH), CONTEMPLATION (MUSHAHADAH)

Awareness is the beginning; then follows disclosure, then contemplation. Awareness [from the same Arabic root as *hudur*, presence], is presence of heart, which may be produced by the coming together of innumerable small proofs of what is real. It is still behind the veil, even if the heart is present with the overwhelming power of the practice of remembrance of God.

After this comes disclosure which is presence which has the quality of proof itself. In this condition the heart has no need of pondering indications or searching for the road, nor for seeking protection from occasions of uncertainty, and it is not screened from the nature of the Unseen.

Then comes contemplation which is the presence of the Real without any remaining doubt. Suddenly the sky of one's hidden inner being (*sirr*) becomes clear of the clouds of the veil, and the sun of vision rises in the sign of honor. The truth of contemplation is as Junayd said: "Finding the Real comes with losing yourself."

The aware person is tied to the signs of God, the person in the state of disclosure is broadened by His attributes, and the contemplative person is overthrown by His essence. The aware person is guided by his intelligence, the person in the state of disclosure is brought close by his knowledge, and the contemplative person is obliterated by his realization.

No one has improved upon the explanation of the achievement of contemplation given by Amr bin Uthman al-Makki. The gist of what he said is that the lights of God's manifestation falling upon the heart one after another without a break, with no veil or disruption intervening among them, resemble flashes of lightning seemingly linked together continuously. For just as the darkest night, through the repetition and persistence of lightning-flashes in it, would take on the brilliance of day, when continual divine manifestation takes place in the heart, the heart is full of daylight, and not night.

They recite:

Through Your Face, my night is growing radiant
Though night's darkness has covered all the people.

Mankind's within the curtains of the darkness
But we are in the brilliance of the day.

Nuri said, "Contemplation is not suitable for the servant while a single vein of him remains." And he said, "When the day breaks, there is no need for lamps." There is a party that imagines that the word contemplation must indicate the limit of the state of separation of the individual existence, because the pattern *mufaalah* from which this noun is derived in the Arabic language [theoretically implies some relation] between two [entities]. But this is merely a supposition on their part. The appearance of the Truth, glory to Him, is the disappearance of created existence, and the *mufaalah* pattern in many cases does not require association of two [entities]—take for example the verb safara, to travel, or *taraqa al-nal*, to hammer a horseshoe, and so forth.

They recite:

When the dawn broke, its lights in their shining
Overcame the lights of the shining of the stars.
He makes them drink such a cup that the Fire, if tried by it
Swallowing it, would pass like the swiftest transient thing.

A cup . . . and what a cup! It overthrows them, annihilates them, seizes them from themselves, does not permit them to endure. A cup . . . . It will not keep them as they are or leave them alone, but effaces them completely, so that not a shred remains of the effects of the human condition. As one of them said,
They departed, and there remained neither form nor trace.

16 GLEAMS (LAWAIH), GOVERNING STARS (TAWALI), FLASHES (LAWAMI)

These expressions are very close in meaning and no great difference is to be found among them. They are attributes of those who have made a beginning, who are making progress in the development of the heart. The brilliance of the suns of realization is not yet continuous for them, but the Truth, may He be glorified and exalted, brings the sustenance of their hearts an instant at a time. As He said, "For them, their sustenance is in it morning and evening" (19:62). So whenever the heart's skies are darkened by the clouds of worldly interest, gleams of discovery (*lawaih al-kashf*) are presented to them and flashes of closeness (*lawami al-qurb*) shimmer, and during the time they are veiled they are awaiting and anticipating the sudden appearance of these gleams. It is like the poet's saying:

O lightning-stroke that flashes
Which part of the sky will you enlighten?

First come gleams, then flashes, and then governing stars. The gleams are like lightning-strokes—no sooner have they appeared than they have vanished. As the poet said,

We were separated a year, and when we met
His greeting to me was a farewell.

And they recite,

O you who visited and did not visit
Like one who has come to take some fire!
He passed by the door of the house hurrying.
How would it have hurt him had he entered the house?

Flashes are clearer than gleams and their end does not come with such speed. Flashes may continue two moments, or three. But as they say,

The eye is weeping; the glance is not satisfied.
And as they say,

The eye does not come upon His beauty

Without growing red from watching, before thirst is quenched. When such a flash occurs it severs you from yourself and joins you to Him, but the light of its day scarcely shines before the armies of night turn and attack it. People who are like this are between joy and mourning, because they are between the disclosure and the veiling of the truth. As they say,

Night folds us in the tatters of a cloak
While day enwraps us in a gilded gown.

Governing stars have a more durable impact, are of greater strength, and persist longer. They chase darkness and expel doubt, but the position they occupy is the western horizon, not the height of the mid-heaven, and their power is not constant. Therefore when they come into play their departure is already imminent, and the conditions of their setting have a wide cusp [that is, their influence begins to diminish long before they actually vanish].

These spiritual impacts, the gleams, flashes, and governing stars, are of different types. There are some which, when they have vanished, leave no effect. Like meteors, when they disappear it is as if the darkness of the night had been continuous. And there are some from which an effect remains—if their mark has ceased, yet the pain of them remains, and if their lights have set, yet the traces of them remain.

After the disturbance of it has quieted, a person who has had this sort of experience lives in the brilliance of its blessing. Until it shines a second time he devotes his moments to awaiting its return, and lives on what he discovered at the time of its existence.

17 SURPRISES (BAWADIH) AND ENCOUNTERS (HUJUM)

Surprises, spontaneous perceptions, come out of the Unseen and suddenly confront the heart with a shock. This may result in either joy or sorrow. Encounters, are effects of the power of the "now" upon the heart that you cannot produce by yourself. They differ in type according to the strength or weakness or the experience. There are some Sufis who are altered by surprises and diverted by encounters, and others whose state and strength are above whatever they meet with unexpectedly. These are the masters of the moment. As it is said:

The misfortunes of time do not find the way to them.
They hold the reins of the serious affair.

18 TRANSFORMATION (TALWIN) AND STABILITY (TAMKIN)

Transformation, is the characteristic of people endowed with mystical states. Stability, is the characteristic of those who have entered into the realities. As long as the servant is on the Way he possesses *talwin*, because he progresses from one state to another and is transported from one quality to another. He leaves a campsite and arrives in a meadow. But when he attains, he stabilizes.

They recite:

With Your love I have entered such campsites
That the soul was amazed at the entering.

The person in the state of transformation is always developing; the person in the state of stability has arrived at union and stayed there. The token of his having entered unbroken union is that through the All, he becomes devoid of everything of his own. One of the shaykhs said, "The seekers' journey comes to an end with their victory over themselves. When they have been victorious over themselves, they have arrived."

The shaykh means the removal of worldly and human influences and the conquest of the power of reality. When this condition becomes constant for the servant, he has stability.

Abu Ali al-Daqqaq used to say, "Moses possessed stability. When he returned from hearing the speech of God he had to veil his countenance, because the situation had acted upon him [and made his face brilliantly radiant]. Our Prophet possessed stability. When he returned [from his entry into the Presence of God, the *miraj*], he was just the same as he had been when he left. Nothing he witnessed that night could affect [the perfection of his condition]."

He used also to cite the story of Joseph where the women who unexpectedly saw Joseph, cut their hands at the impact of the sudden vision of him. But the wife of Pharaoh's officer was more perfect in the love of Joseph than were they, and that day not a hair upon her altered. She was a possessor of *tamkin* in the matter of Joseph.

Know that the reaction produced by the impact of inspiration upon the servant is due to one of two circumstances: either the strength of the experience, or the weakness of the one who experiences it. And the absence of reaction in someone who experiences something is also due to one of two circumstances: either his strength, or the occurrence's weakness.

I heard Abu Ali al-Daqqaq say that the basic views of the Sufis about the possibility of unbroken *tamkin* are of two sorts. The first of them is that it is impossible, because [the Prophet] said, "Were you able to remain in the state you have when you are in my presence, the angels would come and shake hands with you!" Also, he said, "I have a time in which there is no room for anything other than my Lord Almighty and Glorious," thus reporting a particular private moment.

The second view is that continuity of states is proper and possible, because people who have achieved truth do in fact progress beyond the quality of being affected by events. [According to this view the Prophet's] statement in the Tradition, "The angels would shake hands with you," was not linking the matter with an impossible condition. The greeting of the angels is a lesser thing than what is generally acknowledged in the Prophet's saying, "The angels will spread their wings over the seeker of knowledge out of pleasure with what he is doing." As for his saying, "I have a time," he only spoke according to the understanding of the listener; in all his states he was established in reality.

The best point of view is that as long as the servant continues to evolve, he is a possessor of talwin, for whom increase and decrease of state is typical. But when he achieves Truth through nullifying the limitations of the human condition, the Truth, glory to Him, stabilizes him—that is, He does not return him to the illusions of the ego.

A person of this sort is established in his state as befits his place and merit. After that, whatever rare gift the Truth may grant him in each inspiration—and there is no limit to His capacities—he will receive an increase of state, changing, as it were, from color to color. Better, he will be made to change from color to color. But fundamentally his state is stable, and will always stabilize again in a condition higher than the one he was in before. Then he will progress from that condition to one yet higher, since there is no end to all the varieties of the powers of the Truth, glory to Him.

As for the person whose contemplation is overcome, whose perceptions are overwhelmed entirely, for him the human condition is absolutely at an end. When he becomes free of his whole being, his ego, and his senses—and thus from the brands of their captivity — he enters perpetual absence, and is erased. He has then no tamkin, no talwin, no station, and no state. As long as he fits this description he can neither receive any honor nor bear any responsibility — that is, unless he is returned [to ordinary life] with everything that has happened to him and with nothing of himself. Such a servant seems to be acting of his own will, according to the opinions of men, but in fact is the object of the free action of God. God Most High said,"*You would think them awake, but they are asleep, and We turned them on their right and on their left sides*" (18::18). And success is from God.

19 NEARNESS (QURB) AND DISTANCE (BUD)

The first degree of nearness is the nearness of obedience to Him, characterized by service to Him at all times. As for *bud*, distance, it is to be disgraced through opposition to Him and withdrawn from obedience to Him. The first stage of distance from God is to be far from His bounty and assistance. Then it is to be far from reaching the Truth. Indeed, to be far from His assistance is to be far from reaching the Truth. The Prophet reported from the Truth, glory to Him, "Those who are brought close do not approach Me with anything equal to the performance of the duties that I have made binding upon them, and the servant will not cease approaching Me through additional voluntary devotions until he loves Me and I love him; and when I love him, I am for him hearing and sight, so that through Me he sees and through Me he hears . . ."—as the Tradition goes.

The servant's nearness to God, first of all, is a nearness through his faith and its confirmation. It becomes nearness through his spiritual consciousness or 'doing things beautifully,' intentions (*ihsan*) and its actualization. God's nearness to His servants is in the special wisdom and insight for which this world has been chosen and in the immediate vision of Him with which He honors the servant in the next life; meanwhile it is in all the varieties of His kindness and benevolence.

The servant cannot be close to the Truth except by being far from the world. But this pertains to the attributes of the heart, not to the rules of daily life or to the visible existence of things.

The Truth is close to everything and everyone through His knowledge and power. He is close to the believers in particular through His kindness and help. And He is close to His Friends through a special intimacy. God Most High said, "*We are closer to him than his jugular vein*" (50:16) and He said, "*We are closer to him than you are*" (56:85), and "*He is with you wherever you are*" (57:4), and "*Three cannot gath - er in secret without Him as the fourth of them*" (58:7). The lowest state of someone who has made closeness to the Truth a reality is continuous vigilance before God. For over him is the watchman of fear of God, then the watchman of faithfulness, and finally the watchman of the shame produced by an active conscience (*hayyah*). They recite:

It seems one of Your watchmen is guarding my thoughts
And another is guarding my glances and my tongue.
I can't look, after You, toward a sight that vexes You,

Without Your saying they'd complained of me.
No phrase without You has escaped my lips
To anyone else, but You said they'd heard.
After You, there's no thinking one thought of someone other
    within myself; they're hauling at my reins.
I've grown tired of the news of the brotherhood of sincerity
    and I hold back from them my glances and my tongue.
It is not renunciation that turns me from them; rather
I've found You to be witnessed in every place.

There was a shaykh who preferred one of his students over all the others. His followers complained to him about this. He gave a bird to each of them and ordered, "Go and sacrifice this where no one will see!"

They all went and sacrificed the bird in a hidden place, but the favorite student came back, bringing his bird alive. The shaykh questioned him about this. "You ordered me to sacrifice it where no one would see," the student said. "But there is no place where the Truth, glory to Him, will not see! "That is why I give precedence to this one over you," declared the shaykh. "The circumstances of the world have overpowered you, but this one is not heedless of the truth!"

Seeing one's nearness is a veil over nearness, for whoever sees himself as possessing a spiritual level, or makes himself comfortable in one, is misled by it. On this account the Sufis pray, "May God make you alien to His nearness!"—that is, from being aware of His closeness; for seeking to be on easy terms with His nearness is a sign of self-glorification. The Truth, glory to Him, is above every familiarity. Encounters with reality produce amazement and obliteration of self. In reference to this, they say:

My affliction in You is that I am not tortured by Your affliction.
Your nearness is like Your distance; when is the moment of my
    rest?

Abu Ali al-Daqqaq used often to recite:
Your favor is an abandonment and Your love is a rejection
And Your nearness is a distance and Your peace is a war.

Abu-l-Husayn al-Nuri saw one of Abu Hamzah's followers and called to him, "Are you one of the friends of Abu Hamzah, who spoke of closeness? When you see him, tell him that Abu-l-Husayn al-Nuri greets you and says, "Ultimate nearness in our business is ultimate distance." As to nearness to the Essence—far exalted be God, the King, the Truth, above that! He is sanctified beyond limitations, places, direction, and measure. No created thing can unite with Him and no ephemeral being can separate from Him. The majesty of His absoluteness refuses union and separation.

There is one nearness that is intrinsically impossible, and that is the mutual approximation of [human and divine] essences. There is another closeness that is intrinsically necessary, and that is closeness through His knowledge and vision of us. And there is still another closeness that is in nature possible, for which He designates whom He chooses of His servants, and that is the nearness of grace, through His kindness.

20 THE DIVINE LAW (SHARIAH) AND THE TRUTH (HAQIQAH)

The divine Law commands one to the duty of servanthood. The Way the inner reality, is the contemplation of divine lordship. Outward religious practice not confirmed by inner reality is not acceptable. Inner reality not anchored by outward religious practice is not acceptable. divine Law brings obligation upon the creation, while the Way is founded upon the free action of the Real. The divine Law is that you serve Him. The Way is that you see Him.

The divine Law is doing what you have been ordered to do. Haqiqah is bearing witness to what He has determined and ordained, hidden and revealed. I heard Abu Ali al-Daqqaq say that God's saying [in the Opening Chapter] *iyyaka nabudu*—"You we worship"—preserves the outward practice, the divine Law. *Iyyaka nastain*—"to You we turn for help"— establishes the inner reality, the Way.

Know that religious obligation is a spiritual reality in that it was made necessary by His command. And spiritual reality, as well, is a religious obligation, in that the realizations of Him were also made necessary by His command.

21 THE BREATH (NAFAS)

Inspiration, *nafas*—literally "breath," also "breathing space" or ample room—is the refreshment of hearts by subtleties from the Unseen. A person who receives inspirations is finer and clearer than a person who is open to mystical states. The person of the momentary inner experience is at the beginning, the inspired person is at the conclusion, and the person of states is between the two. The states are means and inspirations are the end of progressive development. Moments belong to those who have hearts, states belong to those who possess a spirit (*ruh*), and inspirations belong to the people of inner being (*sirr*). The Sufis have said, "The best act of worship is to count the breaths along with God Glorified and Exalted."

And they have said, "God created the hearts and made them mines of the understanding of Him. After that He created the secret inner awarenesses and made them a place for declaring the Unity. Every breath that occurs without the guide of knowledge of God and the sign of Unity emerges from blind compulsion, and is a dead thing. The one to whom it belongs is accountable for it."

I heard Abu Ali al-Daqqaq say, "No 'breathing space' is granted to the gnostic because no indulgence can take place with him. But the lover in the early stages (*muhibb*) must necessarily have some "breathing space," since were there not a breath for him he would be ruined, because of his lack of capacity.

22 THOUGHTS (*KHAWATIR*)

Thoughts are declarations that arrive in one's awareness. This may result from the dictation of an angel or from the dictation of a devil, or from the operations of the ego or may come from the Truth, glory to Him. If thoughts come from an angel, they are called inspired suggestions, *ilham*. If they are from one's ego, they are called notions, *hawajis*. If they are from satan, they are called imaginations and anxieties, *waswas*. If they are from the Truth, glory to Him, and His dictation to the heart, they are called true thought, *khatir haqq*. And all of these are a kind of talking.

When a thought comes from an angel, its reliability can only be known through the corroboration to be found in religious knowledge. Because of this the Sufis have said, "Every thought unattested by a point of outward practice is in vain." When a thought is from the Devil, the greater part of it will be a summons to disobedience. When it is from the ego, for the most part it will be a call to the satisfaction of a desire or the indulgence of a feeling of vanity, or some other characteristic peculiar to the ego. The shaykhs agree that whoever eats what is forbidden will not be able to distinguish between angelic and demonic suggestion. I heard Abu Ali al-Daqqaq say that when someone receives his food from a worldly source rather than depending directly on God, he will see no difference between inspiration and fantasy. But when true effort silences the ego's notions, the testimony of one's heart grows articulate by virtue of one's suffering.

The shaykhs are agreed that the ego will not tell the truth, while the heart will not lie. Some shaykhs add that indeed, your ego will not be truthful and your heart will not tell lies—but even were you to make every effort to bring your ruh, your soul, to converse with you, it would not address you at all.

Junayd distinguished the ego's notions from the insinuated imaginations of satan in the following way saying that when the ego wants something from you, it is importunate. It will not stop bringing the thing back to your attention, even after time has passed, until it reaches what it wants and attains its object. Even if the integrity of effort [in opposing it] is continuous, it will bring the thing back to you again and again. On the other hand, when satan invites you to a sin and you resist him by abandoning it, will suggest to you some other sin, since all oppositions are the same to him. He wants only to summon you always to some error or another. It does not matter to him at all which particular one it is. It has been said that when a thought comes from an angel, the one who experiences it may sometimes be in harmony with it and may sometimes oppose it. But when a thought comes from the Truth, glory to Him, no resistance will arise to it from the servant.

The shaykhs have discussed whether, when there are two thoughts sent from the Real, the second is more powerful than the first. Junayd said that the first such thought is more powerful, because when it lasts, the one to whom it has come repeatedly meditates upon it, which is a condition of knowledge. The abandonment of the first thought makes the second weaker. Ibn Ata said the second is more powerful, because it is augmented by the strength of the first. Abu Abd allah bin Khafif, a more recent writer, said that the two are the same, because both of them are from the Real, and neither one of them has superiority over the other. The first does not last when the second comes into existence because it is not possible for phenomena to be permanent.

23 KNOWLEDGE OF CERTAINTY (ILM AL-YAQIN), EYE OF CERTAINTY (AYN AL-YAQIN), TRUTH OF CERTAINTY (HAQQ AL-YAQIN)

These are all expressions for sure knowledge. Certainty, *yaqin*, in general linguistic usage, means knowledge of such a sort that no doubt enters into the one who possesses it. (The term is not employed in the description of the Truth, glory to Him, because of the lack of a supportive verse from the Koran.) Knowledge received through information is certainty. Knowledge through experience (*ayn al-yaqin*) is likewise itself certainty. And knowledge through being also is certainty.

According to Sufi terminology, knowledge of certainty (*ilm al-yaqin*) is based upon abstract proof. The Eye of Certainty exists through the force of clear demonstration. The Truth of Certainty (*haqq al-yaqin*) derives from the property of self-evidence. *Ilm al-yaqin* belongs to people who possess intelligence. *Ayn al-yaqin* belongs to people who possess knowledge. *Haqq al-yaqin* belongs to people who possess realization.

To discuss this topic in explicit detail would become redundant. We have here confined ourselves to the essentials.

24 SPIRITUAL FEELINGS (WARID)

The mention of spiritual influences (*waridat*) occurs frequently in Sufi discourse. The term refers to praiseworthy thoughts that arrive (*yaridu*) upon the heart without the intention of the servant, and also to other things not belonging to the category of thoughts. There may be an influence arising from the Truth, and there may be an influence produced by knowledge.

*W*aridat are more general than thoughts, which are specifically a type of speech, or comprehended in the meaning of speech. But waridat may include a feeling of joy, a feeling of sorrow, an influence of qabd, contraction, an influence of bast, expansion; and so forth for other meanings and implications.

25 WITNESS (SHAHID)

Frequently occurring in Sufi discussion is the phrase al-shahid, "the witness." So-and-so is *bi-shahid al-ilm*, "with the witness of knowledge," someone else is *bi-shahid al-wajd*, "with the witness of ecstasy," and someone else is *bi-shahid al-hal*, "with the witness of mystical state." The Sufis use the phrase "the witness" for the thing that inhabits the heart of a human being—that is, the recollection of which preoccupies him, until even when he is away from it, it is as if he were looking upon it. Anything whose remembrance takes possession of a person's heart is his witness. If knowledge is supreme in him, he is "with the witness of knowledge." If ecstasy is supreme in him, he is "with the witness of ecstasy."

The [linguistic] meaning of *shahid*, witness, is "dweller," "that which is present" (*al-hadir*). Everything that dwells in your heart is your witness. Shibli was asked about contemplation (*mushahadah*, witnessing), and replied, "How can we witness the Truth? The Truth is our witness!" He used "the witness of the Truth" to hint that the remembrance of the Truth possessed and dominated his heart, and was always present in it.

When someone's heart grows attached to a created being, it is said that [his beloved] is "his witness," because that person inhabits his heart. Love requires the continuous remembrance of the beloved and the beloved's capturing [the heart of the lover]. Some Sufis have applied themselves to considering the derivation of this usage, and have said that shahid [as "beloved"] comes from *shahadah*, testimony. If a lover looks upon a person who has the quality of beauty, and that person's humanity falls away—so that the act of looking at him does not distract the lover from his state, nor does his company produce an effect upon the lover—then that person is a witness for him, testifying to the passing away of his ego. But if someone is affected by [the natural attractiveness of the beloved], the beloved is a witness against him, testifying to the continued existence of his ego. Whether or not a lover concerns himself with the human qualities [of the beloved] will be a witness either for him or against him.

This is the import of the saying of the Prophet, "I saw my Lord, on the night of the Ascension, in the most beautiful of forms." That is, "Even the most beautiful of the forms I saw that night could not distract me from the vision of Him, may He be exalted; rather, I saw the Former in the form and the Creator in the creation." He means by this the vision of knowledge, not literal visual perception.

26 THE EGO, SOUL (*NAFS*)

The *nafs* of a thing, linguistically, is its being. With the Sufis, what is intended in the use of the expression *nafs* is not being, and not the concrete form of the body. They only mean by *nafs* those qualities of the servant that are diseased, and whatever there is in his character and actions that is blamable.

Diseases of the servant's qualities are of two kinds. The first sort, such as his disobediences and oppositions to God's orders, he brings on himself. The second sort, comprised of low character traits that are intrinsically blameworthy, [he discovers already existing in his nature]. When the servant treats them and combats them, he may expel these traits from himself through a program of concentrated effort, by consistency of habit.

The first part of the constitution of the *nafs* consists of things forbidden by the command of God or by respect for His majesty. The second of its two parts consists of trivialities and vilenesses of character in general. In particular, it is made up of pride, anger, hatred, envy, bad behavior, intolerance, and the other blameworthy characteristics.

The worst and most difficult of the elements of the ego is its supposing that there is something good about itself, or that it has a right to some standing. This quality is counted as secretly attributing equals to God (*shirk khafi*).

The whole cure of character is the abandonment and breaking of the ego through suffering hunger, thirst and wakefulness, and through other sustained efforts, including the breakdown of strength—for that is also part of the general abandonment of the ego.

This implies that the ego is a subtle entity, seated in the physical body, which is the locus of blameworthy characteristics. The ruh, the soul, is likewise a subtle entity, seated in the physical body, which is the locus of praiseworthy characteristics. And the whole is subjugated one part to another, and the totality is one human being.

As far as possessing a subtle body is concerned, the existence of the soul and the ego is like the existence of the angels and the devils. And just as the eye is the proper site of vision, the ear of hearing, the nose of smell, and the mouth of taste, while the hearer, the seer, the smeller, and the taster is only the totality, which is the person, so the site of laudable attributes is the heart and the soul, and the site of condemnable attributes is the ego. The ego is a part of this whole, and the heart is a part of this whole, and the principle and the name refer back to the whole.

27 THE SPIRIT (RUH)

People of experience among the Sunnis have differed on the subject of souls. Some say the soul is the life force; others say souls are subtle essences seated in these physical bodies. God made it a rule for the creation that life should continue in the physical form as long as souls are in their bodies. So the human being is alive through the life force, yet souls are located in bodies. They can progress by degrees in the state of sleep; they separate from the body and then return to it.

The human being is soul and body because God, may He be glorified and exalted, subjected each part of the whole to the other; the resurrection will be for the whole, and that which is rewarded and punished is the whole. The souls are created, and whoever speaks of their pre-eternity is making a very grave error. The Traditions indicate that they are subtle essences.

28 THE SECRET, INNERMOST AWARENESS (SIRR)

The term implies a subtle entity seated in the body, like the soul. Fundamental Sufi teaching declares that the *sirr*, the hidden awareness, is the site of the contemplation of God, just as the soul is the site of love and the heart is the site of spiritual realizations and understandings. They have said, "The *sirr* is that part of you which is ennobled, and the *sirr al-sirr*, the secret of the secret, is that which has no consciousness of anything but the Truth." According to both the terminology of the Sufis and the dictates of their basic teachings, the sirr is subtler than the soul, and the soul is nobler than the heart.

They say, "The *sirr* is liberated from the bondage of the other-than-God, from its fragments and ruins."

The expression *sirr*, secret, designates those states which are guarded and concealed between the servant and the Truth, glory to Him. This is the meaning of the statement of the one who said, "Our secrets are virgin; no speculator's imagination has deflowered them."

The Sufis say, "The breasts of the noble are the graves of secrets." And they have said, "If the button of my coat learned my secret, I would cast it away!"

PART III: STATIONS AND STATES

1 ON REPENTANCE (*TAWBAH*)

God Most High said, "*Turn to God together, O believers, that you may be successful*" [24:31].

Abu Bakr Muhammad bin al-Husayn bin Furak reported to us . . . from Anas bin Malik, that the Messenger of God (ﷺ) said[1] . . . "One who repents from sin is like one who has not sinned at all. When God loves a servant, a sin will not persist in him." Then he recited, "*God loves the repentant and loves those who purify themselves*" (2: 222).

Someone asked, "Messenger of God, what is the sign of repentance?" He replied, "Remorse." Ali bin Ahmad bin Abdan al-Hawari reported to us[2] . . . from Anas bin Malik that the Prophet (ﷺ) said, "There is nothing dearer to God than a repentant youth."

Tawbah, repentance, is the first station for spiritual travelers and the first stage of development in seekers. The root meaning of *tawbah* in the Arabic language is "return"—its associated verb, *taba*, is used to mean "to come back." So repentance is to return from what is blameworthy in the divine law to what is praiseworthy in it.

The Prophet said, "Regret is an act of repentance."

Sunni scholars of the Quran and *Hadith* have said that three things form the conditions for the authenticity of repentance: regret for violations committed against the divine law, immediate abandonment of the error, and the resolve never to go back to the act of disobedience that was performed. And these, indeed, are undoubtedly the prerequisites for the soundness of one's repentance.

These scholars say that the *Hadith*, "Regret is an act of repentance," is only pointing out the most important element of repentance.

When the Prophet said, "The pilgrimage is Arafah," he meant its most important element is Arafah or rather standing in prayer there. He did not mean that there was no other necessity of pilgrimage except standing at Arafah, but that to stand and pray there was of greatest significance. Just so, his saying "Regret is an act of repentance," means that the greatest foundation of repentance is regret.

However, one among the people of realization said, "Regret is sufficient for the authenticity of repentance because the consequence of regret is the other two conditions. An evaluation that would count regret to truly exist while one persisted in similar acts or was resolved to pursue them is absurd." This is the definition and general meaning of repentance.

From an analytical perspective, repentance has causes, degrees, and parts. First comes the heart's awakening from the sleep of heedlessness and the servant's recognizing his negative condition. He will attain this if he manages to pay attention to the reprimands of God, the Truth within him, by listening to his heart. This is found in the hadith, "God's counselor is in the heart of every Muslim," and in the *hadith*, "There is a piece of flesh in the body: if it is sound, the whole body is sound, and if it is corrupt, the whole body is corrupt. It is the heart."

When the servant has reflected in his heart on the evil of what he is doing and has seen the ugliness of his actions, the wish for repentance and for leaving his negative behavior will form in his heart. God will help him by confirming his resolution, his starting to return to good deeds, and his readiness for the steps to repentance.

These steps begin with his leaving bad company—that is, people who would entice him to turn back from his purpose and confuse him about the rightness of his decision. Perfection at this level only comes with the diligent practice of witnessing that increases the servant's longing for repentance and with the dedication of his efforts to accomplish his resolve through the strengthening of his fear and hope of God. Then the knot of his persistence in negative actions will be loosened from his heart. He will stop running after dangerous things. He will rein in his ego from pursuing passions or desires of the flesh. Then he will immediately abandon his sin and confirm his resolution never to return to the like of it in the future. If he proceeds according to his intention and acts in conformity with his will, he has been granted true sincerity in his repentance. But even if his repentance has weakened once or many times and only his force of will induces him to renew it—and this sort of thing occurs very frequently—he must not give up hope of repentance on account of such incidents because "*Surely to each period is a decree established*" (13:38).

It is related that Abu Sulayman al-Darani said, "I attended the meeting of a judge. His words made an impression on my heart. When I rose to go, nothing remained in my heart of it. I went back yet again and the effect of his words stayed in my heart until I returned to my house. I shattered the means of my disobedience and became attached to the Way." When this story was told to *Yahya ibn Muadh*, he remarked, "A sparrow captured a crane!" By the sparrow he meant the judge and by the crane, Abu Sulayman al-Darani.

It is related that Abu Hafs al-Haddad said, "I left the action so many times and I returned to it. Then the action left me, and I did not return to it again."

It is said that at the beginning of his wayfaring, Abu Amr bin Nujayd attended the sessions of Abu Uthman [Said bin Salam al-Harani], whose words affected his heart so that he repented. Then his first enthusiasm faded and he fled from Abu Uthman whenever he saw him and avoided attending his meetings. One day Abu Uthman met him in the street. He turned aside and took another path. Abu Uthman followed him and kept following him until he caught up with him. "My dear son," he said, "you are not in the company of someone who only loves you when you are sinless. And only Abu Uthman can help you in a case like this!" Abu Amr bin Nujayd repented and returned to his intention and fulfilled it.

I heard Abu Ali al-Daqqaq say, "A spiritual seeker repented and then his feelings cooled. He lapsed from his repentance. One day he was wondering what the decision on his case would be if he were to repent again. A voice from the unseen spoke to him and said, 'O so-and-so! You obeyed Us and We thanked you; then you abandoned Us and We gave you time. If you return to Us We will accept you.' The youth returned to his resolve and completed it."

When the servant abandons disobedience and the knot of persistence in it is loosened from his heart, genuine remorse will come into his heart. He will regret his behavior and begin to grieve for what he has done to himself and for the ugly acts he has committed. His repentance is complete and struggle sincere when he has exchanged society for solitude and changed his association with bad friends into alienation and withdrawal from them, when his night passes into day with longing, and when in all his states he is embraced by real sadness.

Then the rightness of the lesson he has learned will cancel the effects of his having slipped. The goodness of his repentance will heal the wounds inflicted by his offense. He will be distinguished from those like him by how emaciated he is which bears witness to the soundness of his state.

The servant will never be able to carry through any of this until he has cleared himself by satisfying those he has wronged and has left behind what still attaches to him from his misdeeds. Certainly the first stage of repentance is the satisfaction of those who have been wronged insofar as the servant has power to give them their due or until their feelings change and they declare the thing lawful and themselves free of it. When this is not possible, the resolve in the servant's heart must be to give them their rights as soon as he can and he must turn to God with sincere supplication and prayer for them.

The characteristics of the repentant include various attributes and states. All of these are counted as within the compass of repentance, for its soundness makes their different qualities shine. The differing remarks of the masters on the meaning of repentance point to this.

I heard Abu Ali al-Daqqaq say, "Repentance has three parts: the first of these is *tawbah*, in the middle is *inaba*, and the last is *awba*." He makes *tawbah* a beginning and *awba* an end, with *inaba* between them. Everyone who repents from fear of the consequences of his actions possesses *tawbah*. Whoever repents from hope of reward possesses *inaba*. And whoever repents out of respect for the divine order, neither from desire of reward nor terror of punishment, possesses *awba*.

It is also said that *tawbah* is the attribute of the believers—God Most High said, "*So turn (tubu) to God together, O believers*" (24:31), *inaba* is the attribute of the Friends of God and those who are brought close to Him. God Most High said, "*Come with a repentant (munib) heart*" (50:33), and *awba* is the attribute of the prophets and Messengers. God Most High said, "*The best of servants is the repentant one (awwab)*" (38:30, 44).

I heard Abu Abd al-Rahman al-Sulami say[3] . . . Junayd said, "Repentance has three meanings. The first is to feel regret. The second is to give up going back to what God has forbidden. The third is to make an effort to repair the wrongs that have been done." Sahl bin Abd Allah al-Tustari said, "Repentance means to stop procrastinating. I heard Muhammad bin al-Husayn say[4] . . . that Harith al-

Muhasibi said, "I have never said, 'My God, I ask You to turn to me,' but I say, 'I ask You for the desire to turn to You [in repentance].'"

Abu Abd allah al-Shirazi informed us that[5] . . . Junayd said that one day he went to Sari al-Saqati. Seeing he was disturbed, he asked him what had happened. Sari said, "A young man came to me and asked me about repentance. So I told him, 'It is that you not forget your sins!' He contradicted me, and said, 'No, rather repentance is that you do forget your sins.'" Junayd said that in his opinion the young man was correct. Sari asked why. Junayd said, "When I was in a state of estrangement from God, He transported me to a state of fidelity and to remember estrangement in a state of purity is itself estrangement." Sari was silent.

I heard Abu Hatim al-Sijistani say that he heard[1] . . . that Sahl bin Abd Allah al-Tustari was asked about repentance and said, "It means not to forget your sins." Junayd was asked about repentance and said, "It means to forget your sins." Abu Nasr al-Sarraj said, "Sahl was referring to the state of disciples and novices which are constantly changing. As for Junayd, he pointed to the repentance of those who have reached the state of truth. They do not recall their sins because the majesty of God Most High has dominated their hearts and they are in continual remembrance of Him." He also observed that this is like when Ruwaym was asked about *tawbah* and said, "It is to repent from repenting," or when Dhu-l-Nun was asked about *tawbah* and said, "The repentance of the majority is from sins, while the repentance of the elect is from forgetfulness."

Abu Husayn al-Nuri said, "Repentance is to turn away from everything other than God Almighty and Glorious." I heard Muhammad bin Ahmad bin Muhammad al-Sufi say that he heard Abd Allah bin Ali bin Muhammad al-Tamimi say, "What great differences there are among those who repent from their sins, among those who repent for moments of heedlessness or forgetfulness, and among those who repent from awareness of their own good deeds!" Al-Wasiti said, "Pure repentance does not allow any trace of disobedience, hidden or manifest, to remain in the one to whom it comes. If someone's repentance is pure, it does not matter where he spends the night or where he spends the day."

I heard Abu Abd al--Rahman al-Sulami say[6] . . . that Yahya bin Muadh used to pray, "My God, because I know my nature, I cannot say, 'I have repented and will not go back on my repentance.' With what I know of my weaknesses, I can take no responsibility for abandoning sin. Instead I say, 'I am not going back to my old ways—maybe I will die before I do!'" Dhu-l-Nun said, "To ask forgiveness from God without leaving the sin is the repentance of liars."

I heard Muhammad bin al-Husayn say that he heard al-Nasrabadhi say that Ibn Yazdanyar was asked, "When the servant abandons the world for God, what should be the principle of his departure?" He said, "Not to return to what he has left, nor to pay attention to anything but the One for Whom he has left, and to protect his inner awareness from giving any notice to the things from which he has freed himself." Someone remarked, "This is the case of someone who is leaving something behind. What about someone who has nothing to leave?' He said, 'Sweetness in the future is compensation for bitterness in the past."

Asked about repentance, al-Bushanji said, "When you remember the sin and do not find pleasure in the recollection, it is repentance." Dhu-l-Nun said, "The reality of repentance is that the world with all its vastness will become narrow for you until you find no rest in it; and then your own self will become narrow for you, as God Most High said in His Book, *'Their selves became narrow for them and they bethought themselves that there was no refuge from God except in Him; then He turned to them so they would turn to Him '* (9:18)."

Ibn Ata said, "There are two sorts of repentance: the repentance of penitence and the repentance of response. The repentance of penitence is when the servant repents for fear of His punishment. The repentance of response is when he repents out of shame at His generosity."

Abu Hafs al-Haddad was asked, "Why does a repentant person hate this world?" He replied, "Because it is the place in which his sins were committed." Someone objected, "But it is also the place in which God honored him with repentance!" "Sins are certain," he returned, "but there is risk in his repentance being accepted!" Al-Wasiti said, "The joy of Prophet David and the sweetness he experienced in obedience to God caused him to fall into a long and deep sadness of repentance. But in this second state his condition was more perfect than it had been before, when his true level was unknown to him." A Sufi there said, "The repentance of liars is on the edge of their tongues," that is, merely saying 'May God forgive me.'" Abu Hafs al-Haddad was asked of repentance. He said, "The servant has no part in repentance! Repentance is extended to him, not obtained from him."

It is said that God Most High revealed to Adam, "O Adam, you have bequeathed to your offspring hardship and disease and you have also bequeathed to them repentance. Whoever among them calls to me as you have, I will respond to him as I have responded to you. O Adam, I will resurrect the repentant from their graves smiling and laughing and their prayer will be answered."

A man said to Rabia, "I have so many sins and acts of disobedience. If I were to repent, would He also turn to me?" "No," said she. "Rather, if He were to turn to you, then you would repent!"

Know that God Most High said, "*God loves the repentant and loves those who purify themselves*" (2:222). When someone yields to a sin, but sincerely believes that he has sinned and has repented, he is in doubt as to the acceptance of his repentance. This is especially so when he knows that the acceptance of his repentance depends on his being worthy of God's love, for there is a long interval between the time of the commission of the sin and the time when he will find signs of God's love for him in his nature. When the servant becomes aware that he has done something requiring his repentance, constant contrition, with persistent renunciation of the fault and asking of forgiveness, is a necessity. In fact, it is said that he should be continuously worried until his time comes. God said [speaking of and through His Prophet], "*Say: If you love God, follow me: God will love you*" (3:31).

Continuous asking of forgiveness was part of the way of life of the Prophet. He said, "Something comes over my heart so that I ask forgiveness of God seventy times a day."

I heard Abu Abd Allah al-Sufi say[7] . . . that Yahya bin Muadh said, "One slip after repentance is uglier than seventy before it." I heard Muhammad bin al-Husayn say that Abu Uthman said concerning the word of God Almighty and Glorious, "*Certainly to Us is their return*" (78:25) that it means "they will be brought back [to God], even though wandering in opposition has given them respite."

I heard Abu Abd al--Rahman al-Sulami say that Abu Amr al-Anmati said, "The vizier, Ali bin Isa, rode in a great procession. It made strangers ask, 'Who is that? Who is that?' A woman standing by the roadside said, 'How long are you going to ask, "Who is that, who is that?" That is a servant who has fallen from God's favor so God is trying him with what you see!' Ali bin Isa heard this. He returned to his house, freed himself of the vizierate, and went to Mecca and remained there."

2 ON STRIVING (*MUJAHADAH*)

God Most High said, "*Those who strive for Us we will certainly guide in Our ways; God is with the doers of good*" (29:69).

Abu-l-Husayn bin Ahmad al-Hawari informed us[1] . . . from Abu Said al-Khudri, "The Messenger of God was asked about the most excellent war for religion and said, 'A word of justice in the face of despotic power.' When he related this, tears came to Abu Said's eyes."

I heard Abu Ali al-Daqqaq say, "If someone beautifies his outer being by struggling against the passions of his ego, God will beautify his inner being with the vision of Him. God Most High said, "*Those who struggle for Us we will certainly guide in Our ways*" (29:69).

Know that whoever does not strive from the beginning will never find the slightest trace of this Way. I heard Abu Abd al--Rahman al-Sulami say that he heard Abu Uthman al-Maghribi say, "If anyone supposes that something of this Way will be opened to him or that something of it will be revealed to him without the necessity of struggle, he is in error." I heard Abu Ali al-Daqqaq say, "Whoever does not stand up in the beginning will not sit down in the end." I also heard him say, "Their saying, 'Movement is a blessing' (*al-harakah barakah*)'—means to bestir oneself outwardly brings on the bestowal of grace inwardly."

I heard Muhammad bin al-Husayn say[2] . . . Abu Yazid al-Bistami said, "For twelve years I was the blacksmith of my ego and for five years the mirror of my heart. One year I was looking between the two of them and there around my waist was an obvious belt of dualism! So for twelve years I worked to cut it. Then I looked again, and inside me was another belt of dualism. So I worked to cut that. For five years I looked for how it could be done and it was revealed to me. Then I looked at the people and saw them to be dead. So I said 'God is Greater' (*Allahu akbar*) over them four times [as at the funeral prayer]."

I heard Abu Abd al--Rahman al-Sulami say[3] . . . that Sari al-Saqati said, "O assembly of young men! Be serious before you reach my age and become feeble and incapable as I have." At that time none of the young men were anywhere near comparison to him for divine service. I heard him say[4] . . . that al-Hasan al-Qazzaz said, "This undertaking is built upon three things: that you do not eat except for need, that you do not sleep except when you are overpowered, and that you do not talk except as necessary." And I heard him say[5] . . . that Ibrahim bin Adham said, "A man is never granted the degree of the righteous before six difficult things become possible for him: the first, that he close the door of ease and open the door of difficulty; the second, that he close the door of honor and open the door of humiliation; the third, that he close the door of comfort and open the door of effort; the fourth, that he close the door of sleep and open the door of wakefulness; the fifth, that he close the door of wealth and open the door of poverty; the sixth, that he close the door of imagining the future and open the door of readiness for death."

I heard Abu Abd al--Rahman al-Sulami say that he heard his grandfather Abu Umar bin Nujayd say, "Anyone whose ego has been honored has had his religion debased!" And I heard him say[6] . . . that Abu Ali al-Rudhbari said, "If a Sufi said after five days [without food], 'I am hungry,' they would order him to the market and command him to earn a living!"

Know that the foundation and rationale of struggle or striving (*mujahadah*) is to wean the ego from what is familiar to it and to induce it to oppose its desires (passions) at all times. The ego (animal soul) has two traits that prevent it from good: total preoccupation with cravings (attraction to pleasure) and refusal of obedience (avoidance of pain/harm). When the ego is defiant in the pursuit of desire, it must be curbed with the reins of awe of God. When it stubbornly refuses to conform with God's will, it must be steered toward opposing its desires. When it rages in anger [at being opposed], its state should be controlled—no process has a better outcome than the breaking of the power of anger by developing good character traits and by extinguishing its fires by gentleness. And if the soul finds sweetness in the wine of arrogance, it will have become incapable of anything but showing off its great deeds and preening itself before anyone who will look at it and notice it. It is necessary to break it of this habit, dissolving it with the punishment of humiliation by means of whatever will make the soul remember its paltry worth, its lowly origin, and its despicable acts.

The struggle of the majority of people is to bring their works to full development. The struggle of the elite is to purify their states because the endurance of hunger and wakefulness is simple and easy. The cure of character and the cleansing of its impurities is extremely difficult.

One of the thorniest problems of the soul is its inclination to find great pleasure in praise. Anyone who drinks a mouthful of this wine bears the weight of the heavens and the earths on his eyelids! A sign of the weight of this burden is that when this drink of praise is withheld from such a soul, its state reverts to laziness and cowardice in its striving.

There once was a shaykh who had prayed in the first [and most honorable] row of his mosque for many years. One day an obstacle hindered him from arriving early at the mosque, so he prayed in the last row. After that he was not seen for awhile. When asked the reason, he said, "I had performed my prescribed prayer for so many years and while doing so I held that I was devoting myself exclusively to God. The day that I was late to the mosque, a sort of shame came over me because people saw me in the last row. So I knew that my whole lifetime's zeal had derived only from offering my prescribed prayer where I could be seen. I had to redo all my prescribed prayers."

It is told that Abu Muhammad al-Murtaish said, "I used to perform the pilgrimage on foot without taking any provisions with me. I realized all of my effort was defiled by the sense of pleasure I received in the way that I performed it. One day my mother asked me to draw a jar of water for her and my ego found that hard. I knew then that my ego's compliancy on the pilgrimages had been for the sake of show and was in fact a blemish in it. For if my ego had truly passed away from itself, it would not have found difficult something that was a duty according to the divine law."

A woman who had grown very old was asked about her situation. She replied, "When I was young I found liveliness in my self and conditions which seemed good to me. I thought it was due to the power of my state. But when I grew old this left me, so I knew that it had been the strength of youth, while I had imagined it to be spiritual states." One of the shaykhs could never hear this story without feeling sympathy for this old lady. He said, "She was certainly a woman of principle."

I heard Muhammad bin al-Husayn say[7] . . . Dhu-l-Nun al-Misri said, "God honors a servant with no greater honor than to show him the vileness of his ego. He humiliates a servant with no greater humiliation than to hide from him the vileness of his ego." I heard him say[8] . . . that Ibrahim al-Khawwas said, "There was not a thing that horrified me which I did not commit." And I heard him say[9] . . . that Muhammad bin al-Fadl said, "Rest is liberation from the ego's demands."

I heard Abu Abd al-Rahman say that he heard Mansur bin Abd Allah say that he heard Abu Ali al-Rudhbari say, "Disaster comes upon people through three things: diseased constitution, attachment to habit, and bad company." I asked him, "What is diseased constitution?" He said, "Eating the forbidden." I asked, "What is attachment to habit?" He said, "To look and listen for forbidden things and slander." I asked, "And what is bad company?" He replied, "Whenever the ego is roused by a desire, you go and pursue it."

I heard him say that he heard al-Nasrabadhi say, "Your ego is your prison. When you have escaped from it, you find yourself in eternal ease." I heard him say[10] . . . that Abu-l-Husayn al-Warraq said, "Our most sublime principles in the beginning of our undertaking are: [to act as] if the mosque of Abu Uthman al-Hiri were to prefer to give to others whatever gifts were given to us; not to pass the night knowing what our sustenance would be; and, if someone were to confront us with a distasteful action, not to avenge ourselves but to excuse him and behave humbly towards him. If disdain for someone came into our hearts, we would involve ourselves in serving him and doing good to him until it passed."

I heard Abu Hafs say, "The self is entirely darkness. Its lamp is its secret (*sirr*). The light of its lamp is inner direction from God. The result of success is prayer (*tawfiq*). Whoever is not accompanied in his secret self by such direction from his Lord is in total darkness."

Saying, "Its lamp is its secret," alludes to the secret (*sirr*) between the servant and God Most High that forms the center of the servant's sincerity by means of which he knows that events take place through God and not through nor from himself so that he is free at all times from pretensions to divine power and strength. Then, by the success that God grants, the servant is preserved from the evils of his ego. If this gift of success does not reach someone, neither his knowledge of himself nor his knowledge of his Lord will profit him. Because of this the shaykhs have said, 'He who does not have the secret (*sirr*) will be insistent on following his own desires."

Abu Uthman al-Maghribi said, "As long as a person finds anything good in the self, that person will never be able to see his faults. Only one who blames the ego at all times will be able to see his faults." Abu Hafs al-Haddad said, "How swift is the destruction of the one who does not know his own faults! Disobedience is the high road to unbelief." Abu Sulayman al-Darani said, "I did not find a single good work coming from my ego. Why should it count for anything with me?" Sari al-Saqati said, "Beware of those who visit the rich, those who recite the Koran in market places, and those who act as scholars for princes."

Dhu-l-Nun al-Misri said, "Corruption only comes upon the people through six things. First, weakness of intention in working for the next world; second, their bodies' captivity to their lusts (attraction to pleasure); third, elaborate anticipation of the future despite the shortness of life; fourth, choosing to please creatures rather than the Creator; fifth, following their own whims and casting the *Sunnah* of their Prophet behind their backs; sixth, basing excuses for themselves on tiny slips of our noble predecessors, while burying many of their wonderful deeds."

3 ON RETREAT AND SECLUSION (*KHALWAH* AND *UZLAH*)

Abu-l-Hasan Ali bin Ahmad bin Abd Allah told us[1] . . . from Abu Hurayrah that the Messenger of God said, "The best of all human modes of life is that of a person who takes hold of the reins of his horse in the way of God. If he hears an alarm or an uproar, he is on his horse's back looking for death or battle wherever it is to be found. Or it is that of a person living on what he has won by warfare on the top of some mountain or at the bottom of some valley, who stands in prayer, gives charity, and serves his Lord until the certainty of death overtakes him. He comes not among people except for good."

Khalwah, retreat, belongs to the purified, while *uzlah*, withdrawal from the world, marks the people of union. The seeker needs to withdraw from his own kind in the beginning stages. Then, in the last stages, he needs to retreat in order to confirm himself in intimacy with God.

If the servant chooses to withdraw, his intention must be to separate himself from people so that they will be safe from his evil—he must not be looking to protect himself from their evil. For the first of these attitudes comes from thinking little of one's own ego, while the second comes from making oneself out to be better than other people. A person who thinks little of himself is humble, while a person who sees himself as better than anybody else is arrogant.

A Christian monastic was asked, "Are you a monk?" He replied, "No, I am the guardian of a dog. My ego is a dog that injures people, so I have taken it out from among them so that they may be safe from it."

A man passed by one of the righteous and that shaykh gathered his garment away from him. The man said to him, "Why are you pulling your clothes away from me? My clothes are not defiled!" The shaykh answered, "I thought that you would think that my clothes were defiled so I pulled them away from you—in order not to defile your clothes, not so that you would not defile mine!"

One of the rules of withdrawal is that whoever goes into seclusion must acquire the knowledge that makes his commitment to unity (*tawhid*) firm, so that satan cannot seduce him through the imagination. Then he should acquire enough knowledge of the divine law that he is able to fulfill his religious duties so that his undertaking may be built on definite and sure foundations.

Withdrawing from the world does not mean going away from inhabited places. The essence of seclusion is to isolate blameworthy traits in order to substitute the divine names for them. Thus it was asked, "Who is the gnostic (*arif*)?" and they replied, "A creature distinguished," that is, someone who appears to be together with people, but is inwardly separated from them.

I heard Abu Ali al-Daqqaq say, "When you are with people, wear what they wear, eat what they eat and be separated from them by what is within you." I heard him say, "A man came to me and said, 'I have come to you from far away.' I said, 'That is not the way it is done. To really cross distances and endure the difficulties of travel, leave yourself. If you are successful, you will attain your object."

It is related that Abu Yazid al-Bistami said, "I saw my Lord Almighty and Glorious in a dream and asked, 'How shall I find You?' He said, 'Leave yourself and come!'" I heard Abu Abd al--Rahman al-Sulami say that he heard Abu Uthman al-Maghribi say, "Whoever chooses retreat over companionship must be free of every recollection but the remembrance of his Lord, free of every wish but the pleasure of his Lord, and free of every variety of the ego's demands. If he does not have these qualities, his retreat will plunge him into inner conflict or disaster."

It is said, "Solitude in retreat contains all one could ask of comfort." Yahya bin Muadh said, "Look and seek whether your intimacy with God is through retreat or whether your intimacy is through Him, but in retreat. If your intimacy is through retreat, it will vanish when you leave the retreat. But if it is through Him, in retreat, then any place you may be, in the desert or on the plains, will be the same to you."

I heard Muhammad bin al-Husayn say[2] . . . he heard that Muhammad bin Hamid say, "A man paid a visit to Abu Bakr al-Warraq. When he wanted to go back home, he asked him, 'Advise me.' Abu Bakr said, 'I found the good of this world and the next in retreat and having little, while [I found] evil in this world and the next in having much and mixing with people." And I heard him say[3] . . . that he heard al-Jurayri say when asked about seclusion, "It is to go among the crowd, while your secret prevents them from crowding you and to withdraw your ego from sins while your inner awareness is bound to the Real."

It has been said, "Whoever prefers seclusion has attained seclusion." Sahl al-Tustari said, "Retreat will not work unless one's sustenance is lawful. Eating lawful sustenance will not work unless one carries out one's duties to God."

Dhu-l-Nun al-Misri said, "I see nothing more productive of purity of faith than retreat." Abu Abd Allah al-Ramli said, "Make retreat your companionship, hunger your food, and intimate prayer your conversation until you either reach God or die." Dhu-l-Nun said, "Someone who is concealed from the people by retreat is not like someone who is concealed from them by God."

I heard Abu Abd al-Rahman al-Sulami say[4] . . . Junayd said, "The suffering of seclusion is easier to bear than the sociability of mixing with people." Makhul said, "There is some good in associating with people, but in seclusion there is safety." Yahya bin Muadh said, "Solitude is the table companion of the truthful."

I heard Abu Ali al-Daqqaq say he heard Shibli cry, "'Bankruptcy! Bankruptcy, O people!' They asked him, 'Abu Bakr, what is the sign of bankruptcy?' He replied, 'One of the signs of bankruptcy is familiarity with people.'"

Yahya bin Abi Kuthayr often said, "Whoever mixes with people tries to influence them, and whoever tries to influence them attempts to impress them." Shuayb bin Harb said, "I went to see Malik bin Masud in Kufa. He was in his house by himself. I asked, 'Why do you isolate yourself here alone?' He answered, 'I do not think of anyone as isolated who is together with God.'"

I heard Abu Abd al-Rahman al-Sulami say[5] . . . that Junayd said, "Whoever wants to secure his religion and rest his body and his heart, let him withdraw himself from people. This is a difficult time and the intelligent person will choose solitude in it." And I heard him say[6] . . . that Abu Yaqub al-Susi said, 'Only the strong have the strength to manage separation from people. For the likes of us, community is more fortunate and more useful. Some will work because of seeing the efforts of others." And I heard him say[7] . . . that Abu Abbas al-Damghani said that Shibli advised him saying, "Cling to solitude.

Efface your name from among the people and face the prayer niche until you die."

A man went to Shuayb bin Harb. "What brings you here?" he asked. The man said, "I want to be with you!" "My brother," Shuayb told him, "Worship should not depend on companionship. Someone who enjoys no closeness with God will not be brought close by anything external."

Some people asked a Sufi, "What is the strangest thing you have encountered in your travels?" He told them, "Khidr came to meet me and sought my company, but I was afraid that it would spoil my trust in God alone." Another Sufi was asked, "Is there anyone here with whom you would be close?" "Yes," he said. He stretched out his hand to his copy of the Quran and placed it against his heart. "This." With this meaning they have recited,

> Your Book is my strength; it does not leave my couch,
> And in it is healing for that which I conceal.

A man asked Dhu-l-Nun, "When will withdrawing from the world be the right course for me?" He answered, "When you are capable of withdrawing from yourself." Ibn al-Mubarak was asked, "What is the remedy of the heart?" He replied, "Few encounters with people."

It is said that when God wants to transport a servant from the humiliation of disobedience to the honor of obedience, he makes him familiar with solitude, enriches him with contentment, and brings him to see the shameful deeds of his own ego. So whoever has been given this has been given the best of this world and the next.

4 ON CONSCIOUSNESS OF GOD (*TAQWA*)

G od Most High said, *"The noblest of you in the sight of God is the one who is most God-wary"* (49:13).

Abu-l Husayn Ali bin Ahmad bin Abdan reported[1] . . . that Abu Said al-Khudri said that a man went to the Prophet and said, "O Prophet of God, advise me." He said, "'Be wary of God for in it is gathered all good.' (3:102). Take upon yourself war for God's sake, for it is the monasticism of a Muslim. Take upon yourself the remembrance of God, for it is a light for you."

Ali bin Ahmad bin Abdan reported[2] . . . that Anas said that someone asked, "Prophet of God, who are the Family of Muhammad?" He said, "Everyone who is God-wary, for in the fear of God is gathered all good."

The basic meaning of *ittiqa* (or *taqwa*), fear of God, is protection, by obedience to God, from His punishment. In ordinary usage it is said, "So-and-so was protected (*ataqqa*) by his shield." The foundation of this fear or awe is to guard yourself from attributing equals to God. After that, it manifests in guarding yourself from acts of disobedience and offenses, then in guarding yourself from doubtful situations, and later still in guarding yourself from omitting to do what is good.

Thus I heard Abu Ali al-Daqqaq say, "To every part of God-wariness there is a door. This has come to us in the explanation of His saying, *'Be wary of God with the respect that is due Him'* (3:102), which means that the servant obey and not revolt, remember and not forget, give thanks and not be ungrateful."

I heard Abu Abd al-Rahman al-Sulami say[3] . . . that Sahl bin Abd Allah al-Tustari said, "There is no helper but God, no guide but the Messenger of God, no provision but being wary of Him, and no work but patience in worship." And I heard him say[4] . . . that al-Kattani said, "The share of this world is trouble. The share connected to the next world is God-wariness." And I heard him say[5] . . . that al-Jurayri said, "No one who fails to institute fear and inner attention as the principles of his relations with God will arrive at the disclosure of secrets and the contemplation of Him."

Al-Nasrabadhi said, "Fear means that the servant fear what is other than God Almighty and Glorious!" Sahl al-Tustari said, "Whoever wants fear of God as his proper state must abandon sins altogether." He also said, "Someone who adheres to God-wariness yearns for separation from this world, for God Most High has said, '*In the next world is good for those who fear Him—do you not under - stand?*' (6:32)."

A Sufi said, "When someone makes God-wariness a reality, God makes avoidance of this world easy on his heart." Abu Abd Allah al-Rudhbari said, "Being wary of God is to shun what distances you from God." Dhu-l-Nun al-Misri said, "The one who is God-wary is the one who does not stain his exterior with acts of resistance nor his interior with delusions and who stands in a position of agreement and conformity with God."

I heard Muhammad bin al-Husayn say he heard Abu-l- Hasan al-Farisi say, "God-wariness has an outside and an inside. Its outside is to preserve the limits set by God on behavior. Its inside is intention and sincerity."

Dhu-l-Nun said:

There is no living except with people
Whose hearts long for God-wariness
And who are happy in remembrance
Content are they with the spirit of certainty
    and its goodness
Like the nursing infant in its mother's arms.

It is said that a person is judged to possess God-wariness on the basis of three things: the beauty of his trust in God for what has not been granted; the beauty of his satisfaction with what has been granted; the beauty of his patience toward what has passed him by. Talq ibn Habib said, "God-wariness is to work in obedience to God with light from God, wary of the penalty of God."

I heard Abu Abd al-Rahman al-Sulami say[6] . . . that Abu Hafs al-Haddad said, "'God-wariness means the lawful alone and nothing else." And I heard him say[7] . . . that Abu 'l-Husayn al-Zanjani said, "If someone's capital were fear of God, tongues would grow tired describing his profit." Al-Wasiti said, "God-wariness is that one be wary of being wary—that is, of seeing one's own fear of Him."

The one who respects God's right over him is like Ibn Sirin. He bought forty jars of butter. His servant took a mouse out of one of them. Ibn Sirin asked, "Which jar did you take it from?" The man replied, "I don't know!" So he dumped all of them onto the ground. Or he is like Abu Yazid al-Bistami. He bought a measure of oats in Hamadan, and a little of it was left over. When he returned to Bistam he spied two ants in it so he returned to Hamadan and set down the ants.

It is said that Abu Hanifa used to avoid sitting in the shade of a tree that belonged to someone to whom he had loaned money. He would say, "This derives from the *hadith*, 'Every loan drawing interest is usury.'"

It is told that Abu Yazid al-Bistami washed his robe in the desert. He had a companion with him. The man said, "Let's hang up your robe to dry on the wall of this vineyard." He answered, "No, don't drive a peg into somebody's wall." His companion said, "Then we'll hang it on a tree." "No," he returned, "it may break the branches." "We'll spread it out on the grass." "No, the animals eat it. We will not block it off from them." So he turned his back to the sun, with his robe on his back, until one side of it dried. Then he turned it until the other side dried.

Abu Yazid al-Bistami went into the congregational mosque one day and drove his staff into the ground. It slipped and rested on the staff of an old man next to him who had also stuck his staff in the ground and knocked it down. The old man leaned over and picked up his staff. Abu Yazid went to his house and asked his forgiveness. He said, "The reason you bent over was my negligence in driving in my staff which made it necessary for you to do so."

He was once seen at the doorstep of a bathhouse server. When asked why, he answered, "It is the place where I disobeyed my Lord!" On being questioned further, he said, "I removed from this wall a bit of clay with which a guest of mine cleaned his hand and I did not ask the permission of its owner so that it would be lawful."

Ibrahim bin Adham said, "I spent a night under the Rock in Jerusalem. When part of the night had passed, two angels descended. One of them said to his fellow, 'Who is here?' 'Ibrahim ibn Adham,' answered the other. 'That is the one whom God, glory be to Him, lowered by a degree!' 'Why?' 'Because he bought some dates in Basra and one of the dates belonging to the grocer fell in among his dates. He did not return it to its owner.' Ibrahim said that he went back to Basra, bought dates from that man and let fall a date into the man's dates and then returned to Jerusalem and spent the night at the Rock. When part of the night had passed, suddenly he found himself with two angels descended from heaven. One of them said to his companion, 'Who is here?' 'Ibrahim bin Adham,' the other replied, and added, 'He is the one whom God returned to his place and whose degree was raised!'"

It is said that God-wariness has various aspects. For the common people it is to guard against attributing equals to God. For the elect it is to guard against acts of disobedience. For the saints, it is to guard against attempting to gain things through actions. For the prophets, it is to guard against the attribution of actions to themselves, since their fear of Him is from Him and towards Him.

Ali, the Commander of the Faithful said, "The most noble of humanity in this world are the generous, and the most noble in the next world are the God-wary."

Ali bin Ahmad al-Ahwazi reported[8] . . . from Abu Umamah from the Prophet, "If someone has looked upon the beauty of a woman and lowered his eyes without looking again, God has created an act of service for him whose sweetness he will find in his heart." I heard Muhammad bin al-Husayn say[9] . . . he heard Muhammad bin Abd Allah al-Farghani say, "Junayd was sitting with Ruwaym, al-Jurayri and Ibn Ata. Junayd said, 'No one who is saved is really saved except by sincerity in taking refuge. God Most High said, *"And upon three who were opposed until the earth with its expanse became narrow for them. . ."*—and so on, to the end of the verse (9:118).

Ruwaym said, "No one is saved except by sincere carefulness of the rights of God. God Most High said, *'God will rescue those who have been careful with their gains'* (39:61)." Jurayri said, "No one who is saved is really saved except by the respect which comes of loyalty. God Most High said, *'Those who are loyal to the covenant of God and do not violate the pact, for them is the final abode'* (13:20-22)."

Ibn Ata said, "No one who is saved is really saved except by actualizing the shame that comes from real awareness of one's state. God Most High said, *'Does he not know that God sees?'* (96:14)."

No one who is saved is really saved except by the judgment and decision of God. God Most High said, *"Those to whom good has come from Us previously will be removed far [from hell]"* (21:101)." No one who is saved is really saved except by being chosen beforehand. God Most High said, *"We chose them and guided them to the straight path"* (6:87).

5 ON ABSTAINING (WARA)

Abu-l-Husayn Abd al-Rahman bin Ibrahim bin Muhammad bin Yahya al-Mazaki reported[1] . . . from Abu Dharr that the Messenger of God said, "Part of the beauty of Islam is that a person leaves what does not concern him."

As for *wara*, abstaining from unlawful acts,, it means to leave everything whose rightness is doubtful. Thus Ibrahim bin Adham said, "Abstaining from the unlawful is to leave every doubtful situation and to leave what does not concern you. It is the abandonment of the superfluous."

Abu Bakr al-Siddiq said, "We used to pass by seventy lawful situations for fear that we would find ourselves in one situation that was forbidden." And the Prophet said to Abu Hurayrah, "Be heedful of the lawfulness of your acts. You will be the most worshipful of people."

I heard Abu Abd al-Rahman al-Sulami say[2] . . . that Sari said, "The people who abstained from unlawful acts in their era were four— Hudhayfah al-Murtaish, Yusuf bin Asbat, Ibrahim bin Adham and Sulayman al-Khawwas. They looked into how to care for the lawful and when matters became difficult for them they took refuge in needing little."

And I heard him say[3] . . . that Shibli said, "Abstaining from the unlawful means to refrain from everything other than God Most High." And I heard him say[4] . . . that Ishaq bin Khalaf informed us, "To be scrupulous in speaking is harder than to be scrupulous with gold and silver. To renounce social position is harder than to renounce gold and silver because you spend both of them in search of social position."

Abu-l-Sulayman al-Darani said, "Abstaining from the unlawful is the beginning of renunciation of the world, just as contentment with one's lot is a branch of satisfaction with the will of God."

Abu Uthman said, "The reward for abstaining from the unlawful is an easy accounting on the Last Day." Yahya bin Muadh said,

"Abstaining from the unlawful means to stop at the limit of religious knowledge without making interpretations."

I heard Muhammad bin al-Husayn say[5] . . . that Abd Allah ibn al-Jalla said, "I knew someone who stayed in Mecca thirty years and would not drink any other water than Zamzam which he drew himself with his own pitcher and a rope and would not eat food imported from an outside city." I heard him say[6] . . . that Ali bin Musa al-Tahirati said, "A small coin belonging to Abd Allah bin Marwan fell into a polluted well. He paid thirteen dinars to have it brought out. When asked about this, he said, 'The name of God Most High is upon it.'" And I heard him say[7] . . . that Yahya bin Muadh said, 'Abstaining from the unlawful has two aspects: Exterior abstaining, which is not to make a move except for the sake of God Most High and interior abstaining, which is not to admit anything other than God Most High into your heart." Yahya bin Muadh said, "Whoever does not look into the fine points of abstaining from the unlawful will not attain the sublimity of the gift." And it is said, "The one whose attention to religion is meticulous is the one whose importance at the resurrection will be great."

Ibn al-Jalla said, "Someone who takes up the dervish life unaccompanied by fear of God eats what is totally unlawful." Yunus bin Ubayd said, "Abstaining from the unlawful is to leave the doubtful and to call the ego to account for its every glance."

Sufyan al-Thawri said, "I never saw anything easier than abstaining from the unlawful. Leave everything that makes a mark upon you conscience." Maruf al-Karkhi said, "Guard your tongue from praise as you have guarded it from blame." Bishr bin al-Harith said, "The hardest works are three: to be generous when you have little, to be scrupulous about what is lawful when in retreat from the world and to tell the truth before someone from whom you hope for benefit or fear harm."

It is told that the sister of Bishr al-Hafi went to Ahmad bin Hanbal and said, "We spin on our terrace while torches pass by us outside and their beams fall upon us. Is it permissible for us to spin in their rays?" Ahmad asked, "Who are you? May God Most High forgive all your sins!" She answered, "I am Bishr al-Hafi's sister." Ahmad wept and said, "From your house issues true care for the divine law! No, do not spin in their rays."

Ali al-Attar said, "I passed through the streets in Basra. Old men were sitting there while boys played around them. I asked, 'Aren't you ashamed to show so little respect for these elders?' One of the boys answered, 'These old men had little care for the lawful, so they have inspired little respect.'"

It is said that Malik bin Dinar made his home in Basra for forty years, but it never felt right to him to eat any of the dates of Basra, dry or fresh. He died without having tasted them. Each time the date harvest would pass, he would say, "People of Basra! This stomach of mine has not shrunk any. Has anything of yours increased?"

Ibrahim bin Adham was asked, "Don't you drink Zamzam water?" He answered, "If I had a bucket of my own, I would drink it."

I heard Abu Ali al-Daqqaq say, "When Harith al-Muhasibi passed his hand over food whose lawfulness was in doubt, a vein in his fingertip would throb and he would know it was not permissible." Bishr al-Hafi, it is told, was invited to a banquet. Food was placed before him. He tried to stretch his hand out to it, but his hand would not reach. This happened three times. A man who knew something about him said, "His hand will not stretch towards food that has anything doubtful in it! What use is it for the one who is holding this dinner to invite this shaykh?"

Ahmad bin Muhammad bin Yahya al-Sufi reported[8] . . . that Ahmad bin Muhammad bin Salim said in Basra that Sahl bin Abd Allah al-Tustari was questioned about the purely lawful. He said, "It is that in which there is nothing producing disobedience to God Most High." Sahl also said, "The purely lawful is that in which there is nothing producing forgetfulness of God Most High."

Hasan al-Basri entered Mecca and saw a young man, one of the children of Ali bin Abi Talib, who was resting his back against the Kabah while preaching to the people. Hasan got hold of him and asked, "What is the foundation of religion?" The youth replied, "Abstaining from the unlawful." Hasan asked, "And what is the disaster of religion?" He said, "Ambition!" Hasan marveled at him. Hasan said, "An atom's measure of sound abstaining from the unlawful is better than a thousand measures of fasting and prayer."

God, glory to Him, revealed to Moses (﷽), "Those who draw near do not come near to Me with anything that can compare to abstaining from the unlawful and renunciation of the world."

Abu Hurayrah said, "Those who will sit with God Most High tomorrow are the people who abstain from the unlawful and practice renunciation." Sahl bin Abd Allah al-Tustari said, "A person unattended by the ability to abstain from the unlawful could eat the head of an elephant and not be full!"

It is said that Umar bin Abd al--Aziz was brought some musk that had been taken as spoils of war. He held his nose closed. He said, "The only benefit of this is its scent. I would hate to discover its scent without the rest of the Muslims."

Abu Uthman al-Hiri was questioned about abstaining from the unlawful. He said, "Abu Salih Hamdun al-Qassar was with a friend of his at his last moment. The man died. Abu Salih blew out the lamp. Asked why, he replied, 'Up until now the oil in the lamp was his. From now on, it belongs to his heirs.' So they looked for other oil."

Kuhmus said, "I committed a sin for which I have wept for forty years. A brother of mine visited me. I bought some fried fish for him. When he had finished, I took a bit of clay from my neighbor's wall so that he could clean his hand with it. I did not ask my neighbor to make it lawful."

It is said that a man wrote a note while he was living in a rented house. He wanted to blot what he had written with dust from the wall of the house. It occurred to him that the house was rented, but then it came to his mind that it was of no importance, so he blotted the letter. Then he heard a voice from the unseen say, "The one who thinks little of dust shall learn what a long accounting he will face tomorrow!"

Ahmad bin Hanbal left a copper pot as security with a grocer in Mecca. When he wanted to redeem it, the grocer took out two pots and said, "Take whichever of them is yours." Ahmad said, "I am not sure which is my pot, so it is yours, and the money is also yours." The grocer said, "This one is your pot. I wanted to put you to the test!" He replied, "I will not take it." And he went away and left the pot with the grocer.

It is said that Ibn Mubarak let loose a horse of great value while he prayed his noon prescribed prayer. The animal pastured in the field of a village whose revenues belonged to a king. Ibn Mubarak abandoned the beast and would not ride it. It is said that Ibn Mubarak returned from Merv to Damascus because of a pen he had borrowed and not returned to its owner.

Al-Nakhai hired a riding animal. His whip dropped from his hand. He descended, tied the animal and went back and picked up his whip. It was said to him, "If you had ridden your mount back to the place where you dropped your whip in order to pick it up, it would have been easier for you." He answered, "I only hired it to travel from such-and-such a place to such-and-such a place!"

Abu Bakr al-Daqqaq said, "I was lost in the desert of the Children of Israel for fifteen days. When I found the road, I encountered a soldier who gave me a drink of water. Because of this, a covering came over my heart from which I suffered for thirty years."

It is said that Rabia-l-Adawiyyah mended a tear in her shirt by the light of a sultan's lamp. For awhile she lost knowledge of her heart. Then she remembered, ripped her shirt, and found her heart.

Sufyan al-Thawri was seen in a dream. He had two wings with which he was flying from tree to tree in paradise. He was asked, "By virtue of what were you granted this?" and said, "By abstaining from the unlawful."

Hasan bin Abi Sinan stopped with the companions of Hasan al-Basri and asked, "What thing is most difficult for you?" He replied, "To be scrupulous about the lawful." "Nothing is easier than that for me," he said. "How can that be?" they asked. "I have not drunk from this river of yours for forty years," said he.

Hasan bin Abi Sinan used never to sleep reclining nor to eat any sort of oil nor to drink cold water for sixty years. After he died he was seen in a dream and asked, "How has God treated you?" "Well," he said, "but I am veiled from paradise by a needle I borrowed and did not return."

Abd-l-Wahid bin Zayd had a slave who had waited upon him for many years and spent forty years in worship. In the beginning he [the salve] had been a grain measurer. When he died, he was seen in a dream and asked, "How has God treated you?" "Well," he replied, "except that I am veiled from paradise. I measured forty measures of grain and did not clean the dust that collected at each measure. This giving of short measure was counted against me."

Jesus son of Mary passed by a grave and called a man out of it. God Most High brought him back to life. Jesus asked, "Who are you?" The man said, "I was a porter who carried things about for people. One day I carried firewood for someone. I broke off a splinter and used it as a toothpick, and I have been paying for it since I died."

Abu Said al-Kharraz was discoursing on abstaining from the unlawful when Abbas bin al-Muhtadi passed by. He said, "Abu Said, aren't you ashamed? You sit under the roof of a miserly sultan, drink from the well of a queen, do your business with false coin, and you talk about abstaining from the unlawful?"

6 ON RENUNCIATION (*ZUHD*)

Hamzah bin Yusuf al-Sahmi al-Jurjani related to us[1] . . . from Abu Khilad, who sat with the Prophet, that the Prophet said, "If you see a man who has been gifted with renunciation of the world and who has eloquence, seek to approach him, for wisdom has been instilled in him."

The Sufis have differing opinions in the matter of renunciation (*zuhd*). Some of them say that one need only renounce the unlawful, because the lawful has been made permissible by God Most High. When God benefits His servant with lawful property and the servant in turn worships Him with gratitude for it, it is not preferable for him to leave it with his own will rather than keeping it with God's permission.

Other Sufis say that renunciation of the unlawful is an obligation, while renunciation of the lawful is a virtue. From this point of view, as long as the servant is patient with his state of little property, satisfied with what God Most High has apportioned for him, and content with what he has been given, he is more perfect than one who lives richly and comfortably in the world. God Most High has urged people to abstain from the world by His saying, "*Say: The provision of this world is but small, while the next is better for whoever is God-wary*" (4:77) and in many other verses that may be cited disparaging the world and recommending abstention from it.

Some of them say that if the servant spends his wealth in works of obedience, his state being marked by patience and, in difficult times, by not raising objections to what the law forbids, then his renunciation of lawful property is the more preferable.

Others say that the servant must neither attempt to abandon the lawful by his own effort nor to seek superfluous wealth, but that he should respect his apportioned share. If God Exalted and Glorified has provided him with the sustenance of lawful income, he should thank

Him. If God Most High has appointed to him enough to take care of all his needs, he should not strive to seek out excess property. Patience is the better course for the poor man. Gratitude is more suitable for the possessor of lawful wealth.

They have discoursed on the meaning of renunciation. Each of them has spoken of his own time and pointed to its particular character. I heard Abu Abd al-Rahman al-Sulami say[2] . . . that Sufyan al-Thawri said, "Renunciation of the world means to give up placing your hope in it, not to eat coarse food or wear the robe of an ascetic." And I heard him say[3] . . . Sari al-Saqati said, "God strips the world from His Friends, denies it to His purified ones, and removes it from the hearts of those He loves because He is not satisfied with that for them."

It is said that the principle of renunciation derives from His Word, "*So that they may neither mourn over what has escaped them, nor exult over what has been granted them,*" (57:23) because the renunciater does not exalt in what he has of the world nor grieve over what he does not have.

Abu Uthman said, "Renunciation is to give up the world and then not care who gets it." I heard Abu Ali al-Daqqaq say, "Renunciation is to leave the world as it is and not to say, 'I will construct a shelter,' or 'I will build a mosque.'" Yahya bin Muadh said, "Renunciation makes one generous with property, while love makes one generous with spirit."

Ibn al-Jalla said, "Renunciation is to look at the world with an eye for its transience, so that it becomes small in your eyes and avoiding it becomes easy for you."

Ibn Khafif said, "The sign of renunciation is that ease exists when wealth departs." He also said, "When the heart has forgotten apparent causes and the hands have withdrawn themselves from wealth, it is renunciation."

It has been said, "Renunciation exists when the ego genuinely dislikes the world." I heard Abu Abd al-Rahman al-Sulami say that he heard al-Nasrabadhi say, "The ascetic is a stranger in this world, and the gnostic is a stranger in the next."

It is said, "If someone is sincere in his renunciation, the world comes to him despite himself." And about this they say, "If a crown were to fall from heaven, it would only fall on the head of someone who didn't want it."

Junayd said, "Renunciation is that the heart be free of whatever the hand is free of." Abu Sulayman al-Darani said, "To wear wool is a sign of renunciation, but it is not right for a reenunciate to wear it if he has three dirhams and the wish for five dirhams is in his heart."

Our predecessors have held varying views in the matter of renunciation. Sufyan al-Thawri, Ahmad bin Hanbal, Isa bin Yunus and others have held that to renounce the world is to abandon ambition and be satisfied with one's lot, which they say is one of the signs, motivations and consequences of renunciation.

Abd Allah bin al-Mubarak said, "Renunciation is trust in God Most High together with love of poverty." So say also Shaqiq al-Balkhi and Yunus bin Asbat. This is also one of the guideposts of renunciation, for the servant has no strength to renounce except by means of trust in God Most High. Abd al-Wahid bin Zayd said, "Renunciation is to leave both the dinar and the dirham." Abu Sulayman al-Darani said, "Renunciation is to abandon whatever distracts you from God Glorified and Exalted."

I heard Muhammad bin al-Husayn say[4] . . . when Ruwaym asked about renunciation, Junayd said, "It is seeing the world as insignificant and erasing its vestiges from the heart." Sari said, "The life of an ascetic is not good while he is distracted from himself. The life of a gnostic is not good while he is distracted by himself."

Junayd, questioned about renunciation, said, "It is that the hand be free of property and the heart of pursuing it." Shibli was asked about renunciation and said, "It is to abstain from what is other than God Most High."

Yahya bin Muadh said, "No one attains the reality of renunciation until there are three characteristics in him: work without attachment, speech without personal motives, and honor without seeking position."

Abu Hafs said, "One can only renounce the lawful, and there is nothing lawful in the world, so there is no renunciation." Abu Uthman said, "God Most High gives to the ascetic more than what he desires. He gives to the desirous one less than what he desires. He gives to the one on the middle and straight path exactly in accordance with his desires."

Yahya bin Muadh said, "The ascetic makes you snuff up vinegar and mustard. The gnostic lets you smell ambergris and musk." Hasan al-Basri said, "Renunciation of the world is that you loathe its people, and you loathe what it contains." A Sufi was asked, "What is renunciation of the world?" He answered, "To abandon whatever is in it to whoever is in it."

A man asked Dhu-l-Nun al-Misri, "When will I renounce the world?" He replied, "When you have renounced yourself."

Muhammad bin al-Fadl said, "The predilection of ascetics is for having no needs and the predilection of spiritual warriors (*fityan*) is for being in need. God Most High said, '*And they prefer others over themselves, even though they may be in need*' (59:9)."

Al-Kattani said, "The thing about which the Kufan, the Medinese, the Iraqi, and the Damascene do not differ is abstinence from the world, generosity of nature, and giving good counsel to people. Not one of all those sorts of people would call these traits anything but laudable."

A man asked Yahya bin Muadh, "When will I enter the tavern of trust in God, put on the cloak of renunciation and sit with the ascetics?" He said, "When the secret training of your ego progresses to such an extent that if God cut off your sustenance for three days, you would not be weakened in yourself. Inasmuch as you have not matured to this degree, your sitting on the prayer carpet of ascetics would only be ignorance. And I could not guarantee that you would not be exposed among them!"

Bishr al-Hafi said, "Renunciation is a king who dwells only in a free and empty heart." I heard Muhammad bin al-Husayn say[5] . . . that Muhammad bin Muhammad bin al-Ashath al-Bikandi said, "If someone discourses on renunciation and preaches to the people and then desires what they have, God Most High removes the love of the next world from his heart."

It is said that when the servant has renounced the world, God Most High sets an angel over him who will plant wisdom in his heart. A Sufi was asked, "Why did you renounce the world?" He replied, "It renounced me!"

Ahmad bin Hanbal said, "Renunciation has three phases. The first is abandonment of the unlawful which is the renunciation of the majority of people. The second is abandonment of excess in the lawful which is the renunciation of the elite. The third is abandonment of whatever distracts the servant from God Most High, which is the renunciation of gnostics."

I heard Abu Ali al-Daqqaq say, "A Sufi was asked, 'Why do you abstain from the world?' He answered, 'When most of the world renounced me, I disdained to take an interest in the rest of it.'"

Yahya bin Muadh said, "The world is like an unveiled bride. The one who seeks her waits upon her like a maid while the ascetic blackens her face, tears out her hair, and sets fire to her raiment. But the gnostic is occupied with God Most High and does not even notice her."

I heard Abu Abd Allah al-Sufi say[6] . . . that Sari said, "I exercised every aspect of renunciation and was granted what I wished, except for renunciation of other people— I have not attained it, nor am I capable of it." It is said, "Ascetics leave nothing but for their own sake. They give up a temporal benefit for an eternal one."

Al-Nasrabadhi said, "Renunciation spares the blood of the ascetics, but sheds the blood of the gnostics." Hatim al-Asamm said, "The ascetic exhausts his purse before he exhausts his ego. The would-be ascetic exhausts himself before he has exhausted his purse!"

I heard Muhammad bin Abd Allah say[7] . . . that Fudayl bin Iyad said, "God put everything bad in one house and made its key the love of this world. He put everything good in another house and made its key renunciation."

7 ON SILENCE (*SAMT*)

Abd Allah bin Yusuf al-Ispahani informed us[1] . . . through Abu Hurayrah that the Messenger of God said, "Whoever believes in God and the last day, let him not trouble his neighbor. Whoever believes in God and the last day, let him be generous to his guest. Whoever believes in God and the last day, let him say what is good, or let him be silent."

Ali bin Ahmad bin Abdan informed us[2] . . . that Ukbah bin Amir said, "I asked, 'O Messenger of God, what is salvation?" He said, 'Keep your tongue to yourself, stay home, and weep over your sins.'"

Silence is security. That is the root of the matter. This can be cause for remorse on occasions when keeping quiet is blameworthy. What is necessary is that one choose speech or silence according to the divine law and the obligation of a Muslim to command what is good and forbid what is evil. To say nothing at the proper time is a characteristic of true men, just as to speak at the proper occasion is one of the noblest of qualities. I heard Abu Ali al-Daqqaq say, "Whoever holds back from speaking the truth is a devil without a tongue."

One should be silent in the presence of God. God Most High said, "*When the Quran is recited, hearken to it and give ear so that you may receive mercy*" (7:204). And He said, referring to the *jinn* who were in the presence of the Messenger, "*When they were present with him, they said, 'Listen!'*" (46:29), and "*Voices will be lowered for the Beneficent, so that nothing will be heard but a whisper*" (20:108).

What a difference is there between a servant who is silent to protect himself from lying and gossiping and a servant who is silent because he is overwhelmed by the power of the awe he feels! With this sense they recite:

I ponder over what to say when we are apart,
And judge myself addicted to proving by the word.

But when we are together, I lose all from the start,
And if I say a single thing, say only the absurd.

And they recite:

O Layla, how many proofs have been my task!
When I come to you, O Layla, I don't know what that
    means.

And they recite:

And how many speeches to you!
But when I was set before you, I forgot them all.

And:

I realize that speech adorns a noble youth,
But silence is the better course for one who can keep
    silent.
On how many an occasion has the alphabet brought
    death,
And how many a speaker has wished he had been
    quiet?

Silence has two parts, outer quiet and the quiet of heart and mind.
Someone who trusts in God stills his heart as a way of laying claim to
his sustenance. The gnostic stills his heart in acceptance of destiny
through the quality of harmony with God. The one relies upon the
fineness of His work. The other is content with the totality of His
decrees. With this meaning they have said:
His misfortunes came over you,
And the cares of your inner being were relieved.

Sometimes silence is caused by the amazement of spontaneous
understanding. When the unveiling of a divine attribute occurs suddenly, all expressiveness is struck dumb. There can be no explanation
or discourse, and all demonstrative evidences are blotted out so that
there is neither knowledge nor sensation. God Most High said, *"On the
day [of judgment] God will gather the Messengers and ask, 'What
answer have you received?' They will reply, 'We have no knowledge'"*
(5:109).

As for the predilection of the masters of inner struggle for silence, it is because they know what disasters there are in speech; that is, it involves the pleasure of the ego, the display of qualities for praise, and the inclination to discriminate among people on the basis of how well they speak, and other catastrophes of human nature. Thus silence is a trait of practitioners of inner discipline. It is one of the pillars of the conduct of their campaign and of their training of character. It is said that Dawud al-Tai, when he wanted to seclude himself in his house, decided to attend the sessions of Abu Hanifa, whose student he had been, sit with his fellow scholars, and not discuss a single question. When he had steeled himself by putting this quality into practice for an entire year, he secluded himself in his house and chose solitude. Umar bin Abd al-Aziz, if he wrote something and embroidered in its expression, tore it up and wrote something else.

I heard Abu Abd al-Rahman al-Sulami say[3] . . . Bishr bin al-Harith said, "When speech makes you conceited, be silent. When silence makes you conceited, speak." Sahl ibn Abd Allah al-Tustari said, "Silence is not appropriate for a person until his ego has been compelled to retreat. Repentance is not appropriate for a person until his ego has been compelled to silence."

Abu Bakr al-Farisi said, "He whose native country is not silence is excessive even when he keeps quiet. Silence does not pertain exclusively to the tongue but to the heart and all of the limbs." A Sufi said, "The one who does not value silence, when he speaks, speaks nonsense."

I heard Muhammad bin al-Husayn say[4] . . . that Mumshad al-Dinawari said, "The wise inherit wisdom through silence and reflection." Abu Bakr al-Farisi was asked about the silence of the inner being, the secret (*sirr*), and said, "It is the abandonment of occupation with the past and the future." He also said, "When the servant speaks about what concerns him and about what he must, he is within the bounds of silence."

It is related that Muadh bin Jabal said, "Speak to people little and speak to your Lord much. Perhaps your heart will see God Most High." Someone asked Dhu 'l-Nun al-Misri, "Who among people best protects his heart?" He replied, "The one among them who best controls his tongue."

Ibn Masud said, "Nothing is worthier of a stay in prison than the tongue." Ali bin Bukkar said, "God Most High made two doors for everything, but He made four doors for the tongue—the lips are two leaves of a door, and the two jaws are two leaves of a door. It is said that Abu Bakr al-Siddiq, for many years used to hold a stone in his mouth in order to limit his speech.

It is said that Abu Hamzah al-Baghdadi was a fine orator. Then a voice form the unseen spoke to him and said, "You have spoken, and you have done it well. He is waiting for you to be silent and to do it well." He did not speak afterwards until he died which was more or less a week after this occurrence.

Sometimes silence will come over a speaker in order to discipline him, because his conduct has been bad in some respect. When he sat with his circle and they did not ask him about anything, Shibli used to say, *"The decree came upon them because of how they had sinned, and they do not speak"* [27:85].

Sometimes silence will come over a speaker because someone with greater right to speak is among those present. I heard Ibn Sammak say that Shah al-Kirmani and Yahya bin Muadh were friends. Although they lived in the same city, Shah would never attend Yahya's sessions. Asked about this, he would insist that it was the proper course. People continued to pursue him, however, until one day he went to the sessions. He sat on one side so that Yahya bin Muadh would not be aware of him. When Yahya began to speak, he fell silent. Then he said, "There is someone here who should speak before me," and he remained speechless. Shah said, "I told you that the right thing was for me not to come to his sessions."

Sometimes silence falls upon a speaker for a reason having to do with those present; that is, because there is someone there who is not worthy to hear that discourse. In such a case God Most High restrains the tongue of the speaker out of jealousy, to preserve that discourse from those to whom it does not belong.

Sometimes the reason for silence affecting a speaker is that God Most High knows the state of a member of the audience to be such that, if he were to hear such a discourse, it would become a test for him. Either he might imagine that what he heard applied to his own case, while it did not, or the matter of the discourse might oblige him to take on something of which he was incapable. So God Almighty and Glorious has mercy upon him by protecting him from hearing that discourse, either to guard him or to hinder him from error.

The shaykhs of this Way have said that sometimes the cause may lie in the presence of *jinn* who are not fit to hear, for the sessions of Sufis are not devoid of the presence of a congregation of *jinn*. I heard

Abu Ali al-Daqqaq said, "One time I fell ill in Merv. I longed to return to Nishapur. I had a dream in which it seemed a voice was saying to me, 'It is not possible for you to leave this city, for a gathering of *jinn* is enjoying your discourse and is present at your sessions, so for their sake, remain here.'"

A wise man said that the human being was created with only one tongue, but with two eyes and two ears so that he may hear and see more than he says. Ibrahim bin Adham was invited to a banquet. When he sat down, the guests began to gossip. He remarked, "It is our custom to eat the meat course after the bread, but you have begun by eating the meat!" (He was pointing to the saying of God, "*Would one of you like to eat the dead flesh of his brother? No, you would abhor it*" (59:12)).

A Sufi said, "Silence is the tongue of forbearance." Another said, "Learn silence as you have learned speech. Speech will guide you, and silence will protect you." It is said, "The chastity of the tongue is its silence." And it is said, "The tongue is like a beast of prey. If you do not tie it up, it will attack you."

Abu Hafs was asked, "Which is better for the Friend of God, speech or silence?" He replied, "If the one who speaks knew what disasters there are in speech, he would be silent even if he lived as long as Noah, and if the one who keeps silent knew what disasters there are in silence, he would pray to God Most High twice as much as Noah did until he could speak."

It is said that the silence of ordinary people is of the tongue, the silence of the gnostics is of the heart, and the silence of the lovers is to protect the secrets of their inner selves. A Sufi was told, "Speak!" He said, "I don't have a tongue!" "Then listen!" "There is no place within me where I can listen!"

One of the Sufi's said, "I lived thirty years in which I did not hear my tongue except from my heart. Then I lived another thirty years in which I did not hear my heart except from my tongue." Another said, "Even if you silenced your tongue, you would not be saved from the talk of your heart. Even if you became old and dried up, you would not be purified from the chatter of your ego. Even if you strove with every effort, your soul would not speak to you, for it is the concealer of the inner secret."

It is said, "The tongue of the ignorant is the key of his destruction." And it is said, "When the lover keeps silent, he perishes. When the gnostic keeps silent, he rules."

I heard Muhammad bin al-Husayn say[5] . . . that Fudayl bin Iyad said, "Whoever counts his talk as part of his work will talk little except in what concerns him."

8 ON FEAR (*KHAWF*)

God Most High said, *"They call upon their Lord fearing and desiring"* (32:16).

Abu Bakr Muhammad bin Abd al-Hiri al-Adl informed us[1] . . . through Abu Hurayrah that the Messenger of God said, "No one who weeps from the fear of God Most High can enter the fire any more than milk can re-enter the udder. The dust of the Way of God and the smoke of hell will never be mingled in a servant's nostrils."

Abu Naim bin Muhammad bin Ibrahim al-Muhrijani related[2] . . . through Qatadah that the Messenger of God said, "If you knew what I know you would laugh little and weep much." Fear is an emotion connected to the future. A person only fears that something hated will befall him or that something loved will escape him and this cannot happen except with future events. Fear does not attach to what exists now.

Fear of God Most High means that one fears that God will punish him, either in this world or in the next. God, glory to Him, has obliged the servants to fear Him. He said, *"So fear, if you are believers"* (3:175) and He said, *"So let it be Me that you are afraid of"* (16:51). And He has praised the believers for fear, *"They fear their Lord above them"* (16:50).

I heard Abu Ali al-Daqqaq say, "Fear has degrees: Fear (*khawf*), dread (*khashiyah*), and awe (*haybah*). Fear is a condition and an effect of faith. God Most High said, *"So fear Me if you are believers"* (3:175). Dread is a condition of knowledge. God Most High said, *"Only those among His servants who know, dread God"* (35:28). Awe is a condition of realization. God Most High said, *"Be wary of God Himself"* (3:28).

I heard Abu Abd al-Rahman al-Sulami say[2] . . . that Abu Hafs said, "Fear is the whip of God with which he drives vagrants from His door." Abu-l-Qasim al-Hakim said, "Fear is of two sorts, fright (*ruhba*) and dread (*khashiya*). The frightened person takes refuge in flight when he has become afraid. The person who senses dread takes refuge in the Lord."

He said, "'To stand in terror' (*rahaba*) and 'to flee' (*haraba*) may properly be said to have a single meaning, like 'he attracted' (*jadha - ba*) and 'he drew' (*jabadha*). When someone flees, he has been drawn by his own desires like those monks (*ruhban*) who follow their instincts or desires [in devising a form of religious life that flees from the world]. But when they have been reined in by the reins of knowledge and are established in the truth of the divine law, it is dread (*khashiya*)."

I heard Muhammad bin al-Husayn say[3] . . . that Abu Hafs said, "Fear is the lamp of the heart by means of which whatever is good and bad in it is made visible." I heard Abu Ali al-Daqqaq say, "Fear is when your ego does not make excuses with 'perhaps' or 'later'." I heard Muhammad bin al-Husayn say[4] . . . that Abu Umar al-Dimashqi said, "The man of fear is the one who fears his own ego more than he fears satan." Ibn al-Jalla said, "The one who fears is the one who finds security amid fearful things."

The person of fear, it is said, is not a person who weeps and rubs his eyes. The person of fear is only he who abandons that for which he is afraid he will be punished.

Fudayl was asked, "Why do we never see anyone who fears God?" He answered, "If you were fearers, you would see fearers. The fearer is not seen except by those who fear. It is the woman who has lost a child who likes to see another woman who has lost a child."

Yahya bin Muadh said, "How sad is the case of the son of Adam! If he feared the fire as he fears poverty, he would have entered the garden." Shah al-Kirmani said, "The sign of fear is perpetual sadness." Abd al-Qasim al-Hakim said, "Someone who is afraid of something runs away from it, but someone who is afraid of God Almighty and Glorious runs to Him."

Dhu-l-Nun al-Misri was asked, "When will the way of fear become easy for the servant?" He replied, "When he assigns himself the position of a sick person and abstains from everything for fear of lengthening his illness."

Muadh bin Jabal said, "The heart of the believer is not at rest and his alarm is not quieted until he puts the bridge of hell behind him." Bishr al-Hafi said, "Fear of God is a king who will only dwell in the heart of a pious one." Abu Uthman al-Hiri said, "The shame of the fearer in his fear is reliance upon his fear, for it is a hidden affair." Al-Wasiti said, "Fear is a veil between God Most High and His servant." This statement contains an ambiguity. It means that the one who fears looks toward a moment other than the present, while the Sufis, the sons of the moment, pay no attention to the future. "The virtues of the righteous are the flaws of those brought close."

I heard Muhammad bin al-Husayn say[5] . . . that Nuri said, "The fearer flees from his Lord to his Lord." A Sufi said, "The sign of fear is amazement and standing before the door of the unknown." I heard Abu Abd Allah al-Sufi say[6] . . . when Junayd was questioned about fear, he said, "It is the expectation of punishment with every breath." I heard Abu Abd al-Rahman al-Sulami say[7] . . . that Abu Sulayman al-Darani said, "Fear does not leave a heart without destroying it." And I heard him say[8] . . . that Abu Uthman said, "Integrity in fear is to be scrupulous about faults both outer and inner." Dhu-l-Nun said, "Fear never leaves people of the Way. If fear disappears from them, they have strayed from the Way." Hatim al-Asamm said, "Everything has an ornament and the ornament of worship is fear. The sign of fear is the cutting short of worldly hope."

A man exclaimed to Bishr al-Hafi, "I find you to be afraid of death!" "To come before God Almighty and Glorious," replied Bishr, "is a serious matter."

I heard Abu Ali al-Daqqaq say, "I went to visit Abu Bakr bin Furak in his last illness. When he saw me, tears came to his eyes. I said, 'If God Most High wills, He will cure and heal you.' 'Do you believe me to be afraid of death?' he asked to me. 'I am only afraid of what is beyond death!'"

Ali bin Ahmad al-Ahwazi informed us[9] . . . on the authority of Abd al-Rahman bin Said bin Mawhib from Ayisha that she said, "O Messenger of God, *'Those who will bring what they have brought while their hearts are full of dread'* (23:60)—is this the man who steals, commits adultery, and drinks wine?" "No," he said, "Rather the man who fasts, prays, and gives alms, and fears that they will not be accepted from him."

Ibn Mubarak said, "This means the person whom fear agitates until continuous self-observation dwells in his heart in private and in public." (I heard Muhammad bin al-Husayn[10] . . . say that Ibn Mubarak said this). I heard Muhammad bin al-Husayn said [11] . . . that Ibrahim bin Shayban said, "When fear dwells in a heart it sets fire to the places of lust within it and drives away from it the wish for the world."

It is said, "Fear is the power of the knowledge of how God's decrees come into effect." And it is said, "Fear moves and troubles the heart because of the majesty of the Lord."

Abu Sulayman al-Darani said, "It is necessary that nothing over-power the heart but fear. When hope overpowers the heart, it becomes corrupted." Then he said [to one of his followers], "Ahmad, it is through fear that they advanced. When they allowed it to perish, they stopped!"

Al-Wasiti said, "Fear and hope are two ropes that hold people back from falling into egotism." And he said, "When the Truth manifests to one's inner being, no space remains in it for hope or fear."

There is an ambiguity in this statement. It means that when the evidences of Truth have torn up the foundations of someone's inner being, they take it over. No possibility remains for the recollection of ordinary things. Hope and fear, however, are signs of the persistence of perception according to the ordinary limitations of mortality.

Husayn bin Mansur al-Hallaj said, "When anyone fears some-thing other than God Almighty and Glorious, or hopes for something other than Him, the doors of everything are locked against him. Anxiety and imagination are given power over him. He is veiled with seventy veils, the least of which is doubt."

The Sufis feel an intense fear produced by thinking about the con-sequences of actions and dreading the loss of their state. God Most High said, *"And there appeared to them from God what they never counted upon"* (39:47), and He said, *"Have We not informed you of the greatest losers in regard to works? Those whose efforts go astray in the life of this world, while they hold they are producing well"* (18:103-104). Who could wish for the state of someone whose condition is reversed, who is afflicted by the taint of ugly actions, who has traded intimacy with God for alienation from Him and presence for absence? I often heard Abu Ali al-Daqqaq recite:

You thought well of the days when things went well,
Had no fear of the evil that destiny brings.
The nights made excuses, and you were fooled.
In the clarity of night, the clouds appear.[12]

I heard Mansur bin Khalaf al-Maghribi tell of two men who were spiritual students together for some time. Then one of them traveled and became separated from his friend. A long while passed and nothing was heard of him. In the meantime, the other student entered the border wars against the Byzantines where a masked man in armor came out against the Muslims in search of duels. One of the Muslim heroes engaged with him, and the Byzantine killed him. Then a second—he killed him. Then a third arose, and he killed him as well. Finally the Sufi came out to him, and they fought. The Byzantine uncovered his face—and it was his friend with whom he had shared so many years of training and service! The Sufi asked, "What is your story?" His friend answered that he had turned away from Islam and mixed with the Byzantines, that children had been born to him, and that he had accumulated property. "And all the Quran that you used to recite?" "I do not remember a letter of it," he replied. "Do not do this," urged the Sufi. "Come back!" "That I will not do," he said, "for among the Byzantines I have rank and wealth. So turn back or I will certainly do to you what I have done to these others!" "Know that you have killed three Muslims," the Sufi said. "It is not for you to be disdainful about turning back! Turn back yourself, and I will give you time!" But the man turned and fled so that the Sufi followed him, stabbed him, and killed him. After all that effort and the endurance of all that discipline, he was killed as a Christian!"

It is said that when the events involving Iblis took place, the angels Gabriel and Michael began to cry. They wept for a long time. Then God Most High asked them, "Why do you cry all these tears?" "O our Lord," they said, "We are not safe from Your plot!" "This whole creation," said God Most High, "is not safe from My plot."

It is related that Sari al-Saqati said, "I look at my nose so many times a day for fear that it will have turned black from the punishment I dread!" Abu Hafs said, "For forty years it has been by private belief that God Most High looks upon me with displeasure, and my works point to that." Hatim al-Asamm said, "Do not be fooled by a sound position, for no place is safer than paradise, and there Adam encountered what he encountered. Do not be fooled by many acts of worship, for Iblis, after the length of his service, encountered what he encountered. Do not be fooled by much knowledge, for Balam used to know the greatest name of God, and see what he encountered! Do not be fooled by the sight of the righteous, for no personality was of greater worth than Prophet Muhammad, but meeting him did not profit his relatives and enemies."

One day Ibn Mubarak went out to his companions and said, "Yesterday I was bold towards God Almighty and Glorious! I asked Him for His paradise."

It is said that Jesus traveled with one of the righteous of the Children of Israel. A sinner notorious among the Jews for corruption, followed after them. He sat down a little away from them and, contrite, prayed to God Most Glorious, "O God, forgive me." The righteous man prayed as well, and said, "O God, do not join me together tomorrow with that disobedient man." God Most High revealed to Jesus, "I have answered the prayers of both of them at once. I have turned back that righteous one from religion, and I have pardoned that sinner!"

Dhu-l- Nun al-Misri said, "I asked a man of knowledge, 'Why are you called insane?' He told me, 'When I had been held back from Him for a long time, I became mad for fear of permanent separation from Him in the next world.'" With this meaning they have recited:

If what is in me were of rock, He would dissolve it,
So how is a creation of clay to endure Him?

A Sufi said, "I have not seen a man with greater hope for this community or greater fear for himself than Ibn Sirin."

It is told that Sufyan al-Thawri became ill. When his diagnostic sample was presented to the doctor for examination, he remarked, "This is a man whose liver has been disrupted by fear." He came and felt his pulse and said, "I did not know that there was the like of him in the religion."

Shibli was asked, "Why does the sun grow pale when it sets?" He answered, "Because it is being removed from a public place, and it grows pale from fear of the situation. Thus, when his departure from the world draws near, the believer's complexion becomes pale, for he is frightened by the situation. And when the sun rises, it rises radiant. Likewise the believer: when he is resurrected he will come forth from his grave with a shining face."

It is related that Ahmad bin Hanbal said, "I asked my Lord Almighty and Glorious to open to me a door of fear. It was opened, and I feared for my sanity. So I said, 'O Lord, give to me to the extent that I can bear.' So that passed off from me."

9 ON HOPE (*RAJA*)

God Most High said, "*Whoever hopes to meet with his Lord—the reward of God is nigh*" (29:5).

Abu-l Husayn bin Ahmad al-Ahwazi informed us[1] . . . that al-Ala bin Zayd said, "I came in to see Malik bin Dinar and found that Shahr bin Hawshab was with him. When we left his company, I said to Shahr, 'May God Most High have mercy upon you. Enrich me. God Most High has enriched you!' 'Certainly,' he said. 'My aunt, Umm al-Darda, related to me from Abu-l- Darda, from the Prophet that Gabriel said, "Your Lord Almighty and Glorious said, 'My servant who has worshiped Me, hoped in Me, and not associated anything with Me, I have forgiven you for whatever proceeded from you. Were you to meet Me with errors and sins enough to fill the whole earth, I would meet you with the same amount of forgiveness and forgive you and not care."

Ali bin Ahmad informed us[2] . . . through Anas bin Malik that the Messenger of God said, "On the day of judgment God Most High will say, 'Bring out of the fire anyone in whose heart is faith to the amount of a grain of barley.' Then He will say, 'Bring out of the fire anyone in whose heart is faith to the amount of a mustard seed.' Then He will say, 'By My Power and Majesty, I will not make anyone who has believed in Me for one moment, night or day, like someone who has not believed in Me at all.'"

Hope is the attachment of the heart to something loved that may occur in the future. Just as fear falls upon future time, so hope arises because of something to which one looks forward. The livelihood and freedom of hearts is through hope.

The difference between hope and expectation is that expectation causes laziness in the one who has it so that he does not travel the road of effort and endeavor, while the one who has hope is the opposite. Thus hope is praiseworthy, and expectation is condemnable.

The shaykhs have discoursed on hope. Shah al-Kirmani said, "The sign of hope is good obedience." Ibn al-Khubayq said, "Hope is of three kinds. One kind of person will do good and hope for acceptance. A second kind will do evil, then repent and hope for forgiveness. The third kind is the lying person who persists in sin and says that he hopes for forgiveness. If someone knows himself to be doing wrong, his fear must predominate over his hope." It is said, "Hope is trust in the liberality of the Generous and Loving One." And it is said, "Hope is seeing Majesty with the eye of Beauty." Hope is said to be "the heart's nearness to the benevolence of the Lord," and "the joy of the innermost heart at the goodness of the hereafter," and "to regard the breadth of God's mercy."

I heard Abu Abd al-Rahman al-Sulami say[3] . . . that Abu Ali al-Rudhbari said, "Fear and hope are like the two wings of a bird. When they are balanced, the bird is balanced and its flight is perfect. When one of the two is defective, its flight is defective, and if they both go, the bird is at the edge of death."

And I heard him say[4] . . . that Ahmad bin Asim al-Antaki was asked, "What is the sign of hope in the servant?" and said, "When virtue and excellence surround the servant he is inspired to gratitude, hoping for the perfection of blessing from God Most High upon him in this world and the perfection of His forgiveness in the next." Abu Abd Allah bin Khafif said, "Hope is to rejoice in the existence of His grace." And he said, "Hope is the heart's finding rest in seeing the generosity of the hoped-for Beloved."

I heard Abu Abd al-Rahman al-Sulami say he heard Abu Uthman al-Maghribi say, "If someone excites hope in himself, he is idle. If he excites fear in himself, he despairs. Best is sometimes some of the one and sometimes some of the other." And I heard him say[5] . . . from Bakr bin Sulaym al-Sawwaf, "We went to see Malik bin Anas on the night he died and said, 'Abu Abd Allah, how are you?' 'I don't know what to tell you,' he said, 'except that you will see things beyond reckoning from the forgiveness of God Most High!' We did not leave him then until we had closed his eyes."

Yahya bin Muadh prayed, "The hope I place in You when I sin almost drowns the hope I place in You when I am performing good works. In the course of good works I find I rely upon sincerity. How am I to preserve that when I am well-known for calamities? But in sin I find I rely upon Your forgiveness. How will You not forgive, when Your quality is generosity?"

They were talking to Dhu-l--Nun al-Misri during his last illness. He said, "Don't worry about me. I am amazed by how many kindnesses God Most High has shown me!" Yahya bin Muadh said, "My God, the sweetest gift in my heart is hope of You. The most pleasant word on my tongue is praise of You. My dearest hour is the hour of meeting You."

In a commentary on the Quran it is written that the Messenger of God came in on his Companions from the Gate of Bani Shaybah and saw them laughing. He said, "Do you laugh? If you knew what I know, you would laugh little and weep much." He left, but then he came back and said, "Gabriel descended to me with the word of the Most High, *'Tell My servants that I am the Forgiving, the Compassionate.'* (15:49)."

Abu-l- Husayn Ali bin Ahmad al-Ahwazi related to us[6] . . . that Ayisha said, "I heard the Messenger of God say, 'God Most High laughs at the hopelessness and despondency of the servants when mercy is so near them.' 'By my father and mother, Messenger of God,' I asked, 'does our Lord Almighty and Glorious then laugh?' 'By Him in Whose Hand I am, He certainly laughs!' he said. She said, 'Good things beyond reckoning come to us when He laughs.'"

Know that the laughter used to describe Him is a quality of His action. It means the manifestation of His grace as in the saying, "The earth laughs with vegetation." His laughter at their despondency manifests the reality of His grace by doubling the bounties His servants had awaited from Him.

It is said that a fire-worshiper sought the hospitality of Abraham the Friend of God who said to him, "If you become a Muslim, I will grant you my hospitality." The fire-worshiper exclaimed, "If I become a Muslim? What kind of a favor is that for you to do?" God Most High revealed to Abraham, "O Abraham, will you not feed him unless he changes his religion? For seventy years We have fed him in his unbelief—if you were to show him hospitality for one night, what is it to you?" Abraham went in pursuit of the fire-worshiper and offered his hospitality. The man asked him, "What brought on this change?" So he recounted what had happened. The fire-worshiper marveled, "Is it thus that He deals with me?" Then he said, "Spread Islam before me!" And he became a Muslim.

I heard Abu Ali al-Daqqaq say that Abu Sahl al-Suluki saw Abu Sahl al-Zajjaj, who used to speak of the threat of eternal punishment, in a dream. He asked him, "How are you? What is your condition?" Al-Zajjaj replied, "We have found the matter easier than we had imagined."

I heard Abu Bakr bin Ishkib say, "I saw Abu Sahl al-Suluki in a dream in the shape of indescribable beauty. I said to him, 'O Master, through what have you been granted this?' He answered, 'Through my thinking well of my Lord.'"

Malik bin Dinar was seen in a dream. He was asked, "What has God done with you?" "I was brought before my Lord Almighty and Glorious with many sins," he replied. "My good thoughts of Him made them vanish from me."

It is related that the Prophet said, "God Almighty and Glorious said in a sacred Tradition, 'I am present with My servant's thought of Me, and I am with him when he remembers Me. If he remembers Me in himself, I remember him in Myself. If he remembers Me in company, I remember him in a company better than his. If he draws near to Me by a hand's length, I draw near to him by an arm's length. If he draws near to Me by an arm's length, I draw near to him by a span. If he comes to Me walking, I come to him running.'" Abu Naim Abd al-Malik bin al-Hasan al-Isfarayani informed us[7] . . . through Abu Hurayrah that the Prophet said this.

It is told that once Ibn Mubarak was fighting an idolater when the time for the idolater's prayer arrived. He asked for a respite. It was granted. When he prostrated himself to the sun, Ibn Mubarak wanted to strike him with his sword, but he heard something speaking in the air that said, *"Keep your agreements if an agreement is made"* (17:34), so he restrained himself. When the fire-worshiper had finished praying, he asked, "Why did you hold back from what you had in mind?" Ibn Mubarak recounted to him what he had heard. The fire-worshiper cried, "What an excellent lord is a lord who will reprove his friend for the sake of his enemy!" So he became a Muslim, and made good his Islam.

It is said that God only involved believers with sin when He had named Himself the Forgiver. If He were to say, "I will not forgive sins," no Muslim would sin at all. Thus as He said, *"God will not forgive that anything be set equal to Him,"* (4:48). No Muslim will ever set anything equal to Him, but as He said, *"And He will forgive what is less than that to whom He will"* (4:48), they hope for His forgiveness.

It is told that Ibrahim bin Adham said, "I had waited a long time

for the holy precincts of the Kabah to be empty of all but me. One dark
night when there was a heavy rain, the precincts were deserted, so I
began to make the circumambulation, saying, 'O God, make me free of
sin! O God, make me free of sin!' Then I heard a voice from the unseen
say to me, 'O Ibn Adham, you are asking Me for freedom from sin.
Everybody is asking Me for freedom from sin. If I were to free you
from sin, to whom would I be Merciful?'"

It is said that in his last illness, Abu-l- Abbas bin Shurayh had a
dream. It was as if the resurrection had arrived when the All-Powerful
will say, "Where are the people of knowledge?" Abu-l- Abbas said,
"They came," and He demanded, "What have you done with what you
knew?" We answered, "O Lord, we have fallen short and done ill."
Again the question was asked as if He were not satisfied and wanted
another answer. So I said, "As for me, there is no setting of equals to
You in my record. You promised to forgive what is less than that!" "Go
forth all." He said, "I have forgiven you!" Abu 'l- Abbas died three
nights later.

It is said that a heavy drinker gathered a drinking party and gave
a young slave four dirhams, ordering him to buy some fruit for the
company. The slave passed by the door of one of Mansur bin Ammar's
meetings. The shaykh was asking something for a poor man, and saying, "Whoever turns four dirhams over to me, I will pray for him four
prayers." The slave gave him the dirhams. "For what do you wish me
to pray?" Mansur asked. "I have a master," he replied. "I want to be
free of him! Pray for me about that, Mansur!" "What else?" "That God
Most High recompense me for my dirhams. Pray for me about that."
"And what else?" "That God turn to my master [so that he might
repent]." He prayed. "And what else?" "That God forgive me, my master, you, and this company." So Mansur prayed for that. The slave
returned to his master. "What took you so long?" he demanded. The
young man told him the story. "For what did he pray?" asked his master. "I asked emancipation for myself." "Go. You are free," his master
said. "What was the second?" "That God recompense me for the
dirhams." "There are four thousand dirhams for you," he said. "What
was the third?" "That God turn to you." "I turn in repentance to God
Most High. What was the fourth?" "That God Most High forgive you
and me and the gathering and the one I have mentioned." "This alone
I cannot do!" he said. That night when he went to sleep he dreamed
that a voice said to him, "You have done what you could do. See if I will

not do what is for Me to do! I have forgiven you, the slave, Mansur bin Ammar and all those who were present."

It is said that Raja al-Qaysi made many pilgrimages. One day, while he had stopped under the rainspout of the Kabah, he said, "My God, I give such-and-such a number of my pilgrimages to the Messenger, ten of them to his ten companions, two of them to my parents, and the remainder to the Muslims." He did not retain anything from them for himself. Then he heard a voice from the unseen say, "O you who show Us generosity! We will certainly forgive you, your parents and whoever has made a true profession of Islam."

It is related that Abd al-Wahhab bin Abd al-Majid al-Thaqafi said, "I saw a funeral in which the bier was being carried by three men and a woman so I took the place of the woman. We went to the graveyard, prayed over the coffin, and buried the person. I asked the woman, 'What relation did this person have to you?' 'He was my son,' she told me.' 'Have you no neighbors to attend the funeral?' I asked. 'Yes,' she said, 'but they thought little of him.' 'Why should that be?' I asked. She said, 'He was effeminate!' I felt pity for her, so I brought her to my house and gave her money, grain, and clothing. That night when I slept I seemed to see a person come to me. Dressed in white clothes, he resembled the moon at its full. He began to thank me. 'Who are you?' I asked. 'I am that effeminate one you buried today,' he said. "My Lord has forgiven me because of people's contempt for me.'"

I heard Abu Ali al-Daqqaq say, "Abu Amr al-Bikandi one day passed by a side street and saw a group of people who wanted to expel a youth from the neighborhood because of his corrupt ways while a woman cried. He was told she was his mother. Abu Amr felt pity for her. He interceded with them for the youth, saying, 'Give him his liberty this time. If he returns to his corruption, then do as you like.' So they let him go, and Abu Amr left. After some days he was crossing that lane again and heard an old woman crying behind the same door. 'Perhaps the youth has returned to his corruption,' he said to himself, 'and they have banished him from the district.' So he knocked on her door and inquired about the youth's situation. The old woman came out and said, 'He has died!' He asked her about his state. She said, 'When his time approached, he said, "Don't tell the neighbors of my death. I have made trouble for them—they will be glad and will not come to my funeral. But when you bury me, bury with me this ring of mine on which is written, 'In the Name of God,' and when you have finished the burial, make intercession for me with my Lord Almighty and Glorious.'" She continued, 'I did as he wished, and when I turned from the head of the grave I heard his voice saying, "Leave me, Mother—I have come before a generous Lord."'

It is said that the inspiration from God Most High came to Prophet David, "Say to them that I did not create them in order to place My hopes in them—I only created them so that they would hope in Me!"

I heard Muhammad bin al-Husayn say[8] . . . that Ibrahim al-Utrush said, "We were sitting in Baghdad with Maruf al-Karkhi on the banks of the Euphrates when some young people passed by us in a boat, beating tambourines, drinking, and making merry. We said to Maruf, 'Look at them, how flagrantly they disobey God Most High! Pray to God against them!' He opened his hands and said, 'My God, as you have made them joyful in this world, make them joyful in the next.' 'But we asked you to curse them!' we cried. 'If He makes them joyful in the next world, He will have brought them to repentance,' replied Maruf."

I heard Abu-l- Hasan Abd al-Rahman bin Ibrahim bin Muhammad al-Mazaki say[9] . . . that Abu Abd Allah al-Husayn ibn Abd Allah ibn Said said, "Judge Yahya bin Aktham was a friend of mine. He loved me, and I loved him. Yahya died and I longed to see him in a dream and ask him, 'What has God Most High done with you?' One night I did see him. I asked, 'What has God Most High done with you?' 'He has forgiven me,' he said, 'except that He rebuked me and then said to me, "Yahya, you confused Me with things in the world." I said, "Yes, Lord." I trusted in a hadith related to me by Abu Muawiyah al-Darir[10] . . . through Abu Hurayrah that the Messenger of God said that You had said, 'I would be ashamed to punish a grey head with the fire.' "He said, 'I have forgiven you, Yahya, and My Prophet spoke the truth. Nevertheless, you confused Me with things in the world!'"

10 ON SORROW (*HUZN*)

God Most High has said, "*And they said, 'Praise be to God Who has made sadness depart from us'*" (35:34).

Ali bin Ahmad bin Abdan informed us[1] . . . through Abu Said al-Khudri that the Messenger of God said, "Nothing afflicts a believing servant, whether sickness or fatigue or sadness or pain that troubles him, without God Most High removing some of his evils from him."

Sadness, *huzn*, is a state that contracts the heart from being scattered in the valleys of unconsciousness. Sadness is one of the characteristics of those involved in active search. I heard Abu Ali al-Daqqaq say, "The sorrowful person experiences in the Way of God in a month what, without his sorrow, he would not experience in years."

A *hadith* says, "God loves every sorrowing heart." And in the Torah, "When God loves a servant, He puts a mourner in his heart and when He is dissatisfied with a servant, He puts a festive flute in his heart." It is related that the Messenger of God was in continuous sorrow and reflection. Bishr bin al-Harith said, "Sadness is a king who, when he dwells in a place, does not please to have anyone else dwell there." It is said that a heart that has no sadness in it is as a house with no one living in it; it falls into ruins.

Abu Said al-Qarshi said, "The tears of sorrow blind, while the tears of yearning make the sight dim but do not blind." God Most High said, "*And his [Jacob's] eyes grew white from sorrow and he fell into silent melancholy*" (12:84).

Ibn Khafif said, "Sadness deters the ego from the pursuit of pleasure." Rabia-Adawiyyah heard a man lamenting, "What great sorrow!" "You should cry, 'What little sorrow!'" she returned. "If you were really sorrowful, you would not be able to breathe!"

Sufyan bin Uyaynah said, "If a sorrowful person in this community wept, God Most High would have mercy on the whole community for the sake of his tears." Dawud al-Tai was dominated by sadness. He used to say, at night, "My God, concern for You ruins other concerns for me and comes between me and sleep." And he used to say, "How should a person for whom every moment means grave misfortune seek to be distracted from sorrow?"

It is said that sorrow prevents one from eating, while fear prevents one from sinning. A Sufi was asked, "What indicates a person's sorrow?" He replied, "The extent of his groaning." Sari-al-Saqati said, "I would love for the sadness of all humanity to be cast upon me."

Many people have discussed sadness. All of them have said that only sadness for the sake of the next world is praiseworthy. Sadness for the sake of this world is not commendable. Only Abu Uthman al-Hiri disagrees. He said that every sort of sadness that is not the result of a sin has merit and increase in it for the believer. If it does not necessarily make him one of the spiritual elite, still it must purify him.

There was a shaykh who, when one of his companions went on a journey, used to say, "If you see any sorrowing person, send him my greetings." I heard Abu Ali al-Daqqaq say, "There was a Sufi who used to ask the sun when it set, 'Did you rise today upon one who sorrows?'" No one was able to see Hasan al-Basri without thinking that he had been newly afflicted by troubles. Waki said when Fudayl died, "Today sorrow has left the earth."

One of our predecessors said, "The majority of the good deed the believer will find in his record on the last day will be care and sorrow." I heard Abu Abd Allah al-Shirazi say[2] . . . that Fudayl bin Iyad said, "Those who came before us used to say that everything owes a tithe and the tithe of the mind is long sadness."

I heard Abu Abd al-Rahman al-Sulami say[3] . . . that Abu l-Husayn al-Warraq said, "One day I asked Abu Uthman al-Hiri about sorrow. He said, 'A sorrowful person has no leisure for questions about sorrow. Strive to find sorrow—then ask!'"

11 ON HUNGER (*JU*) AND THE ABANDONMENT OF LUST (*TARK AL-SHAHWAH*)

God Most High has said, "*And We shall try them with something of fear and hunger*" (2:155), and at the end of the verse, "*and give good news to the patient.*" So He sent them good news of a beautiful reward following patience in the endurance of hunger. And He has said, "*And they prefer [others] over themselves even though they may be in need.*" (59:9).

Ali bin Ahmad al-Ahwazi informed us[1] . . . that Anas bin Malik said, "Fatimah went to the Messenger of God with a bit of bread. 'What is this morsel, Fatimah?' he asked. 'A piece of flat bread [or barley bread] I baked,' said she. 'I could not feel at ease in myself until I had brought it to you.' 'It was the first food that had entered your father's mouth for three days,' he told her."

On this account hunger is one of the characteristics of the Sufis. It is the first pillar of spiritual struggle. Travelers on the Way are graded according to how habituated they have become to hunger and forsaking food. They have found springs of wisdom in hunger and there are many stories told of them about this.

I heard Muhammad bin Ahmad bin Muhammad al-Sufi say[2] . . . that Ibn Salim said, "The proper conduct with regard to hunger is for a person to diminish what he is accustomed to eating by an amount no larger than a cat's ear." It is said that Sahl bin Abd Allah ate food only once every twenty-five days. When the month of Ramadan came he did not eat until the next new moon and broke his fast every evening only with water.

Yahya bin Muadh said, "If hunger were a thing sold in the marketplace, it would not have been right for people who hope for the hereafter to buy anything else there."

We have been told that Muhammad bin Abd Allah bin Ubayd said[3] . . . that Sahl bin Abd Allah said, "When God Most High created the world, he placed sin and ignorance in satiation and knowledge and wisdom in hunger." He also said, "For novices, hunger is an act of discipline. For the repentant, it is an experiment. For ascetics, it is a policy. For gnostics, it is a gift."

I heard Abu Ali al-Daqqaq say, "A Sufi visited a shaykh and found him crying. He asked, 'What makes you weep?' The shaykh replied, 'I am hungry.' 'How could someone like you cry out of hunger?' the dervish exclaimed. 'Be silent!' returned the shaykh. 'Don't you know that His object in my hunger is for me to cry?'"

I heard Abu Abd Allah al-Shirazi say[4] . . . that Mukhallad said, "Hajjaj bin Farafisah, who was with us in Damascus, would go fifty nights without drinking or satisfying his hunger with something to eat." And I heard him say[5] . . . that Abu Abd Allah Ahmad bin Yahya al-Jalla said, "Abu Turab al-Nakhshabi left to go to Mecca through the desert. Afterwards we asked what he had eaten on the way. He answered, 'When I left Basra I ate once at Nabaj and once in Dhat Irq. From Dhat Irq I came to you.' He had crossed the desert eating only twice."

And I heard him say[6] . . . that Abd al-Aziz bin Umayr said, "A certain type of bird would fly forty mornings without eating anything. When these birds came back after many days, the fragrance of musk would emanate from them." Sahl bin Abd Allah used to gather strength when he was hungry and weaken when he ate. Abu Uthman al-Maghribi said, "The one who attaches himself to divine Lordship will not eat for forty days. The one who attaches himself to Absolute Plenitude will not eat for eighty days."

I heard Abu Abd al-Rahman al-Sulami say[7] . . . that Abu Sulayman al-Darani said, "The key of this world is satiation and the key of the next world is hunger." I heard Muhammad bin Abd Allah bin Ubayd Allah say[8] . . . that Abu Muhammad al-Istikhari said, "Sahl bin Abd Allah was asked the state of a person who eats one meal a day. "It is the meal of the sincere." And two meals a day? "It is the meal of the believers." And three? "Tell your family to build a trough for you!" said he." And I heard him say[9] . . . Yahya bin Muadh said, 'Hunger is a light while satiation is a fire. Desire is like the firewood from which the conflagration is generated. Its flame will not be extinguished until it burns the one who keeps it." I heard Abu Hatim al-Sijistani say that he heard Abu Nasr al-Sarraj al-Tusi say, "A Sufi once visited a shaykh who presented him food and then asked him, 'For how many days have you not eaten?' 'For five days,' the man replied. 'Your hunger is the hunger of a miser,' the shaykh told him. 'You are wearing [decent] clothing while you go hungry? This is not the hunger of dervishes!'"

I heard Muhammad bin al-Husayn say[10] . . . that Abu Sulayman al-Darani said, "To give up one bite of my supper is dearer to me than to stand in prayer until the end of the night." And I heard him say that he heard Abu-l-Qasim Jafar bin Ahmad al-Razi say, "For years Abu-l Khayr al-Asqalani had a craving for fish. Then one day it appeared to him in a lawful context. When he stretched out his hand in order to eat it, the point of a fishbone caught his finger and entered that hand. He cried, "O Lord, this is what happens to someone who reaches for a desire that is lawful—what will happen to someone who reaches for an unlawful desire?"

I heard Abu Bakr bin Furak say, "The result of following lawful desire is preoccupation with one's family. What do you suppose is the outcome of unlawful desire?" I heard Rustam al-Shirazi say, "Abu Abd Allah bin Khafif was at a banquet when one of his companions, because of the need he was in, reached for food before the shaykh did. Some of the shaykh's other companions wanted to reproach him for the fault thus displayed in his behavior, so one of them set just a bit of something to eat in front of that dervish. The dervish knew that he had been reproached for his bad conduct, so he resolved not to eat for fifteen days as a punishment and discipline for his lower self and a manifestation of his repentance for his fault—and he had already been in need before that." I heard Muhammad bin Abd Allah al-Sufi say[11] . . . Malik bin Dinar says, "When someone conquers the desires of this world, satan is afraid of his shadow!" And I heard him say[12] . . . that Abu Ali al-Rudhbari said, "When a Sufi said, after five days without food, 'I am hungry'—they would send him to the marketplace and command him to earn a living!"

I heard Abu Ali al-Daqqaq tell of a shaykh who said that the lust of the people of the fire had overcome their honor and manifested itself in their being assigned to the fire. And I heard him say, "Someone asked a dervish, 'Do you desire nothing?' He said, 'I desire, but I abstain.'"

A Sufi was asked, "Aren't you hungry?" He replied, "I hunger not to hunger." And it is just so. I heard Abu Abd al-Rahman al-Sulami say[13] . . . that Abu Nasr al-Tammar said, "One night Bishr [al-Hafi] came to see me. I said, 'Praise be to God Who has brought you to me! Cotton reached us from Khurasan, so I gave it to my daughter, and she sold it and bought us meat. So break your fast with us.' He said, 'Were I to eat with anyone, I would eat with you.' Then he said, 'For years I have wished for eggplant and it has never fallen to me to eat it!' 'Surely in all that time there must have been eggplant that was lawful,' I objected. 'Not until the love of eggplant becomes pure for me,' he replied."

I heard Abd Allah bin Bakawiya al-Sufi say that he heard Abu Ahmad al-Saghir say, "Every night Abu Abd Allah bin Khafif ordered me to set before him ten raisins with which he would break his fast. One night I worried for him and put out fifteen raisins. He looked at them and said, 'Who ordered you to do this?' He ate ten of them and left the rest."

I heard Muhammad bin Abd Allah bin Ubayd Allah say[14] . . . that Abu Turab al-Nakhshabi said, "Only once did I grant my lower self its desires. It wanted bread and eggs. I was traveling. I turned off toward a village. Someone stood up and grabbed me and said, 'This one was with the thieves!' So they beat me seventy blows. Then one of them recognized me and cried, 'This is Abu Turab al-Nakhshabi!' They apologized. A man took me to his house out of hospitality and sympathy and laid before me bread and eggs. So I said to my lower self, 'Eat, after seventy blows!'"

12 ON HUMILITY (*KHUSHU*) AND SUBMISSIVENESS (*TAWADU*)

God Most High has said, *"The believers, who are humble in their prayers, have prospered"* (23:1-2).

Abu-l- Hasan Abd al-Rahim bin Ibrahim bin Muhammad bin Yahya al-Mazaki informed us[1] . . . through Abd Allah bin Masud that the Prophet said, "No one in whose heart is a grain of pride will enter the garden and no one in whose heart is a grain of faith will enter the fire."

A man asked, "O Messenger of God, what of a man who likes his clothes to be fine?" He said, "God Most High is beautiful and loves beauty. Pride is refusing the truth and showing disdain to people."

Ali bin Ahmad al-Ahwazi informed us[2] . . . that Anas bin Malik said, "The Messenger of God used to visit the sick, attend funerals, ride a donkey, and respond to the invitations of slaves. The day of the conquest of Qurayzah and al-Nadir he rode upon a donkey whose halter and saddle were of common rope."

Kushu, humility, is to yield to the truth. *Tawadu*, lowliness, modesty in submission, is to abandon oneself to the truth and give up opposition to God's decrees. Hudhayfah said, "The first thing you will lose out of your religion will be humility."

Asked about humility, a Sufi replied, "Humility is the heart's standing before the Truth with total attention." Sahl bin Abd Allah said, "Satan will not come near someone whose heart is humble." One of the signs of the presence of humility in the servant is that when he is angered, opposed or rejected, he takes it upon himself to meet that with acceptance.

A Sufi said, "Humility is to restrain the eyes from looking." Muhammad bin Ali al-Tirmidhi said, "The man of humility is he in whom the fires of lust (attraction to pleasure) have been extinguished and the smoke of his breast abated, while the light of glorification has dawned in his heart. Since his lust has died and his heart has come to life, his limbs are humble."

Hasan al-Basri said, "Humility is perpetual fear attached to the heart." Junayd was asked about humility and said, "It is the abasement of hearts before the signs of the unknowable."

God Most High has said, *"The servants of the Beneficent are those who walk upon the earth with humility"* (25:63). I heard Abu Ali al-Daqqaq say that the meaning of that was [to act] submissively and humbly. And I heard him say that these servants are people who, when they walk, do not reckon the soles of their shoes to be good.

The shaykhs have agreed that the place of humility is the heart. One of them saw a man of depressed and dejected appearance whose shoulders were knit and tense. "O so-and-so!" he said. "The place of humbleness is here"—pointing to his heart—"not here!"—pointing to his shoulders. And it is related that the Messenger of God saw a man who was absent-mindedly playing with his beard during his prayers. "If his heart possessed humility," he said, "then his limbs would manifest it."

It is said that the defining condition of humility in the prescribed prayer is that one does not know who is on one's right or one's left. This implies, as it is said, that humility is bowing one's head to attend to one's inner state in accordance with the proper conduct for bearing witness to the Truth.

It is said that humility is a fading that comes over the heart when it becomes aware of the Lord, or else that it is the heart's melting and drawing back before the power of reality. Or, it is said, humility is the conquering vanguard of awe or a shudder that comes upon the heart suddenly with the shock of the unveiling of reality.

Fudayl bin Iyad said that he used to hate to see a man behaving as if he had a humility greater than what was actually in his heart. Abu Sulayman al-Darani said, "If all the people were to gather to humble me as I am humbled when I am alone, they would not be able to do it." It is said that someone who has no humbleness when he is alone does not have it with others either. Umar bin Abd al--Aziz [one time ruler of the entire Islamic world] never made a prostration of prayer except upon the dust of the earth.

Ali bin Ahmad al-Ahwazi informed us[3] . . . from Ibn Abbas that the Messenger of God said, "No one in whose heart there is pride to the extent of a grain of mustard seed will enter the garden." Mujahid said, "When God, glory to Him, drowned the people of Noah, all the mountains loomed up, while Mount Judi was lowly, so God made it the resting-place for Noah's ship."

Umar bin al-Khattab used to hurry as he walked. He used to say that he hurried to his work to take himself far away from haughtiness.

Umar bin Abd al-Aziz was writing something one night while he had a guest with him. The lamp had almost gone out. The guest said, "I will climb up to the lamp and put it right." "No," said Umar. "It is not hospitality that a guest should be put to work!" "Then I will rouse the slave," he proposed. "No, he is sleeping the best part of his sleep," said Umar. He climbed up to the oil-flask and put oil in the lamp. "You yourself climb up there, Commander of the Faithful?" the guest exclaimed. "I went as Umar and I have come back as Umar," Umar said to him.

Abu Said al-Khudri has related that the Messenger of God used to feed his donkey, sweep the house, mend his sandals, patch his clothes, and milk the ewe. He would eat with his servant and labor along with him when he grew tired. He was not ashamed to carry merchandise home from the market for his family. He would shake hands with rich and poor and was the first to offer a greeting. He did not scorn anything that was offered to him to eat, even unripe dates. He made things easy. He was of a gentle disposition and possessed a natural generosity. It was wonderful to keep company with him. He had an open, cheerful face. He smiled without laughing loudly, was sad without becoming gloomy, humble without abasing himself, and liberal without being extravagant. He was soft-hearted and compassionate to every Muslim. He never belched from satiation or stretched his hand toward an object of selfish interest.

I heard Abu Abd al-Rahman al-Sulami say[4] . . . that Fudayl bin Iyad said, "The Quran-reciters of God are humble and lowly. The Quran-reciters of the magistrates are haughty and proud." He also said, "He who sees any value in himself has no share in the modesty of submission (*tawadu*)." Asked about lowliness, Fudayl said, "It is humbleness before the truth, yielding to it, and accepting it from whoever speaks it." He said, "God Glorious and Exalted revealed to the mountains, 'I will speak to a prophet upon one of you [mountains]!' So the mountains towered up. But Mount Sinai made itself low, so upon it God, glory to Him, spoke to Moses."

I heard Muhammad bin al-Husayn say[5] . . . Junayd was asked of lowliness and said, "It is taking others under one's wing and behaving graciously towards them." Wahb said, "It is written in one of the books revealed by God Most High, 'I brought out the atoms [of future generations] from the loins of Adam and found no heart with fiercer modesty than the heart of Moses, so for that reason I chose him and spoke to him.'"

Ibn al-Mubarak said, "Haughtiness toward the rich and humility toward the poor is part of the modesty of submission." Abu Yazid al-Bistami was asked, "When is a man a possessor of lowliness?" He replied, "When he does not feel himself to possess either station or state and does not see among other people anyone worse than he."

It is said that humility is a blessing no one envies, while pride is a misfortune no one pities. Grandeur is in humility, and anyone who searches for it in pride will not find it. I heard Abu Abd al-Rahman al-Sulami say[6] . . . Ibrahim bin Shayban said, "Nobility is in humility, grandeur in awe of God, and freedom in contentment." And I also heard him say[7] . . . that Ibn al-Arabi said, "I have been told that Sufyan al-Thawri said that the greatest men are of five kinds: a reenunciate scholar, a Sufi jurist, a humble rich man, a contented poor man, and a descendant of the Prophet who follows his practice and claims no special prestige."

Yahya bin Muadh said, "Humility beautifies everyone, but it is more beautiful in the rich; pride makes everyone repulsive, but it is more repulsive in the poor!" Ibn Ata said, "Lowliness is to accept the truth from anyone."

It is told that Zayd bin Thabit was riding. Ibn Abbas descended and took hold of his stirrup. "Uncle of God's Messenger, stop that!" Zayd cried. "This is the way we have been ordered to treat the learned ones among us," was the reply. So Zayd bin Thabit grabbed the hand of Ibn Abbas and kissed it. "This is the way we have been ordered to treat the family of the Messenger of God!" said he.

Urwah bin al-Zubayr said, "I saw Umar bin al-Khattab with a full waterskin upon his shoulder. 'Commander of the Faithful! That is not suitable for you!' I exclaimed. 'Delegations of obedient subjects approached me. A feeling of superiority came into my ego. I wish to break it,' he answered. He went with the waterskin to the rooms of a woman who was one of the early Muslims of Medina and emptied it into her cistern."

I heard Abu Hatim al-Sijistani say that Abu Nasr al-Sarraj al-Tusi said that Abu Hurayrah, while he was commander of Medina, was seen with a bundle of firewood on his back, saying "Make way for the prince!" Abd Allah bin al-Razi said, "Lowliness is to give up making distinction in service."

I heard Muhammad bin al-Husayn say[8] . . . that Abu Sulayman al-Darani said, "Whoever sees any value in himself has not tasted the sweetness of service." But Yahya bin Muadh said, "To show haughtiness to one who, on account of what he possesses, shows haughtiness to you is lowliness."

Shibli said, "My humiliation makes idle the humiliation of the Jews." A man came to Shibli, who asked, "What are you?" "Master, I am the dot under the letter '*b*'," he replied. "May you be my example," said Shibli, "since you do not assign yourself any station!" Ibn Abbas said, "It is part of lowliness that a man drink from the dregs of his brother." Bishr said, "Give greetings to the sons of this world by giving up greeting them."

Shuayb bin al-Harb said, "I was circumambulating the Kabah when suddenly a man shoved me with his elbow. I turned to face him. It was Fudayl bin Iyad. 'If you thought that someone worse than we two would attend the holy season, Abu Salih,' he said, 'how evil is what you thought!'"

A Sufi said, "During the circumambulation of the Kabah I saw a man preceded by people thanking and praising him so that because of him people were prevented from making the circumambulation. Some time later I saw him on the embankment in Baghdad begging. I was amazed. He said to me, "I made much of myself in a place where people humble themselves, so God, glory to Him, has tried me by humiliating me in a place where people give themselves airs."

Umar bin Abd al-Aziz heard that one of his sons had bought a ring-stone for a thousand dirhams. Umar wrote to him, "I have been told that you bought a ring-stone for a thousand dirhams." When this letter of mine reaches you, sell the ring and fill a thousand stomachs. Get a ring for two dirhams and make its bezel of Chinese iron, and write there, 'God has mercy upon a man who knows his own worth.'"

A slave was offered to a prince for a thousand dirhams. When the price was named, the prince thought it more than seemed right for the purchase and put the money back in its coffer. The slave said, "O my master, buy me. In me is a trait worth a thousand dirhams for each of those dirhams there!" "What is it?" the buyer asked. "The smallest and least of it is that were you to buy me and set me over all of your slaves, it would not coarsen me. I would know that I am your servant." So the man bought him.

Raja bin Haya has related that the clothes worn by Umar bin Abd al-Aziz while delivering a public address were valued at twelve dirhams, including robe, turban, shirt, trousers, shoes, and cap.

It is said that Abd Allah bin Muhammad bin Wasi paraded himself [in a way] that invited disapproval. His father said to him, "You are aware that I bought your mother for three hundred dirhams and your father—may God not make many more fathers like yours among the Muslims! Yet you walk like that?"

I heard Muhammad bin al-Husayn say[9] . . . that Hamdun al-Qassar said, "Lowliness is that you see no one in need of you either in this world or the next." Ibrahim bin Adham said, "I only rejoiced in my submission to God on three occasions. One time I was on a ship where there was a man given to laughter and ridicule. He used to say, 'We seized the infidels in the land of the Turks like this: we took hold of the hair of their head and shook them. That pleased me because there was no one on the ship more contemptible in his eyes than myself. On another occasion I was in a mosque, sick. The *muezzin* entered and said, 'Get out!' I was not able, so he grabbed my feet and dragged me outside of the mosque. On the third occasion I was in Syria. I was wearing skins and when I looked at them I could not tell whether there were more hairs or more lice upon them, and that made me happy."

In another account Ibrahim bin Adham said, "Nothing has ever delighted me as I was delighted one day when I was sitting down and a man came and urinated on me." It is said that Abu Dharr and Bilal quarreled. Abu Dharr insulted Bilal about being black. Bilal complained to the Messenger of God who said, "Abu Dharr, something of the pride of the days of ignorance remains in your heart." Abu Dharr threw himself on the ground and swore that he would not raise his head until Bilal trod on his cheek with his foot. And he did not get up until Bilal had done that.

Hasan bin Ali passed by two boys who had a few crusts of bread. They invited him to be their guest. He stopped and ate with them. Then he took them to his house and fed and clothed them. He said, "They are the ones who were generous, because they had nothing but what they fed me, and I had more than that."

It is said that Umar bin al-Khattab was distributing clothing, taken as spoils of war, among the Companions. He sent a Yemeni garment to Muadh. Muadh sold it and bought six slaves whom he set free. Umar heard of this while he was dividing the clothes that remained, so he sent him a lesser garment beside the first. Muadh scolded him. Umar said, "Don't scold me! It is because you sold the first one." "Who cares?" said Muadh. "Give me my share—I swear I will hit you over the head with it!" "This head of mine is in front of you," replied Umar. "Perhaps an old man will treat an old man gently."

13 ON OPPOSING THE EGO (*MUKHA - LAFAT AL-NAFS*) AND REMEMBERING ONE'S FAULTS (*DHIKR UYUBIHA*)

God Most High has said, "*As for him who fears to stand before his Lord and restrains the ego [animal soul] its desires, the garden is shelter*" (79:40).

Ali bin Ahmad bin Abdan informed us[1] . . . through Jabir that the Messenger of God said, "The worst of what I fear for my community is the pursuit of passion and ambition for the future, for the passions leads away from the truth, while ambition makes one forget the next world." So know that opposing the ego (*nafs ammarah*, the animal soul, the passions throughout the chapter) is the beginning of worship.

The shaykhs, asked about submission to God—Islam—have said that it means to slaughter the ego with the swords of opposition to it. You should know that when the disasters of the ego rise in a person, the glories of intimacy with God set.

Dhu-l--Nun al-Misri said, "The key to worship is reflection. The sign of attaining the mark is to oppose the ego and its desires. To oppose the ego is to abandon what it craves." Ibn Ata said, "The ego is disposed to bad conduct while the servant is commanded to observe the rule of behavior, so the ego falls by its nature into the arena of things to be actively resisted, and the servant with effort can turn it back from the evil of its wishes. He who gives it free rein is partner to its corruption."

I heard Abu Abd al-Rahman al-Sulami say[2] . . . Junayd said, "The ego [animal soul] summons to dangers, assists enemies, pursues whims, and is to be suspected of every sort of wickedness." Abu Hafs said, "Whoever does not suspect his ego at every moment, oppose it in all circumstances, and drag it toward what it hates for all his days, has been fooled. Whoever looks at it expecting any good from it has caused his ruin."

How can an intelligent person be satisfied with himself while the noble, son of the noble, son of the noble, son of the noble—Joseph the son of Jacob, the son of Isaac, the son of Abraham the Friend of God—says, "*I do not absolve myself, for the ego [animal soul] commands to wrongdoing*" (12:53)!

I heard Muhammad bin al-Husayn say[3] . . . that Junayd said, "One night I could not sleep. I got up to make my private devotions but was unable to find the sweetness and delight I usually find in conversations with my Lord. I was troubled and amazed. I wanted to sleep but was not able. I sat but could not endure the sitting. So I opened the door and went outside. There in the street lay a man wrapped in a cloak. When he felt my presence he raised his head and said, 'O Abu-l-Qasim, finally!' 'Sir,' I said, 'no appointment was made.' 'Rather I asked the Mover of Hearts to move your heart towards me,' he replied. 'He has done that,' I told him. 'What is your need?' 'When does the disease of the ego [animal soul] become its cure?' he asked. 'When the ego [animal soul] opposes its desire, its disease becomes it cure,' I answered. Directing himself to his ego, he said, 'Listen! I have given you this answer seven times and you refused to hear it except from Junayd. So now you have heard it!' He turned away from me. I did not know him, and I have never come across him again.

Abu Bakr al-Tamastani said, "The greatest blessing is to escape from the ego, because the ego is the greatest veil between you and God Almighty and Glorious." Sahl bin Abd Allah said, "There is no way to worship God equal to opposing the ego and its caprice."

I heard Muhammad bin al-Husayn say[4] . . . that Ibn Ata was asked what thing most quickly brings on God's wrath. He said, "Looking upon the ego and its states, the worst of which is the expectation of compensation for its acts." And I heard him say[5] . . . that Ibrahim al-Khawwas said, "I was on the mountain of al-Lukam [in Damascus] when I saw some pomegranates and wanted them. I came up, took one, and broke it open, but finding it sour I went away and left them. Then I saw a man lying on the ground. He was covered with hornets. Peace be upon you,' I greeted him. 'And upon you be peace, Ibrahim!' he replied. 'How do you know me?' I asked. 'Nothing is hidden from one who knows God Most High,' said he. 'I see that your state is with God Most High,' I said. 'If only you would ask Him to shelter and protect you from the torment of those hornets!' 'And I see that your state is with God Most High,' he returned. 'If only you would ask him to protect you from the desire for pomegranates! For a man but finds the pain of the sting of hornets in this world, while he finds the pain of the sting of pomegranates in the next!' So I left him and went away.

It is told that Ibrahim bin Shayban said, "I did not sleep under my own roof or in any place that had a lock upon it for forty years. Many times I desired to eat a meal of lentils, but it did not come about. Then one time when I was in Damascus, an earthen vessel full of lentils was presented to me. I ate out of it and was leaving when I saw glasses to which were clinging what seemed to be drops of liquid. I had thought the vessel clean, but somebody said to me, 'What are you looking at? Those are wine dregs, and that jug is a wine jug!' 'I must carry out a duty,' I said to myself. So I went into the wineseller's shop and kept pouring out that jug. He supposed I was emptying it by order of the Sultan. When he knew that it was not so, he dragged me to the judge Ibn Tulun who ordered that I be flogged with 200 lashes and thrown me into prison. There I stayed for awhile, until my teacher, Abu Abd Allah al-Maghribi, came to that city. He interceded for me. When his eyes fell upon me, he asked, 'What have you done?' 'A meal of lentils and two hundred lashes,' I said. 'You have been protected by shields against the true punishment,' he told me.'"

I heard Abu Abd al-Rahman al-Sulami say[6] . . . that Sari al-Saqati said, "My ego has been pleading with me for thirty or forty years to dip a carrot into date syrup, and I have not fed it!" And I heard him say that he heard my grandfather say, "The bane of the servant is his satisfaction with himself as he is." I also heard him say[7] . . . that Husayn bin Ali al-Qirmisini said, "I am ibn Yusuf, the Amir of Balkh, who sent a gift to Hatim al-Asamm, who received it from him." Asked why he did so, he said, "In accepting it I found humiliation for me and honor for him, while in returning it was honor for me and humiliation for him, so I chose his honor over mine and my humiliation over his."

Someone told a Sufi, "I want to go on the pilgrimage free of material support." He answered, "First free your heart from distraction, your ego from frivolity, and your tongue from nonsense—then travel however you wish!"

Abu Sulayman al-Darani said, "Whoever does good at night is rewarded during the day and whoever does good during the day is rewarded at night. Whoever is sincere in abandoning a desire is saved from catering to it. God is too noble to punish a heart that has abandoned a desire for His sake."

God, glory to Him, revealed to David, "O David, beware! Warn your companions about devouring the objects of desire. When people's hearts are tied to the desires of this world, their intelligence is veiled from Me."

A man was seen seated in mid-air. Someone asked him, "Why were you granted this?" "I gave up idle desire (*hawa*)," he said, "and the air (*hawa;* a play on words because *hawa* means both) became subject to me."

It is said that if a thousand desires were presented to a believer he would drive them away through fear of God, while if a single desire were presented to a libertine, it would drive fear of God away from him. It is said, "Do not give your bridle into the hand of caprice, for it will lead you into darkness."

Yusuf bin Asbat said, "Nothing will extinguish desires from the heart except an unsettling fear or a troubled yearning." Al-Khawwas said, "Whoever gives up a desire and does not find the recompense for it in his heart is lying about having given it up."

Jafar bin Nisar said, "Junayd gave me a dirham and said, 'Go and buy me Waziri figs.' I bought them, and when he broke fast he took one and put it in his mouth. Then he spit it out, wept, and said, 'Take them away!' I asked him about this. He said, 'A voice spoke in my heart saying, "Aren't you ashamed? A desire you gave up for My sake—now you are returning to it!"'"

They recite:

> The last letter of disgrace has been stolen from
>   desire.
> The victim of every desire is a victim of disgrace.

Know that the ego possesses contemptible characteristics, and one of them is envy.

14 ENVY (*HASAD*)

God Most High said, "*Say: I seek refuge with the Lord of Daybreak from the evil of what He has created.*" After this, He said, "*and from the evil of the envious one when he envies*" (113:1, 5). So He ended the *surah* that He made a protection with the mention of envy.

Abu-l-Husayn al-Ahwazi informed us[1] . . through Ibn Masud, that the Prophet said, "Three things are the origin of every error so shield yourself from them and beware of them. Beware of pride, for pride made satan not prostrate himself to Adam. Beware of ambition, for ambition made Adam eat from the tree. Beware of envy, for one of the sons of Adam killed his brother out of envy." A Sufi said, "The envious person is an infidel for he is not satisfied with the judgments of the unique One." And it is said, "The envious man will not prevail."

It is stated in the Word of the Most High, "*Say: My Lord has only forbidden indecencies, outer and inner.*" (7:33). "Inner" indecency is said to be envy. According to another holy book, "The envious person is the enemy of My blessing."

It is said that the effect of envy becomes visible in you before it becomes visible in your enemy. Al-Asmai said, "I saw a Bedouin who had lived 120 years. 'How long your life has been!' I marveled. 'I gave up envy and endured,' he replied." Ibn Mubarak said, "Praise be to God Who has not put into the heart of the man who commands me what He has put into the heart of the man who envies me."

According to the ancient traditions, in the fifth heaven is a certain angel. A deed shining like the sun passes before him, and the angel says to it, "Stop! For I am the angel who deals with envy. I will strike the one whose work this is in the face with it, for he was an envier!"

Muawiyah said, "It is possible to please everyone except an envier, for he is not pleased except by the disappearance of good fortune." And it is said, "The envious is a tyrannical oppressor: he will not let you be or leave you alone." Umar bin Abd al-Aziz said, "I never saw a tyrant who more resembled a victim of tyranny than does an envier: Constant trouble with each successive breath!" One of the marks of the envier is that he will flatter someone when he is present, slander him when he is absent and gloat over misfortune when it befalls. Muawiyah said, "No bad characteristic is more just than envy—it destroys the envier before it destroys the object of his envy."

It is said that God, glory to Him, revealed to Prophet Solomon son of Prophet David, "I will counsel you about seven things. Do not criticize one of My righteous servants and do not envy any of My servants." Solomon said, "O Lord, that is enough for me!"

It is said that Prophet Moses saw a man by the Throne of God and wished for his state. He asked what the man's characteristic had been that he had been granted such a state and was told that he would never envy people for the graces God bestowed upon them.

The envier, it is said, when he sees a blessing criticizes, and when he sees an error, gloats. It is said, "If you wish to be safe from the envier, conceal your affairs from him. The envier is enraged at people who do not sin and miserly about what he does not possess. Beware of exhausting yourself seeking the affection of one who envies you, for he will never accept your gift. When God Most High wishes to give power over a servant to an enemy who will show him no mercy, He gives that power to the one who envies him.

The Sufis have recited:

It is enough for you to say of a man
That you see his enviers merciful to him.
And they have recited:

You may hope for the end of all enmity
But that of the hater from envy.

Ibn Mutazz said:

When you see the envier pant with envy;
Say: 'O tyrant who appears tyrannized
May your lungs burst!'

They recited:

When God wants an open virtue hidden
He assigns it an envier's tongue.

Another contemptible characteristic of the ego is habitual back-biting.

15 ON BACKBITING (*GHIBAH*)

God, glory to Him, said, *"Let not some of you criticize others. Would one of you like to eat the dead flesh of his brother? You would abhor that. Fear God for God is most forgiving, merciful"* (49:12).

Abu Said Muhammad bin Ibrahim al-Ismaili informed us[1] . . . from Abu Hurayrah, "A man who had earlier been seated with the Messenger of God stood up and left. Some people said, 'How weak and helpless is so-and-so!' The Prophet said, 'You have devoured and back-bitten your brother.'"

God, glory to Him, revealed to Prophet Moses, "He who dies having repented from backbiting will be the last to enter paradise, and he who dies persistent in it will be the first to enter hell."

Awf said, "I went to see Ibn Sirin and talked against the tyrant Hajjaj. Ibn Sirin said, 'God Most High arranges things justly. As God will ask the rights of others from Hajjaj, He will ask the rights of Hajjaj from others. If you were to meet God Almighty and Glorious tomorrow, the smallest sin you have committed would be worse for you than the greatest sin committed by Hajjaj.'"

It is said that Ibrahim bin Adham was invited to a banquet and attended. The other guests mentioned someone who was not among them. "What a disagreeable man!" they said. "This ego of mine has only worked upon me so that I would be present in a place where people are criticized!" Ibrahim declared. He left, and would not eat for three days.

A person who maligns other people is like someone who sets up a catapult with which he throws his good deeds East and West. He criticizes one person from Khurasan, another from Damascus, another from the Hijaz, another from Turkistan—he scatters his good deeds, gets up, and has nothing left!

It is said that the servant may be given his book on the resurrection day and not see a good deed in it. He will ask, "Where is my prayer, my fasting, my obedience?" and will be told, "All of your work disappeared through your maligning of people." It is said that God will forgive half the sins of anyone who is attacked with slander.

Sufyan bin al-Husayn said, "I was sitting with Iyas bin Muawiyah and talking about somebody. He said to me, 'Have you made any forays against the Turks or the Byzantines this year?' 'No,' I said. 'The Turks and the Byzantines are safe from you,' he exclaimed, 'but not your Muslim brother!'"

It is also said that a man may be given his book and see in it good deeds that he did not perform. He will be told, "This is through people's criticism of you of which you were unaware." Sufyan al-Thawri was asked about the saying of the Prophet, "God hates the carnivorous household." He said, "They are those who malign people and eat their flesh."

Backbiting was mentioned to Abd Allah bin al-Mubarak. He said, "If I were to criticize anybody, I would criticize my parents—they have the greatest right to my good deeds!" Yahya bin Muadh said, "Let the believer's share from you be three traits, 'If you cannot help him, then do not harm him. If you cannot make him happy, then do not make him unhappy. If you cannot praise him, then do not blame him.'"

Hasan al-Basri was told, "So-and-so has talked against you." He sent that person a tray of sweets, and said, "It has come to my attention that you have directed your good deeds to me, so I thank you!"

Ali bin Ahmad al-Ahwazi informed us[2] . . . through Anas bin Malik that the Messenger of God said, "To criticize someone who casts the veil of shame from his face is not unlawful." I heard Hamzah bin Yusuf al-Sahmi say[3] . . . that Junayd said, "I was sitting in the Shuniziyyah mosque waiting for the arrival of a coffin I was to pray over, along with citizens of Baghdad of all ranks who were sitting waiting for the funeral, when I saw a dervish upon whom were the marks of piety. He was begging from people. 'Were he to do some work that would sustain him, it would be more becoming,' I said to myself. When I returned to my house I had some of my night's devotions to do—weeping and prayer and so forth—but all of them weighed heavily upon me. I sat awake, but sleep overcame me and I saw that dervish. They were bringing him spread out upon a table, and they said to me, 'Eat his flesh! You have slandered him!' 'What slander?' I objected. 'I only said something to myself.' 'You are not a person from whom that sort of thing is acceptable,' I was told. 'Go and resolve it.' So in the morning I went out and did not come back until I had seen him. He was in a place where, through the pooling of water, leaves that had been discarded in the washing of vegetables were collected. I offered him a greeting. 'Will you return to what you have done, Abu-l-Qasim?' he asked. 'No,' I replied. 'May God forgive us and you,' said he."

I heard Abu Abd al-Rahman al-Sulami say[4]. . . that Abu Jafar al-Balkhi said, "There used to be a young man from Balkh with us who would make great efforts and devote himself to worship. But he was always criticizing people, saying this person is like this, that person is like that, someone else is some other way. I saw him one day among the homosexuals in the baths. He came out from among them and I asked him, "What is happening to you?" "That which I brought down upon people has brought this down upon me," he said. "I have been afflicted with passion for one of these — so now, because of him, I am the one who serves them. All my old states have vanished so ask God to forgive him."

16 ON TRUST IN GOD (*TAWAKKUL*)

God Almighty and Glorious said, "*Whoever trusts in God, He suf-fices him*" (65:3), and "*In God let the believers place their trust*" (5:23).

Abu Bakr Muhammad Allah Ahmad bin al-Hasan bin Furak related to us[1] . . . through Abd Allah bin Masud, "The Messenger of God said, 'I was made to see the religious communities at the time of pilgrimage. I saw that my community filled the plain and the mountain. I marveled at their number and appearance. I was asked, "Are you pleased?" And I said, 'Yes.'"

He said, "Together with these were seventy thousand who will enter paradise without any reckoning. They do not cure by cauterization (surgery) nor practice divination nor cure by spells. They trust in their Lord."

Ukashah bin Muhsin al-Asadi got up and said, "O Messenger of God, pray to God that He place me among them." The Messenger of God said, "O God, place him among them." Someone else got up and said, "Pray to God that he place me among them!" "Ukashah has preceded you in this," the Prophet replied.

I heard Abd Allah bin Yusuf al-Ispahani say[2] . . . that Abu Ali al-Rudhbari said, "I asked Amr bin Sinan, 'Tell me something about Sahl bin Abd Allah al-Tustari." Amr answered, "He said, 'Three signs show someone who trusts in God: not begging from anyone, not rejecting anything that is given, and not accumulating whatever comes to hand.'"

I heard Abu Abd al-Rahman al-Sulami say[3] . . . that Abu Musa al-Dabili said that Abu Yazid was asked, "What is trust?" "What do you say?" he inquired of me. I answered, "Our companions say that if there were lions and poisonous snakes on your right and your left, your inner being would not be disturbed by it." Abu Yazid said, "Yes, that is close. But if you were to see the people of the garden in bliss in the garden and the people of the fire in torture in the fire and it then occurred to you to have a preference, you would have left the category of trust."

Sahl bin Abd Allah said, "The first station of trust is when the servant in the hands of God Almighty and Glorious be like a corpse in the hands of the washer who turns him however he wishes, while he has neither motion nor self-will." Hamdun al-Qassar said, "Trust is clinging to God Most High."

I heard Muhammad bin al-Husayn say[4] . . . that Ahmad bin Khadruyah said that a man asked Hatim al-Asamm, "From whence do you eat?" He replied, "*To God belong the treasures of the heaven and the earth, but the hypocrites do not understand*' (63:7)."

Know that the place of trust is in the heart. Outward action does not contradict trust in the heart. Once the servant has become sure that the ordering of things is from God Most High, he knows that if something is difficult, He has ordained it, and if it is agreeable, He had made it easy.

I heard Ali bin Ahmad bin Abdan related[5] . . . from Anas bin Malik that a man came to the Prophet on his camel, and said, "O Messenger of God, I will leave her loose and trust in God." He said, "Tie up [the camel]—and trust in God."

Ibrahim al-Khawwas said, "He who properly trusts God with his own self will also entrust everything else to Him." Bishr al-Hafi said, "Some dervishes say, 'I trust in God Most High,' while they are lying to God Most High. If they really trusted, they would be satisfied with what God does with them." Yahya bin Muadh was asked, "When is a man one of those who trust?" He replied, "When he is satisfied with God Most High as a trustee."

I heard Abd al-Rahman al-Sulami say[6] . . . that Ibrahim al-Khawwas said that while he was journeying in the desert, suddenly a voice called out from he knew not where. He turned and there was a traveling bedouin! The bedouin said to him, "Ibrahim, we possess trust. Stay with us until your trust is sound. Don't you know that you are being sustained by looking forward to entering a town where there is food? Cut off your hope of towns, and trust!" And I heard him say[7] . . . that when Ibn Ata was asked the meaning of trust, he said, "Though you are in great need, you feel no anxiety about means of subsistence. Though you find means, you do not lose the peace there is in reliance upon the Truth." I heard Abu Hatim al-Sijistani say that he heard Abu Nasr al-Sarraj say, "The condition for trust is what Abu Turab al-Nakhshabi has said—abandoning the flesh in servanthood, attaching the heart to the divine lordship, and serenity through feeling the all-sufficiency of God. So if He gives, one is thankful, and if He forbids, one is patient."

As Dhu-l-Nun said, "Trust in God is to give up directing oneself, to divest oneself of ability and power. The servant will only have the strength for trust when he knows that God, glory to Him, knows and sees his situation."

I heard Muhammad bin al-Husayn say[8] . . . that Abu Jafar bin Abu Ōl-Faraj said he saw a man known as "Ayisha's camel" among outcasts being beaten with whips. He asked him, "When will the pain of the beating be eased for you?" He said, "When He for Whose sake we are beaten has looked upon us." And I heard him say that he heard Abd Allah bin Muhammad say "Husayn bin Mansur al-Hallaj asked Ibrahim al-Khawwas, 'What have you accomplished with these journeys, the crossing of these deserts?' 'I maintained the condition of trust and confirmed myself in it,' he said. 'You have made your life vanish in the culture of your inner self,' said Husayn. 'Where is vanishing into unity (*tawhid*)?'"

I heard Abu Hatim al-Sijistani say that he heard Abu Nasr al-Sarraj say, "Trust is what Abu Bakr al-Daqqaq said, 'Reducing livelihood to one day's worth and dropping concern about tomorrow'—and what Sahl bin Abd Allah al-Tustari said, 'Trust is to be at ease with God Most High about what He wishes.'"

I heard Abu Abd al-Rahman al-Sulami say[9] . . . that Abu Yaqub al-Nahrajuri said, "Trust in God, in the true meaning of the word, is what occurred in Prophet Abraham at the moment when he was about to be thrown into the fire. Gabriel came and asked, 'Do you need anything' and he said to Gabriel, 'Not from you!' For Abraham's ego [animal soul] was absent with God Most High and he could not see anything other than God along with Him.' And I heard him say[10] . . . that Said bin Uthman al-Khayyat said that a man asked Dhu-l--Nun al-Misri, 'What is trust in God?' I heard him reply, 'Deposing lords and cutting off means.' 'Tell me more,' the questioner said. 'Casting the ego into servanthood and driving it out of lordship,' said he.'

And I heard him say[11] . . . when asked about trust, Hamdun al-Qassar said, "If you had ten thousand dirhams and owed one penny of debt, you would not feel that it was safe for you to die while it remained in your pocket. But if you owed ten thousand dirhams of debt, the payment of which you could not leave to another, you would not despair of God Most High's discharging it for you."

Abu Abd Allah al-Qarshi was asked about trust. He said, "Clinging to God Most High in every state." "Say more," the inquirer asked. He said, "It is to give up relying on any means leading to livelihood until the Truth becomes your guide."

Sahl bin Abd Allah said, "Trust is the state of the Prophet while earning is his practice. Who can remain in his state and not establish his practice?" Abu Said al-Kharraz said, "Trust is uncertainty without rest and rest without uncertainty." And it is said, "Trust means that having much and having little are the same to you." Ibn Masruq said, "Trust is to give oneself up to the course of God's judgments and decisions."

I heard Muhammad bin al-Husayn say[12] . . . that Abu Uthman al-Hiri said, "Trust is contentment with God Most High together with confidence in Him." And I heard him say[13] . . . that Husayn bin Mansur al-Hallaj said, "The true man of trust will not eat a thing while there is anyone around who has a greater right to it than he does." And I heard him say[14] . . . Umar bin Sinan said, "Ibrahim al-Khawwas stopped with us. We asked him, 'Tell us the strangest thing you have seen in your travels.' 'Khidr met with me and asked for my companionship,' he said, 'but I was afraid my trust would be spoiled by staying with him, so I left him.'"

Sahl bin Abd Allah was asked of trust. He said, "It is a heart that lives with God Most High without attachment to anything else." I heard Abu Ali al-Daqqaq say, "Those who trust possess three degrees: trust (*tawakkul*), surrender (*taslim*), and self-abandonment (*tafwid*). The man of trust relies upon His promise. The man of surrender finds His knowledge sufficient. The man of self-abandonment is well-satisfied with His judgment." And I heard him say, "Trust is a beginning, surrender a middle, and self-abandonment an end."

Al-Daqqaq was asked about trust and said, "Eating without greed." Yahya bin Muadh said, "To wear wool like a dervish is a shop to keep, to speak of asceticism is a trade, and to seek the company of caravans is a venture. All of these are worldly attachments."

A man came to Shibli and complained to him that his family was too numerous. He said, "Go back to your house. Anyone there whose sustenance does not come from God—chase him away!

I heard Abu Abd al-Rahman al-Sulami say[15] . . . that Sahl bin Abd Allah said that he recited over Muhammad bin al-Husayn, "Whoever talks against working for a living is talking against prophetic practice. Whoever talks against trust in God is talking against faith." And I heard him say[16] . . . that Ibrahim al-Khawwas said, "I was on the road to Mecca when I saw a wild-looking person. 'Jinn or human being?' I wondered. 'Jinn!' said he. 'Where are you going?' 'To Mecca.' 'Without provisions?' 'Yes. Among us also are those who travel in the way of trust.' 'What is trust?' I asked. 'To receive from God Most High,' he said." And I heard him say[17] . . . that al-Farghani said, "Ibrahim al-Khawwas lived detached from the world in a condition of trust. He was meticulous about this. Yet he was never without a needle and thread, a water flask, and a scissors. Someone asked, 'Abu Ishaq al-Fazari, why do you carry these, while you abstain from everything else?' 'This sort of thing does not contradict trust,' he said. 'There are obligations that we owe to God. A poor dervish has no more than one garment and sometimes his garment tears. If he does not have a needle and thread with him, the parts of his body that should be covered will show and his prayer will not be accepted. If he has no water flask with him, he cannot perform his ritual ablution when he needs it. If you see a dervish without flask or needle or thread, suspect the perfection of his prayers.'"

I heard Abu Ali al-Daqqaq say, "Trust is the attribute of believers, surrender the attribute of the friends of God, and self-abandonment the attribute of those who know unity (*tawhid*). Thus trust is the attribute of the majority, surrender is that of the elite, and self-abandonment is that of the elite of the elite." And I heard him say, "Trust is the attribute of the prophets, surrender the attribute of Prophet Abraham and self-abandonment the attribute of our Prophet Muhammad."

I heard Muhammad bin al-Husayn say[18] . . . that Abu Jafar al-Haddad said, "I lived some dozen years tied to trust in God. I was employed in the market. Every day I would receive my pay. I did not use it for a drink of water or to enter a public bath, but would bring it to the dervishes in Shuniziyyah mosque. I continued uninterrupted in my state." And I heard him say[19] . . . that Husayn, the brother of Sinan, said, "I made fourteen pilgrimages barefoot in the way of trust. When a thorn would enter my foot, I would remember that I had bound my lower self to trust, so I would scratch it out in the earth and walk on." And I heard him say[20] . . . that Abu Hamzah said, "I am ashamed before God Most High to enter the desert with a full belly when I have bound myself to trust, lest my effort be dependent upon the provision of satiety with which I have equipped myself."

Hamdun al-Qassar was asked of trust and said, "I have not yet reached that degree. How is someone whose state of faith has not become sound supposed to speak about trust?" It is said that the one who trusts is like an infant. He knows nothing to resort to but his mother's breast. Just so, the one who trusts is guided to nothing but his Lord."

A Sufi said, "I was in the desert at the head of a caravan when I saw someone in front of me. I hurried to catch up. It was a woman! She had a staff in her hand and was walking slowly and deliberately. I supposed her to be exhausted, so I put my hand in my pocket, took out twenty dirhams, and said, 'Take this, and wait until the caravan joins you. You can engage it, then spend the night, until your situation has improved.' She reached her hand—thus!—in the air. Suddenly there were dinars in her palm. 'You take dirhams from your pocket,' she said, 'while I take dinars from the unseen!'"

Abu Sulayman al-Darani saw a man in Mecca who would not accept any food whatsoever except a sip of Zamzam water. Day after day he passed by him. One day Abu Sulayman said to him, "If Zamzam were to dry up, what would you drink?" The man stood up and kissed him upon the head. "May God reward you, for you have guided me well!" he exclaimed. "I have been worshipping Zamzam for days!" And he went away.

Ibrahim al-Khawwas said, "On the road to Damascus I saw a young man of beautiful appearance. He asked, 'Will you keep company with me?' 'I am going hungry,' I said. 'If you go hungry, I will go hungry with you,' he replied. We continued that way for four days. Then something came our way. 'Have some!' I urged. He answered, 'I have committed myself not to receive anything from an intermediary.' 'Young man, you are fastidious!' I complained. 'Ibrahim, don't make yourself out to be something you're not!' said he. 'If you are a critic of patience, what trust can you possess?' Then he added, 'The least degree of trust is that when times of need come upon you, your ego aspires to nothing but the One Who is All-Sufficient. Trust is negation of doubts, and giving oneself up to the King of Kings.'"

It is told that a group of people went to Junayd and asked, "Where shall we seek our sustenance?" "If you know the place where He is," he said, "go and seek it there." "Request this of God Most High for us," they asked. "If you know Him to have forgotten you, then you remind Him!" he returned. "We have entered the House and trusted," they said. "To make trial of God is doubt," he replied. "Then what is the means?" "To abandon means."

Abu Sulayman al-Darani said to Ahmad bin Abu-l-Hawari, "Ahmad, the roads to the next world are many. Your shaykh is familiar with many of them, but not with this blessed trust. I have not smelled the fragrance of it."

It is said that trust is confidence in what is in the hands of God and giving up hope of what is in the hands of men. And it is called removing from your inner being any thought of seeking sustenance by laying claim to it. Harith al-Muhasibi was asked whether appetite afflicts the one who trusts in God. "Dangers reach him by way of his natural disposition," he answered, "but they do him no harm. Giving up hope of what is in the hands of men empowers him to let go of his ego and its desires."

It is told that Nuri was hungry in the desert when a voice called out to him, "Which is dearer to you, the normal means of receiving your sustenance or to find what is sufficient?" "Sufficiency has no goal above it," he said. So he continued seventeen days without eating.

Abu Ali al-Rudhbari remarked, "If a dervish says, after five days, 'I am hungry,' let him go to the market and busy himself with work and earning a living.'" It is said that Abu Turab al-Nakhshabi looked at a Sufi who, after three days, stretched his hand toward a watermelon rind in order to eat it and told him, "Sufism is not suitable for you! Go to the marketplace!"

Abu Yaqub al-Aqta al-Basri said, "One time at the Kabah I went hungry for ten days and became weak. My ego spoke to me, so I went out to the valley in order to find something that might quiet my weakness. I saw a discarded turnip and picked it up. I found a kind of wildness in my heart from this, as if someone were saying to me, 'You have gone hungry ten days and after all that your portion is some old turnip?' So I threw it away, and went back to the mosque and sat down. All of a sudden a stranger came up to me. He sat in front of me, put down a satchel, and said, 'This is for you.' 'Why have you singled me out?' I asked. He said, 'For ten days we were at sea and the ship was on the verge of foundering. Every one of us vowed that if God Most High were to save us we would give something in charity. I swore that if God rescued me I would give this to the first person my eyes fell upon at the holy place. You are the first whom I have met.' 'Open it,' I said. He opened it and there were Egyptian wheat cakes, shelled almonds, and pearl sugar. I took a handful of each and said, 'Take the rest back to your children. It is a gift from me to you. I have received the charity you intended.' Then I said to my ego, 'Your sustenance has been coming to you for ten days, and you go out looking for it in the valley!'"

I heard Abu Abd al-Rahman al-Sulami say that he heard Abu Bakr al-Razi say, "I was with Mumshad al-Dinawari when there was talk of debt. He said, 'I owe a debt,' and this troubled my heart. Then I dreamed that someone was saying to me, 'O miser, you hold this amount against Us! Take! It is for you to take, and it is for Us to give!' After that I asked neither grocer nor butcher nor anybody else for an accounting."

It is related that Bunnan al-Hammal said, "I was on the road to Mecca going from Egypt, and I had provisions with me. A woman came up to me and said, 'Bunnan, you are a baggage carrier (*hammal*) indeed—you carry provisions on your back and imagine that He will not sustain you!' So I threw my provisions away. Afterward there came upon me three days without food. Then I found an anklet in the road and said to myself, 'I will carry this until its owner appears. Maybe he will give me something for returning it to him.' Suddenly, there was that woman! 'You are a merchant,' she accused. 'You say, "...until its owner appears, so I will get something from him!"' She threw a few dirhams at me, and said, 'Spend them!' So I contented myself with these until I was almost at Mecca."

It is also related that Bunnan had need of a maidservant to wait on him. News of this spread to his brethren who collected the cost for him, saying, "Here it is. A caravan is coming, so buy whatever suits you." When the caravan arrived, the opinions of all agreed on one woman. They said, "She is the one for him!" They asked her owner, "How much is this one?" And he said, "She is not for sale." They insisted, and he said, "But she is for Bunnan al-Hammal! She has been given to him by a woman of Samarkand." She was taken to Bunnan, and the story was recounted to him.

I heard Muhammad bin al-Husayn say[21] . . . that Hasan al-Khayyat reported, "I was with Bishr al-Hafi when a group of travelers came in. They greeted him, and he asked, 'Where are you from?' 'We are from Damascus,' they said. 'We have come to greet you and we wish to make the pilgrimage.' 'May God reward you,' he said. 'Will you come out with us?' they asked. 'On three conditions: if we do not carry anything with us, if we do not ask anything from anyone, and if, should anyone offer us anything, we decline to accept it.' 'As for not carrying anything, yes,' they said. 'As for not asking anything, yes. But as for not accepting anything given to us, that we cannot do.' 'You have gone forth placing your trust in the provisions of the pilgrims!' he said. He spoke again. 'Hasan, there are three kinds of dervishes: there is a dervish who will not ask and, if he is given something, will not accept it. This sort has real spiritual substance. There is a dervish who will not ask, but if he is given something accepts because of what has been appointed for him. These are protected within the enclosures of paradise. And there is a dervish who will ask, and, if he is given something, he will take to the point of repletion. The penance of this sort is charity.'"

Habib al-Ajami was asked, "Why did you give up trade?" He said, "I found that giving surety was placing trust in creatures."

Long ago a man went on a journey carrying a loaf of bread. "If I eat this up, I will die of hunger!" he said. So God Most High assigned an angel to him, saying, "If he eats it, give him sustenance, but if he does not eat it, give him nothing!" The loaf stayed with him until he died. He did not eat. They laid his bread next to him in his grave. It is said, "He who falls into the arena of self-abandonment is conducted to the object of his desire as a bride is conducted to her husband."

The difference between neglect and self-abandonment is that neglect means neglecting the rights of God Most High. That is blameworthy. Abandonment means abandoning your own rights. That is praiseworthy. Abd Allah bin al-Mubarak said, "He who takes a penny that is unlawful has no trust in God."

I heard Muhammad bin Abd Allah al-Sufi say[22] . . . that Abu Said al-Kharraz said, "Once I went into the desert without provisions, and need beset me. I saw an oasis at a distance. I rejoiced that I had reached it. Then I thought to myself, 'I have been reassured by and dependent upon other than He!' so I swore that I would not enter the oasis unless I was carried in. I dug a hole for myself in the sand and concealed my body in it up to the chest. In the middle of the night the villagers heard a voice from on high saying, 'People of the oasis! God Most High has a friend who has confined himself in this sand—go and fetch him!' So they all came to me together, brought me out, and carried me to the town."

I heard Abu Abd al-Rahman al-Sulami say[23] . . . that A b u Hamzah al-Khurasani said, "One year I went on the pilgrimage. While walking on the road, I fell into a hole. I fought with my ego over whether to try and get help. 'No, by God,' I said, 'I will not look for human assistance!' Scarcely was this thought completed when two men passed by the mouth of the hole. One of them said to the other,

'Come on, let's block off the mouth of this pit so that no one will fall into it.' They came with cane and matting and covered over the opening. I was about to call out when I said to myself, 'Call out to the One who is closer!' So I remained silent. After about an hour, suddenly something was there with me. It uncovered the mouth of the pit, let its foot hang down, and seemed to say, 'Grab hold of me!'—in its muttering I understood that much. So I took hold of it, and it drew me out. It was a lion! Then it went away. A voice from nowhere said to me, 'O Abu Hamzah, isn't this better? We have saved you from destruction by means of a destruction!' So I walked on, all the while saying:

> I was afraid to show my need to You Who are Most
>   Hidden,
> But my soul shows forth what my sight says to it.
> My shame before You forbade me; I restrained my
>   desire
> And through understanding from You, discovery
>   became needless.
> You dealt subtly with my case. You showed my state
> To be not plain, but hidden—the fire is grasped by
>   the fire —
> You revealed Yourself in a hidden way; it was as if
> You gave word in that hidden place—You were in the
>   lion's paw!
> I saw You, and in me from awe of You was wildness.
> You tamed me with Your loving sympathy.
> You gave life to a lover when You were his death in
>   love.
> Life together with death—a marvelous thing!

I heard Muhammad bin al-Husayn say[24] . . . that Hudhayfah al-Murashi, who was the servant and companion of Ibrahim bin Adham, when asked, "What was the most amazing thing you saw around him?" said, "We endured on the road to Mecca for days without finding anything to eat. Then we came to Kufa and took shelter in a ruined mosque. Ibrahim bin Adham looked at me and said, 'Hudhayfah, I see a sign of hunger in you!' 'It is as the Shaykh has seen,' I said. 'I have an inkwell and pen with me,' he said. So I brought them, and he wrote: 'In the Name of God, the the Merciful, the Compassionate. You are that which is sought in every state, and that which is indicated by every idea.'"

I am the praiser, the thanker, the rememberer.
I am the hungry, the thirsty, the naked. These are
six qualities: I am responsible for half.
Be You responsible for the other half, O Maker!
My lauds for other than You are a flame of fire
　　into which I have rushed.
Hold back Your worshiper from entering the fire!
The fire, to me, is begging.
Do not compel me to enter the fire.

Then he handed the scrap of paper to me and said, 'Go out not attaching your heart to anything other than God Most High and hand this paper to the first person whom you meet.' So I went out, and the first person I met was a man riding a mule. I gave it to him and he took it, and he wept. He asked, 'What is the owner of this paper doing?' 'He is in such-and-such a mosque,' I said. He gave me a purse in which were six hundred dinars. Then I met another man and asked him, 'Who was the man on that mule?' 'He is a Christian,' he told me. I went back to Ibrahim bin Adham and told him the story. 'Don't touch that purse,' he said. 'He will come within the hour.' When an hour had passed the Christian appeared, prostrated himself before Ibrahim ibn Adham, and accepted Islam.

17 ON CONTENTMENT (*QANAAH*)

G od Most High said, "*Whoever does good works, whether man or woman, and is a believer, We will certainly cause to live a good life*" (16:97). Many commentators have said that the "good life" in this world is contentment with one's lot.

Abu Abd al-Rahman al-Sulami related[1] . . . through Jabir bin Abd Allah that the Messenger of God said, "Contentment is an inexhaustible treasure." Abu-l-Hasan al-Ahwazi related[2] . . . through Abu Hurayrah that the Messenger of God said, "Be one who abstains and you will be the most thankful of men. Wish for others what you wish for yourself, and you will be a believer. Treat your neighbors well, and you will be a Muslim. Laugh little, for much laughter kills the heart."

It is said, "The poor are as dead, except those whom God Most High gives life with the honor of contentment." Bishr al-Hafi said, "Contentment is a king who dwells only in a believing heart." Muhammad bin al-Husayn said[3] . . . that Abu Sulayman al-Darani said, "Contentment is to satisfaction as the station of abstinence is to renunciation. Contentment is the beginning of satisfaction, while abstinence is the beginning of renunciation." It is said, "Contentment is to remain calm when facing that to which one is not accustomed." Abu Bakr al-Maraghi said, "The intelligent person is the one who treats the affairs of this world with acceptance and deferment, the affairs of the next with ambition and hurry, and the affairs of religion with knowledge and effort." Abu Abd Allah bin Khafif said, "Contentment is not to wish for what you lack and not to need what you have."

It is said that the meaning of His saying, "*God will provide them with a beautiful sustenance*" [22:58] is contentment. Muhammad bin Ali al-Tirmidhi said, "Acceptance is one's satisfaction with one's allotted sustenance." And it is said, "Acceptance means to find what exists sufficient and to stop hoping for what is not obtainable." Wahb said,

"Honor and riches went out wandering in search of a friend. They ran into contentment and settled down with it." It is said, "He whose contentment is fat finds every broth good." He who turns to God in every circumstance, God provides with contentment. Abu Hazim passed by a butcher who had good fat meat. He said, "Take some, Abu Hazim, it is fat." "I don't have a dirham with me," he replied. "I will wait for it," said the butcher. "It seems better to me that my ego should wait than that you should," said he.

A Sufi was asked, "Who is the most contented of men?" He answered, "The one who gives people the most help and who asks the least." In the Psalms of David it says, "The contented person is rich even if he goes hungry." It is said that God Most High put five things in five places: honor in obedience, humiliation in disobedience, awe in standing in prayer at night, wisdom in an empty belly, and wealth in contentment.

I heard Abu Abd al-Rahman al-Sulami say[4] . . . that Ibrahim al-Maristani said, "Take revenge on your ambition with contentment as you take revenge on your enemy with retaliation." Dhu-l-Nun al-Misri said, "He who is contented is at rest from his contemporaries and towers over his fellows." And it is said, "He who is contented is at rest from preoccupation and towers over everything." Al-Kattani said, "Whoever sells ambition for contentment has triumphed in honor and moral goodness (*muruwa*)." And it is said, "For the one whose eyes follow what is in people's hands, sorrow and care grow long." They recite:

> Generosity and hunger — better for a true person
> Than a day of disgrace that brings cash!

Someone saw a wise man eating discarded vegetables from a gutter. He said, "If you were to wait on the sultan, you would not need to eat this!" "And were you content with this, you would not need to wait on the sultan!" the wise man replied.

It is said that the flying eagle is mighty. Neither the hunter's eye nor the attraction of his bait can rise to it. It is only when the eagle has an appetite for carrion that it becomes entangled in the snare. It descends from its flight and is trapped in a net. When Prophet Moses spoke mentioning appetite—"*If you wished, you could get a reward for that*"—Khidr said to him, "*This is the parting between you and me*" (18:77-78). And it is told that when Prophet Moses had said that, a gazelle stopped in front of he and Khidr. They were both hungry. The side which faced Prophet Moses was not roasted, while the side which faced Khidr was roasted.

His saying, *"The righteous are in bliss"* (82:13) refers to contentment in this world, while *"and the corrupt are in hellfire"* [82:14] refers to avidity in this world. His saying, *". . . the emancipation of a slave . . ."* (90:13) is said to mean freeing him from the humiliation of greed. His saying *"God only wishes to remove impurity from you, People of the Household,"* (33:33) means miserliness and appetite. *"And to cleanse you in purification"* [33:33] means with generosity and selflessness. And it is said that His saying, *". . . give me a kingdom which is not appropriate for anyone after me . . ."* (the prayer of Prophet Solomon) [38:35] means, "a station in contentment by which I would be singled out from those like me. In it I would be satisfied with Your judgment." And it is said that His saying, *"We will certainly punish him with a severe punishment"* (27:21) means "We will strip him of contentment and try him with ego desires"—that is, he would ask God to inflict such punishment.

Abu Yazid was asked, "Through what did you reach what you have reached?" He answered, "I gathered together all the ways and means of this world, bound them with the rope of contentment, set them in the catapult of truthfulness, and cast them into the sea of resignation—and I was at rest." I heard Muhammad bin Abd Allah al-Sufi say[5] . . .that Abd al-Wahhab, the uncle of Farhan of Samarrah, said, "I was sitting with Junayd during the pilgrimage season while all around us was a gathering of many foreigners and strangers. A man came with five hundred dinars, placed them before him, and said, 'Distribute these among your dervishes.' 'Do you have more than this?' Junayd asked. 'Yes, I have many dinars,' he said. 'Do you desire more than what you possess?' 'Yes,' he said. 'Take these,' Junayd said to him. 'You have greater need of them than we do.' And he would not accept them."

18 ON THANKFULNESS (*SHUKR*)

God Almighty and Glorious said, "*If you are grateful, I will give you more*" (14:7).

Abu-l-Hasan Ali bin Ahmad bin Abdan reported[1] . . . from Ata that he went to see Ayisha together with Ubayd bin Umayr and asked, "Tell us the most wonderful thing you ever saw from the Messenger of God." She wept and said, "What affair of his was not wonderful? One night he came to me and came in under the bedclothes with me (or perhaps she said 'under the blanket') until his skin touched mine. Then he said, 'O daughter of Abu Bakr, let me worship my Lord.' 'I love your being close,' said I, and I gave him permission. He arose and went over to a waterskin and made ablution, pouring a great deal of water. Then he stood and prayed and wept until his tears flowed upon his chest. Then he bowed and wept, then made prostration and wept, then raised his head and wept. He continued like this until Bilal came to give him the announcement of morning prayer. I said to him, 'O Messenger of God, what has made you weep? God has forgiven you your sins, whether they came before or might come later.' 'Shall I not be a grateful servant?' he said. 'And why should I not do this, when God has sent down upon me the verse, "*In the creation of the heavens and the earth . . .* are signs for people who reflect' (2:16)."

The true meaning of *shukr*, thankfulness, according to the ones who know, is acknowledging the benefactor's gift with humility. Thus the Truth, glory to Him, is described as Thankful (*shakur*) by extension, not in reality. The sense of this is that He rewards His servants for thankfulness. The recompense of thankfulness is called thankfulness, just as in the saying of the Most High, "*The recompense of an evil is an evil like it*" (42:40). It is said that the gratitude of the Most High is His giving much as a reward for just a few good deeds. This sort of usage is found in the expression, a "grateful" mount, which means that the animal shows itself to be fatter than the amount of fodder it is given.

It is also possible to say that the proper meaning of gratitude is to praise the one who does good by mentioning the good he does in his presence. In that case the servants' gratitude toward God Most High is their praising Him by recollecting His goodness before Him, and the gratitude of the Truth, glory to Him, towards His servants is His praising them by recollecting their goodness before them. The goodness of the servant, then, is his obedience to God Most High, and the goodness of the Truth is His grace towards the servant in enabling him to offer Him thanks.

The thankfulness of the servant, in reality, is only to tell with the tongue and confirm in the heart the blessings of the Lord. Thankfulness is subdivided into thanksgiving of the tongue, which is recognition of the blessing together with humility; thanksgiving of the body and the limbs, which is characterized by loyalty and service; and thanksgiving of the heart, which is to withdraw oneself into contemplation of God's attributes with a continual preservation of reverence.

The thankfulness common to everybody pertains to what one says; the thankfulness proper to devoted worshippers pertains to what one does; the thankfulness proper to gnostics pertains to perseverance throughout one's states.

Abu Bakr al-Warraq said, "Thankfulness for a blessing is to see it as grace and maintain respect." Hamdun al-Qassar said, "Thankfulness for a blessing is to see yourself, in relation to it, in the position of an uninvited guest." Junayd said, "In thankfulness there is an ill: someone who cultivates gratitude seeks increase for himself and clings to the portion of his ego as well as to God, glory to Him."

Abu Uthman said, "Thankfulness is the realization of the inability to give thanks." It is said that thankfulness for thankfulness is more perfect than thankfulness itself—that is, you see your gratitude as being through His enabling, and that enabling becomes the most profound blessing to you so that you give thanks to Him for your thanksgiving, then for your thankfulness for your thanksgiving, and so on without end.

It is said that thankfulness is to connect the blessing to its Bestower and feel your lowliness. Junayd said, "Thankfulness is that you not see yourself as deserving of the blessing." Ruwaym said, "Thankfulness is to expend every effort to demonstrate your gratitude."

The ordinary thankful person, it is said, is he who gives thanks for that which exists. The deeply grateful person is he who gives thanks for that which is lacking. The ordinary thankful one gives thanks for God's permission, while the deeply grateful one gives thanks for His refusal. Or, the ordinary thankful one gives thanks for benefit, while the deeply grateful one gives thanks for prohibition. Or, the one gives thanks for the gift while the other gives thanks for the trial. Or the one gives thanks for free generosity while the other gives thanks for the postponement of his hopes.

I heard Abu Abd al-Rahman al-Sulami say[2] . . . that Junayd said, "Once I was playing in front of Sari al-Saqati. I was seven years old. Before him was a congregation engaged in the discussion of thankfulness. He asked me, 'My boy, what is thankfulness?' I said, 'It means that you do not disobey God with what He has given you.' He said, 'It seems that your portion from God will be your tongue!' Junayd said, 'I have never stopped crying over that saying of Sari's.'"

Shibli said, "Thankfulness is seeing the Giver, not seeing the gift." It is said that thankfulness securely ties up that which is and then goes hunting for that which is lacking. Abu Uthman said, "The gratitude of the majority is for the stuff of food and clothing. The gratitude of the elite is for the insights that have reached their hearts."

It is told that the Prophet David said, "My God, how can I thank You, while my gratitude to You is a gift from You?" God revealed to him, "Now you have truly thanked Me." Prophet Moses is said to have asked in his intimate prayers, "My God, You created Adam by Your own hand, and did this and did that—how can one thank You?" He replied, "Know that all that is from Me. Your realization of that is your thanks to Me."

A dervish had a close friend who was imprisoned by a sultan. He sent word of this to the dervish who answered his companion, "Give thanks to God Most High." Then the man was beaten. He wrote to the dervish who said, "Give thanks to God Most High." Then they brought a Zoroastrian who had a intestinal ailment and chained him up. One shackle was linked to that man's foot and the other to the foot of the Zoroastrian. The Zoroastrian had to get up many times at night. The man was obliged to stand in front of him until he was finished. He wrote this to his friend, who answered, "Give thanks to God Most High." "How long are you going to be saying this?" he asked. "What trial is worse than this one?" His friend replied, "Suppose the belt, the sign of dualism, which is around his waist, was placed around yours, as the shackle which is on his foot has been placed upon yours? Then what would you do?"

It is said that a man came in to Sahl bin Abd Allah al-Tustari and told him, "A thief came into my house and took my possessions!" "Give thanks to God Most High," he said. "What if the thief—satan—had come into your heart and spoiled your knowledge of unity (*tawhid*)? What would you do?"

The gratitude of the eyes, it is said, is that they cover over the shame they see in your companion and the gratitude of the ears is that they cover over the shame they hear from him. It is said that thankfulness is to take delight in praising Him for those gifts that He was not obliged to give.

I heard al-Sulami say[3] . . . that Junayd said that when Sari wanted to give him a benefit, he used to ask him a question. One day he said to him, "Abu-l- Qasim, what is thankfulness?" He replied, "It is not to make use of any blessing of God Most High in order to disobey Him." "Where did you get this from?" he asked. "From your sessions," he told him.

It is told that the grandson of the Prophet, Hasan bin Ali, clung to the corner of the Kabah and said, "My God, You have done good to me and have not found me grateful. You have tested me and have not found me patient. Yet You have not taken Your blessings away from me for all my lack of gratitude, nor made difficulty continue, for all my lack of patience! My God, nothing comes from the Generous except generosity."

It is said that if you cannot stretch your hand to give recompense, you should stretch your tongue to give thanks. And it is said that there are four whose labors are fruitless: anyone who whispers to a deaf man, sets a benefit before the unthankful, sows in a salt marsh, or lights lamps in the sunshine.

When Prophet Idris was given the good news of God's forgiveness, he requested a long life. Asked why, he said, "In order to thank Him, for before this I was working for forgiveness." The angel unfurled his wings and carried him off to heaven.

One of the prophets passed by a little rock from which was issuing great amounts of water. He wondered at that, so God caused it to speak to him. "Since I heard God Most High say, '*A fire whose fuel is men and stones*' (66:6) it said, 'I have wept.'" So that prophet prayed to God to protect that rock. God Most High revealed to him that He had indeed protected it from the fire. The prophet went on. When he came by again he found the water gushing from it as before. He wondered, and God caused the rock to converse with him. "Why are you crying," he asked it, "When God has forgiven you?" "Those were tears of grief and fear," it said. "These are tears of gratitude and joy."

It is said that the grateful person is present with God's bounty, because what he sees is the blessing. God Most High said, "*If you are thankful, I will give you more*" (14:7). The patient person, though, is present with God Most High, because what he sees is the One who is putting him to the test. God, glory to Him, said, "*Certainly God is with the patient*" (2:153; 8:46; 8:66).

It is said that a delegation came before caliph Umar bin Abd al-Aziz. There was a young man among them who began to speak, but Umar cried, "Seniority, seniority! [Let the elders speak!]" "O Commander of the Faithful," the youth said to him, "If command were a matter of age, there are those among the Muslims who are older than you!" "Speak on," he said. "We are not a delegation of desire," he said, "nor are we a delegation of fear. Our desire has been conveyed to us by your graciousness, just as we have been made secure against our fear by your justice." "Who are you, then?" "We are a delegation of gratitude. We have come to you to thank you and go away." He recited:

> It would be a disaster if my gratitude were silent
> About what you have done, while your goodness is
>   eloquent.
> To see the benefit from you and keep it secret—
> That would make me a thief from the hand of the
>   Generous.

It is said that God Most High revealed to Prophet Moses, "Be compassionate to My servants, both those who are in tribulation and those who are protected from it." "What troubles have the protected?" Prophet Moses asked. "The smallness of their gratitude for My protection of them!" God Most High replied.

And it is said, "Praise is due for the breaths you draw, gratitude for the capacities of your body." It is also said, "Words of praise are a beginning and come to you from Him, while thankfulness is an imitation that comes to Him from you." According to a sound tradition, "The first who will be summoned to paradise are those who have praised God in every circumstance." And it is said, "Praise is due for what He has prevented, but thankfulness is due for what He has done."

It is related that a Sufi said, "In one of my journeys I saw a reverend man who had grown very old. I asked him about his state. He said, 'Early in my life I fell in love with the daughter of my uncle, and she likewise with me, so it was arranged that she be wed to me. The night of the wedding we said, "Come, let us enliven this night with thanks to God Most High that He has brought us together." So we prayed that night, and neither of us turned our attention to the other. When the second night came we said the same thing. It is now seventy or eighty years that we have been this way every night. Is it not so, my dear?' 'It is just as the shaykh says,' the old lady replied."

19 ON CERTAINTY (*YAQIN*)

God Most High said, *"Those who believe in what has been sent down to you and what has been sent down before you, and about the afterlife they are sure"* (2:2-4).

Abu Bakr Muhammad bin al-Hasan bin Furak related to us[1] . . . from Abd Allah bin Masud that the Prophet said, "Do not try to satisfy any person by risking the displeasure of God Most High. Do not praise any person for the grace that comes from God Almighty and Glorious. Do not blame any person for what God has not given you— the greed of the greedy will not drive God's sustenance to you, nor will the hater's hatred turn it away from you. God, with His justice and equity, has set rest and joy in being satisfied with Him and in certainty. He has set worry and grief in doubt and discontent."

Abu Abd al-Rahman al-Sulami reported[2] . . . that Abu Abd Allah al-Antaki said, "The smallest amount of certainty on reaching the heart fills it with light and denies it all doubt. Through it the heart is filled with gratitude and fear of God Most High."

Abu Jafar al-Haddad said, "Abu Turab al-Nakhshabi saw me while I was in the desert sitting by a spring. I had gone sixteen days without eating or drinking. He asked me, 'Why are you sitting here?' 'I am poised between religious knowledge and spiritual certainty, waiting to see which one will dominate so that I can bring myself together with it. For if knowledge gains control over me, I will drink, and if certainty gains control over me, I will go away.' 'A great undertaking will be yours,' he said to me."

Abu Uthman al-Hiri said, "Certainty means to care little about tomorrow." Sahl bin Abd Allah al-Tustari said, "Certainty comes from increase of faith and its actualization." Sahl also said, "Certainty is a branch of faith and comes before attestation to truth." A Sufi said, "Certainty is knowledge deposited in hearts." This speaker is pointing out that it is not to be acquired by human effort but is given by the

Truth.

Sahl said, "The beginning of certainty is discovery of the hidden—thus one of our ancestors said, 'If the veil were lifted, my certainty would not increase.' Next comes direct vision, and then contemplation."

Abu Abd Allah bin Khafif said, "Certainty is the confirmation of the secrets pertaining to the order of the hidden mysteries." Abu Bakr bin Tahir said, "Knowledge is the opposite of doubt, but in certainty there is no doubt." He was hinting at acquired and intuitive knowledge: the Sufi sciences are acquired in the beginning, but at the end become intuitive.

I heard Muhammad bin al-Husayn say, "A Sufi declared that the first stage is knowledge of God. Then comes certainty, then confirmation, then sincerity, then bearing witness, then obedience in action, and the name of all of these together is faith."

The Sufi who said this was pointing out that the first thing one requires is the knowledge of God. Knowledge does not come about except by the prior fulfillment of its conditions—that is, one must examine things in a pertinent and relevant way. Then when hints of the divine have become continuous and clear demonstrative evidence has been obtained, the perceiver, through this succession of lights and his deep reflection upon them, becomes seemingly independent of the consideration of proof. This is the state of certainty. After this comes the power of confirming things about the future actions of God that one has heard reported from the divine messages brought by the Prophet—for confirmation can only relate to transmitted information. Next comes sincerity in all that follows from fulfilling God's commandments. After that, the divine response manifests by creating within one a beautiful witness to faith. Then comes carrying out the acts of obedience He has ordered and stripping oneself of what He has banished—but all within the unity.

Abu Bakr Muhammad bin Furak hinted at the same idea when I heard him say, "Verbal remembrance of God is the surging up of the grace in the heart to the tongue." Sahl ibn Abd Allah said, "It is unlawful for a heart to smell the fragrance of certainty while relying upon what is other than God Most High." Dhu-l--Nun al-Misri said, "Certainty calls one to drop ambitions. Dropping ambitions calls one to renunciation. Renunciation bequeaths wisdom. Wisdom bequeaths seeing the consequences of acts."

I heard Muhammad bin al-Husayn say[3] . . . that Dhu-l-Nun al-

Misri said, "Three signs of certainty are: mixing little with people; not praising them when they give something; not blaming them when they withhold something. Three signs of the supreme degree of certainty are: looking toward God Most High in everything; returning to Him in every matter; seeking His help in every state."

Junayd said, "Certainty is the establishment in the heart of knowledge that does not reverse itself, transform, or alter." Ibn Ata said, "Whatever certainty people obtain corresponds to the measure of their closeness to real fear of God. The foundation of this real fear is to stand opposed to what is prohibited. To oppose the prohibited is to oppose the ego. To the extent to which they separate themselves from the ego, they arrive at certainty."

A Sufi said, "Certainty is discovery, and discovery has three aspects: discovery of the meaning of transmitted information, of the manifestation of divine power, and of the realities of faith."

Know that discovery, *mukashafah*, when used in Sufi discourse, means the appearance of a thing to the heart with the force of something remembered, so that no doubt can remain. Sometimes the Sufis mean by the term 'discovery' an event resembling a dream between wakefulness and sleep, but usually they use the term *thibat*, 'sureness,' for this condition.

I heard Abu Bakr bin Furak say that he asked a question of Abu Uthman al-Maghribi. "What is this thing you are saying?" he inquired. "I saw such-and-such people, and they said it," he told me. "Did you see them by ocular vision or by inward discovery?" I asked. "By discovery," he replied.

Amir bin Abd Qays said, "Were the veil to be lifted, my certainty would not increase." Certainty, it is said, is looking at evident things with the force of faith. It is called "the disappearance of resistance." Junayd said, "Certainty is the elimination of doubt by witnessing of the unseen."

I heard Abu Ali al-Daqqaq say about the saying of the Prophet about Jesus the son of Mary, "Had his certainty increased, he would have walked on the air, as I did." The Prophet thus indicated his own state on the night of his Nocturnal Journey because it was regarding the subtleties of the Nocturnal Journey that he said, "I saw that the celestial steed al-Buraq would stay, so I walked on."

I heard Muhammad bin al-Husayn say that Sari asked about certainty, saying, "Certainty is your stillness in the face of the wandering among expedients that takes place in your breast because you are sure that your own action will neither benefit you nor turn aside from you anything appointed." And I heard him say[4] . . . Ali bin Sahl said, "The peace in being present with the Truth is superior to certainty because presence is a place to settle, while certainty is a place of danger."

He seems to make of certainty the beginning of presence with the Truth and presence with the Truth, the continuity of certainty. Thus he holds it possible to acquire certainty while devoid of presence, but holds it absurd to conceive of presence without any certainty. Regarding this, Nuri said, "Certainty is contemplation." That is, in contemplation is certainty without doubt, because no one can contemplate God without placing reliance in what comes from Him.

Abu Bakr al-Warraq said, "Certainty is the foundation of the heart and through it comes the perfection of faith. By certainty one knows God Most High, while by intellect one understands things from God Most High." Junayd said, "By certainty some men have walked on water, while those of greater certainty have died of thirst."

I heard Abu Abd al-Rahman al-Sulami say that Ibrahim al-Khawwas said that he met a youth like a silver ingot in the desert waste. "Where are you going, young man?" he asked. "To Mecca." "Without provisions, or a caravan, or any money for your support?" "O you whose certainty is weak!" he said to me. "Is not the One Who is able to preserve the heavens and the earth able to bring me to Mecca without attachment?" When I entered Mecca, while circumambulating the Kabah, I suddenly found myself with him. He was saying:

> O eye that is tearful always, O ego dead and dark
> Do not love anyone except the Sublime, the Absolute!

When he saw me, he asked, "O Shaykh, is your certainty still so weak?" And I heard him say[5] . . . that al-Nahrajuri said that when the servant has perfected the inner dimensions of certainty, trouble becomes a blessing for him and ease becomes a misfortune.

Abu Bakr al-Warraq said, "Certainty has three faces: the certainty of a received report, the certainty of a piece of evidence and the certainty of seeing for oneself." Abu Turab al-Nakhshabi said, "I saw a youth walking in the desert without provisions. 'If he has no certainty with him, he is destroyed,' I said to myself. So I called, 'Young man! To be in a place like this without any supplies6[9] . . . .' 'O Shaykh,' he said, 'raise your head! Do you see anything but God Almighty and Glorious?' 'Now go howsoever you will,' said I."

I heard Muhammad bin al-Husayn say[7] . . . that Abu Said al-Kharraz said, "Knowledge is what urges you to work. Certainty is what carries you." And I heard him say[8] . . . that Ibrahim al-Khawwas said, "I worked for a living in order to eat lawfully. I was a fisherman. One day a fish fell into the net, so I drew it out and cast the net into the water. Another fell in. I threw it out too, and then went back home. An unseen voice said to me, 'You only find your living in catching those who remember Us, so kill you them!' He said, I tore the net and gave up fishing."

20 ON PATIENCE (*SABR*)

God Glorified and Exalted said, *"Be patient; and you cannot be patient except through God"* (16:127).

Ali bin Ahmad al-Ahwazi reported[1] . . . from Abu Hurayrah from Ayisha that the Messenger of God said, "Patience is the forbearance shown at the initial shock." (The same Tradition is reported by Ali bin Ahmad[2] . . . from Anas bin Malik).

Thereafter patience is of different sorts. There is patience with what the servant has brought on himself and patience with what has come to him independently of his will. Patience with things for which he is responsible is itself in two parts: patience in what God Most High has commanded him to do and patience in what He has forbidden him from doing. As for patience in what the servant has not earned, it consists of enduring whatever hardship attaches itself to him by the decree of God.

I heard Abu Abd al-Rahman al-Sulami say[3] . . . that Junayd said, "The journey from this world to the next is smooth and simple for the believer, but leaving ordinary life for the sake of God is difficult. The journey from the ego to God Most High is extremely difficult, and patience in God is more difficult still." Junayd was asked about patience. He said, "It means swallowing gall without a frown."

Ali bin Abi Talib said, "Patience in relation to faith is like head in relation to the body." Abu-l- Qasim al-Hakim said, "The saying of the Most High, 'Be patient' is a command relating to worship, while His saying, *'You cannot be patient except through God'* (16:127) relates to servanthood itself. Whoever progresses from the degree of 'for You' to the degree of 'through You' has been transported from the level of worship to the level of servanthood. The Prophet said, 'Through You I live and through You I die.'"

I heard Abu Abd al-Rahman al-Sulami say[4] . . . that Ahmad bin

Abil-Hawari said he asked Abu Sulayman al-Darani about patience. "By God, we are not patient with what we love!" he told him. "How shall we be patient with what we hate?"

Dhu-l-Nun said, "Patience is to keep your distance from acts of opposition to God, to keep silent while swallowing choking lumps of distress, and to show independence although poverty afflicts you in the fields of daily life." Ibn Ata said, "Patience is to dwell in tribulation with the finest of conduct." And it is described as vanishing into trouble without manifesting complaint.

Abu Uthman said, "The continuously patient one is he whose ego has been accustomed to unpleasant things by the surprises of life. It is said that patience is to settle down with tribulation in good fellowship, as one settles down with well-being." He also said, "The best reward granted for any act of worship is that which is given for patience. There is no reward higher. God Almighty and Glorious has said, '*We shall grant those who are patient their recompense according to the best of what they have done*' (16:96)."

Amr bin Uthman al-Makki said, "Patience means standing firm with God Glorified and Exalted, meeting trials with equanimity and welcome." Al-Khawwas said, "Patience is to persevere in the principles of the Book and the *Sunnah*." Yahya bin Muadh said, "The patience of lovers is harder than the patience of ascetics. I am amazed that they keep patient!" And he recited:

Patience is to be praised in every realm
Except in wanting You.
That is not to be praised!

Ruwaym said, "Patience is to stop complaining." Dhu-l-Nun said, "Patience is to seek help through God Most High." I heard Abu Ali al-Daqqaq say, "Patience is like its name. [*Sabr* also means aloes, an important medicine that is very bitter].

Abu Abd al-Rahman al-Sulami recited to me[5] . . . what Ibn Ata recited to himself:

I will be patient, if it pleases You, and be ruined by
    sorrow.
It is enough for me that You are satisfied,
    though my patience destroy me.

Abu Abd Allah bin Khafif said, "Patience has three phases: there is the person who attempts patience (*mutasabbir*), the patient person (*sabir*), and the continuously patient or steadfast person (*sabbar*)." Ali bin Abi Talib said, "Patience is a mount that does not stumble." Muhammad bin al-Husayn said he heard Ali bin Abd Allah al-Basri say that a man stopped before Shibli and asked, "What sort of patience is hardest on the one who is patient?" "Patience for God's sake," he replied. "No," said the man. "Then patience toward God." "No." "Then patience in God." "No!" "Then what thing is it?" "Patience away from God," the man said. And Shibli screamed such a scream that his spirit might have departed! And he heard him say[6] . . . that Abu Muhammad al-Jurayri said, "Real patience means making no distinction between hardship and ease, together with peace of mind in both states. The effort of patience is to be tranquil despite tribulation, despite the agony of the weight of trouble.

One of them recited:

I was patient, and the desire of You
    did not break upon my patience.
I concealed what I felt toward You
    from the place of patience,
Out of fear that my soul
    would complain of my longing
To my tears, in secret,
    and they flow without my knowing.

I heard Abu Ali al-Daqqaq say, "The patient win the glory of both worlds because they obtain from God His company. God Most High has said, '*God is with the patient*' (2:153).

It is said that the meaning of His saying, "*Be patient, and strive in patience, and take a fighting position*" (3:200) is that patience is less than striving in patience (*musabirah*), which is less than taking a fighting position (*murabita*). It is said "*Be patient*"—with your ego in maintaining obedience to God Most High; "*strive in patience*"—with your heart, in troubles for God's sake; "*and take a fighting position*"— with your innermost being, in yearning for God. And it is also said, "*Be patient*" for God, "*strive in patience*" through God, "*and take a fighting position*" in God.

God Most High revealed to Prophet David, "Qualify yourself with My qualities. One of My qualities is that I am the Most Patient." And we are told, "Drink patience! For if He kills you, He will kill you as a martyr and if He allows you to live, He will make you live honorably."

Patience toward God is a form of hardship, while patience through God is a form of abiding in Him. Patience for God's sake is a trial, while patience together with God is loyalty. Patience away from Him is alienation!

They recited:

Patience away from You—its results are
blameworthy,
While patience in everything else is deserving of
praise.

And they recited:

How patience, away from one who is as free of me
as the place of the right hand is free from that of
the left?
While men have amused themselves with everything,
I have seen that Love amuses itself with men!

"Patience in quest," it is said, "is the token of victory, patience in trouble the sign of release."

I heard Mansur bin Khalaf al-Maghribi say, "Once a dervish was beaten with whips. When he was returned to prison, he called over one of his companions and spit into his hand. Some bits of silver fell from his mouth into the man's hand. Asked about this, he said, 'I had two dirhams in my mouth. I did not want to cry out while in the sight of a certain person who is on the fringes of my circle, so I bit on the dirhams. They broke in my mouth.'"

It is said that your state is your fortress, and all things below God Most High are your enemies so take up a good fighting position in the fortress of your state! And it is said that "striving in patience" is patience upon patience, patience drowned in patience, and patience overpowered by patience. As it is said:

He who is patient with patience, patience seeks help
from him.
Patiently the lover gives patience its due.

It is told that Shibli was once held in an insane asylum. A group of people went to see him. "Who are you?" he asked. "Your friends who have come to visit you," said they. So he started to throw stones at them, and they ran away. "O liars!" he called. "If you were my friends, you would have been patient with my trial!"

According to some reports God Most High has said, "By My Essence, what the sufferers endure is for My sake." God Most High said, *Be patient with the decision of your Lord; you are in Our sight'* (52:48)."

A Sufi said, "In Mecca I saw a dervish circumambulating the House of God. He took a scrap of paper out of his pocket, looked at it and went away. The next day he did the same thing. I observed him for many days, and he always performed the same action. One day he made the circumambulation, looked at the scrap, then moved away a little and fell down dead! I took the scrap from his pocket. It said, *"Be patient with the decision of your Lord; you are in Our sight* (52:48)."

A young man was seen striking an old man in the face with his sandal. "Aren't you ashamed? Hitting an old gentleman in the face like that!" people asked. "His crime is great," the youth replied. "And what is that?" "This old man claims that he longs for me, but for three days he hasn't been to see me!"

A dervish said, "I went to India, and saw there a man with one eye who was called 'The Patient One'. I asked about his condition. They told me that in the prime of his youth a dear friend of his left on a journey. As he returned from saying farewell, tears flowed from one of his eyes, but the other did not weep. He said to his dry eye, 'Why are you not crying over my separation from my friend? I will forbid you to look on this world!' He shut his eye, and for sixty years he has not opened it."

It is said that the expression "beautiful patience" in the saying of the Most High, *"So be patient with a beautiful patience"* (70:5) refers to a person who suffers trouble and distress, yet cannot be told apart from other people. Umar bin al-Khattab said, "If patience and thankfulness were two camels, I would not care which one of them I rode."

When trials came upon him, Ibn Shubrumah used to say, "It is only a cloud—soon it will scatter." In a hadith, the Prophet, when asked about faith, replied, "Patience and generosity of action." (Abu Abd al-Rahman al-Sulami reported this *hadith*[7] . . . from the great-grandfather of Umayr).

Sari al-Saqati was asked about patience. He had begun to speak of it when a scorpion stung him in the foot, striking him with its tail many times. He kept quiet. When asked, "Why didn't you brush it away?" he replied, "I would have been ashamed before God to speak of patience and not be patient."

According to one *hadith*, the patient poor will sit with God Most High on the day of judgment. God Most High revealed to one of the prophets, "I sent My trials upon My servant, so he prayed to Me and I was long in answering him. Then he complained to Me, and I said, 'O My servant, how shall I deliver you from something which is in itself the means of delivering you?'"

Ibn Uyaynah commented on the meaning of the Quranic verse, *"When they were patient, We made them leaders guided by Our com - mand"* (32:24), saying, "Because they took hold of the chief thing, We made them chiefs."

I heard Abu Ali al-Daqqaq say, "The definition of patience is that one not resist the ordainment of destiny. To talk about trouble without complaining about it does not invalidate patience. God Most High said in the story of Job, *"We found him patient. How excellent a servant! Surely he turned to Us,"* (38:44) although He also reported that Job had said, *"Trouble has touched me"* (21:83). And I heard him say, "God drew this statement out of him (that is, his saying, *'Trouble has touched me,'*) in order that it might be a relief for the weak ones of this community.

A dervish said, "*'We found him patient'*—He did not say 'totally patient'! For not all of his states were patience. In some conditions he used to seek pleasure from trials and find sweetness in them, and in this state of finding delight he was not enduring with patience. Therefore he was not called 'totally patient'."

I heard Abu Ali say that the essence of patience is that one leave trouble as one entered into it. The example is Prophet Job. At the end of his trials he said, *"Trouble has touched me, and You are the most merciful of the merciful"* (21:83). Thus he maintained the best conduct in addressing God, for in saying "You are the most merciful of the merciful" he only hinted, rather that making a plain declaration and saying "Have mercy upon me."

Know that patience is of two sorts: the patience of servants and the patience of lovers. The best thing is for the patience of servants to be preserved and for the patience of lovers to be abandoned.

With this meaning they have recited:

It was clear, on the day of separation:
His promise of patience was a lie from the start!
And with this meaning I heard Abu Ali al-Daqqaq say that when

Prophet Jacob had sworn himself to patience, he began by saying, "*And so a beautiful patience*" (12:83). That means, "So my business is a beautiful patience." After that, he could not be moved until he cried, "O *my grief for Joseph!*" (12:84).

21 ON VIGILANCE (*MURAQABAH*)

God Most High has said, *"God over everything is Vigilant"* (33:52).

Abu Naim Abd al--Malik bin al-Hasan bin Muhammad bin Ishaq reported[1] . . . from Jurayr bin Abd Allah al-Bajli that Gabriel appeared to the Prophet in the form of a man. "O Muhammad," he said, "What is faith (*iman*)?" The Prophet replied: "To believe in God, His angels, His books, His messengers, and destiny—its good and bad, its sweet and bitter, come from God." "You have spoken the truth," said the visitor. We were surprised that someone would corroborate the Prophet, both questioning him and confirming what he said. "And inform me: What is *islam* (submission to God's will)?" he continued. "Islam is to establish prayer, give the poor-due, fast during the month of Ramadan and make the pilgrimage to the House of God." "You have spoken the truth," he said again. "So tell me about doing what is beautiful (*ihsan*)?" "Doing what is beautiful is to worship God as if you see Him, and if you do not see Him, certainly He sees you." "You have spoken the truth," he said.

What the Prophet has here spoken—"And if you do not see Him, certainly He sees you"—points to the state of vigilance, for vigilance is the servant's knowledge that the Lord is aware of him. Perseverance in this knowledge is vigilant awareness of the Lord which is the foundation of every good for the servant.

One can hardly attain to this degree until one has emptied oneself through *muhasabah*, self-observation and inner accounting. The person who has taken account of what he has done in the past and improved his state in the present has attached himself to the path of the Truth. In his relationship with God Most High, he has learned how to keep a heedful heart. He has guarded his breaths for God and turned his attention to God in all his states. So he knows that God is watchful over him—close to his heart, knowing his states, seeing his acts, hearing his words. Whoever is neglectful of all of this is far from the beginning of contact—how far, then, from the realities of nearness to Him?

I heard Abu Abd al-Rahman al-Sulami say[2] . . . that al-Jurayri said that whoever does not establish awe of duty and vigilance in his relationship to God will not arrive at disclosure of the unseen or contemplation of the divine. I heard Abu Ali al-Daqqaq say, "A prince had a vizier who, while attending upon his sovereign one day, turned his regard to some serving youths who were standing there, not because of any misgiving, but because some motion or sound from them had caught his attention. It so happened that the prince looked at his vizier at that moment. The vizier feared the prince would suppose that he had looked at the youths with suspicion and begin to look at him in the same way. After that day that vizier would always come into the prince's presence looking to the side until the prince supposed that his physical disposition had changed. Such was the attentiveness of a creature toward a creature—what then should be the vigilance of the servant towards his Lord?

I heard a dervish tell the following story. A prince possessed a serving youth whom he admitted to his presence more often than his other slaves. This youth was not more valuable than they, nor was he fairer of form. The others therefore were curious about it. The prince wanted to demonstrate to them the young man's superiority in service. One day he was out riding together with his entourage. In the distance was a snow-capped mountain. The prince looked toward the snow and bowed his head. At this, the youth raced off on his horse and nobody knew why! After awhile he returned, bringing some snow with him. "What made you know that I wanted the snow?" asked the prince. "You looked at it," said the youth, "and the sultan's looking at anything can only arise from a clear intention." "I have selected him for my hospitality and acceptance," said the prince "because while everyone has some occupation, his occupation is to consider my glances and attend upon my states."

A Sufi said, "Whoever is vigilant towards God Most High in his thoughts will be made blameless by God in his acts." Abu-l-Husayn bin Hind was asked, "When does the shepherd use his staff to drive the flock away from dangerous pastures?" "When he knows that someone is watching," he replied.

It is said that while traveling, Ibn Umar saw a young man keeping watch over a flock. He asked him, "Would you sell me one of these sheep?" "They do not belong to me," the youth replied. "Tell their owner that the wolf took one of them!" he suggested. "And where is God during all of this?" the servant asked. For a long time afterward Ibn Umar would repeat, "That servant said, 'And where is God during all of this?'"

Junayd said, "If someone has made vigilance to God a reality, he will fear how far his worldly fortune is from his Lord—nothing else."

Once a shaykh chose to keep company with one of his students more often than he received the others. They complained to him about this and he said, "I will make it clear to you." He handed a bird to each of them and said, "Go and kill this where no one can see." He gave one to his favorite as well. They went away and each one of them came back having slaughtered his bird. Then the favorite came back with his bird still alive. "Did you not kill it, then?" the shaykh asked. "You ordered me to kill it where no one could see," explained the student, "but I didn't find any place where Someone could not see!" "This is why I have singled him out for my company," announced the shaykh.

Dhu-l-Nun al-Misri said, "The sign of vigilant awareness is to prefer what God Most High prefers, to hold to be important that which He holds to be important, and to see as trivial that which He sees as trivial." Al-Nasrabadhi said, "Hope moves you to acts of obedience. Fear removes you from acts of disobedience, and vigilance directs you to the paths of the realities."

I heard Muhammad bin al-Husayn say he heard Abu-l-Abbas al-Baghdadi say that Jafar bin Nisar was asked what vigilance was. He said, "Watchfulness over your inner being because of awareness of God's gaze with every thought." And I heard him say[3] . . . al-Jurayri said, "This business of ours is constructed in two parts: that you oblige yourself to devote your attention to God Most High and that your outer aspect be in conformity with religious knowledge." And I heard him say[4] . . . al-Murtaish said, "Vigilance means watchfulness over the innermost because of attentiveness to the unseen with every glance and expression."

Ibn Ata was asked, "What is the best act of obedience?" He replied, "Vigilance of God at all times." Ibrahim al-Khawwas said, "Attentiveness bequeaths vigilance. Vigilance bequeaths purity of being and openness to God Most High."

I heard Abu Abd al-Rahman al-Sulami say that he heard Abu

Uthman al-Maghribi say, "The best thing to which a person can attach himself in this Way is self-observation, attentiveness, and governance of his works by knowledge." And he heard him say[5] . . . that Abu Uthman said that Abu Hafs said to him, "When you sit with people, be a warner of your heart and your ego, and their company will never lead you astray. Remember that they are looking at your exterior, but God is looking at your interior." And he heard him say[6] . . . that Abu Said al-Kharraz said, "One of my shaykhs told me, 'Your duty is reverence of soul and vigilance towards God.' Afterwards, as I was traveling one day in the desert, I was terrified by a noise behind me. I wanted to turn around but did not. Then I saw something over my shoulder so I turned, and was appalled. I turned full around and there I was with a tremendous lion!"

Al-Wasiti said, "The best act of obedience is to guard your every moment—that is, the servant should not study beyond his limit, attend to anything but his Lord, or keep company with anything but the present moment."

22 ON SATISFACTION (*RIDA*)

God Most High has said, "*God is pleased with them and they with Him*" (98:8).

Ali bin Ahmad al-Ahwazi reported[1] . . . that Jabir said that the Messenger of God said, "While the people of paradise are sitting together, a light will shine upon them from the gate of paradise. They will raise their heads and lo! the Lord Most High will be looking down upon them. He will say, 'O people of paradise, ask of Me!' They will say, 'We ask that You be pleased with us.' The Most High will say, 'You have entered My House because I am pleased with you. This is the time when I will honor you with My gifts, so ask of Me.' They will say, 'We ask You for increase.' So they will be given camels of red ruby with halters of red ruby and green emerald. They will travel upon them, and each step that they set their hoofs will be as far as the eye can see. God, glory to Him, will command trees with fruit upon them. The maidens of paradise will come to them and say, 'We are tender virgins who do not fade. We are eternal and we do not die—mates for a noble believing people!' And God, glory to Him, will order a sand dune of fragrant white musk, and the wind called 'The Arouser' will rouse them to excitement, until ultimately they come to the garden of Eden, which is the citadel of paradise. Then the angels will say, 'O Our Lord, the people have come!' And God will say, 'Welcome, O truthful ones! Welcome, O obedient ones!' The veils will be lifted for them, and they will look upon God Almighty and Glorious. They will be provided with the light of the Beneficent, so much so that one of them will not see another. Afterwards He will say, 'Return them to the palaces with rare gifts.' So they will be returned and will recognize each other again. And the Messenger of God said, 'That is the meaning of the saying of the Most High, "*A provision from a Forgiving and Merciful One*' (41:32).'"

The Iraqis and the Khurasanis disagree over whether full satisfaction in God should be counted among the spontaneously granted spiritual states (*ahwal*) or the earned stations of development (*maqa - mat*). The people of Khurasan say that full satisfaction belongs to the stages and that it is the highest evolution of trust. This means that it is one of those things that the servant may reach as a result of his own efforts. The Iraqis, however, say that such satisfaction belongs to the states, that the servant cannot acquire it, but that it is an event that befalls the heart like the rest of the states. Agreement is possible between these two positions, for it is said that the beginning of pleasure in God's will can be obtained by the servant and is one of the stages, while its end belongs to the states and cannot be acquired.

Many people have talked of full satisfaction in God, each one expressing his own state and his own experience of it. Their statements vary since their experiences and portions of it are dissimilar. According to religious knowledge, the necessary definition of the condition of full satisfaction is: someone who is satisfied with God Most High and does not oppose what He has destined.

I heard Abu Ali al-Daqqaq say, "Satisfaction does not mean that you do not feel difficulties. Satisfaction only means that you do not oppose God's decision and judgment."

Know that the thing with which the servant must be pleased is destiny itself. He has been commanded to be satisfied with this. It is neither necessary nor possible for the servant to be pleased with much of what destiny contains, such as acts of disobedience or the various sorts of trials that Muslims undergo. The shaykhs have said, "Satisfaction with the divine will is the greatest gate of God."

They mean that whoever is ennobled by satisfaction has been fully welcomed by God and been honored by the the most exalted proximity. I heard Muhammad bin al-Husayn say[2] . . . that Abd al-Wahid bin Zayd said, "Satisfaction with the divine will is the greatest gate of God and the paradise of this world."

Know that the servant can hardly be satisfied with the Truth, glory to Him, until the Truth is satisfied with him because God Almighty and Glorious has said, *"God is pleased with them and [then] they with Him"* (98:8). I heard Abu Ali al-Daqqaq say that a student asked his master, "Is the servant aware when God Most High is pleased with him?" "No. How should he know that," his master said, "while His pleasure belongs to the unseen?" "But indeed, he does know that!" the student rejoined. "How?" inquired the master. "When I find my heart to be satisfied with God Most High," the student said, "I know that He is satisfied with me." "Well done, my boy!" said the master.

It is said that Prophet Moses prayed, "My God, show me a work such that if I performed it, You would be pleased with me on account of it." God replied, "You are not capable of that." Moses fell to the ground, prostrating himself in entreaty and God Most High revealed to him, 'O son of Imran, My satisfaction is in your satisfaction with My judgment!'"

Abu Abd al-Rahman al-Sulami reported[3] . . . that Abu Sulayman al-Darani said, "When the servant thinks no more about desires, he is satisfied." And I heard him say that al-Nasrabadhi said, "Whoever wishes to reach the place of full satisfaction should cling to that in which God has set His satisfaction." Muhammad bin Khafif said, "Satisfaction has two parts: satisfaction in Him and satisfaction with Him. Satisfaction in Him is to be pleased with Him as Orderer of affairs. Satisfaction with Him pertains to what He has decided."

I heard Abu Ali al-Daqqaq say, "The seeker's road is long. It is the road of training the ego. The road of the elite of God's servants is shorter but also harder. On that road one's acts must correspond to satisfaction in God, and one's satisfaction must correspond to one's destiny." Ruwaym said, "Full satisfaction means that if God were to place hell at someone's right hand [in the direction of paradise], he would not ask Him to move it to his left." Abu Bakr bin Tahir said, "Full satisfaction means that negativity leaves your heart until there is nothing in it but happiness and delight." Al-Wasiti said, "The state of satisfaction in God has a use for your effort. Do not stop its making use of you, or you will become veiled by its delight and vision from the reality of what it reveals."

Know that this saying of al-Wasiti is a thing of great importance. It contains a warning against a hidden trap for Sufis. For them, settling into states is a veil over the transformer of states. If you seek the pleasure of satisfaction and find in your heart the ease and rest of satisfaction, you will be veiled by your state from witnessing the Truth. Therefore al-Wasiti has also said, "Beware of seeking the sweetness of devotions—it is deadly poison!" Ibn Khafif said, "Full satisfaction is the heart's peace in relying upon His judgments and the heart's agreement with and preference for that which pleases God." Rabia-Adawiyyah was asked, "When is the servant truly satisfied?" She replied, "When bad fortune pleases him as well as does good."

In front of Junayd, Shibli spoke the formula used when something disturbs one, "There is no power nor strength save in God!" Junayd said, "Your saying that comes from distress of the heart, and distress of the heart comes from abandoning satisfaction with the decision of God!" Shibli was silent.

Abu Sulayman al-Darani said, "Taking pleasure in God's will means that you neither ask God Most High for the garden nor seek refuge with Him from the fire!"

I heard Muhammad bin al-Husayn say[4] . . . that Dhu-l-Nun al-Misri said, "Three of the signs of satisfaction are: having no preference towards God's decision, feeling no bitterness after His decision, and the passion of love in the midst of trials." And I heard him say that[5] . . . Muhammad bin Yazid al-Mubarrid said that Husayn bin Ali bin Abi Talib heard that Abu Dharr said, "Poverty is dearer to me than wealth, and sickness is dearer to me than health." He said, "May God have mercy upon Abu Dharr! As for me, I say that whoever trusts in the goodness of God's choice for him has no wish for anything but what God Almighty and Glorious has chosen for him."

Fudayl bin Iyad said to Bishr al-Hafi, "Satisfaction is better than asceticism in this world because the satisfied person does not wish for what is above his station." Abu Uthman al-Hiri was asked about the prayer of the Prophet, "I ask You for satisfaction after the decision." He said, "To be satisfied before a trial takes place is the intention to be satisfied, whereas satisfaction after it takes place is really satisfaction."

I heard Abu Abd al-Rahman al-Sulami say[6] . . . that A b u Sulayman al-Darani said, "I hope I know a little bit about being pleased with God. If He sent me into the fire, I would be satisfied with that." Abu Umar al-Dimashqi said, "Full satisfaction is the disappearance of anxiety, whatever the judgment may be." Junayd said, "Full satisfaction is the suspension of preference." Ibn Ata said, "Full satisfaction means the heart looks at the eternal dimension of God Most High's choice for the servant. It is abandoning resentment." Ruwaym said, "Full satisfaction is meeting the judgments of God with joy." Al-Muhasibi said, "Satisfaction is quietness of heart in the midst of troubles." Nuri said, "Full satisfaction is happiness of heart in the bitterness of destiny."

I heard Muhammad bin al-Husayn say that[7] . . . that al-Jurayri said, "If someone is satisfied with less than his due, God will raise him beyond his utmost goal." And I heard him say[8] . . . that Abu Turab al-

Nakhshabi said, "Satisfaction in God is not granted to anyone in whose heart the world finds scope."

Abu Abd al-Rahman al-Sulami reported[9] . . . from Abbas bin Abd al-Muttalib that the Messenger of God said, "Whoever is satisfied with God as Lord has tasted the sweetness of faith." It is told that Umar bin al-Khattab wrote to Abu Musa al-Ashari, "In satisfaction is the whole of good. If you are able, be satisfied—if not, be patient."

It is said that Utbah al-Ghulam spent a whole night until morning saying, "If You punish me, know that I love You, and if You have mercy upon me, know that I love You!" I heard Abu Ali al-Daqqaq say, "The human being is earthenware. Earthenware does not have enough value that it should resist the judgment of the Truth, may He be exalted.

Abu Uthman al-Hiri said, "For forty years God Almighty and Glorious has not established me in a state that I hated or transported me to another that I resented." I heard Abu Ali al-Daqqaq say, "A man was angry with his slave. The slave asked someone to intercede with his master. He forgave him, and the slave began to cry. The one who had interceded asked, 'Why are you crying when your master has forgiven you?' "He seeks my pleasure alone, and he cannot reach that," the master told him. "It is only because of this that he cries."

23
ON SERVANTHOOD (*UBUDIYAH*)

God Almighty and Glorious has said, "*So serve your Lord until that which is certain [death] comes to you*" (15:99).

Abu-l-Hasan al-Ahwazi reported[1] . . . from Abu Hurayrah, that the Messenger of God said, "Seven are they whom God will shade with His shade on the day when there will be no shade but His shade: a just leader; a youth raised in the service of God Most High; a man whose heart clings to the mosque from the time he leaves it until he returns to it; two men who love each other in God, coming together and parting from each other for the sake of God; a man who remembers God in solitude so that his eyes stream with tears; a man who is invited by a charming and beautiful woman but says, 'I fear God, the Lord of the Worlds'; a man who gives charity and conceals it so that his left hand does not know what his right hand has spent."

I heard Abu Ali al-Daqqaq say, "Servanthood is more perfect than worship (*ibada*). First comes worship, then servanthood, then total adoration (*ubuda*)." Thus worship is for ordinary believers, servanthood for the elite, and total adoration for the elite of the elite. I heard him say, "Worship is for the one who has received true information about God. Servanthood is for the one who has seen the truth. Total adoration is for the one who has truth of being." And I heard him say, "Worship belongs to people engaged in the struggle against the lower self, servanthood belongs to the masters of endurance in that fight, while total adoration is an attribute of those who have reached the contemplation of God. Whoever does not spare his own ego is involved in worship. Whoever does not withhold his heart is involved in servanthood. Whoever is not miserly with his soul is involved in adoration."

It is said that servanthood means to fulfill the duties of obedience unstintingly, to look at what proceeds from you as insufficient, and to view what is produced by your virtues as ordained by God. And it is said that servanthood means to give up your own will for the sake of the manifest orders of God. Servitude or servanthood is to free yourself from pretensions to strength and power and to affirm that prosperity and favor have but been entrusted to you. Servanthood is to embrace that to which you have been commanded and to leave that against which you have been warned.

Muhammad bin Khafif was asked, "When is servanthood sound and whole?" He replied, "When one has cast one's weight upon one's Master, and is patient with Him under His trial." I heard Abu Abd al-Rahman al-Sulami say[2] . . . that Sahl bin Abd Allah al-Tustari said, "Concentrated devotion is not right for anyone until four things cease to worry him: hunger, wearing rags, poverty, and humiliation."

Servanthood means that you surrender all of yourself to Him and let Him carry your burden. One of its signs is that you abandon planning and precaution and bear witness to destiny. Dhu-l-Nun al-Misri said, "Servanthood is that you are His servant at all times, as He is your Lord at all times."

Al-Jurayri said, "The servants of benefit are many, but the servants of the Benefactor are precious." I heard Abu Ali al-Daqqaq say, "You are the slave of the one who holds you in bondage and captivity. If you are in bondage to your ego, you are the slave of your ego, and if you are in bondage to your worldly life, you are the slave of your worldly life."

The Messenger of God said, "How wretched is the servant of the dirham! How wretched is the servant of the dinar! How wretched is the servant of the fine garment!"

Abu Zayn saw a man and asked him, "What is your trade?" "Donkey server," the man replied. "May God Most High kill your donkey so that you may be the servant of God, not the servant of the donkey!" said he.

I heard Abu Abd al-Rahman say that his grandfather Abu Amr bin Nujayd said, "You are not truly ready for the first step in servanthood until you can testify that as far as you are concerned, your works are all show and your states pretension."

I heard him say[3] . . . that Abd Allah bin Munazil said, "Only the servant who does not seek others to serve him is a real servant. If he has looked for a servant for himself, he has fallen outside the bounds of servanthood and abandoned its behavior." And I heard him say[4] . . . Sahl bin Abd Allah al-Tustari said, "It is not appropriate for the ser-

vant to pursue a life of exclusive devotion until he is such that no trace
of wretchedness is visible upon him in a time of poverty nor any trace
of luxury in a time of wealth."

It is said that servanthood is the witnessing of the divine lordship.
I heard Abu Ali al-Daqqaq say that al-Nasrabadhi said, "The value of
a worshiper is determined by what he worships, just as a knower is
ennobled by what it is that he knows." Abu Hafs said, "Servanthood is
the ornament of the servant. Whoever abandons it lacks all adornment."

I heard Muhammad bin al-Husayn say[5] . . . that al-Nibaji said,
"The foundation of worship is three things: refusing none of His decisions, withholding nothing from Him, and not letting Him hear you
ask what you need from anyone else." I heard him say[6] . . . that Ibn
Ata said, "Servanthood is in four traits: keeping your promise; staying
within the bounds of the divine law; being pleased with what you
have; being patient with what you lack." And I heard him say[7] . . . Amr
bin Uthman al-Makki said, "I never saw anyone, among all those I
met in Mecca or elsewhere or those who reached us at the pilgrimage
season, who made a fiercer effort in God's service or worshiped more
continuously than al-Muzani [student of the great codifier of the
divine law, al-Shafii]. Neither have I seen anyone who took more seriously the grandeur of God's commands nor anyone harder on himself
and more liberal towards other people than he was."

I heard Abu Ali al-Daqqaq say, "There is nothing nobler than servanthood nor any name more perfect for a believer than having a
name for servanthood. Thus God Most High, describing the Prophet
on the night of the nocturnal journey, which was the moment of his
highest honor in this world, said, "*Exalted is He Who transported His
servant by night from the Sacred Mosque,*" (17:1) and "*And revealed to
His servant that which He revealed*" (53:10). If there had been a name
more glorious than that of servanthood, He would have called him by
it.

With this meaning they recite:

O Amr, to avenge my blood is Zahra's right
As anyone who hears and sees will know.
Call me by no name but, "O her servant!"
It is my noblest title.

One of the Sufis said, "There are only two obstacles: Finding peace in one's own pleasure and relying upon one's own actions. When these two things fall away from you, you truly become a servant." On this subject Al-Wasiti said, "Beware of the bliss that comes with God's gifts. It is a veil for the pure."

Abu Ali al-Juzjani said, "Satisfaction with God's will is the house of servanthood. Patience is its door. Self-abandonment is its inner room. One knocks at the door, is free of labor in the house and finds comfort in the inner room."

I heard Abu Ali al-Daqqaq say, "Just as Lordship is an eternal attribute of the Truth, so servanthood is a continuous attribute of the servant, which can never leave him.

The Sufis recite:

If you ask me, I say I am His slave.
If He is asked, He says He is my master.

I heard Abu Abd al-Rahman al-Sulami say, "Worship performed in search of pardon and forgiveness for one's shortcomings is closer to being real service than is worship performed in hopes of compensation and reward." And I heard him say that al-Nasrabadhi said, "Servanthood is losing sight of one's attempts at service in the vision of the One served." And I heard him say[8] . . . that Junayd said, "Servanthood is to give up every sort of occupation and employment for the sake of a work which is the root of freedom from your own work."

24 WILL POWER (*IRADAH*)

God Almighty and Glorious said, "*Do not drive away those who call upon their Lord in the morning and evening, wishing for His Face*" (6:52).

Ali bin Ahmad bin Abdan related[1] . . . through Anas that the Prophet said, "When God Most High wishes good to a servant, He makes use of him." He was asked, "How does He make use of him, O Messenger of God?" He replied, "By making him successful in a righteous work before death."

Iradah, the will to find God, is the beginning of the path of spiritual travelers, the first title given to those who are determined to reach God Most High. This attribute is only called *iradah* because will is the preface to every undertaking. What the servant does not will, he does not carry out. Since this is the start of the enterprise of one who travels the path of God Almighty and Glorious, it is called 'will' by analogy to the resolution involved at the beginning of everything else.

According to etymology, the disciple is 'he who possesses will,' just as the knower is 'he who possesses knowledge' because the word belongs to the class of derived nouns. But in Sufi usage, the disciple is he who possesses no will at all! Here, one who does not abandon will cannot be called a disciple, just as, linguistically, one who does not possess will cannot be called a disciple.

Many people talked about the meaning of will, each expressing the extent it has manifested to his heart. Most shaykhs say that will means the abandonment of what has become habitual. What is habitual for people, in the vast majority of cases, is dwelling in the realms of unconsciousness, basing one's life upon he pursuit of the passions and inclining toward whatever one's desires call for. The spiritual aspirant is someone who has cast off all of this. His emergence becomes a token and a guide to the soundness of his wish. This condition is called spiritual wish: it means the emergence from the habitual.

While the abandonment of what is habitual is the mark of spiritual wish, its inner reality is the activation of the heart in searching for the Truth. Thus is is called 'a pain of love' which sets at every object of fear. I heard Abu Ali al-Daqqaq give an account that Mumshad al-Dinawari said, "Since I learned that the states of the dervishes are entirely serious, I have never joked with them."

Once a dervish presented himself to me. He said, "O shaykh, I wish you would get me some candy." "Wish," I said involuntarily, "together with candy?" The dervish disappeared without my noticing it. I ordered candy to be fetched and went to search for him, but I could not find him. On seeking news of him, I was told that his mind had become disordered, so that he would say to himself, "Wish—and candy? Wish—and candy?" He wandered about aimlessly and finally went into the desert and never stopped saying those words until he died.

One of the shaykhs said, "I was alone in the desert. My heart was so distressed that I was saying, 'O human beings, talk to me! O *jinns*, talk to me!' A voice from the unseen addressed me. 'What do you wish?' 'I wish for God Most High,' I said. 'When are you wishing for God?' it said. 'Somebody who says to people and spirits, "Talk to me!"—when is he a seeker of God Almighty and Glorious?'"

Through the whole night and day the aspirant does not slacken his endeavors. Outwardly he has the characteristics of struggle, inwardly the attributes of endurance. He has separated himself from his bed and bound himself to concentration. He bears difficulties and defies pains. He treats the ills of his character and applies himself to problems. He embraces terrors and leaves outward appearances. As it is said,

Then I passed the night in a desert,
Fearing neither wolf nor lion.
Overcome by desire, I travel the night quickly.
The one who desires continues overwhelmed.

I heard Abu Ali al-Daqqaq say, "Spiritual wish is a pain of love in the soul, a burning in the heart, a passion in the mind, an agitation of inward being. Fires that blaze in hearts!" I heard Muhammad bin al-Husayn say[2] . . . that Yusuf bin al-Husayn said, "There was a pact between Abu Sulayman al-Darani and his dervish, Ahmad bin Abu-l-Hawari, that Ahmad would not oppose Abu Sulayman in anything that he might order him to do. One day Ahmad went to the shaykh while he was giving a discourse to his circle and said, "The baking oven is hot. What do you command?" Abu Sulayman did not answer him. He repeated it two or three times. Finally Abu Sulayman said, "Go and sit in it!" Abu Sulayman was distracted, and he forgot about Ahmad for an hour. Then he remembered and said, "Go and find out if Ahmad is in the oven, because he promised himself that he would never disobey me!" So they looked, and he was indeed in the oven and not a hair of him was singed.

I heard Abu Ali say, "In my early youth I was on fire with spiritual wish. I used to say to myself, 'If only I knew what the real meaning of spiritual wish might be!' It is said that among the qualities of the aspirant is such love of extra devotions as: sincerity in offering counsel to the community; intimacy with God in retreat; patience with the difficulties of the divine judgments; preferring His command to everything; shyness in the face of His vision; lavishing what he has struggled for on what he loves and risking every means that might bring him to it; contentment with obscurity; and restlessness of heart until he attains to his Lord.

Abu Bakr al-Warraq said, "Three things are the bane of the student: marriage, writing down hadiths, and journeying." He was asked, "Why have you given up collecting hadiths?" He said, "Spiritual wish has prevented me from it."

Hatim al-Asamm said, "If you see a Sufi aspirant wishing for something other than his goal, know that this has manifested from his baseness." I heard Muhammad bin al-Husayn say[3] . . . that al-Kattani said, "Among the principles of the spiritual student are three rules: to sleep only when overwhelmed, to eat only at need, and to speak only when obliged to it."

And I heard him say[4] . . . that Junayd said, "When God Most High wishes the aspirant well, He throws him among the Sufis and prevents him from the company of professional reciters of the Quran." And I heard him say[5] . . . that al-Raqqi said that he heard al-Daqqaq say, "The object of spiritual wish is that you point toward God Most High, so that you may find Him with the pointing." He asked, "So what thing is large enough to comprehend spiritual wish?" He said, "Your finding God Most High without any pointing."

I heard Muhammad bin Abd Allah al-Sufi say[6] . . . that Abu Bakr al-Daqqaq said, "The spiritual aspirant is not truly an aspirant until the angel on his left [who records transgressions] has not written anything against him for twenty years. Abu Uthman al-Hiri said, "If someone does not have a firm wish in the beginning, the passing days will only advance him in falling back."

Abu Uthman said, "When an aspirant hears some Sufi knowledge and acts upon it, it becomes wisdom in his heart until the end of his life. He benefits from it, and if he talks about it, it benefits whoever hears him. But if someone hears some of their knowledge and does not act upon it, it becomes a story that he remembers for a few days, and then forgets."

Al-Wasiti said, "The first stage for the spiritual aspirant is to wish for the Truth by abandoning his own will." Yahya bin Muadh said, "The hardest thing for Sufi students is the company of people who oppose the Sufi way." I heard Abu Abd al-Rahman al-Sulami say[7] . . . that Yusuf bin al-Husayn said, "If you see a spiritual student occupying himself with indulgences and the earning of benefit, nothing will come of him."

And I heard him say[8] . . . that Jafar al-Khuldi said Junayd was asked, "What can students find in the telling of anecdotes and stories with which Sufi discourse is often concerned?" He said, "Such stories are one of the armies of God Most High with which he strengthens aspirants' hearts." "Have you an authoritative proof of this?" he was asked. "Yes," he said. "It is the saying of the Almighty and Glorious, *'We have related to you from the stories of the Messengers things through which We have made firm your heart'* (11:120)." And I heard him say[9] . . . that Junayd said, "The true spiritual student has no need of the learning of the learned."

The difference between the disciple (*murid*) [is that he is] the one who wishes for God, while the shaykh (*murad*) is the one for whom God wishes. In reality, everyone who wishes is wished-for. If it were not the object of God's wish that someone should wish for Him, that person could not be an aspirant, since nothing exists but what God Most High has willed. And every wished-for one is likewise one who wishes because when the Truth wanted him among the elite, He suited him for spiritual wish.

However, the Sufis do make a difference between the *murid* and the *murad*. According to them, the *murid*, the wisher, is the beginning; the *murad*, the wished-for one, is the end. It is the *murid* who is exhausted by toil and plunged into the endurance of hardships. It is the *murad* who is saved by command from further difficulty. The *murid* is a laborer. The *murad* is soothed and gently treated.

God's treatment of those who aspire to Him is of different kinds. Most of them He prepares for struggles. Then after the endurance of all sorts of things they attain to the splendor of the realm of meaning. But many of them have the sublimity of the spiritual realm revealed to them in the beginning and attain to that which the majority of those engaged in self-training and discipline have not reached. However, most of these are returned to effort after this kindness in order that He may give them a full share of the principles of the people of discipline, which would otherwise have escaped them.

I heard Abu Ali al-Daqqaq say, "The *murid* bears. The *murad* is borne." And I heard him say, "Prophet Moses was a *murid*, one who wished for God, for he said, *'My Lord, expand my breast for me'* (20:25). Our Prophet was a *murad*, one for whom God wished, so that God Most High said, *'Have I not expanded your breast for you and lifted from you the burden that galled your back, and exalted for you your recollection?'* (94:1-4). Thus Moses prayed, *"My Lord, show Yourself to me so that I may look upon You."* God replied, *"You shall not see Me"* (7:143). But to our Prophet He said, *"Have you not seen your Lord, how He extends the shadow?"* (25:45).

Abu Ali used to say that what God intended by saying "Have you not seen your Lord?" and "How He extends the shadow" was a veil and a barricade to protect the inner and outer meaning from those who would not be able to understand it.

Junayd was questioned about the *murid* and the *murad*. He said, "The *murid* is governed by the policy of knowledge. The *murad* is governed by the guardianship of the Truth. So the *murid* journeys, while the *murad* flies. When has a wayfarer ever overtaken a bird?"

It is said that Dhu-l-Nun sent a man to Abu Yazid with the instruction, "Ask him, 'How long will he sleep and rest, while the caravan passes on?'" Abu Yazid replied, "Tell my brother Dhu-l-Nun, 'A true man sleeps the whole night, yet the morning finds him in the oasis before the caravan arrives!'" Dhu-l-Nun said, "Very good. In our present state we cannot answer this."

25 ON STEADFASTNESS (*ISTIQAMAH*)

God Most High has said, *"Those who say, 'Our Lord is God,' and then be steadfast, the angels descend upon them'"* (41:30). Abu Bakr Muhammad bin al-Husayn bin Furak reported from Thawban, the client of the Prophet, that the Prophet said, "Even if you cannot do it perfectly, be steadfast on the straight path. Know that the best of your religion is prescribed prayer and that no one but a believer will ever maintain a constant state of ablution."

Steadfastness, continuing straight ahead without deviation, is a level that contains the perfection and completion of everything. By its existence the good things are attained and their balance and harmony kept. If someone lacks the quality of steadfastness, his effort is weak and his exertion fails. God Most High has said, *"Do not be like the woman who unravels the thread she has spun"* (16:92). If someone does not possess this directness as his attribute, he will not progress from the stage he is occupying to another, for his undertaking has not been firmly founded. One of the conditions for the future development of the beginner is that he remains steadfast in the conduct that pertains to the goal.

One of the marks of steadfastness in beginners is that their ordinary daily conduct is not adulterated by apathy. One of its marks in those of the middle stages is that they do not indulge themselves in the stages they reach. And one of its marks in the advanced is that no veil interrupts their transactions with God.

I heard Abu Ali al-Daqqaq say, "Steadfastness on the path has three steps: first, preparation (*taqwim*), then performance (*iqamah*) and then steadfastness (*istiqamah*). Preparation is the disciple of the ego, performance is the refinement of the heart; and steadfastness is the drawing near to God."

Abu Bakr commented that His saying, "Those who say, '. . . *and then be steadfast* . . .(41:30),'" means that they do not attribute partners to Him." Umar said that it meant that they do not swindle as foxes do. Abu Bakr al-Siddiq refers to the observance of the fundamental principles of unity (*tawhid*). The statement of Umar refers to the search for interpretations that obscure the clear sense of the Quran and commitment to the terms of one's responsibilities. Ibn Ata said, "They *'then continue steadfast'* in singleness of heart with God Most High."

Abu Ali al-Juzjani said, "Be content with the state of steadfastness; do not be a seeker of miracles. It is your ego that is excited by the search for miracles, while your Lord Almighty and Glorious calls for you through steadfastness."

I heard Abu Abd al-Rahman al-Sulami say that Abu Ali al-Shabbuwi said, "I saw the Prophet in a dream and asked him, 'It is related, O Messenger of God, that you said, "Sura Hud has turned my hair white." Which part of it affected you like that? The stories of the prophets and the destruction of nations?' 'No, none of these,' he said to me. "It was the saying of the Most High, *'Continue steadfast as you have been ordered.'"* (11:112)

It is said that only the great have the capacity for undeviating travel because it means leaving familiar things and separation from outward forms and customs and standing before God Most High in true candidness and integrity. It was thus that the Prophet said, "Even if you cannot do it perfectly, be steadfast on the straight path."

Al-Wasiti said, "Direction is the trait through which good qualities are perfected and through lack of which they are corrupted." The story is told that Shibli said, "Steadfastness on the path is to see the day of judgment now."

It is said that steadfastness in speech is to abandon backbiting; in actions, to prohibit deviation; in spiritual works, to forbid apathy; and in states, getting rid of the veil." I heard Abu Bakr Muhammad bin al-Husayn bin Furak say, "The letter *sin* in *istiqamah* is grammatically the *sin* of asking for something. People with *istiqamah* request that the Truth establish them first in unity (*tawhid*), then in constancy in fulfilling their promise to Him and adhering to the guidelines of the divine law."

Know that steadfastness on the straight path necessarily produces continuous miracles and acts of grace. God Most High said, "If they had continued steadfast on the path, We would have brought them to the drinking of abundant water." He did not say, "We would have given them a drink," but rather, "we would have brought them to the drinking." The form, "I brought him to the drinking," implies "I gave him that which provides water." This indicates it to be perpetual.

I heard Muhammad bin al-Husayn say that Junayd said, "I met a young seeker in the desert under an acacia tree. 'What has brought you to sit here,' I asked. He said, 'A treasure I have lost.' I continued on and left him. When I returned after the pilgrimage, I found myself again with this young seeker. He had moved off to a place nearby the bush. 'What is the meaning of your sitting here?' I asked. 'I found what I had been searching for in this place,' he said, 'so I will remain here.' Junayd said, 'I don't know which was the more noble, his attachment to the search for his state or his attachment to the place in which he was granted his desire.'"

26 ON SINCERITY (*IKHLAS*)

God Most High has said, *"Does not sincere religion belong to God?"* (39:3).

Ali bin Ahmad al-Ahwazi reported[1] . . . from Anas bin Malik that the Messenger of God said, "Three things prevent the heart of a Muslim from betrayal: sincerity of effort for God's sake; giving good counsel to leaders; attachment to the community of Muslims."

Sincerity, *ikhlas*, is to give one's obedience, with firm intention, exclusively to the Truth—that is, above all one wishes one's good works to bring one closer to God. One does not engage in them to impress someone, to acquire a good reputation in society, out of the love of people's praise, or for any other reason than to come closer to God Most High. It is truly said that sincerity is the purification of action from the consideration of created beings. And it is also well-said that sincerity means to guard against giving attention to the opinions of others.

There is an authenticated tradition that the Prophet reported from Gabriel that God Glorified and Exalted said, "Sincerity is a secret from My secret. I have bestowed it upon the hearts of the ones I love among My servants." When I asked him "What is sincerity?" I heard Abu Abd al-Rahman al-Sulami say[2] . . . that the Lord of Power said this. I heard Abu Ali al-Daqqaq say, "Sincerity is to guard against paying attention to the opinions of other people, while true integrity, *sidq*, is to be cleansed from looking at one's own ego. Thus the man of sincerity has no hypocrisy, while the man of integrity has no spiritual pride."

Dhu-l--Nun al-Misri said, "Sincerity is only perfected by truthfulness in it and patience with it, while truthfulness is only perfected by sincerity in it and continuous perseverance with it." Abu Yaqub al-Susi said, "When people see sincerity in their sincerity, their sincerity is in need of sincerity!"

Dhu-l-Nun said, "Three of the signs of sincerity are that praise and blame from ordinary people become equal to you; that you forget to watch yourself performing good deeds while you are performing them; and that you forget the necessary reward for good works in the next world."

I heard Abu Abd al-Rahman al-Sulami say that Abu Uthman al-Maghribi said, "Sincerity is that in which the ego takes no pleasure whatever. Such is the sincerity of ordinary people. The sincerity of the elite is something that comes upon them, not from them, so that they manifest acts of obedience to God while remaining detached, without seeing or relying upon these acts. Such is the sincerity of the elite."

Abu Bakr al-Daqqaq said, "The flaw in the sincerity of every sincere person is that he sees his own sincerity. When God Most High wants to purify someone's sincerity, He will cause that person's sight of his sincerity to fall away from the sincerity itself. Thus he becomes a 'purified one' (*mukhlas*) rather than a 'possessor of purity' (*mukhlis*)." Sahl al-Tustari said, "Only a sincere person knows what hypocrisy is."

I heard Abu Hatim al-Sijistani say[3] . . . that Abu Said al-Kharraz said, "The hypocrisy of gnostics is superior to the sincerity of students." Dhu-l-Nun said, "Sincerity is that which is preserved from the corruption of the enemy." Abu Uthman said, "Sincerity is to forget to see the creation while continually looking at the goodness of the Creator." Hudhayfah al-Marashi said, "Sincerity means that the actions of the servant are inwardly and outwardly the same." Sincerity is called, "that which is intended for the Truth and aims at truthfulness," and it is called "blindness to one's own good deeds."

I heard Muhammad bin al-Husayn say[4] . . . that Sari al-Saqati said, "Whoever decks himself out before people with what he does not possess has fallen from God's grace." And I heard him say[5] . . . that Fudayl said, "To give up working for people's sake is pretension, while to work for people's sake is to set up partners to God. Sincerity is when God release you from both of these."

Junayd said, "Sincerity is a secret between God Most High and His servant. Even the recording angel knows nothing of it to write it in the recording of one's deeds. Satan does not know it to corrupt it, nor is passion [animal soul] aware of it that it might influence it." Ruwaym said, "Sincerity in the performance of good deeds means that a person wishes no compensation for his deeds in this world or the next, nor any favors from his recording angels." Sahl bin Abd Allah was asked, "What thing is hardest on the ego?" He said, "Sincerity— because the ego has no share in it." Questioned about sincerity, a Sufi said, "It means not showing your deeds to anyone but God."

Another Sufi said, "I came to see Sahl bin Abd Allah at his house one Friday before the time of congregational prayer. I saw a snake in his house. I started forward on one foot but pulled back the other. 'Come in!' he said. 'No one attains the reality of faith while he is afraid of anything on the face of the earth.' Then he added, 'Do you want to make the congregational prayer [at the Prophet's Mosque]?' 'There is a day's and night's journey between us and the mosque!' I said. But he took my hand and in a short while I saw the mosque. So we entered it, prayed with the congregation and left. He stopped to look at the people as they went out and remarked, 'The people of "There is no god but God!" are many, but the sincere among them are few.'"

Hamzah bin Yusuf al-Jurjani reported[6] . . . that Makhul said, "If a servant be sincere for forty days, the springs of wisdom will well up from his heart to his tongue." I heard Abu Abd al-Rahman al-Sulami say[7] . . . that Yusuf bin al-Husayn said, "The most powerful thing in the world is sincerity; yet how often have I striven to drive hypocrisy from my heart, while it has sprouted up again in another form?"

And I heard him say[8] . . . that Abu Sulayman al-Darani said, "When the servant acts with sincerity, it cuts off most of imagination and pretense from him."

27 ON TRUTHFULNESS (*SIDQ*)

God Most High has said, "*O you who believe, fear God and be together with the truthful*" (9:119).

Abu Bakr Muhammad bin Furak reported[1] . . . from Abd Allah bin Masud that the Prophet said, "If the servant is unceasingly truthful and strives for truthfulness, it will be written down that he is a truthful person. If he lies unceasingly and strives for the lie, it will be recorded that he is a liar.

Sidq, truthfulness, is the supporting pillar of Sufism. In truthfulness this Way finds its perfection and balance. It is a degree next to prophethood. God Most High said, "*Such are together with those whom God has blessed—the prophets and the truthful . . .* " as the verse runs (4:69).

Sadiq, a person who tells the truth, is the noun derived from *sidq*, and *siddiq*, a person of total integrity, in its intensive form. *Siddiq* means someone who has a great deal of truthfulness, in whom truthfulness is the dominant characteristic, just as *sikkir* (of the same intensive form) means a drunkard, or *khimmir,* one who is overcome by wine, and so forth. The minimum of truthfulness requires that what one is in private and and in public be the same. The *sadiq* shows this truthfulness in his words, while the *siddiq* is truthful in all of his words, his actions, and his states.

Ahmad bin Khadruyah said, "Whoever wants God to be with him should attach himself to truthfulness. For God Most High has said, '*Certainly God is with the truthful ones*' (2:153). I heard Abu Abd al-Rahman al-Sulami say[2] . . . that Junayd said, "The truthful person is transformed forty times in a single day, while the hypocrite is stuck in a single state for forty years." Abu Sulayman al-Darani said, "Even if the speaker of truth wanted to describe what is in his heart, his tongue could not articulate it."

It is said that real truthfulness means to speak the truth in times of peril. It is also called the agreement of inner being and outer expression. Qannad said, "Truthfulness forbids the jaw unlawful things," while Abd al-Wahid bin Zayd said, "Truthfulness is loyalty to God in action." I heard Muhammad bin al-Husayn say[3] . . . that Sahl bin Abd Allah said, "A servant who flatters himself or others will never smell the fragrance of truthfulness." Abu Said al-Qurashi said, "The truthful person is prepared to die and would not be ashamed of his secret if it were revealed. God Most High said, '*So long for death, if you are truthful*' (2:94)."

I heard Abu Ali al-Daqqaq say that Abu Ali al-Thaqafi was giving a talk one day when Abd Allah bin Munazil said to him, "Abu Ali, get ready for death! It is inevitable!" Abu Ali said, "You too, Abd Allah! Get ready for death, it is inevitable!" Abd Allah laid his head down on his arm and said, "I have died." And he died. Abu Ali stopped short because he was not able to do what Abd Allah had done. For Abu Ali had worldly attachments, while Abd Allah was unattached, without any worldly concern.

I heard Abu Abd al-Rahman al-Sulami say that Abu-l- Abbas al-Dinawari was giving a talk when an old woman in the assembly let out a shout. Abu-l- Abbas al-Dinawari said to her, "Die!" She got up, took a few steps, then turned to him and said, "I have died!" And she fell dead.

Al-Wasiti said, "Truthfulness is sound belief in the unity along with conscious intention." It is told that Abd al-Wahid bin Zayd looked at a youth among his companions whose body had become emaciated and asked, "Young man, are you constantly fasting?" "I am not constantly breaking my fast," he replied. "Do you always stay up at night to pray?" "I do not always sleep," said he. "What is it that drives you?" "A continual love and a continual secrecy about it." Abd al-Wahid said, "Be silent! What boldness is this?" The youth stood up, took a few steps, and said, "My God, if I am truthful, take me!" And he fell down dead.

It is related that Abu Amr al-Zujjaji said, "My mother died and left me a house, so I sold it for fifty dinars and went on the pilgrimage. When I reached Babel I was met by one of those rough men who works as a professional guide and water-finder. 'What do you have with you?' he asked. "I said to myself, 'Truthfulness is best.'" 'Fifty dinars,' I replied. 'Give it to me,' he said. So I gave him the purse, and he counted it, and indeed it was fifty dinars. 'Take it!' he said. 'Your truthfulness has captured me.' Then he got off his mount and said, 'Ride!' 'I don't want to,' I said.'You must!' said he. And he insisted until I rode. 'I am following in your track,' he said. For the next year he kept close by me and attached himself to me until he died."

I heard Muhammad bin al-Husayn say[4] . . . that Ibrahim al-Khawwas said, "You will not see the truthful person engaged in anything but a religious duty that he is fulfilling or an act of excellence upon which he is working."

And I heard him say[5] . . . that Junayd said, "Real truthfulness is to tell the truth in a situation from which only lying can save you." It is said that three things are never missing from a truthful person: gentleness, reverence, and inward beauty.

It is told that God revealed to the Prophet David, "O David, if someone confirms Me as truthful in his interior life, I will confirm him as truthful before the people in his exterior life."

Ibrahim bin Dawhah and Ibrahim bin Sitanba went into the desert together. Ibrahim bin Satanbah said, "Cast off whatever attachments you have with you." Ibrahim bin Dawhah tells, "So I threw away everything except one dinar. Then he said to me, 'Ibrahim, don't distract my awareness. Cast off whatever attachments you have with you!' So I threw away the dinar. And he said again, 'Ibrahim, cast off whatever attachments you have with you!!' Then I remembered that I had some thongs for my sandals and threw them away. And on the road I never had need of a shoelace without finding one in front of me. Ibrahim ibn Satanbah said, 'That is the way of one who deals with God Most High with integrity.'"

Dhu-l- Nun al-Misri said, "Truthfulness is the sword of God. It never falls upon anything without cutting through it." Sahl bin Abd Allah said, "The beginning of disloyalty in the truthful is their discussing things with their egos." Fath al-Mawsili was questioned about integrity. He thrust his hand into the blacksmith's forge, brought out the hot iron, and placed it on his palm. "That is integrity," he said. Yusuf bin Asbat said, "One night spent working for God Most High in truthfulness is dearer to me than wielding my sword for God's sake."

I heard Abu Ali al-Daqqaq say, "Truthfulness means to be with others as you are by yourself or to be by yourself as you are with others. Harith al-Muhasibi was asked about the signs of truthfulness. He said, "Because of the integrity of his own heart, the truthful person does not care if all sense of his value leaves the hearts of others. He does not want people to find out an atom's worth of the goodness of his actions nor does he hate people finding out what is bad in them. To object to this would indicate his wanting something more from people, and that is not one of the characteristics of the truthful."

A Sufi said, "If someone does not fulfill a religious obligation that is always due, obligations due at particular times will not be accepted from him." He was asked, "What obligation is always due?" and replied, "Integrity."

It is said that if you seek God with integrity, He will give you a mirror in which you will see all the wonders of this world and the next. And it is said, "Keep to the truth, though you fear that it will harm you, for you will benefit from it. Do not lie, though you believe that it will benefit you, for it will do you harm."

"Everything is something," it is told, "but the friendship of a liar is nothing at all." And, "The mark of a liar is that he offers many oaths without anyone asking him to swear." Ibn Sirin said, "Speech has too much range for an eloquent man to have to lie." And it is said, "An honest merchant is never bankrupt."

28 ON SHAME (*HAYAH*)

God Most High has said, *"Does he not know that God sees?"* (96:14).

Abu Bakr Muhammad Abd al-Hiri al-Mazaki related[1] ... from Ibn Umar that the Messenger of God said, "Shame is part of faith."

And Abu Said Muhammad Ibrahim al-Ismaili related[2] ... from Ibn Masud that the Prophet of God one day said to his companions, "Be ashamed before God with shame that is real." They said, "We are ashamed, O Prophet of God, and praise be to God!" He said, "It is not that. If someone is ashamed before God with shame that is real, he should guard his head and what it holds and his belly and what it craves and remember death and tribulation. Whoever wants the next life, abandons the adornment of the life of this world. Someone who has done this has been ashamed before God with shame that is real."

I heard Abu Abd al-Rahman al-Sulami say[3] ... that a wise man said, "People keep their sense of shame alive by seeking the company of those before whom they feel ashamed." And I heard him say[4] ... that Ibn Ata said, "The greatest knowledge is awe and shame, for if awe and shame leave, no good remains in one." And I heard him say[5] ... that Dhu-l- Nun al-Misri said, "Shame is the existence of reverence in the heart together with the feeling of desolation caused by how badly you have dealt with your Lord." Dhu-l- Nun al-Misri said, "Love makes one speak, while shame makes one remain silent and fear makes one agitated."

Abu Uthman al-Hiri said, "Whoever discourses on shame without being ashamed before God Almighty and Glorious because of what he is talking about is being drawn to destruction by seemingly acceptable acts." I heard Abu Bakr ibn Ishkib say that Hasan bin al-Haddad went to see Abd Allah bin Munazil, who asked, "Where have you come from?" "From Abu-l- Qasim the preacher's meeting," he replied. "What was he speaking about?" "About shame." "Amazing!" Abd Allah said. "Someone who is not ashamed before God Most High—how can he talk about shame?"

I heard Muhammad bin al-Husayn say[6] . . . that Sari al-Saqati said, "Shame and intimacy with God knock upon the door of the heart. If they find renunciation of the world and careful action to be at home, they camp there. If not, they pass by." And I heard him say[7] . . . that al-Jurayri said, "The first generation of Muslims dealt with each other on the basis of religion, until religion grew thin. Then the second generation dealt with loyalty, until loyalty departed. The third generation dealt with spiritual chivalry, until spiritual chivalry departed. The fourth generation dealt with shame, until shame departed. Then people came to deal with each other on the basis of desire for reward and fear of punishment."

It is told about the saying of the Most High, "*She desired him, and he (Joseph) would have desired her, were it not that he saw the evi-dence of his Lord*" (12:24), that the "evidence" was this: Zulaykha (the wife of Pharaoh's minister who was attempting to seduce Joseph) cast a garment over the face of the idol that was in a corner of the house. Prophet Joseph asked, "What are you doing?" "I am ashamed before it," she told him. "I have more right than you to be ashamed before God Most High!" said Prophet Joseph.

And it is told concerning His saying "*One of the two (maidens) came to him (Moses) walking with shyness*" (28:25) that she was shy before him because she was inviting him to hospitality and was afraid that Prophet Moses might not respond. Shyness is a characteristic of the hospitable. It is the bashfulness of generosity.

I heard Muhammad bin al-Husayn say[8] . . . that Abu Sulayman al-Darani said, "God Most High said, 'O My servant, as long as you are ashamed before Me, I will make the people forget your shameful acts and the places of the earth forget your sins. I will erase your errors from the original Book and will not examine your account on the day of judgment.'"

It is told that a man was seen praying outside of a mosque. He was asked, "Why don't you go into the mosque to pray?" "I am ashamed to go into His house while I have disobeyed him!" said he.

It is said that one of the signs of the possessor of shame is that he is not to be seen in a place that would make him ashamed. A Sufi said, "We went out one night and, passing through a forest, found a man lying asleep, his horse grazing by his head. So we woke him up and asked him, 'Aren't you afraid to sleep in a fearful place like this full of wild beasts?' "He raised his head and said, 'I am ashamed before the Most High to fear anything but Him.' He put his head back down and went back to sleep."

God, glory to Him, revealed to Jesus, "Warn yourself, and if you take warning, then warn others—otherwise be ashamed before Me while you are warning others."

It is said that shame has different aspects. There is shame for the commission of a fault, like that of Adam when it was said to him, "In flight from Us!" and he replied, "Rather, ashamed before You!" There is the shame of one's shortcomings, as when the angels said, "Glory to You, we have not worshiped You with the worship of which You are worthy!" There is the shame of reverence as with Israfil's wrapping himself in his wings out of shame before God Almighty and Glorious. There is the shame of generosity, like that of Prophet Muhammad who used to be ashamed to say, "Go home!" to his community, so that God said, *"(Leave his house after the meal to which you have been invited) . . . do not seek to listen to talk"* (33:53). There is the shame of bashfulness, like that of Ali bin Abi Talib when he asked al-Miqdad bin al-Aswad to ask the Messenger about what ablution was necessary in the case of the emission of seminal fluid, rather than asking himself because of the position of Fatimah. There is the shame of distaste, as when Prophet Moses said, "If some need of this world were to befall me, I would be ashamed to ask it of you, Lord!" and God Almighty and Glorious replied, "Ask of Me even the salt for your bread and the fodder for your donkey!" And there is also the shame of beneficence, which is the shame of the Lord, glory to Him. After the servant has crossed the the narrow bridge into paradise, God will present him with a sealed book, saying, "You did what you did, and I would be ashamed to manifest it to you. So go! I have forgiven you."

I heard Abu Ali al-Daqqaq say about this *hadith* that Yahya bin Muadh commented, "Glory to Him against whom the servant sins—and He is ashamed of it!" I heard Muhammad bin al-Husayn say[9] . . . that Fudayl bin Iyad said, "Five signs of spiritual failure are: cruelty of heart, an eye incapable of tears, small conscience, love of the world, and elaborate ambition." And in a certain holy book, "My servant does not treat Me well. When he calls upon Me I am ashamed to turn him away, but when he disobeys Me, he is not ashamed of it!"

Yahya bin Muadh said, "If someone is ashamed before God when he is obedient, God will be ashamed before him when he is a sinner." Know that shame requires melting (to "die of shame"). It is said,

"Shame is one's insides dissolving because of the awareness of the Lord." And it is said, "Shame is the heart's shrinking because of feeling the Lord's grandeur."

When a man sits down to preach and give admonition to people, two angels call out to him, "Preach to yourself that which you would preach to your brother! And if not, be ashamed before your Master! He sees you!" Junayd, questioned about shame, said, "There is the vision of His gifts and there is the vision of your shortcomings. Between the two of them a state is generated which is called *hayyah*, shame."

Al-Wasiti said, "Someone who is close to transgressing a guideline or violating a promise will not taste the burnings of conscience." He also said, "Sweat pours from the man of conscience, which is the excellence in him. As long as there is any substance to the ego, one is distracted from conscience."

I heard Abu Ali al-Daqqaq say, "Shame means to abandon pretensions before God Almighty and Glorious." I heard Muhammad ibn al-Husayn say[10] . . . that Abu Bakr al-Warraq said, "Sometimes I pray two cycles of ritual prayer to God and leave them feeling such shame that I might have just returned from robbing a house."

29 ON FREEDOM (*HURRIYAH*)

God Almighty and Glorious has said, "*And they prefer others over themselves even when they are destitute*" (59:9).

They only prefer others to themselves in order to strip themselves of what they have abandoned anyway and preferred to leave to others. Ali ibn Ahmad al-Ahwazi reported[1] . . . from Ibn Abbas, that the Messenger of God said, "That which minimally satisfies the needs of your flesh is sufficient for any one of you. Finally it comes down to four cubits and a span (the size of a grave). The whole business returns to its end."

Freedom means that the servant is not a slave to created beings and that things and events do not exercise control over him. The sign that it is sound and whole is that preferring one thing to another drops from a person's heart so that it makes no difference whatever may chance to occur.

Harithah said to the Messenger of God, "I have turned myself away from this world and its stones and its gold are all the same to me." I heard Abu Ali al-Daqqaq say, "If someone comes into this world and is independent of it, he will be transported to the next and be independent of it." I heard Muhammad bin al-Husayn say[2] . . . from al-Daqqaq, "Whoever is free of this world in this world will be free of the next world in the next world.

Know that the reality of freedom is the perfection of servanthood. When you are sincere in being a servant to God Most High, your independence will save you from bondage to anything other than Him. If anyone imagines that the servant surrenders to God in order to throw off the restraints of servanthood at some other time and turns his attention away from the guidelines of what is commanded and what is forbidden—which are proper to this realm of responsibility—he is casting off the religion. God, glory to Him, said to His Prophet, "*Serve your Lord until that which is certain comes to you"* (15:99). That means the end of life, and upon this all the commentators are agreed.

What the Sufis have indicated by *hurriyah*, freedom, is that the servant is not under the domination of any created thing, whether it pertains to this world or the next. He belongs solely to the One. He is not enslaved by any pressure of this world, by the occurrence of any desire, by any future fate—not by a want nor by an intention nor by a need nor by a worldly fortune.

Shibli was asked, "Do you not know that He is the unconditionally Merciful?" He said, "Indeed, but since I have realized His mercy I have not asked Him to have mercy upon me!"

The station of freedom is one of great power and dignity. I heard Abu Ali say that Abu-l- Abbas al-Sayyari used to say that if there were anything but recitation of the Quran that would make a prayer complete, it would be this verse:

I always desire an impossible thing—
That my eyes should see as the eyes of a free man.

Here are the sayings of the shaykhs about freedom.

Husayn bin Mansur al-Hallaj said, "If someone wishes for freedom, let him attain servanthood." Junayd was asked about the case of someone who had no more of this world than could be sucked off a date pit. He replied, "When a servant contracts to buy his freedom from his master, as long as he owes one dirham, he is still a slave." Abu Abd al-Rahman al-Sulami said [3]. . . that Junayd said, "You will not attain to pure freedom while any remnant of the reality of servanthood remains for you to achieve."

Bishr al-Hafi said, "Whoever wants to taste the food of freedom and find rest from being a slave, let him purify the secret understanding that exists between him and God Most High." Al-Husayn bin Mansur said, "When the servant has fulfilled all the stations of servanthood he becomes free of all the toil of being a slave and pursues servanthood without care or ceremony. That is the station of the prophets and the truthful. It means that they are borne rather than having to bear. Such a one encounters no difficulty in his heart, even if he is made to appear to be in difficulty."

Abu Abd al-Rahman recited to us[4] . . . what Mansur al-Faqih recited of his own composition:

In all humanity no free man remains.
None. And none is free among the *jinn*.
The free of these two groups have passed away.
The savor of life has passed.
Know that the greater part of freedom is found in
      service to the dervishes.

I heard Abu Ali al-Daqqaq say, "God Most High revealed to Prophet David, 'If you see anyone who seeks Me, be his servant.' The Prophet said, 'The master of a people is their servant.'"

I heard Muhammad bin al-Husayn say[5] . . . that Yahya bin Muadh said, "The sons of this world are served by slaves and slave girls, while the sons of the next are served by the righteous and the free." And I heard him say[6] . . . that Ibrahim bin Adham said, "The generous free man gets out of this world before he is taken out of it." Ibrahim bin Adham also said, "Keep company with no one except a generous free man: he listens and does not lecture."

30 ON REMEMBRANCE (*DHIKR*)

God Most High has said, "*O you who believe, remember God with much remembrance*" (33:41).

Abu-l- Husayn Ali bin Muhammad bin Abd Allah bin Bushran in Baghdad reported[1] . . . from Abu Darda that the Messenger of God said, "'Have I not told you about the best of your works and attested to it before your King and exalted it in your ranks? It is better than the gift of gold and silver or encountering your enemies and beheading them while they are beheading you.' 'What is that, O Messenger of God?' they asked. 'The remembrance of God,' he replied."

Abu Naim Abd al-Malik bin al-Hasan reported[2] . . . from Anas that the Messenger of God said, "The hour (of the end of the world) will not come while there is one person saying, 'God, God!'" And Ali bin Ahmad bin Abdan reported from Anas bin Malik that the Messenger of God said[3] . . ., "The hour will not come until 'God, God!' is no longer said upon the earth."

Dhikr, the practice of remembering God, is a strong pillar in the way of the Truth. Indeed, it is the mainstay of this Way. No one attains to God except through continuous remembrance.

There are two kinds of remembrance: that of the tongue and that of the heart. By means of the tongue's remembrance, the servant reaches constant remembrance of the heart. Its object and result is the remembrance of the heart. If the servant becomes one who remembers both with his tongue and with his heart, the state of his spiritual search is described as perfect.

I heard Abu Ali al-Daqqaq say, "The practice of remembering God is a proclamation of office. Whoever has been made successful in remembrance has been granted the proclamation and whoever has been denied remembrance has been dismissed from office."

It is told that in the beginning of his practice Shibli lived each day upon the road. He would carry with him a bundle of sticks, and if some unconsciousness entered his heart, he would beat himself with a stick until he broke it upon himself. Sometimes the bundle would be gone before evening came, so he would strike his hands and feet against a wall.

Remembering God with the heart is called the sword of seekers. With it the seeker slays his enemies and drives off troubles that are headed for him. Even if difficulty should overshadow the servant, his fleeing to God Most High in his heart immediately turns away from him the thing he hates.

Al-Wasiti was asked about the practice of remembrance and said, "It is leaving the enclosed court of unconsciousness for the vast space of contemplation through the power of fearing Him and the intensity of loving Him."

I heard Abu Abd al--Rahman al-Sulami say[4] . . . that Dhu-l- Nun al-Misri said, "Whoever really remembers God Most High forgets everything else at the time of his remembrance. God Most High takes care of everything for Him and sets Himself in the place of everything." And I heard him say[5] . . . that Ahmad al-Masjidi said that Abu Uthman was asked the question, "We practice remembering God Most High (with our tongues), but we do not find any sweetness in our hearts." He answered, "Give praise to God that He has adorned one of your limbs with obedience to Him!"

There is a famous *hadith* that the Messenger of God said, "When you see the gardens of paradise, feast in them." He was asked, "What are the gardens of paradise?" and said, "The congregations for remembrance."

Abu-l- Hasan Ali bin Bushran in Baghdad reported[6] . . . that Jabir bin Abd Allah said, "The Messenger of God came out among us and said, 'O people, feast in the gardens of paradise!' 'Messenger of God, what are the gardens of paradise?' we asked. 'The congregations for remembrance,' he said."

So go about your business and remember. Whoever would like to know his place with God, let him look at God's place with him! For certainly God, glory to Him, gives rank to a servant according to the rank the servant assigns God himself. I heard Muhammad bin al-Husayn say[7] . . . that Shibli said, "Hasn't God Most High said 'I am the companion of the one who remembers Me?' What is it that you have profited from the society of the Truth?" And I heard him say[8] . . . that Shibli recited in his gathering:

I spoke Your remembrance—not that I had
    forgotten You for an instant—
But my tongue's recollection eased the remembrance
    itself.
Without ecstasy I nearly died of desire;
My heart was frantic with heartbeats within me.
When ecstasy showed me that You were there
I bore witness that You exist in every place.
So I announced something existent without any
    discourse
Perceived something known, without seeing it.

One of the special features of the practice of remembrance is that it has no assigned time. Indeed, there is no moment in which the servant is not commanded to the remembrance of God, whether it be an obligatory duty or a recommended one. The ritual prayer, though it is the noblest of all devotions, is not possible at some times, while the heart's remembrance is continuous in all circumstances.

God Most High has said, *"Those who remember God standing and sitting and lying on their sides . . . "* (3:191). I heard Abu Bakr bin Furak say, "Standing is true remembrance, while sitting is pretending to it." I heard Abu Abd al-Rahman ask Abu Ali al-Daqqaq, "Which is more perfect, the practice of remembrance (*dhikr*) or meditation (*fikr*)?" Abu Ali inquired, "What do you say?" Abu Abd al-Rahman said, "It seems to me that *dhikr* is more perfect than *fikr* because remembrance is known to be an attribute of the Truth, whereas meditation is not. Whatever is an attribute of the Truth is more perfect than something that is specific to the creation." Abu Ali was pleased with this.

I heard Abu Abd al-Rahman al-Sulami say[9] . . . that al-Kattani said, "Were my practice of remembrance not an obligation that I owe, I would not do it out of respect for Him. The likes of me, remembering Him! Someone who has not even cleansed his mouth with a thousand acts of accepted repentance!"

I heard Abu Ali recite to a dervish:

I would not have remembered You, but a care drove
    me—
Heart and soul and secret—into Your remembrance.

It was as if Your watcher was whispering to me
"Beware, O Rememberer! Woe to you! Beware!"

Another special feature of remembrance is that it produces remembrance in response. God Most High has said, *"Remember Me— I will remember you!"* (2:147). According to a *hadith*, Gabriel said to the Messenger of God, "God Most High says, 'I have given to your community what I have not given to any other community.'" "What is that, O Gabriel?" the Prophet asked. "It is the saying of the Most High, 'Remember Me—I will remember you.' He has not said that to anyone outside this community." It is said that the angel of death consults with the one who remembers God before taking his soul.

In one of the holy books it is written that Prophet Moses said, "O Lord, where do You dwell?" God Most High revealed to him, "In the heart of My believing servant." The meaning of this is the indwelling of remembrance in the heart, for the Truth, may He be glorified and exalted, transcends every kind of inhabiting and incarnation. It is only the affirmation and attainment of remembrance that is intended here.

I heard Muhammad bin al-Husayn say[10] . . . that Thawri said, "I asked Dhu-l- Nun about remembering God. He told me, 'It is the absence of the one who remembers from the act of remembrance.' Then he extemporized:

It's not from forgetting You that I remember You so
    much.
Only, that is what comes off my tongue!

Sahl bin Abd Allah al-Tustari said, "There is no day when the Sublime One is not calling, 'O My servant, you do not treat Me justly! I remember you and you forget Me. I call you to Me, and you go to something else. I drive trials away from you, while you are addicted to sins! O son of Adam, what will you have to say when you come to Me tomorrow?'" Abu Sulayman al-Darani said, "There are plains in paradise and when anyone starts to practice the remembrance of God, the angels begin to plant trees there. Sometimes an angel stops. When they ask him, 'Why did you stop?' he answers, 'The one for whom I am planting this tree has grown lax.'"

Hasan al-Basri said, "Seek sweetness in three things: in prayer, in the remembrance of God, and in the recitation of the Quran. If you find it, good. If not, know that the door is shut." Hamid al-Aswad said, "I was on a journey with Ibrahim al-Khawwas. We came to a place that was full of snakes. He set down his cooking pot and sat down, so I sat down too. When the night grew cold, with a cold wind, the snakes came out. I cried out to the shaykh, and he said, 'Remember God!' So I began to practice remembrance, and they went back. Then they returned, so I cried out again, and he said the same thing. I carried on until morning in that way. When day broke upon us, he got up and walked and I walked along with him. Out of his bedroll fell an enormous snake! It had wrapped itself all around him. "Didn't you feel that?" I exclaimed. "No," he said. "It is a long time since I spent a night as pleasant as the last!"

Abu Uthman said, "Whoever has not tasted the loneliness of unconsciousness will not find the food of the intimacy of remembrance." I heard Muhammad bin al-Husayn say[11] . . . that Sari al-Saqati said, "It is written in one of the Books sent down by God, 'If what dominates My servant is My remembrance, then he loves Me and I love him.'" Through the same chain of narrators, God Most High revealed to Prophet David, "In Me rejoice, and in My remembrance take pleasure."

Thawri said, "For everything there is a punishment, and the punishment for the gnostic is to be kept from practicing remembrance." In the Gospel, it says, "Remember Me when you are angry. I will remember you when I am angry. Be satisfied with My aid to you, for My aid to you is better for you than your aid to yourself."

A monk was asked, "Do you fast?" He answered, "I fast by remembering God. When I remember something other than Him, I have broken my fast." It is said that when remembrance of God has taken possession of a heart, if satan comes close to it he falls into a fit—just as a person may fall into a fit when satan comes close to him. All the little satans gather around him asking, "What is this?" And it is said, "A human being has touched him!"

Sahl al-Tustari said, "I know no disobedience uglier than forgetfulness of the Lord." It is said that no angel presents to God the act of interior remembrance because no angel has any awareness of it. It is a secret between the servant and God Almighty and Glorious.

A Sufi said, "People described to me a man who practiced remembrance in the midst of the forest. I went to see him. While he was seated, suddenly a huge beast struck him a blow and tore a piece out of him! He fainted and so did I. When I regained consciousness, I asked,

"What was that?" "God's grace has set this beast upon me," he said. "Every time some laxness enters into me it takes a bite out of me, as you have seen."

I heard Abu Abd al-Rahman al-Sulami say[12] . . . that al-Jurayri said, "There was a man among my companions who was always chanting, 'God, God!' One day a tree fell on his head and fractured his skull. Blood flowed, and it wrote upon the earth, 'God, God!'"

31 On Spiritual Chivalry (*FUTUWAH*)

God Most High has said, *"They were spiritual warriors who believed in their Lord and He increased them in guidance"* (18:13).

The essence of *futuwa*—noble, generous, and honorable conduct—is that the servant should always be working for the sake of something other than himself. The Prophet said, "God Most High never ceases to be concerned with the need of a servant while the servant is concerned with the need of his Muslim brother."

Ali bin Ahmad bin Abdan related to us[1] . . . from Zayd bin Thabit that the Messenger of God said that he heard Abu Ali bin al-Daqqaq say, "This characteristic (*futuwa*) only reached its perfection in the Messenger of God. At the resurrection everyone will be saying 'Myself, myself!', but he will be saying, 'My people, my people!'"

I heard Abu Abd al-Rahman al-Sulami say[2] . . . that Junayd said, "Spiritual chivalry is in Damascus, eloquence in Iraq and truthfulness in Khorasan." And I heard him say[3] . . . that Fudayl said, "Spiritual chivalry is pardoning the slips of brothers."

It is said that spiritual chivalry means not to see in yourself any superiority over other people. Abu Bakr al-Warraq said, "The spiritual warrior is he who has no enemy." Muhammad bin Ali al-Tirmidhi said, "Spiritual chivalry is to fight for your Lord against yourself." And it is said, "The spiritual warrior is he who is not the enemy of anyone else."

I heard Abu Ali al-Daqqaq say that al-Nasrabadhi said, *"The Companions of the Cave were called 'spiritual warriors'* (18:13) because they placed their faith in their Lord without intermediary.

The *fata*—the spiritual warrior, the person of honor—is called "he who breaks the idol." God Most High has said, *"'We heard a spiritual warrior named Abraham speak of them (the idols Abraham broke)"*

(21:20). And He said, *"And he made them fragments"* (21:60). The idol of every person is his own ego, so in reality, whoever opposes his own desires is a "spiritual warrior."

Harith al-Muhasibi said, "Spiritual chivalry is to deal fairly with others while not demanding fairness for yourself." Umar bin Uthman al-Makki said, "Spiritual chivalry is good character." Junayd, when asked about noble conduct, said, "It means not to avoid a poor man nor imitate a rich one." Al-Nasrabadhi said, "Moral goodness (*muruwah*) is a branch of spiritual chivalry. It means turning away from this world and the next and having disdain for them both."

Muhammad bin Ali al-Tirmidhi said, "Spiritual chivalry means that native and foreigner are the same to you." I heard Muhammad bin al-Husayn say[4] . . . that Abd Allah bin Ahmad bin Hanbal said, "I asked my father (Ahmad bin Hanbal, the great jurist and champion of the divine law), 'What is spiritual chivalry?' He told me, 'To give up what you want because of what you fear.'"

A Sufi was asked, "What is spiritual chivalry?" He said, "That it make no difference whether a saint or an unbeliever is eating with you." I heard a scholar say that a Magian asked hospitality from Prophet Abraham, the Friend of God, who said, "On the condition that you surrender to God (accept *islam*)." So the Magian went his way. Then God Most High revealed to Abraham, "For fifty years I have fed him in his unbelief. Is it too much for you to give him a morsel without requiring that he change his religion?" Abraham followed the Magian's track until he caught up with him and apologized to him. Asked the reason, he told the man. The Magian surrendered to God.

Junayd said, "Spiritual chivalry means to restrain yourself from causing trouble while giving freely." Sahl bin Abd Allah said, "Spiritual chivalry is to follow the practice of the Prophet."

It is called:

— Loyalty and guarding what is precious.
— A virtue you attain without seeing it in yourself.
— Not running away when a beggar approaches.
— Not hiding yourself from those who come to you
    in need.
— Not hoarding and not making excuses.
— Manifesting blessing and concealing trouble.
— Inviting ten people and not caring whether nine
    or eleven come.
— To abandon making distinctions.

I heard Abu Abd al-Rahman al-Sulami say that Ahmad bin Khidruya said to his wife, Umm Ali, "I want to have a feast and invite so and so (a spiritual warrior who was head of the neighborhood watch)." "Are you worthy to invite the chivalrous to your table?" she asked. "Certainly," said he. "If you would do it," she advised, "slaughter sheep and cattle and donkeys and distribute them to the neighbors from the door of your guest's house to your own door." "Sheep and cattle I understand, he said, "but what is this about donkeys?" "You are inviting a man of honor to your house," she said. "The least one can expect is that there be some good in it for the dogs of the neighborhood!"

It is told that a dervish gave a feast. Among the guests was Shaykh Shirazi. After they had eaten, at the time of the spiritual concert, sleep overcame them all. Shaykh Shirazi asked the host, "What is the reason for this sleep of ours?" "I have no idea," he replied. "I worked hard that all of what I fed you (would be lawful)[5] . . . except the eggplant! About that I did not inquire." When morning came they questioned the seller of the eggplant. "I had nothing," he said, "so I stole the eggplant from the premises of so-and-so and sold it." They took the thief to the owner of the land so that he might make the eggplant lawful. "You are asking of me a thousand eggplants!" said he. "I am giving him this land, two garments, a donkey, and the tools of agriculture so that he will never return to the like of what he has done!"

It is told that a man arranged marriage with a woman and before the time of consummation she contracted smallpox (and became disfigured). "My eyes have been injured!" the man declared, and then, "I have gone blind." So the woman entered into the marriage. After twenty years she died and the man opened his eyes. Asked about this, he said, "I was not blind but I pretended to be for fear that she would be saddened." "You have surpassed all the chivalrous!" they told him.

Dhu-l-Nun al-Misri said, "Whoever wants to know elegance, let him look at the water-sellers of Baghdad!" "How is that?" he was asked. He replied, "When I was brought before the caliph because of the heresy attributed to me, I saw a water-carrier wearing a turban wrapped about with Egyptian kerchiefs. In his hands were two jugs of fine porcelain. 'This must be the sultan's cupbearer,' I said. 'No,' they told me, 'It is the public water-bearer.' So I took the jug and drank. Then I said to the one accompanying me, 'Give him a dinar.' But the man would not accept it! 'You are a prisoner,' he insisted, 'and it is not chivalrous that I should take anything from you!'"

It is also not chivalrous to make a profit on a friend. One of our friends said, "There was a spiritual warrior named Ahmad bin Sahl the Merchant. I bought a white cloak from him. He took as price the amount it had cost him. "Won't you take some profit?" I asked. "I have accepted its price," he told me. "I am not going to make you bear the weight of having received a favor because this is not of sufficient importance that my relations with you should be shaped by it. I am not going to take any profit because it is not according to spiritual chivalry to make a profit from your friend."

A man who lay claim to chivalry left Nishapur for Nisa. There another man, who was accompanied by a number of adherents to the code of honor, invited him to dinner. When they had finished the food, a serving-maid came out and poured water over their hands. The Nishapuri held back from washing his hands. "It is not according to spiritual chivalry that women should pour water over the hands of men!" he said. "I have been coming to this house for two years," one of the company commented, "and I didn't know whether the water was poured by a woman or a man!"

I heard Mansur al-Maghribi say that someone wanted to put the hero, Nuh al-Nishapuri, to a test. He sold him a serving-maid dressed as a boy, stipulating that she was in fact a boy. She had a shining face, so Nuh bought her as a boy, and she remained with him for many months. "Did he know that you were a woman?" she was asked. "No," she said. "He never touched me, for he supposed that I was a youth."

It is told that some villains demanded that Nuh give up to the Sultan a youth who served him. He refused. They flogged him with a thousand lashes, but he did not surrender the lad. That night it was intensely cold, and it so happened that Nuh experienced one of those dreams that requires a total ablution. When he got up he immersed himself in the icy water. "You risked your life!" people told him. "I was ashamed before God to have been patient under a thousand lashes for the sake of a creature," he said, "and not to be patient under the pain of a cold ablution for His sake!"

It is told that a party of men of honor arrived to visit a man who lay claim to spiritual chivalry. "Boy, prepare the table!" ordered the man. But the youth did not prepare it. The man said the same thing to him a second, and then a third time. The guests looked at one another, saying, "It is not according to spiritual chivalry that the man should employ someone who would disobey him like this in the matter of setting the table!" So the man asked, "Why are you so slow about the table?" "There is an ant on it!" the youth answered. "It is not courtesy to set the table for spiritual warriors together with an ant, but it is not according to spiritual chivalry to throw the ant off the table. So I am waiting until it crawls off." "Proceed, young man!" they said. "It is the likes of you that should serve great-hearted men!"

A man who had come to Medina for the pilgrimage fell asleep. He imagined that his purse had been stolen. He went out and saw Jafar al-Sadiq, grabbed hold of him, and said, "You took my purse!" "What was in it?" Jafar asked him. "One thousand dinars!" So Jafar took the man to his house and counted out for him a thousand dinars. The man went back home, entered his house, and saw in his house the purse he had thought stolen. He went back to Jafar to apologize and return him the dinars, but Jafar refused to accept them. "A thing I have sent forth from my hand I shall not take back into it again," he said. The man asked, "Who was that?" and was told it was Jafar al-Sadiq.

Shaqiq al-Balkhi asked Jafar al-Sadiq about greatness of heart. "What do you say?" the other inquired. "When God gives something to us, we are thankful," Shaqiq replied, "and when He withholds something from us, we are patient." "The dogs in our city do that!" exclaimed Jafar. "O son of the Prophet's daughter," Shaqiq asked, "what is spiritual chivalry according to you?" "When God gives something to us, we prefer it for others, and when He withholds something from us we are thankful," Jafar said.

I heard Abu Abd al-Rahman al-Sulami say[6] . . . that al-Jurayri said, "One night Abu-l- Abbas bin Masruq invited us to his house. We met with a friend of ours and urged him, "Come back with us! We are accepting the hospitality of the shaykh." "But he hasn't invited me!" he protested. "We will ask permission for you," we told him, "just as the Messenger of God used to for Ayisha." So we brought him with us. When he came to the shaykh's door, we informed the shaykh of what he had said and what we had said. "The place I hold in your heart should bring you here without an invitation," declared the shaykh. "I vow that you shall walk to your seat upon my cheek!" And he insisted, placing his cheek upon the ground! So the man was lifted up and set his foot upon the shaykh's cheek without hurting him, while the shaykh dragged his face along the floor until he reached the man's seat.

Know that it is part of spiritual chivalry to cover over the shames of one's friends, especially when there is something in them that would give malicious pleasure to enemies. I used to hear Abu Abd al-

Rahman al-Sulami say to al-Nasrabadhi, "Ali, the Singer, drinks by
night and attends your sessions by day!," but al-Nasrabadhi would not
listen to what was said. It so happened that one day the shaykh was
walking with one of those who used to talk to him that way about Ali,
the Singer, when they came across Ali, the Singer, lying on the ground
somewhere. He was clearly intoxicated and in need of washing out his
mouth. "How many times have we told the shaykh about this, but he
would not listen!" the man said. "This Ali, the Singer, is just as we
have described him!" Al-Nasrabadhi looked at the critic and said,
"Carry him on your shoulders and take him to his house!" And the
man could not escape from obeying him in this.

I heard him say[7] . . . that al-Murtaish said that he went with Abu
Hafs to see a sick man whom they were tending. There was a whole
group of them. Abu Hafs asked the sick man, "Would you like to recover?" "Yes!" said he. So Abu Hafs said to his companions, "Take this
away from him and upon yourselves." The invalid stood up and went
out with us! The next day all of us were in bed under treatment.

32 ON SPIRITUAL INSIGHT (*FIRASAH*)

God Most High has said, "*In that are signs for those who read the signs*" (15:75). "By those who read the signs" means "for those who can see the inward state of things" or "those who have insight."

Abu Abd al-Rahman al-Sulami reported[1] . . . from Abu Said al-Khudri that the Messenger of God said, "Fear the spiritual insight of the believer, for he sees by the light of God."

Firasah, the precise insight of people, comes suddenly upon the heart and negates whatever might contradict it. It has a kind of jurisdiction over the heart. The term is derived from "prey (*farisa*) of a lion." The ego cannot oppose the spiritual insight of that which is usually regarded as correct and possible. It exists to the same degree as one's strength of faith: whoever has stronger faith has sharper insight.

Abu Said al-Kharraz said, "One who sees with the light of spiritual insight, sees with the light of the Truth. The very substance of his knowledge comes from God, unmixed with either negligence or forgetfulness. Indeed, it is a judgment of Truth flowing from the tongue of a servant." Abu Said's expression "looking with the light of the Truth" means seeing by a light with which the Truth has favored him. Al-Wasiti said, "Spiritual insight means the rays of light that gleam in hearts and the solid establishment of a spiritual knowledge that conveys secrets of the invisible realm from one hidden place to another. Thus the possessor of insight witnesses things in the way that the Truth brings him to witness them, and he speaks what is in people's minds."

It is related that Abu Hasan al-Daylami said, "I went into Antakya for the sake of a black man whom they told me could speak of secrets. I waited there until he came down the mountain of Likam with some lawful goods to sell. I had gone hungry for two days, having not eaten anything at all. 'How much is this?' I asked him, to lead him to believe that I would buy what he had before him. 'Sit over there,' he said, 'until we have sold it, and we will give you some money to buy something to satisfy your hunger.' I left him and went on to someone else to convince him that I was only a customer. Then I came back to him and said, 'If you are going to sell this, then tell me how much it is!' 'You have gone hungry for two days! Sit over there until we have sold it, and we will give you some of what you would have bought!' he said. So I sat down. When he had sold it, he gave me something and went away. I followed him, and he turned and told me, 'When a need befalls you, take it to God Most High. But if your ego has some share in it, you will be prevented from your need.'"

I heard Muhammad bin al-Husayn say[2] . . that al-Kattani said, "Spiritual insight is the disclosure of certainty and the direct witnessing of the unseen. It is one of the stages of faith." Once al-Shafii and Muhammad bin Hasan al-Shaybani, his teacher, were at the Kabah when a man came in. Muhammad bin al-Hasan said, "It comes to me that he is a carpenter," and al-Shafii said, "It comes to me that he is a blacksmith!" So they asked him and he said, "I used to be a blacksmith, but now I do carpentry!"

Abu Said al-Kharraz said, "The one who draws out knowledge is one who constantly observes the unseen. It is not invisible to him. Nothing is hidden from him. It is he to whom the saying of the Most High points, '. . . *Those of them who can search out knowledge of it would have known it*' (4:83)." The close examiner is one who knows the sign. He is familiar with what is in the depths of the heart through indications and signs. God Most High has said, '*Indeed in that are signs for those who read the signs*' (15:75). The person of insight looks with the light of God Most High—that is, with the rays of light that gleam in his heart by which he becomes aware of the meaning of hidden things. This is one of the special characteristics of faith. Those who have a greater share of this are called "those learned in God." God Most High said, '*Be ones learned in God*' (3:79), meaning knowers, wise men, qualified with the attributes of the Truth in perception and character. Such people possess no information concerning what is hidden in other people or any perception of them or any business with them."

Once Abu-l- Qasim al-Munadi fell ill. He was of great importance among the shaykhs of Nishapur so Abu-l- Hasan al-Bushanji and Hasan al-Haddad came to see him, having bought an apple on credit for half a dirham. They brought it to him, and when they sat down Abu-l- Qasim said, "What is this darkness?" They left. "What have we done?" they asked each other. So they thought about it and said, "Perhaps it is that we did not pay for the apple!" They gave the grocer its price and then went back to Abu-l- Qasim. "This is amazing!" he said, when his eye fell upon them. "Is it possible for a person to get out of the darkness with such speed? Tell me what has been happening with you!" So they related the story to him, and he said, "Yes. Each of you had relied upon his companion to pay and the man was ashamed to call you to account. Yet the responsibility remained, and I was the cause of it. But I saw that in the two of you."

Abu-l- Qasim al-Munadi, the Crier, used to go into the market every day to cry his wares. When what he needed—from a penny to half a dirham—came into his hands, he would leave, and return to his main occupation and the observation of his heart. Abu-l- Husayn bin Mansur al-Hallaj said, "When the Truth takes possession of one's secret, He grants possession of secrets so that one sees them directly and can tell of them."

A Sufi was asked about spiritual insight and said, "There are souls that are at home in the realm of invisible causation, so that they look down over unseen meanings and speak of people's secrets with the speech of direct vision, not that of thinking or approximation."

It is told that before his repentance Zakariya al-Shakhtani had intimate relations with a woman. One day—after he had become one of Abu Uthman al-Hiri's special students—this situation came into the head of the shaykh. Zakariya was thinking about her. Abu Uthman raised his head and asked him, "Aren't you ashamed?"

In the early days when I had found Abu Ali al-Daqqaq, he appointed me to hold a session in the mosque of Mitraz. From time to time I would ask permission of him to travel to Nisa, and he would give it to me. One day I was walking with him on the way to his teaching session. The thought in my mind was, "If only he would take my place in my meetings for the days I am gone!" He turned to me and said, "I will stand in for you and hold meetings the days you are away." So I walked a little further, and the thought came to my mind that he was not well and it would be difficult for him to stand in for me two days a week. If only he would shorten it to one day a week! He turned to me and said, "Two days a week is not possible for me. I will substitute for you once a week." So I walked with him a little further and the thought of a third thing came to my mind, and he turned to me and gave me explicit information about it.

I heard Abu Abd al-Rahman al-Sulami say that his grandfather,

Abu Amr bin Nujayd, said that Shah al-Kirmani had keen spiritual insight. He did not err. He would say, "Whoever casts down his eyes before forbidden things, restrains his ego from lusts (attraction to pleasure), fills his inner being with continuous attentiveness and his outer being with adherence to the Sunnah, and accustoms himself to eating what is lawful, will make no mistakes with his insight.

Abu-l- Hasan al-Nuri was asked, "What is the origin of spiritual insight in the one who has it?" He answered, "It comes from the saying of the Most High, *'And I breathed into him (Adam) of My Spirit'* (15:29). If someone's share of this light is more perfect, his vision is wiser and his judgment based on his insight is truer. Do you not see how the breathing of the Spirit into Adam made it necessary for the angels to prostrate before him? For the Most High said, *'I formed him and I breathed into him of My Spirit, so fall down before him in pros - tration'* (15:29)."

This statement of Abu-l- Hasan al-Nuri is somewhat difficult, so be careful with it. In this mention of the breathing of the Spirit he was aiming to correct those who say that souls are uncreated. The situation is not as it might occur to the hearts of the weak. That to which this breathing (and union and separation) are properly attributed is liable to influence and alteration, which are signs of the transitoriness of created things. Yet God Glorious and Exalted has chosen the believers for perceptions and lights through which they come to possess insight. In essence, these are forms of the knowledge of God. This is the import of the Prophet's saying, "The believer sees by the light of God"—that is, by a knowledge and inner vision for which God Most High has specially chosen him and by means of which He has distinguished him from others like him. To call these kinds of knowledge and perceptions "lights" is not an innovation, and to describe that process as "breathing" is not reaching far afield. What is intended is one's created nature. Husayn bin Mansur said, "The man of spiritual insight hits his target with the first shot. He does not turn to interpretation or opinion or calculation."

It is said that the spiritual insight of students is a thought that demands verification, but the insight of gnostics is a verification that demands a reality. Ahmad bin Asim al-Antaki said, "When you sit with the people of truthfulness, sit with them in truthfulness, for they are the spies of hearts. They will enter and leave your heart without your feeling it." I heard Muhammad ibn al-Husayn say[3] . . . that Abu Jafar al-Haddad said, "Spiritual insight appears as a spontaneous initial thought that nothing can challenge. If contradictions arise, it is a simple thought, an event of the ego."

It is related that Abd Allah bin Muhammad al-Razi (later of Nishapur), said, "Ibn al-Anbari invested me with a cloak of wool. I saw on Shibli's head an elegant cap that went well with that cloak. I wished to myself that I could have the two of them together. When Shibli stood up after the meeting he turned to me so I followed him, for it was his custom when he wanted me to follow him to turn to me like that. When he went into his house, I went in too. 'Take off the cloak!' he said. I took it off. He folded it and threw the cap on it, then called for fire and burnt the both of them."

Abu Hafs al-Nishapuri said, "It is not for anyone to lay claim to direct spiritual insight, but be careful of the spiritual insight of others. The Prophet said, 'Beware the spiritual insight of the believer.' He did not say, 'Try to practice spiritual insight into people!' How can pretensions to this sort of vision be appropriate for someone who is obliged to be wary of it?"

Abu-l- Abbas bin Masruq said, "I went to visit an old man, one of our companions. I found him in a state of destitution and said to myself, 'How does this shaykh make a living?' 'Put away from you these base thoughts, Abu-l- Abbas!' he said to me. 'God possesses hidden kindnesses!'"

It is related that al-Zabidi said, "I was in a mosque in Baghdad with a congregation of dervishes. No lawful means of subsistence had presented itself to us for days so I went to al-Khawwas in order to ask him for something. When his eyes fell upon me he said, 'The need for the satisfaction of which you came—does God know of it or not?' 'Of course,' I said. 'Be silent,' he said, 'and do not reveal it to any created being.' So I returned, and after only a short wait, more than we needed was provided for us."

Sahl bin Abd Allah al-Tustari was in the congregational mosque one day when such fierce heat and discomfort struck the place that a dove fell dead inside. Sahl said, "Shah al-Kirmani has died this very hour. (That is the meaning of this), God willing." So they wrote inquiring about that, and it was just as he said.

Once Abu Abd Allah al-Turughandi—he was one of the great men of his time—traveled to Tus. When he reached Khurr he told his companion, "Buy some bread." The man bought enough for the two of them, but Abu Abd Allah said, "Buy more than that." So his companion deliberately bought enough for ten people. It was as if he did not expect the word of that shaykh to be fulfilled. The man said, "When we climbed the mountain we came upon a group of people who had been bound by thieves.

They had not eaten for some time. They begged food from us, and the shaykh said, 'Prepare the table for them.'"

One day I was with Abu Ali al-Daqqaq when there was talk of how Abu Abd al-Rahman al-Sulami would stand up in the spiritual concert just like the dervishes. Abu Ali said, "The likes of him, in his state—perhaps stillness would be more suitable for him." Then in the midst of the gathering he said, "Go to him. You will find him sitting in his library. On top of the books will be a little volume bound in red containing poems of Husayn bin Mansur al-Hallaj. Take the volume without saying anything to him, and bring it to me." It was midday. I went to see him, and there he was in his library, with the volume placed just as it had been described. When I sat down Abu Abd al-Rahman deduced what had been said. "There used to be someone who forbade that a gnostic should move in the spiritual concert," he remarked. "One day that man was seen alone in his house spinning in circles as if he were trying to bring on an ecstasy. When he was asked about his state, he said, 'A certain spiritual question had been difficult for me. Its meaning became clear. I could not restrain my joy so finally I stood up and turned.' He was told, 'The state (of those you have criticized) is like that.' When I saw the thing that Abu Ali had ordered me to do and saw what he had described to me just as he had said it—and when there came from the tongue of Abu Abd al-Rahman the very thing that he had mentioned—I was confounded. 'How shall I deal with the two of them?' I wondered. Then I thought to myself, 'There is nothing for it but to tell the truth.' 'Abu Ali described this volume to me,' I told him, 'and told me to bring it without asking permission of the shaykh. I am afraid of you, but it is not possible for me to disobey him. To what do you command me?' He took out another volume of the works of Husayn in which was an essay called *Al-Sayhur fi naqd al-duhur*, and said, 'Take this to him and tell him that I am studying the other book and taking some verses from it for my own notebooks.' So I left."

It is related that Hasan al-Haddad said, "I was in the presence of Abu-l- Qasim al-Munadi while a group of dervishes was with him. He told me, 'Go out and get them something to eat.' I was delighted that he had permitted me to exert myself for the dervishes and bring them something, although he knew of my poverty. 'Take a basket!' he said and I left. When I came to the street of Siyyar I saw a magnificent old man. I greeted him and said, 'A group of dervishes is in such-and-such a place. Do you have anything to give them?' He gave orders and bread and meat and grapes were brought out for me. When I reached the door of the shaykh's house, Abu-l- Qasim called out to from behind it, 'Return that to the place from which you took it!' So I went back, apologized to the old man and said, 'I did not find them.' I hinted that they had left and gave back the food. Then I went to the market and came across something so I brought that. 'Come in!' said Abu-l- Qasim. I told him the story. 'Yes,' he said, 'that was Ibn Sayyar, one of the sultan's men (and therefore his wealth, if acquired without right, could be unlawful). When you come to dervishes with something, bring them the likes of this, not the likes of that!'"

Abu-l- Husayn al-Qarafi said, "I visited Abu-l- Khayr al-Tinati. When I was taking leave of him, he went out with me to the door of the mosque and said, 'Abu-l- Husayn, I know that you do not carry with you any regular sustenance to rely upon but take with you these two apples.' So I took the two of them, put them in my pocket and was happy, for nothing had come my way for three days. I took out one of them and ate it. Then I went to take out the second—and there were both of them together in my pocket! So I would eat of them, and they would keep coming back. But at the gate of Mosul I said to myself, 'They are corrupting my state of trust in God since they have become a known source of sustenance for me.' So I took them both out of my pocket at the same time, looked around, and there was a dervish wrapped in a cloak, saying, 'I crave an apple!' I gave them both to him. When I had covered some distance it occurred to me that the shaykh had actually meant the apples for him. They had just kept me company on the road. I turned back to the dervish, but I could not find him."

I heard Muhammad bin al-Husayn say[4] . . . Abu Amr bin Ulwan said that there was a youth who kept company with Junayd who used to speak people's thoughts. This was mentioned to Junayd, who asked him, "What is this thing that has been said about you?" "Hold something in your mind," he told Junayd. "I am holding it," he said. "You are holding such-and-such a thought." "No!" said Junayd. "Try it a second time," said the youth. So he did. "You are holding such-and-such a thought," the youth said. "No!" "A third time!" The same sort of thing was said. "This is very strange," said the youth. "You are a truthful man, but I know my heart!" "You spoke the truth the first, second, and third times," said Junayd, "but I wanted to test whether your heart would change!"

And I heard him say that Abd Allah bin Muhammad al-Razi said that Ibn al-Raqqi fell ill. Medicine was brought to him in a cup. He took it and then said, "Something has happened in the country today. I will not eat or drink until I know what it is." Several days after this the news came that the Carmatians had entered Mecca on that day and perpetrated in it their dreadful massacre.

I heard Abu Abd al-Rahman al-Sulami say that Abu Uthman al-Maghribi said that this story was mentioned to Ibn al-Katib. "That's amazing!" he said. "No, it isn't amazing," I told him. "So what is the news of Mecca today?" Abu Ali bin al-Katib asked me. "It is this," I said. "The Talhiyun and the Bani Hasan are fighting with each other. The Talhiyun are being led by a black man in a red turban. In Mecca today there is a cloud over the whole sacred precinct." So Abu Ali wrote to Mecca, and it was just as I had told him.

It is told that Anas bin Malik said, "Before I went to see Uthman bin Affan, in the street I had looked at a woman, gazing at her charms. Uthman said, 'One of you has come in upon me with the marks of fornication clear upon his eyes!' 'Can there be revelation after the Messenger of God?' I exclaimed to him. 'No,' he said, 'but there is enlightenment, proof and insight.'"

Abu Said al-Kharraz said, "I entered the Sacred Mosque and saw a dervish, who wore two Sufi cloaks, begging from people. 'This sort of thing is tiresome for people!' I said to myself. He looked at me and said, '*And know that God knows what is within you, so beware of Him!*' (2:235)' So I asked forgiveness in my secret being, and he called to me, "*And it is He who accepts the repentance of His servants*" (42:25).'"

It is related that Ibrahim al-Khawwas said, "I was in Baghdad in the Medina mosque, where there was a congregation of dervishes. An elegant young man approached us, sweetly perfumed, showing goodly respect, and with a handsome face. I said to our companions, 'It comes to me that he is a Jew!' They were all displeased by this so I went out. The young man went out also, then returned to them. 'What did the shaykh say about me?' he asked. They were ashamed to tell him, but he insisted so they said, 'He said that you were a Jew.' Thereupon he came to me, prostrated before me, and became a Muslim. When asked the reason, he said, 'We find in our books that the insight of a man of real integrity does not err. So I said, 'I will put the Muslims to the test.' I considered them closely and felt that if there were a man of true integrity among them, he would be in this group because they talk of

Him. So I dressed myself like one of you. When this shaykh became aware of me and had insight into me, I knew that he was indeed a man of true integrity.' The young man became a great Sufi."

I heard Abu Abd al-Rahman al-Sulami say[5] . . . that Muhammad bin Dawud said, "We were with al-Jurayri. He asked, 'When the Truth wants to bring about some event in the country, is there any man among you whom He informs of this before He makes it manifest?' 'No,' we said. 'Then weep for hearts that find out nothing from God Most High!' said he."

Abu Musa al-Daylami said, "I asked Abd al-Rahman bin Yahya about trust in God. He said, 'Even if you thrust your hand into the mouth of a viper up to the wrist, do not fear anything outside of God along with Him.' So I went out to Abu Yazid to ask him about trust in God. I knocked on his door and he said, 'Isn't there enough for you in the saying of Abd al-Rahman?' 'Open the door!' I cried. 'Don't visit me,' he said. 'I have given you the answer from behind the door.' So I went away. I waited a year, then went to see him again. 'Welcome!' he said, 'Now you have come to me as a visitor.' I was with him for a month. Nothing used to enter my heart without his telling me about it. When I was taking leave of him, I asked, 'Profit me with a lesson.' He said, 'My mother told me that when she was carrying me, if lawful food came near her, her hand would reach out to it, but if there were anything doubtful about it, her hand would hold back.'"

Ibrahim al-Khawwas said, "I traveled into the desert and was besieged by difficulties. So when I reached Mecca a certain amount of spiritual pride took hold of me. Then an old woman called out to me, 'O Ibrahim! I was with you in the desert, but I didn't speak to you because I didn't want to distract your inner being. Cast out of yourself these vain imaginings!'"

It is related that al-Farghani used to go out on the pilgrimage every year. He would pass Nishapur, but he never went in to see Abu Uthman al-Hiri. He said, "One time I did go to see him. I greeted him, and he did not return my greeting. I said to myself, 'A Muslim comes to see him and greets him and he does not give greeting in return?' Abu Uthman said,'The likes of this goes on pilgrimage, leaves his mother behind, and takes no care of her?' I went back to Farghanah and stayed with my mother until she died. Then I went straight to Abu Uthman. When I came in he received me and made me sit down. From then on al-Farghani attended upon Abu Uthman. He asked of him the job of taking care of his horse and was entrusted with that duty until the shaykh died."

Khayr al-Nassaj said, "I was sitting in my house when it struck me that Junayd was at the door. I denied what was in my heart, but it came to me a second and a third time. Finally I went out, and there was Junayd! 'Why didn't you come out at the first thought?' he asked."

Muhammad bin al-Husayn al-Bistami said, "I went to see Abu Uthman al-Maghribi, saying to myself, 'Perhaps he will want me to do something.' Abu Uthman said, 'It isn't enough for people that I accept them—they want me to ask of them, too!'"

A Sufi said, "I was in Baghdad when it struck me that al-Murtaish was bringing me fifteen dirhams to buy a small pot, a rope and sandals, and that I would go into the desert. There was a knock on the door. I opened it, and there was al-Murtaish, holding a purse. 'Take this,' he said. 'O Master, I don't want it!' I protested. 'Why are you troubling us? How much do you want?' 'Fifteen dirhams.' 'It is fifteen dirhams,' said he."

Concerning the saying of the Most High, "*Or one who was dead— we have brought him to life*" (6:122), a Sufi said, "Someone who was dead of mind, but God Most High brought him to life with the light of insight, and set for him the light of divine manifestation and direct vision—he will not be like someone who walks, unconscious, with the people of unconsciousness." It is said that when insight becomes sound, its possessor progresses to the level of contemplation.

I heard Abu Abd al-Rahman al-Sulami say[6] . . . that Abu-l-Abbas bin Masruq said that a shaykh approached them and used to speak to them about Sufism with beautiful words. He possessed a sweet tongue and an excellent mind. In one of his talks he said to them, "Whatever thought strikes you, tell it to me." It struck my heart that he was a Jew. The thought became powerful and unceasing. I mentioned this to Jurayri, and it seemed of great importance to him. 'It is inevitable that I will tell the man about this,' I said to myself. So finally I told him, 'You have urged us, "Whatever thought strikes you, tell it to me."' It has occurred to me that you are a Jew.' He bowed his head in silence for an hour. Then he raised his head and said, 'You have spoken the truth. I testify that there is no god but God and that Muhammad is the Messenger of God! I tried all the schools, and said, "If something is to be found with any group of them, it will be found with these." So I came to you to experiment with you, and you are in the right.' And he made good his Islam."

It is related of Junayd that his teacher, Sari, used to say to him,

"Address the people!" Junayd said, "There was shyness in my heart about speaking to people, for I had doubts whether I was worthy of this. One night I saw the Prophet in a dream. It was a Thursday night (preceding the day of congregational prayer, when groups would meet in the mosque for discourse). 'Address the people!' he said to me. I woke up, and went to Sari's door before morning and knocked on it. 'So you would not attest to our truthfulness until it was told to you!' he said." The next day Junayd sat down with the people in the congregational mosque, and word began to spread that he was holding sessions and giving discourse. So a Christian youth, who was in disguise, stopped by him and asked, "O Shaykh, what is the meaning of the saying of the Messenger of God, 'Fear the spiritual insight of the believer, for he sees with the light of God?' Junayd bowed his head, then raised it and said, 'Surrender to God! The time for your Islam has arrived!' So the youth became a Muslim."

33 ON MORAL CHARACTER (*KHULUQ*)

God Most High has said, "*Verily you (the Prophet) are of a moral character*" (68:4).

Ali bin Ahmad al-Ahwazi reported[1] . . from Anas that the Messenger of God was asked, "Which of the believers has the most excellent faith?" He replied, "The one who has the best (most moral) character."

Thus moral character is the best of the servant's virtues. In it the substance of humanity is manifest. The real human being, who is masked by his old worn-out garment is made known by his nature. I heard Abu Ali al-Daqqaq say, "God Most High specially distinguished His Prophet as He did but then praised none of his traits the way He praised his character. He said—mighty is He Who spoke—"*Verily you are of the (highest moral) character*" (68:4).

Al-Wasiti said, "God Most High described him as 'of a the highest moral character' because both the worlds were lavished upon him, but he was content with God." Husayn bin Mansur al-Hallaj said, "It means 'harshness had no effect on you after your acquaintance with the Truth.'" Abu Said al-Kharraz said, "It means that you possess no concern beyond God Most High." I heard Abu Abd al--Rahman al-Sulami say[2] . . . that al-Kattani said, "Sufism is morality. Whoever surpasses you in morality surpasses you in Sufism." It is related that Ibn Umar said, "If you ever hear me say to a slave, 'God shame you!' bear witness that he is free."

Fudayl said, "Even if a man beautifully performs every act of religious merit, if he has a hen and treats it badly, he is not one of the doers of good." It is said that when Ibn Umar saw one of his slaves performing the prescribed prayer well, he would free him. The slaves were familiar with this side of his character. They used to offer the prescribed prayer well with an eye towards him, and he would set them free. He was advised of this and said, "Anyone who deceives us in God—we let ourselves be deceived by him!"

I heard Muhammad bin al-Husayn say[3] . . . that Harith al-Muhasibi said, "We are lacking three things: a beautiful face accompanied by chastity, beautiful speech accompanied by trustworthiness and beautiful companionship accompanied by loyalty." And I heard him say that Abd Allah bin Muhammad al-Razi said, "Character is to count as little what proceeds from you toward Him and to count as great what proceeds from Him toward you."

Ahnaf was asked, "From whom did you learn character?" He said, "From Qays bin Asim al-Munaqqari." "What out of his character impressed you?" "He was sitting in his house when a serving-woman of his came with a skewer of broiled meat. It dropped from her hand and struck one of his sons, who died. The woman was appalled, but he said, 'Don't be afraid. You are free, for God's sake.'" Shah al-Kirmani said, "The sign of moral character is to hold back from giving offense and to bear burdens."

The Messenger of God said, "If you cannot improve people's condition with your property, improve it with an open face and a moral character." Dhu-l--Nun al-Misri was asked, "What person has the most troubles?" He replied, "The one who has the worst character." Wahb said, "If someone imitates a good habit for forty days, God will make that good characteristic a part of his nature." Hasan al-Basri remarked about the saying of God Most High, "*And your garment purify*" (74:4), "That means, 'Make your character moral.'"

A hermit had a ewe. One day he saw her with only three legs. "Who has done this to her?" he cried. "I did," said his servant. "Why?" "To make you grieve because of her!" "That you cannot do," he said. "But I will bring grief to the evil one who made you do this. Go! You are free."

Ibrahim bin Adham was asked, "Have you found any pleasure in this world?" "Yes, on two occasions," he answered. "The first of these was a day when I was sitting and a man came and urinated on me. The second was once when I was sitting and a man came and slapped me." When children saw Uways al-Qarani, they would throw stones at him. He used to say, "If you must do that, throw the little ones so that you don't hit my leg and keep me from offering my prescribed prayers!"

A man reviled Ahnaf bin Qays while following him through the streets. When they came close to his quarter he stopped and said, "Noble youth, if there is anything left to say, say it! Otherwise some of the fools of the neighborhood may hear you and answer you back."

Hatim al-Asamm was asked, "Is a man to put up with everyone?" "Yes," he said, "Except himself." It is related that the Commander of the Faithful, Ali bin Abi Talib called his manservant, who did not answer. He called him a second time and a third, and still he did not answer. So he got up and found him lying down. "Didn't you hear me, boy?" he asked. "Yes, I did." "Then what induced you not to answer me?" "I felt safe from your punishment," the boy said, "so I was lazy." "Go!" Ali cried. "You are free, for God's sake!"

Maruf al-Karkhi went down to the Euphrates to make ablution. He set down his copy of the Quran and its wrappings. A woman came and carried them off. Maruf followed her and said, "O sister, I am Maruf—no harm will come to you. Do you have a son who can read the Quran?" "No," she answered. "Or a husband?" "No." "Then give back my copy and take my robe instead!"

One time thieves entered the house of Abu Abd al-Rahman al-Sulami in Mukabirah. They took whatever they found. I heard one of our companions tell that he had heard Abu Abd al-Rahman say, "I was passing through the market and came across my cloak on someone who had bought it at auction. I turned aside and did not approach him."

I heard Abu Hatim al-Sijistani say[4] . . . that al-Jurayri said, "When I came back from Mecca (may God protect it!), I went immediately to see Junayd to save him the bother of visiting me (since returned pilgrims are customarily honored with visits). So I gave him greeting and then went home. When I offered the morning prescribed prayer in the mosque, I found that he was with me. He was behind me in the row. "I came to you yesterday so that you would not have to be bothered (with honoring me like this)," I said. "That was your goodness," said he, "and this is your right."

Abu Hafs was asked about moral character. He said, "It is that which God Glorious and Exalted chose for His Prophet in His saying 'Accept forgiveness and enjoin what is good' (7:199)[4] . . . as the verse runs."

Character, it is said, is to be a friend to people and a stranger to their business. And it is also said that character means to accept without vexation or alarm whatever human cruelty or divine judgment may reach you.

Abu Dharr was at a a fountain watering his camels when a man came up in a hurry and broke the spout. Abu Dharr sat down and then lay prostrate. Asked why he did that, he answered, "The Messenger of God ordered that if a man became angry, he should sit down until it passed off, and if it did not pass, that he should prostrate himself."

It is written in the Gospel, "My servant, remember Me when you are angry. I shall remember you when I am angry." Malik bin Dinar's wife yelled at him, "Hypocrite!" "O wife," he replied, "You have found a name of mine that all the people of Basra have lost!" Luqman said to his son, "There are three that are only made known by three: the gentleman by anger, the hero by war, and the true brother by need of him."

Prophet Moses prayed, "O my God, I beg of You that what is not in me not be attributed to me." God, glory to Him, revealed, "I do not even do that for Myself—how should I do it for you?" Yahya bin Ziyad al-Harithi had a bad servant. "Why do you hold onto that boy?" they asked. "To learn forbearance through him," he replied.

It is said that in the saying of the Most High, "*He has granted you His favors complete, outwardly and inwardly*" (31:20), "outwardly" means a harmonious physical being and "inwardly" means a purified character. Fudayl said, "The company of a good-natured libertine is dearer to me than that of a bad-natured devotee."

Good nature is to bear unpleasant things pleasantly. It is related that Ibrahim bin Adham went out into the steppe, where a soldier hailed him. "Where is human civilization?" he asked. Ibrahim pointed to a graveyard. The man hit him over the head and wounded him. After he left him, the soldier learned that the man he had met had been Ibrahim ibn Adham, the ascetic of Khorasan. The soldier went back to Ibrahim to apologize. "When you struck me," said Ibrahim, "I asked God Most High to grant you paradise!" "But why?" "I knew that God would compensate me for the blow, and I did not want my share from you to be good, while your share from me was bad."

It is related that a man invited Abu Uthman al-Hiri to be his guest. When Abu Uthman appeared at the door of his house, the man said, "O Master, this is not the time for you to come in! I am so sorry! Go back!" So Abu Uthman went home. When he reached his own house, the man came to him again, saying, "O Master, I am sorry!" and began excusing himself. "Come now," he urged. So Abu Uthman got up and went, but when he reached the door, the man said the same sort of thing he had said the first time. He kept on like this a third and a fourth time, while Abu Uthman went back and forth. After a number of repetitions of this behavior, the man confessed, "O Master, I wanted to put you to the test!" And he began to apologize and praise him. "Do not praise me for a character that one finds in dogs," Abu Uthman said. "When you call a dog, he comes, and when you drive him off, he runs away!"

Abu Uthman was crossing the street at midday when a basin of ashes was thrown on him from a roof. His companions were furious and unleashed their tongues against the one who had thrown them. "Don't say anything!" said Abu Uthman. "If someone deserves to have fire poured upon him and a compromise is reached with ashes, he cannot be angry!"

A dervish came to stay with Jafar bin Hanzalah, and Jafar served him assiduously. "What a fine man you would be," the dervish would say, "if only you were not a Jew!" "Do not vilify my belief," Jafar said, "when you rely upon it to be served! Ask a cure for yourself and guidance for me."

Abd Allah the tailor had a Magian client for whom he sewed clothes. The man would give him counterfeit dirhams, and Abd Allah would accept them. It so happened that one day Abd Allah left his shop on some business. The man came with the counterfeit coins and presented them to Abd Allah's apprentice, who would not take them. So the Magian gave him real ones. When Abd Allah returned he asked his apprentice, "Where is the Magian's shirt?" The story was recounted to him. "You have done very badly!" he exclaimed. "For a long time he has been dealing with me like this. I have been patient with him and thrown the coins into the river for fear that he would use them to deceive someone other than me!"

Bad character, it is said, narrows the heart of the one who possesses it. There is no room in it for anything but what he wants, just as a narrow room is not big enough for anyone but its owner. Good character means that it makes no difference to you who stands in the prayer row beside you. It is part of your own bad character to let your eyes fall upon the bad character of someone else. The Messenger of God was asked about bad luck, and said, "Bad character."

Abu-l-Hasan Ali bin Ahmad al-Ahwazi reported[5] . . from Abu Hurayrah that someone said, "O Messenger of God, pray to God Most High against the polytheists!" He replied, "I was only sent as a mercy; I was not sent as a punishment."

34 ON BOUNTIFULNESS (*JUD*) AND GENEROSITY (*SAKHA*)

God Most High has said, "*And they prefer others over themselves, even if they are destitute*" (59:9).

Ali bin Ahmad bin Abdan reported[1] . . . from Ayisha that the Messenger of God said, "The generous person is close to God, close to people, close to paradise, and far from hell, while the miser is far from God, far from people, far from paradise, and close to hell. Someone ignorant of faith who is generous is dearer to God Most High than a stingy devotee."

There is no difference, in Sufi usage, between *jud*, bountifulness, and *sakha*, generosity. However the Truth, glory to Him, is not described with the words *sakha* or *samaha*, magnanimity, for lack of an authoritative text. The real essence of generosity is that one does not find it difficult to give freely.

According to the Sufis, *sakha* is the first degree. *Jud* comes after it, and then *ithar*, preferring others to oneself. Whoever gives a part and keeps a part (of his wealth) possesses *sakha*. Whoever freely distributes most of it, but keeps something for himself possesses *jud*. The one who suffers need but prefers that someone else have enough possesses *ithar*. Thus Abu Ali al-Daqqaq says that Asma bin Kharijah commented, "I do not like to refuse anyone a need that he has asked of me. If he is noble, I guard his honor, and if he is base, I guard my honor from him."

It is told that Muwarriq al-Ijali used to introduce gifts among his spiritual brothers with great refinement. He would leave a thousand dirhams with them, saying, "Hold onto this until I come back," and then send a message to them, "You have it at your disposal."

A man of Minbaj met a man of Medina and asked where he came

from. "From the people of Medina," he replied. "One of your men came to us," said the first. "He was called al-Hakam bin Abd al-Muttalib and he made us rich." "How?" asked the Medinian. "He didn't go to you with anything but a woolen gown!" "He did not enrich us with property, but he taught us generosity. So our rich gave to our poor until we all became rich."

I heard Abu Ali al-Daqqaq say that when Ghulam al-Khalil slandered the Sufis before the caliph, the caliph ordered that their heads should be cut off. Junayd was protected from this penalty by the study of law, for he used to make juridical decisions in the school of Abu Thawr. As for al-Shahham, al-Raqqam, Nuri, and the rest of the congregation, however, they were arrested. The leather mat was spread for their decapitation. Nuri stepped forward. "Do you know what you are hurrying to?" the executioner asked. "Yes." "Then what makes you impatient?" "I prefer that my friends, rather than myself, should live a little longer."

The executioner was amazed and sent word to the caliph, who turned the prisoners over to a judge who could investigate their state. The judge threw some legal questions at Abu-l- Husayn al-Nuri. He answered them completely and then began to say, "And beyond this, God has servants who when they stand, stand in God, and when they speak, speak in God[4] . . ." Sayings came, one after the other, that made the judge weep. So the judge sent to the caliph, saying, "If these are heretics, there is no Muslim on the face of the earth."

Ali bin al-Fudayl bin Iyad used to buy from neighborhood merchants. "You would find it less expensive in the bazaar," people told him. "But these have settled near us hoping we would bring them profit!" he said.

While Jibalah bin Suhaym was among his companions, a man sent him a woman servant as a gift. "It is an ugly thing for me to accept her for myself while you are here," he said, "and I don't like singling out one of you while each of you has a right and a respect that is due him. And she will not bear dividing!" They were eighty, and he ordered a handmaiden or a page for each one.

One day Ubayd Allah bin Abi Bakra grew thirsty in the street. He asked for water at the house of a woman. She brought him out a jug, but stood behind the door and said, "Stand away from the door and let one of your serving boys come and take it, for I am an Arab woman, and my servant died some time ago." Ubayd Allah drank the water and said to his young servant, "Take her 10,000 dirhams!" "God is supreme! Are you making fun of me?" she exclaimed. "Take her 20,000 dirhams." "May God give me strength!" "Boy, take her 30,000 dirhams!" She shut the door, saying, "Shame on you!" But he brought her 30,000 dirhams. She accepted them, and before long she had many suitors.

Generosity, it is said, is to respond to the first thought. I heard one of the companions of Abu-l-Hasan al-Bushanji say, "Abu-l-Hasan al-Bushanji was in retreat. He summoned one of his students and told him, 'Take this shirt off of me and give it to so-and-so.' 'Couldn't you have waited until you came out of retreat?' he was asked. 'I had no confidence that my state would not be changed by the consequences of withholding this shirt!' said he.

They asked Qays bin Sad bin Ubadah, "Have you ever seen anyone more generous than yourself?" "Yes," he said. "In the desert we came upon a woman. Her husband was nearby. 'Two guests have come to us,' she told him. So he brought a she-camel, slaughtered it, and said, 'Help yourself!' "When the next day came, he brought another one and slaughtered it too. 'Help yourself!' he said again. 'But we have not eaten more than a little of what you killed for us yesterday!' we protested. 'I am not going to feed my guests leftovers!' said he. We stayed with him two or three days while there was a rain from heaven, and he acted thus. When we wanted to continue traveling we left a hundred dinars for him in his house, told the woman, 'Apologize to him for us,' and left. It was well into the day when suddenly the man was with us, yelling from behind us, 'Stop, vile riders! You gave me a fee for my hospitality!' When he overtook us, he said, 'Take this, or I will pierce you with this lance of mine!' So we took it. He turned back, reciting,

> To accept a reward for what was given
> Would be sufficient insult to a giver!

I heard Abu Abd al-Rahman al-Sulami say that Abu Abd Allah al-Rudhbari went to the house of one of his students, but found him away, and the door of the house locked. "A Sufi, and his door is locked!" he exclaimed. "Break the lock!" So they broke the lock. He ordered that everything that was found on the premises be conveyed to the market, where they sold it, using the price for whatever was useful at the moment. Then they went and sat in the house. When the master of the place came back, he was incapable of speech. Next his wife came home wearing a cloak. She entered the house and threw down the cloak, saying, "Friends, this is also part of the household goods! Sell it!" "Why have you taken this upon yourself by your own choice?" her husband complained. "Hush!" said she. "A shaykh like this acts openly with us—if he judges against us, shall we keep something that we have withheld from him?"

Bishr ibn al-Harith said, "Even to look at a miser hardens the heart." Qays bin Sad bin Ubadah fell sick. He waited a long time for his brethren to come. He asked about them and was told, "They are ashamed because of the debts they owe you." "May God shame money that prevents brothers from visiting!" he cried. Then he ordered the town crier to proclaim, "Whoever owes a debt to Qays is free of it!" By evening his threshold was broken by the number of those who came to see him.

Abd Allah bin Jafar was told, "You lavish much when you are asked—but you won't ask the slightest thing from those to whom you have given!" "I give my money freely," he said, "but I'm stingy with my mind." Abd Allah bin Jafar went out to his country estate. He stopped by somebody's palm garden where a young black slave was working. When the boy got his food a dog came into the enclosure and approached him. The boy threw him a piece of bread and he ate it. Then he threw him a second, and a third, and the dog ate those too. Abd Allah bin Jafar watched this. "Young man, how much of your food meets this fate every day?" he asked. "As you see." "Why do you prefer this dog to yourself?" "This is not dog country," the boy said. "He must have come a great distance out of hunger, and I hate to turn him away." "And how do you fare the day?" "Today I will go hungry." "Am I scolded for too much generosity?" Abd Allah bin Jafar exclaimed. "This fellow is more generous than I am!" So he bought the youth, the garden and the tools that were in it, then freed the boy and gave it all to him.

A man went to his friend's house and knocked on the door. On coming out to him his friend asked, "For what have you come?" "I am in debt for four hundred dirhams." So the friend went into his house, counted out four hundred dirhams and brought them out to him. Then he went back into the house crying. "Why didn't you make some excuse if the request caused you difficulty?" his wife asked. He said, "I am only crying because I didn't pay any attention to his condition so that he found it necessary to speak to me about this."

Mutrif bin Sukhayr said, "When one of you wants something from me, write me a note, for I would hate to see the humiliation of need in your face."

A man wanted to do some harm to Abd Allah bin al-Abbas. He went to the dignitaries of the city and announced to them, "Ibn al-Abbas says to you, 'Come have dinner with me tomorrow!'" They all came, filling the house. "What is this?" he asked, and the thing was related to him. He immediately sent for fruit to be bought and ordered bread, hot dishes, and the matter was set right. When they were finished eating, he asked his retainers, "Do we have this available every day?" "Yes," they told him. "Then let all of these dine with us every day!" he said.

I heard Abu Abd al--Rahman al-Sulami say, "One day Abu Sahl al-Suluki was making ablutions in the courtyard of his house when a man came in and asked him for charity. He had nothing with him. "Be patient until I finish," he said. So the man waited. When Abu Sahl finished his ablutions he told him, "Take this water-bottle and go." The man took it and went. Abu Sahl waited until he knew the man was far away. Then he cried, "A man came and took the water-bottle!" So they walked after him but didn't catch up with him. He only did that because his family used to reproach him about how much he would give away. And I heard him say, "One winter Abu Sahl gave away his robe. He would wear a woman's robe when he went out to teach because he didn't have another. A delegation of notables arrived from Persia that included experts of every sort—leaders among lawyers, theologians, and grammarians. The army commander, Abu-l- Hasan, sent to him and ordered him to ride out to meet them. So he put on a cloak over that woman's robe and rode. 'He is scorning me before the whole country to ride in a woman's robe!' the commander said. But Abu Sahl engaged the lot of them in scholarly argument, and his discourse triumphed over the discourse of them all in every field. And I heard him say that Abu Sahl would not give anyone anything from his own hand. He would cast it on the ground so that the one who received it would pick it up from there. He used to say, 'This world is of too little importance that for its sake I should see my hand set over the hand of someone else.' The Prophet used to say, 'The hand that is above is better than the hand that is beneath.'"

Abu Marthad was the first of the generous. A poet composed a panegyric in praise of him. "I have nothing to give you," he said, "but take me before the judge and claim 10,000 dirhams. I will confess it.

Then have me cast into prison. My family will not let me stay in jail." So the poet did that, and before evening he was given 10,000 dirhams, and Abu Marthad went free.

A man asked alms of Hasan bin Ali bin Abu Talib. He gave him 50,000 dirhams and 500 dinars. "Bring a porter to carry it to you," he said. So the man brought a porter and al-Hasan gave him a head scarf, saying, "The porter's fee is on me."

A woman asked Layth bin Sad for a bowl of honey. He ordered a whole skein of honey for her. Asked about that, he said, "She asked according to the extent of her need, but we gave according to the extent of our charity."

A dervish said, "One morning I prayed in al-Ashath's mosque in Kufah. I was looking for a debtor of mine. When the final salutations of prescribed prayer were made, a suit of clothes and a pair of sandals were placed in front of everyone, and in front of me as well. 'What is this?' I asked, 'Al-Ashath has just returned from Mecca,' I was told, 'and he ordered this for the members of the congregation of his mosque.' 'But I only came looking for someone who owes me money!' I said. 'I don't belong to his congregation.' 'It is for everyone present,' they said."

When al-Shafii's death drew near, he said, "Get so-and-so to give me the funeral ablution." The man was away at the time of the death, but when he came back he was told about this request. So he called for al-Shafii's book of accounts and found outstanding against him a debt of seventy thousand dirhams. He paid it, saying, "This is my ablution for him."

It is said that when al-Shafii went to Mecca from Sana he was carrying 10,000 dinars. "Buy a property," people told him. But he struck a tent outside of Mecca and poured out the dinars, which he gave to everyone who came in to see him, by the handful. When the time of noon prescribed prayer came around, he stood up and tore the cloth of the moneybag, and not a thing remained.

Sari went out one holiday and was greeted by a man of importance. Sari gave him only a short salutation. "But this is a man of stature!" he was told. "I am aware of that," he said, "but it is related through a reliable transmission that when two Muslims meet a hundred mercies are divided between them and ninety go to the friendlier of the two. I wanted the greater number to go to him." The Commander of the Faithful Ali bin Abi Talib was crying one day. "Why are you weeping?" they asked him. "No guest has come to me for seven days," he replied, "and I am afraid that God Most High has scorned me." It is related that Anas bin Malik said, "The tithe of the house is that a room in it be used for hospitality."

In regard to the saying of the Most High, *"Has the account of the guests honored by Abraham reached you?"* (51:24), they are called honored because he attended upon them himself, and the guests of the generous are honored by generosity." Ibrahim ibn Junayd said, "It used to be said that there are four things a noble man must not hold himself above, even if he be a prince: rising from his place for his father, waiting upon his guest, serving the learned man who taught him, and asking about what he does not know."

Ibn Abbas commented about the saying of the Most High *"There is no sin upon you whether you eat together or separately"* (24:61), that the Companions used to be distressed when one of them ate by himself, and it was made easier for them by this revelation. Abd Allah bin Amir bin Kurayz offered hospitality to a man and entertained him very well. But when the man was leaving, Abd Allah did not send his servants to assist him. Asked about that, Abd Allah said, "They will not help anyone who leaves us." Abd Allah bin Bakawiya al-Sufi recited, saying that al-Mutanabbi recited to us about this:

If you leave those who have the means to keep you —
They are the ones who are leaving.

Abd Allah bin al-Mubarak said, "The generosity involved in relinquishing what is in human hands is greater than the generosity involved in giving freely."

A dervish said, "I went to see Bishr bin al-Harith on a day of extreme cold. He had taken off his clothes and was shivering. 'Abu Nasr,' I said, 'On a day like this people put on more clothes! Why have you removed them?' 'I thought of the poor and what this day is like for them,' he said. 'I do not have the means to help them, but I wanted myself to keep company with them in the cruelty of the cold.'"

I heard Abu Abd al-Rahman al-Sulami say[2] . . that al-Daqqaq said, "It is not generosity when the one who has, gives to the one who has nothing, but it is generosity when the one who has nothing gives to the one who has."

35 ON JEALOUSY (*GHAYRAH*)

God Most High has said, "*Say: My Lord has only forbidden inde* - *cencies—those of them which are evident and those which are hidden.*" (7:33).

Abu Bakr Muhammad bin Ahmad bin Abd al-Mazaki reported[1] . . . from Abd Allah bin Masud that the Messenger of God said, "No one is more jealous than God Most High and out of His jealousy he has forbidden indecencies—those of them which are evident and those which are hidden."

Ali bin Ahmad al-Ahwazi reported[2] . . . that Abu Hurayrah recounted the Messenger of God saying, "God is jealous and the believer is jealous. God Most High is jealous that the believing servant should approach that which God has forbidden him."

Ghayrah is an aversion against admitting the partnership of others (*al-ghayr*). When God, glory to Him, is described as possessing jealousy, it means that it does not please Him for anything else to share with Him in the obedience of the servant, which is due to Him alone.

It is related that the verse "*When the Koran is recited ,We set a veil as a covering between you and those who do not believe*" (17:45) was recited before Sari al-Saqati, Sari said to his companions, "Do you know what this veil is? It is the veil of jealousy, and there is no one more jealous than God Most High." The meaning of his saying, "It is the veil of jealousy" is that God does not make disbelievers privy to the understanding of the truth of religion.

Abu Ali al-Daqqaq said, "The people who are lazy in worshipping the Most High are those whose feet the Truth has bound with the shackles of spiritual failure. He has chosen for them to be distant from Him and delayed their reaching the place of closeness. Because of that, they delay their worship and service."

They recite:

I am enamored of the one I desire,
But my wiles are not for the evil eye of outsiders.

And with the same meaning they also say, "The sick one who is not healed is a seeker who is not sought."

I heard Abu Ali say that Abbas al-Zawzani said, "I had a good spiritual beginning and used to know how much distance remained between me and the attainment of my goal, the victory of my intention. One night in a dream it seemed to me that I was rolling down a mountain, though I wanted to arrive at its peak. I was saddened. Sleep overtook me, and I saw someone who said, 'O Abbas, the Truth does not want you to reach what you have been seeking. But He has opened wisdom for your tongue.' When morning came I received inspiration for wise words."

I heard Abu Ali say, "There was a shaykh who had a state and a moment with God Most High. For awhile he was hidden and not seen among the dervishes. When he reappeared after that, the moment that had once come upon him no longer did. He was questioned about it, and said, 'Alas, the veil has fallen!'"

Whenever something happened in the course of a spiritual gathering that disturbed the hearts of the participants, Abu Ali used to say, "This is from the jealousy of the Truth, glory to Him. He wished that whatever flowed from the purity of this moment should not flow upon them."

With this sense they recited:

She cared for our coming till she looked in the
     mirror.
Her lovely face forbade her such concern.
A Sufi was asked, "Do you want to see Him?"
"No."
"Why not?"
"I deem that beauty to be above the glance of the
     likes of me!"

They recited with this meaning:

I am envious of my glance at You
So I cast down my eyes when I look at You.

I see You pass proudly with all those qualities
That enthrall me, and I jealously guard You for You.

Shibli was asked, "When will you find rest?" "When I don't see anyone remembering Him!" he said.

I heard Abu Ali discuss the matter of a horseman who came to pledge himself to the Messenger of God. He spoke to him as if he did not recognize him. The Messenger of God spoke to him without identifying himself. "May God grant you long life!" said the bedouin. "Who are you?" The Prophet said, "A man of the Quraysh." One of the Companions present said to the bedouin, "It is enough suffering for you that you do not know your Prophet!"

Abu Ali used to say, "He only said 'A man of the Quraysh' out of jealousy, lest he be obliged to acquaint everybody with who he was. Then God, glory to Him, caused this identification to flow from the tongue of that Companion to the bedouin by his saying, "It is enough suffering for you that you do not know your Prophet!"

Some people say that jealousy is a trait of beginners, and that a person who truly affirms the unity bears no witness to jealousy and is not characterized by any preference. He has no authority to judge what takes place in the land. The Truth brings to pass what He requires, as He requires.

I heard Abu Abd al-Rahman al-Sulami say that Abu Uthman al-Maghribi said, "Jealousy is the work of students, not of those who know the realities." And I heard him say[3] . . . that Shibli said, "Jealousy is two jealousies: human jealousy, which is hard upon egos, and divine jealousy, which is hard upon hearts." Shibli also said, "Divine jealousy concerns the breaths lost on what is other than God Most High."

It is rightly said that jealousy is two jealousies: there is the Truth's jealousy of the servant that the servant should not give himself over to created things but withhold himself from them; and the servant's jealousy for the Truth, that he will not give over any of his states and breaths to what is not the Truth. One does not say, "I am jealous of God Most High," but one says, "I am jealous for God." To permit jealousy of God is ignorance that may lead to the abandonment of religion. But jealousy for God makes you hold His rights to be great and purifies your works for His sake.

Know that it is God's custom with His Friends that if they dwell upon what is other than Him or give their attention to something else or cleave to something else in their hearts, He will put that thing into disorder. For He is jealous that their hearts should again be purely His, devoid of whatever they dwelt upon or paid attention or clove to. Thus when Prophet Adam settled down to immortality in paradise, God drove him out of it. And when Prophet Abraham delighted in Prophet Ishmael, He ordered that the boy be sacrificed. But when Abraham took his son out of his heart *"and they both submitted and he threw him down on his forehead"* (37:103), and he had purified his inner being of him, God commanded the child's redemption by the substitution of the sacrificial ram.

I heard Abu Abd al--Rahman al-Sulami say that[4] . . . Muhammad bin Hassan said, "While I was wandering the mountains of Lebanon a man suddenly came across us—a young man, parched by the hot winds. When he saw me, he turned and ran. So I followed him, and asked, 'Give me some advice!' 'Beware!' he said to me. 'He is jealous and does not like seeing anything but Himself in the heart of His servant!'"

I heard Abu Abd al-Rahman say that Nasrabadhi said, "The Truth is jealous. Part of the jealousy is that He he has not left a road to Himself that is other than Himself." It is told that God, glory to Him, revealed to one of His prophets, "A certain person needs something of Me and I also need something from him. If he satisfies My need, I will satisfy his need."

In his private prayers that Prophet asked, "My God, how can it be that You have a need?" "His heart has dwelt upon something other than Me," God revealed. "Let him empty his heart of it and I will satisfy his need."

Abu Yazid al-Bistami dreamed of a gathering of the maidens of paradise and gazed upon them. For days he was stripped of his state. Then again he saw a group of them in his dreams. He refused to turn to them, saying, "You are distractions!"

Rabia-Adawiyyah fell sick. "What is the reason for your illness?" she was asked. "My heart looked toward paradise," she said, "and He has reprimanded me. Reproof belongs to Him. I shall not return to it."

It is related that Sari said, "For a long time I sought a man to be a friend. I was passing through some mountains and came upon a gathering of diseased, blind and ailing people. I asked what they were doing. They told me that once a year a man came out there, prayed for them, and they would be healed. So I waited for him to come. He prayed for them, and they were indeed cured. I followed after him and clung to him and told him, 'I have an inner sickness! What is the cure?' 'O Sari,' he said, 'get away from me! For the Most High is jealous to see you find rest in anything other than Him, and you will fall from His eye.'"

There are some Sufis whose jealousy is such that when they see people mentioning the Most High in unconsciousness they are unable to look at that and find it unbearable. I heard Abu Ali al-Daqqaq say, "When the bedouin entered the Prophet's mosque and urinated in it, the Companions fell upon him to throw him out. The bedouin had only displayed bad behavior, but embarrassment overcame the Companions and they were upset when they saw someone who had cast off all decency."

Thus the servant, when he knows the majesty of God's Omnipotence, finds it painful to hear the remembrance of someone who mentions Him in unconsciousness or to see the obedience of someone who does not serve Him with respect. It is related that Abu Bakr al-Shibli had a son by the name of Abu-l- Hasan who died. His mother, mourning for him, cut off her hair. Shibli went to the baths and shaved off his beard. Everyone who came to him to offer condolences would say, "O Abu Bakr, what is this?" "It is in sympathy with my wife," he would say. But one of them said to him, "Abu Bakr, tell me the real reason that you have done this."

"I knew," he said, "that they would come with their condolences, saying 'May God recompense you' in unconsciousness. So I sacrificed my beard as a ransom for their mentioning God unconsciously."

Nuri heard a man make the call to prescribed prayer and exclaimed, "Slander and deadly poison!" Then he heard a dog barking and cried, "At your service and pleasure!" "This is the abandonment of religion!" people said, "that he should say to a believer in his act of witness 'Slander and deadly poison,' and give the pilgrim's cry of service in reply to the barking of dogs!" Nuri was queried about this. He said, "As for that man, his remembrance of God was the very essence of unconsciousness, and as for the dog, God has said, *'There is nothing that does not glorify His praise'* (17:44)."

One time Shibli was making the call to prescribed prayer, and when he had completed the two acts of witness to the unity of God and the messengership of Muhammad, he said, "Were it not that You had commanded me, I would not mention together with You anyone other than You!"

A man heard another man use the common exclamation, "God is

greater!" He told him, "I wish you would hold Him to be greater than that!" I heard one of the dervishes say that Abu-l- Hasan al-Khazafani said, "There is no god but God" from the depths of the heart—"Muhammad is the Messenger of God" from the behind the earlobe!

Someone who looked at the outward aspect of this expression might imagine that it devalues the divine law. It is not the way that it might occur to him. But in reality, importance given to others is trivial in comparison with the omnipotence of the Truth.

36 ON SAINTHOOD (*WILAYAH*)

G od Most High said, *"The Friends of God—no fear is upon them, nor do they grieve"* (10:62).

Hamzah bin Yusuf al-Sahmi reported[1] . . . from Ayisha that the Prophet said that God Most High said, "Whoever harms a friend of Mine has declared war upon Me. The servant has no means to approach Me equal to the performance of what I have made his duty. The servant will not stop drawing close to me through voluntary devotions until I love him. I do not hesitate in anything that I do as I hesitate in taking the soul of My believing servant because he hates death, and I hate to trouble him, but it is necessary for him."

The word *wali*, "saint," "Friend of God," has two etymological senses. The first assigns the word the meaning of a passive participle. The *wali* is then the person of whose affairs God, glory to Him, takes charge. God Most High has said, *"He has charge over the doers of good"* (7:196). God does not leave such a person with his own ego for even a moment. He Himself takes care of him."

The second sense assigns the word the meaning of an intensive active participle. In this sense the *wali* takes the service and worship of God into his care, so that his service flows uninterruptedly without any disobedience intervening. Both of these descriptions are necessary for a *wali* to be truly a *wali*—his discharge of the rights due to God Most High through close study and full performance and God's continual protection of him in joy and sorrow. It is part of the definition of being a saint that one be protected, just as it is part of the definition of being a prophet that one be made incapable of sin. And anyone who objects to the statement that obedience to the religious law is required of a saint is mistaken and deceived.

I heard Abu Ali al-Daqqaq say that Abu Yazid al-Bistami went to see someone who had been described as a saint. When he arrived at the man's mosque, Abu Yazid sat and waited for him to come out. The man came out and spit in the direction of the mosque. Abu Yazid left without greeting him. "The man is not trustworthy regarding a point of behavior of the divine law," Abu Yazid said. "How shall he be trustworthy regarding the secrets of the Truth?"

The Sufis differ over whether or not it is possible for the saint to know he is a saint. Some of them say that is not possible. According to them, a saint looks upon himself with an eye that sees his own smallness. When any sort of miraculous grace appears to him, he is afraid that it may be a test of deception. He is constantly filled with fear—the fear of falling from where he is, of his end becoming the opposite of his current state. Those who take this position hold that one of the conditions of sainthood is the carrying out of one's duty until the end.

In this section many stories of the saints have been met with, and a countless number of Sufi shaykhs have held this opinion. If we were to occupy ourselves with recounting what they said, we would exceed the bounds of brevity. Of the shaykhs whom we have met personally, Abu Bakr bin Furak took this point of view.

Some Sufis say that it is possible for the saint to know he is a saint, and that carrying out one's duty to the end is not a condition for the actualization of sainthood now. Given that this faithfulness at death is a defining characteristic of sainthood, a saint might still be chosen by God for the grace of knowing that his final state is secure for we must admit the possibility of the miracles granted to the saints. No matter how the saint may fear his end, his actual state of awe, magnification, and glory is more effective and perfect. Hearts find more peace in a little bit of awe and glorification than in a lot of fear. And (if uncertainty about one's end is a necessity for sainthood), why did the Prophet say, "Ten of my Companions are in paradise?" The ten undoubtedly believed the Messenger of God spoke the truth and knew the safety of their end. That knowledge could not have nullified their state.

One of the conditions for a proper understanding of prophethood is an awareness of the nature of prophetic miracles. To know the reality of the special graces granted the saints is a part of this awareness. If a saint saw such graces manifested upon him, he would have to be able to distinguish between them and other sorts of events. And when he saw them, he would know that his current state was true. Therefore it is possible that he could know that in the end he would remain in the same condition, for the knowledge would be a grace granted to him, and to speak of the miraculous graces granted the saints is sound religion.

Many Sufi stories suggest this view is correct. We shall recount some of them in the section on the miracles of the saints, if God so wills. Among the shaykhs whom we have met, Abu Ali al-Daqqaq takes this point of view. Ibrahim bin Adham asked a man, "Would you like to be a Friend of God?" "Yes," he said. "Do not concern yourself with anything of this world or the next, but devote yourself to God Most High. Turn your face toward Him so that He will turn His face toward you and befriend you."

Yahya bin Muadh said, characterizing the saints, "They are servants who, after suffering, have been clothed in intimacy with God Most High and who have embraced ease after struggle through their attainment of the station of Friendship."

I heard Abu Abd al-Rahman al-Sulami say[2] . . . that Abu Yazid said, "The saints of God Most High are God's brides. Brides are not seen except by members of the family. They are secluded with Him behind the curtain of intimacy. They are not seen by anyone of this world or the next."

I heard Abu Bakr al-Saydalani, who was a righteous man, say, "Many times I rebuilt the marker at the grave of Abu Bakr al-Tamastani in the cemetery at Hira and wrote his name upon it. The marker was torn up and stolen! Nothing like that happened to any of the other graves. This astonished me so I asked Abu Ali al-Daqqaq about it one day. He said, "That shaykh preferred secrecy in this world. With the marker that you made, you wanted to make his grave known. The Truth, glory to Him, chose to hide his grave just as he had preferred to veil himself."

Abu Uthman al-Maghribi said, "The saint may be famous, but he is not dazzled." I heard Abu Abd al-Rahman al-Sulami say that al-Nasrabadhi said, "The saints ask for nothing—their state is only waning and extinction." He also heard him say, "The end of saintship is the beginning of prophethood."

Sahl bin Abd Allah said, "The saint is he whose acts are continuously in harmony with God's will." Yahya bin Muadh said, "The saint does not act for show and is not a hypocrite. There are so few friends with such character!"

Abu Ali al-Juzjani said, "The saint has passed away from his own state and abides in the contemplation of the Truth. God takes charge of the governance of his life, and the lights of this care continuously fall upon him. He possesses no information about himself and no home with what is other than God."

Abu Yazid said, "The worldly destinies assigned the saints, together with their explanations, come from four divine Names. The support of every party of them derives from one of these four. They are: 'the First,' 'the Last,' 'the Outer,' 'the Inner.' When a saint passes away from these after having known them intimately, he is perfect and complete. Whoever draws a share from God's Name 'the Outer' takes as his portion the wonders of divine Omnipotence. Whoever draws a share from God's Name 'the Inner' takes as his portion the divine lights that shine upon souls. Whoever draws a share from God's Name 'the First' is occupied with what preceded Creation, and whoever draws a share from God's Name 'the Last' has been stationed with what will come to pass. Each receives knowledge according to what he can bear, except the one of whom the Truth, in His goodness, has taken charge. That one He supports through Himself."

This saying of Abu Yazid's points to the elite of God's servants who have progressed beyond these categories. There are no consequences for them to remember, no origins for them to think upon, no calamities for them to be captured by. Thus those who have entered into the truth are erased from the qualities of created beings. As God Most High has said, *"You would reckon them awake, while they are asleep"* (18:17).

Yahya bin Muadh said, "The saint is the sweet herb of God Most High in the earth. The truthful smell him and his fragrance reaches their hearts so that they yearn for their Lord and increase their worship according to their different characters."

Al-Wasiti was asked, "How is the saint nourished in his sainthood?" He said, "In the beginning, through his devotions. In his maturity, through God's concealing the graces He has bestowed upon him. Then God draws him to the qualities and attributes destined for him and makes him taste the pleasure of living every moment for God's sake."

It is said that the saint has three signs: he is occupied with God, he flees to God, and he cares for God. Al-Kharraz said, "When God Most High wants to befriend one of His servants, He opens for him the door of His remembrance. When remembrance gives him delight, He opens for him the door of closeness and in that way raises him to the circles of intimacy. Then he seats him upon the throne of the recognition of unity. Then removes the veil from him and causes him to enter the house of singularity. Then He reveals to him the divine Majesty and Grandeur. When his sight rests upon that Majesty and Grandeur, he loses himself. At that time the servant becomes crippled, annihilated, and falls under the protection of God, and he is freed from the pretenses of his ego."

I heard Muhammad bin al-Husayn say[3] . . . that Abu Turab al-Nakhshabi said, "When the heart is fond of turning away from God, its speech is the vilification of the Friends of God."

The Sufis say that one of the traits of the saint is that he has no fear. Fear is the anticipation of something hated coming about in the future or the anxiety that something liked will pass away in the future, but the saint is the son of his moment. He has no future that he should be fearful of anything. And just as he has no fear ,he has no hope because hope is the expectation that something liked will come about or that something hated will be taken away, and that also refers to a second moment. Thus also he has no grief, for grief comes of the difficulty of the heart. Someone who is in the radiance of contentment and the soothing coolness of harmony with the divine will—how should he grieve? God Most High has said, "The Friends of God—no fear is upon them, nor do they grieve."

37 ON SUPPLICATION (*DUA*)

G od Most High said, *"Call upon your Lord humbly and secretly"* (7:55), and He said, *"Your Lord says, 'Call upon Me; I will answer you"* (40:60).

Abu Ali bin Ahmad bin Abdan reported[1] . . . from Anas bin Malik that the Messenger of God said, "Supplication is the core of worship." *Dua*, supplication, is the key of need, the comforter of the distressed, the refuge of the destitute, the breath of relief for those who are in want. God Glorious and Exalted has condemned a people who abandoned such prayer, saying *"And they close their hands"* (9:67)—that is, "They do not stretch them toward Us, asking." Sahl bin Abd Allah al-Tustari said, "God Most High created the Creation and said, 'Confide in Me, and if you do not, then look toward Me, and if you do not, then listen to Me, and if you do not, then be at My door, and if you are not, then lay upon Me what you need of Me.'"

I heard Abu Ali al-Daqqaq say that Sahl bin Abd Allah said, "The prayer that is closest to being answered is the prayer expressed in one's state. 'The prayer expressed in one's state,' means that the one who prays is in absolute need and has no other recourse.

I heard Hamzah bin Yusuf al-Sahmi say that Abu Abd Allah al-Makanisi said he was with Junayd when a woman came to them and said, "Pray to God that He return my son to me. I have a son who is lost." "Go away, and be patient," he said. She left. Again she came back and said the same thing to him. "Go away and be patient," Junayd told her. So she went away but later came back. She did this many times, while Junayd said to her, "Be patient." Finally she said to him, "Enough of patience! I have no more capacity for it. Pray for me!" "If things are as you say," Junayd said, "then go home. Your son has returned." So she left and found him. Later she came back to thank the shaykh. "How did you know that?" they asked Junayd. Said he: "God Most High said, *'Or, Who answers the distressed one when he calls upon Him, and removes the evil . . . ?' (27:62)."*

People differ over whether it is better to ask things in prayer or to keep silent and be satisfied with one's lot. Some say that to ask is in itself an act of worship—the Prophet said "Supplication is the core of worship"—and to perform an act of worship is better than to abandon it. Moreover, supplication is the right of God Most High over His servants. Even if God does not accept the servant's supplications and the servant does not receive the thing he wants, still he is performing his duty in rendering the right of his Lord. For supplication is the manifestation of the need proper to servanthood. Abu Hazim al-Araj said, "Being forbidden to ask would be harder on me than being refused an answer."

Another party says that silence and indifference to whatever happens is the more perfect course, and that satisfaction with what God has already chosen is superior. Thus al-Wasiti said, "To prefer what has been coming to you since before time began is better for you than to resist what is happening now. The Prophet gave news that God Most High said, 'If My remembrance distracts someone from asking things of Me, I will give him more than I give those who ask.'"

Yet another group says that the servant should have supplication on his tongue and satisfaction in his heart so that he brings both sides of matter together.

The best opinion is that situations vary. In some states supplication is better than silence so that supplication is the best behavior, while in other states silence is better than supplication so that silence is the best behavior. This is something that can only be understood in the moment, for the knowledge of the moment only comes to exist in that moment. If someone finds an indication for supplication in his heart, then supplication is most suitable for him. If he finds there an indication for silence, then silence is most suitable for him.

It is correctly said that the servant must not forget to look to his Lord when he supplicates. Then he must observe his own state. If he finds that the supplication is increasing the openness of his heart, supplication is better for him. But if something like a rebuke or a tightening comes over his heart at the moment of supplication, then it is better for him to give up the petition at that time. If he finds neither an increase of openness nor the occurrence of a rebuke, then supplicating or giving it up are at that point alike. If the thing that governs him at that moment is religious knowledge, then supplication is better because of its being an act of worship. If the thing that governs him at that moment is divine realization and spiritual state and silence, then silence is better.

It is correctly said that in the case of things that are the rightful lot of a Muslim or that involve some service to the Truth, asking is better. When supplication involves asking something for one's lower self, silence is more perfect.

According to a transmitted hadith, "When a servant is supplicating God and God loves that servant, He says, 'O Gabriel, delay My servant's need, for I love to hear his voice.' And when a servant is supplicating God and God is angry at that servant, He says, 'O Gabriel, satisfy My servant's need, for I hate to hear his voice!'"

It is related that Yahya bin Said al-Qattan saw the Truth, glory to Him, in a dream and said, "My God, how often have I supplicated You and You have not answered me!" He said, "O Yahya, it is because I love to hear your voice."

The Prophet said, "By Him in Whose hand is my life, the servant will supplicate God Most High while God is angry with him, and God will turn away from him. Again he will supplicate, and God will turn away and again he will supplicate, and God will turn away. Then again he will supplicate, and God Most High will say to the angels, 'My servant refuses to call upon anything other than Me so I have answered him.'"

Abu-l-Husayn Ali bin Muhammad bin Abd Allah bin Bushran of Baghdad reported[2] . . . from Anas bin Malik, "There was a man who had made an arrangement with the Messenger of God to trade between Damascus and Medina and between Medina and Damascus. Placing his trust in God Almighty and Glorious, he would not have the caravans accompanied by guards. He said that he was coming from Damascus intending to go to Medina when suddenly a brigand on horseback appeared and shouted, 'Halt, halt!' So the merchant stopped and said to him, "Your business is with my property so let me go free.' 'The property is my property anyway,' said the brigand. 'I want your life!' 'What do you want with my life?' the merchant asked him. 'Your business is the merchandise. Let me go free!' But the brigand replied to him with the same speech as before. So the merchant said, 'Wait until I perform ablution and a prescribed prayer and call upon my Lord.' 'Do what has occurred to you,' said the thief. So the merchant stood up, performed ablution and offered four cycles of prescribed prayer. Then he raised his hands to heaven and said in his supplication, "O Loving One, O Loving One, O Owner of the Glorious Throne, Beginner of things and Returner of everything to its proper state, constant Doer of what He wills—I ask You through the light of Your Countenance that floods the pillars of Your Throne, through Your Omnipotence by which You have total power over Your Creation, and through Your Mercy which encompasses everything—there is no god but You—O Granter of help, help me! (three times).' When he had finished his prayer, suddenly there appeared a rider upon a grey horse wearing green garments and holding in his hand a spear of light! When the thief saw the rider, he left the merchant and began to edge toward him. But when he had drawn close, the horseman charged the thief and pierced him with a stab that threw him away from his horse. Then he came to the merchant and said, 'Rise and kill him!' 'Who are you?' the merchant asked him. 'I never killed anyone in my life, and his death is not sweet to me!' The rider went up to the brigand and killed him. Then he came to the merchant and said, 'Know that I am an angel of the third heaven. When you prayed the first time, we heard the doors of heaven shake and said, "Something is happening!" When you prayed the second time, the doors of heaven opened with sparks like flames of fire. Then when you prayed the third time, Gabriel descended to us from the height of heaven and cried, 'Who is for this man in distress?' Then I prayed to my Lord that He assign me to kill the one who threatened you. And know, O Servant of God, that whoever offers this supplication of yours in any difficulty, any danger, any calamity, God Most High will liberate him from it and help him.' So the merchant proceeded safe and sound until he entered Medina, where he went to the Prophet, told him the story and told him the supplication. The Prophet said to him, 'God Almighty and Glorious has instilled in you those Beautiful Names of His which, when you call upon Him by them, He answers, and when you ask of Him by them, He gives.'"

Part of the conduct proper to supplication is presence of heart—that you are not inattentive while you supplicate. It is related that the Prophet said, "God Most High will not answer the supplication of a servant whose heart is heedless."

Another one of the conditions of supplication is that your food be lawful. The Prophet said to Sad, "Earn your livelihood lawfully so that your supplication will be answered." It has been said that supplication is the key of need, and the teeth of that key are lawful morsels.

Yahya bin Muadh used to supplicate, "My God, how can I supplicate You while I am disobedient? And how can I not supplicate You while You are the Generous One?"

Prophet Moses passed by a man who was supplicating and imploring. "My God," Prophet Moses said, "If his need were in my hand, I would satisfy it!" God Most High revealed to him, "I am more compassionate toward him than you are, but he has a herd of sheep, and while he is calling upon Me, his heart is with his sheep! I do not answer a servant who calls upon Me while his heart is with something else." So Prophet Moses recounted this to the man, who then devoted his heart completely to God Most High and his need was satisfied. Someone asked Jafar al-Sadiq, "Why is it that when we supplicate we are not answered?" "Because you are calling upon someone whom you do not know!" he said.

I heard Abu Ali al-Daqqaq say, "An illness appeared in Yaqub bin al-Layth for which the physicians could find no cure. They told him, 'In your domain is a righteous man named Sahl bin Abd Allah al-Tustari. If he supplicates for you, perhaps God will answer him." So he summoned Sahl and said, "Supplicate God Almighty and Glorious for me." "And how will he answer my prayer on your behalf," said Sahl, "while the victims of oppression are in your prisons?" Yaqub freed everyone whom he was holding. Sahl prayed, "My God, as You have shown him the humiliation of disobedience, show him also the dignity of obedience and remove this from him." And he was cured. Yaqub sent money to Sahl, but Sahl refused to accept it. "Why didn't you take it and distribute it among the dervishes?" he was asked. He looked toward some desert pebbles. Suddenly they were jewels! "Does someone who has been granted the likes of this," he asked his companions, "stand in need of the money of Yaqub bin al-Layth?"

Salih al-Murri often would say, "Someone who applies himself to knocking at the door is on the verge of having it opened." Rabia asked him, "How long are you going to keep on saying this? When has the door ever been closed that one needs to seek for it to be opened?" "An ignorant shaykh," said Salih, "and a woman who knows!"

I heard Abu Abd al-Rahman al-Sulami say[3] . . . that Sari al-Saqati said, "I was present at one of Maruf al-Karkhi's meetings when a man stood up and said, 'Abu Mahfuz, pray to God Most High that my purse be returned to me! It was stolen, and there were 1,000 dinars in it!'" Maruf was silent. The man reiterated what he had said. Maruf remained silent, and the man repeated it again. Finally Maruf said, "What shall I say? Shall I say, 'That which You have removed from Your prophets and sincere friends, give it back to him?'" "Just supplicate God Most High for me!" the man said. Maruf supplicated, "O God, give him whatever is good for him."

It is related that al-Layth said, "I saw Uqbah bin Nafi blind and later I saw him with his vision. 'By what means did God return your sight?' I asked him. 'A visitation in my dreams,' he told me. 'It was said, "Say: O Near One, O Answerer, O Hearer of prayers, O You Who are Gracious toward what You will, restore to me my sight!" I said it and God Glorious and Exalted gave me back my vision.'"

I heard Abu Ali al-Daqqaq say, "When I first returned to Nishapur from Merv, I developed pain in my eyes. For a period of some days I could not sleep. One morning I was lying awake when I heard a voice say to me, *'Isn't God sufficient for His servants?'* (39:36). So I understood and the inflammation left me. The pain immediately disappeared. Pain in my eyes has not troubled me since then."

It is related that Muhammad bin Khuzaymah said, "When Ahmad bin Hanbal died, I was in Alexandria. I was grieved. Then I saw him in a dream. He was strutting! 'O Abu Abd Allah,' I said, 'What kind of a bearing is this?' 'It is the bearing of the servants in the House of Peace,' said he. 'What has God Glorious and Exalted done with you?' I asked. 'He forgave me, set a crown on my head, sandals of gold on my feet and said, "Ahmad, this is for saying that the Quran is My speech." Then He said, "Ahmad, call upon Me with those supplications that came to you from Sufyan al-Thawri and that you used to supplicate with in the lower world." So I supplicated, 'O Lord of everything, by Your power over everything, forgive me everything and don't ask me about anything!' "O Ahmad," He said, "this is paradise. Enter it!" So I went in.'"

A young man clung to the drapery of the Kabah and said, "My God, You have no partner to influence You nor any minister to be bribed. If I have obeyed You, it is through Your grace, and the praise belongs to You. If I have disobeyed You, it is through my ignorance, and the argument against me is Yours. For the sureness of Your argument against me and the disruption of my argument before You, there is no help but that You forgive me!" A voice from nowhere was heard to say, "The noble youth is freed from the fire!"

It is said that the point of supplication is that it manifests need before the Most High. Otherwise, the Lord does what He wills. The supplication of ordinary people, it is said, is made with words. The supplication of ascetics is made with actions. The supplication of the gnostics is made with states. The best supplication is that which provokes sadness.

A Sufi said, "If you ask God Most High for something you need and it comes easily, then ask Him after that for paradise. Maybe it is your day to be answered!" The tongues of novices, it is said, utter supplications, but the tongues of the gnostics are mute.

Al-Wasiti was asked to supplicate. He said, "I am afraid that if I supplicate, I will be told, 'You have asked Us for what was already yours according to Us. You have doubted Us!' Or else, 'You have asked Us for what does not belong to you, according to Us. You have behaved badly toward Us! If you had remained content, in time We would have brought things to pass so that you would have been satisfied.'"

It is reported that Abd Allah bin Munazil said, "For fifty years I have asked nothing in supplication, nor have I wanted anyone to supplicate for me." Supplication, it is said, is the ladder of sinners. Supplication is communication. As long as communication continues, the business is still beautiful.

It is said that the tongue of sinners is their supplications. I heard Abu Ali al-Daqqaq say, "When the sinner cries, he is in contact with God Glorious and Exalted." And with this sense they recited:

The tears of the youth spell out what he has hidden,
And his sighs show forth what his heart conceals.
A Sufi said, "Prayer is to give up sinning."
Prayer is the voice of yearning for the Beloved.
Permission to pray is better for the servant than
          receiving the gift.

Al-Kattani said, "God Most High never opens the tongue of the believer to ask for pardon without opening also the door of forgiveness."

It is said that supplication makes one be present with God, while receiving the gift makes one go away. To stand at the door is more perfect than to go elsewhere. Supplication is to speak personally to the Truth with the tongue of shame. The prerequisite of asking in supplication is to abide with God's destiny in contentment. How can you be waiting for an answer to your supplication when you have blocked its road with sin? Someone asked a dervish, "Supplicate for me." He replied, "It is enough foreignness to your Lord that you set a mediator between yourself and Him!"

I heard Hamzah bin Yusuf al-Sahmi say that[4] . . Abd al-Rahman bin Ahmad said, "A woman came to Taqi bin Mukhallad and said, 'My son has been captured by the Byzantines. My only property is a little house that I cannot sell. Could you direct me to someone who would ransom him with something? I know neither day nor night, sleep nor rest!' 'Yes,' he told her. 'Go back home until I look into his affairs, God willing.' The shaykh bowed his head, and his lips moved. We waited some time. The woman came back, and with her was her son. She began to pray for the shaykh, and said, 'My son has returned safe and sound, and he has a story to tell you.' Her son said, 'I was in the hands of one of the Byzantine kings together with a group of other prisoners. He had a man who would set us to work every day. He used to send us out into the desert to labor and then bring us back. We were in chains. While we were leaving work after sunset with the official who would oversee us, the shackle on my foot opened and fell onto the ground. He described the day and hour, and it agreed with the time when the woman had come to us and the shaykh had prayed. So the overseer pounced on me and yelled at me, 'You have broken the chain!' 'No,' I told him. 'It fell from my foot.' He was amazed and summoned his companion. They summoned the blacksmith, who set a new shackle on me. But when I walked a few steps, it fell from my foot again. They were astounded by the affair so they called their monks. 'Do you have a mother?' they asked me. 'Yes,' I said. 'Her supplication has attained an answer and God Almighty and Glorious has set you free,' they said. 'It is not possible for us to keep you captive.' So they provisioned me and sent to accompany me someone who could lead me to the borders of the Muslims.'"

38 ON SPIRITUAL POVERTY (*FAQR*)

God Most High has said, "*Charity is for the poor who are con -fined in the way of God. They cannot go about in the land. The ignorant man thinks them to be rich on account of their abstaining from begging. You can recognize them by their mark—they beg not of people importunately. And whatever good thing you spend, surely God is Knower of it*" (2:273).

Abu Abd Allah al-Husayn bin Shuja bin al-Husayn bin Musa al-Bazzaz in Baghdad reported[1] . . through Abu Hurayrah from the Prophet, "The poor will enter paradise 500 years before the rich: that is half a celestial day."

Abu Bakr Muhammad bin Ahmad bin Abd al-Hiri reported in Baghdad[2] . . . from Abd Allah, "The Messenger of God said, 'The utterly poor one is not the one who goes from door to door for a morsel or two, or a date or two.' 'Who is the utterly poor one, O Messenger of God?' they asked. 'The one who cannot find what would free him of need and who is ashamed to beg from people so no one notices him to give him alms.'"

The meaning of his saying, "They are ashamed to beg from people" is that they are ashamed before God Most High, not ashamed before the people. Poverty is the badge of the saints, the adornment of the pure, and the state the Truth chooses for His elect among the pious and the prophets. The poor are the cream of God's servants, the repositories of His secrets amidst His creation. Through them the Truth maintains the creation, and by the strength of blessing they accumulate He expands its sustenance.

According to the report that has reached us from the Prophet, on the day of judgment, the poor who are full of patience will be the close companions of God Most High. Abu Abd al-Rahman al-Sulami reported[3] . . . from Umar bin al-Khattab that the Messenger of God said, "Everything has a key. The key of paradise is the love of the wretched and the patient poor. They will be the close companions of God Most

High on the day of judgment."

A man gave Ibrahim bin Adham 10,000 dirhams, but he refused to accept them. "You want to erase my name from the register of the poor with 10,000 dirhams!" he exclaimed. "I won't have it!" Muadh al-Nasfi said, "God Most High will not destroy a people, even though they continue in their evil practices, as long as they do not humiliate and abase the poor."

If the poor man had no merit beyond his wish and desire that God should grant abundance to Muslims and that prices should be low— because he needs to buy while the rich man needs to sell—it would be enough for him. Such are the common run of the poor. What then must be the state of their elect?

I heard Abu Abd al-Rahman al-Sulami say[4]. . . that when Yahya bin Muadh was asked about poverty, he said, "Its essence is that the servant is not enriched except by God, and its form is the lack of all means whatsoever." And I heard him say[5] . . . that Ibrahim al-Qassar said, "Poverty is a gown bequeathed by satisfaction in God when the servant has made that a reality." A poor dervish arrived from Zuzan to see Abu Ali al-Daqqaq in the year 394 or 395 AH (1004 or 1005 AD). He was wearing a worn-out haircloth robe and a haircloth hat. Jokingly, one of the company asked him, "How much did you pay for that robe?" "I bought it for the price of this world," he said, "and I have been offered the next world for it—but I wouldn't sell!"

I heard Abu Ali al-Daqqaq say, "A poor dervish stood up in a Sufi gathering to ask for charity. 'I have gone hungry for three days,' said he. A shaykh who was there called out, 'You lie! Poverty is God's secret. He is not going to entrust His secret to somebody who will carry it to anyone he feels like!'

I heard Muhammad bin al-Husayn say[6] . . . that Hamdun al-Qassar said, "When satan and his armies get together, nothing makes them happier than three things: a believing man who has killed another believer, a man who dies in unbelief, and a heart in which there is fear of poverty. And I heard him say[7] . . . that Junayd said, "O company of the poor! You know God. You give honor to God—see how you will fare with God when you are alone with Him!"

I heard Abu Abd al--Rahman al-Sulami say[8]. . . that Junayd was asked which is more perfect, the state of being in need of God or the state of being enriched by Him. He said, "If the state of poverty before God is sound, if the state of wealth through God is sound, and if wealth through God is properly the perfection of independence from the world that He grants, then it cannot be asked, 'Which is more perfect, poverty or wealth!' For these are two states neither of which is complete without the other." And I heard him say[9] . . . that Ruwaym, when asked about the quality of the poor dervish, said, "Giving oneself over to the decisions of God Most High." It is said that the character of the poor dervish is three things: protecting his secret, performing his obligations, and guarding his poverty.

Abu Said al-Kharraz was asked, "What keeps the kindness of the rich from reaching the poor?" He answered, "Either that which is in the hands of the rich is not good or God has not accepted them for service or the poor have been intended for trial."

It is told that God Almighty and Glorious revealed to Prophet Moses, "When you see the poor, inquire after them as you inquire after the rich. If you will not do it, then put everything that I have taught you under the dust!"

It is related that Abu Darda said, "I would rather fall from the top of a castle and be shattered to bits than to sit with wealth. For I heard the Messenger of God say, 'Beware of sitting with the dead!' And when it was asked, 'O Messenger of God, who are the dead?' he said, 'The rich.'"

They complained to Rabi bin Haytham, "The prices have gone beyond bounds!" "We are too insignificant to God that he should make us go hungry," he replied. "It is only His friends that He keeps hungry." Ibrahim bin Adham said, "We sought poverty and met with riches. Most people seek riches and meet with poverty."

I heard Muhammad bin al-Husayn say[10] . . . that al-Husayn bin Ulluyah said that Yahya bin Muadh was asked, "What is poverty?" He answered, "Fear of poverty." He was asked, "What is wealth?" He answered, "Security coming from God Most High."

And I heard him say[11] . . . that Ibn al-Karini said, "The genuine poor man is on guard against wealth for fear that wealth will overtake him and spoil his poverty, just as the rich man is on guard against poverty for fear that it will overtake him and spoil his wealth." Abu Hafs was asked, "With what does the poor man approach his Lord?" He said, "The poor man has nothing with which to approach his Lord except his poverty."

God Most High revealed to Prophet Moses, "Would you like to have the equivalent of all the good deeds of all of humanity together on the day of judgment?" "Yes!" said he. "Visit the sick and rid the clothes of the poor of lice!" So Prophet Moses established for himself a week every month to circulate among the poor, cleanse their clothes of lice and visit the sick.

Sahl bin Abd Allah al-Tustari said, "Five things come from the essence of the self: a poor person who appears rich, a hungry person who appears satisfied, the sad who appear happy, a man who is at enmity with another man but shows him affection, and a man who fasts during the day and supplicates during the night without showing weakness!" Bishr ibn al-Harith said, "The best of stations is to hold firmly to patience in poverty until the grave." Dhu-l--Nun said, "The sign of God's displeasure with His servant is the servant's fear of poverty."

Shibli said, "The lowliest sign of true poverty is this: if someone owned the whole world and spent it in a day and then thought, 'I should have kept one day's sustenance!' —his poverty would not be genuine."

I heard Abu Ali al-Daqqaq say, "People talk about poverty and wealth. They ask which of the two is better? As far as I am concerned, the best thing is for a person to be given what is sufficient to him and then be preserved in it."

I heard Muhammad bin al-Husayn say[12] . . . that Abu Muhammad bin Ya Sin said that Ibn al-Jalla was asked about poverty. He remained silent until he had gone off by himself and then shortly returned. He said, "I had four pennies on me and I was ashamed before God Almighty and Glorious to speak on poverty. So I went and got rid of them." Then he sat down and talked about poverty. And I heard him say[13] . . . that Ibrahim bin al-Muwallid said that he asked Ibn al-Jalla, "When does the dervish become worthy to be called poor?" He said, "When no remnant of poverty remains." "How is that?" I asked again. "If a dervish possesses poverty, he is not poor. When poverty does not belong to him, he is truly poor."

Poverty is sound, it is said, when the poor man seeks no wealth but in the One of whom he is in need. Abd Allah bin al-Mubarak said, "To appear rich while being poor is better than poverty."

I heard Muhammad bin Abd Allah al-Sufi say[14] . . . that Bunnan al-Misri said, "I was sitting across from a young man in Mecca when a fellow came and brought the youth a purse of dirhams, setting it down in front of him. 'I have no need of it,' he said. 'Distribute it among the poor.' Yet when evening came I saw him in the valley searching for something to eat. 'If only you had left yourself something out of what you had,' I said. 'But I didn't know that I would live until this moment!' said he."

I heard Abu Abd al-Rahman al-Sulami say[15] . . . that Abu Hafs said, "The best connection between the servant and his Lord is to be in continuous need of Him in all circumstances, to attach oneself to the Sunnah in all acts, and to seek one's livelihood in a lawful way." And I heard him say[16] . . . that al-Murtaish said, "The poor dervish's aspiration must not run ahead of where he sets his feet." And I heard him say[17] . . . that Abu Ali al-Rudhbari said, "In their time, they were four."

One would not accept anything from the brethren or from the sultan. That was Yusuf bin Asbat, who inherited 70,000 dirhams from his father and did not take a thing from it, but used to work with his hands, weaving palm leaves. Another would receive from brethren and the sultan both. That was Abu Ishaq al-Fazari. What he would get from the brethren he would distribute among contemplatives who had withdrawn from the world, and what he got from the sultan he would give out to the needy of the people of Tarsus. The third would take from the brethren but not from the sultan. That was Abd Allah bin al-Mubarak, who used to accept things from the brothers and give things in return. The fourth used to take from the sultan but not from the brethren. That was Mukhallid bin al-Husayn. He used to say, "The sultan is not doing a favor, but the brothers would be doing a favor."

I heard Abu Ali al-Daqqaq say, "It has come in a hadith, 'Whoever humbles himself to a rich man on account of his wealth has lost two-thirds of his religion.'" It is like that because a man is heart, tongue and ego. When he has humbled his tongue and his ego before a rich man, two-thirds of his religion have gone. If he were to believe in that man's superiority in his heart as he abased himself in ego and tongue, all of his religion would have left.'"

It is said, "The poor man in his poverty should hold on to at least four things: a knowledge that governs him, a scrupulousness that restrains him, a certainty that carries him, and a remembrance that makes him intimate with his Lord." Whoever wants poverty because of the nobility of poverty dies a poor man, but whoever wants poverty so that he may occupy himself with God Most High dies rich. Al-Muzayyin said, "The roads reaching to God were more than the stars of the sky and not one of them remains except the road of poverty, the soundest road."

I heard Muhammad bin al-Husayn say[18] . . that Nuri said, "The poor dervish's quality is to keep silent when he has nothing and to give to others when he has something." And I heard him say[19]. . . that when asked about the essence of poverty, Shibli said, "It is that the servant is not enriched by anything except God Almighty and Glorious." And I heard him say that Mansur bin Khalaf al-Maghribi said that Abu Sahl al-Khashshab al-Kabir said to him, "Poverty: poverty and abasement." He said, "No, rather poverty and honor." Mansur said, "Poverty and the dust." He said, "No, rather poverty and a throne."

I heard Abu Ali al-Daqqaq say, "I was asked about the meaning of the saying of the Prophet, 'Poverty is close to unbelief.' I answered thus, 'The ruination and opposite of a thing is commensurate with its virtue and scope. The more it is in itself excellent, the more its ruination and opposite are defective. Thus with faith—since it is the noblest of personal qualities, its opposite is the worst, unbelief. And since the danger attached to poverty is disbelief in God, this indicates that it is the noblest of conditions.'"

I heard Abu Abd al-Rahman al-Sulami say[20] . . . that al-Murtaish said that Junayd said, "When you encounter a poor dervish, show him kindness. Do not show him your knowledge because kindness makes him intimate with you, but knowledge will make him a stranger." "Abu-l- Qasim," I asked him, "Is the poor dervish then alienated by knowledge?" "Yes," he told me. "If the poor one is sincere in his poverty and you set your knowledge before him, it will melt just as lead melts in a fire." And I heard him say that[21]. . . Muzaffar al-Qirmisini said. "The poor one is he who has no need of God."

Abu-l-Qasim said, "This expression contains the deepest mystery for someone who hears it without awareness of the aim of the Sufis. The speaker is only alluding to the falling away of all objects of desire, the absence of individual choice, and satisfaction with whatever the Truth, glory to Him, might send."

Ibn Khafif said, "Poverty is lack of possessions and exiting the realm controlled by attributes." Abu Hafs said, "Poverty is not appropriate for anybody until giving is dearer to him than receiving. It is not generosity for someone who has to give to someone who lacks. It is only generosity for someone who lacks to give to someone who has."

I heard Muhammad bin al-Husayn say[22]. . . that Ibn al-Jalla said, "If humility were not an honor due to God, it would be the right of the poor dervish to swagger when he walks." Yusuf bin Asbat said, "For forty years I have not owned anything except two shirts."

A Sufi said, "I had a vision that the day of judgment had come. It was announced, 'Malik bin Dinar and Muhammad bin Wasi, enter paradise!' I looked to see which of them would go first, and it was Muhammad ibn Wasi who preceded. I asked the cause of his precedence and was told, 'It is because he had one shirt, and Malik had two!'"

Muhammad al-Musuhi said, "The poor dervish is he who does not see himself as in need of means." Sahl bin Abd Allah was asked, "When will the poor dervish find rest?" He replied, "When he cannot visualize for himself any other moment than the one he is in."

People were discussing wealth and poverty before Yahya bin Muadh. He commented, "Neither poverty nor wealth will be weighed tomorrow, only patience and gratitude. It is said, 'Be thankful and be patient.'"

It is told that God Most High revealed to one of the prophets, "If you want to know the degree of My satisfaction with you, look at how far the poor are satisfied with you." Abu Bakr al-Zaqqaq said, "Whoever is not accompanied by the fear of God in his poverty eats what is totally unlawful." In the gatherings of Sufyan al-Thawri, it is said, the poor were treated like princes.

I heard Abu Abd al-Rahman al-Sulami say[23] . . . that Abu Bakr bin Tahir said, "One of the principles of the poor dervish is that he should have no desire for this world. And if he does, if it is inescapable, then his desire must not exceed what is sufficient for him."

Abu Abd al-Rahman al-Sulami recited what[24]. . . Ahmad bin Ata recited to some dervishes, "They ask, 'Tomorrow is a holiday. What will you wear?' I say, 'The robe of honor of a cupbearer whose love is deep draughts.'"

> Poverty and patience—these are my two garments.
>   Under them is a heart
> That sees its darling holidays and days of prayer.
> The most fitting apparel is that given by the Beloved
> On the day of visitations, in garments that are robes
>   of honor!
> If You are not there, my hope, all life is just
>   mourning
> A holiday when You are not mine is merely an event.
>   (It is said that these are verses of Abu Ali al-
>   Rudhbari.)

When questioned about the genuine poor one, Abu Bakr al-Misri said, "One who does not possess and is not so inclined." Dhu-l- Nun al-Misri said, "Continual need of God, though one mixes with the world, is dearer to me than continual purity together with spiritual pride." I heard Abu Abd Allah al-Shirazi say[25] . . . that Abu Abd Allah al-Husri said, "For twenty years Abu Jafar al-Haddad worked each day for one dinar, distributed it to the poor, and fasted. Between sunset and night prayer he would go and seek alms for himself at the public gates."

I heard Muhammad bin al-Husayn say[26]. . . that Nuri said, "The characteristic of the poor dervish is silence when he has nothing and free giving and preference for others when he has something." And I heard him say[27]. . . that Muhammad bin Ali al-Kattani said, "When we were in Mecca there was a spiritual warrior who wore old rags who would neither visit us nor keep company with us. Love for him came into my heart. Two hundred dirhams reached me from a lawful source. I took them to him, set them by the side of his prayer mat, and said, 'This has come to me lawfully: spend it on your affairs.' He looked at me askance. Then he revealed what had been hidden from me. 'I bought this sitting with God Most High by giving up 70,000 dinars free of profit and loss,' he told me. 'And you want to dupe me out of it with these!' He got up and scattered them. I sat picking them up off the ground. I never saw the like of his dignity when he passed by nor the like of my humiliation while I gathered them up. Abu Abd Allah bin Khafif said, "For forty years I did not own enough to pay the alms due at the end of Ramadan, though I received a warm welcome from high and low."

I heard Abu Abd Allah bin Bakawiya al-Sufi say that he heard Ibn Khafif say that he heard Abu Ahmad al-Saghir said, "Abu Abd Allah bin Khafif was asked what was to be said about a poor dervish who went hungry for three days, and after the three days passed went out and begged the amount that would suffice him. He said, "It should be said about him that he was exhausted. Eat and be silent! If a poor dervish were to enter this door, he would shame the lot of you!"

I heard Muhammad bin al-Husayn say[28] . . . that al-Duqqi was asked what constituted bad behavior toward God in the states of poor dervishes. He said, "It is their falling from spiritual reality back to indirect religious knowledge." And I heard him say[29]. . . Khayr al-Nassaj said, "I entered a certain mosque. In it was a poor dervish. When he saw me, he attached himself to me. 'O Shaykh,' he said, 'turn to me with sympathy, for my affliction is great!' 'What is it?' I asked. 'I have lost trouble,' he said, 'and have grown strong in well-being.' I looked and saw that he had been given some alms." And I heard him say that Muhammad bin Muhammad bin Ahmad said that Abu Bakr al-Warraq said, 'Happy is the dervish who is poor in this world and the next.' Asked about this, he explained, 'The sultan does not seek taxes from him in this world, and the Sovereign shall not seek an accounting from him in the next!"

39 ON SUFISM (*TASAWWUF*)

Purity, *safa*, is praised by every tongue; its opposite, impurity, is condemned.

I heard Abd Allah bin Yusuf al-Ispahani report[1] . . . that Abu Juhayfah, "The Messenger of God came out to us with his color changed. He said, 'The earth's purity has gone and only impurity remains. Death, today, is a blessing for every Muslim.'" Thereafter this title came to be widely applied to this group so that a person might be called *sufi*—its plural being *sufiyya*. Someone who is attempting to reach this level is called *mutasawwif*—in plural, *muta - sawwifa*.

In respect of Arabic philology, there is no other word in the Arabic language to be drawn from the name *sufi*. The most obvious one would be that it resembles a descriptive surname, as if someone were to say, "He is of wool." Then *tasawwaf* could be said to mean "he wears wool," just as *taqammasa* means "he wears a shirt." That is one possibility. But the Sufis are not distinguished by the wearing of wool!

Some say the Sufis are named from their relation to the bench (*suffa*) of the mosque of the Messenger of God. But the attributive name derived from *suffa* does not come anywhere near to being *sufi*. Others say that the name is derived from purity, *safa*. But to derive *sufi* from *safa* is a long stretch according to the rules of the language. Then there is the proposition that the name comes from the word "rank," *saff*, because the hearts of the Sufis are, as it were, in the first rank. The meaning is sound, but the language does not permit such a derivative adjective from *saff*. However, this group is certainly too famous to have to be defined by a linguistic model or vindicated by means of a derivation.

Many people have discussed "What is the meaning of Sufism?" and "Who is a Sufi?," each one expressing what most struck him. A close examination of all this material would take us far from our aim of brevity. Here we will mention only some of the statements on this topic, with the aim of fostering understanding, if God Most High so wills.

I heard Muhammad bin Ahmad bin Yahya al-Sufi say[2] . . . that Abu Muhammad al-Jurayri was asked about Sufism and said, "Sufism means to take on every sublime moral characteristic from the life of the Prophet and to leave behind every lowly one."

I heard Abd al-Rahman bin Yusuf al-Ispahani say[3] . . . that when questioned about Sufism, Junayd said, "To be a Sufi means that the Truth causes you to die to yourself and to live through Him." I heard Abu Abd Rahman al-Sulami say[4]. . . that when asked about the Sufi, al-Husayn bin Mansur al-Hallaj said, "The Sufi is a person whose essence is one. No one admits him, and he admits no one." And I heard him say[5]. . . that Abu Hamzah al-Baghdadi said, "The sign of the genuine Sufi is that he is poor, after having been rich, abased after having been honored, hidden, after having been famous. The sign of the false Sufi is that he has worldly wealth, after having been poor is honored after having been abased, and becomes famous after having been obscure."

Amr bin Uthman al-Makki was asked about Sufism. He said, "It is that the servant be engaged at every moment in what is best for him at that moment." Muhammad bin Ali al-Qassab said, "Sufism is noble traits manifested at a noble time in a noble individual among noble people." Sumnun, asked about Sufism, said, "Sufism means that you own nothing and nothing owns you." Ruwaym answered, "It means giving the self over to God Most High for whatever He wants of it." Junayd answered, "It means that you are together with God Most High, without other attachments."

I heard Abd Allah bin Yusuf al-Ispahani say[6] . . . that Ruwaym bin Ahmad al-Baghdadi said, "Sufism is founded on three traits: clinging to spiritual poverty and the need of God; confirming oneself in generosity and concern for others; abandoning resistance to God's will and (abandoning) personal preference."

Maruf al-Karkhi said, "Sufism is to seize the realities and despair of what is in the hands of creatures." Hamdun al-Qassar said, "Keep company with the Sufis. With them the ugly person has all sorts of excuses!" Asked about the people of Sufism, Al-Kharraz said, "People who are made to give until they are exhilarated, who are blocked and frustrated until they lose themselves, who then are summoned away from intimate secrets—why, weep for us!"

Junayd said, "Sufism is force without compromise. The Sufis are people of one household. No outsider enters among them. Sufism is a remembrance of God and a uniting of parts, an ecstasy and a listening to guidance, an individual work and an emulation of the Prophet. The Sufi is like the earth. Every ugly thing is cast upon it, yet nothing grows out of it but what is pleasant. The Sufi is like the earth upon which walk the righteous and the libertine alike or like the cloud that shades everything or like the rain that gives everything drink. When you see a Sufi whose outward aspect is wealthy, know that his inner aspect is in ruins."

Sahl bin Abd Allah al-Tustari said, "The Sufi is one whose blood may be shed with impunity and whose property is open to all." Nuri said, "The characteristic of the Sufi is to keep silent when he has nothing and to prefer others over himself when he has something." Kattani said, "Sufism is morality. Whoever is superior to you in morality is superior to you in Sufism."

Abu Ali al-Rudhbari said, "Sufism is to stay at the door of the Beloved even if you are driven away." He also said, "It is the purity of nearness to God after the impurity of distance from Him." It is said, "The most repulsive of all repulsive things is a stingy Sufi." And, "Sufism is an empty palm and a good heart." Shibli said, "Sufism is to sit with God without concerns." Abu Mansur said, "The Sufi is a pointer from God Most High while the rest of Creation are pointers to God Most High."

Shibli said. "The Sufi is cut off from the creation and put in contact with the Truth. He has said (to Moses), '*I have attached you to Myself*' (20:41).God severs the Sufi from everything else, then says to him, '*You shall never see Me*' (7:143)! The Sufis are children in the lap of the Truth. Sufism is scorching lightning. Sufism is to be protected against seeing the universe."

Ruwaym said, "Sufis do not disappear due to the virtue of their correcting each other. When they become reconciled to the way they are, there is no good in them." al-Jurayri said, "Sufism is self-observation and holding fast to right behavior." Al-Muzayyin said, "Sufism is yielding to the Truth." Abu Turab al-Nakhshabi said, "The Sufi is polluted by nothing and purifies everything." The Sufi, it is said, is he whom no search wearies nor any cause upsets.

I heard Abu Hatim al-Sijistani say[7] . . . that Dhu-l- Nun al-Misri was asked about the Sufis. He said, "They are a people who prefer God over everything and whom God prefers over everything." Al-Wasiti said, "The Sufis have hints. Then these become actions. Then nothing remains but sorrows!"

Nuri, questioned about the Sufi, said, "He is the one who listens to the spiritual concert and prefers lawful means." I heard Abu Hatim al-Sijistani say that Abu Nasr al-Sarraj said, "Al-Husri was asked, 'In your view, who is a Sufi?' He replied, 'He whom the earth does not bear nor the heavens shade.'"

This points to the state of *mahw*, erasure from the world. It is said that the Sufi is one who, if he meets with two states or two characteristics that are both good, will choose the better of the two.

Shibli was asked, "Why are the Sufis called by that name?" He answered, "Because of the last remaining remnant of their egos. If not for that, no name would attach to them!"

I heard Abu Hatim al-Sijistani say[8] . . . that Ibn al-Jalla was asked, "What is the meaning of calling someone a Sufi?" He said, "We will not recognize this person by the condition of his formal learning. We will recognize that someone who is poor, stripped of means, who is with God Most High and without worldly place, but whom the Truth, glory to Him, does not prevent from the knowledge of every place, is to be called 'a Sufi'."

A dervish said, "Sufism is falling from dignity and blackness of face in this world and the next!" Abu Yaqub al-Mazabili said, "Sufism is a state in which the hallmarks of humanity melt away." Abu-l--Hasan al-Sirwani said, "The Sufi is someone who is concerned with inner spiritual conditions as well as outer devotional exercises."

I heard Abu Ali al-Daqqaq say, "The best thing that has been said on this topic is the statement of the one who said, 'This is a path that is only suitable for people whose souls God has used to sweep away their dunghills.'"

In reference to this, he said one day, "If the poor dervish had nothing but a soul and he laid it before the dogs of this gate, no dog would look at it." Abu Sahl al-Suluki said, "Sufism is the resistance to resistance." Al-Husri said, "The Sufi is not to be found after his nonexistence and does not cease to exist after he has come to be."

There is some ambiguity in this. The meaning of his statement, "He is not to be found after his nonexistence," is that when the calamities of his nature have passed away, those calamities do not return. His statement, "He does not cease to exist after he has come to be," means that when he is occupied with the Truth he does not collapse, like the rest of creation, for the events of life do not affect him.

The Sufi, it is said, is the one who has lost himself in what he has glimpsed of the Truth. And it is said, "The Sufi's will is overpowered by direct divine action, but he is veiled by the conduct proper to servanthood." And, "The Sufi is not altered, but if he is altered, he is not polluted."

I heard Abu Abd al--Rahman al-Sulami say[9]. . . that al-Kharraz said, "I was in the mosque of Kairouan one Friday, the day of congregational prescribed prayer, when I saw a man passing among the ranks, saying, "Be charitable to me! I used to be a Sufi, but I was weak. I gave him some money, but he said, 'Go away; for shame! That is not the thing for this problem!' And he would not accept it."

40 ON MODEL BEHAVIOR (*ADAB*)

God Almighty and Glorious has said, *"The sight (of the Prophet, at the time of his Ascension), did not deviate nor overstep the bounds"* (53:17). This is said to mean, "He maintained the conduct proper to the Divine Presence."

The Most High also said, *"Save yourselves and your families from the fire"* (66:6). According to the commentary of Ibn Abbas, this means, "Teach them the stipulations of the divine law and refined behavior."

Ali bin Ahmad al-Ahwazi informed us[1]. . . from Ayisha that the Prophet said, "The child owes it to his parent to make good his name, his upbringing, and his education in conduct." It is related that Said bin al-Musayyib said, "Whoever does not know what rights God Almighty and Glorious has over him and has not been educated in His command and prohibition is cut off from right behavior." It is reported that the Prophet said, "God Almighty and Glorious had educated me in refined behavior and made good my education."

The essence of *adab*, the most beautiful and fitting, refined behavior, is the gathering together of all good traits. The *adib*, the refined person, is he in whom are gathered all these good characteristics. From this is taken the word *maduba*, banquet, a name for the coming together (of such people).

I heard Abu Ali al-Daqqaq say, "Through his obedience the servant attains to paradise. Through refined conduct in obedience he attains to God. I also heard him say, "I saw someone who, during the prescribed prayer before God, wanted to stretch his hand to his nose to remove something that was in it. His hand was seized!"

He could only have been hinting that it was himself because it is not possible for a human being to know that someone else's hand was seized. Abu Ali used never to lean on anything. One day when he was at a gathering, I saw that he was without any support. I wanted to put a pillow behind his back. He drew a little away from the pillow, and I imagined that he was wary of it because there was neither a dervish robe nor a prayer carpet over it. But he said, "I do not want to lean." After this I marveled at his state, for in fact he never did lean on anything.

I heard Abu Hatim al-Sijistani say[2]. . . that al-Jalajili al-Basri said, "For the testimony of unity (*tawhid*) to be in force, faith is prerequisite, for whoever has no faith cannot testify to the unity. For faith to be in force the divine law is prerequisite, for whoever does not hold to the divine law has no faith and cannot testify to the unity. For the divine law to be in force refined conduct is prerequisite, for whoever has not refined his conduct cannot hold to the divine law, has no faith, and cannot testify to the unity.

Ibn Ata said, "*Adab*, refined behavior, is to hold fast to the commendable things." When asked, "What is the meaning of this?" he replied, "It means that you behave properly toward God both in secret and in public. If you are like that, you are a man of refined culture even if you are a foreigner." Then he recited:

When she conversed, her speech was all graciousness,
And when she kept silent, her silence was all fair.

Muhammad bin al-Husayn informed us[3]. . . that Abd Allah al-Jurayri said, "For twenty years, in my times of sitting in solitude, I have not stretched out my feet. It is better to act beautifully toward God." I heard Abu Ali al-Daqqaq say, "If someone keeps company with kings and lacks refined behavior, his ignorance will consign him to death!"

It is related that Ibn Sirin was asked, "What way of behaving brings one closest to God Most High?" He replied, "Realization of His Lordship, work in obedience to Him, praise to Him in happy times, and patience in times of trouble."

Yahya bin Muadh said, "When the gnostic abandons his courtesy in the presence of the One he knows, he has been ruined like all the rest of the spiritually ruined."

I heard Abu Ali say, "To abandon good conduct brings about expulsion. Someone who behaves badly upon the carpet of contemplation is sent out to the gate, and someone who behaves badly at the gate is sent out to look after the animals."

Hasan al-Basri was asked, "People have got hold of much knowledge of forms of refinement. What will give them profit and bring them to union later?" "Acquiring knowledge in religion," he said, "renouncing this world, and understanding the rights of God over you."

Yahya bin Muadh said, "Whoever is educated in the conduct of God Most High joins the people who love God Most High." Sahl said, "The Sufis are those who seek help from God, for the sake of God's business and persevere with God's forms of conduct."

It is related that Ibn al-Mubarak said, "We have greater need of a little bit of refinement than of a lot of knowledge." I heard Muhammad bin al-Husayn say[4] . . . that bin al-Mubarak said, "We sought for right conduct once the teachers of right conduct had left us."

It is said that if one has three traits, one is never a stranger. They are avoiding doubters, behaving well, and restraining oneself from causing harm. On this topic, Abu Abd Allah al-Maghribi recited this to us:

Three things adorn the stranger far from home:
First, fine conduct, second, fine character,
Third, leaving doubters alone.

When Abu Hafs entered Baghdad, Junayd said to him, "You have trained your companions to the conduct of sultans!" "Beautiful outward behavior is the model for beautiful inward behavior," Abu Hafs told him.

Abd Allah bin al-Mubarak said, "Refined behavior is to the gnostic what repentance is to the beginner." I heard Mansur bin Khalaf al-Maghribi say, "A dervish was addressed, 'O uncultured one!'" 'I am not uncultured!' he said. 'Why, who has taught you culture?' they asked. 'The Sufis taught me!' said he.

I heard Abu Hatim al-Sijistani say that Abu-l- Nasr al-Tusi al-Sarraj said, "People have three levels of refinement. For the people of this world, refinement largely consists of eloquent speech and rhetoric, along with the memorization of sciences, of the names of kings, and of the poetry of the Arabs. For the people of the next world, refinement largely consists of training the ego and disciplining the body, preserving the limits of the law and abandoning desires. For the elite, refinement largely consists of cleansing the heart of vices, guarding inner secrets, being faithful to one's promises, protecting the present, not turning aside in thought along with refined behavior in the stations of the search, in the moments of presence with God, and in the stages of closeness to God."

It is told that Sahl bin Abd Allah al-Tustari said, "Whoever over-powers his ego through refining conduct is serving God with sinceri-ty." The perfection of refined conduct, it is said, is not unimpaired except in the prophets and the possessors of true integrity. Abd Allah bin al-Mubarak said, "People have had much to say about fine con-duct. As for us, we say that it is the real understanding of the ego."

Shibli said, "To be carefree about speaking with the Truth, glory to Him, is to abandon right conduct." Dhu-l- Nun al-Misri said, "The culture of the gnostic is above all other culture, for it is the One he knows Who is the educator of his heart."

A Sufi said, "The Truth, glory to Him, said, 'When I sustain some-one with My names and attributes, I attach him to right or refined conduct. When I show someone part of the reality of My Essence, I attach him to his own destruction. Choose whichever of the two you will: refinement (*adab*) or destruction (*atab*)!'"

One day while he was with his companions Ibn Ata stretched out his feet. "Not putting emphasis upon one's refined behavior is itself considered refined behavior among the people who have attained refinement," said he. A *hadith* has been related that testifies to this story. The Prophet had Abu Bakr and Umar with him. Then Uthman entered, and he covered up his leg, saying, "Shall I not be ashamed before a man in front of whom the angels are ashamed?" He was point-ing out that even though he held the modesty of Uthman in great esteem, the affection that existed between himself, Abu Bakr and Umar had been more pure. It is with nearly this meaning that they recited:

> I act with restraint and modesty,
> But sitting with loyal and generous men
> I open myself spontaneously
> And say what I say without reticence.

Junayd said, "When love is sound, the rules of behavior are dropped." Abu Uthman al-Hiri said, "When love is sound, attachment to good behavior in the lover is assured." Nuri said, "Whoever has not been educated for the present, his present is disaster!" Dhu-l- Nun al-Misri said, "When the student abandons the exercise of refined behav-ior, he returns whence he came."

I heard Abu Ali al-Daqqaq discuss God's saying, ". . . *Job, when he called to His Lord, 'Trouble has touched me, and You are the Most*

Merciful of the Merciful" (21:83).*"* He said, "Because Job maintained the correct refinement of address (and would not presume to tell his Lord what to do), he did not say, 'Have mercy upon me!' For the same reason Jesus said, *'If You punish them, they are Your servants'* (5:121). Jesus also said, *'Had I said it, You would have known it'* (5:121). Because he was aware of the conduct proper to the divine presence, he could not insult divine Omniscience by saying, 'I did not say it.'"

I heard Muhammad bin Abd Allah al-Sufi say[5] . . . Junayd said, "A righteous man came to me one Friday and asked, 'Would you send along with me a poor dervish who would bring happiness to my house and eat something with me?' I looked around and saw that among those present was a poor dervish in whom the signs of need were visible. So I extended him the invitation and told him, 'Go with this gentleman and bring him happiness.' So he went. But it was not long before the man came back to me and said, 'O Abu-l--Qasim, that poor man ate nothing but a mouthful and left!' 'Perhaps you said some rough word to him,' I suggested. 'I said nothing!' he assured me. I looked around and saw that the poor dervish was back again sitting with me! 'Why did you not complete his happiness?' I asked him. 'O Master,' he told me, 'I left Kufa and came to Baghdad without anything to eat, but I hated the idea that because of need, bad behavior should appear from me in your presence. When you gave me the invitation, I was happy because it originated with you. So I went, but I had no heart for it. When I sat at his table, he set a meal before me and told me, "Eat, for it is dearer to me than 10,000 dirhams!" When I heard that from him, I knew that his aspiration was low, and I shied away from eating his food.' 'Did I not say to you that you had behaved badly toward him?' I said. 'Abu-l- Qasim, I repent!' he cried. So I asked the dervish to go with him and make him happy."

PART IV: OTHER SUFI CHARACTERISTICS

1 ON SUFI RULES OF TRAVEL (*SAFAR*)

God Almighty and Glorious said, "*He it is Who causes them to travel on the land and the sea . . .*" as the verse goes (10:22). Ali ibn Ahmad ibn Abdan reported . . . that Ibn Umar taught, "When the Messenger of God mounted a camel to go out on a journey he would say "God is Greater" (*Allah akbar*)—three times, and then say, "Glory to the One Who has subjugated this beast to us; we could not do it of ourselves. To our Lord we return." Then he would pray, "O God, We ask You to grant us righteousness and the fear of You during this journey, and we ask that the results of this undertaking receive Your pleasure. O God, make our journey easy for us. O God, You are the Master of the journey and the One responsible for the family we leave behind. O God, I take refuge in You from the hardships of travel, from sorrow upon returning, and from the sight of trouble in our property and family." When he returned he would say these things also, and add to them, "Repenting, returning, and praising our Lord."

Since the attitude of many Sufis has been to choose travel, we have set aside a chapter in this Treatise (*Risalah*) to speak of it, for it is one of their greater undertakings.

The Sufis are of various opinions in this matter. There are some who prefer staying in one place to traveling about, and who never travel unless it is an obligation, as for instance in order to perform the obligatory greater pilgrimage, which is a requirement of Islam. For these, staying in one place has pre-eminence. Such were Junayd, Sahl ibn Abd-Allah (al-Tustari), Abu Yazid al-Bistami, Abu Hafs (al-Haddad), and many others.

Then there are some who prefer to travel, and are engaged in it until they are taken out of this world. Such were Abu Abd-Allah al-

Maghribi, Ibrahim ibn Adham, and others.

Most, however, travel at the beginning of their training, in the time of their youth, making many journeys; then at the end of their states they cease to travel. Among them were Abu Uthman al-Hiri, Shibli, and others. All of them have a set of principles upon which they have founded their path.

Know that there are two kinds of travel: travel with the body, which is to move about from place to place, and travel with the heart, which is to ascend from attribute to attribute. You will see thousands who travel in their person, but few who travel in their hearts.

I heard Abu Ali al-Daqqaq say, "In a village called Farakhk, outside Nishapur, lived a Sufi shaykh who had written books on the theme of travel. Somebody asked him, "Have you traveled, O Shaykh?" "Traveled in the earth, or traveled in the heavens?" he inquired. "Traveled in the earth—no. But traveled in the heavens—yes, indeed!" And I heard him say that one day while he was in Merv a dervish came to him and said, "I have crossed great distances with the aim of meeting you!" "One footstep would have been sufficient for you," he told him, "if you had travelled away from your ego."

The stories about Sufis' traveling vary, as we have mentioned, with their types and states. I heard Abu Abd al-Rahman al-Sulami say[2] . . . that Ahnaf al-Hamadhani said, "I was alone in the desert, and I fell ill. I raised my hands in prayer and said, 'O Lord, I am old and feeble, and I am depending upon Your hospitality.' It struck my heart that I was asked, 'Who invited you?'
'O Lord,' I said, 'This is a country that puts up with the uninvited guest!' Suddenly I heard a voice from behind me. I turned around, and there was a Bedouin on a riding camel. 'O foreigner,' he said, 'Where are you going?' 'To Mecca.' 'Did He invite you?' 'I don't know.' 'Hasn't He said, "*Let he who is able find a way to it*" (3:97)?' 'Bountiful is the country that puts up with the uninvited guest,' I replied. 'A fine uninvited guest you are!' said he. Do you know how to manage a camel?' 'Yes.' He got off his mount and made her kneel. 'Ride!' said he."

I heard Muhammad ibn Abd-Allah al-Sufi say[3] . . . that when a dervish asked him, "Advise me," al-Kattani said, "Every night try to be the guest of some mosque, and try not to die elsewhere than between two stops on the road."

It is told that al-Husri used to say, "To sit down once is better than to make a thousand prescribed pilgrimages." He meant to sit down and concentrate all one's force in contemplation. And upon my life, such as sitting is more perfect than a thousand prescribed pilgrimages made in absent mindedness.

I heard Muhammad ibn Ahmad al-Sufi say that Muhammad ibn Ismail al-Farghani was related to have said, "We traveled for some twenty years, Abu Bakr al-Daqqaq, al-Kattani and I, neither mixing nor associating with anyone. When we would arrive in a city in which there was a shaykh we would give him greetings and sit with him until night came. Then we would retire to a mosque. Al-Kattani would make the ritual prayer from the beginning of the night until its end, offering a complete recitation of the Quran. Al-Daqqaq would sit facing the direction of prayer. I used to lie down and contemplate. When morning came we would perform the dawn obligatory prayer with our ablution of the previous night intact. If it happened that in the mosque with us was a man who was sleeping, we saw him as better than ourselves.

I heard Muhammad ibn al-Husayn say[4] . . . that Ruwaym, asked about the proper conduct for travel, said, "The traveler's concerns do not go beyond his steps, and wherever his heart stops, he stops."

It is related that Malik ibn Dinar said, "God Most High revealed to Moses, 'Take two sandals of iron and a staff of iron, and travel the earth seeking signs and examples until the sandals are worn out and the staff breaks.'"

They say that Abu Abd-Allah al-Maghribi used to travel constantly together with his students. He would keep himself in the pilgrim's state of consecration, and if his state became invalidated, he would reconsecrate himself anew. Yet his single garment (which a pilgrim is not permitted to change) never became dirty, and his fingernails and hair (which a pilgrim is not permitted to cut) never grew long. He used to walk at night with his companions behind him, and if one of them would stray from the path he would say, "To your right, so-and-so!" or "To your left, so-and-so!" He never used to stretch his hand toward the things for which ordinary people would reach. He made his food from the root of some green plant he would find and pull up for that purpose.

The saying goes, "If you say to a friend, 'Come along!' and he says, 'Where to?'—he is not your friend!" With this meaning they recite:

When their help was sought they did not ask of him
    who summoned them
"To which battle?" or "To what place?"

It is related that Abu Ali al-Ribati said that he was one of the companions of Abd-Allah al-Marwazi. Before he joined him, he used to go into the desert without any supplies or any mount to ride. When he became his student he asked him, "Which would you like better, that I should be the leader, or you?" "Rather yourself," Abu Ali al-Ribati said. "And you will be obliged to obey?" "Yes." He picked up a bag, filled it with provisions, and put it on his back. When I said, "Give it to me, so that I can carry it," he told me, "I am the leader, and you must obey!" That night it began to rain upon us. He stood at my head until morning with a cloak over him, protecting me from the rain. All the while I was saying to myself, "I wish I had died before I said, "You be the leader!" Afterwards he said to me, "When you keep company with a person, be his companion as you have seen me be yours."

A youth came to see Abu Ali al-Rudhbari. When he wanted to leave, he asked, "Perhaps the shaykh will give me some teaching." "Young man," Abu Ali said, "The Sufis never used to gather merely because they had made an appointment, or to separate simply because they had agreed to do so. (All aspects of their association were strictly for God's sake.)"

Al-Muzayyin al-Kabir said, "One day I accompanied Ibrahim al-Khawwas on one of his journeys. Suddenly a scorpion ran across his leg. I got up to kill it, but he forbade me, saying, 'Stop! Everything is in need of us, but we are not in need of anything.'"

Abu Abd-Allah al-Nasbini said, "I traveled for thirty years without sewing a patch on my ragged robe, and without turning toward any place in which I knew I had a friend, and without abandoning anyone who needed something from me."

Know that when through inner struggles the Sufis have fully developed the conduct suitable to the divine presence and have wished to add something further to this, they have taken on the rules of travel as a discipline for their egos. In this way they remove it from comfortable and familiar things and make it endure separation from what it knows. So they live with God without attachment and without intermediary.

They do not give up anything of their devotions in their travels. They say, "The lawful relaxation of the requirements for obligatory prayer is for people who travel by necessity. We are neither on business nor have we any need to travel."

I heard Abu Sadiq ibn Habib say that al-Nasrabadhi said, "One time I grew weak in the desert, and despaired of myself. Then my eyes fell upon the moon—this was the daytime—and I saw written upon it, "*So God will them*" (2:137). And I was freed from my troubles. From that moment the meaning of that saying was opened to me."

Abu Yaqub al-Susi said, "The traveler has need of four things in his travelling: a knowledge that governs him, a scrupulosity that restrains him, an ecstasy that carries him, and a character that protects him."

It is said, "Travel—*safar*—is so called because it uncovers (*yus - firu*) the character of people."

When a poor dervish traveled to Yemen and then returned to it a second time, al-Kattani ordered the brothers to break their association with him. He only did that because at that time people used to travel to Yemen for profit.

Ibrahim al-Khawwas used never to carry anything on his travels, but he could not be parted from a needle and a small pot. The needle was for sewing his clothes in case the covering for the parts of the body that must be covered should become torn; the little pot was for washing himself. He did not view this as attachment or as a known source of sustenance.

It is related that Abu Abd-Allah al-Razi said that he left Tarsus barefoot. A friend came together with him. When they entered one of the villages around Damascus a dervish came to him with some shoes, but he refused to accept them. His friend said to him, "Wear them—I can't. God has provided you with these sandals because of me." "What do you mean?" I asked him. "I stripped myself of my sandals (when we set out) to be in harmony with you, and out of respect for the duties of companionship."

Al-Khawwas was travelling with three other people. They arrived at a mosque in the desert and spent the night there. The mosque had no door, and it was very cold, but they slept. When morning came they saw al-Khawwas standing in the doorframe. They asked him about this, and he said, "I was afraid that you would find it cold." He had stood there the whole night.

Once al-Kattani asked permission of his mother to perform the prescribed pilgrimage. She gave him permission, so he left. But in the desert his garment became soiled by urine. "This is through some defect in my state," he said to himself, and he turned back. When he knocked at the door of his house his mother answered him, and opened the door. He saw that she had been sitting behind the door. He asked her why she had been sitting there, and she said, "When you went away, I vowed that I would not leave this spot until I saw you again."

I heard Muhammad ibn al-Husayn say[5] . . . that Ibrahim al-Qassar said, "I traveled for thirty years to set people's hearts in order for the dervishes." A man visited Dawud al-Tai and said, "Abu Sulayman, my ego has been challenging me to meet you for a long time." "That's all right," he told him. "When bodies guide and hearts are silent, the meeting is easier."

I heard Abu Nasr al-Sufi, who was one of the companions of al-Nasrabadhi, said that he left the ocean at Oman. Hunger had affected his mind. He was drawn to the marketplace. He reached a food shop and saw there roast lamb and sweetmeat. He grabbed a man and said, "Buy me some of that!" "Why?" he asked, "Do I owe you a favor or a debt?" "You must buy me some of that!" A man saw him and said, "Leave him be, young man — come to me, not him! Ask it of me! Decide what you want." Then he bought me what I wanted, and went away.

It is related that Abu-l-Husayn al-Misri said that in travelling from Tarabulus he fell in with al-Shajra. We went on for days without eating anything. Then he saw a cast-off gourd, and he picked it up to eat it. But the shaykh looked at him without saying anything, so he threw it away, knowing that he disapproved of it. After that five dinars came to them. They entered a village, and he thought, "The shaykh will buy, without a doubt." But he passed right through, and didn't do it. Then he remarked, "Perhaps you are saying to yourself, 'We are walking hungry, and he didn't buy us anything! What is this?' Trust me until Yahudiyyah—there you will find a man of family who, when we go in to see him, will occupy himself with us. Give him the dinars to spend on us and his family." So we reached it, and he gave the dinars to the man, who spent them. When we were leaving, he said to me, "Where are you heading, Abu-l-Husayn? I will travel with you." "No," he said, "You were disloyal to me over a gourd while you were my companion. Don't do it." And he refused to let me accompany him.

I heard Muhammad ibn Abd-Allah al-Shirazi say[6] . . . that Abu Abd-Allah ibn Khafif said, "In my youth I met a dervish who saw the signs of hardship and hunger in me, invited me to his house, and placed before me meat cooked with dumplings, and all kinds of other meat. I had been eating bread and milk and had avoided meat out of preference. He fed me a morsel and I ate it with an effort. Then he fed me a second one and I was overcome by difficulty. When he saw that in me he became embarrassed, and I was embarrassed on account of him. So I left, and was immediately moved to travel. I sent a man to my mother who would give her the news and bring me my patched robe, and my mother did not prevent me, but approved of my going. So I traveled from Qadisiyyah with a group of dervishes. We got lost, and lost everything that we had with us. We were on the brink of destruction when we reached one of the Bedouin tribes. Yet we did not find any help from them. We were forced to buy a dog from them for ourselves, at a price of some dinars, and roast it. They gave me a piece of its meat, and when I found myself wanting to eat it I thought about my condition. It occurred to me that this was the outcome of the embarrassment of that dervish. So I repented within myself. They led us to the road, so I left, performed the prescribed pilgrimage, and then returned and apologized to the dervish.

2 ON HUMAN COMPANIONSHIP FOR GOD'S SAKE

God Almighty and Glorious said, "(Abu Bakr al-Siddiq was) the second of two when they were in the cave, when he said to his companion, *'Do not grieve; God is with us'*" (9:40).

When God, glory to Him, wishes to attest to the quality of *suhbah*, companionship, in al-Siddiq, He shows him manifesting sympathy, "When he said to his companion, 'Do not grieve; God is with us.'" The free man is in sympathy with the one whom he accompanies.

Ali ibn Ahmad al-Ahwazi reported[1] . . . from Anas ibn Malik: The Messenger of God wondered, "When will I meet my dear ones?" His Companions exclaimed, "You are more precious to us than our mothers and fathers. Are we not your dear ones?" "You are my Companions," he said. "My dear ones are a people who have not seen me, but have believed in me, and I am more to them than their hearts' desires."

True companionship is of three sorts: keeping company with those who are above you, which in essence is service; keeping company with those who are below you, which requires sympathy and compassion in the one who is followed and harmony and respect in the follower; and keeping company with peers and equals, which is based upon preferring others to oneself and maintaining the standards of chivalry.

The behavior proper to someone who keeps company with a shaykh whose degree is above his own is to give up opposing him, to treat everything that appears from him as beautiful, and to accept his states with faith in him.

One of our companions asked Mansur ibn Khalaf al-Maghribi, "How many years did you keep company with Abu Uthman al-Maghribi? "He looked at him askance. Then I heard him reply, "I could not be his companion. But I served him for awhile."

When someone who is beneath you in development keeps company with you (as if you were both of the same degree), you betray that companionship if you do not let him know that this will diminish his own state. Thus Abu-l-Khayr al-Tinati wrote to Jafar ibn Muhammad ibn Nusayr, "The responsibility for the ignorance of the dervishes falls upon you, for you have been distracted by personal interactions from their education, so that they have remained ignorant."

When you keep company with someone who is at your own level, the proper course is to try to be blind to his faults. You should give what you see in him a beautiful interpretation insofar as it is possible. If you cannot find such an interpretation, you should keep your suspicions to yourself and look at your own faults, as you are obliged to do.

I heard Abu Ali al-Daqqaq say that Ahmad ibn Abil-Hawari said, "I said to Abu Sulayman al-Darani, "So-and-so has not made much of an impression on my heart!" "He has not made much of an impression on my heart either," said Abu Sulayman. "But Ahmad, perhaps we are ruined: perhaps we are not of the righteous, so that we do not love them!"

A man kept company with Ibrahim ibn Adham, and when he wanted to depart, asked, "If you have seen any fault in me, please let me know of it." "I have not seen any fault in you," said Ibrahim, "because I have looked upon you with the eye of love, so that everything I saw of you seemed good to me. Ask somebody else about your faults!"

With this meaning they recite:

The eye of good pleasure, like the night, hides every shame
But the eye of displeasure shows up all alike!

It is told that Ibrahim ibn Shayban said, "We used not to keep company with anyone who said 'my sandal'."

I heard Abu Hatim al-Sufi say[2] . . . that *Abu Ahmad al-Qalanasi*, who was one of the teachers of Junayd, said, "I kept company with some people in Basra, who did me much honor. Then one time I asked one of them, 'Where are my trousers?' And my status fell in their eyes."

And I heard Abu Hatim say[3] . . . that al-Zaqqaq said, "In the forty years I have been with these companions, I have seen no friendship shown to any of them unless it came from one of them toward another, or from someone who loved them. Whoever is not accompanied by fear of God and moral watchfulness in this business eats what is totally unlawful."

I heard Abu Ali al-Daqqaq say that a man said to Sahl ibn Abd-Allah (al-Tustari), "Abu Muhammad, I want to keep company with you." "If one of us died, who would be the companion of the one who remained?" "God." "Then let Him be his companion now!"

For awhile one man made himself the student and companion of another, but then he began to think of leaving, and asked permission to go. "On condition that you do not seek the company of anyone unless his level is above mine," his guide said. "And even if he is above me, don't keep company with him, because I was your companion first!" "The wish to leave has disappeared from my heart," said the man.

I heard Abu Hatim al-Sufi say[4] . . . that al-Kattani said, "A certain man associated with me, but I disliked his company. I gave him a gift, hoping that what was in my heart might pass off, but it did not go away. So I brought him to my house and said to him, 'Set your foot upon my cheek.' He refused. 'You must!' I said. So he did it. I intended that he should not raise his foot from my cheek until God raised from my heart the weight I had found there. When what I had discovered vanished from my heart, I said, 'Now lift your foot.'"

Ibrahim ibn Adham used to work as a harvester and an orchard watchman and so forth, and spend what he earned upon his companions. It seems that he would labor each day and then distribute the earnings to a group of companions who, having fasted all day, would gather each night in a certain place. He used to be late in returning from work, and one night they said, "Come on, let's break our fast and eat without him. Maybe after this he will come back more quickly." So they broke their fast and slept.

When Ibrahim came back and found them sleeping, he said, "Poor things! Maybe they have not had any food!" So he applied himself to a bit of flour that there was in the place, kneaded it, kindled the fire, and cast the hot embers over it to bake it. They woke up and found him blowing on the fire, with his beautiful face pressed against the dust.

They asked him what he was doing. "I said to myself that perhaps you had not found anything with which to break your fast," he told them. "You were sleeping. I wanted you to wake up when the ashes had done their work." "Look at what we have done," they said to one another, "and look at how he has treated us!"

Ibrahim ibn Adham used to lay down three conditions for anyone who wanted his company: that he should be the one to serve, that he should act as *muezzin* at prayers, and not as imam, and that he and his companions should share without distinction in whatever worldly sustenance God might provide. One day one of his students told him, "I am not capable of this." "I marvel at your truthfulness," said he.

Yusuf ibn al-Husayn said, "I asked Dhu-l-Nun, 'With whom should I associate?' "He said, 'With someone from whom you would not hide anything that God Most High knows about you.'"

Sahl ibn Abd-Allah (al-Tustari) told a man, "If you are one of those people who is afraid of wild beasts, don't associate with me!"

I heard Muhammad ibn al-Husayn say[5] . . . that Bishr ibn al-Harith said, "The legacy of the company of bad people is to think evil of the good."

It is related that Junayd said, "When Abu Hafs (al-Haddad) entered Baghdad he brought with him a bald man who never spoke. I asked Abu Hafs's companions about his situation, and they said, 'This is a man who provided (Abu Hafs) with a hundred thousand dirhems, and took a loan of a hundred thousand dirhems and spent them upon him, but Abu Hafs will not permit him to utter a word.'"

Dhu-l-Nun said, "Do not attempt to keep company with God unless you conform to His will, nor with people unless you give them good counsel, nor with your ego unless you oppose it, nor with satan unless you are his enemy."

A man asked Dhu-l-Nun "With whom should I associate?" He said, "With some one who will visit you when you are sick, and turn to you with forgiveness when you sin."

I heard Abu Ali al-Daqqaq say, "A tree that grows by itself and is not cultivated by anyone will put forth leaves but not fruit. Just so, if a seeker has no master to educate him, nothing will come of him."

Abu Ali used to say, "I received this Way from al-Nasrabadhi, al-Nasrabadhi from Shibli, Shibli from Junayd, Junayd from Sari, Sari from Maruf al-Karkhi, Maruf al-Karkhi from Dawud al-Tai, and Dawud al-Tai had met the Followers of the Prophet's Companions." And I heard him say, "I would never frequent the gatherings of al-Nasrabadhi unless I had previously made a total ablution."

I myself, when I was a beginner, never used to go in to see Abu Ali unless I was fasting and had made a total ablution beforehand. Many times I used to go right to the door of his school but then turn back, too much in awe of him to go in. One time I gathered my courage and went into the school. By the time I reached the middle of the school grounds I was overcome by a sort of numbness, so that if a needle had been stuck into me I might not have felt it at all. When I sat down in the shaykh's presence, a question came to my mind. But I did not need to ask him about the matter with my tongue, for just as I was sitting down he began to give an explanation of the thing that had occurred to me. Many times I have seen the like of this from him with my own eyes. And I often used to think to myself that even if God had sent a Messenger to people in my own time, it would not have been possible for me to feel more awe and shyness in my heart than I felt toward Abu Ali. That did not seem even conceivable to me. And I do not recall that in the whole time I attended his gatherings, or later when I was with him after having been accepted as a personal student, that any opposition to him ever entered my heart or crossed my mind, until he left this world, may God have mercy upon him.

Hamzah ibn Yusuf al-Sahmi al-Jurjani reported[6] . . . from Muhammad ibn al-Nadr al-Harithi, "God, glory to Him, revealed to Moses, 'Wake up! Be an explorer. Be close friends with yourself. Drive away every friend who affords you no happiness, and do not associate with him, for if he makes your heart harden, he is your enemy. Most remembrance of Me merits My thanks, and what is beyond that is from My grace.'"

I heard Abu Abd al-Rahman al-Sulami say[7] . . . that Abu Bakr al-Tamastani said, "Keep company with God, and if you are not able, then keep company with those who keep company with God. Then the blessing of their companionship may draw you to the companionship of God."

3 ON MONOTHEISM: AFFIRMATION OF UNITY (*TAWHID*)

God Almighty and Glorious said, *"Your God is One God"* (2:123). Abu Bakr Muhammad ibn al-Husayn ibn Furak reported[1] . . . from Abu Hurayrah, that the Messenger of God said, "Once there was a man, belonging to the peoples who came before you, who had done no good whatsoever except to profess God's unity. He said to his family, 'When I die, burn me up and crush me and scatter half of me over the land and half over the sea on a windy day.' So they did that. Then God Almighty and Glorious said to the wind, 'Bring what you have taken!' When the man was before Him, He asked him, 'What moved you to do what you did?' The man replied, 'I was ashamed to face You!' So God forgave him."

Monotheism (*tawhid*) is the principle that God is One. The knowledge that a thing is one is also a type of monotheism.

One says *wahhadtuhu* (using the verbal form that produces the noun *tawhid*), "I attested to its oneness," when one has described a thing as a unity, just as one says, "I attested to his courage" (using the same verbal form) when one has ascribed courage to someone. One uses in language the basic form *wahada*, present tense *yahidu*, to produce the meanings "single" (*wahid*), "solitary" (*wahd*), and "unique" (*wahid*), just as one uses *farada* to generate "alone" (*farid*), "individual" (*fard*), and "matchless" (*farid*). The root of the word "one" (*ahad*) is also *wahada*. The "w" has been transformed into the opening *hamzah* of *ahad*, for a "w" with an "a" vowel may transform into *hamzah* just as it may with an "i" or a "u" vowel. Thus one says of a woman that she is *asma*, comely, with the meaning of "*wasma*," from *wasamah*, charm.

In learned discourse, the meaning of God's being *wahid*, One, is that it is not proper to describe Him as admitting additions and subtractions. In the case of a human being, it is possible to subtract a part of him—say a hand or a foot—and still properly say of that person, "The human being is a unity." But the Truth, glory to Him, is absolutely and essentially single, rather than being a sum of parts.

Some of those whose know say that the meaning of saying that God is One is to deny any division in His essence, deny that anything else might resemble His reality and attributes, and deny the existence of a partner to Him in His actions and creations.

Affirmation of unity or monotheism (*tawhid*) is of three kinds. First there is the affirmation of Unity that proceeds from the Truth to the Truth, which is His own knowledge that He is One, and His informing Himself of that. Second is the affirmation of Unity that proceeds from the Truth to the creation, which is God's command that the servant should profess His Unity, together with His creation of this profession of faith in the servant. Third is the affirmation of Unity that proceeds from the creation to the Truth, which is the servant's knowledge that God Almighty and Glorious is One, and his conviction and declaration that He is One.

These are all of the meanings of affirmation of unity permitted to us by the demands of brevity. The sayings of the shaykhs on the meaning of affirmation of unity are various.

I heard Abu Abd al-Rahman al-Sulami say[3] . . . that Dhu-l-Nun, when asked of affirmation of unity, said, "Professing Unity means that you know that the power of God Most High in things is without admixture, that His making of things is without means, that the cause of everything is His doing while His doing has no cause, and that whenever you imagine a thing within yourself, God is other than that."

And I heard him say[5] . . . that Jurayri said, "There is nothing for the knowledge of Unity except the tongue of Unity."

Junayd was asked about monotheism and said, "To declare the Unity is to declare the uniqueness of the One Whose Unity is affirmed by attesting to His singularity in the perfection of His Oneness—that only He is the One that does not beget and is not begotten—and by denying all opposites, equals, and resemblances, without comparison, qualification, representation, or likening of Him to anything else. *'Nothing is like unto Him, and He is the Hearing and Seeing'* (26:110)."

Junayd said, "When the minds of the intelligent reach a high degree in professing Unity, they come to bewilderment."

I heard Muhammad ibn al-Husayn say[4] . . . that Jafar ibn Muhammad said he had heard Junayd say this, and that asked about the affirmation of unity (*tawhid*), Junayd also said, "The affirmation of unity is a spiritual condition in which all forms vanish and into which all knowledges are incorporated, and God Most High becomes what He always was."

Al-Husri said, "Our principles in affirming the Unity are five: discarding the ephemeral, singling out the eternal, fleeing from brothers, renouncing homelands, and forgetting what is known or not known."

I heard Mansur ibn Khalaf al-Maghribi say that he was in the courtyard of the congregational mosque in Baghdad while al-Husri was talking about affirming Unity, when he (Mansur) saw two angels ascend into the sky. One of them said to his companion, "What this man is saying is the knowledge of Unity, but Unity itself is something else." I was between wakefulness and sleep.

Faris said, "To profess Unity is to drop all means and relations in the immediacy of one's state, but to return to them in the matter of operating principles, and to know that good deeds do not alter one's destined shares of happiness and sadness."

I heard Muhammad ibn al-Husayn say[5] . . . that Shibli said, "The affirmation of Unity, in reality, is an attribute of the One whose Unity is affirmed, but in form it is an adornment of the affirmer."

Junayd was asked about the profession of Unity of the spiritual elite. He said, "It means that the servant is but a phantom shape before God, glory to Him. Over him flow the currents of God's direction of the changing play of His power. Through passing away from himself, the call of the world to him, and his response with his own being and individuality, he comes to reside in the depths of the seas of God's Unity. Through leaving his own sensation and action in order to be maintained by the Truth according to His wish, he comes to reside in real closeness to Him. The end of the servant returns to his beginning, so that he becomes as he was before he was."

Al-Bushanji, asked of the affirmation of unity, said, "It is neither likening the divine essence to the human nor denying God His attributes."

I heard Abu Abd al-Rahman al-Sulami say[6] . . . that Sahl ibn Abd-Allah (al-Tustari), questioned about the Essence of God Almighty and Glorious, replied, "The Essence of God may be described through religious knowledge, but it is not to be grasped by intellectual comprehension nor seen by the eyes in this world. It exists in the realities of faith without restriction, containable neither by the mind nor by the body. In the Next Life the eyes will see Him manifest in His kingdom and power. He has veiled the creatures from realizing the true nature of His Essence, while guiding them to Him with His signs. Hearts know Him, but intellects cannot attain Him. (In the Next World) the believers will see Him with their eyes without the limits of mental conception and without ever coming to an end.

Junayd said, "The nobles saying on monotheism was uttered by Abu Bakr al-Siddiq, 'Glory to Him Who has not made for His creation any way of knowing Him except the inability to know Him!'"

Abu-l-Qasim said that al-Siddiq does not mean that God is not known. Among people of experience, "inability" means that one is unable to accomplish something that exists, not that something does not exist. Thus a chair is incapable of sitting, since it can neither acquire nor perform this action. Yet sitting exists in it. Just so, the gnostic is incapable of His knowledge, but that knowledge exists in him, necessarily.

According to the Sufis, true knowledge of God is finally a necessary and inalienable attribute of being, but in the beginning it is acquired. Yet even if this acquired knowledge is essentially a realization of God, al-Siddiq has not counted it as anything in comparison with that realization which is necessary and intrinsic. It is like a lamp when the sun rises and shines its rays upon it.

I heard Muhammad ibn al-Husayn say[7] . . . that Junayd said, "The profession of Unity peculiar to the Sufis is discriminating the eternal from the ephemeral, leaving homelands, cutting connections to well-loved things, abandoning what one knows and does not know—and setting the Truth, glory to Him, in the place of all."

Yusuf ibn al-Husayn said, "Whoever falls into the oceans of Unity only increases in thirst with the passing of time."

Junayd said, "The knowledge of Unity contradicts its existence, and its existence contradicts its knowledge." He also said, "The knowledge of Unity rolled up its carpet twenty years ago. People are holding forth on its footnotes!"

I heard Muhammad ibn al-Husayn say that Muhammad ibn Ahmad al-Ispahani said that a man stopped before al-Husayn ibn Mansur (al-Hallaj) and asked, "What is this Truth to which you point?" "The reason for humanity," he replied, "that needs no reason itself." And I heard him say[8] . . . that Shibli said, "Whoever comes into possession of an atom of the knowledge of Unity, because of the weight of what he carries, becomes to weak to carry a fly."

I heard Abu Hatim al-Sijistani say that Abu Nasr al-Sarraj said that Shibli was asked, "Give us a pure affirmation of Unity with the language of a unique truth." "Woe to you!" he said. "Whoever answers about Unity with an explanation is a heretic. Whoever hints with allusions is a dualist. Whoever gestures to it is an idol-worshiper. If someone speaks about it he is unconscious, and if someone keeps silent about it he is ignorant. If someone imagines that he has reached it, he has not attained it. One sees it as near while it is far. The one who strives for ecstasy is destitute of it. Everything that you single out with your speculations and seize with your intellect in the most perfect of your ideas turns aside and comes back to you, a created phenomenon like yourselves."

Yusuf ibn al-Husayn said, "The profession of Unity of the spiritual elite is that in one's innermost being, in one's ecstasy, and in one's heart, one should be as if standing before God Most High. In the oceans of Unity, the changing currents of God's will and the principles of His power flow through the servant who has passed away from himself and left his own sensations. For the Truth, glory to Him, maintains that servant according to His Own wish, and he becomes as he was before he was, in the flow of God's control through him."

The real affirmation of Unity belongs to the Truth, it is said—the creatures are but infants. And it is said, "To affirm the Unity is to drop the 'me'"—not to say "mine," "through me," from me," "to me."

Abu Bakr al-Tamastani was asked, "What is the declaration of Unity?" He replied, "The declaration of Unity, the declarer, and the One Whose Unity is declared—these are three!"

Ruwaym said, "The affirmation of Unity is the erasure of the traces of the human condition, and the sole existence of the divine."

At the end of his life, when his illness had become severe, I heard Abu Ali al-Daqqaq say, "One of the tokens of divine assistance is that the profession of Unity is preserved in moments of decision." Then he spoke like a commentator, pointing to his own condition, "That is, while God is cutting you into pieces with the scissors of His omnipotence in the execution of His decision, you are grateful and full of praise."

Shibli said, "Whoever imagines that he has affirmed the Unity has not smelt the odor of affirming the Unity!"

Abu Said al-Kharraz said, "The first station for someone who discovers the knowledge of Unity and makes it a reality is the disappearance of the recollection of all other things from his heart, so that he is in solitude with God Almighty and Glorious."

Shibli asked a man, "Do you know why your profession of Unity is not sound?" "No," said he. "He told him, "Because you are seeking Him through yourself."

Ibn Ata said, "The sign of the reality of one's profession of Unity is to forget professing the Unity. That is, he who performs a real declaration of oneness becomes one."

It is said, "To certain people, the divine actions are revealed. Such a person sees phenomena through God Most High. To certain people, the reality is revealed. For such a person, the perception of what is other than God vanishes, and he witnesses the unification as a secret, by means of a secret, though his outward aspect may still be described as separate from his Lord."

I heard Muhammad ibn Abd-Allah al-Sufi say[9] . . . that al-Qunfadh said, "Junayd was asked about the profession of Unity. He answered, 'I heard someone say:

He sang to me from my heart
And I sang as He sang.
And we were wherever they were
And they were wherever we were!

The questioner exclaimed, "So are the Quran and Traditions not worth quoting?" "No," said Junayd. "But the one who knows His Unity finds the highest of declarations in the lowest and simplest of speech."

4 ON THE STATES OF THE GREAT SUFIS UPON THEIR DEATHS

God Most High said, "*Those whom the angels cause to die in puri - ty . . .*" (27:32). Abd-Allah ibn Yusuf al-Ispahani reported[1] . . . from Anas ibn Malik, that the Messenger of God said, "The servant will certainly labor under the difficulty and agonies of death. His joints will bid each other farewell, saying, 'Peace be upon you! You are parting from me and I am parting from you until the Day of Judgment.'"

Abu Abd al-Rahman al-Sulami reported[2] . . . from Anas, "The Prophet went to see a young man who was dying. 'How do you find yourself?' he asked. 'I hope in God and fear my sins,' the young man replied. The Messenger of God said, 'These two things do not come together in the heart of a believing servant at this point unless God has granted him what he hopes for and saved him from what he fears.'"

Know that at the moment of death, the states of the Sufis vary. Some of them are overcome by awe, some by hope; to some in that condition something imposing silence and a beautiful trust is disclosed.

It is related that Abu Muhammad al-Jurayri said, "I was with Junayd when death came to him. It was a Friday, New Year's Day. He was reciting the Quran. When he completed the recitation, I asked, 'Abu-l-Qasim, will it be now?' 'Who could be readier than I?' he said. 'This will close my book.'"

I heard Abu Hatim al-Sijistani say[3] . . . that word has reached me that Abu Muhammad al-Harawi said, "I was staying with Shibli on the night he died. The whole night long he recited these two lines:

No house in which You dwell has need of lamps.
Your longed-for face will be our excuse on the day

when people bring excuses.

It is said that Abd-Allah ibn Munazil said, "Hamdun al-Qassar charged his companions that at the time of his death they not leave him among women."

While Bishr al-Hafi was struggling with death, someone exclaimed, "Can it be, Abu Nasr, that you love life?" "The approach to God Almighty and Glorious," he replied, "is most terrible!"

When one of Sufyan al-Thawri's companions was going to travel and would ask him, "Can I do something for you?", Sufyan would answer, "If you find death, buy it for me!" But when his time drew near, he said, "We used to yearn for this . . . and it is very hard."

When death approached al-Hasan ibn Ali ibn Abi Talib, he wept. "Why are you crying?" they asked. "I am going to a Master that I have not seen," he replied.

When death drew near to Bilal, his wife mourned, "O what grief!" "Rather, 'O what joy!'" he told her. "Tomorrow we shall meet the dear ones and the forces of Muhammad."

At the moment of his death Abd-Allah ibn al-Mubarak opened his eyes and laughed. "For the like of this," he cried, "let the workers work!"

Makhul al-Shami used to be overwhelmed by sadness, but when people came to visit him in his last illness, they found him laughing. They asked about this. "Why should I not laugh," he told them, "when I am about to leave everything I have feared, about to approach to all I have hoped and dreamed of?"

Ruwaym said, "I was present at the death of Abu Said al-Kharraz. With his last breath he recited:
Knowers' hearts long to remember.
Secretly they remember, in intimate speech.
Winecups of death pass from hand to hand
So like drunkards they slumber from the world.
Their cares wander unsettled in darkness—
Like shining planets are the lovers of God.
Their bodies are in the earth, slain by His love
But their spirits, within the veil, travel by night
      to the highest.
No dismounting for them except near the Beloved,
No turning from suffering and pain.

They asked Junayd if Abu Said al-Kharraz strove greatly for ecstasy in the presence of death. He said, "It is not surprising that his soul was beside itself with desire."

When his death was close, a Sufi said, "Young man, tie me tightly and cast my cheek into the dust!" Then he said, "The journey is close at hand. I have no remission for my sins nor any excuse to excuse me, nor any strength to help myself. There is only You for me! There is only You for me!" Then he gave a great cry, and died. People heard a voice say, "The servant gave himself up to his Lord, and his Lord accepted him."

On the point of death, Dhu-l-Nun al-Misri was asked, "What do you desire?" He said, "To know Him by a glance before I die."

A dervish in his death-agony was told, "Say 'God!'" He retorted, "How long will you be telling me to say 'God!' while I am burning in God?"

A Sufi said, "I was with Mumshad al-Dinawari when a poor dervish came and said, 'Peace be upon you.' The people present returned the greeting. 'Is there anywhere around here a clean place that a man could die in?' the dervish asked. They pointed out a spot to him. There was a spring of water nearby, so he renewed his ablution and offered some cycles of prayer as God willed, then went over to the place they had indicated, stretched out his legs, and died."

I heard Abu Abd al-Rahman al-Sulami say that one day Abu-l-Abbas al-Dinawari was speaking in one of his gatherings when a woman cried out, seeking for ecstasy. "Die!" he said to her. So the woman got up, and when she reached the door she turned to him and said, "I have died!" And death overtook her.

A Sufi said, "I was with Mumshad al-Dinawari close to his death. They asked, 'How is your illness?' 'Ask my illness about me, how I am!' he replied. 'Say: 'There is no god but God' they urged. He turned his face to the wall, and said, 'I have been annihilated totally by Your Totality. That is the portion of one who loves You.'"

Abu Muhammad al-Dubayli, when people urged him in the presence of death to say 'there is no god but God,' said, "This is a thing that we have long known, and by which we are annihilated." Then he began to recite:

Wrap yourself in the garb of the wilderness
    when you desire Him.
He rejected and was not pleased by His servant.

When Shibli, at his death, was told, "Say: 'There is no god but God,' he said:

The Sultan he loved said: "I do not accept bribes!"
Ask Him by His truth if my death annoys Him!

I heard Muhammad ibn Ahmad al-Sufi say[4] . . . that a dervish said, "We were sitting all around Yahya al-Istakhri as he was dying. One of our number reminded him, "Say, 'I bear witness that there is no god but God.' Yahya sat erect. He took one of us by the hand and said to him, "Say, 'I bear witness that there is no god but God.' Then he took the hand of another until he had set the affirmation of faith before everyone present. And then he died.

It is related that Fatimah, the sister of Abu Ali al-Rudhbari, said, "When my brother Abu Ali al-Rudhbari's time drew close his head was in my lap. He opened his eyes and said, 'Such doors of heaven have opened, and such gardens have been bedecked! Someone is saying to me, "O Abu Ali, We have brought you to the ultimate degree even though you did not reach it yourself!" He began to recite:

By Your Truth, I did not look at any but You
With eyes of love, until I saw You.
I see You afflicted with a slackening vision
And a cheek reddened by Your love.

Then he said, 'Fatimah, the first verse is obvious, the second ambiguous!'"

I heard one of the poor dervishes say, "When Ahmad ibn Nasr's time came, someone said to him, 'Say "I bear witness that there is no god but God."' He looked at him and said, 'Don't abandon respect!'"

A Sufi said, "I saw a poor dervish yield up his life in a strange way. There were flies on his face, and I sat brushing the flies away from it. He opened his eyes and said, 'Who is that? For so many years I have been in search of a moment given over completely to me, and it never happened until now. So you come and stick yourself into it! Go away!' May God have mercy upon him!"

Abu Imran al-Istakhri said, "I saw Abu Turab (al-Nakhshabi) standing upright in the desert, dead. Nothing touched him."

I heard Abu Hatim al-Sijistani say that Abu Nasr al-Sarraj said that the cause of Abu-l-Husayn Nuri's death was that he heard this verse:

> For love of You I kept camping in place after place.
> Hearts are bewildered that He should enter a place.

Nuri fell into ecstasy and wandered into the desert. He came to a stand of cane that had been cut down so that its stumps remained, sharp as swords. He walked over them reciting this verse until morning, while the blood poured from his feet; then he dropped like a drunkard. His feet swelled up and he died.

It is related that when in his death-agony he was told, "Say 'There is no god but God,'" he replied, "Is it not to Him I am returning?"

Ibrahim al-Khawwas fell ill in the congregational mosque in Rayy. He was afflicted with dysentery. When a group of dervishes gathered, he would go into the water and make ablution. On such an occasion when he had gone into the water, his soul departed.

I heard Mansur al-Maghribi say that Yusuf ibn al-Husayn went to visit al-Khawwas in his illness, after countless days had passed in which he had not been cared for. When Yusuf saw him, he asked him, "Do you want anything?" "Yes," answered al-Khawwas. "A bit of fried liver!"

Perhaps what this indicates is that he meant, "I want a heart that takes pity on the poor, and a liver that is fried and burnt for the stranger"—a rebuke for Yusuf ibn al-Husayn, since he had not taken care of him.

The cause of Ibn Ata's death, it is said, is that he was brought before the vizier, who spoke harshly to him. Ibn Ata said to him, "Be quiet, man!" The vizier struck him on the head with his shoe, and he died of it.

I heard Muhammad ibn Ahmad ibn Muhammad al-Sufi say [5] . . . that Abu Bakr al-Duqqi said that one morning when we were with Abu Bakr al-Zaqqaq he said, "My God, how long You have kept me here!" Before the following morning he was dead.

It is related that Abu Ali al-Rudhbari said, "In the desert I came across a youth. When he saw me, he asked, 'Is it not enough for Him to have filled me with His love until I have fallen sick of it?' Then I knew that he was surrendering up his spirit. I told him, 'Say: "There is no god but God." He began to say, "O One from Whom there is for me—even if He torture me—no escape! O He Who has granted from my heart a gift that is without end!"

Junayd was told, "Say: 'There is no god but God.' He retorted, "I have not forgotten Him, that I should have to remember Him!" Then he said:

> He was there in my heart, making it live—
> I never forgot Him, that I should remember Him now.
> He is my Master and my support.
> How rich is my portion from Him!

I heard Muhammad ibn Ahmad ibn Muhammad al-Sufi say that Abd-Allah ibn Ali al-Tamimi said that Jafar ibn Nusayr Bukran al-Dinawari used to serve Shibli. I asked him what he had observed of him. He said, "Shibli told me, 'In a dirham there is wrong, but I have always received it in alms. My heart holds no concern greater than this.' Then he said, 'Give me the ablution for prayer.' So I did it, but I forgot to run my fingers through his beard. He said nothing, but grasped my hand and placed it in his beard. Then he died." Jafar wept. He said, "What can you say of a man who, even at the end of his life, would not leave a single one of the practices of the divine Law?"

I heard Abd-Allah ibn Yusuf al-Ispahani say[6] . . . that al-Muzayyin al-Kabir said, "I was in Makkah (may God Most High protect it) when a state of spiritual agitation befell me, and I left, intending to go to Madinah. When I reached the well of Maymunah I suddenly came upon a young man lying on the ground. I went over to him; he was on the point of death. I told him, 'Say: "There is no god but God."' He opened his eyes and recited:

> If I die, my heart is filled with passion.
> Declaring passion makes the noble die.

He gave a moan, and expired. I bathed him, shrouded him, and prayed over him. When I had finished his burial, the wish for travel that had been in me was stilled, so I returned to Makkah."

A Sufi was asked, "Do you love death?" "It is better to go to somebody from whom you hope for good," he said, "than to remain with somebody from whose evil you cannot be safe!"

It is related that Junayd said, "I was with my master, Ibn al-Karnabi, when he was giving up his soul. I looked toward the heavens, and he said, 'Far!' Then I looked toward the earth, and he said, 'Far!'

That is, 'It is nearer to you than your looking toward the heavens or the earth—it is on the spot.'"

I heard Abu Hatim al-Sijistani say[7] . . . that Abu Yazid (al-Bistami) said at his death, "I only remembered You out of unconsciousness, and You only restricted Your gifts because of my slackness."

Abu Hatim al-Sijistani said[8] . . . that Abu Ali al-Rudhbari said, "In Egypt I saw a gathering of people. 'We are the funeral party of a noble man,' they said. When he heard someone say:

Great is the servant's ambition.
It strives to see You!
he heaved a sigh, and died.

A group of people came to Mumshad al-Dinawari in his final illness and asked, "What has God done with you? How has He acted?" "For thirty years paradise and all that is in it have lain open to me," he said, "and I have not given it a glance." At his death agony, they asked, "How do you find your heart?" "It is thirty years since I lost my heart!" said he.

I heard Muhammad ibn Ahmad ibn Muhammad al-Sufi say [9] . . . that al-Wajihi said, "Ibn Bunnan died because of a spiritual influence that came over his heart so that he wandered aimlessly. His people caught up with him in the middle of the desert of the Children of Israel, in the sand. He opened his eyes and said, "Feast! For this is the rich pasture land of lovers!" Then his soul departed.

Abu Yaqub al-Nahrajuri said, "I was in Makkah when a dervish came to me with some dinars and said, 'When tomorrow comes I will die, so with half of this arrange me a proper grave. The other half will take care of what I will need.' I said to myself, 'The man is disturbed; the poverty of the Hijaz has afflicted him.' The next day he came, made a circumambulation of the Kabah, then went and stretched himself out on the ground. I called, 'Hey, you who are playing dead!' Then I went over to him and shook him—and he had died! So I buried him as he had ordered."

When Abu Uthman al-Hiri's condition took a turn for the worse, his son Abu Bakr tore his shirt. Abu Uthman opened his eyes and said, "My son, to violate an outward rule of faith is the sign of some inward hypocrisy."

Ibn Ata went in to Junayd when he was surrendering his spirit. He greeted him, but Junayd was slow in giving the reply. Finally he returned the greeting, and said, "Forgive me—I was in the midst of my devotions." Then he died.

Abu Ali al-Rudhbari said, "A dervish came to visit us. He died, so I buried him. I unshrouded his face when placing him in the earth so that God Most High might have mercy upon his being a stranger. He opened his eyes and said, 'O Abu Ali, will you then show me favors before the One Who has shown me such favors?' 'What, sir, alive after death?' I exclaimed. 'Indeed,' he said to me, 'I am alive, as every lover of God Almighty and Glorious is alive, in order to help you tomorrow by my position, Rudhbari!'"

It is related that Ibn Sahl al-Ispahani said, "Look—I am dying as everybody does, with sickness and visits of the doctor. Only I claim that if someone calls, 'O Ali!' I will answer." He was out walking one day when he suddenly cried out, "Here, I am, Lord!" (the cry of the pilgrims at Makkah)—and then he died.

I heard Muhammad ibn Abd-Allah al-Sufi say[10] . . . that Abu-l-Hasan al-Muzayyin said, "When Abu Yaqub al-Nahrajuri contracted his fatal illness and he was on his deathbed, I said him, "Say: 'There is no god but God.'"

He smiled at me and said, "Are you worried about me? By the might of Him Who tastes not death, there is nothing between me and Him but the veil of Power!" His light was instantly extinguished.

So Al-Muzayyin tore his beard, and cried, "A mere cupper like me, to teach the saints of God the profession of faith? I am so ashamed!" When he recalled this story, he began to weep.

Abu-l-Husayn al-Maliki said, "I kept company with Khayr al-Nassaj for many years. Eight days before his death he said to me, "I am going to die Thursday at sunset, and I will be buried on Friday, before the congregational prayer. You are going to forget this—but don't forget!'"

Abu-l-Husayn said, "I was made to forget it until Friday. Then I ran into someone who told me that Khayr al-Nassaj had died. I went out to be present at his funeral. I found people on the way back, saying, 'He will be buried after the prayer,' but I stayed there and did not leave. I found that the funeral was held before the prayer, just as he had said. "I questioned someone who had been with the shaykh when he died. He said, 'He lost consciousness, then came to himself, turned in the direction of the Holy House, and said, "Stop, may God forgive you! You are a servant under orders, and I am a servant under orders. That to which you have been ordered has not left you, while that to which I have been ordered is leaving me!" He called for water, renewed his ablution, and prayed. Then he stretched out and closed his eyes.' He was seen in a dream after his death, and asked, 'How is your state?' 'Don't ask me!' he replied. 'But I have been freed from this filthy world of yours.'"

Abu-l-Husayn al-Humsi, the author of *The Book of the Splendor of Secrets*, said that when Sahl ibn Abd-Allah (al-Tustari) died, people flocked to his funeral. In the city lived a Jew who was perhaps seventy years old. He heard the clamor and went out to see what it was about. When he looked at the funeral he gave a cry and asked, "Do you see what I see?" "No," they answered. "What do you see?" "I see companies of folk descending from the heavens and washing themselves for the funeral!" Then he made the profession of faith, became a Muslim, and made good his Islam.

I heard Abu Abd al-Rahman al-Sulami say[11] . . . that Abu Said al-Kharraz said that he was in Mecca, and one day passed by the Gate of the Banu Shayban. He saw a young man with a beautiful face lying dead. I looked into his countenance—and he smiled in my face! "O Abu Said," he said to me, "Didn't you know that the lovers are alive, even if they have died? They are only transported from one abode to another."

And I heard him say[12] . . . al-Jurayri said: It came to my attention that Dhu-l-Nun, in his death agony, was asked, "Counsel us!"

"Do not distract me!" said he. "I am amazed at the beauties of His grace!"

And I heard him say[13] . . . Abu Uthman al-Hiri said:

At the point of death, Abu Hafs (al-Haddad) was asked for his advice.

"I have no strength to say," he said.

Then he found strength in himself, so the questioner urged, "Speak, so that I can relate it from you."

"My advice," he said, "is that every heart should break, for falling short."

5 ON THE HEART'S DIRECT KNOWLEDGE OF GOD (*MARIFAH BILLAH*)

God Most High said, "*And they honor not God with the honor due Him*" (6:91). According to commentary, this means, "They do not know God as He deserves to be known."

Abd al-Rahman ibn Muhammad ibn Abd-Allah al-Adl related[1] . . . from Ayisha that the Messenger of God said, "The support of a house is its foundation, and the support of religion is the direct knowledge of God Most High, certainty, and the taming intellect." I asked, "By my father and mother, what is the taming intellect?" "Abstinence from disobeying God and eagerness in obeying God," he said.

Marifah—gnosis, intuition, realization, true familiarity—in the language of scholars means *ilm*, knowledge. Thus every gnosis is a form of knowledge and every knowledge is a form of gnosis. Everyone learned in God knows Him and everyone who knows Him is learned. But according to the Sufis, *marifah* is the trait of someone who knows the Truth in His Names and Attributes and then bears witness to the Divine in all his actions.

The gnostic is purified of base characteristics and the disasters of his nature. He stands patiently at the door of God and remains secluded in his heart. He enjoys the good graces of God and corroborates Him in all of his states. He has cut off the whims of his own self. He does not permit a thought in his heart that would summon to other than God. He becomes a stranger to the creation and is liberated from the catastrophes of his ego. He is cleansed of attachments and distractions and in his secret being is always conversing with God Most High. His every glance returns to God Most High. The Truth inspires him with the intuition of His secrets—the secrets of the course of His Omnipotence. That is why such a person is called an *arif*, a gnostic, and his state is called *marifah,* direct knowledge.

In general, it is to the measure of one's alienation from one's own ego that one attains direct knowledge of one's Lord. Each of the shaykhs who has spoken of direct knowledge has discussed what has happened to him and hinted at what he has found in his own experience.

I heard Abu Ali al-Daqqaq say, "One of the tokens of the gnosis of God is the achievement of deep awe and reverence for God. If someone's realization increases, his awe increases." And I heard him say, "Gnosis requires stillness of heart, just as learning requires outward quiet. If someone's gnosis increases, his tranquility increases."

I heard Abu Abd al-Rahman al-Sulami say[2] . . . that Shibli said, "The gnostic has no worldly attachment. The lover has no complaint of his Beloved. The servant has no pretension. The one who fears God has no rest. No one has any escape from God."

And I heard him say[3] . . . that Shibli, when asked about gnosis, said, "Its beginning is God Most High, and its end is endless." And I heard him say[4] . . . that Abu Hafs al-Haddad said, "Since I came to know God, neither truth nor falsehood has entered my heart."

What Abu Hafs has here expressed is somewhat ambiguous. Its greatest implication is that among the Sufis, direct divine knowledge requires that the servant be absent from himself and so overwhelmed by the remembrance of God that he witnesses only God Almighty and Glorious. He refers to nothing outside of God.

When events occur to an ordinary intelligent person or he has some kind of experience, he refers to his own heart, his own thoughts and recollections. The gnostic refers only to his Lord. Since he is occupied only with his Lord, he cannot turn to his heart. How shall meaning enter the heart of a person who no longer possesses one? There is a difference between someone who lives through his heart and someone who lives through his Lord.

Abu Yazid al-Bistami was asked about realization. He quoted, "'Kings, when they enter a city, ruin it, and make the high among its people to be low.' (27:34)" This is the meaning hinted at by Abu Hafs.

Abu Yazid also said, "People have states, but the gnostic has no state. His form has been erased and his identity annihilated in the identity of Another. All trace of him has vanished into the traces of Another."

Al-Wasiti observed, "While the servant is satisfied with God and in need of God, direct knowledge of God is not appropriate for him."

What al-Wasiti means is that this satisfaction and need are signs of the servant's sobriety and the persistence of his own form. Both traits pertain to the servant. The gnostic, however, is effaced in the One he knows. And how could this be—that someone should be overcome by God's existence or drowned in His vision—while the servant has not reached a state of being in which he is kept from the perception of any trait that might be called his own?

Thus al-Wasiti also stated, "He who knows God Most High is stopped short—rather, he is struck dumb and subdued." The Prophet said, "I cannot count the praises due to You." Such are the qualities of those who hit the far target, but those who have descended from this limit have spoken about realization and at length.

Muhammad ibn al-Husayn related[5] . . . that Ahmad ibn Asim al-Antaki said, "He who knows God best fears Him most."

A Sufi said, "He who knows God Most High tires of his own continuing existence, and the world with all its breadth becomes narrow for him." It is said, "When someone knows God, his livelihood is serene, and life is sweet to him. Everything honors him. The fear of created things leaves him, and he is intimate with God Most High. The fear of worldly things leaves the one who knows God. He does without union and separation. Gnosis produces shame and the glorification of God, just as affirming the unity (*tawhid*) produces satisfaction with His will and surrender to Him."

Ruwaym said, "To the gnostic, divine knowledge is a mirror. When he looks into it, his Lord appears to him." Dhu-l- Nun al-Misri said, "The spirits of the prophets raced in the arena of divine knowledge, and the spirit of our Prophet was first to the fountain of union." Dhu-l- Nun al-Misri also said, "The company of the gnostic is like the company of God Most High. He will tolerate your ways and be gentle to you because he is qualified with the qualities of God."

Ibn Yazdanyar was asked, "When does the gnostic see the Truth?" He said, "When the witness appears but things witnessed disappear, when the senses depart and sincerity vanishes."

Husayn ibn Mansur al-Hallaj said, "When the servant reaches the stage of direct knowledge, God inspires his thoughts and protects his inmost being from fabricating any thought but the truth." And he said, "The mark of the gnostic is that he is empty of this world and the next."

Sahl ibn Abd-Allah al-Tustari remarked, "The goal of realization is two things: perplexity and amazement." I heard Muhammad ibn al-

Husayn say[6] . . . that Dhu-l- Nun al-Misri said, "The person who knows God Most High best is the one who is most amazed in Him." And I heard him say[7] . . . that Abu Umar al-Antaki said, "A man mentioned to Junayd, 'Some esotericists say that abandoning all action is the door of righteousness and fear of God.' Junayd said, 'This is the speech of people who talk of dropping religious works. To me this is very grave. Someone who steals or commits adultery is in a better state than whoever says this. The gnostics receive their works from God Most High and return with them to Him. If I were to live for a 1,000 years, I would not diminish the works of goodness by an atom's weight.'"

Someone asked Abu Yazid, "Through what thing did you find this gnosis?" He replied, "Through an empty belly and a naked body." Abu Yaqub al-Nahrajuri said, "I asked Abu Yaqub al-Susi, 'Does the gnostic lament over anything but God?' He answered, 'Does he see anything else that he should lament over it?' I asked, 'With what eye does he look at things?' He answered, 'With the eye of annihilation and passing away.'" Abu Yazid said, "The gnostic is a bird, the ascetic a wayfarer." "The gnostic's eye weeps," they say, "but his heart laughs."

Junayd said, "The gnostic is not really a gnostic until he is like the earth upon which walk righteous and wicked alike or like the clouds which shade everything or like the rain which gives water to the loved and the unloved." Yahya ibn Muadh commented, "The gnostic goes forth from this world with two goals yet unfulfilled: his weeping over himself and his praise for his Lord."

Abu Yazid said, "People only reach gnosis by squandering what is theirs and holding fast to what is His." I heard Abu Abd al-Rahman al-Sulami say[8] . . . that Yusuf ibn Ali said, "The gnostic is not truly a gnostic until if he were given a kingdom like Solomon's, it would not distract him from God for the blink of an eye." And I heard him say9[8] . . . that Ibn Ata said, "Direct knowledge has three pillars: awe, shame, and intimacy."

I also heard him say[10] . . . that Yusuf ibn al-Husayn said, "Dhu-l-Nun al-Misri was asked, 'How do you know your Lord?' He replied, 'I know my Lord by my Lord. Were it not for my Lord, I would not know my Lord.'"

"The learned man imitates examples," it is said, "but the gnostic receives living guidance." The gnostic gives no attention to anything but God," Shibli remarked. "He does not speak of anything else for even a sentence and sees no protector for himself but God Most High."

They say that the gnostic is friendly with the remembrance of God but estranged from His creation, dependent upon God but independent of His creation, abased before God but exalted over His creation. Abu-l-Tayyib al-Samiri said, "Direct knowledge is the Truth's approach to people's inward hearts by means of lights." Is is said that the gnostic is more than what he talks about, while the scholar is less than what he talks about.

Abu Sulayman al-Darani said, "God Most High reveals to the gnostic lying upon his bed more than He reveals to anyone else standing in prayer." Junayd said, "The gnostic: God speaks from his inner being, while he himself is silent."

Dhu-l-Nun said, "Everything has a punishment and the punishment for the gnostic is to be cut off from the remembrance of God." I heard Abu Hatim al-Sijistani say[10] . . . that Ruwaym said, "The hypocrisy of gnostics is better than the sincerity of students." Abu Bakr al-Warraq observed, "The gnostic's silence is more profitable to him, but his speaking is sweeter and more delicious." Dhu-l-Nun said, "Ascetics are the kings of the next world, but they are the poor among the gnostics."

Junayd was asked about the gnostic. He replied, "The color of the water is the color of the vessel." (That is, the gnostic is under the rule of his immediate state.)

Asked about the gnostic, Abu Yazid said, "Sleeping he sees nothing but God. Waking he sees nothing but God. He conforms to nothing but God. He studies nothing but God."

I heard Muhammad ibn al-Husayn say that he heard Abd-Allah ibn Muhammad al-Dimashqi say that one of the shaykhs was asked, "By what means do you know God Most High?" He replied, "By means of a flash signaling news gathered by an established discernment and an utterance coming forth from a lost and ruined tongue." (The shaykh is hinting at a manifest ecstasy and giving word of a hidden secret. He is himself insofar as he is manifested and something else insofar as he is hidden). Thus they recited:

I spoke without any speech that was speech.
That speech was Your expression — or it's
    manifestation in speech.
You showed Yourself to hide me. While You were
    hidden from me
You made lightning flash upon me, and lightning
    made me speak.

And I heard him say[11] . . . that al-Jurayri said that Abu Turab al-Nakhshabi was asked about the character of the gnostic. He said, "The gnostic is polluted by nothing and purifies everything." And I heard him say that Abu Uthman al-Maghribi said, "The lights of knowledge shine upon the gnostic, and with them he sees the wonders of the unseen. I also heard him say that Abu Ali al-Daqqaq said, "The gnostic is drowned in the seas of realization. As one of them said, 'Divine know-ledge is plunging waves: they ebb and flow.'"

Yahya ibn Muadh was asked about the gnostic and replied, "He is a man existent, separate." Another time he said, "He exists and yet is separate." Dhu-l-Nun said, "The gnostic has three marks: the light of his gnosis does not extinguish the light of his moral care; he does not believe any piece of esoteric knowledge that is contradicted by an exoteric rule; the many blessings of God upon him do not move him to tear the veils of God's forbidden things."

Direct knowledge is not attributed to the gnostic by people who seek the next world, they say. How then should it be attributed to him by people who seek this one? Abu Said al-Kharraz said, "Realization proceeds from a generous eye and the expenditure of effort."

I heard Muhammad ibn al-Husayn say[12]. . . that Jafar said that Junayd was asked about the saying of Dhu-l-Nun al-Misri describing the gnostic, "He was here, but he left." He commented, "The gnostic is not held back by any one state from any other. No station veils him from roaming freely among the stations. When he is with the people of any place, he finds in it the same things that they find. While he is there he articulates that place's qualities so that its people may profit." And I heard him say[13]. . . that Muhammad ibn al-Fadl said, "Direct knowledge is the life of the heart with God Most High." I also heard him say[14]. . . that al-Kattani said, "Abu Said al-Kharraz was asked, 'Does the gnostic come to a state that turns him away from weeping?' He said, 'Yes. Weeping belongs to the time of their journey to God. When they dismount at the realities of closeness, and through His goodness, they taste the flavor of union, weeping passes away from them.'

6 ON LOVE OF GOD (*MAHABBAH*)

God Almighty and Glorious said, "*O you who believe, if anyone among you turns back from His religion—God will bring a peo - ple whom He loves and who love Him*" (5:54).

Abu Naim Abd al-Malik ibn al-Husayn reported[1]. . . from Abu Hurayra that the Messenger of God said, "Whoever loves to meet God, God loves to meet him. Whoever does not love to meet God, God does not love to meet him." Abu-l-Husayn Ali ibn Ahmad ibn Abdan report-ed[2]. . . from Anas ibn Malik that the Messenger heard from Gabriel that his Lord said, "Whoever humiliates a friend of Mine has declared war upon Me. I do not hesitate in anything that I do as I hesitate in taking the soul of My believing servant who hates death, and I hate to trouble him—but it must be. My servant does not come close to Me with anything that is dearer to Me than the performance of the things that I have made his duty. My servant will not stop coming close to Me with extra devotions until I love him, and when I love him I become his hearing and his sight and his hand and his support."

Ali ibn Ahmad ibn Abdan reported[3]. . . from Abu Hurayra that the Prophet said, "When God Almighty and Glorious loves the servant, He says to Gabriel, "O Gabriel, I love so-and-so. You love him too." So Gabriel loves him. Then Gabriel calls to all the heavenly folk, 'God Most High loves so-and-so. You love him too!' So all the denizens of the heavens love him, and they prepare a welcome for him in the earth. When God hates the servant, he says, 'What is wrong with you?' It seems that in His displeasure He says nothing more than that."

Love is a noble condition that the Truth has acknowledged to the servant. He has informed the servant of the existence of His love. The Truth, glory to Him, may be described as loving the servant, and the servant may be described as loving the Truth.

In scholarly usage, love, *mahabbah*, means will, *iradah*, but the Sufis do not mean will when they speak of love. For human will does not connect to the Eternal—unless one understands it as the will to draw close to Him and glorify Him. We shall mention here just a fraction of the examination of this subject, if God Most High so wills.

The love of the Truth—glory to Him—for the servant is His will to bestow special blessings upon that servant. Just so, His mercy is also His will to bless, but mercy is more particular than will, and love is more particular than mercy. For the will of God Most High, when it brings reward and blessing to the servant, is called mercy. And when that will selects the servant for closeness and exalted states, it is called love. God's will is a single attribute, but through the variety of aims to which it attaches itself, it takes on different names. When it concerns punishment, it is called anger. When it concerns general blessings, it is called mercy. When it concerns special blessings, it is called love.

One party holds that God's love for the servant means His praise and beautiful approval. The meaning of His love, in that case, comes back to His speech—and His speech is eternal. Another party holds that God's love for the servant is one of the attributes of action. It is then a special virtue through which the servant encounters God and a special state to which he ascends. As one holding this view has said, "God's mercy to the servant is a blessing that accompanies him." A party of our respected forebears simply said that God's love is one of the divine attributes related in the Traditions so they permitted the use of the expression but refrained from commenting upon it.

As for traits in excess of this—the well-known attributes of human love, such as sympathizing with the beloved object and seeking to be intimate with it or the creaturely state the lover experiences when with his beloved—the Eternal, glory to Him, is exalted above all that.

If we turn to the love of the servant for God, it is a condition found in the servant's heart that is too fine and subtle to be expressed. This condition moves him to the glorification of God, the preference for God's good pleasure above all else, a lack of patience away from Him, a passionate excitement about Him, and an inability to rest anywhere short of Him. It shows itself in the existence of a desire to draw close to Him through continuously remembering Him within the heart. The servant's love for God contains no sympathetic identification and lays no claim to possessing the Beloved. How should it? For the reality of His Absolute nature is hallowed beyond being overtaken, perceived or comprehended. The lover, drowned in the Beloved, is closer to Him than he would be if he could be said to possess the Beloved.

Love cannot be described with any clearer attribute or defined with a more understandable definition than to say that it is love. One makes a close study of what has been said about it in order to resolve ambiguities. When this abstruseness and obscurity pass away, the need to immerse oneself in the explanation of statements can be dropped. People have offered a great many explanations of love, including discussions of its linguistic roots.

Some say that *hubb*, love, is a name for purity of affection, because the bedouins when speaking of the pure whiteness and regularity of someone's teeth use the expression *habab al-asnan*. Others say that since *hubab* is a word for the excess water that results from a heavy rain, *mahabbah* came to mean the heart's boiling and stirring with the thirst and excitement of meeting the Beloved. Still others say the word is derived from *habab al-ma*, the greater part of a body of water, because love is the object of most of the heart's concerns. Another derivation draws the word from necessity and fixity, for one says *ahabba al-baghir* of a camel that kneels and refuses to stand. In just this way the lover's heart refuses to leave the remembrance of his Beloved. *Hubb* is also said to come from *hibb*, an earring. The poet says:

> The snake showed its flicking tongue at the place of
>   his earring;
> Stealthily listening to secrets.

The earring is called *hibb* either because of its clinging to the ear or because of its jangling sound; both of these meanings are acceptable (as original associations) for love.

Other derivations are from *habb* (the plural of *habbah*), bread, and *habbat al-qalb*, the heart's blood, meaning the thing that sustains it. So love would be called *hubb* from the name of its location. *Habb* and *hubb* are said to be like *amr* and *umr*, (synonyms, both of which mean "lifetime"). *Hubb* is also said to be taken from *hibbah,* the seeds of desert plants, and so named because it is the kernel of life, just as a seed is the kernel of vegetation. *Hubb* is also the name of the four planks upon which one sets a jar. Love is then called *hubb* because it supports everything that comes from the beloved, whether it be humiliating or exalting.

Again, the name of love comes from that *hubb* which is a vessel that contains water. The vessel holds what is in it, but has no room for anything but what fills it. Like this, when the heart is full of love, it has no space for anything but the Beloved.

As for the sayings of the shaykhs, they have said that love is the perpetual inclination of the enraptured heart; preference for the Beloved over every friend; harmony with the Beloved in what is seen and what is unseen; the effacement of the attributes of the lover and the affirmation of the essence of the Beloved; the heart's agreement with the wishes of the Lord; the fear of abandoning reverence together with established service.

Abu Yazid al-Bistami said, "Love is to count it as little when a great deal comes from yourself and to count it as much when a little bit comes from your Beloved." Sahl al-Tustari said, "Love is to embrace obedience and leave disobedience." Junayd, asked about love, said, "It is to enter into the attributes of the Beloved in exchange for the attributes of the lover."

Junayd was indicating the state of being overwhelmed by the remembrance of the Beloved until nothing can dominate the lover's heart except the recollection of the attributes of the Beloved. Then everything that pertains to the traits of the ego and the very sense of it is forgotten.

Abu Ali al-Rudhbari said, "Love is harmony." Abu Abd-Allah al-Qurayshi said, "The essence of love is to give all of yourself to the one you love so that nothing of yourself remains to you." Shibli said, "Love is called love because it erases from the heart everything except the Beloved." Ibn Ata said, "Love is to always be blameworthy."

I heard Abu Ali al-Daqqaq say, "Love is a delight, and occasions of reality are an amazement." And I heard him say, "Passionate desire (*ishq*) means to exceed the bounds in love. The Truth, glory to Him, cannot be described as exceeding bounds and so passion is not attributed to Him. And if all of the loves of all of creation converged in one person, that love would not reach the degree of love that is due to the Truth—so it cannot be said that a servant exceeds the bounds in the love of God."

So passion cannot be attributed to the Truth and cannot be attributed to the servant in his love of the Truth. Thus passion is disqualified. It is not possible in the description of the Truth. It does not proceed from the Truth to the servant nor proceed from the servant to the Truth.

I heard Abu Abd al-Rahman al-Sulami say[4] . . . that Shibli said, "Love means you are jealous that anyone else like you should love the

Beloved." And I heard him say[5] . . . that Ibn Ata, when asked about love, said, "Love's branches are planted in the heart and bear fruit according to one's mind." And I heard him say that al-Nasrabadhi said, "There is a love that demands the sparing of blood, and there is a love that demands the spilling of blood." I also heard him say[6] . . . that Sumnun said, "The lovers of God Most High have carried off the honors in this world and the next; for the Prophet said, 'A man is together with the one he loves'—so they are together with God Most High."

Yahya ibn Muadh said, "The essence of love is not decreased by harshness or increased by kindness." And he said, "That person is not truthful who claims to love God yet does not respect the limits He has set." Junayd said, "When love is sound, the rules of behavior fall away." With this meaning Abu Ali recited:

When people's love is pure, their ties are constant
Speeches of praise sound ugly.

He used to say, "You don't see a kindly father showing elaborate respect when he talks to his son. People may stand on ceremony when they address a man, but his father just calls him by name." Al-Kattani said, "Love is to prefer the beloved to oneself."

I heard Muhammad ibn al-Husayn say that[7] . . . Bundar ibn al-Husayn said, "Majnun ibn Amir was seen in a dream. He was asked, "What did God do with you?" He replied, "He forgave me and set me as evidence against the lovers."

Abu Yaqub al-Susi said, "The essence of love is that the servant forgets what he has received from God and forgets what he needs from Him." Husayn ibn al-Mansur said, "The essence of love is that you stand with your Beloved stripped of your attributes."

I heard Abu Abd al-Rahman al-Sulami say that Nasrabadhi was told, "People say you have not experienced love." He said, "People have spoken the truth, but I have their griefs and in that I am inflamed." And I heard him say that Nasrabadhi said, "Love is to avoid solace in every circumstance." Then he recited:

One whose passion is prolonged tastes a kind
     of forgetting
But I taste no forgetfulness of Layla.
The closest I came to union with her

Consisted of wishes that did not come true,
    passing like a lightning flash.
Muhammad ibn al-Fadl said, "Love means that every love falls
from the heart except the love of the Beloved."
Junayd said, "Love is an excess of attraction without fulfillment."
Love, it is said, is a disturbance of hearts occasioned by the beloved.
And it is said to be a trial imposed upon the innermost heart by the
object of one's desire.
    Ibn Ata recited:

I planted a branch of desire for the people of love.
No one before me knew what desire was.
As a branch it came to leaf. It ripened as the
    infatuation of youth
Then bitterness was born to me from the sweet fruit.
The desire of all of the lovers, every one—
If they look for its history, that is its origin.
It is said that the beginning of love is deception, and
    its end is slaughter.

    I heard Abu Ali say (concerning the meaning of the saying of the
Prophet, "'Your love of a thing makes you blind and deaf). It makes
you blind to all but the Beloved out of jealousy and to the Beloved out
of awe." Then he recited:

When what appears to me is His Grandeur
I turn back as if I had not arrived.

    I heard Abu Abd al-Rahman al-Sulami say[8] . . . that Harith al-
Muhasibi said, "Love is your attraction to a thing with your entire
being; then your preference for it over your own self, your soul, and
your possessions; then your harmony with it privately and publicly;
then your knowledge that you have fallen short in the love of it." And
I heard him say[9] . . . that Sari said, "Love between two is not sound
until the one says to the other, "O I!"
    Shibli said, "The lover is destroyed if he keeps silent. The Knower
is destroyed if he does not keep silent." It is said:

Love is a fire in the heart that burns all but the wish
    of the Beloved."

Love is to spend all effort while the Beloved does
what He wills."

Nuri said, "Love tears veils and reveals secrets." Abu Yaqub al-
Susi said, "Love is not sound until one leaves off seeing love and,
instead, sees the Beloved through the annihilation of the knowledge of
love." Jafar said that Junayd said, "Sari gave me a scrap of paper and
said, 'This is better for you than 700 stories or traditions of the
Companions.' On it was written:

When I claimed to love, she said, "You lie to me!
"How should I see your limbs still clothed in flesh?
"It isn't love till your heart cleaves to your guts,
"And you waste away past answering any caller—
"You waste away till no desire remains
"But an eye to cry with and a secret shared!"

Ibn Masruq said, "I saw Sumnun speak about love; every lamp in
the mosque shattered." I heard Muhammad ibn al-Husayn say[10] . . .
that Ibrahim ibn Fatik said, "Sumnun was seated in the mosque discoursing upon love when a little bird came in. It came closer and closer to him never stopping its approach, until it was sitting upon his
hand. Then it struck its beak upon the earth until the blood flowed
and it died." Junayd said, 'Every love pertains to an object. When the
object vanishes, that love vanishes.'"

Shibli, it is told, was committed to an asylum. A number of people
went to see him. "Who are you?" he asked. "We are people who love
you, Abu Bakr," they replied. He began to throw stones at them, and
they ran away. "If you claim to love me," he called, "then you should
be patient under my trial!"

Shibli recited:

O Generous Lord, the love of You
     never ends inside me.
O You who take sleep from my eyes
You know what has happened to me.

I heard Abu Abd al-Rahman al-Sulami say[11] . . . that Ali ibn
Ubayd said, "Yahya ibn Muadh wrote to Abu Yazid, 'I am intoxicated
with how much I have drunk from the cup of love.' Abu Yazid wrote

back to him, 'Someone else has drunk the oceans of the heavens and the earth and his thirst is not yet quenched. His tongue is hanging out and he is asking, "Is there any more?"'

They recited:

> I'm amazed at someone who says, "I've remembered
>   my darling."
> Have I ever forgotten, that I should have to
>   remember?
> I die remembering You, then come back to life.
> Were it not for my good thought of You, I would not
>   have revived.
> Desire's object lives when I die to desire.
> How many times have I lived for you, how many
>   times died?
> I drink love, glass after glass.
> The glass is not empty. My thirst is not sated.

God Most High revealed to Jesus, "When I look upon the heart of a servant and do not find in it the love of this world or the next, I fill it with the love of Me." I saw in the handwriting of Abu Ali al-Daqqaq, in an inspired book, "My servant, I love you as a right due to you. So love Me as is My right." Abd-Allah ibn al-Mubarak said, "Whoever is given something of love and has not been given the same amount of fear is deceived." Love, it is said, is that which obliterates all trace of you. Love is said to be a drunkenness from which one never recovers except through seeing the Beloved. And the drunkenness that then comes of that vision cannot be described. They recite:

> The people grew drunk from passing the cup,
> But the One who passed it made them drunker still.

Abu Ali al-Daqqaq often recited:

> I have two intoxications; the regretful have but one.
> The thing by which I am distinguished from them is
>   One.

Ibn Ata said, "Love is to perish continuously." Abu Ali had a woman servant named Fayruz whom he used to love because she would often wait upon him. I heard him say, "One day Fayruz was bothering me and speaking sharply to me. Abu-l-Hasan al-Qari said,

'Why are you troubling this shaykh?' She replied, 'Because I love him!'"

Yahya ibn Muadh said, "A mustard seed's worth of love is dearer to me than seventy years of loveless worship." A young man looked down over the people gathered on the festival day and said:

Whoever dies of love, let him die thus.
There is no good in love without death!
Then he cast himself from a high terrace and fell down dead.

It is said that a Hindu loved a maidservant. She moved away and the man went out to say farewell. Tears fell from one of his eyes but not the other. For eighty-four years he kept shut the eye that did not weep. He would not open it in order to punish it for not crying over the departure of his beloved. With this meaning they recited:

My one eye wept on the morn of departure.
The other was miserly toward us with tears.
I punished the tear-miser by closing it tight
On the day when we met again.

A Sufi said, "We were discussing love among ourselves in the presence of Dhu-l- Nun al-Misri. He said, 'Drop this topic. The lower self cannot hear of it and so it pretends to it.' Then he began to recite:

Fear and sadness best befit the sinner when he
    worships.
Love is for the pious and the purified of filth.

Yahya ibn Muadh said, "Whoever spreads talk of love among those not suited for it is an impostor in what he claims." It is said that a man claimed to have been totally overcome by the love of a particular person. "How can that be?" the youth asked him. "My brother here has a more handsome face than I and a more perfect beauty!" The man raised his head to see and the youth threw him off the balcony upon which they were standing. "That is the reward of whoever pretends to love me but looks at someone else!" said he.

Sumnun used to give love priority over inner knowledge, but most of the shaykhs have given inner knowledge priority over love. Among those who know the true meanings of things, love means to be overwhelmed with delight, while inner knowledge means to bear witness with wonder and to lose oneself in awe.

Abu Bakr al-Kattani said, "The topic of love arose in Mecca during the pilgrimage season, and all the shaykhs were talking about it. Junayd was the youngest present. 'Share with us what you know about it, O Iraqi!' the others urged. "He cast down his head, and his eyes were full of tears. He said, 'There is a servant who has left himself behind, who is attached to the remembrance of his Lord, who is steadfast in performing the duties due Him, who looks to Him in his heart, a heart burning with the lights of His Essence. God has purified the draught he has drunk from the cup of His love. The All-Powerful has raised for him the veils of the unseen. If he discourses, it is through God. If he speaks privately, it is from God. If he moves, it is by the order of God. If he keeps still, it is together with God. He is by God, for God, with God.' The shaykhs wept and said, 'There is nothing to be said beyond this. May God grant you strength, O Crown of the Knowers!'"

God Most High revealed to Prophet David, "O David, I have forbidden My love to enter hearts while the love of something else is in them." Hamzah ibn Yusuf al-Sahmi related that[2] . . . Abu Abbas, the servant of al-Fudayl ibn Iyad, said, "Fudayl suffered from retention of the urine. He raised his hands and prayed, 'My God, by my love for You, unless You relieve me of this, I won't go away until I am cured!'"

Love, they say, is to prefer the other above oneself. Thus the wife of Pharaoh's minister, when her love for Joseph became great, said, "*I tried to tempt him, but he is surely one of the truthful*" (12:51). In the beginning, though, she had said, "*What should be the requital of one who wished to do evil to your wife, except imprisonment or a painful punishment?*" (12:25). In the beginning she attributed the sin to him, but in the end she admitted the treachery was hers.

I heard Abu Ali say that it is related that Abu Said al-Kharraz said, "I saw the Prophet in a dream and said, 'Messenger of God, forgive me! Loving God has distracted me from loving you.' He replied, 'O blessed one, whoever loves God Most High loves me.'" In her private prayers, Rabiah asked, "My God, would You burn in the fire a heart that loves You?" A voice from the unseen replied, "We would not do such a thing. Do not think bad thoughts about Us!"

The word for love, *hubb*, is made of two letters, "*h*" and "*b*." This is said to indicate that whoever loves must leave behind both soul (*ruh*, symbolized by its final letter) and body (*badan*, symbolized by its initial letter).

In summary, the Sufis have said that love, overall, is harmony, and that the strongest form of harmony is the harmony of the heart. Love requires the absence of all discord. The lover is always together with his Beloved. Thus we have received the following hadith: Abu Bakr ibn Furak reported[12] . . . that Abu Musa al-Ashari said, "The Prophet was asked, 'If a man loves a people, will he not overtake and join them?' The Prophet answered, 'A man is with the one he loves.'"

I heard Abu Abd al-Rahman al-Sulami say[13] . . . that Abu Hafs said, "Most corruption of states comes from three things: the dissoluteness of gnostics, the faithlessness of lovers, and the dishonesty of seekers."

Abu Uthman said, "The dissoluteness of gnostics means freeing their glances, tongues, and hearing to follow worldly causes and benefits. The faithlessness of lovers means their choosing their own whims over the pleasure of God Almighty and Glorious in whatever they encounter. The dishonesty of seekers means their being occupied with the remembrance and vision of people to the exclusion of the remembrance of God." And I heard him say[14] . . . that Abu Ali Mumshad ibn Said al-Ukbari said, "Inside the dome of Solomon's temple, a male swallow courted a female swallow. She refused to have anything to do with him. He asked her, 'Why do you reject me? If you wished, I would pull down this dome on top of Solomon!' Prophet Solomon summoned the bird to him. "What is the meaning of this?" he demanded. "O Prophet of God," pleaded the bird, "lovers are not to blame for the things they say!" "You have spoken the truth!" said the king.

7 ON LONGING (SHAWQ)

God Almighty and Glorious said, "*Whoever hopes to meet his Lord—God has delayed the meeting*" (29:5).

Ali ibn Ahmad ibn Abdan al-Ahwazi reported[1] . . . that al-Saib said, "Ammar ibn Yasir prayed with us. He made the prayer short. 'You have made a simple prayer, Abu Yaqzan!' I exclaimed. 'That is not my doing,' he replied. 'I have prayed to God with prayers that I heard from the Messenger of God. Once when he stood up after finishing his private prayer, a man who was there at the time followed him and asked him what he had said. He told him, "My God, by Your knowledge of the unseen and Your power over the Creation, make me live the life You know to be best for me. Make me die the death You know to be best for me. My God, I ask You for the middle course between wealth and poverty. I ask You for a blessing that does not diminish and a comfort that is unbroken. I ask You for satisfaction after Your judgment and ease of existence after death. I ask to look upon Your Generous Face, and for the longing to meet You without painful distress, without misleading trials. My God, adorn us with the adornment of faith. My God, make us leaders of the well-guided."'

Longing, *shawq*, is the heart's excitement to meet the Beloved. One's longing is to the extent of one's love.

I heard Abu Ali al-Daqqaq discriminate between longing, *shawq*, and passionate desire, *ishtiyaq*. He said: Longing is quieted by meeting and seeing the Beloved, but passionate desire does not cease with the meeting. With this sense they recited:

> The glance turns not away from Him when He is
> seen
> Save to come back ardently to Him.

I heard Abu Abd al-Rahman al-Sulami say that al-Nasrabadhi said, "Every person has some share of longing, but not everyone has a share of passionate desire. Whoever enters into the state of ardent yearning wanders distracted in it until no trace of him remains to be seen." It is said that Ahmad ibn Hamid al-Aswad went to Abd-Allah ibn Munazil and said, "I saw in a dream that you will die in a year. Are you ready to go?" "Have you delayed us for so long a time?" Abd-Allah ibn Munazil cried. "How shall I manage to live for a whole year? I feel so close to that verse I heard from al-Thaqafi (that is, Abu Ali):

O you who complain of desire because the
      separation from Him has been long,
Be patient in your illness. You shall meet your
Beloved tomorrow.

Abu Uthman said, "The sign of longing is to love death with ease." Yahya ibn Muadh said, "The sign of longing is the weaning of the body away from lusts." I heard Abu Ali al-Daqqaq say, "One day Prophet David went out into the desert alone. God Most High revealed to him, "How is it that I see you solitary, O David?" "My God," he replied, "Longing to meet You possesses my heart and comes between me and the society of men." God Most High revealed, "Return to them. If you guide one servant who has strayed to Me, I will put your name on the Guarded Tablet as a great sage."

An old woman, it is told, went out to meet a relative who had arrived after a long journey. All of her people were showing great joy, but the old lady wept. They asked her, "Why are you crying?" and she replied, "The arrival of this young man reminds me of the day of arrival before God Most High."

Ibn Ata was asked about longing and said, "The burning of guts, the blazing of hearts, the laceration of livers!" Then they asked him which was higher, longing or love. He said, "Love—because longing is born of it."

A Sufi said, "Longing is a flame generated in the folds of the bowels and produced by separation. If there is meeting, that flame is extinguished. When what dominates one's innermost being is the witnessing of the Beloved, longing does not befall one." A dervish was asked, "Do you yearn?" "No," said he. "Longing is only for someone absent. He is here!"

I heard Abu Ali al-Daqqaq say, concerning God's word, "*And I has -*

tened to You, my Lord, to please You" (20:84). The meaning of this is, "Out of longing for You." It is veiled by the expression "good pleasure."

And I heard him say, "One of the signs of longing is to wish for death when everything is going well. Thus Prophet Joseph did not say, "Take me to You!" when he was cast into the well nor when he was put into prison. But when his parents came to him and his brothers fell down prostrate before him, and wealth and dominion were his, then he said, *"Take me to You in full submission"* (12: 101). With this sense the Sufis recited:

We have the most perfect of joys,
But only with you will joy be complete.
Our joy is shame, people of love,
Since you are absent, though we are here.

They also recited:

Whom does the new holiday bring joy?
I've found no joy in it.
My happiness would be perfect
Were my Beloved here with me.

Ibn Khafif said, "Longing is the heart's finding rest in ecstasy and the love of that meeting with God that takes place through closeness to Him." Abu Yazid said, "God has servants who, if He veiled them from seeing Him in paradise, would seek rescue from paradise the way that the people of hell seek rescue from the fire."

Muhammad ibn Abd-Allah al-Sufi reported[2] . . . that al-Husayn al-Ansari said, "In a dream it seemed to me that the day of judgment had come. There was a person standing under the Throne of God. The Truth said, "O My angels, who is this?" "God knows best!" they replied. He said, "This is Maruf al-Karkhi, drunken with My love. He will not recover except by meeting with Me."

In another relation of a dream like this it is said, "This is Maruf al-Karkhi. He left the world out of yearning for God so God Almighty and Glorious permits that he look upon Him." Faris said, "The hearts of those full of ardent yearning are illuminated with the light of God Most High. When their yearning is awakened, that light illumines all that exists between heaven and earth. God displays them to His angels, and says, "These are they who passionately desire Me. I call you to witness that I desire them more!"

I heard Abu Ali al-Daqqaq comment on the prayer of the Prophet, "I ask You for the longing to meet You." Longing had a hundred parts. Ninety-nine of them were given to him and one part was distributed among the people. But he wanted that one part to be his also, out of jealousy that there should be even a fragment of longing for anyone else. The longing felt by people who are close to God is more complete than that felt by those who are still veiled. If those who yearn for God sip at the sweetness of death when it comes, it is because they have been shown that the comfort of meeting Him is sweeter than honey.

I heard Muhammad ibn al-Husayn say[3] . . . that Sari said, "Longing, when it is thoroughly actualized, is the greater station for a gnostic. When he attains longing, he becomes oblivious to whatever might turn him away from the object of his longing."

Abu Uthman al-Hiri commented on the divine words, "*God has delayed the meeting*" (29:5), saying, "This is a consolation for those who yearn for Him. It means, 'I know your desire for Me has overcome you, while I have put off the meeting with you until its appointed time. But soon you will reach the One Whom you desire.'"

It is told that God Most High revealed to Prophet David, "Tell the young men of Israel, 'Do not occupy yourselves with anything but Me. I am yearning for you—what sort of coarse behavior is this?'" It is also said that God Almighty and Glorious revealed to Prophet David, "If those who oppose Me knew how I watch over them, knew of My friendship toward them and My longing for them, they would abandon their disobedience and die out of longing for Me—though I have cut their connection to My love! O David, if this is My wish for people who oppose Me, what then shall be My wish for people who turn to Me?"

It is written in the Torah, "We set yearning in you, but you have not yearned. We set fear in you, but you have not feared. We set mourning in you, but you have not mourned."

I heard Abu Ali al-Daqqaq say, "Shuayb wept until he went blind, so God Almighty and Glorious returned his vision to him. Again he wept until he went blind, and again God returned his sight. A third time he wept until he was blinded." God Most High revealed to him, "If this weeping were for paradise, I would ensure it to you. If it were on account of hell, I would secure you from it." "No," said Shuayb. "It is out of desire for You." God revealed, "Since it is for the sake of that, I have appointed you My prophet, one who shall speak to Me over ten years."

They say everything yearns for the one who yearns for God. It comes in a hadith: "Paradise longs for three: Ali, Ammar, and Salman." I heard Abu Ali say that one of the shaykhs said, "I entered into longing and all things longed for me, but I was free of all of them." I heard Abu Abd al-Rahman al-Sulami say[4] . . . that Malik ibn Dinar said, "I read in the Torah, 'I set yearning in you, but you did not yearn. I played for you, but you did not dance.'" I heard Muhammad ibn Abd-Allah al-Sufi say that Muhammad ibn Farhan said, "Junayd was asked, 'Why does the lover cry when he meets the Beloved?'"

He replied, "That is only out of joy, and out of ecstasy from the intensity of the longing for Him. "I have heard that once two brothers embraced. One of them exclaimed, 'O, what longing!' "The other one cried, 'O, what bliss!'"

8 On Showing Consideration for the Hearts of the Shaykhs and Abandoning Opposition to Them

God Most High, in the story of Moses and Khidr, said, *"Shall I follow you so that you will give me good guidance out of what you know?"* (18:66).

When Moses wanted the companionship of Khidr, he followed the prescribed behavior. First he asked permission to keep company with Khidr. Then Khidr specified that Moses should not oppose him in anything, or offer resistance to any decision. When Moses did object to Khidr's actions, Khidr ignored this the first and second times. Then when the third time came—and three is the end of "a little" and the beginning of "a lot"—Khidr insisted that they part company. He said, *"This is the parting between me and you"* (18:78).

I heard Abu-l-Husayn al-Ahwazi say[1] . . . from Anas ibn Malik, that the Messenger of God said, "No young man honors an old man (shaykh) in his old age without God Most High appointing someone to show him honor in his own old age."

I heard Abu Ali al-Daqqaq say, "The beginning of all separation is opposition." By this he meant that whoever opposes a shaykh cannot continue in his path. The bond between them is severed even though they come together in the same place. Whoever keeps company with any shaykh and then resists him in his heart has wronged the vow of companionship. Such a person must repent, although the shaykhs have said, "There is no repentance for disobeying teachers."

I heard Abu Abd al-Rahman al-Sulami say, "During the lifetime of my shaykh, Abu Sahl al-Suluki, I traveled to the city of Merv. Before I left he was holding sessions for reading the Quran on Friday mornings between dawn and sunrise. When I came back I found that he had left that mosque. Instead, at the same hour, he was meeting with

Abu-l-Ghufani for singing sessions. I wondered at this, and began saying to myself, "How could he want to substitute singing for reading the Quran?"

One day he said to me, "Tell me, Abu Abd al-Rahman, what are people saying about me?" "They are saying, 'He has given up Quran sessions for singing sessions!'" I replied. "Whoever asks his teacher 'Why?' will never prosper!" said he.

It is well known that Junayd said, "One day I went to see Sari and he ordered me to do something. I immediately carried out the thing he needed. When I returned, he handed me a slip of paper and said, 'This belongs to the place where you did what I needed so quickly!' I read the paper. On it was written:
'I heard a camel-driver urge on his camel in the desert, singing:

I wept—did you hear what made me weep?
I wept for fear that you would leave me
Would cut my halter and not see me again!'"

It is told that Abu-l-Hasan al-Hamadani al-Alawi said, "One night I was with Jafar al-Khuldi. I had ordered a bird to be baked in the oven, and my heart was taken with that. Jafar said to me, 'Stay and pray with us tonight!' but I made some excuse and went back to my house, took the bird out of the oven, and set it before me. Then a dog came in the door, and when no one was paying attention, he carried off the bird! So they brought the pastry that had been baked under the bird, but somehow the hem of the serving woman's dress got stuck to it. And so it was all wasted.

"The next morning I went to see Jafar. When his eyes fell upon me, he said, 'Those who show no consideration for the hearts of shaykhs have dogs set over them to torment them!'"

I heard Abu Abd al-Rahman al-Sulami say[2] . . . that the grand-uncle of al-Hasan al-Damghani said, "Shaqiq al-Balkhi and Abu Turab al-Nakhshabi went to visit Abu Yazid. A table was prepared. There was a youth waiting upon Abu Yazid. "Come, eat with us, young man!" the two of them urged. "I am fasting," said he. "Eat, and you will have the reward of a month's fast!" said Abu Turab. The youth refused. "Eat, and you will have the reward of a year's fast!" said Shaqiq. Still he refused. "Pray for someone who has fallen from God's grace," Abu Yazid said to them. In a year that young man had begun to steal, and his hand was cut off!

I heard Abu Ali say that Sahl ibn Abd-Allah described a certain man as a saint. He was a baker in Basra. Another man heard this from the members of Sahl's circle, and began to yearn after this saint. So he went to Basra and came to the baker's shop. There he saw the man baking bread. His face was wrapped to protect him from the fire of the oven, as is the custom of bakers. The traveler said to himself, "If this man were really a saint, his hair would not burn, even if he had no protection!" He offered the baker greetings and asked him something. The baker said, "Since you think so little of me, why should I benefit you with my talk?" And he refused to speak to him.

I heard Abu Abd al-Rahman al-Sulami say that Abd al-Rahman al-Razi heard Abu Uthman al-Hiri describe Muhammad ibn al-Fadl al-Balkhi, praising him highly. So he conceived a desire to see him, and went to pay him a visit, but Muhammad ibn al-Fadl did not make the impression on his heart that he had expected. He went back to Abu Uthman and asked him about this. "How did you find him?" asked Abu Uthman. "I did not find him to be what I thought he should be!" said Abd al-Rahman. "You did not profit from him because you belittled him," said Abu Uthman. "When a person thinks little of another person, that person's special value and usefulness is denied him. Go back to Muhammad ibn al-Fadl with respect." So Abd al-Rahman went back, and benefited from his visit.

There is a famous story that Umar ibn Uthman al-Makki saw al-Husayn ibn Mansur (al-Hallaj) writing something. "What is this?" he asked. "Why, I am competing with the Quran!" said Husayn. Umar cursed him and broke off relations with him. The shaykhs say that what eventually befell Husayn was the result, after a long interval, of the curse of that shaykh.

I heard Abu Ali al-Daqqaq say, "When the people of Balkh threw Muhammad ibn al-Fadl out of the city, he prayed against them. 'My God,' he prayed, 'forbid them integrity!' And no man of real integrity has come out of Balkh since."

I heard Ahmad ibn Yahya al-Abiwardi say, "If someone's shaykh is pleased with him, he will not be rewarded for that during his lifetime, lest reverence for the shaykh should leave his heart. But when the shaykh dies, God Almighty and Glorious will manifest the reward for having pleased him."

If someone alienates the heart of his shaykh, that too will not be requited during the lifetime of that shaykh, lest the shaykh have sympathy for him, for shaykhs are prone to be generous. But when the shaykh dies—then it will be paid for.

9 ON SPIRITUAL CONCERT (SAMA)

God Almighty and Glorious said, *"So give good news to My ser - vants who listen to the Recital and follow what is best in it"* (39:18).

The definite article used in His saying "the Recital" implies generality and comprehensiveness. The proof of this is that He praises those who follow "the best" (and not all of it, as would be appropriate if the Recital meant were exclusively that of the Quran). And He says, *"They are in a garden, delighting"* (30:15). It has come in a commentary that this is the sama, the spiritual concert.

Know that listening to poetry with beautiful melodies and delightful intonation—when the one who listens does not believe it to be forbidden, does not hear anything that is blameable according to divine Command, is not driven by the reins of his lusts, and does not gather together with others for the sake of lusts—is wholly permissible.

There is no denying that poetry was recited before the Messenger of God, and that he listened to it and did not censure those who recited it. So if hearing it without beautiful melody is licit, how should the rule be altered by hearing it with melody?

This is the obvious side of the matter. What comes next is that the one who listens should find his wish to perform acts of devotion increased. He should remember the degrees that God Most High has prepared for His servants who fear Him. This should lead him to guard against sins, and immediately convey to his heart the purity of feeling and impression required by the religion and preferred in the divine Law.

There has come upon the tongue of the Messenger of God that which is nearly poetry, although his intention was not to make poems.

Abu-l-Husayn Ali ibn Ahmad al-Ahwazi reported[1] . . . that Anas said, "While the Helpers were digging the trench to defend the city of Madinah, they began to sing:

We are the ones who have sworn to Muhammad
To fight as long as any of us remain!

Then the Messenger of God answered them:

My God, there is no life but the life of the Herafter
So honor the Helpers and the Emigrants!

This phrase of his did not have the measure of poetry, but it was very close to it.

Our forefathers and great predecessors listened to verses with melody. One of those who spoke for the allowability of this was Malik ibn Anas. All the people of the Hijaz permit singing, and as for the songs used to urge on camel caravans, there is universal consensus that they are licit. Traditions have been received, and the ancient accounts attesting to this are exhaustive.

It is related that Ibn Jurayj danced when hearing spiritual music. Someone asked him, "When the day of judgment comes upon you, and your good and evil deeds are brought forward, in which category will you find your spiritual concert?" He said, "Among neither the good nor the evil deeds, but among the harmless neutral ones."

Al-Shafii did not rule listening to music to be forbidden. In most cases, he counted it disapproved. Even if someone practiced singing as a profession, or constantly listened to music for entertainment rather than as a statement of faith, al-Shafi'i identified the act as one of those that cause the loss of manly virtue. He did not count it as one of those prohibited by God.

However, we are not discussing this sort of listening to music. The degree of the Sufis is too great for them to listen to vanity, or to sit down together to hear while inattentive, or to ponder nonsensical meanings in their hearts, or to listen to any unsuitable thing. Ibn Umar is reported to have allowed listening to music, and likewise Abd-Allah ibn Jafar ibn Abi Talib and Umar, both in camel caravans and otherwise.

Poetry was recited before the Prophet, and he did not turn away from it. It is also related that he asked for it to be recited. A widely famous report tells that he entered the house of Ayisha and found two young women singing, and did not stop them.

Abu Abd al-Rahman al-Sulami reported[2] . . . from Aisha, " Abu

Bakr al-Siddiq came to see me while two girls were visiting. They were singing what the Helpers had sung back and forth to each other on the day of the battle of Buath, in the times before the Prophet. Twice Abu Bakr exclaimed, "Satan's pipe!" But the Prophet said, "Abu Bakr, let them be. Every people has a festival, and our festival is today."

Ali ibn Ahmad al-Ahwazi reported[3] . . . from Ayisha, "I was planning a wedding for a relative among the Helpers. The Prophet came and asked, "Are you making a bridal procession for the girl?" "Yes," I said. "Have you sent for someone to sing?" "No," I said. "The Helpers have love songs," remarked the Prophet. "If you were to send, someone would recite:

> We come to you, we come to you
> So greet us, we are greeting you!

Abu Bakr Muhammad ibn al-Husayn ibn Furak reported[4] . . . from al-Bira ibn Azib, that the Messenger of God said, "Beautify the Quran with your voices, for a beautiful voice increases the beauty of the Quran."

This Tradition indicates the excellence of a beautiful voice. Ali ibn Ahmad ibn Abdan al-Ahwazi reported[5] . . . from Anas ibn Malik, that the Messenger of God said: Everything has an ornament, and the ornament of the Quran is a beautiful voice.

Ali ibn Ahmad al-Ahwazi reported[6] . . . from Anas ibn Malik, that the Messenger of God said, "Two sounds are accursed: the sound of wailing in difficulty, and the sound of the reed-pipe in prosperity."

This statement is understood to imply that all other sounds in all other circumstances are permissible; detailed specification would be pointless. Hadith reports pertaining to this are numerous. To increase them beyond what we have already recalled would take us beyond the bounds of brevity.

It is related that a man recited before the Messenger of God:

> Joy to her! She turned to me
> Her two cheeks like black pearls.
> Then she fled. I said to her
> My heart in a blaze,
> "Woe to you! Can I be wrong
> To love a thing denied?"

The Messenger of God said, "No."

A beautiful voice is a blessing of God upon the people who possess it. God Almighty and Glorious said, "*He increases (His blessings) upon people as He wills*" (35:1). According to a commentary, part of this is a beautiful voice. God has condemned an ugly voice. He said, "*The most hateful of voices is the voice of the donkey*" (31:19).

The yearning of hearts for lovely sounds, the pleasure taken in them, and the refreshment they bring, cannot be produced by any effort. Children are quieted by a sweet voice. The camel endures the hardships of travel and the difficulty of bearing burdens when the driver soothes it with song. God Most High said, "*Have you not looked at the camel, how it is created?*" (88:17).

Ismail ibn Aliyyah said, "Once I was walking with al-Shafi^{c}i at midday, and we passed by a place where someone was singing. 'Come with me over there,' he said. Then he asked, 'Doesn't this move you?' 'No,' I replied. 'You have no sensibility!' said he."

The Messenger of God said, "God Most High does not listen to anything the way He listens to a prophet singing the Quran." Ali ibn Ahmad al-Ahwazi reported[7] . . . from Abu Hurayrah that the Messenger of God said this.

It is said that the *jinn* and men and birds and animals used to listen to the prophet David when he would chant the psalms. Four hundred funeral processions would issue from his gatherings—all people who died (of ecstasy) when hearing him recite.

The Prophet said to Abu Musa al-Ashari (known for his fine voice), "You have been given one of the flutes of the family of David."

Muadh ibn Jabal said to the Messenger of God, "If I had known you were listening (to my recitation of the Quran), I would have embellished it for you."

Abu Hatim al-Sijistani reported[8] . . . that Abu Bakr Muhammad ibn Dawud al-Dinawari al-Raqqi said, "I was in the desert when I came upon one of the Bedouin tribes. One of the men of the tribe offered me hospitality. When I went to his dwelling, I saw in the courtyard a black slave, bound, and a camel that had died. The slave said to me, 'Tonight you are a guest, and my master will honor you over himself. Intercede for me! He will not refuse you.' So I told the master of the house, 'I will not eat any of your food unless you release that slave.' 'That slave has impoverished and ruined me!' he exclaimed. 'What did he do!' I asked. 'He has a sweet voice,' he said. 'I made my living from the back of that camel, using her to transport heavy burdens. Singing, he drove her to cross three days' distance in one day's time. When he got down from her back, she dropped dead. But I will give him to you.' And he untied him. When morning came, I wanted to hear the slave's voice. I requested it of my host, and he ordered the slave to sing to a camel that was drinking at a watering trough. So he sang, and the camel broke its halter and wandered off in a daze. I do not think that I have ever heard a voice finer than his until his master signaled him to be silent.

I heard Abu Abd al-Rahman al-Sulami say[9] . . . that Abu Amr al-Anmati said, "Junayd was asked, 'What is the condition of a man who is peaceful until he hears music, and then becomes greatly moved?' He replied, 'At the time of the original pact with humanity, God Most High addressed the atoms of all the souls that would be. He said, '*Am I not your Lord?*' They said, '*Yes, indeed!*' (7:172). The delight of hearing this divine speech exhausted the capacity of the souls. When they hear music, it excites in them the memory of this."

I heard Abu Ali al-Daqqaq say, "The spiritual concert is forbidden to ordinary people because of the continued maintenance of their egos. It is permissible for renunciates because of their pursuit of inner struggle. It is recommended for our companions, for the sake of the life of their hearts."

I heard Abu Hatim al-Sijistani say[10] . . . that al-Harith ibn Asad al-Muhasibi said, "Three things, when found, are useful, and we have lost them all: A beautiful face together with chastity, a beautiful voice together with piety, a beautiful fellowship together with loyalty."

Dhu-l-Nun al-Misri was asked about beautiful voices, and said, "They are sermons and signs entrusted by God to every good man and good woman." On another occasion he was asked about the spiritual concert. He said, "True feeling excites hearts toward the truth. Whoever listens to music truthfully gives true testimony of faith, and whoever listens to it with the ego commits heresy."

Jafar ibn Nusayr relates that Junayd said, "Divine mercy descends upon the dervishes in three circumstances: during the spiritual concert, for they hear only truth, and speak only in ecstasy; while eating, for they eat only out of need; in the pursuit of learning, for they recall nothing but the qualities of the saints."

I heard Muhammad ibn al-Husayn say[11] . . . that Junayd said: Spiritual music is a trial for the one who seeks it out, but a comfort for the one who happens upon it.

It is related that Junayd said, "Spiritual concert requires three things: The right time, the right place, and the right company."

Shibli was asked about the spiritual concert. He said, "Outwardly it is a test, but inwardly it is a lesson. If someone understands signs, it is lawful for him to listen to the lesson. Otherwise he is asking for trials and risking trouble."

It is said that listening to music is only right for a person whose ego is dead and whose heart is alive—whose ego has been slain by the sword of inner struggle, and whose heart is vivified by the light of harmony with God.

Abu Yaqub al-Nahrajuri, asked about the spiritual concert, said, "It is a state that demonstrates the return to inner secrets through being burnt up."

Spiritual concert, it is told, is a grace which is the food of souls for the people of inner knowledge.

I heard Abu Ali al-Daqqaq say, "Listening to music is carnal unless it derives from the divine Command. It is a violation of what is right unless it is from the truth. It is a trial unless it is a lesson.

Spiritual concerts are said to be of two kinds. One sort depends upon knowledge and sobriety. The condition required of participants in this kind of concert is an understanding of the divine names and attributes. Without this, they fall into pure infidelity.

The other sort depends upon state. What is required of participants in this kind of concert is the annihilation of all ordinary human states, and purification from all traces of personal pleasure by the appearance of the principles of reality.

It is related that Ahmad ibn Abil-Hawari said, "I asked Abu Sulayman (al-Darani) about the spiritual concert. He said, 'Of two things, it is dearer to me than one.'"

Abu-l-Husayn al-Nuri was asked, "Who is a Sufi?" He replied, "He who listens to spiritual music and prefers lawful means."

One day Abu Ali al-Rudhbari was asked about the hearing of spiritual music. He remarked, "Would that each and every one of us could be free of it!"

I heard Abu Abd al-Rahman al-Sulami say that Abu Uthman al-Maghribi said, "Whoever claims to participate in the spiritual concert, yet does not hear the sound of the birds, the creaking of the door, or the blowing of the winds, is a presumptuous dervish."

I heard Abu Hatim al-Sijistani say[12] . . . that Jafar said that Ibn Ziri was an excellent shaykh and a member of the circle of Junayd. Sometimes he would be present in a place where a spiritual concert was held. If the proceedings pleased him, he would spread out his garment and sit down, and say, "The Sufi is together with his heart." If they did not please him, he would say, "Spiritual concert is for the lords of hearts!" and leave, taking his shoes.

I heard Muhammad ibn al-Husayn say[13] . . . that Abd-Allah ibn Abd al-Majid al-Sufi said, "Someone asked Ruwaym about what the Sufis experience in the spiritual concert."

He said, "They witness meanings that escape from other people, but that call to them, 'Come to me, come to me!' So they are blessed by this joy until the veil is rent, and joy becomes weeping. Then some of them tear their clothing, and others cry out, and others weep—each person according to his capacity."

I heard Muhammad ibn Ahmad ibn Muhammad al-Tamimi say[14] . . . al-Husri said in one of his discourses, "What have I to do with a spiritual concert that isolates the one who listens to it? Your spiritual concert must be a thing that joins, not one that severs." He also said that al-Husri said, "It must be a constant thirst—each time your drinking increases, your thirst must increase."

Mujahid gave a commentary on the saying of God, *"They are in a garden, delighting"* (30:15). He said that they are listening to the houris of Paradise singing with their lovely voices, "We are eternal so we never die; we are blessings so we never harm!"

The spiritual concert, it is said, is a summons. Ecstasy is the aspiration to respond.

I heard Muhammad ibn al-Husayn say that Abu Uthman al-Maghribi said, "The hearts of the Sufis are hearts that are present; their ears are ears that are open." And I heard him say: Abu Sahl al-Suluki said, "The participant in spiritual concert is between veiling and manifestation. Veiling requires burning; manifestation bequeaths rest. Veiling produces the physical movements of students. It is the place of weakness and incapacity. Manifestation produces the stillness of those who have attained. It is the place of direction and stability."

Such is the characteristic of gatherings for remembrance through music. They contain nothing but melting under the impact of awe. God Most High said, *"And when they came to it, (the jinns who listened to recitation of the Koran) said, 'Be silent!'"* (46:29)

Abu Uthman al-Hiri said, "There are three aspects to the spiritual concert. The first belongs to students and beginners, who use the concert to attempt to call up noble states. One may fear that they will encounter trials and hypocrisy in so doing. The second belongs to the truthful ones who seek to increase the states they already possess, and hear during the concert what is in harmony with their own experience. The third belongs to gnostics who possess steadfast direction. Whether God Most High sends movement or stillness to their hearts, they do not choose otherwise than as He has chosen."

I heard Abu Abd al-Rahman al-Sulami say[15] . . . that Abu Said al-Kharraz said, "If someone alleges that he is overcome with emotion though still in possession of his understanding—that is, during the spiritual concert — and that his moving to the music is the result of that, the proof of it is the good opinion of the people among whom he entered his ecstasy.

Shaykh Abu Abd al-Rahman said: When I recalled this account to Abu Uthman al-Maghribi, he said, "That's the least of it! The true proof of such a person's claim is that there is not a sincere person in the gathering who does not feel close to him, nor an insincere one who does not feel alienated from him."

Bundar ibn al-Husayn said, "Spiritual concert has three aspects. Sometimes people listen to music for the sake of their natural inclination. At other times they listen for the sake of their inner state. At still other times they listen for the sake of the Truth. Listening out of natural inclination is something shared by both ordinary people and the spiritual elite, for it is human nature to take delight in sweet sounds. The person who listens for the sake of his inner state meditates upon a recollection aroused by the music: the recollection of a rebuke or a piece of advice, a union or a separation, a time of closeness or a time of distance, a sorrow over something past or a desire for something yet to come, faithfulness to a promise or the proving of a pledge or the breaking of a promise, restlessness or yearning or fear of parting or joy of reunion or wariness of division—and so forth and so on. The one who listens for the sake of the Truth listens to God and through God. Such a person cannot be described according to states that are intermingled with ordinary human concerns, states that are maintained together with defects. Such people listen out of the purity of Unity, objectively and not subjectively."

Participants in the spiritual concert are said to fall into three grades. When listening to spiritual music, those who are the children of the realities hear the discourse that the Truth has addressed to them. People of another sort use the meanings expressed in what they hear to address God Most High in their hearts, seeking with sincerity the direction they have been shown toward Him. A third sort are dervishes free of attachments who have cut their connections to the world and its calamities. They listen for the well-being of their hearts, and these are the closest of all to security.

I heard Muhammad ibn al-Husayn say[16] . . . that Abu Ali al-Rudhbari, when asked about spiritual concert, said, "It is the uncovering of secrets until the Beloved is beheld."

Al-Khawwas was asked about the condition of a person who was roused to movement when hearing music and poetry that was not the Quran, but was not so affected when he heard the Quran. He said, "Listening to the Quran is a shock. Because of the intensity of the force that overwhelms him, it is not possible for someone to move when he hears it. Hearing spiritual song is ease and comfort. In it one is able to move."

I heard Muhammad ibn al-Husayn say[17] . . . that Junayd said, "When you see a student who loves the spiritual concert, know that there is a remnant of foolishness still in him.

And I heard him say[18] . . . that Sahl ibn Abd-Allah said, "The spiritual concert is a knowledge that God Most High claims for Himself. No one knows it except Him."

It is told that Ahmad ibn Muqatil al-Akki said, "When Dhu-l-Nun al-Misri entered Baghdad, all of the Sufis gathered around him. Among them was a spiritual singer. They asked Dhu-l-Nun if the man might sing something in his presence, and he agreed. So the man began:

The little love you bear for me torments me.
What would it be if your love for me were total!
My heart's desires were scattered.
You've drawn them all to you.
Won't you mourn for a poor wretch who weeps
While the one who is free of him laughs?

Dhu-l-Nun stood up and then fell down on his face. Blood trickled from his forehead, but did not drop upon the earth. Then a man of the company stood up and tried to bring on an ecstasy. Dhu-l-Nun said to him: '. . . the One who sees you when you stand up!' The man sat back down."

I heard Abu Ali al-Daqqaq comment on this account that Dhu-l-Nun was exercising supervision over that man, because he advised him that what he was doing was not proper for him. And the man was one who knew what was right, because he accepted that from Dhu-l-Nun, and returned and sat down.

I heard Muhammad ibn Ahmad ibn Muhammad al-Tamimi say[19] . . . that Ibn al-Jalla said, "There were two shaykhs in North Africa who kept circles of companions and students. One of them was named Jiblah, and the other Ruzayq. One day Ruzayq visited Jiblah among his students. A member of Ruzayq's group recited something, and one of Jiblah's companions cried out and died. When morning came, Jiblah said to Ruzayq, "Where is the man who was reciting yesterday? Let him recite again!" So the man began to recite. Jiblah cried out, and the reciter died! "One for one," said Jiblah, "and the one who started it is the worse tyrant!"

Ibrahim al-Maristani was asked about actions in which people engage during the spiritual concert. He replied, "I have heard that Moses was telling parables to the Children of Israel when one among them tore his shirt (out of grief). God Most High revealed to Moses, *'Say to him: "Tear your heart for Me, do not tear your garment!"'*

Someone said to Abu Ali al-Mughazili al-Shibli, "Sometimes a verse from the Book of God strikes my ear and urges me to abandon material things and turn away from this world. Then afterwards I turn back to my old states and to people." Shibli said, "That which draws you to Him is a movement of sympathy from Him toward you, and a grace. And that which returns you to yourself is an act of kindness that He shows to you. For it is not appropriate for you to be devoid of power and strength and to wholly face Him."

I heard Abu Hatim al-Sijistani say[20] . . . that Ahmad ibn Muqatil al-Akki said, "One night in Ramadan I was with Shibli in a mosque. He was praying behind an imam, and I was next to him. The imam recited, *"And if We willed . . . what We have revealed to you"* (17:86). And then he screamed! I said, "His spirit has flown." Shibli was trembling. He said, "This is the way that lovers converse!" And he repeated it over and over. It is related that Junayd said, "One day I went to visit Sari. With him I found a man who had fainted. 'What happened to him?' I asked. 'He heard a verse of the Book of God,' Sari told me. 'Have someone recite another one,' I suggested. So it was done, and the man came to himself. 'Where did you learn that?' Sari asked. 'From the shirt of Joseph,' I replied. 'On its account Jacob's vision vanished, and then again on its account, his vision returned. So that made this approach seem a good one to me.'"

I heard Abu Hatim al-Sijistani say[21] . . . that Abd al-Wahid ibn

Ulwan said, "There was a young man in Junayd's circle who used to cry out when he heard music in the remembrance of God. One day Junayd said to him, 'If you do that one more time, leave my company!' After that, when he participated in the spiritual concert he would be visibly affected, but would hold back, and every hair of his body would become soaked in sweat. Finally the day came when he screamed a great scream—and his lower self was destroyed!

I heard Abu Hatim al-Sijistani say[22] . . . that Abu-l-Husayn al-Darraj said, "I set out from Baghdad to visit Yusuf ibn al-Husayn al-Razi. When I entered the city of Rayy I inquired where he was to be found, but everyone I asked exclaimed, "What do you want with that heretic?" This made me lose my enthusiasm, and I made up my mind to turn back. So I spent that night in a mosque. Then I said to myself, "I have come to this city—at least I should call on him."

So I kept asking after him until I happened upon his mosque. And there he was, sitting in the prayer-niche, with a Quran-stand in front of him, and upon it a copy of the Quran from which he was reading. And lo and behold, he was a radiant old man, with a beautiful face and beard!

I approached him and gave him greeting. He returned my greeting and asked, "From where have you come?" "From Baghdad," I said. "I set out to visit the shaykh." "Did some person in some part of the land invite you, 'Stay with me!' until he had sold you a house or a slavegirl? Did he try to prevent you from visiting me?" he inquired. "Master," I confessed, "God Most High did not test me with anything like that. If He had, I don't know what I would have done!" "Would you like to recite something?" he asked. "Certainly," I said. And I recited:

I watched you build with effort in my realm.
If I were stouthearted, I'd tear down what you built.

He closed the book. He did not stop crying until his hair and robe were covered with tears, until I felt pity for how much he wept. Then he said to me, "My son, do not blame the people of Rayy for saying, 'Yusuf ibn al-Husayn is a heretic.' For at the time of prayer, when the Quran is recited, not a tear falls from my eye—but the day of judgment has broken upon me with this verse!"

I heard Muhammad ibn Ahmad ibn Muhammad al-Sufi say[23] . . . that al-Darraj said, "Ibn al-Quwati and I were traveling along the Euphrates between Basra and Ubalah when we came across a beautiful castle with a tower. Upon the tower was a man, and before him was a slavegirl, singing. She sang:

> For God's sake I have lavished love upon you.
> Yet every day you change.
> Something else would be more fitting!

At the bottom of the tower there happened to be a youth who carried a small pot in his hand and wore the patched robe of a dervish. He heard this song, and called out, "O maid! By your master's life, repeat:

> 'Yet every day you change.
> Something else would be more fitting!'"

So she repeated it. "Sing!" cried the youth. She sang it again. "By God," the dervish said, "this paints my picture, in truth!" Then he uttered a groan, and his spirit departed. The owner of the castle said to the slavegirl, "You are free, for God's sake!"

The people of Basra came out and buried the dervish, and offered his funeral prayer. Then the master of the castle stood up and said, "Would that you had not known me! I bear witness to you that all of my property is given in the way of God, and all of my slaves are free." Then he wrapped a cloth around his waist and put on a cloak, gave the whole castle as alms, and left. He was never seen or heard of again.

I heard Muhammad ibn Ahmad ibn Muhammad al-Sufi say [24]. . . that Yahya ibn al-Rida al-Alawi said, "Abu Sulayman al-Dimashqi heard a street peddler crying his wares, 'Wild thyme from the desert!' He fell down unconscious! When he awoke, someone asked him what had happened. He said, "I reckoned him to be saying, 'Be generous—you will see My goodness."

Utbah heard a singer sing to a man:

> Great is the Lord of the Heavens
> The lover is in pain!

Utbah said, "You have spoken the truth!" Another man heard the same verse and said, "You lie!"

Each of them heard in accordance with what he was.

I heard Abu Hatim al-Sijistani say[25] . . . that Abu-l-Hasan Ali ibn

Muhammad al-Sufi said, "Ruwaym was asked about shaykhs whom he had met during the spiritual concert." He said, "They were like a flock when the wolf falls upon them."

It is told that Abu Said al-Kharraz said, "I saw Ali ibn al-Muwaffaq in a spiritual concert. "Help me to stand!" he said. So they supported him, and he stood and moved to the music in pursuit of ecstasy. Afterward he commented, "I am the dancing shaykh!" One night al-Raqqi stood in devotion until morning. While he was standing he hit upon a verse, and all the people wept. The verse was:

By God, repeat:
A grieving heart has no substitute for its Beloved.

I heard Muhammad ibn Ahmad al-Tamimi say[26] . . . that al-Husayn ibn Muhammad ibn Ahmad said, "I served Sahl ibn Abd-Allah (al-Tustari) for many years, and I never saw him to be at all affected during the spiritual concert, whether he was listening to the remembrance of God, or the Quran, or anything else. But toward the end of his life, someone recited before him, "*Today compensation shall not be accepted from you*" (57:15). I saw his appearance alter, and he trembled and nearly fell. When he had returned to his usual sober condition, I asked him what had happened. "My dear," he said, "we grew weak."

Ibn Salim is reported to have said, "I saw him on another occasion when *'The true kingdom, today, belongs to the Merciful'* (25:26) was recited before him, and his faced changed and he nearly fell. When I spoke to him about that, he said, 'I weakened.' And that is the characteristic of the great. No feeling or impression, strong though it may be, comes over them without their being stronger still."

I heard Shaykh Abu Abd al-Rahman al-Sulami say, "I went to visit Abu Uthman al-Maghribi. Someone there was drawing water from a well by means of a pulley. "Abu Abd al-Rahman," he asked, "do you know what the pulley says?" "No," I confessed. "It says 'God! God!' said he.

I heard Muhammad ibn Abd-Allah al-Sufi say[27] . . . that Ruwaym said, "It is related that Ali ibn Abi Talib heard the sound of a church bell and asked his companions, "Do you know what that is saying?" They said, "No." He said, "It is saying: 'Great is God—truly, truly—the Lord, Eternal—He abides.'"

I heard Muhammad ibn Ahmad al-Tamimi say[28] . . . that Ahmad ibn Ali al-Karkhi al-Wajihi said, "A congregation of Sufis had gathered in the house of al-Hasan al-Qazzaz. There were singers among them, and people were singing and moving to the music in search of ecstasy. Then Mumshad al-Dinawari looked down over them, and they fell silent. 'Go back to what you were doing,' he said. 'Were all the instruments in the world to gather in my ear, my will would not distracted, and no part of my condition would be cured!'

According to the same line of transmission from al-Wajihi, he said he heard Abu Ali al-Rudhbari say, "In this business we have reached a place like the edge of a sword. If we incline that much to either side—into the fire!"

Khayr al-Nassaj said, "Moses son of Imran was telling parables to some people when one of them screamed. Moses scolded him. God Most High revealed to him, 'O Moses, it is with My sweetness they bleed, with My love they show themselves, with My ecstasy they cry out. Why do you refuse this to My servants?'"

Shibli heard somebody call, "The goods are ten for a penny!" He let out a cry, and said, "If the goods be ten for a penny—what price the evils?" When the houris sing, it is said, roses bloom on the trees of paradise. Awn ibn Abd-Allah used to order his sweet-voiced handmaiden to sing in sad tones until people wept.

Abu Sulayman al-Darani was asked about the spiritual concert. He said, "Every heart wants the beautiful voice. It is weak, and is treated as a child is treated when it wants to sleep." Then he added, "A beautiful voice introduces nothing into the heart: it only activates what is already there."

Ibn Abil-Hawari said, "Abu Sulayman spoke the truth, by God." Jurayri said, "'Be men of God'—that is, those who listen to God, and speak through God."

A dervish, asked about spiritual concert, said, "Bolts of lightning flash and then fade. Lights appear and vanish. How sweet it would be if they stayed for the blink of an eye!" Then he recited:

A thought of Him occurred within
A lightning-thought began and dwindled.
Which of Your visitors purposely traveled?
Who that knows You, really, has done it?

The spiritual concert is said to provide a share for every limb. What falls to the eye is to weep. What falls to the tongue is to cry out.

What falls to the hand is to tear the clothes and strike the breast. What falls to the foot is to dance.

A foreign king died, and left as his successor a tiny son. His people wanted to pledge their fealty to the heir, but they wondered, "How shall we arrive at an understanding of his mental capacity and intellect?" Then they agreed to bring a singer and have him sing something. If the child paid good attention, they would know he was intelligent. They brought the singer, and when he sang, the infant laughed. So they kissed the ground before him and pledged themselves.

I heard Abu Ali al-Daqqaq say that Abu Amr ibn Nujayd and al-Nasrabadhi met together somewhere with a group of Sufis. Nasrabadhi declared, "According to me, when dervishes gather and one of them sings, it is better for the others to remain silent than for them to speak evil of anybody."

Abu Amr replied, "If you had been spoken against for thirty years, it might have saved you from showing in spiritual concert something that was not yours to show!"

I heard Abu Ali al-Daqqaq say, "Three sorts of people participate in spiritual concerts: the first one hears the music according to the immediate conditions (*mutasammi*); the second hears according to his state (*mustami*); and the third hears according to the truth (*sami*).

More than once I questioned Abu Ali al-Daqqaq, looking for an easing of the rules of behavior during spiritual concert. He used to answer me in terms of the need to restrain that wish. After many such replies he finally said, "The shaykhs have taught that whatever joins your heart to God—glory to Him— is all right."

Abu-l-Hasan Ali ibn Ahmad al-Ahwazi reported[29] . . . from Ibn Abbas that God revealed to Moses, "I have placed in you ten thousand ears so that you might hear My word, and ten thousand tongues so that you might answer Me. And what is dearest and closest to Me in you is your calling down many blessings upon Muhammad."

A dervish saw the Prophet in a dream. He spoke and said, "The mistakes in this are many." He meant the spiritual concert.

I heard Abu Abd al-Rahman al-Sulami say[30] . . . that Abu-l-Harith al-Ulasi said that he saw the satan (may God curse him) in a dream. He was up on one of the roofs of the town of Ulas, and I was on another roof. On his right was a congregation, and on his left was a congregation, all wearing clean garments. He said to a group of them, "Speak!" and they recited and sang. The sweetness of his voice startled me so much that I wanted to throw myself from the roof. Then he said "Dance!" and they danced, as nicely as can be. Then he turned to me. "Abu Õl-Harith," he said, "I could find no means to invade you but this!"

I heard Muhammad ibn al-Husayn say that he heard Abd-Allah ibn Ali say that one night he was in a gathering with Shibli. A singer was singing something, and Shibli cried out and moved to the music, but remained sitting. "Abu Bakr," they asked, "what does this mean, your sitting in the middle of the congregation?" So he got up and moved, and said:

> I have two intoxications, the regretful have but one.
> The thing that separates me from them is One.

And I heard him say[31] . . . that Abu Ali al-Rudhbari said that he passed by a castle and saw a youth with a beautiful face who had fallen upon the ground. People were gathered around him, so he asked about him. They told him that he too had passed by the castle. In it a handmaiden was singing:

> Great is the wish of the slave
> Who desires to see You.
> Isn't it enough for an eye to see someone who has seen You?
> The youth heaved a sigh, and died.

10 On The Miracles of Saints

It is admissible that miracles may be manifested in the saints. The proof of its admissibility is that it is a thing that may be postulated, conceivable by the intellect, whose happening would not mean the suspension of any basic principle. The description of God requires that He have complete power over what He has created. When the existence of a thing is necessarily under the power of God, nothing can prevent the possibility of its occurrence.

The manifestation of miracles is a sign of truthfulness of state in the person in whom they are manifested. If someone has not this truthfulness, nothing like a miracle can appear in him. It is conceivable that a person's being pointed out in this way might be an instruction from God to the rest of us. In that way we could discern the difference between someone whose states are truthful and someone whose arguments are vain. This would not be feasible unless the true saint were distinguished by something not to be found in the pretender. That thing is the miracle that is revealed to us.

The miracle must then be an act violating the habitual structure of this universe and manifesting in someone who has the qualities of sainthood, that serves to attest to his state.

Sufis have spoken about the difference between miracles granted to the saints (*karamat*), and evidentiary miracles unique to the prophets (*mujizat*).

Abu Ishaq al-Isfarayani said, "Evidentiary miracles are proofs of the truthfulness of the prophets, and a proof of prophethood is not to be found in anyone but a prophet. It is like the case of a precise intellect: when it exists, its very existence is proof that someone is learned, because it is not to be found in anyone who is not learned." He used to say, "The saints have miracles that resemble the answering of a prayer. But anything like the evidentiary miracles of the prophets— no."

As for Abu Bakr ibn Furak, he used to teach, "The evidentiary miracles of the prophets are proofs of their truthfulness. Thus if someone in whom they appear claims to be a prophet, evidentiary miracles indicate the truth of what he says. And if a person points to his state of sainthood, evidentiary miracles indicate the truth of what he is. Yet we call this simply a miracle, (*karamah*), not an evidentiary miracle (*mujizah*), even if it is the same sort of event as the evidentiary miracles, in order to make a distinction."

About the distinction between evidentiary and simple miracles, he taught, "The prophets were commanded to display miracles. The saint is required to cover them and hide them. The Prophet laid claim to his miracles, and used them to cut off dispute. But the saint does not lay claim to them, and is not convinced by his own miracle, because it is possible that it might be a test."

That prodigy, Qadi Abu Bakr al-Ashari, said, "Evidentiary miracles are unique to the prophets, while simple miracles belong to the saints. Prophets but not saints possess evidentiary miracles because one of the defining conditions of the evidentiary miracle is its association with a claim of prophethood.

"The miracle is not evidentiary in and of itself. It is only evidentiary when it fulfills numerous requirements. If just one of these conditions is not fulfilled, it cannot be an evidentiary miracle. Since one such condition is the claim of prophethood, and the saint makes no such claim, what manifests in him cannot be an evidentiary miracle."

This is the statement upon which we rely and which we teach; indeed, we profess it. All or many of the requirements for evidentiary miracles may be found in the miracles of the saints, with the exception of this one condition.

The saint's miracle is an action that undoubtedly originates in time (for what is outside time cannot be attributed to an individual), but which violates the customary order of things. It takes place in this world, and manifests upon a servant as a mark of his distinction and excellence. It might or might not happen through his choice and request. In some circumstances it might happen without his will.

The saint is not commanded to call people to himself, though if something like this manifests in the right person, it is permissible. The shaykhs differ over whether or not it is possible for the saint to know he is a saint.

Abu Bakr al-Furak says that it is not possible, because such knowledge would remove fear and make one feel safe. Abu Ali al-

Daqqaq says that it is possible. It is his view that we prefer and teach.

Such a knowledge is not a requirement for all saints, so that a saint would necessarily have to know he was a saint. But it is possible that some saints could know, just as it is possible that some might not know. If someone knew that he was a saint, that very realization would be the miracle that distinguished him.

It is not necessary that each miracle of a given saint be found to occur in all saints. Indeed, a saint might not have any miracle manifest through him in this world, yet its absence would not detract from his sainthood.

The case of prophets is different. It is necessary that they should display miracles, because a prophet is sent as an emissary to the creation, and people need evidence to realize that he speaks the truth. This cannot be directly known except through the evidentiary miracle. The saint's state is the opposite of this. Thus it is necessary neither to humanity, nor to the saint himself, that he should know he is a saint.

The Messenger of God reported that ten of his Companions would enter paradise, and they confirmed this. Some say that it is impossible for a person to know he is a saint because the knowledge would remove him from fear, but while there is no harm in fearing a change in one's final destination, the awe, praise, and magnification of the Truth that these ten found in their hearts exceeded in effect even a great deal of fear.

Know that the saint may not rely upon the miracle that manifests in him, and that he has no control over it. Sometimes, when such things occur, the saints may have the power of certainty or an increased inner vision that confirms for them that the thing is an act of God. From this they conclude that the principles of faith which they hold are correct.

In general, to state that the manifestion of miracles to the saints is possible is a religious necessity, and upon this the vast majority of those who know are agreed. By and large, the number of hadiths and other accounts in wide circulation makes the existence of miracles, and their appearance in the saints, a strong knowledge capable of repelling doubts. If anyone should come among the Sufis and hear their reports, no uneasiness in this regard would remain in him, overall.

One of the proofs of all of this is the Quranic text dealing with the companion of Solomon, who said, "*I will bring it (the throne of the Queen of Sheba) to you before your glance returns*" (27:40)," though he was not a prophet. And there is the widely-known and established account of the Commander of the Faithful, Umar ibn al-Khattab. In the middle of his Friday sermon he called out "Sariyah! The mountain!" and the sound of his voice instantly reached Sariyah, so that he guarded against the ambush that the enemy had set in the mountain at that very hour.

Someone might inquire, "How is it possible that miracles should be manifested to the saints that are more substantial than the evidentiary miracles of the prophets? How can the excellence of the saints be greater than that of the prophets?"

The answer is that these miracles are an adjunct to the evidentiary miracles of our Prophet. If someone has no sincerity in Islam, miracles will not manifest in him. Every prophet has had miracles manifest upon members of his community, and these are counted among his own evidentiary miracles, for if that prophet were not truthful, the miracles would not have appeared in someone who followed him.

As far as the spiritual degree of the saints is concerned, it does not surpass the degree of the prophets, and there is firm universal agreement that this is so.

Thus when Abu Yazid al-Bistami was asked about this matter, he said, "What has been attained by the prophets is like a skin full of honey from which a single drop of honey has oozed forth. That drop is what belongs to all the saints, while what is in the vessel is what belongs to our Prophet.

*****

These miracles might take the form of an answer to a prayer, or the appearance of food in time of need without any apparent cause, or the occurrence of water in a time of draught, or the easy crossing of a great distance in a short time, or liberation from an enemy, or the hearing of speech from an invisible voice, or others of the many types of acts that violate the customary order of things.

Know that many of the events now known to occur only under the absolute power of God cannot possibly appear as miracles in the saints. By necessity or something very like it we know that to be so. Among these are the production of a human being without two parents and the transformation of a stone into a monster or an animal. There are many similar cases.

*****

Someone might ask, "What is the meaning of 'saint', or Friend of God (*wali*)?" The term bears two interpretations. The first construes the word as an intensive active participle, like alim or qadir and so forth. Under this construction its meaning is "the one whose obedience continues uninterruptedly (*tawalat*), without any disobedience intervening."

It is also possible to construe the word as a passive participle, like *qatil* with the sense of *maqtul*, or *jarih* with the sense of *majruh*. Then the saint is the one of whom the Truth constantly and uninterruptedly takes care (*yatawali*). God does not create for such a person the state of being forsaken, which is itself the capacity for disobedience. Rather He perpetuates His acceptance, which is the capacity for obedience. God Most High said, *"He constantly cares for the righteous"* (7:196).

*****

Someone might ask, "Is the saint free of sin?" If one means necessarily and essentially free of sin, as is said of the prophets, then the answer is no. But if one means protected to the extent of being unable to decide in favor of sins, whether trifles or disasters or mistakes, then nothing forbids the saints being so described. Junayd was asked, "Abu-l-Qasim, does a gnostic commit adultery?" He remained silent for a long time. Then he raised his head and said, "The order of God is a destiny decreed" (33:38).

*****

Someone might ask, "Does fear leave the saints?"

If one means fear as the dominant force in great shaykhs, we have spoken of this earlier as something rare but not impossible. Thus Sari al-Saqati said, "If someone were to enter an orchard in which were many trees, and on every tree was a bird that said to him in the clearest language, 'Peace be upon you, O Friend of God!'—if he does not fear that it is a deception, he is truly deceived!"

There are many similar statements in the accounts of the saints.

*****

Someone might ask, "Is seeing God with the physical eyes, today, in this world, a possible miracle?" The answer is, that the strongest opinion holds that it is not possible, for consensus has been arrived at upon this question. But I heard Imam Abu Bakr ibn Furak relate that Abu-l-Hasan al-Ashari said two different things about it in his book *The Great Vision (al-Ruyat al-kabir)*.

*****

Someone might ask, "Is it possible that a person might be a saint now, but change at the end?" According to those shaykhs who make a good end to one's life one of the defining conditions of sainthood, it is not possible. According to those who say that one may truly be a believer now, though possibly one's state might change later, it is not unlikely that someone might now sincerely be a Friend of God, and later alter. This is the view we prefer.

It is possible for the miracles of a saint to include the knowledge that his end is secure and that his condition will not change. This question may be met with in our previous discussion of whether the saint can know that he is a saint.

*****

Someone might ask, "Does the saint ever stop being afraid of deception by God?" If the ordinary consciousness of the saint is overthrown and his perceptions dazzled by his state, so that he is overwhelmed by what takes possession of him, this may be so. Fear is a characteristic of those who are present with ordinary awareness.

*****

Someone might ask, "What is dominant in the saint in his state of sobriety?" This answer is: First, his sincerity in fulfilling his duties to God. Next, his friendship and sympathy toward the creation, whatever his state. Next, the expansion of his compassion to the whole of creation. Next, his constant good-natured tolerance of people; his spontaneously seeking the blessings of God for them without any request on their part; a fixed aspiration to rescue them along with the abandonment of revenge; a wariness of any feeling of hatred for people along with abstinence from their property; the abandonment of any form of ambition toward them; the restraint of his tongue from speaking any evil of them; guarding himself from seeing their evils. The saint is not the adversary of anyone in this world or the next.

*****

Know that one of the sublimest miracles vouchsafed to the saints is God's perpetual acceptance of their acts of obedience, and their full preservation from acts disobedience and opposition.

Among the Quranic evidences of the appearance of miracles in the saints is God's saying, in His description of Mary—who was neither prophet nor messenger—*"Whenever Zachariah came to her place of prayer, he found sustenance with her." He would say, "Whence has this come to you?" and she would reply, "It is from God"* (3:37). God also said to her, *"Shake the branch of the palm tree, and it will drop upon you fresh dates"* (19:25), though it was not the season for dates.

Similarly, there is the story of the Companions of the Cave and the wonders that appeared them, such as their dog's speaking to them, and so forth. There is also the story of Dhu-l-Qarnayn, whom God strengthened as He had strengthened no one else. Another evidence is what appeared through the hand of Khidr, both the setting up of the fallen wall and other marvels, and the things he knew that were hidden from Moses. All of these were matters violating the customary order of things, matters for which Khidr was specially chosen—yet he was not a prophet, he was only a saint.

Another similar account that has been related is the *hadith* of "Jurayj the Monk." Abu Naim Abd al-Malik ibn al-Hasan al-Isfariyani reported it through Abu Iwanah Yaqub ibn Ibrahim ibn Ishaq[1] . . . from Abu Hurayrah, and Abu Iwanah said al-Sinani and Abu Umayyah (related it to him through another route)[2] . . . from Abu Hurayrah, that the Prophet said, "Only three have ever spoken in the cradle: Jesus son of Mary, an infant at the time of Jurayj, and another infant. As for Jesus, you are familiar with him. As for Jurayj, he was a devout man of the Children of Israel. He had a mother, and one day while he was praying his mother longed to see him, and called, 'O Jurayj!' 'O Lord,' he said in prayer, 'is it better to pray, or to go to her?' And he kept praying. She called him again, and he asked the same thing, and still kept praying. His mother found this hard, so she prayed, 'O God, do not take him in death until You have made him behold the faces of harlots!'" Now there was an adulteress among the

Children of Israel. She said to the people, 'I am going to tempt Jurayj until he commits adultery!' She went to him, but was not able to accomplish anything. A shepherd was sheltering for the night by the foundation of Jurayj's cell. When Jurayj rejected her, she seduced the shepherd. He came to her, and she bore a child. Then she announced, 'This baby of mine belongs to Jurayj!' The Children of Israel attacked him, destroyed his hermitage, and reviled him. He prayed and asked of God, and then produced the little boy." Muhammad ibn Sirin said that Abu Hurayrah said, 'I was looking at the Prophet when he said this, gesturing with his hand.' 'Boy, who is your father?' 'The shepherd!' said the child. Then the people regretted what they had done, and apologized to Jurayj. 'We will build you a new cell out of gold!' they said. (Or maybe he said, 'Out of silver.') But Jurayj refused this, and they built it again as it had been before.

"As for the other infant—a woman was holding her suckling child when a handsome and attractive young man passed by. 'My God,' she prayed, 'make my son be like that!' The child exclaimed, 'My God, don't make me like that!' Muhammad ibn Sirin said that Abu Hurayrah said, 'I was looking at the Prophet when he said this, and he imitated the boy suckling.'

"Then someone else passed by the mother and child—a woman whom the people said stole, and committed adultery, and had been punished. 'My God,' she prayed, 'don't make my son be like that!' The child exclaimed, 'My God, make me like that!' His mother asked him what he meant. He said, 'The young man is a tyrant among tyrants. But the woman—they say she committed adultery, but she did not, and they say she stole, but she did not, and she says, 'God is sufficient for me!'"

This *hadith* is reported in the fully authenticated collection. Another such is the hadith of the cave, which is famous in its entirety. Abu Naim Abd al-Malik ibn al-Hasan al-Isfariyani reported[3] . . . from Abu Salim, that the Messenger of God said, "A group of three people got separated from the rest of the party that had gone before them, and they took shelter for the night in a cave. When they had gone inside, a boulder fell down from the mountain and trapped them in the cave. 'By God,' they agreed, 'there is no way we will escape from this boulder unless we implore God Most High for the sake of the goodness of our deeds.' One of them said, 'My two parents were very old, and I would never give a sip to drink to anyone—either a member of my family or any of my livestock—before offering something to them. One day I was out looking for firewood and got distracted, and did not get back to them before they had fallen asleep. I drew some milk and prepared their drink and brought it to them, and found them both sleeping. I didn't want to wake them up, and I didn't like it that anyone or anything in the household should eat before them. So I stood with the drinking bowl in my hand, waiting for them to wake up, until dawn. Then they arose and drank their meal. 'My God, if I did that for Your sake, then save us from the trouble we are in!' A crack opened in the wall, but they were not able to go out through it.

"Then the second man said, 'O God, I had a cousin who was the dearest of people to me. I tried to seduce her, but she resisted. Then a year of crop failure made her suffer. She came to me for help, and I gave her a hundred and twenty dinars on condition that she would let me have my way with her. She agreed, until when I had her in my power she said, "It is not right for you to break the seal unless it is lawful!" So I was prevented from sleeping with her, and turned away, and she was the dearest of people to me. I gave up the gold that I had given her. 'My God, if I did that for Your sake, then save us from the trouble we are in!' The boulder moved a little farther, but they were still unable to get out through the crack.

"The third said, 'O God, I hired some laborers and paid them their wages, all except one man, who abandoned what was due him and went away. So I invested the money that would have gone to pay him. After awhile he returned and demanded, "Abd-Allah, give me my wage!" 'All of what you see is part of your wage,' I said, '—camels, sheep, cattle, and slaves!' 'Don't make fun of me, Abd-Allah,' he complained. 'I'm not making fun of you,' I said. So he took it all and went far away, and I never saw any of it again." 'My God, if I did that for Your sake, then save us from the trouble we are in!' The boulder moved aside, and they left the cave and went their way." This is a sound *hadith*, agreed upon by all.

Related to this is the account given by the Prophet of the ox who spoke. Abu Naim al-Isfariyani reported[4] . . . from Abu Hurayrah, that the Prophet said, "While a man was watering his ox, he sat upon its back. The ox turned its head and said, 'I was not created for this! I was only created to plow!' People exclaimed, 'Glory to God!' The Prophet said, 'I believe this—I, and Abu Bakr, and Umar."

Also related to this is the account of what Umar ibn al-Khattab saw of the state and history of Uways al-Qarani—for instance, his meeting with Hazim ibn Hayyan and their greeting each other personally without there having been any previous acquaintance between them. All of these states were in violation of the customary order of things, and we have left off detailing the story of Uways because of its fame.

Miracles have appeared in our predecessors among the Companions and the Followers, and then among those who came after, to an extent bordering on profusion. Numerous books have been written about them; for the sake of brevity we will only point out a few, God willing.

Thus: Once when Ibn Umar was traveling, he came across a group of people who had halted on the road for fear of a lion. He drove the lion off the road, and said, "Only the thing he fears has power over the son of Adam. If he fears nothing but God, then nothing has mastery over him." This is a well-known account.

And it is related that the Messenger of God sent al-Ila ibn al-Khadrami out on a raid, and an arm of the sea came between him and the place to which he was sent. He beseeched God by His Greatest Name, and they walked over the water.

It is said that Attab ibn Bashir and Asid ibn Khadir left the presence of the Messenger of God (one dark night), and the head of the staff of one of them glowed as if it had been a lamp. There was a large bowl in front of Salman and Abu 'l-Darda. It praised God so that they heard its praise.

The Prophet said, "How many a one there is with matted hair, covered with dust, with two old garments to his name, unnoticed by all—who, if he adjured God, would be answered, and it would make no difference to God what he had asked Him for." We have not mentioned the chains of transmission of these accounts because of how widely they are known.

Sahl ibn Abd-Allah said, "If anyone renounces the world for forty days—truthfully, from the heart, sincerely—miracles will manifest in him. If they do not manifest, it is from lack of truthfulness in his renunciation." Somebody asked Suhayl, "What form did the miracle take in him?" He replied, "He received what he wanted, the way he wanted it, from wherever he wanted."

Ali ibn Ahmad ibn Abdan reported[5] . . . from Abu Hurayrah, that the Prophet said, "While a certain man was reciting a word, he heard thunder in a cloud. He heard a voice in the cloud, saying, 'Water the garden of so-and-so!' Then that cloud moved over a garden plot and emptied its water upon it. The man followed the cloud, and in the garden he found another man, standing in prayer. 'What is your name?' asked the first man. 'So-and-so, son of so-and-so,' answered the second. The first man asked, 'What are you doing with this garden of yours? You have harvested the trees.' 'Why do you ask about that?' 'I heard a voice in the cloud say, "Water the garden of so-and-so." 'Since you ask, I have divided it into thirds: I took a third for myself and my family, left a third to the land, and set aside a third for travelers and the poor.'"

I heard Abu Hatim al-Sijistani say that he heard Abu Nasr al-Sarraj say that they entered Tustar and saw in the compound of Sahl ibn Abd-Allah a building that people called "The Lion House." They asked them about that, and they told them that lions used to come to Sahl and he would bring them into that house and make them his guests, feed them meat, and send them away. Abu Nasr said that all the people of Tustar agreed on this and none of them denied it, and they are a large community."

I heard Muhammad ibn Ahmad ibn Muhammad ibn Ahmad ibn Muhammad al-Tamimi say[6] . . . that Hamzah ibn Abd-Allah al-Alawi said that he went to see Abu-l-Khayr al-Tinati. He had made a decision to greet him and leave, and not eat anything with him. After he left his presence, he walked for awhile. Suddenly he found him behind him, carrying a tray full of food. "Noble youth," he said, "Eat this!" He immediately changed my decision.

Abu-l-Khayr al-Tinati was famous for miracles. It is said that Ibrahim al-Raqqi said, "I set out to offer greetings to (Abu-l-Khayr). He was praying the evening prayer, and he did not recite the Opening Chapter (*Fatihah*) very well. 'I have wasted my trip,' I said to myself. After I greeted him I went outside to perform the ablution. A lion headed right for me. I went back and said, 'A lion chased me!' He went outside and yelled at the lion, 'Haven't I told you not to trouble my guests?' And the lion went away! So I performed my ablution. When I returned, he said, 'You have concerned yourself with the correction of outer forms, so you are afraid of the lion. But we have concerned ourselves with the correction of the heart, so the lion is afraid of us!'"

Jafar al-Khuldi had a ring. One day it fell into the Euphrates. He knew a special prayer for the discovery of lost things, so he offered the prayer, and found the ring in the middle of a stack of papers that he was leafing through.

I heard Abu Hatim al-Sijistani say that he heard Abu Nasr al-

Sarraj say that the prayer was, "O You Who will bring mankind together on the Day concerning which there is no doubt, bring me together with what I have lost!"

Abu Nasr al-Sarraj said that Abu-l-Tayyib al-Akki showed him a text in which it was recalled that whoever invoked this prayer over a lost object found it. The text had a great many pages (of cases).

I asked Ahmad al-Tabarani al-Sarakhsi, "Have any miracles manifested to you?" He told me, "When I was a student at the beginning of my undertaking, sometimes I would look for a stone with which to cleanse myself at the privy, and not be able to find one. So I drew something out of the air. It would turn out to be a jewel, and I used that and threw it away." Then he asked, "What is this concern with miracles? The only point to them is that they increase certainty in the Unity. If someone sees that nothing but God is to be found in the universe, whether the act he witnesses conforms to the usual order of things or violates it, it is all the same."

I heard Muhammad ibn Ahmad al-Sufi say[7] . . . that Abu-l-Hasan al-Basri said, "In Abadan there was a poor black man who lived in the ruins. I brought something with me and sought him out. When his eyes fell upon me, he smiled and gestured with his hand toward the earth. I saw the whole ground turn to glittering gold! 'Give me what you brought!' he said. So I handed it to him, but his state so terrified me that I ran away."

I heard Mansur al-Maghribi say that he heard Ahmad ibn Ata al-Rudhbari say, "I used to give exaggerated care to the matter of ablutions. One night I was depressed because I had poured out too much water when making an ablution. My heart would not rest. 'Lord, Your forgiveness!' I prayed. Then I heard an invisible voice say, 'Forgiveness is in knowledge!' My condition left me."

I heard Mansur al-Maghribi say, "One day I saw (al-Rudhbari) sitting on the ground in the desert, in the midst of sheep tracks, without a prayer carpet. 'O shaykh, these are sheep tracks!' I objected. 'The legal scholars differ upon it,' said he."

I heard Abu Hatim al-Sijistani say[8] . . . that Husayn ibn Ahmad al-Razi said that Abu Sulayman al-Khawwas said, "One day I was riding a donkey. Flies were bothering it, so it kept shaking its head. I hit it on the head with the stick I had in my hand. The donkey looked up and said, 'Strike! There is someone over your head to strike you too!' I asked Abu Sulayman, "Did this really happen to you?" "Yes, just as I have told you," he confirmed.

Ibn Ata is recalled to have said that he heard Abu-l-Husayn al-Nuri say, "I have had one of these miracles in myself. I took a pole from a couple of boys and stood among the boats. 'By Your Might,' I swore, 'If You do not bring out for me a two-pound fish, I'll drown myself!' And a two-pound fish emerged. This story reached Junayd. He said, 'He deserved to have a snake come out and bite him!'"

I heard Abu Abd al-Rahman al-Sulami say[9] . . . that Abu Jafar al-Haddad, the teacher of Junayd, said, "I was in Makkah. My hair had grown long, and I had no iron instrument with me with which to cut off my hair so I went to the barber, hoping for the best. 'Will you cut off my hair for God's sake?' I asked. 'Yes,' said he, 'and a miracle, too!' There was a worldly fellow there in front of him, but he sent him away and sat me down instead. He shaved my head, then passed me a dirhem wrapped in a bit of paper. 'Use this for some of your needs.' I took it, but made up my mind to give him the first gift that reached me because of it. I went into the mosque and met a student of mine. 'One of your brethren has brought you this packet from another brother of yours in Basra,' he told me. It contained three hundred dinars. I took the packet back to the barber. 'Here are three hundred dinars,' I said. 'Spend them on your affairs.' 'Shaykh, aren't you ashamed?' he exclaimed. 'I told you I'd shave your head for God's sake—should I take something for it, then? Go away, and may God forgive you!'"

I heard Abu Hatim al-Sijistani say[10] . . . that Ibn Salim said, "When Ishaq ibn Ahmad died, Sahl ibn Abd-Allah went to his hermitage and found a basket containing two long-necked bottles. In one of them was something red, and in the other something white. He also found a bit of gold and a bit of silver. He threw the two pieces of precious metal into the Euphrates and poured out the two bottles into the dust. Now, Ishaq had been in debt. "What was in those bottles?" I asked Sahl. "If you cast a dirham's weight of one of them upon several measures of copper, the copper would become gold," he said. "If you cast a measure of the other upon several measures of lead, the lead would turn into silver." "Why didn't he use this to settle his debt?" I wondered. "My friend," said Sahl, "he was afraid for his faith."

It is said that Nuri went out one night to the banks of the Euphrates. When he got there he bestrode the river, touching both banks at once. Then he turned aside. "By Your Might," he said, "I won't cross otherwise than in a boat!"

I heard Abu Hatim al-Sijistani say[11] . . . (according to) a story related of Muhammad ibn Yusuf al-Banna, he said, "Abu Turab al-

Nakhshabi displayed many miracles. One year I traveled with him, along with forty people he had with him. A time of need afflicted us. Abu Turab turned off the road and came back with a bunch of bananas, which we ate. A young man who was with us, however, refused them. 'Eat!' urged Abu Turab. 'To give up known and reliable sources of sustenance is the state in which I believe,' replied the youth. 'To me, you have now become just such a reliable source. I cannot keep company with you after this!' 'Be together with the state that has befallen you,' Abu Turab advised."

Abu Nasr al-Sarraj related that Abu Yazid said that Abu Ali al-Sindi (who was the teacher of Abu Yazid) one day came in to see me with a traveling bag in his hand. He emptied it out, and it was full of jewels. "Where did you get these?" I asked. "I came across a riverbed here. It was shining like a lamp," he said. "So I took these." "What state were you in when you reached that riverbed?" I wondered. "It was a moment when I had lapsed from my spiritual state!" he confessed. Someone said to Abu Yazid, "So-and-so walked all the way to Makkah in a single night!" "The Devil walks from East to West in an hour," Abu Yazid retorted. "And such-and-such a man walks on water, and flies in the air!" "Birds fly in the air, and fish cross the face of the water," said he.

Sahl ibn Abd-Allah said, "The greatest of miracles is to change one of your blameworthy traits." I heard Muhammad ibn Ahmad ibn Muhammad al-Tamimi say[12] . . . that Salim said, "There was a man named Abd al-Rahman ibn Ahmad who kept company with Sahl ibn Abd-Allah. One day he told Sahl, 'Sometimes when I am making my ablution before offering prayers, the water dissolves before me into branches of gold and silver.' 'Don't you know,' said Sahl, 'that when children cry they are given little twigs to distract them?'"

I heard Abu Hatim al-Sijistani say[13] . . . that Junayd said, "One day I went to visit Sari. He told me, 'Every day a little bird used to come here, so I would crumble some bread for it and it would eat from my hand. Then a time came when it would not perch upon my hand. I tried to recall what the cause of that might be, and I remembered that I had eaten some spiced salt. 'I will not eat it anymore,' I said to myself. 'I am sorry I ate it.' Then the bird perched upon my hand and ate."

Abu Amr al-Anmati related, "I was with my teacher in the desert when rain started to fall. We went into a mosque to seek shelter. The ceiling leaked, so we climbed up to the roof, bringing with us a board to fix the ceiling. The board was too short to reach the wall. 'Stretch it!' ordered my teacher. So we stretched it, and it covered the enclosure from one side to the other."

I heard Muhammad ibn Abd-Allah al-Sufi say[14] . . . that Abu Bakr al-Daqqaq said, "I was passing through the desert of the Children of Israel, my mind occupied with contradictions between esoteric knowledge and the divine Command. An invisible voice called to me from beneath a tree, 'A truth that does not conform to the divine Command is unbelief!' A dervish said, 'I was with Khayr al-Nassaj when a man came in and confessed, "O shaykh, I saw you yesterday. You had sold some thread for two dirhems. I came up behind you and removed them from a fold of your garment. But my hand has cramped shut over the two dirhems in my fist!" Khayr laughed. He gestured at the hand, and it opened. 'Go and buy something for your family with them,' he said, 'and don't do this sort of thing again!'"

It is related that Ahmad ibn Muhammad al-Sulami said, "One day I came in on Dhu-l-Nun and saw before him a basin full of gold, with two kinds of incense burning around it. "Are you one of those people who drops in on kings when they are feeling expansive?" he asked. Then he gave me a dirhem, and I spent from that dirhem all the way to Balkh."

Abu Said al-Kharraz said, "During one of my journeys there were three days when every day something to eat appeared to me. I ate, and it sufficed me. Then came three days when nothing whatsoever came, and I grew weak. I sat down, and an invisible voice called, 'Which do you prefer, means or power?' 'Power!' I said. Immediately I stood up. Then I walked for twelve days without tasting a thing, and without losing my strength."

According to al-Murtaish, al-Khawwas said, "I had been wandering in the desert for days when a person came, greeted me, and asked, 'Lost?' 'Yes,' I said. 'Won't I lead you to the road, then?' said he. He walked in front of me for a few steps, then disappeared from sight. I found myself on the main road! Since then, I have never been lost or suffered from hunger or thirst on a journey.

I heard Muhammad ibn Abd-Allah al-Sufi say[15] . . . that Ibn al-Jalla said, "After my father died, he laughed at the man who came to wash his body! So no one would wash him, for they all said he was alive. Finally one of his close friends came and washed the body."

I heard Muhammad ibn Ahmad al-Tamimi say[16] . . . that al-Munayhi, the companion of Sahl ibn Abd-Allah, said that Sahl abstained from food for seventy days. When he ate, he would grow weak, and when he went hungry, he would grow strong.

At the beginning of the month of Ramadan, Abu Ubayd al-Basri would go into a room and tell his wife, "Lock the door behind me, and throw me in a loaf of bread through the window every night." When the day of festival came at the end of the month, the door would be unlocked and his wife would go in. There would be thirty loaves in a corner of the room. He had neither eaten, nor drunk, nor slept, nor missed a single cycle of prayer."

Abu-l-Harith al-Ulashi said, "I lived thirty years during which my tongue spoke of nothing but my inmost heart. Then my state changed, and I lived another thirty years when my inmost heart spoke of nothing but my Lord."

I heard Muhammad ibn Abd-Allah al-Sufi say[17] . . . that Ali ibn Salim said, "At the end of his life, Sahl ibn Abd-Allah was afflicted with a chronic illness. When the time of prescribed prayer would come, he would be able to move his hands and feet, but as soon as the obligatory portion of the prayer was finished, his illness would return."

It is related that Abu Imran al-Wasiti said, "The ship we were in foundered, and my wife and I kept afloat on a board. Under those circumstances, she went into labor. She cried out to me, saying, 'Thirst is killing me!' 'God sees our state,' I told her. I lifted my head, and there was a man in the middle of the air! He had a chain of gold in his hand, and attached to it was a ruby cup. 'Here you are,' he said. 'Drink!' I took the cup and we drank from it. It was more fragrant than musk, colder than ice, and sweeter than honey. 'May God have mercy upon you—who are you?' I asked. 'A servant of your Lord.' 'How have you attained to this?' 'I gave up my own whim for His good pleasure, and He has seated me in the air,' said he. Then he vanished, and I saw him no more."

Muhammad ibn Abd-Allah al-Sufi reported[18] . . . that Dhu-l-Nun al-Misri said, "At the Kabah I watched a young man bowing and prostrating himself in prayer over and over again. I came up to him and said, 'You are certainly making a lot of prayers!' I am waiting for my Lord's permission to go,' said he. I saw a scrap of paper fall upon him. Written upon it was, 'From the Mighty, the Forgiving, to My sincere servant—Go. All your sins that have come before, and all that shall follow, are forgiven you.'"

A dervish said, "I was in the City of the Prophet, in his mosque, with a group of people who were recounting the signs of God. A blind man nearby us was listening. He came over and said, 'I am quite intimate with what you are talking about. You should know that I had a wife and child, and used to go out to the wasteland full of tree roots, in order to gather firewood. One day I went out and saw there a man wearing a linen shirt, with sandals upon his feet. I supposed that he was lost, and I decided to rob him of his clothes. "Take off what you have on you!" I ordered. "Go away, may God protect you!" he said. I repeated my order a second and third time. Finally he said, "No escaping it?" "No escaping it!" I told him. From some distance away, he pointed his finger at my eyes. They both fell out. "My God," I cried, "who are you?" "Ibrahim al-Khawwas," he said.'"

Dhu-l-Nun al-Misri said, "Once I was on board a ship when a piece of velvet stuff was stolen. People suspected a certain man of the theft. 'Pray to God to be gentle with him' I said. The man was sleeping in his cloak. He stuck his head out of the cloak, and I spoke to him about the suspicions. 'You are speaking this way to me?' he exclaimed. 'My Lord! I swear by You that there's not a single fish that won't come here with a jewel!' We watched the fish come to the surface of the water. In their mouths were jewels. The man threw himself into the sea and went ashore."

Ibrahim al-Khawwas said, "Once I went into the desert and encountered a Christian, who wore the belt of dualism around his waist. He asked for my company, so we walked together for a week. Then 'O Muslim monk,' he said, 'give us what entertainment you have with you, for we are hungry.' I prayed, 'My God, do not disgrace me before this unbeliever!'—and I saw a tray bearing bread, roast meat, fresh dates, and a pitcher of water. So we ate and drank. We walked another week. Then suddenly it occurred to me to say, 'O Christian monk, give us what you have with you. Trouble is over for you!' He leaned upon his staff and prayed, and there were two trays, bearing twice as much as there had been upon my tray! I was amazed and disturbed, and I refused to eat. He insisted, but I would not answer him. Then, 'Eat!' he said. 'I will give you two pieces of good news. The first is that I bear witness that there is no god but God, and I bear witness that Muhammad is the Messenger of God!' And he untied the belt. 'The other is that I prayed, "My God, if this servant here is important to You, then give me something for his sake!" And it was given.' So we ate, and walked, and performed the prescribed pilgrimage, and lived in Mecca for a year. Then he died, and was buried in the valley."

Muhammad ibn al-Mubarak al-Suri said, "I was with Ibrahim ibn Adham on the road to Jerusalem. When it came time for the afternoon nap, we stopped under a pomegranate tree. We offered a few cycles of prayer. Then we heard a voice come from the root of the tree, 'O Abu Ishaq! Honor us by eating something from us!' Ibrahim bowed his his head. The voice repeated its plea three times, and then said, 'Muhammad, intercede with him to eat something from us!' 'Abu Ishaq,' I said, 'you heard.' So he stood up and took two pomegranates. He ate one and gave me the other. They were sour, and the tree was stunted. When we passed by on our way back, that tree was tall, and its pomegranates were sweet. It used to bear fruit twice a year. They called it "The Tree of the Worshippers," and people who were devoted to worship took shelter in its shade."

I heard Muhammad ibn Abd-Allah al-Sufi say[19] . . . that Jabir al-Rahbi said, "Many times the people of Rahbah expressed to me their denial of miracles. So one day I rode a lion into town. 'Where are the people who call God's Friends liars?' I demanded. After that they restrained themselves."

I heard Mansur al-Maghribi say, "A Sufi met Khidr and asked him, 'Have you seen anyone who is higher than yourself?' 'Yes,' he said. ''Abd al-Razzaq ibn Humam was relating *hadiths* in Medina, and the people were gathered around him to listen. I saw a man with his head upon his knees, some distance away. 'It is Abd al-Razzaq who is reporting hadiths of the Messenger of God,' I asked him. 'Why aren't you listening to him?' 'He transmits from the dead,' the man informed me. 'I cannot be absent from God!' 'I challenged, "If you are what you claim—Who am I?' 'He raised his head and stated, 'You are my brother Abu-l-Abbas al-Khidr!' So I knew that God had servants who were unknown to me.'"

It is said that Ibrahim ibn Adham had a friend named Yahya who devoted himself to worship in a room which no ladder nor any staircase reached. When he wanted to make his ablution, he would go to the door of his room, say, "There is no power nor strength save in God," and pass through the air like a bird. Then he would make his ablution, and when he was finished, he would say, "There is no power nor strength save in God," and return to his room.

Muhammad ibn Abd-Allah al-Sufi related[20] . . . that Abu Muhammad Jafar al-Hadhai in Shiraz said, "I was educated by Abu Umar al-Istakhri. When some matter would concern me, I used to go out to Istakhr. Sometimes he would give me the answer I needed without my asking him, and sometimes I would ask him and then he would answer. Later affairs prevented me from making the trip. Then when a question formed within my soul he would answer me from Istakhr and give me advice about what had occurred to me."

A Sufi said, "A poor dervish died in a darkened house. When we wanted to wash his body, we were obliged to search for a lamp. Then a radiance broke through a small window and illuminated the house. So we washed him, and when we were finished the radiance went away, as if it had never been."

Adam ibn Abi Iyyas is reported to have said, "We were in Askalon. There was a young man who would visit us, and sit and converse with us. When we were finished, he would stand and pray. One day he bade us farewell, saying, 'I'm for Alexandria.' I went outside with him. I wanted to give him a few pennies, but he refused to take them. I insisted. So he took a handful of sand and threw it into his water pot, then filled it with seawater. 'Eat this!' he said. I looked—and it was porridge with raisins, and full of sugar! 'If someone's state with God is like this,' he asked, 'is he in need of your money?' Then he recited:

> As for desire—you who love me, understand the voice of my
> being. It is a stranger to existence.
> It is forbidden that anything but Truth should have a share
> In a heart that has refused desire.

And also:

> In heart and soul together
> the Beloved finds no vacant place.
> He is my wish, my longing, my happiness.
> By Him I live, and my life is good.
> When sicknesses visited my heart
> I found no other physician for my ills.

It is said that Ibrahim al-Ajri said, "A Jew came to me to question me about religion. He was a man of eminence. I was sitting by the kiln, which was fired to bake some brick. 'Ibrahim,' said the Jew, 'show me a sign to which I can submit.' 'You will do it?' I asked. 'Yes,' said he. 'Take off your cloak,' I told him. So he took it off. I folded it, and wrapped my cloak around his, and threw them into the fire. Then I went into the kiln and drew out the cloaks from the midst of the fire, and went out the other door. My cloak was untouched, but his cloak, within it, was aflame. The Jew became a Muslim."

Habib al-Ajami, it is said, was seen in Basra on the night preceding the great holy gathering of the prescribed pilgrimage, but on the Day of Arafah itself he was on the plain of Arafat in Makkah.

I heard Muhammad ibn Abd-Allah al-Sufi say that he heard Ahmad ibn Muhammad ibn Abd-Allah al-Farghani say that Abbas ibn al-Muhtadi married a woman, but on the wedding night he felt remorse. When he wanted to approach his bride, he was held back and prevented from embracing her. So he left. After three days it came to light that she already had a husband! This is really a miracle, since the knowledge was preserved for him!

Fudayl ibn Iyad was on one of the mountains of Mina when he said, "If one of the Friends of God ordered this mountain to move, it would move." The mountain began to shake! "Be still!" said Fudayl. "I didn't want you to do this!" And the mountain was still.

Abd al-Wahid ibn Zayd asked Abu Asim al-Basri, "What did you do when you were summoned by Hajjaj?" "I was in my room," he replied. "They knocked on my door and came in, so I gave myself a push, and there I was on the mountain of Abu Qubays in Mecca." "How did you eat?" asked Abd al-Wahid. "Every time it came time to break my fast, an old woman would climb up to me with a couple of loaves of the bread that I had used to eat in Basra." Abd al-Wahid said, "God Most High ordered this world to wait upon Abu Asim."

When Amir ibn Abd Qays received his allotted stipend from the treasury, there was no one he met to whom he wouldn't give something. When he came to his house, he would throw dirhams at it. Yet the amount he had received was never diminished at all.

I heard Abu Abd-Allah al-Shirazi say[21] . . . that Abu Amr al-Zujjaji said, "I went to visit Junayd, having planned to perform the prescribed pilgrimage. He gave me a shiny dirham, and I tied it up in my clothes. I never entered a campsite without finding friends there, and I never needed a penny. When I completed the prescribed pilgrimage, I returned to Baghdad and went to see Junayd. He stretched out his hand and said, "Give it here!" So I gave him the dirham. 'How did it do?' he asked. 'The order was effective,' I told him.

It is related that Abu Jafar al-Awar said, "I was with Dhu-l-Nun al-Misri. We were all trading stories about things' obedience to the saints. Dhu-l-Nun said, 'Part of this obedience is that if I tell this chair to tour the four corners of the room and then come back to its place, it will do it.' And the chair went about the four corners of the room and returned to where it had been! A young man in the company began to weep, and he died on the spot.

Wasil the Hunchback recited, "*In the heavens is their sustenance and what they have been promised*" (51:22). He said, "My sustenance is in the heavens, and I have been searching for it in the earth! By God, I will not search for it anymore!" So he entered a ruined building and lived there for two days, and nothing appeared to him. The situation grew difficult, but when the third day came, suddenly there was a dish full of dates. Now Wasil had a brother whose intention surpassed his own. His brother came out to be with him, and the dish became two dishes. That state of theirs did not cease until they were separated by death.

A Sufi said, "I looked down at Ibrahim ibn Adham from a height. He was in an orchard where he worked as a watchman. Sleep had overcome him. A snake came with a bunch of narcissus in its mouth and fanned their perfume over him."

A group of people was traveling with Ayyub al-Sijistani, and they tired themselves out searching for water. "Will you promise not to reveal this while I am alive?" asked Ayyub. "Yes," they said. So Ayyub turned in a circle, and water came out of the ground, and (we!) drank. When we came to Basrah, Hammad ibn Zayd was told this anecdote, and Abd al-Wahid ibn Zayd confirmed, "I was there to bear witness to him that day."

Bakr ibn Abd al-Rahman said, "We were with Dhu-l-Nun al-Misri in the desert. We camped under a lote-tree and remarked, 'How nice this place would be if there were dates here!' Dhu-l-Nun smiled. 'You have an appetite for dates?' he said. Then he shook the tree and commanded, 'I adjure you by Him Who created you and made you a tree—shower fresh dates upon us!' Then he shook it again, and fresh dates rained down. So we ate until we were satisfied. Then we slept. When we woke up, we shook the tree ourselves, but only thorns came down."

It is related that Abu-l-Qasim ibn Marwan al-Nihawandi said, "Abu Bakr al-Warraq and I were walking along the seacoast near Saydah with Abu Said al-Kharraz. He saw somebody in the distance. 'Sit down,' he said. 'That man is certainly one of the Friends of God.' Before long, a young man with a beautiful face came by. He was carrying a waterpot and an inkwell in his hands, and wore the patched cloak of a dervish. Abu Said turned to him and challenged his carrying an inkwell as well as a waterpot. 'Noble youth,' he said, 'what are the paths to God Most High?' 'Abu Said,' he answered, 'I know two paths to God: the general path, and the special path. As for the general path, that is what you follow. As for the special path—come on!' Then he walked out over the water until he vanished from our sight. Abu Said remained astounded by what he had seen."

Junayd said, "I went to the Shuniziyyah mosque and found there a congregation of dervishes talking of the signs of God. One of them said, 'I know a man who could say to that column, "Be half gold and half silver," and it would happen.' 'Watch!' I said. And half the column was gold, and half was silver.'"

Sufyan al-Thawri performed the prescribed pilgrimage with Shayban al-Rai. A lion threatened them. "Don't you see that lion?" Sufyan asked Shayban. "Don't be afraid," Shayban replied. Shayban took hold of the lion's ear and scratched it, and the lion gave himself a shake and wagged his tail. "What sort of public demonstration is this?" demanded Sufyan. "If I weren't afraid of public demonstrations," Shayban retorted, "I'd have him carry my gear on his back all the way to Makkah!"

It is told that when Sari gave up his business, his sister supported him by selling the yarn she spun. One day she was late returning. "Why were you late?" Sari asked. "My yarn didn't sell," she told him, "People said it was jinxed." Sari held back from eating her food. Then one day, his sister came in on him and found an old woman sweeping his room. And every day that old woman brought him two loaves of bread. Sari's sister was saddened, and complained to Ahmad ibn Hanbal. Ahmad ibn Hanbal spoke to Sari about it. "When I refrained from eating my sister's food," Sari told him, "God assigned this world to feed me and wait upon me!"

Muhammad ibn Abd-Allah al-Sufi reported[22] . . . that Muhammad bin Mansur al-Tusi said, "I visited Abu Mahfuz Maruf al-Karkhi, and he prayed for me. I went back the next day, and there was a mark on his face. Somebody asked, "Abu Mahfuz, we were here with your yesterday and that mark wasn't on your face then. What happened?" "What do you think?" he countered. "By your Lord, you will have to tell me!" the man replied. "Yesterday I was praying here," said Maruf, "and I longed to be circling the Kabah. So I went to Makkah and made the circumambulation. Then I went over to Zamzam in order to drink some of its water, but I slipped at the door and hurt my face, as you see."

It is told that Utbah al-Ghulam used to sit and say, "O turtle dove!

If I am obedient to what God has commanded me, then come and sit on my hand!" And the dove would come and sit on his hand.

It is related that Abu Ali al-Razi said, "One day I was walking along the Euphrates and I found myself wishing for fresh fish. Suddenly the water flung a fish up on the shore beside me! A man passing by asked, 'Shall I fry this for you?' 'Yes!' I said. So he fried it, and I sat and ate it."

Ibrahim ibn Adham was among a group of people who were confronted by a lion. "Abu Ishaq," they told him, "a lion has come upon us!" Ibrahim went out and said, "Lion, if you have been ordered to do something to us, then do it! Otherwise, go away!" The lion went back where it had come from, and the party continued on its way.

Hamid al-Aswad said, "I was with al-Khawwas in the desert. We camped for the night under a tree. A lion came, so I climbed up the tree and stayed there until morning. I couldn't sleep at all. Meanwhile Ibrahim al-Khawwas slept, while the lion sniffed him from head to foot and then went away. The second night we spent in a mosque in a town. A bedbug jumped on Ibrahim's face and bit him, and he groaned. 'This is very strange,' I remarked. 'Yesterday a lion couldn't disturb you, yet tonight a bedbug makes you yell!' 'As for yesterday,' he told me, 'that is the condition I was in with God. And as for tonight, this is the condition I am in by myself!'"

It is related that Ata al-Azraq's wife gave him two dirhams she had earned spinning wool, and sent him out to buy the family some flour. So he left his house, and came across a slave girl, weeping. "What's wrong?" he asked. "My master gave me two dirhams to buy something, and I dropped them," she told him. "Now I am afraid he will beat me!" Ata gave her his two dirhams, and left. He went and sat in the shop of a friend of his who cut teakwood for a living. He recounted both what had happened, and also what he feared from the bad temper of his wife. "Take some of this sawdust home with you in this bag," his friend suggested. "Maybe you will be able to use it to heat the oven, at any rate, since I have no other means of helping you!" So Ata took the sawdust and went home. He opened the door of the house, threw in the bag, shut the door, and went and stayed in the mosque until dark. Perhaps everybody would fall asleep, and his wife would not be mean to him! But when he went back and opened the door, he found the family eating bread. "Where did this bread come from?" he asked. "From the flour that was in the bag," they told him. "Don't ever buy any other flour than this again!" "God willing!" said he.

I heard Abu Abd al-Rahman al-Sulami say[23] . . . that Abu Jafar ibn Barakat say, "I was sitting with the dervishes, and I had received some dinars, so I wanted to give them to them. Then I said to myself, 'But maybe I will need them!' Suddenly I was hit with a toothache. I went and had the tooth pulled. Then I was struck with another toothache, so I had to have that tooth pulled too. A voice from nowhere announced, 'If you don't give them the dinars, you won't have a single tooth left in your mouth!'" As far as miracles go, this is more perfect than if he had received many dinars in violation of the natural order.

Abu Sualyman al-Darani is related to have said, "Amir ibn Qays traveled to Damascus. He had with him a small waterskin. When he wished, water poured from it so that he could make his ablution for prayer, and when he wished, milk poured from it for him to drink."

It is said that Uthman ibn Abi'l-Atikah said, "We were out on a raid into Byzantine territory. The captain sent a detachment off somewhere, and set our rendezvous for such-and-such a day. But the day came, and there was no sign of that detachment. Meanwhile, Abu Muslim (al-Khawlani) was making his prayers with his spear thrust into the earth in front of him when a bird came and perched on the spearhead. 'The raiding party is safe,' announced the bird. 'They are dividing the spoils of battle and will rejoin you on such-and-such a day at such-and-such a time!' 'Who are you, may God have mercy upon you?' Abu Muslim asked the bird. 'I am the one who drives sadness from the hearts of the believers!' it replied. Abu Muslim went to the captain and told him what had happened. When the day the bird had told of arrived, the detachment returned, just as it had said." A dervish said, "We were on board ship when a man who had fallen sick among us died. So we held his funeral, and we wanted to throw him into the sea. But the sea went dry, and the ship ran aground, and we left and dug a grave and buried him in it. When we had finished, the water level rose, and the ship was lifted, and we continued on."

It is told that when the people of Basra were suffering from famine, Habib al-Ajami bought bread on credit and distributed it among the poor. Then he took a sack and placed it under his head. When his creditors came, he took out the sack, and it was full of dirhems. With these he paid what he owed them.

Muhammad ibn Abd-Allah al-Sufi reported[24] . . . that Abu Hamzah Nasr ibn al-Faraj, the servant of Muawiyah al-Aswad, said that Abu Muawiyah lost his vision. But when he wanted to read the Quran, he would open the volume, and God would return his sight to him. When he closed the volume, his sight would leave him.

Ahmad ibn al-Haytham al-Mutatayyib said that Bishr al-Hafi told him, "Tell Maruf al-Karkhi that when I have offered my pre-scribed prayers, I will come to you." So I conveyed this message, and I waited for him. We prayed the noon prescribed prayer, and he did not come. And we prayed the prescribed afternoon prayer, the prescribed evening prayer, and the night prescribed prayer. I said to myself, "God forbid that the likes of Bishr should say something and not do it. It isn't possible that he won't do it!" So I waited. I was up on the roof of the mosque at the cistern when Bishr finally arrived, after half the night had passed. He had his prayer carpet over his head. He came up to the bank of the Tigris and walked over the water. I jumped off of the roof and kissed his hands and feet. "Pray to God for me," I begged. So he prayed, and then said, "Keep this a secret for me." I never spoke of it until after he had died.

I heard Abu Abd-Allah al-Shirazi say[25] . . . that Qasim al-Jari said, "I watched a man circling the Kabah. All that he would say was, 'My God, You fulfill everyone's needs, but You have not fulfilled my need!' So I asked him, 'What is it with you, that you never pray any-thing but this?' He said, 'I will tell you. Know that I was one of seven people from different cities who went and joined the holy war. The Byzantines captured us and held us in order to execute us. I saw seven doors open in the skies, and at each door was a beautiful houri maid. One of us stepped forward, and his head was cut off. I saw one of the maids descend to the earth with a kerchief in her hand, and she received his soul. So it proceeded until six of us had been beheaded. Then one of the Byzantines wanted to keep me alive. 'O bereft one, what a thing you have missed!' exclaimed the houri. And the doors were shut. 'My brother, I am sorrowful and grieving over what has escaped me!' Qasim al-Jari said, 'I saw him to be the best of them all, for he had seen what they did not see, and strove with longing after they had gone.'"

And I heard him say[26] . . . that Abu Bakr al-Kattani said, "I was on the road to Makkah in the middle of the year when I came across a sack full of glittering dinars. I was excited at the thought of carry-ing it away to distribute among the dervishes of Makkah, but a voice from nowhere announced, 'If you take it, we will strip you of your state of poverty!'"

I heard Muhammad ibn Abd-Allah al-Sufi say[27] . . . that al-Abbas al-Sharqi said, "We were on the road to Makkah with Abu Turab al-

Nakhshabi. He turned off to the side of the road, and one of his students told him, 'I am thirsty!' So he stamped his foot upon the ground, and a spring of cold water appeared. 'I would love to drink it from a cup,' said the youth. Abu Turab struck his hand upon the earth, and passed the young man a vessel of white glass, as beautiful as any I have ever seen. He drank, and gave us to drink, and the cup stayed with us all the way to Makkah. One day Abu Turab asked me, 'What do your companions say about these matters with which God honors his servants?' 'I have not seen anyone who did not believe in them,'I told him. 'Whoever does not believe in them is without faith,' he returned. 'I was only inquiring about a perspective on states.' 'I do not know that they say anything about it,' I declared. 'Indeed?' said he. 'Your companions maintain that they are a deception from the Truth. That is not how things are. The only deception lies in relying upon such events. Whoever does not demand them and does not count upon them belongs to the degree of men of God.'"

I heard Muhammad ibn Abd-Allah al-Sufi say[28] . . . that Abu Abd-Allah ibn al-Jalla said, "We were in Sari al-Saqati's room in Baghdad. When much of the night had passed he put on a clean shirt and trousers and a cloak and sandals, and got up to go. 'Where are you going at this hour?' I asked. 'I am going to visit Fath al-Mawsili,' he said. Now Fath had been out walking in the streets of Baghdad, and the night patrol had arrested him and locked him up. The next morning it was ordered that he be whipped along with the other prisoners. When the executioner raised his hand to beat him, his hand froze, and he was unable to move it. 'Strike!' they ordered him. 'There is a shaykh standing in front of me, face to face,' the man exclaimed. 'He is telling me, "Do not hit him!" and my hand is held and cannot move!' So they investigated who the prisoner was and found he was Fath al-Mawsili, and they did not whip him."

Abu Abd al-Rahman al-Sulami reported[29] . . . that Said ibn Yahya al-Basri said, "Some members of Quraysh used to sit with Abd al-Wahid ibn Zayd. One day they came to him and said, 'We are afraid of poverty and need!' Abd al-Wahid raised his face to the heavens and prayed, 'My God, I ask You by Your Name 'The Remover of Trouble' (al-Murtafi) by which You have honored whom You will among Your Friends, and with which You have inspired the pure among Your beloved ones, that You give us a sustenance from Your presence that will cut satan's bonds from our hearts and the hearts of these our companions. You are the Gracious, the Benevolent, the Eternal, the Great

Gift! My God, right now, right now!' And by God, there was some clattering upon the roof, and then dinars and dirhams rained down upon us. 'Be satisfied with God Almighty and Glorious, and free of everything else!' said Abd al-Wahid ibn Zayd. So they took the money, and Abd al-Wahid ibn Zayd touched none of it."

I heard Abu Abd-Allah al-Shirazi say[30] . . . that al-Kattani said, "I saw a Sufi, a stranger of whom I knew nothing, approach the Kabah and say, 'O Lord, I do not know what these people are praying!'— meaning the people circling the Kabah. 'Look over what is upon this paper,' he was told. Then the piece of paper flew into the air and vanished!"

And I heard him say[31] . . . that Abu Abd-Allah ibn al-Jalla said, "One day my mother wanted to have some fish, and asked my father for it. So my father took me with him and went to the market. He bought fish and stood looking for someone to carry it home for him. He noticed a young boy stop in front of him with another lad. 'Uncle,' the boy asked, 'do you want someone to carry that?' 'Yes,' said my father. So he picked it up and walked along with us. Then we heard the call to prescribed prayer. 'The *muezzin* is calling to prayer,' observed the boy. 'I need to make ablution and pray, if that is all right with you. Otherwise, take the fish.' And he put the fish down and went away. 'As for us, it is better that we trust God with this fish,' said my father. So we entered the mosque and prayed, and the boy came and prayed too. And when we came out, there was the fish sitting where it had been left. So the boy took it and went with us to our house. My father recounted all this to my mother. 'Ask him to stay and eat something with us,' she urged. So we asked him, but he said, 'I am fasting.' 'So come back to us tonight,' we said. 'When I have worked as a porter once during a day, I don't do it a second time,' he told us. 'I go and stay in the mosque until evening. But I will come to see you then.' And he went away. When evening came the boy arrived and we ate. We we had finished we showed him the place to make ablution. Then we saw that he preferred to withdraw, so we left him alone in the house. Now one of our relatives had a crippled daughter. Part way into the night she came to us, walking. We asked her what had happened. She said, 'I prayed, "O Lord, cure me for the sake of our guest"— and I stood up!' So we went to look for the boy, and all the doors were locked as they had been, but we could not find him. 'There are some who are little,' remarked my father, 'and then again, there are some who are big!'"

I heard Muhammad ibn al-Husayn say[32] . . . that Said ibn Yahya al-Basri said, "I went to see Abd al-Wahid ibn Zayd, and he was sitting in the dark. 'If you were to ask God to increase your sustenance, I have every hope that He would do it,' I said. 'My Lord best knows the interests of His servants,' he told me. Then he picked up some pebbles off the ground and prayed, 'My God, if it is Your will to make these gold, then do it!' And by God, they were gold in his hand. He threw them at me and said, 'You spend these. There is nothing good in this world except what belongs to the Next!'"

I heard Muhammad ibn Abd-Allah al-Sufi say[33] . . . that Abu Yaqub al-Susi, the master of Ahmad ibn Mansur, told him, "I was giving somebody the funeral ablution. He grabbed my thumb, though he was already in the washing room! 'Let go of my hand, my son,' I said. 'I am aware that you are not dead, but are only moving from one house to another.' So he released my hand."

And I heard him say[34] . . . that Ibrahim ibn Shayban said, "A young man who possessed fine spiritual intent was among my students. He died, and my heart was very distracted on account of it. I took it upon myself to give him the funeral ablution. When I wanted to wash his hands, I was so upset that I began with the left hand. He took it back from me and gave me his right hand! 'You are correct, my son,' I said. 'I have made a mistake.'"

And I heard him say[35] . . . that Abu Yaqub al-Susi said, "In Makkah a student came to me and said, 'Master, I will die tomorrow at the time of noon prayer. Take this dinar. Use half of it to have my grave dug, and half of it to shroud me.' When the next day arrived, he came and circled the Kabah, then went some ways off, and died. So I washed his body, and shrouded him, and set him in the tomb. Then his eyes opened. 'Living after death?' I exclaimed. 'I am alive,' he said. 'All lovers of God are alive!'"

I heard Abu Abd al-Rahman al-Sulami say[36] . . . that Abu Ali ibn Wasif al-Muaddib said that Sahl ibn Abd-Allah (al-Tustari) was talking one day about the remembrance of God. "If the rememberer really remembered God," he remarked, "if he set himself to revive the dead, he could do it." Then he ran his hand over a sick man who was there before him, and the man recovered and stood up."

I heard Abd-Allah al-Shirazi say[37] . . . that Bishr ibn al-Harith said, "When Amr ibn Utbah offered his prescribed prayers, clouds would form over his head, and the lions would gather around him, wagging their tails.

And I heard him say[38] . . . that Junayd said, "I had four dirhams, so I went to see Sari and said, 'Here are four dirhams that I have brought you. I give you good news that you will prosper, boy,' he said. 'I have need of four dirhams!' Then he prayed, 'My God, send these by the hand of one who will prosper with You!'"

And I heard him say[39] . . . that Abu Ibrahim al-Tamimi said, "We went out traveling along the seashore with Ibrahim ibn Adham and ended up at a cane thicket in which was plenty of dry firewood. Nearby was a fortress. So we went to Ibrahim ibn Adham and asked, 'What if we spend the night here and light a fire with this wood?' 'Do it,' he said. So we gathered some fire wood from the forest and set up a campfire. We had some bread with us, so we took it out and ate it. 'What could be better than these coals,' one of us observed, 'if only we had some meat to broil upon them?' 'God Most High is able to feed you with that,' said Ibrahim. Just then a lion appeared, chasing a goat. When it got near to us it attacked the goat and broke its neck. Ibrahim ibn Adham stood up and said, 'Slaughter it! God is feeding you!' So we salughtered it and broiled its meat while the lion sat and watched us.

I heared Muhammad ibn al-Husayn say[40] . . . that Hamid al-Aswad said, "I was with Ibrahim ibn al-Khawwas in the desert for seven days in a single unchanging condition. But when the seventh day came I grew weak and sat down. He turned to me and asked, 'What has happened?' 'I am weakening,' I told him. 'What need has overcome you—water or food?' he asked. 'Water,' I said. 'Water is behind you,' he told me. So I turned around, and there was a spring of water fine as cow's milk. I drank and made my ablutions. Ibrahim watched but did not come near. When I was ready to stand up and go, I meant to take some of the water with me. 'Restrain yourself,' said Ibrahim. 'This is not the sort of thing that can be carried as supplies.'"

I heard Abu Abd-Allah ibn Abd-Allah say[41] . . . that Zaytunah was the servant of Abu-l-Husayn al-Nuri and waited upon him. She also served Abu Hamzah and Junayd. She said, "It was a cold day, so I asked Nuri, 'Shall I bring you something?' 'Yes,' said he. 'What do you want?' I asked. 'Bread in milk.' So I brought it. There was some charcoal in front of him that he was turning with his hand, and it had gotten all over him. He began to eat the bread, and the milk ran down his hand, black with charcoal as it was. 'How filthy are Your Friends, O Lord,' I said to myself. 'There isn't a clean one among them!' Then I left him. Outside, a woman grabbed hold of me and yelled, 'You stole a package of clothes from me!' And she took me off to the policeman. Nuri was told about this. He went and told the policeman, 'Don't mix yourself into this. She is one of the Friends of God Most High.' 'But what am I supposed to do about the woman who lodged the complaint?' protested the man. Then a maid came in carrying the package in question. Nuri called me in. 'Are you going to say, after this, "How filthy are Your Friends?" he inquired. 'I have repented to God,' I told him."

I heard Muhammad ibn Abd-Allah al-Shirazi say[42] . . . that al-Khawwas said, "One one of my journeys I grew so thirsty that I dropped from thirst. Then suddenly I felt the splashing of water on my face. I opened my eyes, and there was a handsome man riding a grey horse. He gave me water, and said, 'Ride behind me.' I was in the Hijaz. It was not more than a short while before he asked me, 'What do you see?' 'I see Medina!' I exclaimed. 'Get down,' he said, 'and go and offer my salutations to the Messenger of God. Say, "Your brother Khidr sends you his greetings."

I heard Abu Abd al-Rahman al-Sulami say[43] . . . that al-Muzaffar al-Khassas said, "One night Nasr al-Khirat and I were somewhere sharing pieces of knowledge with each other. Al-Khirat said, 'When someone begins to remember God, he needs to know that God is remembering him, and that his remembrance exists through God's remembrance.' I disagreed with him. 'What would you say if it were Khidr who were here bearing witness with his fellowship?' he demanded. Suddenly we found ourselves with an old man who traveled between the heavens and the earth until he reached us. He greeted us and said, 'He has spoken the truth—the one who remembers God Most High does so by grace of God's remembering him.' So we knew that he was Khidr."

I heard Abu Ali al-Daqqaq say that a man went to Sahl ibn Abd-Allah and said, "People claim that you walk on water." "Ask the local *muezzin*," Sahl suggested. "He is an honest man who does not lie." The man said, "So I asked him, and the muezzin told me, 'I don't know anything about that. But not long ago he went down to the cistern to make his ablution and fell in the water, and if it hadn't been for me he woud be there still!" Abu Ali al-Daqqaq said, "Sahl in fact possessed the state that had been attributed to him, but God, glory to Him, wants to veil His Friends, so He brought about what happened in the story of the *muezzin* and the cistern as a veil for Sahl's true state. For Sahl manifested miracles."

Very similar in meaning is the anecdote of Abu Uthman al-Maghribi that I saw recorded in the handwriting of Abu-l-Husayn al-

Jurjani. He said, "One time I wanted to go to Egypt, and I thought to travel by ship. Then it occurred to me that I was known here, and I hated celebrity. So the ship sailed, and when it seemed right, I walked over the water and caught up with it and climbed on board. People looked at me, but no one said a thing, whether this was a breach of the natural order or not. So I knew that the friend of God is hidden even when he is famous."

With our own eyes we have witnessed something of the state of Abu Ali al-Daqqaq. He suffered from a urinary disease and had to leave the room more than once an hour. Eventually he was obliged to renew his ablution more than once for two cycles of obligatory prayer. He would carry a bottle with him on the way to the mosque, and sometimes would have to stop on the road several times, both coming and going. Yet when he mounted the pulpit to discourse, he would not need to make an ablution, even if the meeting continued for a very long time. We observed this in him for years, but during his lifetime it never occurred to us that it was something out of the ordinary. Only after his death did it strike me, and only then was I enabled to know him for what he was.

What is related of Sahl ibn Abd-Allah is similar to this. At the end of his life he was afflicted with paralysis, but his strength would return to him at the time of each obligatory prayer, and he would pray standing.

It is well known that Abd-Allah al-Wizan was crippled, but when ecstasy manifested in him during the spiritual concert he would stand up and participate.

I heard Muhammad ibn Abd-Allah al-Sufi say[44] . . . that Ahmad ibn Abil-Hawari said, "Abu Sulayman al-Darani and I performed the prescribed pilgrimage together. While we were traveling I dropped the waterskin I was carrying. 'I have lost the waterskin!' I exclaimed to Abu Sulayman. So we were left without water, and it was very cold. Abu Sulayman prayed, 'O Returner of what is lost, O Guider away from error, return to us what we have lost!' Immediately somebody called, 'Whose waterskin has left him?' 'Me!' I said and took it from him. Again, during our journey we had bundled ourselves in furs against the fierceness of the cold. We found ourselves with a man wearing tatters. He was dripping with sweat. 'Come on, we will give you some of the clothes we are wearing,' said Abu Sulayman. 'Abu Sulayman,' came the rejoinder, 'will you show me asceticism while you find it cold? I have been wandering in this Creation for thirty years and have never shivered nor shook. God dresses me against the cold with heat from His love. In summer He dresses me with the taste of the coolness of His love!' And he went away."

And I heard him say[45] . . . that al-Khawwas said, "Once I was traveling in the desert in the middle of the day. I reached a tree that had water nearby, so I camped. Suddenly I found myself with a tremendous lion. He approached me, and I abandoned myself to what would come. But when he drew close, I saw that he was lame. He whimpered and knelt in front of me and put his paw in my lap. I looked at it. It was swollen with pus and blood. So I took a spinter of wood and lanced the place that was full of pus. Then I bound a scrap of cloth around his paw, and he went away. But after an hour, there he was, back again. With him were two cubs. They rubbed their backs against me and brought me a loaf of bread."

And I heard him say[46] . . . that Ahmad ibn Abil-Hawari said that Muhammad ibn al-Sammak was ailing, so we took a sample of his urine and hurried off to the doctor, who was a Christian. While we were traveling between Hirah and Kufah we met a man with a beautiful face, a sweet fragrance, and immaculate clothes. "Where are you going?" he inquired. "We want to find so-and-so, the doctor, and show him the urine of Ibn al-Sammak," we said. "May God be glorified!" he exclaimed. "You are seeking help for God's friend from God's enemy? Break that on the ground, and go back to Ibn al-Sammak and tell him, 'Put your hand on the place that hurts and say: "By the Truth we have made it diminish, and by the Truth it has abated." Then he vanished, and we could not find him. So we returned to Ibn al-Sammak and told him what had happened. He placed his hand on the painful spot and recited what the man had said, and he was immediately cured. "That was Khidr," he told us.

Muhammad ibn al-Husayn said[47] . . . that al-Bistami, the uncle of Abd al-Rahman ibn Muhammad al-Sufi, said, "We were sitting in Abu Yazid al-Bistami's gathering when he said, "Get up and come with us, we are going to meet one of the Friends of God Most High." So we got up and went with him. When we reached the alley, there was Ibrahim ibn Shaybah al-Harawi. "It occurred to me that I would meet you," Abu Yazid said to him. "I have made intercession for you with your Lord." "If you had interceded for the whole of creation, it would not be much," replied Ibrahim ibn Shaybah. "They are nothing but a handful of dust!" Abu Yazid marveled at this response.

The miracle of Ibrahim ibn Shaybah, that dismissal, was more perfect than Abu Yazid's miracle of foreknowledge. In that condition he spoke the truth about intercession.

I heard Abu Abd al-Rahman al-Sulami say[48] . . . that Salim al-Maghribi asked Dhu-l-Nun al-Misri about the roots of his repentance. He said, "I had gone out from Egypt to one of the villages, and I had fallen asleep on the road. I woke up and opened my eyes, and there beside me was a little blind nestling that had fallen out of a tree and onto the ground. The earth split, and out of it came two vessels, one gold and one silver. In one of them was sesame seed, and in the other, rosewater. The little bird ate and drank from these. 'It is enough!' I said. 'I have repented.' And I stayed at the the door until He received me."

It is said that Abd al-Wahid ibn Zayd was paralyzed on one side. The time of prescribed prayer came and he needed to perform his ablution. "Who is here?" he asked. No one answered, and he was afraid that he would miss the ritual prayer. So he prayed, "My Lord, free me from my shackles until I have completed by ablution. Then the affair and the command are Yours." He was whole and sound until he had fully performed the purification. Then he returned to his prayer carpet and became again as he had been.

Abu Ayyub al-Hammal said, "When Abu Abd-Allah al-Daylami wanted to make camp during a journey, he would go up to his donkey and whisper in its ear, 'I would have wanted to tie you up, but you are not tied up now, and I am sending you into the desert to graze. So when we want to travel, come back.' And when the time came to leave, the donkey would come back."

It is said that Abu Abd-Allah al-Daylami married off his daughter and needed the wherewithal to equip her. He had a robe that he always went out in, that he had bought for a dinar. So he went to see a dealer in clothing. "This is worth more than a dinar!" said the buyer, and the bidding on it did not stop until the price had reached a hundred dinars. So he outfitted his daughter.

Al-Nadr ibn Shumayl said, "I bought a waist-wrapper and found that it was too short. So I asked my Lord Most High to stretch it an arm's length, and He did it." (The word he used for "to stretch" is like the stretching of a bowstring.) "If I had asked for more, He would have given me more," he added.

Amir ibn Abd Qays prayed and asked that ablution be made easy for him in the wintertime, and when he would go to the water, it would steam. He asked his Lord to free his heart from the desire for women, and he was not troubled by them. But when he asked that satan be kept away from his heart while he was making his prayers, he was not answered.

Bishr ibn al-Harith said, "I went into the house and found a man there with me. 'Who are you, to enter my house without my permission?' I demanded. "He said, 'Your brother Khidr.' 'Pray to God for me,' I asked. 'May God make your obedience to Him easy,' He prayed. I urged, 'Give me more than this!' . . . and may He hide it from you!' he added."

Ibrahim al-Khawwas said, "On one of my journeys I entered a ruined building on the road to Makkah, at night. I found a huge lion there with me, and I was frightened. Then a voice from nowhere said, "Stay where you are—there are seventy thousand angels around you to protect you."

Muhammad ibn al-Husayn reported[49] . . . that Jafar al-Daylami said that Nuri went into the water and a thief came and took his clothes. Then he brought the clothes back; his hand had withered. Nuri prayed, "He has returned the clothes to us. Return his hand to him." So he was cured.

Shibli said, "One time I made an intention to eat nothing but what was religiously lawful. I had been wandering about in the desert when I saw a fig tree. I was stretching out my hand to eat from it when the tree called to me, 'Be careful of your promise! Don't eat from me—I belong to a Jew!'"

Abu Abd-Allah ibn Khafif said, "I entered Baghdad intending to perform the prescribed pilgrimage. I had got the haughtiness of the Sufis into my head, so I did not eat bread for forty days, nor go to see Junayd. I left, and drank no water before the town of Zubalah. I was cleansing myself when I saw a gazelle drinking from the lip of a well. I was thirsty, but when I went down to the well, the gazelle fled, and the water level sank. So I walked on. 'O my Master,' I said, 'Don't I have the place with You that this gazelle has?' I heard a voice from behind me say, 'We have tested you, and you have not been patient. Return and take the water!' So I went back, and the well was brimming with water. I filled up my little pot, and with that water I drank and made my ablutions all the way to Madinah. It was never exhausted. But whenever I went to get a drink, I heard a voice say, 'The gazelle came without a pot, without a rope. You came with a pot and a rope!' On my return from the prescribed pilgrimage I went to the mosque. When Junayd's eyes fell upon me, he said, 'If you had only been patient, water would have streamed from beneath your feet. If you had had an hour's worth of patience!'"

I heard Hamzah ibn Yusuf al-Sahmi al-Jurjani say[50] . . . that Muhammad ibn Said al-Basri said, "I was walking in the streets of Basra when I came across a Bedouin driving a camel. As I looked at him, the camel fell down dead, and its saddle and baggage fell off. I walked on, then looked again. The Bedouin was praying, "O Causer of all causes, O Patron of whoever seeks, return to me the camel that has left me, carrying its saddle and baggage!" The camel stood up, and its saddle and baggage were on its back.

It is said that Shabal al-Marwadhi had an appetite for meat, so he got some for half a dirham. In the road, a kite snatched it away from him. Shabal went into the mosque to pray. When he went back to his house, his wife presented him with some meat. "Where did this come from?" he asked. "Two kites were fighting over something," she told him, "and one of them dropped this." "Praise be to God," Shabal exclaimed, "Who has not forgotten Shabal, though Shabal has often forgotten Him!"

Muhammad ibn Abd-Allah al-Sufi reported[51] . . . that the son of Abu Ubayd al-Busra told the story, "One year my father went out to participate in the border raids, together with a troop of men. The colt he was riding died while he was with the troop. He prayed, 'O Lord, lend him to us until we return to Busra'— that is, to his village. And the colt stood up. When the expedition was completed and he returned to Busra, he said, "My son, unsaddle the colt." "He is sweating," I objected. "If I take his saddle off, he will catch cold!" "He is on loan, my son," said he. And when I took his saddle off, he dropped dead.

It is said there was once a dervish who had previously been a grave robber. A woman died. The people prayed over her, and that robber prayed with them, so that he would know her grave. When night hid him, he went and dug it up. "Glory to God!" the deceased woman exclaimed. "A man who has been forgiven, taking the shroud of a woman who has been forgiven?" "Supposing that you have been forgiven," the robber retorted, "where do you get that idea about me?" "God Most High has forgiven me and all those who prayed for me," she said. "You prayed for me!" "So I left her," the robber later told, "and replaced the earth on her grave." The man repented and made good his repentance.

I heard Hamzah ibn Yusuf say[52] . . . that Abu Muhammad Numan ibn Nusa al-Hiri said in Hira, "I saw Dhu-l-Nun al-Misri when two

men were fighting—one of them was one of the sultan's entourage and
the other, a simple subject. The subject attacked the courtier and
broke his tooth. Then a soldier laid hold of the man and said, "The
commander will settle this between us!"

As they walked, they passed by Dhu-l-Nun. "Go and approach the
shaykh," people urged. So they went up to him and acquainted him
with what had happened. He took the tooth, moistened it with his sali-
va, and replaced it in the man's mouth where it had been before. His
lips moved in a prayer. By God's permission, the tooth held. The man
kept examining his mouth, but he could find no difference among his
teeth.

Abu-l-Husayn Muhammad ibn al-Husayn al-Qattan, in Baghdad,
informed us[53] . . . that Abu Subrah al-Nakhai said, "A man came up
from the Yemen, and his donkey died on the road. He stood and made
an ablution, offered two cycles of ritual prayer, and prayed, 'My God,
I have come with effort for the sake of Your good pleasure. I bear witness that You revive the dead and resurrect those who are in the
graves. Do not do my enemies a favor! Today I ask that You resurrect
my donkey.' And the donkey got up, wiggling his ears."

I heard Hamzah ibn Yusuf say[54] . . . that Abu Bakr al-Hamdani
said, "I remained in the desert of the Hijaz for days without eating
anything. I was longing for beans and bread prepared after the fashion of Bab al-Taq. 'I am in the desert, and there is a great distance
between me and Iraq,' I reminded myself. Just as this thought was
completed, a Bedouin cried from afar, 'Beans and bread' So I went up
to him and asked, 'Do you really have beans and bread?' 'Yes,' said he.
He opened the cloak he was wearing and took out beans and bread
and told me, 'Eat.' So I ate. Again he said to me, 'Eat.' And I ate. Still
again he said, 'Eat,' and again I ate. When he said it to me the fourth
time, I insisted, 'By the Truth which sent you to me, you must tell me
who you are!' 'I am Khidr,' he replied. Then he vanished, and I saw
him no more.

I heard Abu Abd al-Rahman al-Sulami say[55] . . . that Abu Jafar
al-Haddad said, "I went to al-Thalabiyyah and found it ruined. I had
gone seven days without eating. I went inside under the dome. Some
Khorasanians came. They were exhausted, and threw themselves
down at the entrance of the dome. Then a Bedouin came on a camel
and poured dates out in front of them. They were engrossed in eating.
No one said anything to me, and the Bedouin did not see me. After he
had been gone about an hour, the Bedouin came back again. 'Is there

anyone with you beside yourselves?' he asked the Khorasanians. 'Yes,' they said, 'this man inside the dome.' The Bedouin came inside and asked me, 'Who are you? Why didn't you say anything? I had gone on, but a man barred my way and told me, "You have left behind a man whom you have not fed!" And he would not permit me to pass. So I retraced my steps and came back here from miles away!' He poured a lot of dates in front of me, and left. So I called the others, and they ate, and I ate."

Hamzah ibn Yusuf said[56]. . . that Ahmad ibn Ata said, "A camel once spoke to me. On the road to Makkah I saw a camel bearing a heavy litter. During the night she had stretched out her neck. 'Exalted is He Who has relieved her of her burden,' I said. The camel turned to me and said, 'Say, "Mighty is God!"' 'Mighty is God!' I agreed."

I heard Muhammad ibn Abd-Allah al-Sufi say[57] . . . that Abu Dharah al-Janabi said that a woman plotted to deceive him. "Won't you come into the house and visit an invalid?" she asked. I went in, and she locked the door. I saw no one there, so I knew what she had in mind. "My God," I prayed, "Turn her black!" So she turned black. She was astounded. She opened the door, and I left. Then I prayed, "My God, return her to her own state." And she returned to what she had been before.

I heard Hamzah ibn Yusuf say[58] . . . that Khalil al-Sayyad said, "My son Muhammad was missing, and we were terribly worried about him. So I went to Maruf al-Kharki and said, 'Abu Mahfuz, my son has vanished and his mother is worried.' 'What do you wish?' he asked. 'Pray to God to send him back,' I begged. 'My God,' he prayed, 'the heaven is Your heaven, and the earth is Your earth, and everything between them is Yours. Bring back Muhammad!' I went to the Damascus gate, and there he was, standing there. 'Muhammad, where have you been?' I asked. 'Just a moment ago I was out in the granaries,' he told me."

Know that anecdotes of this sort are numberless. To add more to what we have already recounted would take us beyond the bounds of the brevity we have intended. What we have already mentioned on this topic is enough.

11 ON THE DREAMS OF THE SUFIS

God Most High said, *"For them is good news in the life of this world, and in the next"* (10:64). This is said to mean the good dreams that a man sees, or that are shown to him. Abu-l-Hasan al-Ahwazi reported[1] . . . from Abu-l-Darda that he asked the Prophet about the verse, *"For them is good news in the life of this world, and in the next."* He said, "Nobody has asked me about this before. This is the good dreams that a man sees, or that are shown to him."

Al-Sayyid Abu-l-Hasan Muhammad ibn al-Husayn al-Alawi reported[2] . . . from Abu Qatadah, that the Messenger of God said, "The dream of vision (*ruya*) is from God; the dream of confusion (*hulm*) is from satan If one of you dreams a dream that he dislikes, let him spit to his left and take refuge in God; the dream will never harm him."

Abu Bakr Muhammad ibn Ahmad Abd al-Mazaki reported[3] . . . from Abd-Allah ibn Masud, that the Messenger of God said, "Whoever sees me in a dream, has seen me. Satan cannot take on my form." The meaning of this hadith is that such a dream is a true dream, that it is to be interpreted as literally true, and that it is one type of miracle.

Dreams may be defined as ideas that come over the heart and states that take shape in the imagination when sleep does not entirely overwhelm perception. When a person is awake, he supposes he was seeing truly. In fact, his seeing is one of the visualizations and imaginings that inhabit people's hearts. When outward sensation disappears, these imaginings are stripped of the objects of sense and the requirements of necessity, and that modality has power over a person. When he awakes, the states he has formulated grow weak in relation to the state of his perception of the objects of exterior consciousness and the achievement of necessary knowledge. The paradigm of this is someone who sits in the glow of a lamp in intense darkness. When the sun rises, that lamp's glow is overpowered and its light dwindles in relation to the radiance of the sun. The state of sleep is like the person in the lamplight, and the waking state is like the person upon whom the day has broken. When awake, the person remembers what took form for him in the state of sleep.

Now these stories and thoughts that come over the heart in the state of sleep may at one time come from satan, another time from the fancies of the ego, and at another time from the ideas inspired by angels. At still another time they may be instruction given by God Most High through His direct creation of those states in one's heart. According to hadith, "The most truthful of you in dreams is the most truthful of you in speech."

Know that sleep is divided into parts. First there are the sleep of unconsciousness and the sleep of habit. Such sleep is not praiseworthy. Indeed, it is diseased, for it is the brother of death—an oft-recounted hadith states this. God Almighty and Glorious said, "*He it is who brings you to Him by night, and he knows what you have earned by day*" (6:20). And he said, "*God brings the selves to Himself at the time of their death, and those who do not die, in their sleep*" (39:42).

It is said that if there were good in sleep, there would be sleep in paradise. When God cast sleep over Adam in Paradise, it is told, Eve was brought out of him—and all his trouble arrived only after Eve arrived!

I heard Abu Ali al-Daqqaq say, "When Abraham said to Ishmail, "*My son, I saw in a dream that I should sacrifice you,*" Ishmail replied, "O father, those are the deserts of someone who sleeps in the presence of his Beloved! If you had not slept, you would not have been ordered to sacrifice your child!"

God Most High revealed to David, "The one who claims to love Me lies! When night covers him, he leaves Me and sleeps!"

Sleep is the opposite of knowledge. Thus Shibli said, "One nap in a thousand years is a disgrace." Shibli also said, "The Truth informed the creation, 'Who sleeps, is unconscious. Who is unconscious, is veiled.'" Shibli used to anoint his eyes with salt so that he would not be taken by sleep. With this meaning the Sufis recite:

It is amazing that the lover should sleep!
All sleep is forbidden to the lover.

The true student, it is said, eats when he has need, sleeps when he is overcome, speaks when he must.

When Adam slept in the divine presence, he was told, "Here is Eve for you to rely upon. That is recompense for one who sleeps in the Presence!"

If you are present with God, it is said, do not sleep. To sleep in the Presence is bad behavior. And if you are absent, you are one of the people of grief and trouble. Sleep does not come to the one who is troubled.

However, for people engaged in the struggle against their own egos, sleep is an alms given by God. God Almighty and Glorious is proud of the servant who falls asleep in prostration. "Look at My servant!" he says. "He sleeps, his spirit with Me, his body before Me." That is, his spirit is in the place of secret conversation with God and his body is upon the prayer-carpet of worship.

It is said that the soul of anyone who goes to sleep with an ablution is summoned to circumambulate the divine Throne and prostrate himself before God Almighty and Glorious. God Most High said, "*We have made their sleep a refreshment*" (78:9).

I heard Abu Ali al-Daqqaq say, "A man complained to one of the shaykhs that he slept too much. 'Go and give thanks to God for your good health!' the shaykh told him. 'How many sick people there are who are longing for a wink of the sleep that you complain of!'"

There is nothing harder on satan, it is said, than the sleep of the sinful person. He complains, "When will this man get up and go out and disobey God?" The disobedient person's best state is when he is asleep—for if the time does not count for him, it also does not count against him!

I heard Abu Ali al-Daqqaq say, "Shah al-Kirmani made a custom of wakefulness. Then one time sleep overpowered him and He saw the Truth, glory to Him, in his sleep. After that he would force himself to sleep. Asked about this, he said, 'I saw the joy of my heart in sleep so I love slumber and sleep.'

There was a man who had two students who had a difference of opinion. One of them said, "Sleep is better, for a human being does not disobey God in that state." The other said, "Being awake is better, because God Most High is known in that state." They appealed to their shaykh for a decision. "You who speak of the superiority of sleep—death is better for you than life," he declared. "And you who speak of the superiority of being awake —life is better for you than death."

A certain man bought a woman slave. When night came, he ordered her, "Prepare my bed!" "O master," she asked, "do you have a Master?" "Yes," he said. "Does your Master sleep?" she persisted. "No!" he replied. "Then aren't you ashamed to sleep," she inquired, "when your Master is not asleep?" His little girl asked Said ibn Jubayr, "Why don't you sleep?" "Hell does not permit me to sleep," he told her. Malik ibn Dinar's daughter also asked him, "Why won't you sleep?" "Your father is afraid of the night visitor," said he.

When al-Rabi ibn Haytham died, a little girl asked her father, "What happened to the pillar there used to be in our neighbor's house?" "That was our righteous neighbor," her father explained. "He would stand in prayer the whole night, from beginning to end!" (The little girl supposed he was a pillar because she would climb up on the terrace at night and always spied him standing.)

A Sufi said, "Sleep has spiritual value not to be found in waking: part of ii is that in sleep one can see al-Mustafa, the Companions, and the forefathers who have passed away, while one cannot see them when awake. In the same way the Truth may be seen in sleep, and this is an enormous advantage."

It is said that Abu Bakr al-Ajri saw the Truth, glory to Him, while he was asleep. "Ask for what you need," he said. "My God," he implored, "forgive all the sins of the community of Muhammad!" "That is more appropriate to Me than it is to you," he was reproved. "Ask for what you need!"

Al-Kattani said, "I saw the Prophet in a dream. He told me, 'If somebody decks himself out with some trait in front of people when God knows that the opposite is true of him, God has disgraced him." He also said, "I saw the Prophet in a dream and begged, 'Pray to God that my heart will not die!' He said, 'Say forty times every day, 'O Living, O Self-Existent One, there is no god but You' and God will enliven your heart."

Hasan ibn Ali saw Jesus the son of Mary in a dream. "I want to adopt a seal ring," Hasan said. "What should I write upon it?" "Write 'There is no god but God, the King, the Clear Truth.' Jesus told him, "because that is the conclusion of the Gospel."

It is related that Abu Yazid said, "I saw my Lord Almighty and Glorious in a dream. 'What is the way to You?' I asked. He replied, 'Leave yourself, and come!'"

Ahmad ibn Khadruyah also saw his Lord in a dream. "Ahmad," He said, "everyone but Abu Yazid seeks something from Me. He seeks Me."

Yahya ibn Said al-Qattan said, "I saw my Lord in a dream and said, 'O Lord, how often have I prayed to You and you have not answered me!' He said, 'Yahya, I love to hear your voice!'"

Bishr ibn al-Harith said, "I saw the Commander of the Faithful, Ali ibn Abi Talib in a dream. 'O Commander of the Faithful, give me some advice,' I asked. He said, 'How good it is that the rich should incline toward the poor in search of the rewards of God Most High! But better than this is that the poor should be haughty toward the rich because of reliance upon God Most High.' 'O Commander of the Faithful,' I asked, 'give me more!' He recited:

You were dead and became alive.
Soon you shall be dead again.
Honor with a verse the ephemeral world
But build you a house in the permanent realm!'"

Someone saw Sufyan al-Thawri in a dream and asked him, "How did God Most High deal with you?" He replied, "He forgave me." He was asked, "What is the state of Abd-Allah ibn Mubarak?" "He is one of those who come into intimacy with their Lord many times a day," he said.

I heard Abu Ali al-Daqqaq say that Abu Sahl al-Suluki saw Abu Sahl al-Zajjaji in a dream—Zajajji used to teach about the threat of eternal punishment—and asked him, "How did God Most High deal with you?" "Matters here are easier than we used to think!" Zajjaji said.

Hasan ibn Asim al-Shaybani was seen in a dream and asked, "How has God treated you?" "Nothing comes from the Generous except generosity," said he.

A Sufi, seen in a dream and asked about his state, recited:

They weighed us well and were exact.
Then they were gracious and set us free.

Habib al-Ajami was seen in a dream. The dreamer exclaimed, "Are you dead, then, Habib al-Ajami?" "Nonsense!" he returned. "Foreignness (*ujmah*) left me, and I remained in bliss!"

Hasan al-Basri, it is told, went into a mosque to pray the evening prayer. He found Habib al-Ajami serving as the imam there. Hasan did not pray behind him, fearing that Habib would recite badly

because of the foreignness of his tongue. That night a voice spoke to
him in a dream and said, "Why didn't you pray behind him? If you had
prayed behind him, all your preceding sins would have been forgiven!"

Malik ibn Anas was seen in a dream and asked, "How did
God deal with you?" He said, "He forgave me with a phrase that
Uthman ibn Affan used to say when he saw a funeral, 'Glory to the
Living One Who does not die.'"

The night that Hasan al-Basri died it was as if all the doors of
heaven were opened and a crier cried, "Has not Hasan al-Basri
approached God Most High? And He is pleased with him!"

I heard Abu Bakr ibn Ishkib say that in a dream he saw Abu Sahl
al-Suluki in a beautiful state. "Master, how did you come upon this?"
I asked. "By thinking well of my Lord," he told me.

Al-Jahiz was seen in a dream and asked, "How has God dealt with
you?" He recited:

Write with your own hand only such things
As you'll be happy to see at the judgment.

In a dream Junayd saw Satan naked. "Don't you feel ashamed in
front of people?" he asked. "These are not people," satan said. "The
only real people are standing in Shuniziyyah Mosque. They have
exhausted my body and burnt my liver!" Junayd said, "Early in the
morning, as soon as I woke up, I went to the mosque and found there
a congregation sitting with their heads upon their knees, contemplat-
ing. When they saw me, they called out, 'Don't let what the evil one
says fool you!'"

After his death, in a dream, al-Nasrabadhi was seen in Makkah.
"How did God Most High deal with you?" he was asked. "I was reprimanded as the noble are rebuked. Then a voice called, 'O Abu-l-
Qasim, after union, is there separation?' 'No, O Majesty!' I replied,
'and I was not placed in the tomb before I had joined with the One!'"

Dhu-l-Nun al-Misri was seen in a dream and asked, "How
has God dealt with you?" "In the world I had asked him for three
things I needed," he said. "He gave me part of that, and now I hope
that he will give me the rest. I asked that He give me one gift of the
ten awaiting under the power of Ridwan, the angel of paradise. He
gave me Himself. I asked that He punish me with ten punishments for
the one awaiting under the power of Malik, the angel of Hell. He made
that continuous. And I asked that He sustain me in eternal remem-

brance of Him ."

After his death Shibli was seen in a dream and asked, "How did God deal with you?" He said, "He did not demand proof for any claims, except for one thing. One day I had said, 'There is no loss greater than the loss of paradise, and entry into hell.' He said, 'What loss is greater than the loss of meeting with Me?'"

I heard Abu Ali say that al-Jurayri saw Junayd in a dream and asked, "How are you, Abu-l-Qasim?" "Those symbolic hints have vanished," he said, "those fine explanations have passed away, and nothing has profited us but the glorifications we used to recite in the morning!"

Al-Nabaji said, "One day I had a craving for something, and in a dream a voice said to me, 'Does it befit the free man who wants a thing to humiliate himself before slaves, while he can find with his Master all that he wants?'"

Ibn al-Jalla said, "I entered Madinah without any money. I went to the Tomb and declared, 'I am your guest, O Prophet of God!' Then I dozed off. In my sleep I saw the Prophet. He gave me a loaf of bread, and I ate half of it. When I woke up, the other half was in my hand."

A Sufi said, "I saw the Prophet in a dream, saying, 'Visit Ibn Awn! He loves God and His Messenger!'"

Utbah al-Ghulam saw a most beautiful *huri* in a dream. "Utbah, I am your lover," she told him. "See that you don't do anything that would come between us!" "I have divorced this world three times," Utbah said to her, "and I cannot return to her until I have met with you!"

I heard Mansur al-Maghribi say, "I saw a venerable and important shaykh in Damascus. Dejection had overwhelmed him. People told me, 'If you want the shaykh to be happy in your company, after you have greeted him, say, "May God provide you with the huris of Paradise!" He will be pleased with you on account of that prayer.' I asked about the reason for that. They said, 'He saw something of the *huris* in a dream, and part of it remained in his heart.' So I went and greeted him and said, "May God provide you with *huris*!" And he was happy with me.

Ayyub al-Sakhtiyani observed the funeral procession of a sinner, and went into a side room lest he be required to offer the funeral prayer. One of the company saw the dead man in a dream and asked him, "How has God dealt with you?" "He forgave me," the man said, "and He told me, 'Tell Ayyub al-Sakhtiyani, '*Say: If you possessed the*

*treasures my Lord's mercy, yet would you hold back for fear of expend -
ing!' (17:100)'"*

The night that Malik ibn Dinar died it seemed as if all the doors
of heaven had opened, and a voice announced, "Has not Malik ibn
Dinar become one of the dwellers in paradise?"

A Sufi said, "The night that Dawud al-Tai died I saw a light, and
angels ascending and descending. 'What night is this?' I asked. 'It is
the night in which Dawud al-Tai has died,' they told me. 'For the
reception of his soul among its denizens, Paradise has been specially
decorated!'"

I saw Abu Ali al-Daqqaq in a dream and asked him, "How has God
dealt with you?" "One need not have great merit to find forgiveness
here!" he told me. "The least meritorious of those dwelling here is so-
and-so, and he was granted such-and-such!" In the dream, it struck
me that the person he had taken an interest in had unlawfully killed
a man.

When Kurz ibn Wibrah died, someone dreamed that the people of
the graves came out of their graves in new white clothes. "What is
this?" the dreamer asked. He was told, "The people of the graves are
wearing new clothes to welcome Kurz ibn Wibrah among them."

Yusuf ibn al-Husayn was seen in a dream and asked, "How has
God dealt with you?" "He forgave me," he said. "For what reason?"
asked the dreamer. "Because I never confused a serious matter with a
joke."

Abu Abd-Allah al-Zarrad, seen in a dream and asked, "How has
God Most High dealt with you?" said, "He reprieved me and forgave
me every sin I admitted to in the world, except for one that I was
ashamed to confess. So He held me sweating until the flesh dropped
from my face!" "So what was it?" he was asked. "One day I gazed at a
beautiful man, and I was ashamed to recall it," he said.

I heard Abu Said al-Shahham say that he saw Abu-l-Tayyib Sahl
al-Suluki in a dream, and called, "O Shaykh!" "Drop this 'shaykh'!" he
reproved. "What of those spiritual states you experienced?" I asked.
He answered, "They were of no use to us at all." "How has God Most
High dealt with you?" I inquired. "He forgave me for the sake of some
questions some old women had asked, which I answered for them," he
said.

I heard Abu Bakr al-Rashidi al-Faqih say, "I saw Muhammad al-
Tusi, the teacher, in a dream. He told me, 'Say to Abu Said al-Saffar,
the teacher of behavior:

It was as if we would not turn aside from love—
And you changed, by love's own life, we did not change!
You were distracted from us by the company of others
And you showed forth separation—not thus were we!
Perhaps He Who decides things by His knowledge
Will bring us together, after death, just as we were.

I woke up and went and told this to Abu Said al-Saffar. "I used to visit his grave every Friday, but I didn't visit it this past Friday," he said.

It is related that a Sufi said, "I saw the Messenger of God in a dream. A congregation of dervishes surrounded him. While he was like that, two angels descended from heaven. In the hands of one of them was a basin, and in the hands of the other, a pitcher. The angel set the basin before the Messenger of God. He washed his hands and ordered the angels to let the others wash their hands. Then the basin was set in front of me. One of the angels said to the other, 'Do not pour water over his hands. He is not one of them.' 'O Messenger of God,' I cried, 'Is it not reported that you said, "A man is together with those he loves?"' 'Yes, indeed,' he replied. 'Well, I love you,' I said, 'and I love these dervishes!' 'Pour water over his hands,' he commanded. 'He is one of them!'"

It is related that another Sufi was constantly calling, "Well-being! Well-being!" "What is the meaning of this prayer?" he was asked. "At the beginning of my undertaking, I was a porter," he said. "One day I had been carrying a heavy burden for a short while, and I set it down to rest. 'O Lord,' I sighed, 'if you were to give me two loaves, free of toil, every day, it would be enough for me!' Just then two men came along, arguing. I went up to try and make peace between them, and one of them struck me over the head with something he had intended for his opponent! Blood ran down over my face. Then the local constable arrived and took charge of them both. When he saw me stained with blood, he took me too, thinking that I was involved in the fight, and threw me in jail. I remained in jail for awhile, and every day they brought me two loaves.

"One night a voice spoke to me in a dream and said, 'You asked for two loaves every day without any exertion on your part. You didn't ask for well-being! I gave you what you asked for!' I woke up and cried, 'Well-being! Well-being!' Someone knocked on the door of the jail. 'Where is Umar the Porter?' they inquired. So I was discharged, and they let me go my way."

It is related that al-Kattani said, "A man in our circle had an inflamed eye. 'Why don't you have that treated?' they asked him. He said, 'I made my mind up not to seek to have it treated until it became free of blemish itself. Then in a dream a voice said to me, "If all the people of hell made such a decision, We would take them all out of the fire!"

It is related that Junayd said, "In a dream I seemed to be discoursing to people, while an angel stood over me. He asked, 'What thing brings those who are brought close to God the closest?' I replied, 'A secret work at a perfect time.' Then the angel turned away from me, declaring, 'A successful speech, by God!'"

A man told al-Ala ibn Ziyad, "I saw you in my dream as one of the people of paradise." Al-Ala said, "Perhaps satan wanted something and I had been protected against it, so he assigned a man to help him to his goal of misleading me!"

Ata-l-Sulami was seen in sleep and asked, "You certainly had long sorrows. How did God Most High deal with you?" He said, "By God, He caused that to be followed by long ease and eternal joy!" "What degree do you occupy?" he was asked. 'With those whom God has blessed,' he recited, *'The prophets, the truthful . . .'* and on to the end of the verse (4:69)."

Al-Awzai was seen in a dream. He said, "I have not seen here a degree more exalted than the degree of the learned. Then comes the degree of those who have sorrowed."

Al-Nabaji said, "I was told in a dream, 'If someone trusts God to provide for him, his good nature will increase, his lower self will become generous, and fewer imaginations will afflict him in prayer.'"

Zubaydah (Harun al-Rashid's queen) was seen in a dream and asked, "How has God Most High dealt with you?" "He forgave me," she said. "Because of the many charities you established on the road to Makkah?" the dreamer asked. "No," she said, "their benefits go to those who run them. He forgave me for the sake of my intention."

Sufyan al-Thawri was seen in a dream and asked, "How did God deal with you?" He said, "I took one step upon the bridge over the abyss, and my second step was in paradise."

Ahmad ibn Abil-Hawari said, "I saw a young woman in my dreams. I have never seen another as beautiful as she. Her face sparkled with light. 'How luminous is your face!' I marveled. 'Do you remember the night in which you wept?' she asked. 'Yes,' I said. 'Your tears were brought to me and I anointed my face with them, and it became like this,' she told me."

Yazid al-Raqqashi saw the Prophet in a dream and recited some verses of the Quran to him. "This is the recitation," the Prophet told him, "but where are the tears?"

Junayd said, "In a dream I seemed to see two angels descending from heaven. One of them asked me, 'What is real truthfulness (*sidq*)?' I answered, 'Faithfulness to the promise.' The other said, 'He has spoken the truth!' Then they ascended again."

Bishr al-Hafi, asked in a dream "How did God Most High deal with you?" replied, "He forgave me, said, 'Bishr, aren't you ashamed before Me, to have been so afraid of Me?'"

Abu Sulayman al-Darani, asked in a dream "How did God Most High deal with you?" said, "He forgave me, and nothing was harder on me than the symbolic hints of the Sufis!"

Ali ibn Muwaffaq said, "One day I had been thinking about the support of my family and the poverty they were in. In a dream I saw a slip of paper on which was written, 'In the Name of God the Beneficent, the Merciful. O Ibn Muwaffaq, are you afraid of poverty while I am your Lord?' Then in the darkest part of the night before the dawn, a man came to me bearing a purse containing five thousand dinars. 'O you of weak certainty, take this!' said he."

Junayd said, "In a dream I saw myself standing before God Most High. 'Abu-l-Qasim,' He said, 'where did you get these words that you say?' 'I say nothing but the truth,' I said. 'You have spoken truly,' said He."

Abu Bakr al-Kattani said, "I saw a young man in a dream, the most handsome I have ever seen. 'Who are you?' I asked. "I am the fear of God (*taqwa*),' he answered. 'Where do you live?' 'In the heart of every sorrowful person.' Then I turned and saw a dark woman, as brutal-looking as could be. 'Who are you?' I asked. "I am laughter!" "And where do you live?" "In the heart of every happy and distracted person.' "Then I woke up, and I resolved never to laugh unless I was overcome."

It is related that Abd-Allah ibn Khafif said, "I saw the Messenger of God in a dream. He said to me, 'Whoever has known a road to God Most High and followed it, and then turned back from it, is punished by God with a punishment suffered by no one else in the universe.'"

Shibli was seen in a dream and asked, "How God Most High deal with you?" He said, "He examined me so closely that I despaired, and when He saw my despair, He covered me with His mercy."

Abu Uthman al-Maghribi said, "I dreamed that a voice said to me, 'Abu Uthman, fear God in poverty, though it be the amount of a sesame seed!'"

Abu Said al-Kharraz had a son who died before him. He saw him in a dream and said, "My son, give me counsel." "Father," the young man said, "do not treat God with cowardice!" Abu Said said, "Son, tell me more." "Do not oppose God Most High in what He asks of you." "Tell me more." "Do not set a shirt between you and God!" Abu Said did not wear a shirt for thirty years.

A certain dervish used to say in his prayers, "My God, if a thing does not harm You and benefits us, do not keep it from us!" Then in a dream someone said to him, "You too! The thing that harms you and does not benefit you, give it up!"

It is related that Abu-l-Fadl al-Ispahani said, "I saw the Messenger of God in a dream and said, 'O Messenger of God, ask God not to deprive me of faith!' He said, 'God Most High has already finished with that.'"

It is related that Abu Said al-Kharraz said, "I saw satan in a dream, and took my staff and beat him! Then I was told, 'He isn't afraid of that. He is only afraid of a light that exists in the heart.'"

A Sufi said, "I used to pray for Rabiah al-Adawiyyah, and so I saw her in a dream. She said, 'Your gifts have come to me on dishes of light, covered with napkins of light!'"

It is said that Sammak ibn Harb said, "I went blind, and I dreamed a voice said to me, 'Take sweet water, and immerse yourself in it, and open your eyes.' So I did that, and my vision was restored."

Bishr ibn al-Hafi was seen in a dream and asked, "How has God dealt with you?" He said, "When I saw my Lord Almighty and Glorious He said to me, 'Welcome, Bishr. I brought you to Me the day that I brought you to Me, and there is no one upon the earth dearer to Me than you.'"

12 ADVICE FOR SPIRITUAL STUDENTS

When we decided to present a few Sufi lives and add chapters on the stages of inner development, it was our intention to complete this *Risalah* with some advice for spiritual students. We hope that God Most High will grant them good success in applying it and will not prevent us from living by it. And may He not make out it an argument against us!

If a student is to take the first step on this Way, he must be truthful and sincere, so that what he builds may be established upon sound foundations. The shaykhs have said, "They were only forbidden attainment through their neglect of fundamentals." Thus I heard Abu Ali say, "The religious belief that binds the beginner to God Most High must be sound and correct, purified of personal opinions and doubts, free of error and deviation, and issuing from proofs and evidences."

It is an ugly thing for a student to attach himself to a school of thought that does not pertain to this Way. A Sufi does not affiliate himself to an outside and opposing school except through ignorance of the teachings of the people of this Way. For their answers to questions are clearer than anyone else's, and the methods of their schools are more powerful. People in general rely either upon tradition and custom or upon intellect and thought. The shaykhs of this Group have progressed beyond all of that. That which is hidden to most people is evident to them.

Knowledge that most people can only aim for has been made real for them by the Truth. They have arrived, while others are seeking directions. They are as the poet has said:

Through Your Face my night has turned to dawn
And its darkness has passed over to the people.
The people are within the folds of darkness
While we are in the brilliance of the day.

As long as Islam has existed, no age has been without a shaykh of this group who possessed the sciences of Unity and the spiritual leadership, and in every age the leaders of the learned have submitted themselves to that shaykh, humbled themselves to him, and sought his blessing. If these shaykhs were without superiority and special distinction, things would have been just the opposite.

Once Ahmad ibn Hanbal was sitting with al-Shafi°i when Shayban al-Rai came in. "Abu Abd-Allah," Ahmad said, "I'd like to point out to this man the imperfections of his knowledge, so that he will occupy himself with religious studies." "Don't do it!" warned al-Shafi°i. Ahmad ibn Hanbal, however, was not convinced. "What would you say?" he asked, posing a question to Shayban. "Suppose a man forgot one of his five daily prayers, but did not know which of the prayers he had forgotten. What should he do, Shayban?" "Ahmad," Shayban replied, "That is a heart unconscious of God Most High. What is necessary is to educate it so that it will not be heedless of its Master again." Ahmad fainted! When he came to himself, Imam al-Shafi°i remarked, "Didn't I tell you not to try that?"

Shayban al-Rai was one of the illiterates among the Sufis. If the state of their illiterates is like this, what, then, must one think of their leaders?

It is said that the teaching circle of one of the great jurisconsults, Abu Imran, was next to the circle of Shibli in the mosque of al-Mansur. Their meetings would come to a halt when Shibli would speak. One day Abu Imran's students asked Shibli a question about menstruation. Their object was to embarrass him, but Shibli spoke and recalled many sayings about the topic, from many points of view. Abu Imran stood up and kissed Shibli upon the head. "Abu Bakr," he said, "I have derived from this question ten points that I had never heard before. Out all of that you said, I knew three statements!"

The jurisconsult Abu-l-Abbas ibn Shurayh passed by one of Junayd's meetings, and heard him speak. Somebody asked him, "What is he saying in this discourse?"

He replied, "I don't know what he is saying, but I see that this talk has force that is not vain force."

Somebody said to Abd-Allah ibn Said ibn Kullab, "You have critiqued everybody's discourse. Here we have a man called Junayd. Go and see if you object to him or not!" So Abd-Allah ibn Said attended a meeting of Junayd's circle and asked him a question about the Unity.

Junayd answered him, and Abd-Allah was amazed. "Repeat to me what you have said," he asked. Junayd repeated the point, but expressed it differently. "This is something else, something that I have not memorized," Abd-Allah said. "Will you repeat it to me one more time?" Junayd stated it yet again, using still another expression. "It is not possible for me to memorize what you are saying," Abd-Allah cried. "Dictate it to us!" "If you had, I would dictate it," said Junayd. Abd-Allah stood up, confessed Junayd's superiority, and acknowledged the greatness of his work.

The principles of the Sufis are the soundest of principles, and their shaykhs are the greatest, their scholars the most learned of men. If the student who has faith in them is a spiritual traveler capable of progress toward their goals, he will share with them in the inner discoveries that distinguish them. He will have no need of childish dependence upon anyone outside this community. If the student is properly a follower without autonomy of state who wishes to advance through the realms of imitation until imitation becomes real, then let him imitate his forefathers. Let him proceed upon the path of the Sufis, for they will serve him better than anyone else.

I heard Abu Abd al-Rahman al-Sulami say[1] . . . (Abu Bakr al-Razi) that Shibli asked, "What do you think of a knowledge about which the learned have doubts?" And I heard him say[2] . . . (Muhammad ibn Abi Ali ibn Muhammad al-Mukharrami— Muhammad ibn Abd-Allah al-Farghani) that Junayd said, "If I knew that God had created any form of knowledge under the face of the heavens nobler than the knowledge of which we speak to our companions and brethren, I would hurry to it and try to attain it."

Once the student has consolidated the bond between himself and God he must acquire sufficient knowledge of the divine Command— either by his own investigation or by asking religious leaders—to enable him to fulfill his obligations. If the opinions of legal scholars differ regarding some point, he must choose the most cautious interpretation, with the intention of keeping out of controversies.

The easing of restrictions in matters of Sacred Law is for people who are to be considered weak and for people who have pressing needs and preoccupations. Sufis, however, have no other occupation than to attend to the duties owed to the Truth, glory to Him. Thus it is said that if a dervish declines from the level of Reality to the level of indulgences in the Law, his bond with God has been nullified and the promise existing between himself and God, violated.

Next it is necessary for the spiritual student to find a shaykh to teach him behavior, for he who has no teacher will never prosper. Thus Abu Yazid said, "He who has no teacher has Satan for a leader."

I heard Abu Ali al-Daqqaq say, "When a tree grows by itself without a gardener, it puts forth leaves but no fruit. Just so, when the student has no teacher from whom to receive this Way breath by breath, he becomes the worshiper of his own whims and never comes to fruition."

If a student wants to make the spiritual journey, next after all these steps it is necessary for him to turn his attention back to God after every error. He must give up all the errors, secret and open, small and great. And first of all, he must make an effort to satisfy all those who hold something against him. For if someone has not appeased those with whom he has quarreled, nothing of this Way will be opened to him. In this fashion the Sufis have proceeded.

Next the student must work to cast off attachments and preoccupations, for this Way is built upon a heart empty of distractions. When al-Husri was at the beginning of his undertaking, Shibli used to say to him, "If from one Friday in which you come to me until the next anything crosses your mind except God Most High, it is unlawful for you to enter my presence!"

When the student has made the intention to leave his attachments, the first to go should be the attachment to property. "Property" is that which turns you away from the Truth. Every student still attached to the world who has entered into this business has, before long, been dragged back to what he had left.

When one has abandoned property, it is then necessary to abandon position, for catering to the love of position is a serious obstacle. If it is not the same to the student whether people accept him or reject him, nothing will come of him. Indeed, it is worse for a student that people should pay attention to him, attesting to his virtue and seeking his blessing, than if they should fail to do anything of the sort. While he cannot even properly be a student, how can anyone properly seek his blessing? So to give up position is a necessity. It is is a deadly poison for students.

When the student has given up property and position, he must correct the relationship between himself and God Most High and make it sound. He must not oppose his shaykh in anything he counsels. If a student to opposes his shaykh at the beginning of the path it is a grave defect, since the beginning of his state indicates the course of the rest of his life. One of the conditions for a student's development is that he find no resistance to his shaykh in his heart.

If it seems to a student that he has any merit or value in this world or the next, or that anyone on the face of the earth is lowlier than he, he cannot correctly take a single step on the path. It is necessary for him to strive in order to know his Lord, not in order to acquire merit for himself. There is a difference between someone who wants God Most High and someone who wants a place for himself, both now and in the Hereafter.

Next, the student must preserve his secret from his own coat-button—from everyone except his shaykh. But if he hides a single one of his breaths from his shaykh, he will have betrayed the right due to his companionship. If he experiences some objection to what his shaykh indicates to him, he must confess it immediately. He must submit himself to whatever punishment his shaykh decides upon for his offense, whether it be assigned travel or some other undertaking that the shaykh directs.

It is not right for shaykhs to overlook the faults of their students, for that would be to neglect the rights of God Most High.

As long as a student is not stripped of all attachments, it is not possible for his shaykh to instill in him the methods for the remembrance of God. Instead, he must give priority to testing him.

When his heart observes right resolution in the student, the shaykh will stipulate that the student must accept and be satisfied with all the difficulties that may befall him in the Way. He will have the student promise not to be turned aside from the Way by anything he encounters, whether harm, humiliation, poverty, illness, or pain. The student must vow that his heart will not incline toward convenience and seek the easy way out under the onslaughts of need, that he will not prefer calm and become filled with laziness.

For the student to come to a halt is worse than for him to grow slack. The difference between the two is that slackness means turning back from the business of being a student and abandoning it, while coming to a halt means to stop progress and take pleasure in the states that come of laziness. No student who comes to a halt at the beginning is of any use.

When the shaykh has thoroughly tested the student, he must then instruct him in one of the methods of remembrance shown him by his own shaykh. He will first order the student to invoke the assigned divine Name verbally. Then he will order him to engage his heart along with his tongue. He will tell him, "Remain with this act of remembrance constantly, as you would if you were always together with your Lord in your heart. Insofar as it is possible, do not let your tongue repeat anything but this Name."

Next the shaykh will order the student to be always in a state of outward ablution, not to sleep unless he is overcome, and to diminish what he eats by degrees, a little at a time, until he has power over that. He will not order him to leave his habits all at once, for as the hadith says, "The one who overloads a pack animal so that it collapses covers no distance and does not save his own back from burdens."

Then the shaykh will order the student to choose retreat and withdrawal from people, and while in that state, above all else, to make an effort to prevent base thoughts and appetites from distracting his heart.

Know that in such circumstances, while in retreat at the beginning of the path, a student is seldom free of destructive imaginings that attack his belief, especially if he is intelligent and subtle. Rare is the student who does not experience this at the beginning of his studentship; it is one of the trials that students encounter. If the shaykh sees that the student is clever, he should turn him toward intellectual proofs, for without a doubt learning frees the one who seeks divine knowledge from imaginations that afflict him.

When the shaykh perceives that the student has developed strength and firmness in following the Way, he will order him to be patient and continuously practice remembrance until the lights of God's acceptance shine in his heart and the suns of arrival at the goal rise in his innermost being, as they will before long. But this will not take place unless students' efforts are concentrated. The main thing is that, to the extent of the need motivating each student, he should be led back to reflection and meditation upon the signs of God, and that reflection should be conditioned by study of the Quran and the *Sunnah*.

Know that students are especially troubled by a particular sort of destructive imagining. When they have withdrawn to the place where they practice remembrance or are attending spiritual concerts or in similar circumstances, base urges arise in their lower selves and repulsive thoughts enter their minds. They know full well that God, glory to Him, is far above such things and have no doubt that it is empty foolishness, but still it continues. It makes students suffer intensely, and may reach the extreme of the worst vilification, the ugliest language, and the most disgusting thoughts, so bad that the student cannot bring himself to utter them or to confess them to anyone. This is the hardest thing that happens to students.

In such a case, it is necessary to stop giving attention to the thoughts and to continue in the practice of remembrance, while making supplication to God to prevent their occurrence.

These thoughts are not the suggestions of Satan. They are the notions of one's own ego. When the servant deals with them by refusing to pay attention to them, it will cut them off.

Part of the behavior proper to the student—indeed, one of the obligations of his state—is that he stay at the place where he has found teaching and not travel about before the Way has accepted him and his heart has arrived at his Lord. Travel at the wrong time is a deadly poison for students, and not one of them who has traveled inappropriately has gained his hopes. When God wants what is good for a student He ties him to the place where he first received teaching, and when He wants what is bad for a student He sends him back to the profession and state he had left. When God wants a student to suffer an ordeal, He drives him away to the ash-heaps of alienation.

All of this applies to students suited to arrival at the goal. There are also those people whose best path is outward personal service to the dervishes, and who rank a degree below them in the Way. They are content with following an outward example. They dedicate themselves to travel, for the goal of their participation in this Way is the Pilgrimages they accomplish, the visitations they make, and the shaykhs they meet and give greeting. They look at the surfaces of things, and travel gives them enough to keep them happy. These should travel constantly, so that they do not have the opportunity to commit errors. When such people rest and settle in, there is the possibility of trouble and disruption.

It is very dangerous for the novice to find himself brought into the midst of advanced students and dervishes. If someone is so tested, he should make it his business to show reverence to the shaykhs and service to the brotherhood. He must give up any opposition to them and concern himself with making the dervishes feel comfortable. He must make an effort not to alienate the heart of any shaykh. In association with dervishes he must always take their part against him, and never his own part against them. He must see that he has an obligatory duty to every single one of them, but that nobody owes him a thing.

The student must not argue with anybody. Even when he knows

that he is right, he must keep silent and remain in harmony with everyone. Nothing will come of a student who laughs, gets angry, or behaves badly.

When the student is among dervishes, whether traveling or in a teacher's circle, he must not go against their outward habit, whether of eating or fasting, stillness or activity. If he must object, let him object secretly in his heart, and entrust his heart to the protection of God Almighty and Glorious. If, for instance, they indicate that he should eat, he should eat a bite or two. But he should not give his lower self the freedom of its appetites.   Multiplying   litanies and outward devotions is not part of the behavior proper to students. The Sufis are engaged in enduring the purification of their thoughts, the treatment of their character, and the expulsion of unconsciousness from their hearts, not in piling up good deeds. But they must absolutely carry out the religious obligations and the binding sunnahs. And if they add blessings upon the Prophet and continuous remembrance of God in the heart, their devotions are complete.

The student's capital, with which he will make his fortune, is in good-naturedly putting up with everyone, being satisfied with whatever he experiences, being patient in hardship and poverty, and not questioning or opposing—either a little or a lot—the share of life that falls to him. If someone cannot persevere in this, let him go back to the marketplace. Whoever craves what people in general crave must gain his desire as everyone else does: through the toil of his hand and the sweat of his brow.   When the student has adopted perpetual remembrance of God and chosen to withdraw from the world, he will find things that he never found before, either asleep, awake, or between the two — messages heard, miracles witnessed. It is important that he not concern himself with these at all. He must not dwell on them or wait for their recurrence, for they are all distractions from the Truth. But he should describe these states to his shaykh until his heart becomes empty of them. The shaykh, on his part, should protect this secret, hide the affair from other people, and make it seem trivial to his student. For all such things are tests, and whoever spends much time upon them has been tricked. So let the student beware of them and of giving importance to them. His aspirations should be higher.

Know that it is a serious problem when students entertain ideas that God is close to them and has shown them special grace. Thoughts like "I have chosen you and singled you out from your fellows" may be cast into their hearts. If the student makes up his mind to drop such ideas, before long he will be torn away from them by genuine spiritual discoveries.

A detailed analysis and documentation of the whole of this topic is not feasible in books.

It is a rule that if the student cannot find anyone to instruct him in behavior where he first lives, he must move and take up residence near someone who is presently assigned to guide students. He must stay with him and never leave his threshold until he is given permission.

Know that one must prefer being acquainted with the Lord of the House to visiting the House. For if one does not know the Lord of the House, visiting there is scarcely necessary. Sufi students who go on Pilgrimage without the instruction of their shaykhs are merely indulging the natural energy of their egos. They are marked men in this Way, and their journeys are without foundation. The proof of this is that the more they travel, the more separation there is in their hearts. To have traveled away from themselves a single step would have been luckier for them than a thousand journeys.

When he visits a shaykh, the student must make it a condition always to enter his presence with respect and look upon him with modesty. If the shaykh makes it possible for him to perform some service, he should count it as pure blessing.

*****

The student is not required to believe that the shaykhs are immune to sin. What is necessary is that he leave their states to them, think well of them, and respect the matters to which his shaykh directs him as he respects the strictures of God Most High. As for learning, it is sufficient to know the difference between what is praiseworthy and what is blameworthy.

*****

As long as the goods of this world retain any scope or value in a student's heart, the name of "student" may be applied to him only metaphorically. As long as any preference remains in his heart for the things he knew before and has given up, so that he wants to be specially endowed with some sort of goodness or thinks that one person is lower than another, it will falsify his state, and there is danger of his rapidly returning to the world. The student's aim when he severs worldly ties must be to leave them behind, not to busy himself with pieties.

It is an ugly thing for a student to give up the money and property he has, and then become a prisoner to his business. Whether wealth comes to him or not must be all the same to him. He must not, for its sake, shun any dervish or cause trouble to anyone, even a fire-worshiper.

*****

When the hearts of the shaykhs accept a student, it is the surest sign of his happiness and the success of his efforts. If someone is rejected by the heart of any shaykh, he will infallibly see the effect of it, though it be after a long interval. When someone shows disrespect to shaykhs in general, he has shown forth the sign of his own misfortune and spiritual failure; there can be no mistake about it.

*****

One of the worst disasters in this Way is the companionship of youths. It is the consensus of the shaykhs that any servant who is so afflicted has been abased and deserted by God Almighty and Glorious. Indeed, he has been alienated from himself, though he may have been made capable of thousands upon thousands of miracles. Even supposing that such a servant has reached the degree of platonic contemplation, there is no hint of this practice in the hadiths. And has not his heart been distracted from the Creator by a creation?

The worst case is when a servant's heart makes little of the practice and considers it easy. God Most High has said, *"You count it to be trivial, while with God it is grave"* (24:15). As al-Wasiti said, "When God wants to disgrace a servant, He casts him among those rotting corpses."

I heard Abu Abd-Allah al-Sufi say[2] . . . (Muhammad ibn Ahmad al-NajjarÑAbu Abd-Allah al-Husri) that Fath al-Mawsili said, "I kept company with thirty shaykhs who were accounted to be of the rank of the deputies (*abdal*). Each one of them gave me the parting advice, "Fear the society of youths and free association with them."

Some people advance association with youths beyond simple immoral behavior. They make out that it is one of the trials of souls, and not harmful. They recount things that various people have imagined about the contemplation of youths and tell stories about certain shaykhs, when they ought better to be drawing the veil over their defects and the catastrophes that issue from them. This kind of talk is the twin of polytheism and the equal of faithlessness.

So let the student beware of sitting with youths and mixing with them, for the mildest consequence of this habit is the opening of the door of spiritual failure and the initiation of the state of abandonment by God. We take refuge in God from evil destiny.

*****

It is a disaster for a student when his ego is stricken with secret envy of his brethren, so that he grows agitated over what God has granted certain of his fellows in the Way and resents that he has not received it himself.

The servant must understand that what comes to people is a matter of destiny. He will only be purified of his preoccupation with the states of others when he grows content with the existence of the Truth, and accepts that his own progress can only be the outcome of God's generosity and grace.

O student, it is the Truth Who has advanced the degree of all those your eyes fall upon! So you must bear this hardship. That is the custom kept by aspirants of refinement.

*****

Let us turn to the behavior proper to students during the spiritual concert. A student is by no means permitted to move as he chooses during the ritual. Yet if the urge to move overtakes him and he has not much power to withstand it, then to the extent that he is really overwhelmed, he may be excused. When he is no longer overcome, he must sit down and keep still. It is not right to continue to move without being forced to it, simply because one likes the sensation of ecstasy. If someone makes a habit of this, his progress will be retarded and nothing of the realities will be revealed to him. In that case the outcome of his states will only be the raising of his spirits.

In general, moving during the ritual detracts from the one who moves, whether he be a novice or a shaykh, and diminishes his state. The exception arises when his movements are a spontaneous response to the promptings of that moment, or result from a force that takes him away from his conscious preference. However, when the shaykh indicates that he should move, the student should move as directed. If the shaykh has authority over people like him, it is all right.

When the advanced dervishes indicate that the novice should

move in solidarity, he should show solidarity by standing up and performing only the minimal actions necessary to guard against offending their hearts. Later, when his state has grown truthful, it will prevent the hearts of the dervishes from asking for this gesture.

Sometimes in the course of the ritual the participants throw off their cloaks. It is the duty of the student under no circumstances to take back anything that he has cast off. If a shaykh directs him to take it back, them let him do so, preserving in his heart the intention of divesting himself. Later he can dispose of it without offending that shaykh.   When a group of dervishes has the custom of throwing off their cloaks and the student knows that they later take them back again, and if there is no shaykh among them to whom he must show modesty and respect, a student's best course is not to retrieve his cloak. The best method is for him to throw off his cloak when they do, and then to give his cloak to the singer when they retrieve theirs. If he were not to participate at all, as is possible when he knows that the habit of this group is to take back what they have discarded, the ugliness would be in their custom, not in his opposition to it. Still, it is better to throw off one's cloak in harmony with the others, and then forbear to take it back.

It is certainly not given to the student to make requests of the singer in a spiritual concert. It is the authenticity of his state that prompts the singer to make repetitions, and that may prompt others to make requests.

Whoever asks a student's blessing does him an injury. Since his strength is small, it can be dangerous for him. It is necessary for the student to avoid cultivating the esteem of anyone who talks that way by leaving him and his assertion.

In the case of a student's being tempted by position, wealth, the company of a youth or the attraction of a woman, or dependence upon some worldly support, if there is no shaykh available to show him the means to free himself, he should travel. He should go away from that place and break up the situation in which he finds himself.

There is nothing more dangerous to the hearts of students than for them to reach a position of esteem before their natures have been transformed.

Right behavior requires that a student's knowledge of this Way should not be in advance of his stage of development. To study the lives of members of this community and then pretend to possess an understanding of their states and of the questions that concerned them, while not having realized them in one's own development and dealings, makes genuine attainment difficult. The shaykhs have said, "When the knower talks of what he knows, call him ignorant." Reports about stages of development are less than inner knowledge. When someone's learning is greater than his station he is a scholar, not a traveler on this Way.

*****

Right behavior also requires that students not get involved with being leaders or take students and disciples of their own. When a seeker becomes sought after before his nature has been transformed and his critical defects have fallen away, he is veiled from reality. His guidance and instruction will not benefit anyone.

*****

When a student serves the dervishes, their thoughts are divine messengers to him. He must not reject ideas for sincere service that come into his mind, but spend all his strength and capacity in carrying them out.

*****

When the student's path is service to the dervishes, it is his business to be patient when they are harsh to him, even if he believes he is exhausting himself in their service and they never praise him at all. He should beg their pardon for his shortcomings and take the offense upon himself in order to mollify their hearts. Even if he knows himself to be blameless, when their harshness increases he must increase his service and dutifulness toward them.

I heard Imam Abu Bakr ibn Furak say: The saying goes, "If you can't be patient under the hammer, why did you become an anvil?"

With this in mind the Sufis recite:

Sometimes I would come to him to apologize
For sins I had not yet been accused of!

*****

The foundation and essential prerequisite of this undertaking is the preservation of the conduct laid down by divine Command. One must guard one's hand against reaching for forbidden things and doubtful ones, protect one's sight from what is dangerous, and take care in each breath to be together with God Most High and not with the various forms of heedlessness. If even in time of need one may not regard as lawful so much as a sesame seed about which there are doubts, how then shall one do so in a time of ease, when other choices are available?

Part of the student's business is the continuous struggle to abandon lusts, for whoever capitulates to his lust is devoid of happiness. It is the ugliest of traits for a student to return to some lust he had left for God Most High.

*****

It is part of the student's business to keep his promises to God Most High. Breaking a promise of the path, in students, is like revolt against religion in people of the outer world. The student must not, of his own choice, make promises that he cannot carry out. In fulfilling the prescriptions of the divine Command he will find enough to occupy all his strength. Describing one group, God Most High said, "*As for monasticism, they invented it; We did not ordain it for them, but it was for the sake of God's pleasure. They did not practice it as it ought to have been practiced*" (57:27).

*****

It is part of the student's business to cut short his ambitions, for the dervish is the son of "now." Nothing will come of the student who makes elaborate plans for the future, gives his attention to something other than the present moment, and sets his hopes on what might happen.

*****

It is part of the student's business not to carry money, even a little, and especially not when he is among dervishes. For the darkness of the money will put out the light of the moment.

*****

It is part of the student's business—in fact, it is part of the business of accomplished travelers of this school—to refuse to accept gifts from women. How should it be possible, then, to actively seek them out? In this way the Sufi shaykhs have proceeded, and so they have advised. Whoever makes light of this will rapidly meet with disgrace.

*****

It is part of the student's business to keep away from worldly people. Their company is a time-tested poison! He will bring them profit, but they will bring him loss. God Most High has said, *"Do not obey the one whose heart We have made heedless of Our remembrance"* (18:28). Ascetics take the money out of their wallets in order to come closer to God Most High; Sufis take the world and worldly knowledge out of their hearts in order to realize God Most High.

*****

This is our counsel for spiritual students. We ask God the Generous to grant them success and not to let bad consequences issue from this advice.

The whole of this *Risalah* was completed at the beginning of the year 1046 AD/438 AH. We ask God the Generous not to make it an argument against us or cause it to produce a bad effect, but to let it be a useful instrument, and a gift. Grace is His custom, forgiveness His quality.

Praise be to God with the praise that is His due. And may His blessings and graces and mercy be upon His Messenger, our master Muhammad the Untaught Prophet, and upon his pure family and his noble and elect companions, and may God grant them abundant peace.

NOTES

NOTES TO QUSHAYRI'S INTRODUCTION

1 Abd-Allah bin Musa al-Sulami

2 Muhammad bin Abd-Allah al-Razi

3 Abd Allah bin Ali al-Tamimi al-Sufi—Husayn bin Ali al-Damgani

4 Muhammad bin Muhammad bin Ghalib—Abu Nasr Ahmad bin Said al-Isfinjani

5 Abu Nasr al-Tusi al-Sarraj

6 Mansur bin Abd-Allah—Abu-l-Husayn al-Anbar

7 Muhammad bin Abd-Allah—Abu Jafar al-Saydalani

8 Abd al-Wahid bin Ali—Qasim bin al-Qasim—Muhammad bin Musa al-Wasiti—Muhammad bin al-Husayn al-Jawhari

9 Abd al-Wahid bin Bakr—Hilal bin Ahmad

10 Abu-l-Husayn al-Farisi—Ibrahim bin Fatik

11 Abd al-Wahid bin Bakr—Ahmad bin Muhammad bin Ali al-Bardai

12 Abu Bakr al-Razi

13 Abu Abbas bin al-Khashshab al-Baghdadi—Abu-l-Qasim bin Musa—Muhammad bin Ahmad—al-Ansari

14 Abu Ali al-Dalal—Abu Abd-Allah bin Qahraman

15 Mansur bin Abd-Allah—Jafar bin Muhammad

NOTES TO PART I: ON THE SHAYKHS OF THIS WAY

1 ABU ISHAQ IBRAHIM BIN ADHAM BIN MANSUR

1 Muhammad ibn al-Husayn ibn Khashshab—Abu-l-Hasan Ali ibn Muhammad al-Misri—Abu Said al-Kharraz

2 Mansur ibn Abd-Allah—Muhammad ibn Hamid—Ahmad ibn Khadruyah

2 ABU-L-FAYD DHU-L-NUN AL-MISRI

1 Said ibn Uthman

2 Said ibn Ahmad ibn Jafar—Muhammad ibn Ahmad ibn Sahl—Said ibn Uthman

3 Abu Bakr Muhammad ibn Abd-Allah ibn Shadhan

4 Ali ibn Umar al-Hafiz—Ibn Rashiq—Abu Dajanah

3 ABU ALI AL-FUDAYL BIN IYAD

1 Abu Bakr Muhammad ibn Jafar—al-Hasan ibn Abd-Allah al-Askari—his nephew Abu Zarah—Muhammad ibn Ishaq ibn Rahuyah

4 ABU MAHFUZ MARUF BIN FIRUZ AL-KARKHI

1 Abu Bakr al-Razi—Abu Bakr al-Harbi

2 Abd al-Rahim ibn Ali, the *hafiz* of Baghdad—Muhammad ibn Umar ibn al-Fadl—Ali ibn Isa.

5 ABU-L-HASAN SARI BIN AL-MUGHALLIS AL-SAQATI

1 Abd-Allah ibn Ali al-Tusi—Abu Amr ibn Ulwan.

2 Abu Bakr al-Razi—Abu Umar al-Anmati.

3 Abu Bakr al-Razi.

4 Muhammad ibn al-Hasan ibn al-Khashshab—Jafar ibn Muhammad ibn Nusayr.

5 Abu Nasr al-Sarraj al-Tusi—Jafar ibn Muhammad ibn Nusayr.

6 Abu-l-Hasan ibn Abd-Allah al-Ghawati al-Tarsusi— Junayd.

7 Abu Bakr al-Razi—al-Jurayri.

6 ABU-L-NASR BISHR AL-HARITH AL-HAFI

1 Muhammad ibn Abd-Allah al-Razi—Abd al-Rahman ibn Abi Hatim

2 Muhammad ibn Abd-Allah al-Razi

3 Abd al-Aziz ibn al-Fadl—Muhammad ibn Said — Muhammad ibn Abd-Allah

4 Abu-l-Fadl al-Attar

5 Ubayd Allah ibn Uthman ibn Yahya—Abu Amr ibn al-Sammak—Abu Bakr ibn Bint Muawiyah—Abu Bakr ibn Affan.

6 Ubayd Allah ibn Uthman—Abu Amr ibn al-Sammak— Umar ibn Said

7 ABU ABD ALLAH AL-HARITH BIN ASAD AL-MUHASIBI

1 Al-Husayn ibn Yahya — Jafar ibn Muhammad ibn Nusayr.

2 Abd-Allah ibn Ali al-Tusi—Jafar al-Khuldi—Abu Uthman al-Baladi

8 ABU SULAYMAN DAWUD BIN NUSAYR AL-TAI

1 Abu Umar ibn Matar—Muhammad ibn al-Musayyib—Ibn Khubayq

2 Muhammad ibn Yusuf—Sad ibn Amr—Ali ibn Harb al-Mawsili

3 Abu Ishaq Ibrahim ibn Muhammad ibn Yahya al-Mazaki—Qasim ibn Ahmad—Maymun al-Ghazzali

9 ABU ALI SHAQIQ BIN IBRAHIM AL-BALKHI

1 Abu-l-Husayn ibn Ahmad al-Attar al-Balkhi—Ahmad ibn Muhammad al-Bukhari

10 ABU YAZID BIN TAYFUR BIN ISA AL-BISTAMI

1 Abu-l-Hasan al-Farisi

2 Mansur ibn Abd Allah—his uncle al-Bistami—his father

3 Abu Nasr al-Sarraj—Tayfur al-Bistami—someone his uncle al-Bistami knew—his father

4 Hasan ibn Ali—his uncle al-Bistami

5 Abd-Allah ibn Ali—Musa ibn Isa—his father

11 ABU MUHAMMAD SAHL BIN ABD ALLAH AL-TUSTARI
1 Abu-l-Fath Yusuf ibn Umar al-Zahid—Abd-Allah ibn Abd-l-Hamid—Ubayd Allah ibn Lulu— Umar ibn Wasil al-Basri
2 Abu-l-Abbas al-Baghdadi—Ibrahim ibn Firas—Nasr ibn Ahmad

12 ABU SULAYMAN ABD AL-RAHMAN BIN ATIYAH AL-DARANI
1 Abd-Allah ibn Muhammad al-Dari—Ishaq ibn Ibrahim ibn Abi Hasan—Ahmad ibn Abi-l-Hawari
2 Al-Husayn ibn Yahya—Jafar ibn Muhammad ibn Nusayr— Junayd
3 Abu Amr al-Jawlasti—Muhammad ibn Ismail

13 ABU ABD AL-RAHMAN HATIM BIN ULWAN
1 Abu Ali Said ibn Ahmad—his father—Muhammad ibn Abd Allah—his uncle Muhammad ibn al-Layth—Hamid al-Liqaf
2 Abu Nasr Mansur ibn Muhammad ibn Ibrahim al-Faqih—Abu Muhammad Jafar ibn Muhammad ibn Nusayr

14 ABU ZAKARIYA YAHYA BIN MUADH AL-RAZI AL-WAIZ
1 Abd-Allah ibn Muhammad ibn Ahmad ibn Hamdan al-Ukbari—Ahmad ibn Muhammad ibn al-Sari—Ahmad ibn Isa.
2 Abu-l-Qasim Abd-Allah ibn al-Husayn ibn Baluyah al-Sufi—Muhammad ibn Abd-Allah al-Razi—al-Husayn ibn Uluyah
3 Abu-l-Husayn Muhammad ibn Abd al-Aziz, the *muezzin*— Muhammad ibn Muhammad al-Jurjani—Ali ibn Muhammad

15 ABU HAMID AHMAD BIN KHADRUYAH AL-BALKHI
1 Mansur ibn Abd-Allah.

16 ABU-L-HUSAYN AHMAD BIN ABI-L-HAWARI
1 Abu Ahmad al-Hafiz—Said ibn Abd al-Aziz al-Halabi.

17 ABU HAFS UMAR BIN MASLAMAH AL-HADDAD
1 Abu-l-Hasan Muhammad ibn Musa—Abu Ali al-Thaqafi

18 ABU TURAB ASKAR BIN HUSAYN AL-NAKHSHABI
1 Abu-l-Abbas al-Baghdadi—Abu Abd Allah al-Farisi—Abu-l-Husayn al-Razi—Yusuf ibn al-Husayn

19 ABU MUHAMMAD ABD ALLAH BIN KHUBAYQ
1 Abu-l-Faraj al-Wirthani—Abu-l-Azhar al-Miyyafarqini

21 ABU-L-SARI MANSUR BIN AMMAR
1 Abu Bakr al-Razi—Abu-l-Abbas al-Qadi.

23 ABU-L-QASIM AL-JUNAYD BIN MUHAMMAD

1 Muhammad ibn al-Husayn al-Baghdadi—al-Farghani

2 Muhammad ibn Abd-Allah al-Razi—Abu Muhammad al-Jurayri

3 Abu Bakr al-Razi—Abu Muhammad al-Jurayri—Muhammad ibn al-Hasan—Abu Nasr al-Ispahani

4 Mansur ibn Abd Allah—Abu Umar al-Anmati

5 Abu Nasr al-Ispahani

6 Abu-l-Husayn ibn Faris

24 ABU UTHMAN SAID BIN ISMAIL AL-HIRI

1 Abu Amr ibn Hamdan

2 Abd al-Rahman ibn Abd-Allah—one of Abu Uthman's companions

3 Abd-Allah ibn Muhammad al-Sharani

4 Muhammad ibn Ahmad al-Malamati—Abu-l-Husayn al-Warraq

5 Abu Amr ibn Nujayd

25 ABU-L-HASAN BIN MUHAMMAD AL-NURI

1 Ahmad ibn Muhammad al-Bardhai—al-Murtaish.

2 Abu-l-Abbas al-Baghdadi—al-Farghani

26 ABU ABD ALLAH AHMAD BIN YAHYA AL-JALLA

1 Muhammad ibn Abd al-Azim al-Tabari—Abu Umar al-Dimashqi

27 ABU MUHAMMAD RUWAYM BIN AHMAD

1 Abd al-Wahid ibn Bakr

28 ABU ABD ALLAH MUHAMMAD BIN AL-FASL AL-BALKHI

1 Ahmad ibn Muhammad al-Furra

2 Abd Allah al-Razi

3 Abu Bakr al-Razi

29 ABU BAKR AHMAD NASR AL-ZAQQAQ AL-KABIR

1 Al-Husayn ibn Ahmad

2 Muhammad ibn Abd-Allah ibn Abd al-Aziz

30 ABU ABD ALLAH AMR BIN UTHMAN AL-MAKKI

1 Muhammad ibn Abd-Allah ibn Shadhan—Abu Bakr Muhammad ibn Ahmad

31 SUMNUN BIN HAMZAH

1 Abu-l-Abbas Muhammad ibn al-Hasan al-Baghdadi—Jafar al-Khuldi

32 ABU UBAYD AL-BUSRA

1 Abd-Allah ibn Ali—al-Duqqi

2 Ahmad ibn Muhammad al-Baghawi—Muhammad ibn Muammar

33 ABU-L-FAWARIS SHAH BIN SHUJA AL-KIRMANI
1 His grandfather, Ibn Nujayd

36 ABU BAKR BIN UMAR AL-WARRAQ AL-TIRMIDHI
1 Muhammad ibn al-Husayn—Muhammad ibn Muhammad al-Balkhi
2 Abu Bakr al-Balkhi

37 ABU SAID AHMAD BIN ISA AL-KHARRAZ
1 Abu Abd-Allah al-Razi—Abu-l-Abbas al-Siyad

40 ABU-L-HASAN ALI BIN SAHL AL-ISFAHANI
1 Abu Bakr Muhammad ibn Abd Allah al-Tabari

41 ABU MUHAMMAD AHMAD BIN MUHAMMAD BIN AL-HUSAYN AL-JURAYRI
1 Abu-l-Husayn al-Farisi

42 ABU-L-ABBAS AHMAD BIN MUHAMMAD BIN SAHL BIN ATA AL-ADMI
1 Abu Said al-Qurashi
2 Abd al-Rahman ibn Ahmad al-Sufi

43 ABU ISHAQ IBRAHIM BIN AHMAD AL-KHAWWAS
1 Abu Bakr al-Razi
2 Ahmad ibn Ali ibn Jafar—al-Azdi

44 ABU MUHAMMAD ABD ALLAH BIN MUHAMMAD AL-KHARRAZ
1 Abu Nasr al-Tusi

45 ABU-L-HASAN BUNNAN BIN MUHAMMAD AL-HAMMAL
1 Hasan ibn Ahmad al-Razi

47 ABU BAKR BIN MUSA AL-WASITI
1 Abu Bakr Muhammad ibn Abd al-Aziz al-Marwazi

51 KHAYR AL-NASSAJ
1 Abu-l-Hasan al-Qazwini

52 ABU HAMZAH AL-KHURASANI
1 Abu-l-Tayyib al-Akki—Abu-l-Hasan al-Misri

53 ABU BAKR MUHAMMAD BIN ALI AL-KATTANI
1 Abu-l-Abbas al-Baghdadi

55 ABU ALI AHMAD BIN MUHAMMAD AL-RUDHBARI
1 Mansur ibn Abd-Allah

56 ABU MUHAMMAD ABD ALLAH BIN MUNAZIL

1 Abd-Allah al-Muallim
2 Abu Ahmad ibn Isa

57 ABU ALI MUHAMMAD BIN ABD AL-WAHHAB AL-THAQAFI
3 Mansur ibn Abd Allah

60 ABU YAQUB ISHAQ BIN MUHAMMAD AL-NAHRAJUR
1 Abu-l-Husayn Ahmad ibn Ali
2 Abu Bakr al-Razi
3 Ahmad ibn Ali

63 ABU-L-HASAN ALI BIN MUHAMMAD AL-MUZAYYIN
1 Abu Bakr al-Razi

64 ABU BAKR ABD ALLAH BIN TAHIR AL-ABHARI
1 Mansur ibn Abd-Allah

66 ABU ISHAQ IBRAHIM BIN SHAYBAN AL-QIRMISINI
1 Abu Yazid al-Marwazi al-Faqih

70 ABU MUHAMMAD JAFAR BIN MUHAMMAD BIN NUSAYR
1 Muhammad ibn Abd-Allah ibn Shadhan

76 ABU ABD ALLAH BIN KHAFIF AL-SHIRAZI
1 Abu-l-Abbas al-Karkhi

78 ABU BAKR AL-TAMASTANI
1 Mansur ibn Abd-Allah al-Ispahani

PART II: AN EXPLANATION OF THE EXPRESSIONS IN USE AMONG THE SUFIS WITH A CLARIFICATION OF WHAT IS OBSCURE IN THEM
4 CONTRACTION (*QABD*) AND EXPANSION (*BAST*)
1 Al-Husayn ibn Yahya—Jafar ibn Muhammad

6 IMITATING ECSTASY (*TAWAJUD*), ECSTASY (*WAJD*), BEING (*WUJUD*)
2 Umar ibn Muhammad ibn Ahmad

NOTES TO PART III: STATIONS AND STATES
1 ON REPENTANCE (*TAWBAH*)
1 Ahmad ibn Mahmud ibn Kharraz — Muhammad ibn Fadl ibn Jabir — Said ibn Abd Allah—Ahmad ibn Zakariya.
2 Abu-l-Husayn Ahmad ibn Ubayd al-Saffar—Muhammad ibn Fadl ibn

Jabir—al-Hakam ibn Musa—Ghassan ibn Ubayd—Abu Atikah Tarif ibn Sulayman.

3 Mansur ibn Abd Allah—Jafar ibn Nusayr.

4 Abu Bakr al-Razi—Abu Abd Allah al-Qurashi.

Abu Abd Allah ibn Masalih of Ahwaz—Ibn Ziri.

Muhammad ibn Ibrahim ibn al-Fadl al-Hashimi—Muhammad ibn al-Rumi.

5 al-Husayn ibn Ali—Muhammad ibn Ahmad—Abd Allah ibn Sahl.

6 Abu Abd Allah al-Razi.

7 Abu Bakr al-Razi.

2 ON STRIVING (*MUJAHADAH*)

1 Ahmad ibn Ubayd al-Saffar—al-Abbas ibn al-Fadl al-Asqati—Ibn Kasib—Ibn Uyaynah—Ali ibn Zayd—Abu Nadrah.

2 Ahmad ibn Ali ibn Jafar—al-Husayn ibn Ulluyah.

3 Abu-l-Abbas al-Baghdadi—Jafar—Junayd.

4 Abu Bakr al-Razi—Abdul-Aziz al-Najrani.

5 Mansur ibn Abd Allah—Muhammad ibn Hamid—Ahmad ibn Khadruyah.

6 Mansur ibn Abdullah.

7 Muhammad ibn Abd Allah ibn Shadhan—Yusuf ibn al-Husayn.

8 Muhammad ibn Abd Allah al-Razi.

9 Abd Allah al-Razi.

10 Muhammad al-Furra.

3 ON RETREAT AND SECLUSION (*KHALWAH WA UZLAH*)

1 Ahmad ibn Ubayd al-Basri—Abd-l-Aziz ibn Muawiyah—al-Qanabi—Abd-l-Aziz ibn Abi Hazim—his father—Bajah ibn Abd Allah ibn Badr al-Jahni.

2 Mansur ibn Abd Allah.

3 Mansur ibn Abd Allah.

4 Abu Bakr al-Razi—Jafar ibn Nusayr.

5 Abu Bakr al-Razi—Abu Amr al-Anmati.

6 Abu Bakr al-Razi.

7 Abu Uthman Said ibn Abi Said.

4 ON CONSCIOUSNESS OF GOD (*TAQWA*)

1 Ahmad ibn Ubayd al-Saghir—Muhammad ibn al-Fadl ibn Jabir—Ibn Abd-l-Ala al-Qurashi—Yaqub the Blind—al-Layth—Mujahid.

2 Ahmad ibn Ubayd—Abbas ibn al-Mufaddal al-Asqati—Ahmad ibn

Yunus—Abu Hurmuz Nafi ibn Hurmuz.

3 Ahmad ibn Ali ibn Jafar—Ahmad ibn Asim.

4 Abu Bakr al-Razi.

5 Abu Bakr al-Razi.

6 Muhammad al-Furra.

7 Abu Bakr al-Razi.

8 Abu-l-Husayn al-Basri—Bishr ibn Musa—Muhammad ibn Abd Allah ibn al-Mubarak—Yahya ibn Ayyub—Ubayd Allah ibn Rahw—Ali ibn Yazid—al-Qasim.

9 Abu-l-Abbas Muhammad ibn al-Husayn

5 ON ABSTAINING (*WARA*)

1 Muhammad ibn Dawud ibn Sulayman al-Zahid—Muhammad ibn al-Husayn ibn Qutaybah—Ahmad ibn Abu Tahir al-Khurasani—Yahya ibn al-Ghayzar—Muhammad ibn Yusuf al-Firyani—Sufyan—al-Ajlah—Abd Allah ibn Buraydah —al-Aswad al-Duala.

2 Abu-l-Abbas al-Baghdadi—Jafar ibn Muhammad—Junayd.

3 Abu-l-Qasim al-Dimashqi.

4 Abu Jafar al-Razi—al-Abbas ibn Hamzah—Ahmad ibn Abil-Hawari.

5 Husayn ibn Ahmad al-Jafar—Muhammad ibn Dawud al-Dinawari.

6 Abu Bakr al-Razi.

7 Abu-l-Husayn al-Farisi.

8 Abd Allah ibn Ali ibn Yahya al-Tamimi.

6 ON RENUNCIATION (*ZUHD*)

1 Abu-l-Husayn Ubayd Allah ibn Ahmad ibn Yaqub al-Muqarri in Baghdad—Jafar ibn Mujashi—Zayd ibn Ismail—Kuthayr ibn Hisham—al-Hakam ibn Hisham—Yahya ibn Said—Abu Farwah.

2 Ahmad ibn Ismail al-Azdi—Imran ibn Musa al-Isfanji—al-Dawarqi—Waki.

3 Said ibn Ahmad—Abbas ibn Isam—Junayd.

4 Ahmad ibn Ali—Ibrahim ibn Fatik.

5 Abu Bakr al-Razi.

6 Abu-l-Tayyib al-Samiri—Junayd.

7 Ali ibn al-Husayn al-Mawsili—Ahmad ibn al-Husayn—Muhammad ibn al-Hasan—Muhammad ibn Jafar.

7 ON SILENCE (*SAMT*)

1 Abu Bakr Muhammad ibn al-Husayn al-Qattan—Ahmad ibn Yusuf al-Sulami—Abd al-Raziq—Muammar—Zuhri—Abu Salamah.

2 Ahmad ibn Ubayd—Bishr ibn Musa al-Asadi—Muhammad ibn Said al-

Ispahani—Ibn Mubarak—Yahya ibn Ayyub—Ubayd Allah ibn Zahr—Ali ibn Yazid—al-Qasim—Abu Umamah.

3 Abd Allah ibn Muhammad al-Razi—Abu-l-Abbas Muham-mad ibn Ishaq al-Sarraj—Ahmad ibn al-Fath.

4 Muhammad ibn Abd Allah ibn Shadhan.

5 Abu Muhammad Abd Allah ibn Muhammad al-Razi—Muhammad ibn Nasr al-Sa'igh—Marduyah al-Saigh.

8 ON FEAR (*KHAWF*)

1 Abu Bakr Muhammad ibn Ahmad ibn Dalluyah—Muhammad ibn Yazid—Amir ibn Abi-l-Furat—al-Masudi—Muhammad ibn Abd al-Rahman—Isa ibn Talhah.

2 Abu Muhammad Abd Allah ibn Muhammad ibn al-Hasan ibn al-Shurayfi—Abd Allah ibn Hashim—Yahya ibn Said al-Qattan—Shubah.

3 Muhammad ibn Ali al-Hiri—Mahfuz.

4 Abd Allah ibn Muhammad al-Razi—Abu Uthman.

5 Abu-l-Qasim al-Dimashqi.

6 Muhammad ibn Ali al-Nihawandi—ibn Fatik.

7 Ali ibn Ibrahim al-Ukbari.

8 al-Husayn ibn Ahmad al-Saffar—Muhammad ibn al-Musayyib—Hashim ibn Khalid.

9 Abd Allah ibn Muhammad ibn Abd al-Rahman.

10 Ahmad ibn Ubayd—Muhammad ibn Uthman—al-Qasim ibn Muhammad—Yahya ibn Yaman—Malik ibn Maghul—Abd al-Rahman ibn Said ibn Muwahhab.

11 Muhammad ibn al-Hasan—Abu-l-Qasim ibn Abi Musa—Muhammad ibn Ahmad—al-Razi.

12 Abu Bakr al-Razi.

9 ON HOPE (*RAJA*)

1 Ahmad ibn Ubayd al-Saffar—Amr ibn Muslim al-Thaqafi—al-Hasan ibn Khalid.

2 Ahmad ibn Ubayd—Bishr ibn Musa—Khalaf ibn al-Walid—Marwan ibn Muawiyah al-Fazawi—Abu Sufyan Turayf—Abd Allah ibn al-Harith.

3 Mansur ibn Abd Allah.

4 al-Nasrabadhi—Ibn Abi Hatim—Ali ibn Shahmardhan.

5 Abu-l-Abbas al-Baghdadi—al-Hasan ibn Safwan—Ibn Abi-l-Dunya.

6 Abu-l-Hasan al-Saffar—Abbas ibn Tamim—Yahya ibn Ayyub—Muslim ibn Salim—Kharijah ibn Masab—Zayd ibn Aslim—Ata ibn Yassar.

7 Yaqub ibn Ishaq—Ali ibn Harb—Abu Muawiyah—Muhammad ibn

Ubayd—al-Amash—Abu Salih.

8 Muhammad ibn Abd Allah ibn Shadhan—Abu Bakr al-Harbi.

9 Abu Zakariya Yahya ibn Muhammad al-Adib—al-Fadl ibn Sadaqah.

10 al-Amash—Abu Salih.

10 ON SORROW (*HUZN*)

1 Ahmad ibn Ubayd—Ali ibn Hubaysh—Ahmad ibn Isa—Ibn Wahb—Usamah ibn Zayd—Muhammad ibn Amr ibn Ata ibn Yassar.

2 Ali ibn Bukran—Muhammad ibn al-Marwazi—Ahmad ibn Abi Ruh—his father.

3 Muhammad ibn Ahmad al-Furra.

11 ON HUNGER (*JU*) AND ABANDNMENT OF LUST (*TARK AL-SHAHWAH*)

1 Ahmad ibn Ubayd al-Saffar—Abd Allah ibn Ayyub—Abd al-Walid al-Tayalisi—Abu Hashim, the companion of al-Zarani—Muhammad ibn Abd Allah.

2 Abd Allah ibn Ali al-Tamimi.

3 Ali bin al-Husayn al-Arjani—Abu Muhammad Abd Allah ibn Ahmad al-Istikhari in Mecca.

4 Muhammad ibn Bishr—al-Husayn ibn Mansur—Dawud ibn Muadh.

5 Abu Bakr al-Ghazzali—Muhammad ibn Ali.

6 Ali ibn al-Nuhas al-Misri—Harun al-Daqqaq—Abu Abd al-Rahman ibn al-Daraqish—Ahmad ibn Abil.

7 Muhammad al-Alawi—Ali ibn Ibrahim al-Qadi in Damascus Muhammad ibn Khalaf—Ahmad ibn Abi-l-Hawari.

8 Ali ibn al-Husayn al-Arjani.

9 Abd a-Aziz ibn al-Fadl—Abu Bakr al-Shathih.

10 Muhammad ibn Ahmad ibn Said al-Razi—al-Abbas ibn Hamzah—Ahmad ibn Abi-l-Hawari.

11 Abu-l-Faraj al-Wirthani—Abd Allah ibn Muhammad ibn Jafar—Ibrahim ibn Muhammad ibn al-Harith—Sulayman ibn Dawud—Jafar ibn Sulayman.

12 Mansur ibn Abd Allah al-Ispahani.

13 Ahmad ibn Mansur—Ibn Mukhallad—Abu-l-Husayn ibn Amr ibn al-Jahm.

14 Abu-l-Abbas Ahmad ibn Muhammad ibn Abd Allah ibn al-Farghani—Abu-l-Husayn al-Razi—Abu-l-Husayn al-Razi—Yusuf ibn al-Husayn.

12 ON HUMILITY (*KHUSHU*) AND SUBMISSIVENESS (*TAWADU*)

1 Abu-l-Fadl Sufyan ibn Muhammad al-Jawhari—Ali ibn al-Husayn—

Yahya ibn Hammad—Shubah—Aban ibn Thalab—Fadl al-Faqimi—Ibrahim al-Nakhai—Ulqamah ibn Qays.

2 Ahmad ibn Ubayd al-Basri—Muhammad ibn al-Fadl ibn Jabir—Abu Ibrahim—Ali ibn Mashar—Muslim al-Awar.

3 Ahmad ibn Ubayd al-Basri—Ibrahim ibn Abdullah—Abu-l-Hasan Ali ibn Zayd al-Faraidi—Muhammad ibn Kuthayr (he was Masisi)—Harun ibn Hayyan ibn Husayf—Said ibn Jabir.

4 Abd Allah ibn Muhammad al-Razi—Muhammad ibn Nasr al-Saigh—Marduyah al-Saigh.

5 Ali ibn Ahmad ibn Ali ibn Jafar—Ibrahim ibn Fatik.

6 Abu Bakr Muhammad ibn Abd Allah.

7 al-Hasan al-Sawiyy.

8 Muhammad ibn Ahmad ibn Harun—Muhammad ibn al-Abbas al-Dimashqi—Ahmad ibn Abil-Hawari.

9 Ahmad ibn Muhammad al-Furra—Abd Allah ibn Munazil.

13 ON OPPOSITION TO THE EGO (*MUKHALAFAT AL-NAFS*) AND REMEMBERING ITS FAILINGS (*DHIKR UYUBIHA*)

1 Ahmad ibn Ubayd—Tamam—Muhammad ibn Muawiyah al-Nisapuri—Ali ibn Abi Ali ibn Utbah ibn Abi Lahab—Muhammad ibn al-Munkadir.

2 Abu Bakr al-Razi—Abu Umar al-Anmati.

3 Ibrahim ibn Muqassim in Baghdad—Ibn Ata.

4 Mansur ibn Abd Allah—Abu Umar al-Anmati.

5 al-Husayn ibn Yahya—Jafar ibn Nusayr.

6 Abu-l-Abbas al-Baghdadi—Jafar ibn Nusayr—Junayd.

7 Muhammad ibn Abd Allah al-Razi.

14 ON ENVY (*HASAD*)

1 Ahmad ibn Ubayd al-Basri—Ismail ibn al-Fadl—Yahya ibn Mukhallad—Muafi ibn Imran—al-Harith ibn Shahab—Muabbid—Abu Qalabah.

15 ON BACKBITING (*GHIBAH*)

1 Abu Bakr Muhammad ibn al-Husayn ibn al-Hasan ibn al-Jalil—Ali ibn al-Hasan—Ishaq ibn Isa ibn Bint Dawud ibn Hind—Muhammad ibn Abi Hamid—Musa ibn Wirdan.

2 Ahmad ibn Ubayd al-Basri—Ahmad ibn Amr al-Qitwani—Sahl ibn Uthman al-Askari—al-Rabi ibn Badr—Aban.

3 Abu Tahir Muhammad ibn Asyad al-Raqqi—Jafar ibn Muhammad ibn

Nusayr.

4 Abu Tahir al-Isfarayani.

16 ON TRUST IN GOD (*TAWAKKUL*)

1 Abd Allah ibn Jafar ibn Ahmad al-Ispahani—Yunus ibn Habib ibn Abdul-Qahir—Abu Dawud al-Tayalisi—Hammad ibn Maslamah—Asim ibn Buhadilah—Zirr ibn Habash.

2 Abu Nasr al-Sarraj—Abu Bakr al-Wajihi.

3 Mansur ibn Abd Allah—Abu Abd Allah al-Shirazi.

4 Abu Bakr Muhammad ibn Ahmad al-Balkhi—Muhammad ibn Hamid.

5 Ahmad ibn Ubayd al-Basri—Ghilan ibn Abd-l-Samad—Ismail ibn Masud al-Jahdari—Khalid ibn Yahya—his uncle al-Mughirah ibn Abi Qurrah.

6 Muhammad ibn Ali ibn al-Husayn—Abd Allah ibn Muhammad ibn al-Samit.

7 Muhammad ibn Ahmad al-Farisi.

8 Abu Faraj al-Wirthani—Ahmad ibn Muhammad al-Qirmisini—al-Kattani.

9 Muhammad ibn Jafar ibn Muhammad—Abu Bakr al-Bardhai.

10 Said ibn Ahmad ibn Muhammad—Muhammad ibn Ahmad ibn Sahl—Said ibn Uthman al-Khayyat.

11 Abd Allah ibn Muhammad al-Muallim—Abd Allah ibn Munazil.

12 Abd Allah al-Razi.

13 Muhammad ibn Muhammad ibn Ghalib.

14 Abd Allah ibn Ali—Mansur ibn Ahmad al-Harbi—Ibn Abi Shaykh.

15 Abd Allah ibn Ali.

16 Ahmad ibn Ali ibn Jafar—Jafar al-Khuldi.

17 Abu-l-Abbas al-Baghdadi.

18 Abu-l-Abbas al-Baghdadi—Muhammad ibn Abd Allah al-Farghani.

19 Abu Bakr Muhammad ibn Abd Allah ibn Shadhan—al-Khawwas.

20 Muhammad ibn Abd Allahh al-Waiz—Khayr al-Nassaj.

21 Muhammad ibn al-Hasan al-Makhzumi—Ahmad ibn Muhammad ibn Salih—Muhammad ibn Abdun.

22 Nasr ibn Abi Nasr al-Attar—Ali ibn Muhammad al-Misri.

23 Muhammad ibn al-Hasan al-Makhzumi—Ibn al-Maliki.

24 Mansur ibn Abd Allah—Abu Sudan al-Tahirti.

17 ON CONTENTMENT (*QANAAH*)

1 Abu Amr Muhammad ibn Jafar ibn Matar—Muhammad ibn Musa al-Hilwani—Abd Allah ibn Ibrahim al-Ghifari—Munkadir ibn Muhammad—his father.

2 Muhammad ibn Ubayd al-Basri—Abd Allah ibn Ayyub al-Muqarri—Abu-l-Rabi al-Zahrani—Ismail ibn Zakariya—Abu Raja— Barad ibn Sinan—Makhul—Wathilah ibn al-Asqa.

3 Abd Allah ibn Muhammad al-Sharani—Ishaq ibn Ibrahim ibn Abi Hassan al-Anmati—Ahmad ibn Abil-Hawari.

4 Nasr ibn Muhammad—Sulayman ibn Abi Sulayman—Abu-l-Qasim ibn Abi Nizar.

5 Muhammad ibn Farhan of Samarrah.

18 ON THANKFULNESS (*SHUKR*)

1 Abu-l-Hasan al-Saffar—al-Asqati—Munjab—Yahya ibn Yala—Abu Khabbab.

2 Master Abu Sahl al-Suluki—al-Murtaish.

3 Muhammad ibn al-Husayn—al-Hasan ibn Yahya—Jafar.

19 ON CERTAINTY (*YAQIN*)

1 Abu Bakr Ahmad ibn Mahmud ibn Kharzad al-Ahwazi—Ahmad ibn Sahl ibn Ayyub—Khalid, known as ibn Zayd—Sufyan al-Thawri—Sharik ibn Abd Allah—Sufyan ibn Utaybah—Sulayman al-Timi—Khaythamah.

2 Abu Jafar Muhammad ibn Ahmad ibn Said al-Razi—Ayyash ibn Hamzah—Ahmad ibn Abi-l-Hawari.

3 Abu-l-Abbas al-Baghdadi.

4 Abd Allah ibn Ali—Abu Jafar al-Ispahani.

5 al-Husayn ibn Yahya—Jafar.

6 Mansur ibn Abd Allah.

7 Abu Nasr al-Ispahani—Muhammad ibn Isa.

8 Abu Bakr al-Razi—Abu Uthman al-Admi.

20 ON PATIENCE (*SABR*)

1 Ahmad ibn Ubayd al-Basri—Ahmad ibn Ahmad ibn Ali al-Kharraz—Asyad ibn Zayd—Masud ibn Sad—al-Ziyat—Abu Hurayrah.

2 Ahmad ibn Ubayd—Ahmad ibn Umar—Muhammad ibn Mardas—Yusuf ibn Atiyyah—Ata ibn Abi Maymunah.

3 Al-Husayn ibn Yahya—Jafar ibn Muhammad.

4 Abu Jafar al-Razi—Iyyashah.

5 Abu Bakr al-Razi.

6 Muhammad ibn Abd Allah ibn Shadhan.

7 Muhammad ibn Ahmad ibn Tahir al-Sufi—Muhammad ibn Ali al-Tijani—Muhammad ibn Ismail al-Bukhari—Musa ibn Ismail—Suwayd ibn Hatim—Abd Allah ibn Ubayd—Umayr—his father.

21 ON VIGILANCE (*MURAQABAH*)

1 Abu Iwanah Yaqub ibn Ishaq—Yusuf ibn Muslim—Khalid ibn Yazid—Ismail ibn Abi Khalid—Qays ibn Abi Hazim.

2 Abu Bakr al-Razi.

3 Abu-l-Husayn al-Farisi.

4 Abu-l-Qasim al-Baghdadi.

5 Abd Allah al-Razi.

6 Muhammad ibn Abd Allah—Abu Jafar al-Saydalani.

22 ON SATISFACTION (*RIDA*)

1 Ahmad ibn Ubayd al-Basri—al-Karimi—Yaqub ibn Ismail al-Sallal—Abu Asim al-Abadani—al-Fadl ibn Isa al-Raqqashi—Muhammad ibn al-Munkadir.

2 Abu Jafar al-Razi—al-Abbas ibn Hamzah—Ibn Abi-l-Hawari.

3 Abu Jafar al-Razi—al-Abbas ibn Hamzah—Ibn Abi-l-Hawari.

4 Abu-l-Abbas al-Baghdadi—Muhammad ibn Ahmad ibn Sahl—Said ibn Uthman.

5 Muhammad ibn Jafar al-Baghdadi—Ismail ibn Muhammad al-Saffar.

6 Abd Allah al-Razi—Ibn Abi Hassan al-Anmati—Ahmad ibn Abil-Hawari.

7 Abu-l-Husayn al-Farisi.

8 Ahmad ibn Ali—al-Hasan ibn Alawayh.

9 Abu Amr ibn Hamdan—Abd Allah ibn Shatruyah—Bishr ibn al-Hakam—Abdul-Aziz ibn Muhammad—Yazid ibn al-Hadi—Muhammad ibn Ibrahim—Amir ibn Sad.

23 ON SERVANTHOOD (*UBUDIYAH*)

1 Ahmad ibn Ubayd al-Saffar—Ubayd ibn Sharik—Yahya—Malik—Habib ibn Abdul-Rahman—Hafs ibn Asim—Umar ibn al-Khattab—Abu Said al-Khudri.

2 Abu-l-Abbas al-Baghdadi—Jafar ibn Muhammad ibn Nusayr—Ibn Masruq.

3 Abd Allahh al-Muallim.

4 Muhammad ibn al-Husayn—Jafar ibn Nusayr—Ibn Masruq.

5 Abu Jafar al-Razi.

6 Abu-l-Husayn al-Farisi.

7 Muhammad ibn Abd Allah ibn Shadhan—al-Kattani.

8 Abu Bakr Muhammad ibn Abd Allah ibn Shadhan—al-Jurayri.

24 ON WILL POWER (*IRADAH*)

1 Ahmad ibn Ubayd—Hisham ibn Ali—al-Hakam ibn Aslam—Ismail ibn Jafar—Hamid.

2 Muhammad ibn Abd Allah—Abu Bakr al-Sabbak.

3 Abu Bakr al-Razi.

4 al-Husayn ibn Ahmad ibn Jafar—Jafar ibn Nusayr.

5 Abd Allah ibn Ali.

6 Abbas ibn Abu-l-Sahw.

7 Abu Qasim al-Razi.

8 Muhammad ibn al-Husayn.

9 Muhammad ibn Khalid—Jafar.

26 ON SINCERITY (*IKHLAS*)

1 Ahmad ibn Ubayd al-Basri—Jafar ibn Muhammad al-Gharyani—Abu Talut—Hani ibn Abu-l-Rahman ibn Abu Uqbah—Ibrahim ibn Abi Iblah al-Uqayli—Atiyyah ibn Wishah.

2 Ali ibn Said and Ahmad ibn Muhammad ibn Zakariya—Ali ibn Ibrahim al-Shaqiqi—Muhammad ibn Jafar al-Khussaf—Ahmad ibn Bashshar—Abu Yaqub al-Shurayti—Ahmad ibn Ghassan—Abdul-Wahid ibn Zayd—al-Hasan—Hudhayfah—the Prophet (ﷺ)—Gabriel (a.s.). (The transmission is given with each transmitter asking the preceding one, "What is sincerity?")

3 Abd Allah ibn Ali—al-Wajihi—Abu Ali al-Rudhbari—Ruwaym.

4 Abu-l-Husayn al-Farisi—Muhammad ibn al-Husayn—Ali ibn Abu-l-Hamid.

5 Ali ibn Bundar al-Sufi—Abd Allah ibn Mahmud—Muhammad ibn Abd Rabbihi.

6 Muhammad ibn Muhammad ibn Abdul-Rahim—Abu Talib Muhammad ibn Zakariyya al-Muqaddisi—Abu Qarsafah Muhammad ibn Abdul-Wahhab al-Asqalani—Zakariya ibn Nafi—Muhammad ibn Yazid al-Qurataysi—Ismail ibn Abu Khalid.

7 Muhammad ibn Abd Allah ibn Shadhan—Abdul-Razzaq.

8 al-Nasrabadhi—Abu-l-Jahm—Ibn Abi-l-Hawari—Abd Allah ibn Ali—al-Wajihi—Abu Ali al-Rudhbari—Ruwaym—Abu-l-Husayn al-Farisi.

27 ON TRUTHFULNESS (*SIDQ*)

1 Abd Allah ibn Jafar ibn Ahmad al-Ispahani—Abu Bishr Yunus ibn Habib—Abu Dawud al-Tiyalisi—Shubah—Mansur—Abu W'il.

2 Mansur ibn Abdullah—al-Farghani.

3 Abu-l-Abbas al-Baghdadi—Jafar ibn Nusayr—al-Juraryi.

4 Mansur ibn Abdullah—Jafar al-Khawwas.

5 Abu-l-Abbas ibn Muqassim—Jafar al-Khawwas.

28 ON SHAME (*HAYAH*)

1 Abu Sahl Ahmad ibn Muhammad ibn Ziyad al-Nahawi, in Baghdad—Ibrahim ibn Muhammad ibn al-Haytham—Musa ibn Hayyan—al-Muqaddimi—Ubayd Allah ibn Umar—Nafi.

2 Abu Uthman Amr ibn Abd Allah al-Basri—Abu Ahmad Muhammad ibn Abd al-Wahhab—Yala ibn Ubayd—Aban ibn Ishaq—al-Sabah ibn Muhammad—Murrah al-Hamadhani.

3 Abu Nasr al-Waziri—Muhammad ibn Abd Allah ibn Muhammad—al-Ghulabi—Muhammad ibn Mukhallid.

4 Abu Bakr al-Razi.

5 Abu-l-Faraj al-Wirthani—Muhammad ibn Ahmad ibn Yaqub—Muhammad ibn Abd-l-Malik.

6 Abu-l-Abbas al-Baghdadi—Ahmad ibn Salih—Muhammad ibn Abdun—Abu-l-Abbas al-Muaddib.

7 Muhammad ibn Abd Allah ibn Shadhan.

8 Abd Allah ibn al-Husayn—Abu Muhammad al-Baladhari—Abu Abd Allah al-Umri—Ahmad ibn Abi-l-Hawari.

9 Abd Allah ibn Ahmad ibn Jafar—Zanjuyah al-Lubbad—Ali ibn al-Husayn al-Hilali—Ibrahim ibn al-Ashath.

10 Muhammad ibn Abd Allah al-Sufi (r.a.)—Abu-l-Abbas ibn al-Walid al-Zuzani—Muhammad ibn Ahmad al-Juzajani.

29 ON FREEDOM (*HURRIYAH*)

1 Ahmad ibn Ubayd al-Basri—Ibn Abi Qummash—Muhammad ibn Salih ibn al-Nitah—Naim ibn Muwarri ibn Tawbah—Ismail al-Makki—Amr ibn Dinar—Tawus.

2 Abu Muhammad al-Muraghi—al-Raqqi.

3 Abu Bakr al-Razi—Abu Amr al-Anmati.

4 Abu Bakr al-Razi.

5 Muhammad ibn Ibrahim ibn al-Fadl—Muhammad ibn al-Rumi.

6 Abd Allah ibn Uthman ibn Yahya—Ali ibn Muhammad al-Misri—Yusuf ibn Musa—Ibn Khubayq—Muhammad ibn Abd Allah—Ibn Abi Qummash—Muhammad ibn Salih ibn al-Nitah—Naim ibn Muwarri ibn Taw

30 ON REMEMBRANCE (*DHIKR*)

1 Abu Ali al-Husayn ibn Safwan al-Bardhai—Abu Bakr Abd Allah ibn Muhammad ibn Abi-l-Dunya—Harun ibn Maruf—Anas ibn Ayad—Abd Allah ibn Said ibn Abi Hind—Ziyad ibn Abu Ziyad—Abu Buhayrah.

2 Yaqub ibn Ishaq Ibrahim—al-Dayri—Abd-l-Razzaq—Muammar—al-Zuhri—Thabit.

3 Ahmad ibn Ubayd—Muadh—his father—Hamid.

4 Abd Allah ibn al-Husayn—Abu Muhammad al-Baladhari—Abd-l-Rahman ibn Bakr.

5 Abd Allah al-Muallim.

6 Abu Ali ibn Safwan—Ibn Abu-l-Dunya—al-Haytham ibn Kharijah—Ismail ibn Ayyash—Amr ibn Abd Allah—Khalid ibn Abd Allah ibn Safwan.

7 Muhammad al-Furra.

8 Abd Allah ibn Musa al-Silami.

9 Muhammad ibn Abd Allah.

10 Abd Allah ibn Ali—Faris.

11 Abd al-Rahman ibn Abd Allah al-Dhabiyani—Jurayri—Junayd.

12 al-Husayn ibn Yahya—Jafar ibn Nusayr.

31 ON SPIRITUAL CHIVALRY (*FUTUWAH*)

1 Ahmad ibn Ubayd—Ismail ibn al-Fadl—Yaqub ibn Hamid ibn Kasib—Ibn Abu Hazim—Abd Allah ibn Amir al-Aslami—Abd-l-Rahman ibn Hurmuz al-Araj—Abu Hurayrah.

2 Muhammad ibn al-Husayn—Abu Jafar al-Farghani.

3 Abd Allah ibn Muhammad al-Razi—Muhammad ibn Nasr ibn Mansur al-Saigh—Muhammad ibn Marduyah al-Sa'igh.

4 Ali ibn Umar al-Hafiz—Abu Sahl ibn Ziyad.

5 Abu Bakr al-Razi.

6 Abu Ali al-Farisi.

32 ON SPIRITUAL INSIGHT (*FIRASAH*)

1 Ahmad ibn Ali ibn al-Husayn al-Razi—Muhammad ibn Ahmad ibn al-Sakan—Musa ibn Dawud—Muhammad ibn Kuthayr al-Kufi—Amr ibn Qays—Atiyyah.

2 Muhammad ibn Abd Allah.

3 Mansur ibn Abd Allah—al-Khuldi.

4 Abd Allah ibn Ali.

5 Abd Allah ibn Ibrahim ibn al-Il'.

6 Muhammad ibn al-Husayn al-Baghdadi—Jafar ibn Muhammad ibn Nusayr.

33 ON MORAL CHARACTER (*KHULUQ*)

1 Abu-l-Hasan al-Saffar al-Basri—Hisham ibn Muhammad ibn Ghalib—Mualla ibn Mahdi—Bashshar ibn Ibrahim al-Numayri—Ghilan ibn Jarir.

2 al-Husayn ibn Ahmad ibn Jafar.

3 Muhammad ibn Abd Allah al-Razi—Abu Muhammad al-Jurayri—

Junayd.

4 Abu Nasr al-Sarraj al-Tusi—al-Wajihi.

5 Abu-l-Hasan al-Saffar al-Basri—Muadh ibn al-Muththani—Yahya ibn Muanna—Marwan al-Fizari—Yazid ibn Kaysan—Abu Hazim.

34 ON BOUNTIFULNESS (*JU*) AND GENEROSITY (*SAKHAH*)

1 Ahmad ibn Ubayd—al-Hasan ibn al-Abbas—Sahl—Said ibn Muslim—Yahya ibn Said—Muhammad ibn Ibrahim—Ulqamah.

2 Abu Bakr al-Razi.

35 ON JEALOUSY (*GHAYRAH*)

1 Abu Ahmad Hamzah ibn al-Abbas al-Bazzaz in Baghdad—Muhammad ibn Ghalib ibn Harb—Abd Allah ibn Muslim—Muhammad ibn al-Firat—Ibrahim al-Hijri—Abu-l-Ahwas.

2 Ahmad ibn Ubayd al-Saffar—Ali ibn al-Hasan ibn Bunnan—Abd Allah ibn Raja—Harb ibn Shaddad—Yahya ibn Abu Kuthayr—Abu Salamah.

3 Abu Nasr al-Ispahani.

4 Abu Zayd al-Marwazi (r.a.)—Ibrahim ibn Shayban.

36 ON SAINTHOOD (*WILAYAH*)

1 Abd Allah ibn Ada al-Hafiz—Abu Bakr Muhammad ibn Harun ibn Hamid—Muhammad ibn Harun al-Muqarri—Hammad al-Khayyat—Abd-l-Wahid ibn Maymun, the client of Urwah—Urwah.

2 Mansur ibn Abd Allah—his uncle, al-Bistami—his father.

3 Mansur ibn Abd Allah—Abu Ali al-Rudhbari.

37 ON SUPPLICATION (*DUA*)

1 Abu-l-Husayn al-Saffar al-Basri—Muhammad ibn Ahmad ibn Abdan al-Awdi—Kamil—Ibn Luhayah—Khalid ibn Yazid—Said ibn Abi Hilal.

2 Abu Amr Uthman ibn Ahmad al-Maruf with ibn al-Sammak—Muhammad ibn Abd Rabbih al-Hadrami—Bishr ibn Abdul-Malik—Musa ibn al-Hajjaj—Malik ibn Dinar—al-Hasan.

3 Abu Bakr al-Razi—Abu Bakr al-Harbi.

4 Abu-l-Fath Nasr ibn Ahmad ibn Abd al-Malik—Abd al-Rahman ibn Ahmad.

38 ON SPIRITUAL POVERTY (*FAQR*)

1 Abu Bakr Muhammad ibn Jafar ibn Muhammad ibn al-Haytham al-Anbari—Jafar ibn Muhammad al-Saigh—Qubaysah—Sufyan—Muhammad ibn Amr ibn Ulqamah—Abu Salamah.

2 Abu Ahmad Hamzah ibn al-Abbas al-Bazzaz, in Baghdad—Muhammad ibn Ghalib ibn Harb—Abd Allah ibn Maslamah—Muhammad ibn Abi-l-Furat—Ibrahim al-Hijri—Abu-l-Ahwas.

3 Ibrahim ibn Ahmad ibn Muhammad ibn Raja al-Fizari—Abd Allah ibn Muhammad ibn Jafar ibn Ahmad ibn Khushaysh al-Baghdadi—Uthman ibn Muabbid—Umar ibn Rashid—Malik—Nafi—Ibn Umar.

4 Abd-l-Wahid ibn Bakr—Abu Bakr ibn Saman—Abu Bakr ibn Masud.

5 Mansur ibn Abd Allah.

6 Muhammad ibn Ahmad al-Furra—Zakariya al-Nakhshabi.

7 Abd Allah ibn Ata—Abu Jafar al-Farghani.

8 Muhammad ibn al-Hasan al-Baghdadi—Muhammad ibn Abd Allah al-Farghani.

9 Mansur ibn Abd Allah—Jafar.

10 Ahmad ibn Ali.

11 Abu Bakr al-Razi—al-Jurayri.

12 Abu Abd Allah al-Razi.

13 Abd Allah ibn Muhammad al-Dimashqi.

14 Hilal ibn Muhammad—al-Naffash.

15 Ali ibn Bundar al-Sayrafi—Mahfuz.

16 Al-Husayn ibn Ahmad.

17 Abu-l-Faraj al-Wirthani—Fatimah, the sister of Abu Ali al-Rudhbari.

18 al-Husayn ibn Yusuf al-Qazwini—Ibrahim ibn Muwallid—al-Husayn ibn Ali.

19 Mansur ibn Abd Allah.

20 Abu Nasr al-Harawi.

21 Abu Abd Allah al-Razi.

22 Abd-l-Wahid ibn Bakr—al-Duqqi.

23 Muhammad ibn Ahmad al-Furra.

24 Abd Allah ibn Ibrahim ibn al-Ala.

25 Abd-l-Wahid ibn Ahmad—Abu Bakr al-Jawwal.

26 Abu Ali al-Husayn ibn Yusuf al-Qazwini—Ibrahim ibn al-Muwallid—al-Husayn ibn Ali.

27 Mansur ibn Abd Allah.

28 Abd Allah ibn Ali al-Sufi.

29 Muhammad ibn Abd Allah al-Tabari.

39 ON SUFISM (*TASAWWUF*)

1 Abd Allah ibn Yahya al-Talhi—al-Husayn ibn Jafar—Abd Allah ibn Nawfal—Abu Bakr ibn Ayyash—Yazid ibn Abi Ziyad.

2 Abd Allah ibn Ali al-Tamimi.

3 Yusuf, father of Abd-l-Rahman al-Ispahani—Abu Abd Allah Muhammad ibn Ammar al-Hamdani—Abu Muhammad al-Murash—his shaykh.

4 Abd al-Rahman ibn Muhammad al-Farisi—Abu-l-Fatik.

5 Abd Allah ibn Muhammad—Jafar ibn Muhammad ibn Nusayr—Abu Ali al-Warraq.

6 Abu Nasr al-Sarraj al-Tusi—Muhammad ibn al-Fadl—Ali ibn Abdul-Rahim al-Wasiti.

7 Abu Nasr al-Sarraj.

8 Abu Nasr al-Sarraj.

9 al-Husayn ibn Ahmad al-Razi—Abu Bakr al-Misri.

40 ON MODEL BEHAVIOR (*ADAB*)

1 Abu-l-Hasan al-Saffar al-Basri—Ghanam—Abd al-Samad ibn al-Numan—Abd al-Malik ibn al-Husayn—Abd al-Malik ibn Umayr—Masab ibn Shaybah.

2 Abu Nasr al-Sarraj— Ahmad ibn Muhammad al-Basri.

3 Abd Allah al-Razi.

4 Muhammad ibn Ahmad ibn Said—al-Abbas ibn Hamzah—Ahmad ibn Abu-l-Hawari—al-Walid ibn Utbah.

5 Abu-l-Tayyib ibn al-Farhan.

PART IV: OTHER SUFI CHARACTERISTICS
1 ON SUFI RULES OF TRAVEL

1 Ahmad ibn Ubayd al-Basri—Muhammad ibn al-Faraj al-Azraq—Hajjaj—Ibn Jurayh—Abu-l-Zubayr—Ali al-Azadi

2 Muhammad ibn Ali al-Uluwi—Jafar ibn Muhammad

3 Muhammad ibn Ahmad al-Najjar

4 Ali ibn Abd Allah al-Tamimi

5 Abd Allah ibn Ali

6 Abd Allah ibn Muhammad al-Dimashqi—Ibrahim ibn al-Muwallid—Abu Ahmad al-Saghir

2 ON HUMAN COMPANIONSHIP FOR GOD'S SAKE

1 Ahmad ibn Ubayd al-Basri—Yahya ibn Muhammad al-Jiyani—Uthman ibn Abd Allah al-Qurashi—Naim ibn Salim.

2 Abu Nasr al-Sarraj

3 Abu Nasr al-Sarraj—al-Duqqi

4 Abu Nasr al-Sarraj—al-Duqqi

5 Muhammad ibn al-Hasan al-Alawi—Abd al-Rahman ibn Hamdan—Abu-l-Qasim ibn Munabbih

6 Muhammad ibn Ahmad al-Abadi-Abu Iwanah—Yunus— Khalaf ibn Tamim Abu-l-Ahwas

7 Abd Allah ibn al-Muallim

3 ON MONOTHEISM: AFFIRMATION OF UNITY (*TAWHID*)

1 Ahmad ibn Mahmud ibn Kharzad—Masih ibn Hatim al-Ukli—al-Hajabi—Abd-Allah ibn Abd al-Wahhab—Hammad ibn Zayd—Sad ibn Sad ibn Hatim—al-Antaki—ibn Abi Sadaqah—Muhammad ibn Sirin

2 Muhammad ibn Abd-Allah ibn Shadhan—Yusuf ibn al-Husayn

Ahmad ibn Muhammad ibn Zakariya—Ahmad ibn Ata— Abd Allah ibn Salih

3 Abu-l-Husayn ibn Muqassim

4 Abu Bakr ibn Shadhan

5 Mansur ibn Abd Allah—Abu-l-Husayn al-Anbari

6 Ahmad ibn Said al-Basri, in Kufah—Ibn al-Arabi

7 Mansur ibn Abd Allah

8 Ali ibn Muhammad al-Qazwini

4 ON THE STATES OF THE GREAT SUFIS UPON THEIR DEATHS

1 Abu-l-Husayn Ali ibn Muhammad ibn Uqbah al-Shaybani in Kufah—al-Khidr ibn Aban al-Hashimi—Abu Hudbah

2 Abu-l-Abbas al-Asamm—al-Khidr ibn Aban al-Hashimi—Suwar—Jafar—Thabit

3 Abu Nasr al-Sarraj

4 Abd Allah ibn Ali al-Tamimi—Ahmad ibn Ata

5 Abd Allah ibn Ali al-Tamimi

6 Abu -l-Hasan ibn Abd Allah al-Tarsusi—Alush al-Dinawari

7 Abu Nasr al-Tusi—one of his companions

8 Abu Nasr al-Sarraj—al-Wajihi

9 Abd Allah ibn Ali al-Tamimi

10 Abu Abd Allah ibn Khafif

11 Mansur ibn Abd Allah—Abu Jafar ibn Qays, in Egypt

12 Abu Bakr al-Razi

13 Abd Allah ibn Muhammad al-Razi

5 ON THE HEART'S DIRECT KNOWLEDGE OF GOD (*MARIFAH BILLAH*)

1 Muhammad ibn al-Qasim al-Ataki—Muhammad ibn Usharis—Sulayman ibn Isa al-Shajri—Ubbad ibn Kuthayr—Hanzalah ibn Abi Sufyan—al-Qasim ibn Muhammad.

2 Ahmad ibn Muhammad ibn Zayd.

3 Muhammad ibn Muhammad ibn Abd al-Wahhab.

4 Abu-l-Abbas al-Dinawari.

5 Abu Jafar Muhammad ibn Ahmad ibn Said al-Razi—Ayyash ibn Hamzah—Ahmad ibn Abil-Hawari.

6 Muhammad ibn Ahmad ibn Said—Muhammad ibn Ahmad ibn Sahl—Said ibn Uthman.

7 Abu Bakr al-Razi.

8 Abu-l-Husayn al-Farisi.

9 Abu-l-Husayn al-Farisi.

10 Muhammad ibn Abd Allah ibn Shadhan.

11 Abu Nasr al-Sarraj—al-Wajihi—Abu Ali al-Rudhbari.

12 Ali ibn Bundar al-Sayrafi.

13 Muhammad ibn Abd Allah.

14 Abd Allah al-Razi.

15 Ahmad ibn Ali ibn Jafar.

6 ON LOVE OF GOD (*MAHABBAH*)

1 Abu Iwanah Yaqub ibn Ishaq—al-Sulami—Abdul-Razzaq—Muammar—Hummam ibn Munabbih.

2 Ahmad ibn Ubayd al-Sighar al-Basri—Abd Allah ibn Ayyub—al-Hasan ibn Musa—al-Haytham ibn Kharijah—al-Hasan ibn Yahya—Sadaqah al-Dimashqi—Hisham al-Kattani.

3 Ahmad ibn Ubayd—Ubayd ibn Sharik—Yahya—Malik—Suhayl ibn Abi Salih—his father.

4 Mansur ibn Abd Allah.

5 Abu-l-Husayn al-Farisi.

6 Muhammad ibn Ali al-Alawi—Jafar.

7 Abu Said al-Arjani.

8 Ahmad ibn Ali—Ibrahim ibn Fatik—Junayd.

9 Ahmad ibn Ali—Abbas ibn Asim—Junayd.

10 Ahmad ibn Ali.

11 Mansur ibn Abd Allah—al-Nahrajuri.

12 Abu Ali ibn Ahmad ibn al-Qasim—Hamim ibn Hammam—Ibrahim ibn al-Harith—Abdul-Rahman ibn Affan—Abu Ali ibn Ayyub.

13 The Qadi Ahmad ibn Mahmud Harzad—al-Husayn ibn Hammad ibn Fudalah—Yahya ibn Habib—Marhum ibn Abd al-Aziz—Sufyan al-Thawri—al-Ammash—Abu Wail.

14 Abd Allah al-Razi—Abu Uthman al-Hiri.

15 Abu Bakr al-Razi—Abu-l-Qasim al-Jawhari.

7 On Longing (*SHAWQ*)

1 Ahmad ibn Ubayd al-Basri—Ibn Abi Qummash—Ismail ibn Zurarah—Hammad ibn Yazid—Ata ibn al-Saib.

2 Abu-l-Abbas al-Hashimi, writing in Al-Bayda—Muhammad ibn Abd Allah al-Khuzai—Abd Allah al-Ansari.

3 Abd Allah ibn Ali—Jafar—Junayd.

4 Abd Allah ibn Jafar—Muhammad ibn Umar al-Ramli—Muhammad ibn Jafar al-Imam—Ishaq ibn Ibrahim—Marhum.

8 On Showing Consideration for the Hearts of the Shaykhs and Abandoing Opposition to Them

1 Ahmad ibn Ubayd al-Basri—Abu Salim al-Qazzaz—Yazid ibn Bayan—Abu Rijal

2 Abd Allah ibn Ali al-Tusi—Abd Allah al-Dinawari—al-Hasan al-Damghani—his uncle al-Bistami

9 On Spiritual Concert

1 Ahmad ibn Ubayd al-Saffar—al-Harith ibn Abi Asamah— Abu-l-Nasr—Shubah—Hamid

2 Muhammad ibn Jafar ibn Muhammad ibn Matar—al-Hubab ibn Muhammad al-Tustari—Abu al-Ashath— Muhammad ibn Bakr al-Bursani—Shubah—Hisham ibn Urwah—Urwah

3 Uthman ibn Umar al-Dammi—Abu Kamil—Abu Iwanah— al-Ajlah—Abu-l-Zubayr—Jabir

4 Ahmad ibn Mahmud ibn Khurzadh—Husayn ibn al-Harith al-Ahwazi—Salamah ibn Said—Sadaqah bint Abi Imran— Ulqamah ibn Murathid—Zadhan

5 Ahmad ibn Ubayd—Uthman ibn Umar al-Dabbi—Abu-l-Rabi Abd al-Salam ibn Hashim—Abd-Allah ibn Muharraz— Qatadah

6 Ahmad ibn Ubayd—Muhammad ibn Yunus al-Karimi—al-Dahhak ibn Mukhallid—Abu Asim—Shubayb ibn Bishr ibn al-Bakhli

7 Ahmad ibn Ubayd—Ibn Milhan—Yahya ibn Bikir—al-Layth—Uqayl—Ibn Shahab—Abu Salamah

8 Abd Allah ibn Ali al-Sarraj

9 Muhammad ibn Abd Allah ibn Abd al-Aziz

10 Abu Nasr al-Sufi—Al-Wajihi—Abu Ali al-Rudhbari

11 Husayn ibn Ahmad ibn Jafar—Abu Bakr ibn Mumshad

12 Abu Nasr al-Sarraj al-Tusi—Abu-l-Tayyib Ahmad ibn Muqatil al-Akki

13 Abd al-Wahid ibn Bakr

14 Abd Allah ibn Ali

15 Abu-l-Faraj al-Shirazi—Abu Ali al-Rudhbari

16 Abu Bakr al-Razi

17 Abd Allah ibn Muhammad ibn Abd al-Rahman al-Razi

18 Abu Abd Allah al-Baghdadi—Abu Said al-Ramli

19 Abd Allah ibn Ali al-Sufi—al-Raqqi

20 Abu Nasr al-Sarraj

21 Abu Nasr al-Sarraj

22 Abu Nasr al-Sarraj—one of his students

23 Abd Allah ibn Ali al-Tusi—al-Raqqi

24 Abd Allah ibn Ali al-Tusi

25 Abu Nasr al-Sarraj

26 Abd Allah ibn Ali al-Sufi—Ali ibn al-Husayn ibn Muhammad ibn Ahmad, in Basra

27 Ali ibn Tahir—Abd Allah ibn Sahl

28 Abd Allah ibn Ali

29 Ahmad ibn Ubayd al-Basri—Ismail ibn al-Fadl—Yahya ibn Yala al-Razi—Hafs ibn Umar al-Umri—Abu Amr Uthman ibn Badr—Harun ibn Hamzah—al-Ghadafira—Said ibn Jubayr.

30 Muhammad ibn Abd Allah ibn Shadhan—Abu Bakr al-Nihawandi—Ali al-Saih

31 Mansur ibn Abd Allah al-Ispahani

50 ON THE MIRACLE OF THE SAINTS

1 Ammar ibn Raja—Wahb ibn Jarir—Jarir—Muhammad ibn Sirin

2 Husayn ibn Muhammad ibn al-Marwadhi—Jarir ibn Hazim — Muhammad ibn Sirin

3 Abu Iwanah Yaqub ibn Ibrahim ibn Ishaq—Muhammad ibn Awn—Zayd ibn Abd al-Samad al-Dimashqi—Abd al-Karim ibn al-Haytham—al-Diraquli—Abu-l-Khusayb ibn al-Mustanir (and?) al-Masisi—Abu-l-Yaman—Shuayb—al-Zuhri—Salim

4 Abu Iwanah—Yunus ibn Abd al-Ala—Ibn Wahb—Yunus ibn Yazid—Ibn Shahab—Said ibn al-Musayyib

5 Ahmad ibn Ubayd al-Saffar—Abu Muslim—Amr ibn Marzuq—Abd al-Aziz ibn Abi Salamah al-Majishun—Wahb ibn Kaysan—Ibn Umar

6 Abd Allah ibn Ali al-Sufi

7 Abd Allah ibn Ali

8 Abu Nasr al-Sarraj

9 Abu-l-Fath Yusuf ibn Umar al-Zahid al-Qawwas ibn Baghdad—Muhammad ibn Atiyyah—Abd al-Kabir ibn Ahmad —Abu Bakr al-Saigh

10 Abu Nasr al-Sarraj

11 Abu Nasr al-Sarraj—al-Wajihi, via dictation

12 Abd Allah ibn Ali al-Sufi—Ibn Salim

13 Abu Nasr al-Sarraj—Jafar ibn Muhammad

14 Muhammad ibn Ahmad al-Najjar—al-Raqqi

15 Umar ibn Yahya al-Ardabili—al-Raqqi

16 Abd Allah ibn Ali—Talhah al-Qasairi

17 Abu-l-Husayn Ghulam Shuwanah

18 Bukran ibn Ahmad al-Jili—Yusuf ibn al-Husayn

19 Muhammad ibn al-Farhan—Junayd—Abu Jafar al-Khassaf

20 Umar ibn Muhammad ibn Ahmad al-Shirazi in Basra

21 Abu Ahmad al-Kabir—Abu Abd Allah ibn Khafif

22 Ali ibn Harun—Ali ibn Abi Muhammad al-Tamimi—Jafar ibn al-Qasim al-Khawwas—Ahmad ibn Muhammad al-Tusi

23 Mansur ibn Abd Allah

24 Abd al-Aziz al-Fadl—Muhammad ibn Ahmad al-Marwazi—Abd Allah ibn Sulayman

25 Abu-l-Faraj al-Wirthani—Ali ibn Yaqub, in Damascus—Abu Bakr Muhammad ibn Ahmad.

26 Abu-l-Najm Ahmad ibn al-Husayn in Khuzistan.

27 Ahmad ibn Yusuf al-Khayyat—Abu Ali al-Rudhbari

28 Abu-l-Faraj al-Wirthani—Muhammad ibn al-Husayn al-Khuldi in Tarsus

29 Harith-al-Khattabi—Muhammad ibn al-Fadl—Ali ibn Muslim

30 Abu Abd Allah Muhammad ibn Ali al-Juzi, in Jondishapur

31 Abd al-Wahid ibn Bakr al-Wirthani—Muhammad ibn Ali ibn al-Husayn al-Muqarri in Tarsus

32 Abu-l-Harith al-Khattabi—Muhammad ibn al-Fadl—Ali ibn Muslim

33 Husayn ibn Ahmad al-Farisi—al-Raqqi—Ahmad ibn Mansur

34 Abu Bakr Ahmad ibn Muhammad al-Tarsusi

35 Abu-l-Najm al-Muqarri al-Bardhai in Shiraz—al-Raqqi— Ahmad ibn Mansur

36 Muhammad ibn al-Husayn al-Baghdadi

37 Ali ibn Ibrahim ibn Ahmad—Uthman ibn Ahmad—al-Husayn ibn Umar

38 Abu Abd Allah ibn Muflih—al-Mughazili

39 Ibrahim ibn Ahmad al-Tabari—Ahmad ibn Yusuf—Ahmad ibn Ibrahim ibn Yahya—his father

40 Abu-l-Qasim Abd Allah ibn Ali—al-Shajari

41 Abu Abd Allah al-Dabbas al-Baghdadi—Fatimah, the sister of Abu Ali al-Rudhbari

42 Muhammad ibn Faris al-Farisi—Abu-l-Hasan Khar al-Nassaj

43 Muhammad ibn al-Hasan al-Baghdadi—Abu-l-Hadid

44 Ibrahim ibn Muhammad al-Maliki—Yusuf ibn Ahmad al-Baghdadi

45 Abu Bakr Muhammad ibn Ali al-Takriti—Muhammad bin Ali al-Kattani, in Makkah

46 Ahmad ibn Ali al-Saih—Muhammad ibn Abd Allah ibn Mutarraf—Muhammad ibn al-Husayn al-Asqalani

47 Abd al-Rahman ibn Muhammad al-Sufi

48 Abu Bakr al-Razi—Yusuf ibn al-Husayn

49 Abu-l-Faraj al-Wirthani—Abu-l-Hasan Ali ibn Muhammad al-Sayrafi

50 Abu Ahmad ibn Ali al-Hafiz—Ahmad ibn Hamzah—Abd al-Wahhab (a righteous man)

51 Abd al-Wahid ibn Bakr al-Wirthani—Muhammad ibn Dawud—Abu Bakr ibn Muammar

52 Abu-l-Hasan Ismail ibn Amr ibn Kamil in Egypt

53 Abu Ali Ismail ibn Muhammad ibn Ismail al-Saffar—al-Husayn ibn Arafah ibn Yazid—Abd Allah ibn Idris al-Awdi— Ismail ibn Abi Khalid

54 Abu Bakr al-Nabulusi

55 Abu-l-Abbas ibn al-Khashshab al-Baghdadi—Muhammad ibn Abd Allah al-Farghani

56 Abu Tahir al-Raqqi

57 Hasan ibn Ahmad al-Farisi—al-Raqqi—Abu Bakr ibn Muammar

58 Abu Muhammad al-Ghitrifi—al-Sarraj—Abu Sulayman al-Rumi

51 ON THE DREAMS OF THE SUFIS

1 Ahmad ibn Ubayd al-Basri—Ashaq ibn Ibrahim al- Munqarri—Mansur ibn Abi Mazahim—Abu Bakr ibn Ayyash —Asim—Abu Salih.

2 Abu Ali al-Hasan ibn Muhammad Zayd—Ali ibn al-Husayn—Abd Allah bin al-Walid—Sufyan—Yahya ibn Said—Abu Salamah.

3 Abu Ahmad Hamzah ibn al-Abbas al-Bazzaz—Ayyash ibn Muhammad ibn Hatim—Abd Allah ibn Musa—Israil—Abu Ishaq—Abu-l-Ahwas and Abu Ubaydah.